CULTIVATING THE MUSE

Cultivating the Muse

Struggles for Power and Inspiration in Classical Literature

EDITED BY

EFROSSINI SPENTZOU

AND

DON FOWLER

OXFORD

UNIVERSITY PRESS

OXFORD
UNIVERSITY PRESS

Great Clarendon Street, Oxford, OX2 6DP

Oxford University Press is a department of the University of Oxford.
It furthers the University's objective of excellence in research, scholarship,
and education by publishing worldwide in

Oxford New York

Athens Auckland Bangkok Bogotá Buenos Aires Cape Town
Chennai Dar es Salaam Delhi Florence Hong Kong Istanbul Karachi
Kolkata Kuala Lumpur Madrid Melbourne Mexico City Mumbai Nairobi
Paris São Paulo Shanghai Singapore Taipei Tokyo Toronto Warsaw

and associated companies in Berlin Ibadan

Oxford is a registered trade mark of Oxford University Press
in the UK and certain other countries

Published in the United States
by Oxford University Press Inc., New York

British Library Cataloguing in Publication Data

Data available

Library of Congress Cataloging in Publication Data

Data applied for

ISBN 0-19-924004-3

1 3 5 7 9 10 8 6 4 2

Typeset in Dante
by Regent Typesetting, London
Printed in Great Britain
on acid-free paper by
Biddles Ltd., Guildford & King's Lynn

Preface

The present volume started its life as a day conference which took place at Wolfson College Oxford on 4 May 1996 entitled: 'Cultivating the Muse: Power, Desire, and Inspiration in the Classical World'. The original contributors to the event were Don Fowler, John Henderson, Micaela Janan, Penny Murray, Alison Sharrock, and myself. The success of the day, and the interest it triggered on both sides of the Atlantic (communicated to us mainly through e-mail by people unable to attend), made the idea of an expanded publication on the subject an intriguing possibility. After the original participants all agreed to commit their contributions to a joint volume, Don Fowler and I started eliciting contributions for a wider project that would explore alternative approaches to the Muses and inspiration throughout Greco-Roman Antiquity. When Ronnie Ancona, Adriana Cavarero, Ismene Lada-Richards, Andrew Laird, and Gianpiero Rosati had all agreed to offer papers we knew that we had a volume that could unsettle and inspire.

Don and I worked through the initial stages of the project, negotiating the exact contributions and the overall message of this rather complex book with a lot of enthusiasm. As the first drafts of the contributions were being handed in to us, Don fell seriously ill. However, for the few months that followed and until his death, he carried on offering unfailing support and advice on a wide range of issues, but sadly he died when the book was still far from completion.

Thanks are due to several institutions and colleagues; to Wolfson College Oxford for supporting and hosting the initial conference; the Oxford Sub-faculty of Classical Languages and Literature and the Craven Committee for financial contributions that made the event possible; the lively audience of the Wolfson conference for giving us food for thought and for being responsible for an interesting and enjoyable day. The British Museum kindly gave permission to publish the cover photograph of the Muses from the Sophilos dinos. I have incurred many debts when the daunting task of the editorship fell exclusively to me. I thank once again all the contributors for their willing co-operation and kind attitude that made the task much easier. Two of them certainly deserve a special mention: John Henderson and Alison Sharrock both did an awful lot more than their contributors' duty and I am deeply grateful to them; without their practical help and moral support this volume would not have emerged. I would also like to express my gratitude to Hilary O'Shea at Oxford University Press, who put her trust in the project from a very early and rather uncertain stage and was always available for advice in the later stages. My sincere thanks are also due to my colleague at Royal Holloway Richard Alston for taking a kind interest in the project and offering a much-appreciated external point of view. Mike Fraser, Manager of the Humbul Humanities Hub at the University of Oxford, saved me from numerous pitfalls regarding word processors, fonts, bibliographical packages etc., with generous and readily available advice on the other end of the phone.

The project's and my own biggest debt is due to my co-editor and doctoral supervisor Don Fowler. It was his wholehearted and unfailing support and encouragement that made the initial conference possible, the idea for such a daring project convincing, the book in its specific parameters a reality. Working together on this was a most enjoyable and instructive experience for me. Subsequently, when faced with dilemmas and decisions, I tried to draw from the very many lessons learned after years of apprenticeship and collaboration, but errors and unfortunate choices are my own responsibility. Don was the deepest inspiration for this volume, from the beginning through to its completion. We are all very conscious of the fact that this project did not benefit from his knowledge and expertise nearly as much as it could and was meant to, but we hope and believe we have produced something he would have both liked and endorsed. This book is offered in memory of him by us all, students and friends.

E.S.

Contents

List of Contributors

RONNIE ANCONA is Associate Professor of Classics at Hunter College and the Graduate Center, City University of New York.

ADRIANA CAVARERO teaches political philosophy at the University of Verona.

DON FOWLER (1953–99) was Fellow and Tutor in Classics at Jesus College Oxford, from 1980 until his death on 15 October 1999.

JOHN HENDERSON teaches Latin at King's College Cambridge.

MICAELA JANAN is Associate Professor of Classical Studies at Duke University.

ISMENE LADA-RICHARDS is Lecturer in Classics at King's College London.

ANDREW LAIRD is Lecturer at the Department of Classics and Ancient History at the University of Warwick.

PENELOPE MURRAY is Senior Lecturer in Classics at the University of Warwick.

GIANPIERO ROSATI is Professor of Latin Literature at the University of Udine.

ALISON SHARROCK is Senior Lecturer in Classics at the University of Manchester.

EFROSSINI SPENTZOU is Lecturer in the Department of Classics at Royal Holloway College London.

Abbreviations

ANRW	*Aufstieg und Niedergang der römischen Welt*, Berlin (1972–)
AP	*Anthologia Palatina*
D-K	H. Diels and W. Kranz (eds.) *Die Fragmente der Vorsokratiker*, 6th edn., Berlin (1951–2)
FGrHist	F. Jacoby (ed.) *Die Fragmente der griechischen Historiker*, Berlin and Leiden (1923–58)
Gow–Page	A. S. F. Gow and D. L. Page (eds.) *Hellenistic Epigrams*, 2 vols., Cambridge 1965
IMagn.	O. Kern (ed.) *Die Inschriften von Magnesia am Maeander* (1900)
KA	R. Kassel and C. Austin (eds.) *Poetae Comici Graeci*, Berlin and New York (1983–)
LIMC	*Lexicon Iconographicum Mythologiae Classicae*, Zurich and Munich (1981–)
LSJ	Liddell and Scott, Greek–English Lexicon, 9th edn., rev. H. Stuart Jones (1925–40)
OCT	Oxford Classical Texts
OLD	*Oxford Latin Dictionary*
Pfeiffer	R. Pfeiffer (ed.) *Callimachus*, 2 vols., Oxford (1949–53)
PKöln	*Kölner Papyri*, vol. 8, Cologne / Opladen (1976–)
Radt	S. Radt (ed.) *Tragicorum Graecorum Fragmenta* vol. 4, Göttingen (1977)
Roscher	W. H. Roscher, *Ausführliches Lexikon der griechischen und römischen Mythologie*, 6 vols., Leipzig (1884–1937)
Sandbach	F. H. Sandbach (ed.) *Plutarchi Moralia*, vol. 7, Leipzig (1967)
Snell–Maeler	*Pindari Carmina cum Fragmentis*, ed. B. Snell, 8th edn., rev. H. Maeler, Teubner (1987–8)
TLL	*Thesaurus Linguae Latinae*, Leipzig (1900–)
Walz	C. Walz (ed.) *Rhetores Graeci*, 9 vols., Stuttgart and London (1832–6)

Clio gesta canens transactis tempora reddit.
dulciloquis calamos Euterpe flatibus urguet.
comica lascivo gaudet sermone Thalia
Melpomene tragico proclamat maesta boatu
Terpsichore affectus citharis movet, imperat, auget.
plectra gerens Erato saltat pede carmine vultu.
Urania motusque poli scrutatur et astra.
carmina Calliope libris heroica mandat.
signat cuncta manu loquiturque Polymnia gestu.
mentis Apollineae vis has movet undique Musas:
in medio residens complectitur omnia Phoebus.

Ausonius, *Nomina Musarum*

The Muses get their name from a root that indicates ardor, the quick-tempered tension that leaps out in impatience, desire, or anger, the sort of tension that aches to know and to do. In a milder version, one speaks of the 'movements of the spirit'. (*Mens* is from the same root.) The Muse animates, stirs up, excites, arouses. She keeps watch less over the form than over the force. Or more precisely: she keeps watch forcefully over the form.

But this force springs up in the plural. It is given, from the first, in multiple forms. There are Muses and not the Muse. Their number may have varied, as well as their attributes, but the Muses will always have been several. It is this multiple origin that must interest us, and it is also the reason why the Muses, as such, are not the subject here; they are merely lending their name, this name that is multiplied from the first . . .

Jean-Luc Nancy, *The Muses*, 1

I

Introduction: Secularizing the Muse

Efrossini Spentzou

I. GREEK IMPRECISIONS

Μουσάων Ἑλικωνιάδων ἀρχώμεθ' ἀείδειν, | αἵ θ' Ἑλικῶνος ἔχουσιν
ὄρος μέγα τε ζάθεόν τε (*Theog.* 1–2), 'From the Muses of Helicon let us
begin our singing, that haunt Helicon's great and holy Mountain':[1] over-
laden with symbolic nuances, Hesiod's encounter with the Muses as he
was pasturing his sheep on Mount Helicon (*Theog.* 22–35) perfectly distils
the Goddesses' essential character: allusive, elusive, and honoured with
a leading position in poetic endeavour. Even those less at home with
Hesiodic didactic poetry will respond with recognition to the Muses'
celebrated self-definition: ἴδμεν ψεύδεα πολλὰ λέγειν ἐτύμοισιν ὁμοῖα,
ἴδμεν δ', εὖτε ἐθέλωμεν, ἀληθέα γηρύσασθαι (*Theog.* 27–8), 'we know to
tell many lies that sound like truth, but we also know to sing reality,
when we will'. And the Muses did not only haunt the great and holy
mountain. Clothed in a cloud of mystery, often evoked in passing
references, metonymical descriptions, symbolic representations, they
have visited poems and art persistently and with assurance, unfailingly
engaging artistic and poetic imagination ever since. Ἔνθεν ἀπορνύμεναι,
κεκαλυμμέναι ἠέρι πολλῷ, | ἐννύχιαι στεῖχον περικαλλέα ὄσσαν ἱεῖσαι
(*Theog.* 9–10), 'From there they go forth, veiled in thick mist, and walk by
night, uttering beautiful voice'. Once started, the Muses' stroll gathered
momentum bringing them fame and popularity that was meant to
last for centuries, surviving into the Roman world, well after Fulvius

---

[1] All translations of the *Theogony* come from West (1988).

Nobilior, Ennius' patron, brought the statues of the Greek Muses across to Italy founding the temple of Hercules Musarum.[2]

And yet, for all their desire for peregrination, the Muses' very existence is inextricably tied to Hesiod. As one reads on in the *Theogony*, one becomes aware that this revisiting is really mandatory for any serious discussion of their wanderlust. It is Hesiod's tidy, conformist, and reassuring imagery which created for the Muses a secure position on the divine pedestal, as the nine talented daughters of Zeus whose mother, Mnemosyne, bestowed upon them a unique connection with memory.

> τὰς ἐν Πιερίῃ . . . τέκε . . .
> Μνημοσύνη . . .
> λησμοσύνην τε κακῶν ἄμπαυμά τε μερμηράων
>
>   .   .   .   .
>
> . . . ἐννέα κούρας ὁμόφρονας, ᾗσιν ἀοιδὴ
> μέμβλεται ἐν στήθεσσιν ἀκηδέα θυμὸν ἐχούσαις
>   τυτθὸν ἀπ' ἀκροτάτης κορυφῆς νιφόεντος Ὀλύμπου,
> ἔνθα σφιν λιπαροί τε χοροὶ καὶ δώματα καλά
>
>   .   .   .   .
>
> . . . ἐρατὴν δὲ διὰ στόμα ὄσσαν ἱεῖσαι
> μέλπονται, πάντων τε νόμους καὶ ἤθεα κεδνὰ
> ἀθανάτων κλείουσιν.   (53–67)

They were born in Pieria to Memory . . . oblivion of ills and respite from cares . . . nine daughters—all of one mind, their carefree hearts set on song—not far from the topmost peak of snowy Olympus. There they have their gleaming dancing-places and fair mansions . . . lovely is the sound they produce from their mouths as they sing and celebrate the ordinances and the good ways of the immortals.

Having secured a place amongst the archaic divinities, the Muses, together with Apollo, as their chaperon and leader,[3] are thus implicated in what has been aptly called a theology of sung speech,[4] within the continuum of archaic thought which knew how to invent and endow deities with the names of feelings, skills, passions, intellectual faculties in order to picture the world. Quite appropriately for the Hesiodic passage just quoted which foregrounds the Muses' devoted celebration of the gods' good deeds, within this magico-religious system of utterance and

---

[2] On this, see Ennius' *Annales* 15 and cf. Barchiesi (1994) 274–76; Hinds (1998) 52–63, who suggests (at 62) that it was an existing temple of Hercules the Guardian which was used to house the imported statues; but on this contrast Richardson (1982) 187.

[3] Cf. here *Theog.* 94.

[4] Detienne (1996) 7.

thought, Zeus' gracious daughters are portrayed as the representatives of Aletheia, the deified absolute Truth, linked not so much with understanding and the acquisition of knowledge as with praise of, and communication with, the divine.[5]

This 'brand of' Muse is a familiar figure for philosophers and historians of culture who have extensively studied her role in the religious rituals and semiology from the archaic period onwards.[6] This make of Muse, as the representative and intermediary of divine knowledge, would often inspire possessed initiates, creating an ambiance of release and redemption.[7] Such an ecstatic belief in the Muses' capacities also accounts for some renowned epic invocations of the Muse. One thinks, above all, of the Homeric Muses' omniscience as they are called upon to explain to the bard the future happenings and causes of events *word by word*,[8] these divine figures who know all things and can bestow this knowledge to the mortals who have only heard rumours and really know nothing.[9] For Claude Calame, archaic inspiration and narration come under the umbrella of performance. And yet, even when looked at from this angle, the archaic Muse still resonates with uncontestable authority, whatever the differences in the acquisition and understanding of knowledge in a culture of orality may be:[10] 'In the whole of archaic Greek literature, from Homeric poetry to Pindar, the utterance of the enunciation is characterised by the projection of the I of the narrator onto a higher authority, an authority assumed by the figure of the Muse or the Muses, daughters of Memory, an authority endowed with poetic power and knowledge.'[11]

And yet, in spite of the reassuring authority of Hesiod's imagery and message, duly picked up by modern critics, later poetry did not indulge in the details of the myth nearly as much, or as wholeheartedly, as it might. The Hesiodic Muses were steadily invoked in moments of lack of inspiration, but the devotional language used to attract their attention did very little to enhance their personal traits and did not, as a rule, dwell on the minutiae of their idyllic life on Mount Helicon. It is in fact

---

[5] Cf. here ibid. 39–52.

[6] See esp. Boyancé (1937); Otto (1956); Roscher s.v. Musen.

[7] Cf. esp. Barmeyer (1968); Schachter (1986); but contrast Murray (1981).

[8] See e.g. *Od.* 8. 479–81.

[9] See e.g. *Il.* 2. 484 ff. For more on the Homeric invocations of the Muses see Minchin (1995) and esp. 25 n. 3.

[10] On this contrast Cavarero and Laird in this volume.

[11] Calame (1995) 77.

generally argued that the multiple features, names, and representations
of the archaic Muses did nothing to enhance their individuality.[12] In
Hesiod and throughout the archaic period, the Muses' various names at
most momentarily bring into focus the different aspects of their collective qualities. For the Muses are just copies of one another, united in
mind, spirit and feeling—ὁμοφρονέουσαι according to Hesiod[13]—and
classical writers as well as modern critics have outdone one another in
getting this message across to us all.[14] So if the Muses were more or less
a device meant to intensify the epiphany (*Erscheinung*) of poetry, as has
been again and again claimed,[15] there is very little space for character
building, for a *Bildungsroman* to trace the development of these subli-
mated figures and allow them to speak for themselves. Reticence and
dearth of material goes hand in hand with lack of precision and consis-
tency: in spite of their sublime position, a cursory glance at Greek and
Roman literature and art will testify that the Muses have not always
been nine, do not always dwell in the same place, have the same function, or even the same parentage.[16] Significantly, the iconography of the
Muses also seems to corroborate the vagueness of the literary imagery.[17]

[12] Cf. here Keith (2000) 109 also refering to Bronfen (1992) 364–5.

[13] *Theog.* 60.

[14] According to Pausanias, the muses, *mousai*, were characteristically and by definition ὁμοῦ
οὖσαι, and e.g. Trimpi (1983) xvii aptly notices: 'For Hesiod, the Muses exist as various aspects
of one another, one implying all the others, and they enable the poet to transmit a general
cultural and artistic inheritance.'

[15] Barmeyer (1968) 64–5, representing a dominant line in many standard approaches to the
Muses.

[16] Cf. e.g. Pausanias 9. 29. 2–5; Cicero, *De natura deorum* 3. 54.

[17] The earliest scene identifying the Muses is the Sophilos' famous *dinos* (round goblet)
where they appear in two groups—one of five and one of three. The group of three is nearly
identical to the Morai and the Charites, who are also grouped as triplets. Each group is
identified by an inscription and functions as an escort for a chariot bearing a pair of Olympian
deities in the wedding procession for Thetis and Peleus. Commonly the Muses appear with
Apollo Citharode in varying numbers from one to eight and are identified by their association
with him and the possession of an attribute such as a flower, a phiale for libation, or a musical
instrument (lyre, crotales, aulos). In late 5th-cent. red-figure pottery the Muses appear in
'garden paradise' scenes where the only feature which distinguishes a muse from the other
female personifications (such as e.g. Peitho) is an identifying inscription. Otherwise, the
personifications and the Muses blend into the lush, languid multi-figured scenes that were
typical of this popular style of vase decoration. The Muses are rarely identified in sculpture, and
when they are it is usually on tenuous grounds. I am indebted to Blanche Menadier for
drawing my attention to, and offering her insight into, the above material and also for several
engaging discussions on Muses in art. For more on the iconography of the Muses see *LIMC* 6. 1.
657–81.

A different pattern starts to emerge once one becomes sensitive to such undecided aspects of the Muses' apparently neat imagery and thinks twice about the 'objective' qualities ascribed to these divinities. How is it possible that such glorified divinities are clothed in so precarious a garment and bestowed with such hesitant looks? Is this no more than a random discord or is it a discrepancy with deeper roots? An altogether different range of questions will emerge if we dwell longer on this representational and symbolic haziness—and this book will dwell on it, more purposefully than its predecessors, in the hope of breaking through the stillness of the stereotyped images that these figures have been charged with. Is this haziness perhaps the signifier of a certain fragility in the seemingly robust foundations of the mythology and theology of the Muses? How solid indeed is the religious system upon which divine knowledge and deified Aletheia determined the presence and the role of the nine daughters of Zeus and Mnemosyne?

In a perceptive study of archaic perceptions of Truth, Marcel Detienne precisely tuned into these questions and came up with illuminating suggestions with a direct bearing on our own concerns: tracing the changes in the perceptions of truth in the passage from archaic to classical Greek culture, Detienne detects a crucial transformation in the nature of knowledge and thinking during the seventh and sixth centuries BC. Contextualizing this alteration within the dominant political and legal practices of those two centuries, he discovers what he calls an increasing secularization of thinking and speech which were later socially and politically probed and ratified, where before they had been symbolically impressed upon people's minds. Detienne promptly associates this transformation with socio-political developments that promoted the value and power of reasoning and argumentation. It was particularly the rise of the aristocracy and the right of the *aristoi* to ἰσηγορία that disentangled the old magico-religious and 'efficacious' speech from its symbolic network. Knowledge and thinking became crucial instruments in the comprehension of the surrounding, secular world with challenges and problems firmly grounded in time and place rather than simply an atemporal and ahistorical attempt to communicate with the divine.

The transition from magic to reason, so to speak, is superbly exemplified in Aeschylus' *Eumenides* and especially in the last scene of Athena's ruling on the fate of Orestes (778–1047). It is the blending of the old theological principles with new political doctrines in the clash

between old and new gods that makes this scene particularly relevant
and expressive of developments in thought which can be traced behind
the new or transmuted configurations of the Muse that this book aims
to focus on. Representing the old awe-inspiring gods, the Furies are
eventually obliged to succumb to the newly potent persuasion represented by Athena and the tribunal of the Athenian citizens. This is the
epoch of the *polis* and, as the vital role of the assembly of the Athenian
citizens in the disentanglement of the plot suggests, the exercise of
speech and expression is the new power to which the divine itself has to
adjust. Truth can no longer seduce its audience and impose itself on
awestricken people. The new ruling principle is the publicly probed dialogue, and the divine as well will have to assert itself through the
accountable and contextualized channels of persuasion, as modelled
by Athena's eloquent speech in front of the old monstrous gods and
the Athenian audience. What Athena with charming and powerful
eloquence promises to the Athenians is that knowledge will from now
on be the adopted child of the city and this storm of rationality which
sweeps up the old divinities, also shakes and questions the privileged
credentials of the archaic Muses.

Rationalism and secularization of thought force the archaic Muses
from their pedestal; political scrutiny and philosophical and religious
incredulity go hand in hand with the increasing conspicuousness of the
'I' in the world of art. So, too, the figure of the poet regularly appears
more autonomous and conscious of his own poetic craft. Born some-
time in the mid-sixth century BC, Simonides seems to have been
registered in history (or at least, the scholiasts' writings) as the first
smikrologos, money-grabber:[18] boldly and rather irreverently introducing a distinctively human, mercenary muse into his song-making,
Simonides (together with Gorgias) is also considered by many as a precursor of the sophists. By the beginning of the fifth century BC,
Bacchylides appears to take this poetic self-assertiveness further as he
daringly declares himself to be 'the divine prophet of the violet-lidded
Muses' (9.2 ff.), a gesture whose confidence is brought into higher relief
when contrasted with the servile and obedient features of the Homeric
and Hesiodic bard. A product of the same disbelieving regime,
Herodotus also decides to provide a *sphragis* for his oeuvre, in the

---

[18] Cf. Ar. *Pax* 695 ff. and scholia ad loc. Cf. also Pindar, *Isthm.* 2.1 ff., recalling the old ethics
before Simonides and his peers had started their secular business of poetic writing: 'For then the
Muse was not yet fond of profit or mercenary'.

celebrated manner of Alcman and Theognis; and so names himself in his
prelude to the *Histories*. Calame observes the determined character
of the gesture and aptly compares it with the old time-honoured
techniques:

In contrast to the epic *I*, which is never explicitly linked to a proper name but
which can be adopted by the person who utters the poem in the present tense of
each enunciation, [Herodotus'] *he* is given the identity conferred by a proper
name; in this case the *I*'s name is Herodotus, who comes from Halicarnassus.
There is no question of an invocation to the Muses; the sphragis has replaced the
appeal to the source of inspiration, previously the explicit sender of the literary
achievement.[19]

Intently focusing on the oral qualities of the performance, Calame had,
at this point, already captured the defining alteration in relationship
between poet and Muses which saw poetic authority gradually emanci-
pate itself from the uncontestable divine: 'The increasing conspicuousness of the affirmation of the "I" in the archaic tradition and of the
poet-artisan's objective function, objectifies the relationship to the
Muse. . . . The Muses contribute to establishing the subject's competence, and the Subject is then involved in the achievement . . .'[20]

Intrigued by the awakenings of (the poetic) subjectivity, critics
revisited and scrutinized the blissfully tidy imagery of the Hesiodic
Muses only to notice Hesiod himself asserting his identity in a similar
manner, right at the point where he also acknowledges the Muses'
poetic omnipotence: Αἵ νύ ποθ' Ἡσίοδον καλὴν ἐδίδαξαν ἀοιδήν
(*Theog.* 22), 'And once they taught Hesiod fine singing, as he tended his
lambs below holy Helicon.' Even while bowing deferentially to the
Muses' authority, the poet cunningly inserts his signature into the poem,
establishing his own _kleos_ in the years to come next to the Muses' omniscience; and the gesture undermines the Muses' omniscience at the very
moment that it seeks to confirm it.[21] Looking back at the Homeric
Muses with the same scrutinizing eye undermines their command even
further: it is characteristic that the invocations to them are rather sparse
in the *Odyssey*, especially when compared with the more consistently
deferential stance of the Iliadic bard and his surrogates in the text, and
this reticence is further noticeable when juxtaposed with the concerns of

---

[19] Calame (1995) 79.
[20] Ibid. 71, 77.
[21] Cf. e.g. ibid. 66 and esp. Pucci (1977) 31–4 with a perceptive critique of the limits of the
Muses' authority.

the self-taught Phemios, whose song casts yet more doubts on the potential of the Muses' narration.[22] Pietro Pucci succinctly summarizes the doubts in respect to the *Odyssey*: 'The *Odyssey* certainly invokes the Muses at the inception of the poem, and yet it reveals by numerous clues a constant striving to limit and circumscribe their responsibility. . . . These features would in fact support the idea that for the *Odyssey*, the Muses—like the Sirens—are personifications of literary practices, of the epic tradition, rather than divine objective inspirers.'[23]

The picture that emerges is hardly encouraging for the role and position of the Muse in the new secular technologies of knowledge, and a concern about the Muses' own literary future is inevitable: borrowing Hesiod's imagery from *Theogony* 30, how safely could the daughters of Mnemosyne hold on to their sceptre, constantly undermined by doubts and the poets' own inflated sense of autonomy? Is it just an innocent need for poetic variation that drives Callimachus in the third century BC to set his own encounter with the Muses in a dream, while apparently faithful to his archaic master? Or is this gesture a subtle but clear pointer to an elusive metaphor, a Muse deprived of flesh and blood? Is the literary life of the daughters of Mnemosyne a slippery path of ever-increasing abstraction?

Rather unsurprisingly, more recent critics have found such scepticism enticing and appropriately expressive of their incredulous, postmodern sensitivities. Indeed, sceptical critical discourse on the Muses has flourished in recent years and managed to dissociate the Muses from the unyielding religious hierarchy into which they had hitherto been firmly engrafted. And yet, for all the nuances they may have gained as their sacred divine status was questioned, the nine maidens of poetry did not also gain substance: freed from the necessity to defer to an awesome divine structure, the critics enthusiastically delved into the task of challenging divine authority and knowledge and its far-ranging possibilities. The less-than-perfect Hesiodic Muses were thus used as a conceptual tool in what was nothing less than an ambitious attempt to shake and redefine the boundaries of mortal and divine knowledge in the archaic world. Several perceptive critics have turned their attention to the Muses' words, considering it a springboard for the exploration of the boundaries of language and imitation as communicative tools, and the discussion was even more heady as postmodern awareness had already

---

[22] Cf. Pucci (1987) esp. 218–21, 230–2.   [23] Ibid. 231.

drawn attention to the ambiguities of reality and the limitations of representation and of truth itself.

And yet, if it does not sound paradoxical, the vast space created by these critical aspirations, for all the insight it offered, also rendered the Muses' voice too feeble to be heard, so to speak. Derek Collins's recent and elaborate work on ὄσσα, the Muses' own divine voice and utterance, offers striking testimony to this peculiarly 'self-effacing' dominance of the Muses.[24] Aligned with the divine purveyors of truth and knowledge, the Muses' ὄσσα places them within the divine realm of communication, a realm which mortals are unable to comprehend and from which they are forever excluded. But if the divine grandeur of their voices glorifies the Muses in a world above the mortals, it is the same grandeur and awesome power that, so to speak, marginalizes them just as it elevates them. Collins's paper testifies to this subtle slippage, arguing at length for the different forms of divine communication in a study where 'the beautiful and lovely [voice] of the Muses' has yielded to considerations of vast cosmic significance such as the harsh battles between Heaven and Earth during Zeus' contest with the Titans or the threatening utterances of awesome divine creatures like the serpent Typhoeus.[25] If Collins's latest approach results in the Muses' aggrandizement, other studies have taken the opposite tack and have tarnished, as we have seen, the Muses' omniscient image. All the scholarship, though, has one common feature: the figures of Mnemosyne's daughters—however eulogized or tainted—ultimately sink under the weight of amibitious philosophical pondering, or heavily rhetorico-linguistic concerns.[26] Simply call to mind how bulky the bibliography triggered by two single lines of the *Theogony* has become—that famous pair of lines where the Muses' ability to tell lies or truth at will is tersely and suggestively communicated (27–8).[27]

And so it is, therefore, that we are now several pages further on and have made an extensive review of the primary and secondary literature on the Muses, but we still have not managed to paint a vivid picture of

---

[24] Collins (1999).

[25] Ibid. 244–6.

[26] See esp. Pucci (1980).

[27] See e.g. Pucci (1977) 8–16; Arthur (1983) 100–6; Walsh (1984) 24–33; Ferrari (1988) whose exploration of the limits of mimesis and poetic language takes him so much further that, as he admits, he even 'has had very little to say about what [he] takes the significance of the couplet to be in its context in the prologue to the *Theogony*' (70). See also Collins (1999) 242 n. 3, who also considers the literature on the passage voluminous.

the nine lofty maidens. Importance did not give them vigour and verve, as one might expect, since the ethereal figures are pushed *to the margin* at the very moment that they are given centre-stage, almost *as a result* of being given centre-stage. The hesitant gaps in Hesiodic and other descriptions, which drew our attention at the beginning of this chapter, spring to mind again, still unresolved and always puzzling. And the question that naturally suggests itself at this stage was eloquently voiced by Steele Commager when he wondered: 'Did Homer's, Hesiod's, and Pindar's "Muse" have an objective divine reality independent of their own use of her? Or was she merely a projection, a familiar and convenient shorthand for the creative process? How can we be sure when "the Muse" has become "my Muse"?'[28] As the title of his subchapter indicates ('Descent of the Muses'), Commager was perfectly capable of recognizing the onset of an ever-increasing schematization in the Muses' literary life; indeed his essay expertly uncovers (yet more) slippages in precision which, put together, create a chart of the Muses' conventional presence in Augustan Latin poetry.[29] Probed in this manner, Roman Muses, having lost their quasi-mystical *gravitas*, appear either relegated to a more or less formulaic and therefore uncontested, but also unimportant existence, or transformed into secular modes of meaning which could only be inferior to the archaic magico-religious ones. In fact, the Muses' fate had been sealed early on in Commager's exposition when he hastened to declare that: 'Such vitality as the Muse possessed was to pale into an abstraction. One might, indeed, characterize her biography as the history of a fading metaphor.'[30]

In this expert formulation, the Muses' demise appears inevitable. But is it? Are the Muses' 'Roman days' an unavoidable decline, just a succession of glittering and fleeting remembrances of old glory, steeped in condescending respect summoned up for old times' sake, but actually devoid of any active significance and intensity? It will take only a few passages to establish that Latin literature does not endorse the death penalty: the next section will briefly 'unpick' this 'chronicle of a death foretold' before summing up the aspirations of this volume to set the scene for the individual contributors to have their say.

[28] Commager (1962) 2.

[29] Ibid. 2–16. For an extensive discussion of the nine Muses' presence in Augustan literature see also Camilloni (1998) 81–180.

[30] Commager (1962) 3.

II. ROMAN INDECISIONS

The first stop in this quest for Roman Muses boldly resisting their death is furnished by Ovid in the fifth book of the *Metamorphoses*.[31] Minerva meets the Muses on Helicon and at first sight the setting seems to be reassuringly familiar. Minerva asks to be shown around the holy place and insists on being taken to the new spring Hippocrene which was reported to have burst from Pegasus' hoofprint. Passing references to an established myth like this give a semblance of respect for the received tradition. Subsequently, Minerva takes a long look—as does the reader—around the well-known grove of the Muses, gazing at the ancient foliage, the caves, and the grottoes covered in luscious greenery. And she concludes her inspection with a reminder of the Muses' blissful existence: 'Blessed, she said, were the Muses, both in their pursuits and in their home' (264–8).[32]

So far so good. And yet, in typically Ovidian fashion, the story swerves when least expected. Quite unlike their legendary forebears, the Muses of this Latin Helicon have specific opinions (and anxieties) about their role and do not hesitate to voice them.[33] One of them undertakes to explain to Minerva:

> o nisi te virtus opera ad maiora tulisset,
> in partem ventura chori Tritonia nostri,
> vera refers, meritoque probas artesque locumque,
> et gratam sortem, tutae modo simus, habemus
> sed (vetitum est adeo sceleri nihil) omnia terrent
> virgineas mentes, dirusque ante ora Pyreneus
> vertitur . . .   (269–75)

Had not your strength, Pallas, led you on to greater tasks, you would be numbered with our company. Your words are true; our arts, our happy home deserve your praises; blessed indeed is our fortune here, so long as we were safe. But crime is so unchecked that everything frightens our virgin hearts. Brutal Pyreneus haunts me.

Learned readers cannot miss the classic Ovidian wink here, as the *enfant terrible* of Latin literature plays games with tradition again. However,

---

[31] Ovid, *Met.* 5. 250 ff.

[32] Translations of Ovid's *Metamorphoses* are adapted from Melville (1986).

[33] Critics have already noticed certain self-deprecating features in the account of this anonymous Muse but have tended to incorporate them within Ovid's witty attack on a wide range of traditional concepts. Cf. e.g. Anderson (1997) ad 5. 269–72.

what concerns us here is not Ovid's wit but the Muses' disturbed and disturbing image: having spread doubts concerning their pursuits, which
is—let us not forget—their divine knowledge, this unnamed Muse
expresses a thought quite unthinkable for anybody who knows their
Hesiod well: the nine ethereal daughters of Mnemosyne are now seen as
vulnerable 'human beings', an overtone missing from the haze of the
sublime imagery bequeathed to them by the archaic tradition, and
Helicon is nowhere near so safe a place for young girls as it once was or
seemed. What follows by way of explanation is the story of attempted
rape by a certain mortal, Pyreneus, in its specifics an invention of Ovid.[34]
Pyreneus had occupied by force the surrounding rural land and lusted
for the Muses, until one day he tricked them into his house taking advantage of a downpour. He locked them in and tried to rape them. The story
ends in failure but not before the Muses' startling (mortal) vulnerability
has been imprinted upon us. In fact, the whole episode has, as it were, an
unreal air of stark reality. The surroundings of Helicon are claimed by an
army of occupation, the Muses get accosted on their way to the temple
of Apollo, they are exposed to rain—it never used to rain on Helicon!—
and finally are threatened by a brute of a mortal. The new element introduced into the story is antagonism, between mortals and gods, but also
amongst mortals—for the Muses are all too much like women, like real
women, in this episode.

In fact, antagonism is the underlying theme throughout this section of
the *Metamorphoses*. As the Muse is about to finish her story of attempted
rape, nine birds perch upon the nearby boughs attracting the Goddesses'
attention with their lamenting voice (294–300). As Minerva gazes in
wonder, the Muse reveals that these lamenting magpies were once
Muses, from the mountain of Pieria. But she hastily adds that they were
characteristically second-rank ones. The description of this lower-class,
yet ambitious, lot is characteristic of the new secular and impious attitude towards the once awesomely perfect creatures.

> intumuit numero stolidarum turba sororum
> perque tot Haemonias et per tot Achaidas urbes
> huc venit et tali committit proelia voce:
> 'desinite indoctum vana dulcedine vulgus
> fallere. nobiscum, siqua est fiducia vobis,
> Thespiades, certate, deae.'   (305–10)

---

[34] However, see Bömer (1976) 289–90 for the Thracian origins of the tale.

This pack of stupid sisters, puffed with pride in being nine, had travelled through the towns . . . and reached us here and challenged us 'Cease cheating with that spurious charm of yours the untutored rabble if you trust your powers contend with us, Thespian goddesses.'

So it is that the Muses are dragged into the contest, and eventually win but not before dealing a heavy blow to the idealizing memories of their archaic selves. Pierides and Heliconian Muses are not simply inter-changeable, as they may have been in all earlier accounts, they are here set against one another competing for eloquence, but also for an under-standing of this world and its divine as well as mortal components.[35] The departure from the Hesiodic Muses' harmonious, all-in-one singing is impossible to miss. Divine knowledge here appears divided and one is left wondering: whose version of the world is ultimately right?—a question not befitting the true admirer or a deferential (or disinterested) guardian of the archaic maidens and their incontestable knowledge and timeless authority. Some sources tell that the Muses inhabited Pieria even earlier than Helicon, and associate them with such famous Thracian bards as Orpheus, Musaeus, and Thamyris. But in Ovid's version, their tale *extenuat magnorum facta deorum* (320), 'belittles all the exploits of the gods', and talks about the gods' *mentitas figuras*, that is the spurious, deceiving shapes that gods took when they disguised them-selves to escape from the monster Typhon (325–6). If the Muses' original mission was to celebrate the immortals' orderly lives, as in the *Theogony*, the Pierides in Ovid's *Metamorphoses* have given this role a very wicked turn. How could they be the privileged communicators of divine truth, when their songs insist on reminding us how difficult it is to look for truth behind the beguiling shapes and deceptive messages of the world all around?

As for the other group of contestants, the Muses themselves, we can try to look up to them as representatives of the elevated sort of know-ledge and inspiration that the Greeks once believed in. But Ovid's tale emphatically denies them any such assured and assuring role. Their con-frontation with Pyreneus has already exposed their vulnerability and their lack of confidence surfaces again when the anonymous representa-tive wonders whether Minerva has time or leisure to listen to her song (333–4). Minerva promptly offers reassurance but the contrast with the overjoyed atmosphere in the mansions of the immortals, as the deities

---

[35] Cf. also here Anderson (1997) ad 5. 308–11, who rightly draws attention to the Hellenistic touch of the Pierides' pride in their learning, and links this passage with Prop. 2. 23. 1.

rejoiced at the goddesses' ever-desired songs, as described in the
Theogony, is already stark and telling.

The embarrassment of the Ovidian Muse in front of Minerva is
another signal of a rift in the gods' ranks. Even though they still retain
their divine insignia—as Ovid remarks with suspicious eagerness, the
Muse speaks to Minerva as one goddess to another (300)—these Muses
do not feel at ease in the fellowship of the gods. Instead, they now share
the uncertainties of the world of mortals, subject to its threat, and
vulnerable to its vicissitudes; they function as faint reminders of the
previous glory rather than symbolic assurances of artistic excellence.
And the question arises quite naturally: has the faltering Muse also
forfeited the poet's unconditional respect and acceptance? The metaphorical structures of the text give us clues, rather than a definitive
answer. As subject-matter of the *Metamorphoses,* the Muses are impeded
'within'; they are products of the poet's master-minded plot, engulfed by
the bigger frame rather than shaping it from the outside, as 'proper'
Muses would do.[36] They can thus be seen in the first instance as relatively ignorant speakers whose position and knowledge is no more
enlightened than any of the other narrators in the polyphonic world of
the *Metamorphoses.* To use a very specific example, the Muses of Book 5
are not significantly more knowledgeable than, say, Arachne in the next
book, whose signature, intertwined with the ivy of her art, reminds us of
her own involved role as a narrator (6. 127–8). In fact, in the light of
Arachne's (in)famous pride, they come across as more hesitant and
much less confident than her. But of course they are both challenged,
the former by Athena and the latter by Pyreneus. A persistent suitor, this
menace to maiden Muses, he is also a daring 'poet', defying his Muse,
just as he is a hubristic artist, demanding divine inspiration, with a brute
show of violence.[37]

Naturally, this is not the only possible hypothesis: one might want to
see the Muses and the Pierides as powerful singers singing their own
songs, finding their own voices and competing for their own stories.
This is a hardly surprising element in a text of the post-Hellenistic
period. The Muses learned to write long before Ovid, as Peter Bing
points out referring us to book-rolls as attributes of the Muses in vase-
painting as early as the mid-fifth century BC.[38] As he also remarks, by the

---

[36] For more on this polarity see also Sharrock and Rosati in this volume, each arguing from
different positions.   [37] Cf. Leach (1974*a*) 111–13 and Sharrock in this volume.
[38] Bing (1988) 16.

first century BC collaboration between the poet and the Muses (or Graces or Passions) is a frequent departure from the commonplace which had presented poets content to be on the receiving end.[39] Such passages bring out the written character of literature in (post-)Hellenistic times, an important theme for this volume; but the crucial point is the arrival of the theme of antagonism, dominant in Book 5 of the *Metmorphoses*.

The Muses' own voices as they slip through Ovid's text tell stories of notoriously subversive potential;[40] but they also speak of the Muses' own will and independent thought. As we have seen, these notions jar with the Goddesses' traditional stereotypes. The Hesiodic Muses are endowed with lovely voices, as we have seen, but there is nothing to suggest that they have the capacity for personal initiative. If Zeus' omnipotence, affirmed so emphatically in the proem to *Theogony*, is anything to go by, the Muses, just like the other immortals, must have been ordained and given their remit with Apollo, as the leader of the group, representing divine supervision from above. It is characteristic indeed that in the archaic and classical periods, the domain and functions of the Muses and Apollo standardly overlap and the poets make no effort to draw other than contingent distinctions between them. By contrast, the Ovidian Muses' defiant first-person storytelling has the potential to overthrow this acquiescent order. And this is only one indication of their impertinent character: as well as being time-honoured goddesses, the two groups of knowledge holders also reveal unmistakable signs of a novel mortality that makes them erratic, incongruous, and unpredictable. And this secularization of the Muse, far from being a gratuitous *tour de force*, speaks eloquently, if figuratively, about the increasing complexity of the provision of inspiration. These Muses are here to envision the making of poetry and the exercise of authority in an increasingly incredulous world; a 'modern' world unable to comprehend the present myth on the old terms.

We cannot be sure when exactly it was that 'safe' knowledge, like the one intimated by Hesiod's overjoyed Heliconian lot, stopped being an adequate source of happiness and contentment for mortals. But we do know that by the time of Ovid and the other Augustan poets, the daughters of Zeus and Mnemosyne can no longer pose as the exclusive communicators of knowledge. To take one characteristic example: see

[39] Ibid. 19–20.
[40] Hinds (1987*a*) gave the first in-depth reading of this book, to be challenged in ways most relevant to our case here by Cahoon (1990); (1996).

how Catullus slips into irreverence in poem 68. Manlius Torquatus is
there experiencing disappointment in love and has asked Catullus to
send him a poem as consolation. The Muses are still duly invoked as
Manlius asks for a gift from the Muses (as well as Venus). And yet, their
description conveys an unfamilar note of inadequacy. As Catullus
admits, the Muses' sweet singing no longer provides comfort and consolation for the wakeful poet (68A. 7–8). One thing is certain—Manlius
and Catullus do not have the Hesiodic Muses in mind, even though they
still respectfully bow before them. Because, in the archaic poet's
account, the bereaved would put aside his sorrows and his family
troubles, when faced with the gifts of songs of the Muses about the
famous deeds of men of past times (*Theog.* 98–103). Catullus refuses to
grant the request because of personal bereavement, but returns at once
with the desired song (c. 68B). He duly addresses the Goddesses at the
outset, and acts as if he will ask for the usual support, but there is a
surprise ahead. However grudgingly, Catullus agrees to recount Allius'
kindnesses so that the Muses learn and in turn tell many thousands,
'keeping this paper talking well into its old age' (68B. 5–6). So, *he* will give
his Muse her subject-matter so that she can tell the rest of the world—
quite an arresting thought. The profession of the Muses surely hangs in
the balance right at this moment. And the threat of redundancy has a
very Hellenistic stamp on it; it comes from the 'paper' and the wisdom
stored on it, which makes the Muses' privileged relationship with
knowledge and the gods quite beside the point.

Let us now pause, resume our thread, and probe for one last
time Ovid's text. We may have left the two rival groups of the 'Muses'
unbecomingly bickering with one another, but if we had followed the
Ovidian contest to the end we would have seen the Muses' legendary
vivacious voice give way to a raucous chattering (*rauca garrulitas*) when
one of their subsets is transformed into so many ugly magpies, punished
for their irreverence by those other, uncharacteristically vindictive,
Muses. And this lesson is there to find in poems far less mischievously
disrespectful than Ovid's. For example, the proem of the *Aeneid* has
Virgil duly invoke the Muse's memory, only then to burst out at the
thought of her hideously grim and dire stories, with his most famous of
challenges to the divine knowledge of the Muses:

> Musa, mihi causas memora, quo numine laeso
> quidve dolens regina deum tot volvere casus

insignem pietate virum, tot adire labores
impulerit. tantaene animis caelestibus irae?   (*Aen.* I. 8–11)

Tell me, Muse, the causes of her anger. How did he violate the will of the Queen of the Gods? What was his offence? Why did she drive a man famous for his piety to such endless hardship and such suffering? Can there be so much anger in the hearts of the heavenly gods?[41]

Throughout the epic, knowledge as well as fate and destiny are both divinely sanctioned as well as deeply troubling and feared by distrustful people. Aeneas knows that the Sibyl entrusts her insight on leaves because Helenus had told him so in Book 3 when enjoining him to visit Cumae.[42] But, risking irreverence, he is not content with this information and worries that the Sibyl's archive of leaves may be shuffled, confused, and carried away by the whirling winds (6. 75); and Helenus' description of this divine intelligence is far from reassuring:

> verum eadem, verso tenuis cum cardine ventus
> impulit et teneras turbavit ianua frondes,
> numquam deinde cavo volitantia prendere saxo,
> nec revocare situs aut iungere carmina curat.
> (*Aen.* 3. 448–51)

But the leaves are so light that when the door turns in its sockets the slightest breath of wind dislodges them. The draught from the door throws them into confusion and the priestess never makes it her concern to catch them as they flutter round her rocky cave and put them back in order to join up the prophecies.

What could be more vulnerable than divine knowledge entrusted to leaves exposed to the winds? The philosophical and cognitive anxiety should not be overlooked in the dramatic tension of the narrative episode: poetry which so openly defies divine word can no longer graciously accept the old Muses to impose and translate the divine will with blissful assurance. In such an epic, alternative and tormented 'muses' of human descent become important symbols of this new epistemology of knowledge, as they struggle to obtain and comprehend themselves the stories that wait to be written about this world. And the 'new', unstable knowledge has natural links with the 'below' and comes through a more direct contact with death, *furor*, and the other chthonic powers who gain control as the upper deities gradually lose centre-

---

[41] Translations of Virgil's *Aeneid* come from West (1988).
[42] Cf. *Aen* 3. 444: *fata canit foliisque notas et nomina mandat.*

stage.[43] The Sibyl of *Aeneid* 6 and, even more markedly, Phemonoe in Lucan's *Civil War* 5 (an epic even more ruthless in its rejection of the established deities) are two such chthonic figures that eloquently speak for some of the new concerns and anxieties, and it is with these two figures, and their (doomed) urge to appropriate the Muse's role, that I would like to conclude the present section.[44]

The Sibyl of Cumae makes her appearance in the *Aeneid* within appropriately disconcerting settings, comfortably residing in a vast, dark cave and inspired by Apollo with power to disclose future things (and future plots) to the wondering people. The prophetic capacity of the Muses was declaimed and enthused over from Pindar's time, but this muse-like woman here possesses inspiration that fills people with awe rather than bliss. Like the traditional Muses, she has Apollo on her side, but their relationship is one of struggle and antagonism, not camaraderie and togetherness. Forcing his way into the Sibyl, Apollo dictates, through her, the way the poem will go. During their vehement fight, the Sibyl has the divine inserted into her but her mortal nature never quits her, making Apollo's stormy approach feel more and more like rape:

> at Phoebi nondum patiens immanis in antro
> bacchatur vates, magnum si pectore possit
> excussisse deum; tanto magis ille fatigat
> os rabidum, fera corda domans, fingitque premendo.
> (*Aen*. 6. 77–80)

But the priestess was still in wild frenzy in her cave and still resisting Apollo. The more she tried to shake her body free of the great god the harder he strained upon her foaming mouth, taming that wild heart and moulding her by his pressure.

At that point the prophecy comes out of the cavern's hundred mouths. And we find ourselves wondering: would it have made any difference if the prophecy had come out of the Sibyl's own mouth, in her own voice

---

[43] Cf. here Schiesaro (1997) *passim* on this dialectics of 'monstrosity' as played out in Seneca's tragedies.

[44] The two priestesses will also feature in Fowler (Sibyl and Phemonoe) and in Sharrock (Sibyl), in this volume. In the present context, the two prophetesses as alternative muses symbolize the striving and the strain that comes with the new forms of knowledge and inspiration that this volume explores. Fowler and Sharrock foreground those aspects of these figures that make them authorial surrogates, and as such exemplify the passivity involved in the very process of creation. The juxtaposition of the two readings illustrates vividly, I think, the intertwining of active and passive in the act of writing.

and words, according to Aeneas' request (*Ipsa canas oro*: 6. 76) following
Helenus' original injunction (*Aen.* 3. 456–7)? Of course, the immediate
explanation for such a request lies with Aeneas' famous worry,
mentioned just above, about prophecies entrusted to leaves in the wind,
but one cannot help wondering: has the text briefly opened up to the
possibility of a distinctively female voice which, however, never slips
through Apollo's and Virgil's text?

However daring, the possibility of such a reading recurs more
strongly in a later epic, namely Lucan's *Civil War,* and specifically when
Appius requires an oracle from Phemonoe, the prophetess of the
obsolete sanctuary of Apollo at Delphi (*Bell. Civ.* 5. 120–97). The
grotesque and gloomy background of this episode is well known.[45]
What concerns us here are those elements in Phemonoe's presentation
which suggest some bold lines of inquiry appropriate for a mortal,
suffering 'muse'. Vividly reminding us of the joyful and young archaic
Muses, Phemonoe wanders at will around the lush landscape surrounding the temple, free from worries,[46] until she is snatched away by
Apollo's priest and ushered into the temple in order to pronounce the
oracle. As in the case of the Sibyl, the struggle between Apollo and his
former protégée is violent and inexorable. Of course, the Imperial style
prevails here and turns the tersely described suffering of the Sibyl into
excessively hideous images of Phemonoe's struggle. Hardly surprisingly
in an epic which has banned gods from its world-view, Phemonoe's
character is here even more stubbornly human, her struggle with Apollo
still more agonizing. And the possibility of a voice of her own surfaces
again, as it did fleetingly in the text of the *Aeneid*. Dreading the invasion
of Apollo, Phemonoe feigns fictitious words in her tranquil breast (*sub
pectore ficta quieto verba refert*, 149–50). It is not long before Appius per-
ceives the ruse and seething with anger bursts into new fits of rage.
Several scenes of violence ensue in the outrageous Lucanian way. And
his furious exhortation reads like this:

> et nobis meritas dabis, inpia, poenas
> et superis, quos fingis,' ait 'nisi mergeris antris
> deque orbis trepidi tanto consulta tumultu
> desinis ipsa loqui.
>
> (*Bell Civ.* 5. 158–61)

---

[45] See e.g. Masters (1992).

[46] *curisque vacan*[s] (5. 126): so very much like the Hesiodic Muses—we need only think of
their ἀκηδέα θυμόν (*Theog.* 61) here.

Wicked woman, to me and to the gods you feign, you will pay the penalty which you deserve unless you plunge into the cave and cease to speak in your own words when consulted about the turmoil so immense of the anxious world.

In the end, the terrified virgin succumbs to her frightening role and receives the power of Apollo. Her former mind is driven out leaving her possessed and exhausted. And yet, in the description of her possession we keep finding references to the potential of her own speech: *accipit et frenos, nec tantum prodere vati | quantum scire licet* (5. 176–7), 'the prophetess submits to the bridle too, and she is not allowed to tell as much as she is allowed to know'. And as soon as her prophecy is concluded the poet adds: *cetera suppressit fauces obstruxit Apollo* (197), 'The rest Apollo stifled and he blocked her throat'.

What is then 'that remainder', Phemonoe's own fictitious words, that Apollo, his priest, and Appius go to such pains to stifle and repress? Phemonoe resisted prophetic enlightenment because she knew that it would condemn her to unbearable exhaustion. But is it also possible that she was resisting the bridling of her own imagination (female imagination?), resisting the men telling her what to say, because their stories would not necessarily be her stories as well? Of course, quite apart from gender preoccupations, the struggle between Apollo and his prophetess-Muse could also thematize the antagonism on a different level: if divine knowledge is no longer an adequate category for mortals (and we know it certainly wasn't for Lucan), is the struggle of Phemonoe (and of the Virgilian Sibyl?) a struggle to break free from the divine and to confine its power? Throughout this introduction we have been working on the hypothesis that inspiration comes both from within and from without.[47] Might it be that any schism between Apollo and his Muses is a symbolic enactment of the rift between the outside (i.e. the gods' insufficient injunctions and knowledge) and the inside (i.e. the poets' own conceptions of poetry-making and the world)? As the rift went progressively deeper, did something get lost in Rome—not necessarily religious faith as such, but a simple idea of what it is to know something securely, now that the world was increasingly dominated by already existing, already told stories, from a past that was lost and gone?

[47] For more on that see esp. Fowler and Sharrock in this volume.

III. CONTEMPORARY FIXATIONS: THE MUSE AS THE PARADIGM OF VULNERABLE STRENGTH

Greek imprecisions followed by Roman indecisions and a certain critical disengagement or perhaps a certain critical vagueness vis-à-vis the daughters of Mnemosyne seem to constitute the theme of the Muses' life in literature. The present volume steps in at the intersection of all these indeterminate and undecided paths. Especially intrigued by the Muses' shapeless collectivity—a lot hardly commensurable with their centrality in the life of mind and creation—it seeks to redeem their shape in other forms, closer or more distant incarnations of the familiar, but ever so elusive, primal figure. As we shall show, it is this very shapeless collectivity which lends the Muses' existence to appropriation, as dearth of features prompts and provokes the imagination of poets and critics to fill in the gaps, and our book rises to the challenge.

Having absorbed the tensions in the critical writing on the Muses and inspiration, our project revisits the 'ever fading metaphor' and would like to follow up possibilities intimated by the Muses themselves and the critical discourse about them. In the post-archaic secular world of reason and debate, that Athena so eloquently described for us and the Athenians in the *Eumenides*, the Muses—together with the other gods of the older generation—change and adapt to the new values, just as the poet finds the courage to assert himself and sign his name. It is this ever-increasing poetic self-awareness that transforms the well-established Goddesses into metaphors of the poet's disquiet, incarnations of a 'purely intellectual principle'.[48] But if the stately daughters of Mnemosyne have given way to figurative statements about the creative process, then one has to be prepared to accept the surprises and twists that these metaphors carry with them: melting leads to rebirth and salvages from oblivion. If the Muses are (at least partly) figments of the poets' own mundane imagination, then inspiration must be something emanating from inside as well as outside. As we saw, the search is then on for images that test and challenge the archetypal representations, images that stem from and capture the beliefs and preoccupations of different ages, genres, and poets. Stripped of their divine privileges, the new purveyors of knowledge have to fight for respect, as Ovid's diffident Muses vividly suggested. But it is exactly this fight, at times agonizing,

[48] As Curtius (1953) 229 would have it, in a classic formulation which effectively stopped critics really getting into the topic of the 'Muses' for decades.

that can divert them from the barren path of abstraction. Disrespect averts schematization and the doubted Muses' biography no longer looks like Commager's doomed history of a fading metaphor. And, additionally, when imagination and creativity that emanate from the 'inside' start to distinguish themselves from imagination and creativity derived from 'outside', the new configurations of the Muse must gain personality—exactly what the archaic Muses lacked for all their carefree lives—and along with personality, the full range of desires, sorrows, and 'a voice of their own', as the story of the Sibyl hinted and as Phemonoe passionately declared.

The fissures on the figures of the Muses show up in this book from the very beginning. Hesiod's Muses already 'brace themselves up' to face their flagging Ovidian counterparts. The claim I am going to make is that the link between all the different stories told in this volume on the Muses and inspiration is to be found in incredulity and disbelief. If this seems a pretty tenuous link for some, let me propose that tenuous guidance is an appropriate feature for a book that seeks to dissociate inspiration from neat description, and especially the peaceful and blissful Hesiodic imagery of the youthful and amiable Muses. Protagonists—or victims—in a delicate game of cultural self-exploration and expression, the Muses (or muses) of this book are manipulated, transformed, simply employed, jeered at, coveted, even abused or effaced, but they also talk, protest, advocate or resist their fate and explore their own powers of persuasion. An apprentice to contemporary scholarship, this book takes over after assurance has given way to dubiety and the Muses have been deprived of their protective and infallible sacral insignia. Inspiration is thus discussed not in its traditional cult environment, but as a discursive and time-bound trope for an ancient culture at given points to talk about power, authority, desire, knowledge, identity, gender, genres of writing, the past, the future. Perhaps even more importantly, inspiration here serves as a trope to talk about the manifold struggle and tough negotiations that tie all these disparate elements together and place them in tune with the surrounding society.

Seeking to surprise and open to surprises, this book looks beyond the nine canonical Muses in order to renew our perceptions of the intricate games played in the name of inspiration: other major or lesser divinities, common people, emperors, mistresses, patrons, the community, the tradition step in across the different chapters. It is our belief that there is good reason to assemble these suggestions: thoughts hinted at one point are voiced explicitly at another; suspicions intimated in one chapter are openly acknowledged or scotched in another; and concerns apparently settled in one essay are yet again revisited and undermined in another. And so it is in this somewhat insidious and even regressive manner that our exploration may perhaps unsettle the generally uncontroversial tenor of the Muses' literary image and shake some (occasionally complacent) responses to the workings of ancient Greek and Roman inspiration. Interestingly, the benign, uncontested, demure, and secure aspects of inspiration regularly revisit the subversive treatments in the various chapters: as we saw at the very beginning of this introduction, Hesiod's Muses may happily dance away at night, but they always come back to their Olympian palace. In spite of fissures, the Muses will always represent a power, a faith. And with all its focus on controversy and contention, this book is still interested in belief and conviction; but it is fixated with their precarious validity and vulnerable strength, in an inevitably postmodern way.[49]

It is therefore consistent with the concerns of this project, as delineated in the previous pages, that there is no chapter exclusively devoted to the archaic Muses to start off the volume; the archetypal imagery is already undermined from the inception of this book which starts with two discussions of the Platonic Muses, plunging straight into a dynamics of antagonism, as the Greek philosopher attempts to harness the powerful image of the nine graceful daughters of Mnemosyne for his own purposes. Penny Murray discusses Plato's efforts to enlist a seemingly irrelevant symbol, the Muse of poetry, into his propaganda for the newly emerging discourse of philosophy. Arguing for Plato's desire to build bridges with the archaic Muses clearly jars with his reputation as the philosopher who notoriously banished poetry from his ideal state. Murray's paper cuts through these sharp dichotomies. However invulnerable to poetry and its Muses, Plato's philosophy is still the highest form of *mousike*, another form of Muse-related activity. Thus, distrustful of but also charmed by the Muses, Plato draws on those aspects of early Greek literature and mythology which speak for the Muses' links with ethical matters and wisdom and thus concocts another

---

[49] I am most grateful to Richard Alston, John Henderson, Alessandro Schiesaro, and Alison Sharrock, who read and very helpfully criticized earlier drafts. Also, a version of this Introduction was presented at a colloquium on 'Representations of the Sacral in Latin Literature' held at Royal Holloway London in May 1999 and I would like to thank all those present there for comments conducive to further thought.

version of a Muse which can inspire his intellectual concerns and deservedly oversee philosophy.

Plato's battles with his sources of inspiration take a different turn in the chapter of Adriana Cavarero, which is designed as a counterfoil to the previous one. According to Cavarero, Plato's hostility towards the archaic Muse is accounted for as competition between himself and Homer, a contest between the philosophical eye of the mind and the musical voice of the epic performance. The Homeric Muse represents the original phonetic source in which the story recounted and the musicality of the voice are inseparable, enchanting and entrapping the audience in this chain of *theia dynamis*. As Cavarero suggests, Plato envies this Muse, and, in spite of his condemnation of poetic mimesis, he imitates the destructive effect of epic songs. This can be traced in the myth of the cave: by transporting the epic practice of phonetic order into a practice of visual order, Plato's contemplative mind enchains the prisoners / spectators in his theatre of visual tricks. Plato's antagonistic obsession with the Homeric Muse includes other divine singers: the Sirens and the cicadas, seductive, dangerous, and irresistible female figures in whose practice the vocal-acoustic register is supreme. They represent the original—and maternal—realm of rhythmic sounds that cannot be reduced to the binary economy of the patriarchal canon. According to Cavarero, unlike Plato, Homer is still closer to this realm, and this is a major explanation for Plato's notorious envy of the Homeric Muses, but also of Homer as well.

As time moves on, incarnations of the Muse become more unpredictable. Ismene Lada-Richards traces and recuperates a significantly different Muse in the multiple political and ritual world of Greek tragedy. As she shows, the emergence of dramatic poetry did not render the functions of the archaic Muse(s) obsolete. Within the context of fifth-century Athenian performances 'the Muse's presence can still be intensely felt, for Drama as a genre has reinscribed and reamalgamated important attributes traditionally attached to her. Much less of a "real life" entity than her archaic predecessor, the classical Muse operates now on the level of metaphor and figurative discourse.' To put it in another way, reshaped by the performative frame of fifth-century Athenian culture, the notion of 'inspired creativity' that the archaic Muses represent becomes an *internal* dimension of Greek drama. A compelling paradox, and one at the heart of this book, is shaping up: as well as being figurative, and as such more of an abstract entity, this Muse, intricately involved in the progress of the drama as she is, also learns to feel, and is directly affected by the proceedings. Figurative configurations instil life into a conventional symbol and the time when intradiegetic characters will take up the role of the Muse is now rapidly approaching.

However distinct in its generic focus, the following chapter is also a direct response to the challenges bequeathed by the classical Muse to Hellenistic times, as depicted in Lada-Richards's chapter. Weeding through the multiple authorial surrogates in Apollonius Rhodius' Book 3 of the *Argonautica*, my chapter turns the spotlight on Medea as the faltering and doubted, but also enduring, human muse. This is the self-conscious and self-reflexive territory of Hellenistic epic, and therefore many protagonists attempt to write their versions of the story in Book 3—amongst them Medea herself. Medea the muse, though, is a different metaphor of creativity, and I follow her closely as a trope that talks about the struggles, entrappings, and regressions of inspiration in an increasingly incredulous world. Toil and labour are paramount, in a properly Hellenistic fashion, and Medea as a paradigm of the human muse faces many struggles, as a muse but also as a woman, in a narration that ties gender and inspiration explicitly and intricately together.

Appropriately situated towards the centre of the volume, and looking both backwards to the archaic oral epic and forwards to epics produced in a culture of writing, Andrew Laird emphasizes the remarkable communality between presentations of the Muses in the epic tradition as a whole. As oral and written tensions begin to be amalgamated in the chapter, a reliable figure of the epic Muse begins to emerge through the continuities, and this figure becomes even more palpable since Laird focuses extensively on the poets' invocations of the Muses as a locus par excellence where the transgeneric community of epic Muses is built: the Muse is literally called upon to remind us of her existence as well as call attention to the discourse and performance of poetry, oral or written. Once again, palpability also brings contention when the Muses as addressees lend themselves to debates and discourses on power and ideology, informed by modern critical thought such as the Bakhtinian concept of the 'superaddressee'.

Opening up the more explicitly Roman section of the book, Don Fowler has more specifically gendered preoccupations related to the workings of inspiration in Latin poetry. Exploring a wide range of texts, he finds the Roman poet engaged in a twofold relation to his Muse and inspiration. According to this scheme, the inspired mind has access to a powerful creative force which drives his poetry and configures his activity as masculine—coming from 'within'. And yet, the inspired poet also appears regularly overcome by external forces of inspiration (his Muse in a wide range of metaphorical representations) and therefore loses manly autarky in the process of writing, succumbing to inspiration that comes from 'outside' and penetrates him. Through its wide-ranging scope, Fowler's chapter establishes concerns that will subsequently be picked up again by Ancona and Sharrock, who also discuss the close-knit interweavings of gender and genre under the tag of inspiration.

Issues of gender but also of poetic tradition and reception mingle in the exploration of Horace's tussles with inspiration in the following chapter. The exemplum chosen by Ronnie Ancona is *Odes* 1. 22 and the often conflicting muses discussed are Sappho, Catullus, and Lalage. Ancona argues that Horace wants both to belong to the Sapphic/ Catullan tradition of the love lyric and at the same time, to revise and resist it. His engagement with his muse(s), therefore, raises issues of the self, boundaries and their transgression, and desire. Building her argument around the word *integer* (untouched), Ancona seeks to offer an understanding of the speaker's desire to exert a kind of masculine control over the self in the love relation. However, the return to Sappho (in *dulce loquentem*) and Lalage's connection with speech suggest that there is a 'voice' in the 'object position' that may destabilize the 'integrity' of the speaker.

Picking up the strand followed in my exploration of Medea the muse, Micaela Janan also puts under the spotlight an 'alternative' human muse, whose unconventional character is even more emphasized: Janan's muse, perhaps anti-muse, is the bawd Acanthis, as portrayed in Propertius 4. 5, deeply and irrationally hated by the narrator. Unresolved gender battles with inspiration are here looked at through an elaborately developed psychoanalytical scheme, which brings in another distinctive strand to the overall experimentation of the volume. According to Janan, Acanthis has an unusual revelation to offer the poet: she is to show him the inadequacy of the cultural system to adequately represent Woman. In this poem, the extremes of Woman's representation (as beloved or hated, beautiful or ugly, innocent or intriguing) prove to be surprisingly interchangeable, because each extreme rests equally on fantasy. Unsurprisingly for the disturbing character of the muse's knowledge, the narrator of the poem seeks to smother this subversive voice.

However, the uncontrollable potential of a non-conformist muse is fully demonstrated.

Tensions between gender and genre, the poet and the Muse, take an interesting turn in the following chapter on Ovid's *Metamorphoses*, where Alison Sharrock explores inspiration as a relationship—full of tensions and creative struggle—between poet and Muse, as well as between individual poem and poetic tradition. Sharrock argues that Ovid invokes the power of the Muse to give himself epic stature, but at the same time constantly regresses and denies the Muse her easy position as the fountain of all knowledge and poetic wisdom. The relationship between poet and Muse is seen in terms of desire, for which the story of Hermaphroditus and Salmacis is taken to be programmatic. The loss of manly autarky which Hermaphroditus suffers through the desire of Salmacis is mapped onto the potential loss of manly control over speech which the epic poet risks in his engagement with the Muses and the power of epic poetry. At the same time, however, Sharrock argues that Ovid as an epic poet tries to stamp his control over his subject-matter and this struggle is the fount of Ovid's (epic) poetry.

The representation of the ancient Muse takes one more startling turn in Gianpiero Rosati's chapter, which examines Statius' poetry and suggests that for this poet the discourse about his dependence on the Muse, and about inspiration in general, is inextricably tied into the discourse about the relationship with political power: a relationship of conflict, between the (creative) freedom of the poet and the control imposed on him by the political authorities, which press him to celebrate the achievements of Domitian. Statius emancipates himself from the poet's divine sources, from the external authority which traditionally validated his work, and yet he revives and emphasizes the inspirational function of a supernatural agent, who nevertheless eludes his control. But it is exactly this ploy of the uncontrollable Muse that provides him with a useful screen to protect himself against the pressures of power and to defer *sine die* a more direct political involvement.

Deliberately placed last, the dance of Copa, a nugget from the Virgiliana, closes down (perhaps opens up?) this ballet around the Muse and inspiration in Graeco-Roman literature. Women, poetic traditions and aspirations, the streets and markets of Rome all come alive in the guidance of the Virgilian Copa, which John Henderson chose to focus on, his own version of the alternative muse in Augustan poetry, his 'motel' muse as he prefers to call it. Spurning conventions and

established topoi, at ease in the seething streets and inns of the metro-
polis, Copa dances in the rhythm of verses and music, unashamedly
advertising her urbanity and her poetic belatedness, and celebrating the
endless possibilities and freedom of poetry. A paradigm of the alternative muse, Copa cannot (and should not) be pinned down, and neither
should any critical description of her. So, this somewhat swirling dervish
of a chapter stands out in this volume, just as its subject-matter also does,
an intimation of the unlimited paths inspiration can be found in, and as
such an indispensable component of a book that seeks to shake some
mainstream thoughts and perceptions on the nine ever elusive, graceful
daugthers of Zeus and Mnemosyne.

2

Plato's Muses:
The Goddesses that Endure

Penelope Murray

Socrates, not known for his devotion to the Muses, begins to write poetry when he is in prison awaiting execution. In the *Phaedo* (60dff.) he tells his friends of a recurrent dream he has had during his life which urges him to compose and practise music (60e6–7). He had always thought that the dream was encouraging him to do precisely what he had spent his life doing, that is 'making music', on the grounds that 'philosophy is the greatest music'. But now as he awaits death he wonders if after all the dream might be urging him to make music in the popular sense (61a7). So he first of all composes a poem to Apollo whose festival it is, and then reflects that a poet, if he is to be worthy of the name, ought to compose *mythoi* ('myths' or 'fictions') and not *logoi* ('true accounts'). But he himself is not *mythologikos* ('good at inventing stories' or 'fictions'), so he avails himself of some of Aesop's fables which he knows off by heart and are ready to hand, and turns these into poetry, that is, by putting them into verse.[1] To make music in the

---

[1] Rowe (1993) ad loc. points out that the verb ἐντείνω at 60d1 (περὶ γάρ τοι τῶν ποιημάτων ὧν πεποίηκας ἐντείνας τοὺς τοῦ Αἰσώπου λόγους does not necessarily imply that Socrates set Aesop's tales to music. What he 'made' (*poiein*) were *poemata*, which suggests composition in verse. Cf. *Symp.* 205c, where Diotima points out that although the terms ποίησις and ποιητής apply to creation in general, and could be used of a wide variety of crafts, they are in fact reserved for the particular field concerned with music and verse (τὴν μουσικὴν καὶ τὰ μέτρα). Aesop's *logoi* were presumably in prose. Socrates may have set them to music as well as putting them into verse, but that is not made explicit: the emphasis in this passage is primarily on poetic rather than musical composition. Cf. Pl. *Hipparch.* 228d ἐντείνας εἰς ἐλεγεῖον, and contrast Pl. *Protag.* 326b ποιήματα . . . εἰς τὰ κιθαρίσματα ἐντείναντες. Plutarch (*Mor.* 16c) confirms the above interpretation, and brings out well the implications of the contrast between μῦθοι and λόγοι in this passage: 'in poetry a convincing fiction (ψεῦδος) produces admiration and satisfaction more than any device of metre or diction deficient in plot and story. This is why

popular sense thus means primarily to compose poetry, and poetry is characterized by two things: metrical form and 'mythical' or 'fictional' subject-matter. Any claims to inspiration, knowledge, or truth that poets might make are effectively debunked by Socrates' casual remarks, and the overall effect of his words is certainly to devalue the 'popular music' of poetry.[2] Furthermore, this Socrates, who claims not to be a myth-maker, nevertheless later declares himself ready to *mythologein* ('tell a story') about what awaits us after death (61e2, cf. 70b6), and brings the dialogue to a close with an extended myth about the other world (107c), which rivals, or rather replaces, the traditional myths of the poets. *Mythoi* may be the stuff of poetry, and therefore an essential part of *mousike*, but they also have their place in Plato's vision of philosophy.

Mousike is a slippery term, especially in Plato's vocabulary. Sometimes it refers to something like music in our sense, that is, melody, rhythm, harmony, etc., as when Socrates says to Glaucon (*Rep.* 398e) 'Which are the mournful *harmoniai*? Tell me: you know about music' (σὺ γὰρ μουσικός). But often it is much broader in its application, and includes all the arts over which the Muses preside—poetry, music, song, dance, and potentially any other activity which could be ascribed to the Muses' sphere of influence. Greek education traditionally consisted of *mousike* for the soul, and *gymnastike* for the body (see e.g. *Rep.* 376e2–4), hence *mousike* can mean something like 'culture' or 'education', and a generally cultivated person can be described as *mousikos*. But what it means to be a truly 'musical' person is a far from simple issue.

The association between philosophy and the province of the Muses is one that recurs in one form or another in several of Plato's dialogues. Thus amongst the fanciful etymologies of the *Cratylus* (406a) we find that 'the Muses and music in general are named, apparently, from μῶσθαι, that is searching and philosophy' (τῆς ζητήσεώς τε καὶ φιλοσοφίας).[3] In the *Republic*, when asked if the ideal state can ever be

Socrates, the life-long striver for truth, found himself, when he set about composing poetry in obedience to a dream, no very convincing or gifted maker of lies (οὐ πιθανὸς ἦν οὐδ' εὐφυὴς ψευδῶν δημιουργός); he therefore put Aesop's fables into verse, on the principle that where there is no fiction there is no poetry (τοὺς δ'Αἰσώπου μύθους ἔπεσιν ἐνήρμοζεν ὡς ποίησιν οὐκ οὖσαν ἧι ψεῦδος μὴ πρόσεστι)' (tr. Russell (1972) 510). For other interpretations of the *Phaedo* passage see e.g. La Fontaine (1966) 27–8; Nietzsche (1993) 70–1. I am grateful to Andrew . Benjamin for these references.

[2] See e.g. Halliwell (1984) 58; Rowe (1993) ad loc., and on the 'musical' imagery of the *Phaedo* in general, Bacon (1990) 152–3. On Plato's use of myth see Murray (1999).

[3] For the persistence of this etymology see Trimpi (1983) 3, who cites Clem. Al. *Against the Pagans* 31; Cassiodorus, *Institutiones* 2. 5; Isidore, *Etymologiae* 3. 15. 1.

realized, Socrates replies that it will only come into existence when the Muse of philosophy takes charge of the city (499d4). Similarly the long process of degeneration will begin when men neglect 'the true Muse and her companions, reason and philosophy' (548b8). The implication, of course, is that any other sort of Muse is inferior to the Muse of philosophy. Indeed in the *Republic* the Muse of poetry, the 'sweetened Muse', as Plato calls it, the Muse that is sweetened or seasoned with metre, rhythm, and melody, is to be resisted at all costs, for if you allow this Muse into your city, pleasure and pain will rule rather than custom and rational principle (607a5–8). This distinction between two types of Muse corresponds to the two types of music of the *Phaedo*, though in the *Phaedo* there is no mention of the Muses as such: at this crucial juncture in Socrates' life it is not the Muses who instruct him what to do, but the commanding figure of their leader, Apollo. Throughout the dialogue Socrates is presented as the servant of Apollo,[4] and *mousike* is portrayed as his province rather than that of the Muses. Nevertheless the contrast that is implied in the *Republic* between the Muse of philosophy and the Muse of poetry is obviously analogous to the *Phaedo*'s distinction between the music of philosophy and the ordinary music of poetry.[5]

A distinction between a higher and a lower Muse is made in the *Symposium* by Eryximachus, the rather pedantic and tedious doctor (187d–e), who contrasts the heavenly Muse Urania with the more vulgar Muse Polymnia, who is particularly associated with pleasure. As Eryximachus explains (187d–e), there are two types of love: the noble heavenly kind associated with virtuous men and with the heavenly Muse Urania; and the vulgar or common love, associated with Polymnia. As Dover explains (1980: 109), the love or eros referred to here is the desire for a given kind of music or poetry which exists in the hearer; once again we have a contrast between a lower and a higher kind of Muse or music. And it is perhaps not fanciful to see an allusion to the heavenly music of Urania in Alcibiades' drunken eulogy of Socrates at

---

[4] See e.g. 60d2, 61b2, 85b, and Bacon (1990) 150–8 on the allusions to Apollo in the dialogue. In general on Plato and Apollo see Schefer (1996).

[5] The connections between philosophy, music, and the Muses in Plato's work have been discussed by e.g. Flashar (1958) 131–2; Dodds (1959) 260; Dalfen (1974) 287–304; Nightingale (1995) 79–85. For further references see e.g. *Theaet.* 175e–176a; *Phlb.* 67b; *Soph.* 259e2; *Laws* 666d with Saunders (1972) 9–10; 689d6; 967e2 with Stalley (1983) 134–5. At *Laches* 188d the μουσικὸς ἀνήρ is one who tunes his life so that words and actions match, in contrast with one who has merely tuned his mode to a lyre. And similarly at *Rep.* 591c–d the intelligent man is one who will attune his body to match the harmony of his mind and character. On the meaning of *mousike* in Athenian culture see also Lada-Richards in this volume.

the end of the dialogue, when he likens the effect that Socrates has on
him to that of supernatural music on its hearers (215a–c7):

ὁμοιότατον εἶναι τοῖς σιληνοῖς τούτοις τοῖς ἐν τοῖς ἑρμογλυφείοις καθημένοις,
οὕστινας ἐργάζονται οἱ δημιουργοὶ σύριγγας ἢ αὐλοὺς ἔχοντας, οἳ διχάδε
διοιχθέντες φαίνονται ἔνδοθεν ἀγάλματα ἔχοντες θεῶν. καὶ φημὶ αὖ ἐοικέναι
αὐτὸν τῷ σατύρῳ τῷ Μαρσύᾳ. ὅτι μὲν οὖν τό γε εἶδος ὅμοιος εἶ τούτοις, ὦ
Σώκρατες, οὐδ' αὐτὸς ἄν που ἀμφισβητήσαις . . . ἀλλ' οὐκ αὐλητής; πολύ γε
θαυμασιώτερος ἐκείνου. ὁ μέν γε δι' ὀργάνων ἐκήλει τοὺς ἀνθρώπους τῇ ἀπὸ
τοῦ στόματος δυνάμει, καὶ ἔτι νυνὶ ὃς ἂν τὰ ἐκείνου αὐλῇ . . . τὰ οὖν ἐκείνου
ἐάντε ἀγαθὸς αὐλητὴς αὐλῇ ἐάντε φαύλη αὐλητρίς, μόνα κατέχεσθαι ποιεῖ καὶ
δηλοῖ τοὺς τῶν θεῶν τε καὶ τελετῶν δεομένους διὰ τὸ θεῖα εἶναι. σὺ δ' ἐκείνου
τοσοῦτον μόνον διαφέρεις, ὅτι ἄνευ ὀργάνων ψιλοῖς λόγοις ταὐτὸν τοῦτο
ποιεῖς.

[Socrates, says Alcibiades,] bears a strong resemblance to those figures of Silenus
in statuaries' shops, represented holding pipes or *auloi*; they are hollow inside,
and when they are taken apart you see that they contain little figures of gods.
He's also like Marsyas the satyr. You can't deny yourself, Socrates, that you have
a striking physical likeness to both of these . . . But you don't play the *aulos*,
you'll say. No indeed, the performance you give is far more remarkable.
Marsyas needed an instrument in order to charm men by the power which pro-
ceeded out of his mouth, a power which is still exercised by those who perform
his melodies . . . his productions alone, executed by a skilled male performer or
by a wretched flute-girl, are capable, by reason of their divine origin, of throw-
ing men into a trance. But you, Socrates, are so far superior to Marsyas that you
produce the same effect by mere words without any instrument.[6]

This image of Socrates as satyr plays on the contrast between inner
and outer: Silenus, the father of the satyrs and companion and educator
of Dionysus, is a grotesque figure with bulging eyes, protruding lips,
and bald head, but nevertheless the traditional repository of wisdom—
open him up and you find little gods inside. The historical Socrates,
according to the ancient sources, is said to have been a strikingly
unattractive man, and his detractors no doubt made fun of him because
of his physical resemblance to a satyr; his admirers, on the other hand,
seem to have made good use of his satyr-like image, as Paul Zanker
(1995) has suggested. Socrates as Silenus embodies the notion that true

---

[6] Translation by W. Hamilton, Penguin (1951) 100–1, with minor adaptations. Cf. *Protag.*
347c–348a for the view that well-bred, educated people do not need to hire flute-girls for their
symposia because they can rely on their own conversation for entertainment. On the
significance of the *aulos* in Athens see Wilson (1999), and esp. pp. 89–92 on the *Symposium*
passage.

philosophy recognizes the seemingness of the external world and leads instead to the perception of actual being. As Zanker puts it (39), 'Socrates' body may be seen as an exemplar of these precepts, for the seemingly ugly form conceals the most perfect soul.' But what we also have here is the figure of Socrates as musician: he's not just like Silenus, he's like Silenus holding pipes or *auloi*; Socrates' music is the music of philosophy, a point that is explicitly made in the extended comparison with Marsyas. He's like Marsyas, *except* that Marsyas needed an instrument, an *aulos*, to charm and bewitch his listeners (215c1–2), whereas Socrates produces the same effect by words alone (215c7). Escaping from Socrates' influence, Alcibiades says, is like trying to escape from the Sirens (216a7)—the only way to do it is to stop up your ears, like Odysseus' men, and run. The magical powers of music are here very obviously appropriated by the philosophical discourse of Socrates.[7]

This brings me to the Sirens, whom we meet again in the *Phaedrus*, probably the most poetic of Plato's dialogues and certainly the most extended demonstration of philosophy as a muse-loving activity.[8] At the transitional point in the dialogue, when we move from the theme of love to that of rhetoric, Socrates draws attention to the cicadas, who are singing above their heads in the heat in their usual manner (259a ff.). He and Phaedrus should beware, he says, of nodding off under the cicadas' spell like most people do in the heat of the day, for the cicadas would simply laugh at them and regard them as no better than slaves having their midday sleep around the spring, like sheep. But if the cicadas see them conversing and resisting their spell, sailing past them unbewitched by their Siren song, they may perhaps respect them and give them that gift which they have from the gods to bestow on men. When Phaedrus asks what that gift is, Socrates replies that a man who loves the Muses certainly ought to know about such things, and then proceeds to tell the cicadas' story:

The story is that these cicadas were once men, belonging to a time before the Muses were born, and that with the birth of the Muses and the appearance of song some of the men of that age were so unhinged by pleasure that in their singing they neglected to eat and drink, and actually died before they realized what was happening to them; from them the race of cicadas was afterwards born, to whom the Muses granted this privilege, that from their birth they have no need of sustenance, but immediately sing, without food or drink, until they

---

[7] See further Belfiore (1980); Rutherford (1995) 202–3.
[8] On this theme see Nussbaum (1982).

die, and after that go and report to the Muses how each of them is honoured here and by whom. To Terpsichore they report those who have honoured her in the choral dance, and thus win her favour for them; to Erato, those who have honoured her in the affairs of love; and to the other Muses similarly, according to the form of honour belonging to each; but to Calliope, the eldest, and to Ourania who comes after her, they announce those who spend their time in philosophy and honour the music which belongs to them—who most of all the Muses have as their sphere both the heavens and talk (*logoi*) both divine and human, and whose utterances are the most beautiful. So there are many reasons why we should say something (*legein*), and not sleep in the mid-day heat.

(259b5–d8) (10)

The dangers of an indiscriminate love of the Muses are clearly implied in this myth. The cicadas are aligned with both Sirens and Muses: if Socrates and Phaedrus are not careful, the effect of the cicadas could be like that of the Sirens, who bewitch men into forgetfulness, just like the cicadas themselves who, when they were still men, actually died before they realized what was happening to them, so bewitched were they by the pleasures of song that were born with the Muses.[9] In the *Odyssey*, Circe warns Odysseus about the Sirens' deadly powers:

> ὅς τις ἀϊδρείη πελάσῃ καὶ φθόγγον ἀκούσῃ
> Σειρήνων, τῷ δ’ οὔ τι γυνὴ καὶ νήπια τέκνα
> οἴκαδε νοστήσαντι παρίσταται οὐδὲ γάνυνται,
> ἀλλά τε Σειρῆνες λιγυρῇ θέλγουσιν ἀοιδῇ,
> ἥμεναι ἐν λειμῶνι. πολὺς δ’ ἀμφ’ ὀστεόφιν θὶς
> ἀνδρῶν πυθομένων, περὶ δὲ ῥινοὶ μινύθουσι.   (12. 41–6)

Whoever draws near to them unawares and hears the Sirens' voice, he never-more returns, that his wife and little children may stand at his side rejoicing, but the Sirens beguile him with their clear-toned song, as they sit in a meadow, and about them is a great heap of bones of mouldering men, and round the bones the skin is shrivelling.'[10]

In Plato's myth what happens to men bewitched by song is that they shrivel up and turn into cicadas whose Siren song threatens to produce the same effect on their hearers as the Muses produced on them. The gifts of the Muses are thus presented in a decidedly ambiguous light, and

[9] For more on the cicadas' story, cf. also Cavarero in this volume.

[10] Translation adapted from the Loeb edition by A. T. Murray, 1919. Heubeck (1989) notes ad loc. that 'what exactly happens to a man entranced by the Sirens is a matter for conjecture. He is probably distracted from steering his course, and shipwrecked; the bodies are later washed up on shore.' But he also gives a useful summary of theories on the origin and nature of the Sirens, with bibliography.

need to be used with caution, for, as Ferrari has pointed out,[11] 'none show better than cicadas the dangers of succumbing to the seductive pleasures of song . . . they indulge indiscriminately in the gifts of the Muses, overwhelmed by pleasure. They become messengers, mere vehicles for conveying to all the Muses how others, but certainly not cicadas themselves, discriminate between them in their devotion.'

Traditionally, of course, Muses and Sirens have much in common: like the Muses who know all things past, present, and future (Hom. *Il.* 2. 485; Hes. *Theog.* 32 and 38), the Sirens too know everything that comes to pass on the fruitful earth (*Od.* 12. 189–91), and both sets of divinities delight their listeners with the sweetness of their voices (Muses: Hes. *Theog.* 39–40; Sirens: Hom. *Od.* 12. 187; and on the association of song with female figures see Cavarero in this volume). But there are some significant differences. For example, Charles Segal[12] has argued that the Sirens, by luring men to their deaths on their remote island, far away from human habitation, are responsible for destroying heroic *kleos* instead of preserving it; in this respect the Sirens can be seen as antitypes of the Muses, whose function is the opposite of the daughters of Mnemosyne and the poets they inspire. More recently Lillian Doherty (1995) has drawn attention to other important differences in the way that the two groups of females are envisaged, which she summarizes thus:

The choir of the Muses in the *Theogony*, though described as lovely and desirable, have no husbands or lovers; they seem to be cast in the mold of the maiden chorus and are closely linked to their father's house (*Theogony* 36–74). The Muses invoked in both the *Iliad* and the *Odyssey* are virtually sexless. By contrast, the Sirens have a decidedly ambiguous sexual status. Like Kalypso, they occupy a flowery meadow (5. 72; 12. 159), a setting connected elsewhere in archaic poetry with sexual encounters. Their song is said to delight (*terpein*, 12. 189) and to charm (*thelgein*, 12. 44) an exclusively male audience of sailors, who are thus prevented, according to Kirke, from returning to their wives and

---

[11] (1987) 28, and see his discussion, 'What the cicadas sang', pp. 25–34. Like all Plato's myths this story is replete with allusions to earlier Greek poetry. Apart from the obvious references to the *Odyssey* and Hesiod's *Theogony*, Plato's picture of the cicadas perhaps recalls Homer's description of the old men of Troy sitting at the Scaean gates at *Iliad* 3. 150–2: 'Because of old age they no longer took part in battle, but they were good speakers, like cicadas, who sit on a tree in a wood and pour forth their lily-like voice'. Cf. also Kirk (1985) ad loc., who suggests that there may be 'an element of humour in the comparison; the cicadas certainly represent the ceaselessness of these old men's talk'. The cicada later became a proverb for garrulity, LSJ s.v. τέττιξ.

[12] (1983). See also Pollard (1965) 137–45; Gresseth (1970); Stehle (1997) 95–9, and for further bibliography, Doherty (1995).

children (12. 41–43). Whereas *terpein* and *thelgein* are commonly used of the pleasure given by poetry, they are also associated with sexual pleasure and help to link the Sirens with other seductive females in the *Odyssey*, including Kirke herself. . . Thus the virginal or sexless Muses may be contrasted with the seductive Sirens. Moreover, like proper virgins, the Muses are clearly identified as daughters of Zeus, whereas the Homeric Sirens are given no lineage. The Muses perform not only on the peaks of Helicon but in the halls of Zeus on Olympos; the Sirens, on their far-flung island, do not associate with the Olympian in any way. Unlike the Muses, whose narrative authority derives from Zeus, the Sirens appeal to no authority but their own knowledge . . . [the Sirens are thus] unauthorised Muses, seductive rather than dependent females who command the language of poetry for their own inscrutable purposes.   (pp. 84–5)

This distinction which Doherty makes is, I think, an important one. For the Muses, unlike the Sirens, are not generally represented as menacingly seductive or threatening figures in early Greek poetry, though, in common with all Greek divinities, they can be dangerous when provoked. We see this in the story of their encounter with the Thracian bard Thamyris, first described at *Iliad* 2. 594–600, where we are told that they met him as he was travelling through lonely places and stopped his singing, 'For he boasted that he would beat the Muses, the daughters of Zeus the aegis-bearer, if they were to sing against him. But they were angry and maimed him, and took away from him his wonderful singing and made him forget his musical ability.'[13] The Muses' punishment of Thamyris is consistent with the general picture which we have of the way in which the Greek gods dealt with overweening mortals, for it is a classic case of hubris. And it ties in with other myths of the misuse of music, for example, the story of Marsyas, flayed alive for challenging Apollo to a musical contest (Pl. *Euthd.* 285c–d),[14]

---

[13] Homer doesn't specify the particular disability which the Muses inflicted on Thamyris, but we learn from other sources that they blinded him (Hes. fr. 65; Apollod. 1. 3. 3. 1; Paus. 4. 33. 7; 9. 30. 2; 10. 30. 8). Thamyris was the subject of a lost play by Sophocles of which few fragments remain (frr. 237–45 Radt and Lloyd-Jones). According to Pollux (4. 141), Thamyris' mask had a grey (sightless) eye on one side and a dark one on the other, suggesting that the Muses struck him blind whilst he was on the stage. The *Rhesus*, attributed to Euripides, speaks of an actual contest between Thamyris and the Muses, after which they blinded him because he had greatly abused their art (924–5). And Thamyris became a popular subject with vase painters in the 5th and 4th cents., on which see the article on Thamyris in *LIMC*. A. Queyrel (*LIMC* 6. 1. 677 s.v. Mousa/Mousai) notes that representations of the contest between the Thracian bard and the Muses are far more common than those of his punishment. For a psychoanalytic interpretation of the Thamyris myth see Devereux (1987).

[14] See also Hdt. 7. 26; Diod. Sic. 3. 59. 2–5; Ovid, *Met.* 6. 382–400; Ovid, *Fast.* 6. 696–710; Paus. 9. 34. 3 records the story that Hera persuaded the Sirens to compete with the Muses in song; the

or of Linus, who was killed by Apollo for rivalling him in song (Paus. 9. 29. 6). There are similar stories about the related art of prophecy. Apollonius Rhodius, 2. 178 ff., for example, tells of how Phineus was given the gift of prophecy by Apollo, but misused the gift by revealing all of Zeus' plans to everyone. Zeus in anger blinded him. Such stories illustrate the ambiguous nature of divine gifts, which by their very nature elevate their recipients and set them apart from other mortals. But if those on whom the gods confer their special powers are foolish enough to believe themselves the equals of the gods, disaster will follow. Divine gifts must be used appropriately, for the gods are jealous of their powers, and what they give they can also take away. The case of Thamyris shows us that the Muses, like all other Greek divinities, are dangerous when their superiority is challenged. Unlike the Sirens, however, who symbolize the seductive threat inherent in song, they don't go out of their way to lure men to their deaths. Another important difference is that in Homer's version of the story the Muses are dangerous qua divinities rather than as females.

In later versions of the legend, however, the Muses' gender becomes a much more crucial issue. According to Apollodorus' *Library of Greek Mythology* (1. 3. 3. 1), Thamyris, who was exceptional for his beauty as well as for his skill in singing to the lyre, challenged the Muses to a contest on the agreement that if he won, he would have sexual intercourse with all nine Muses; if he lost, they would take from him whatever they wished. The Muses duly won the contest, blinded him, and deprived him of his art. In the *Rhesus*, attributed to Euripides, the Muses punish Thamyris in the same way for his foolhardy challenge to their superiority, but Thamyris is himself the cause of suffering. For the unnamed Muse, mother of Rhesus, who appears *ex machina* at the end of the play, blames Thamyris for the death of her son and for all the sufferings that befell her (915–25). Her sorrows began when Thamyris challenged the Muses to a contest and she came to Thrace. Whilst crossing the Strymon, she was raped by the river-god, and in consequence gave birth to Rhesus. If he hadn't been born, he would not have died and she would not be suffering now. In this story the Muse, so far from being a

Muses won the contest, and plucked the Sirens' feathers to make themselves crowns. Ovid, *Met.* 5. 294–331; 662–78 refers to a similarly unsuccessful challenge to the Muses' power by nine maidens, daughters of Pierus, who were turned into magpies for their arrogance; for more on this see also Spentzou in the Introduction, Part II: 'Roman Indecisions'. For other such stories and discussion of their significance see Griffith (1990).

threatening figure, is the victim of violence herself, and her suffering is presented as the direct result of a mortal's challenge to her art.[15]

The motif of the song contest in myth reflects the agonal context in which Greek poetry developed. For, as the great nineteenth-century historian Jacob Burckhardt showed, Greek culture was dominated by the spirit of competition, and contests were a central feature of Greek life.[16] But myths such as that of Thamyris also dramatize the issues of power which surround the relationship between the poet and the Muses. What does it mean for a poet to invoke a Muse? When Homer calls on the goddess to 'sing the wrath of Achilles', is that a command or a request? Who speaks when the poet reports the Muse's words? Is the Muse an external figure who controls the poet, the embodiment of tradition, or a projection of the poet's own authority?[17] Such questions arise every time a Muse is invoked, for Muses can be envisaged in many different ways. Not only are they mythological figures; as the embodiment of inspiration and authority they can take any form the poet wishes. The ambiguity of their status allows each poet to invent them anew, and it is this very flexibility which has ensured their survival.

In mythology the Muses are generally represented as benign figures, who bring pleasure to gods and humans alike. In the divine sphere their function is to sing and dance in honour of Zeus and the other immortals, for ever praising the blessed existence of the gods.[18] According to Pindar, they came into being when Zeus, having imposed order on the world by assigning each god a cosmic domain, asked the gods if there was anything that they lacked. The gods replied that he should create for himself immortals who would celebrate the great deeds and institutions for which he was responsible.[19] The world of the gods is thus seen as incom-

---

[15] For further discussion of this passage see Lada-Richards in this volume. Hall (1999) 97 draws attention to the highly unusual nature of the 'emotional *singing* theophany of this tragic Muse'.

[16] See Burckhardt (1998) 160–213 on 'The Agonal Age'. As Burckhardt observes (182), 'to a great extent the art of poetry develops under the determining influence of the agon', an insight which forms the basis of Griffith's article (1990) on the competitive quality that characterized Greek poetry from the beginning.

[17] Such questions are discussed by e.g. Calame (1995) 1–74; Nuttall (1992); Stehle (1997) 199–210, and by Laird and Cavarero in this volume.

[18] See esp. Hes. *Theog.* 1–21, 36–74; Hom. *Hymn to Apollo* 182–206, and the discussions of these texts by e.g. Thalmann (1984) 135–55; Lonsdale (1995).

[19] Pindar fr. 31 (Snell–Maehler) = Aelius Aristides, *In Defence of Oratory* 420: Πίνδαρος . . . τοὺς θεοὺς αὐτούς φησιν ἀρομένου τοῦ Διός, εἴ του δέοιντο, αἰτῆσαι ποιήσασθαί τινας αὐτῶι θεούς, οἵτινες τὰ μεγάλα ταῦτ' ἔργα καὶ πᾶσαν γε τὴν ἐκείνου κατασκευὴν κατακοσμήσουσι λόγοις καὶ μουσικῆι. For detailed discussion of this fragment see Snell (1953) 71–89; Bacon (1995) 16–17; the remarks of Lada-Richards in this volume.

plete without the singing of the Muses' chorus to celebrate its beauty and order. This celebratory function of the Muses is mirrored on the human level in their role as bringers of *kleos* ('fame'), for *kleos* gives meaning to mortal deeds. But one of the greatest gifts they offer to human beings is forgetfulness from cares. Mnemosyne, when she lay with Zeus, brought forth 'a forgetting of ills and a rest from sorrows' (Hes. *Theog.* 55, cf. 102–3, and Lada-Richards in this volume), a theme which is echoed again and again in early Greek poetry, and which Plato takes up and transforms in the *Laws* (653–4) in his quasi-mythical account of the origins of *paideia* ('education' or 'culture'). The gods, he says, took pity on the human race, and instituted festivals to give us respite from our cares; but they also gave us the Muses with Apollo, their leader, and Dionysus, to show us how to celebrate appropriately with dance and song. All human beings are born with an innate ability to appreciate rhythm and 'harmony', a gift of those gods who lead us in the dance (χορηγεῖν) which enables them to educate us through participation in their choruses. Hence education, *paideia*, comes originally from Apollo and the Muses.

The Muses give pleasure to gods and humans alike, but whereas they delight the gods by celebrating the blessings of their own existence, in the case of mortals they provide solace for their sorrows, allowing them temporarily to forget the hardships and the pains of human life. The Sirens, too, offer forgetfulness, but in their case it's a forgetfulness of who you are: no man who hears their voices will ever return to his home, 'that his wife and little children may stand at his side rejoicing' (*Od.* 12. 42–3). In the story of the cicadas in the *Phaedrus* Plato plays on this motif of forgetfulness, but collapses the distinction between Muses and Sirens; instead he introduces a distinction between different types of Muse. The most beautiful voice (259d7) belongs to the Muses of philosophy, Calliope and Urania, whose province is 'the heavens and *logoi* both divine and human'—the music which belongs to them is philosophy. Urania is an obvious choice for this role: her very name fits her to be the patroness of cosmological matters, and recalls the *ouranos* depicted in Socrates' myth earlier on in the dialogue about the immortality of the human soul (*Phdr.* 245c6 ff., see also 246e4, 247b1, 247c3). The prominence of Calliope recalls Hesiod's *Theogony* 77 ff., where the names of the nine Muses are listed for the first time: 'Clio and Euterpe, Thalia and Melpomene, Terpsichore and Erato, Polymnia, Urania and Calliope', which West translates as 'Fame-spreading, Entertaining,

Festive, Singing, Dance-delight, Lovely, Rich in themes, Celestial, Beautiful voice' (1988: 64). This differentiation between Muses is not important in terms of their individual functions: the notion that each individual Muse presided over a different province is a much later development, dating from Hellenistic and Roman times, though we can perhaps see the beginnings of it in Plato's myth of the cicadas. Indeed Grube[20] suggests that it may well have been Plato who invented the notion of departmentalized Muses. In Hesiod the nine Muses collectively embody all the aspects of poetry and song which came into being when the Muses were born. As far as we know, the names that he gives them seem not to have been traditional, but rather are suggested by the various things he has said about them in the previous lines.[21] Interestingly none of the names of the Muses invokes their truth-telling function, despite the prominence of this motif in Hesiod's account of his own momentous meeting with the goddesses on Mount Helicon (*Theog.* 22–34). However, Calliope, she of the beautiful voice, is singled out as the most senior Muse (79), for she it is who has the special care of βασιλῆες, 'princes'. Having singled her out in this way Hesiod then goes on to attribute the special gifts of princes to the Muses as a body:

> ὅντινα τιμήσουσι Διὸς κοῦραι μεγάλοιο
> γεινόμενόν τ᾽ ἐσίδωσι διοτρεφέων βασιλήων,
> τῷ μὲν ἐπὶ γλώσσῃ γλυκερὴν χείουσιν ἐέρσην,
> τοῦ δ᾽ ἔπε᾽ ἐκ στόματος ῥεῖ μείλιχα. οἱ δέ τε λαοὶ
> πάντες ἐς αὐτὸν ὁρῶσι διακρίνοντα θέμιστας
> ἰθείῃσι δίκῃσιν. ὃ δ᾽ ἀσφαλέως ἀγορεύων
> αἶψά τε καὶ μέγα νεῖκος ἐπισταμένως κατέπαυσεν.
> τοὔνεκα γὰρ βασιλῆες ἐχέφρονες, οὕνεκα λαοῖς
> βλαπτομένοις ἀγορῆφι μετάτροπα ἔργα τελεῦσι

---

[20] (1965) 5–6 and 5 n. 3. Nancy (1996) 1–39 (also quoted by Spentzou in the epigraph of the Introduction to this volume) considers the related issue of the Muses' and the arts' plurality: '[The Muses'] name is multiplied from the first, so that we may give a title to this question: Why are there several arts and not just one?' (p. 1). As he goes on to say, the plurality of the arts is generally taken as a given: 'That is why, most often, one does not question this plurality; one merely submits it to the test of a "classification" or (formerly) a "hierarchy" of the arts. But one is not sure how to order this classification itself, which is, moreover, why it has undergone so many variations in the course of history, not only as regards its internal distribution (how does one order the recognised arts?), but also as regards the extension of its jurisdiction (what must be recognised as an art?)' (p. 2).

[21] For details see West (1966) ad loc. and p. 32. Trimpi (1983) xvii notes that 'For Hesiod, the Muses exist as various aspects of one another, one implying all the others', and Thalmann (1984) 138 that 'Hesiod virtually summons the goddesses into existence'.

ῥηιδίως, μαλακοῖς παραιφάμενοι ἐπέεσσιν.
ἐρχόμενον δ' ἀν' ἀγῶνα θεὸν ὣς ἱλάσκονται
αἰδοῖ μειλιχίῃ, μετὰ δὲ πρέπει ἀγρομένοισιν.
τοίη Μουσάων ἱερὴ δόσις ἀνθρώποισιν.   (81–93)

Whomsoever great Zeus' daughters favour among the princes that Zeus fosters, and turn their eyes upon him at his birth, upon his tongue they shed sweet dew, and out of his mouth the words flow honeyed; and the peoples all look to him as he decides what is to prevail with his straight judgments. His word is sure, and expertly he makes a quick end of even a great dispute. This is why there are prudent princes: when the peoples are wronged in their dealings, they make amends with ease, persuading them with gentle words. When he goes among a gathering, they seek his favour with conciliatory reverence, as if he were a god, and he stands out among the crowd. Such is the Muses' holy gift to men.[22]

Here the Muses' sphere extends far beyond poetry, for the realm of the princes is the world of *logos*.[23] Princes are able to maintain peace and order in society not only because they are figures of authority with the ability to make 'straight judgments', but also because they have the power of persuasion bestowed upon them by the Muses. Song and political discourse are seen as parallel activities because both depend on effective utterance, which the Muses confer on poets and princes alike.

Already in Homer eloquence is regarded as a gift from the gods (see e.g. *Od.* 8. 170), and the mellifluous speaker is described in terms that are equally appropriate to the poet. Thus Nestor's voice 'flows from his tongue sweeter than honey' (*Il.* 1. 249), a phrase which is echoed by Hesiod in his characterization of the persuasive utterance of the singer (*Theog.* 97), the prince (*Theog.* 84), and the Muses themselves (*Theog.* 39–40).[24] Yet despite this affinity between poetry and eloquence, Homer's Muses are never seen as the source of a *speaker*'s words. Even Odysseus, the most bard-like of all Homeric heroes, relies entirely on his own persuasive powers to charm and enthral his audiences, without reference to divine inspiration. Hesiod's extension of the Muses' domain

---

[22] Translation from West (1988).

[23] See Arthur (1983) 109, and the discussions of this passage by e.g. Solmsen (1954); Lanata (1963) 30–1; Thalmann (1984) 140–2.

[24] For detailed discussion of the parallels between Homer and Hesiod see Thalmann (1984) 140 ff. I agree with his observation on p. 229 n. 18: 'We should not be unduly concerned with the question of whether Hesiod invented the connection between rhetoric and song, or feel that his "originality" has been disappointingly lessened if it turns out that he did not do so. The important point is what he made of the idea as part of his overall statement about poetry.'

to include speech as well as song raises the interesting question of why there never was a Muse of rhetoric. There are, to be sure, occasional references to the Muses in connection with the arts of speech,[25] but no strong tradition of rhetoric as a 'musical' activity. This issue is considered by Plutarch in *Questionum Convivalium* book 9, question 14 (*Mor.* 743e ff.), which is entitled 'Unusual observations on the numbers of the Muses'—the whole discussion indicates that the functions and provinces of the different Muses were by no means fixed in Plutarch's time. Herodes, a teacher of rhetoric, refers to the passage from Hesiod's *Theogony* which I've just quoted, and complains that Calliope has been dragged away from her rightful province: orators as well as poets, he suggests, have a claim on the Muses. And another character in the conversation backs him up and comes up with the theory (744c) that there were originally three Muses, of philosophy, rhetoric, and mathematics—and poetry and music are a subdivision of mathematics.[26] But this is hardly a conventional view, and it is no accident that the whole discussion is entitled '*Unusual* observations on the Muses'. I suppose that one reason why there is not a Muse of rhetoric is that rhetoric is always regarded as a *techne* (a 'skill' or 'craft'), designed to be teachable, and *technai* do not need Muses. Another factor may be that, since truth was an irrelevant criterion in rhetoric, the speaker has no need to claim authority from a higher power in order to establish his credentials.[27] The art of speech, in contrast to music and poetry, is thus seen as an entirely human activity.

Hesiod's *Theogony* firmly establishes Calliope as the senior Muse and it is no doubt due to Hesiod that she is cited more frequently than the

[25] See e.g. Paus. 2. 31. 3.

[26] For discussion of this passage see Trimpi xvi–xvii, and on the flexibility of the Muses' functions see Nisbet and Hubbard (1970) on *Odes* 1. 24. 3. The question of what kinds of activities are presided over by Muses (whether in classical antiquity or in the subsequent tradition) has never, to my knowledge, been seriously investigated. But see the suggestive remarks of Nancy (1996) 4–5: 'It will not be pointless to recall what everyone knows: how the West came to speak of "art" and the "arts" after having spoken of the Muses. We have been saying "art" in the singular and without any other specification only recently, only since the romantic period . . . Earlier, at the time of Kant and Diderot, people said the "beaux-arts" or "fine arts", and these were often distinguished from "belles-lettres." (At the same time, there was already a dominant tendency to place the order and essence of these practices under "poetry").' The one activity with which the Muses have never ceased to be associated is poetry. It might be interesting to consider the extent to which the Muses' spheres of influence coincide with activities which could be subsumed under the heading of 'art' or 'the arts', and what that tells us about notions of the aesthetic at different periods.

[27] This point is stressed by Finkelberg (1998) 12 and 176.

other Muses in early poetry,[28] and is also given prominence, for example, on the François vase (*c.*570 BC), where the nine Muses are depicted at the marriage of Peleus and Thetis. So Plato's choice of Calliope as the highest Muse is traditional, though the function that he gives her is not. Commentators on the *Phaedrus* emphasize Calliope's significance as a goddess of poetry: in appropriating her for philosophy Plato implies not only that the philosopher has usurped the poet's role, but also that, at any rate in this dialogue, philosophy can legitimately use poetic methods in order to achieve its goals.[29] But it is also relevant that in pre-Platonic literature Calliope is more than a goddess of poetry, at any rate on any modern understanding of the term. Apart from her association with the βασιλῆες ('princes') in Hesiod, she is also invoked by the pre-Socratic philosopher Empedocles,[30] who calls on her (B131 DK) to stand by him whilst he reveals a good *logon* (speech or account) about the blessed gods. In other fragments he summons an unspecified Muse to tell him what it is right for men to hear (B3, 3–5), or bids his listener accept the trustworthy dicta of his (Empedocles') Muse (B4). Empedocles' invocation to the Muse should remind us of just how wide the Muses' domain could be. Not only are they givers of pleasure and *kleos*, as daughters of Mnemosyne they know everything about the past, and they are also authorities on ethical matters and wisdom generally.

It is perhaps not so surprising after all that Plato wanted to appropriate them for the emerging discourse of philosophy. But there is one crucial difference between Empedocles and Plato: Empedocles is a poet, in the sense that, like many of the early Greek philosophers (e.g. Parmenides and Xenophanes) he expressed himself in verse. Aristotle later objected that it was ridiculous to call Empedocles a poet just because he wrote in metre (*Poetics* 1447[b]), but Aristotle is there explicitly dissociating himself from the standard view (to which Plato subscribes, see *Phaedo* 60d ff., the passage with which I began, and cf. *Symp.* 205c) which defines the poet as a maker of verses. Empedocles invokes the Muse to guarantee the truth of his revelations, and since he is expressing those revelations in poetry, there is nothing particularly odd about his invocation: it is in fact traditional. But Plato wrote in prose, and the crucial move which Plato makes, I think, is to associate the Muses with prose.

---

[28] See e.g. Sapph. fr. 24; Pind. *Ol.* 10. 14; references in *LIMC* s.v. Mousa/Mousai.

[29] See e.g. Ferrari (1987) 30; De Vries (1969) ad loc.

[30] On Empedocles as poet see Lanata (1963) 128–35. The relationship between Hesiod and Empedocles is discussed by Hershbell (1970).

Plato claimed that there was an ancient quarrel between poetry and philosophy, but in reality this quarrel was largely of Plato's own making. This has been pointed out and discussed by several scholars, notably by Nussbaum (1982 and 1986) and Ferrari (1987), and most recently by Andrea Wilson Nightingale in her book *Genres in Dialogue* (1995), in which she argues that philosophy in Plato's time was a genre in the process of constructing itself. Plato was creating a new and specialized discipline which had to define and legitimize itself against the genres of discourse that had authority and currency in democratic Athens. The most ancient and the most authoritative of those discourses is poetry, and in particular the poetry of Homer and the tragedians, whom Plato sees as his main rivals, most obviously in the *Republic*, but also in the *Laws*. When the Athenian is asked in that dialogue whether tragedians will be admitted into their Cretan city he replies: ἄριστοι . . . τῶν ξένων, ἡμεῖς ἐσμὲν τραγῳδίας αὐτοὶ ποιηταὶ κατὰ δύναμιν ὅτι καλλίστης ἅμα καὶ ἀρίστης. πᾶσα οὖν ἡμῖν ἡ πολιτεία συνέστηκε μίμησις τοῦ καλλίστου βίου, ὃ δή φαμεν ἡμεῖς γε ὄντως εἶναι τραγῳδίαν τὴν ἀληθεστάτην (817b), 'we [i.e. the lawgivers] are tragedians ourselves, and our tragedy is the finest and best we can create. At any rate, our entire state has been constructed so as to be a representation of the finest and noblest life—the very thing which we maintain is most genuinely a tragedy'. As for the sons of the μαλακῶν Μουσῶν ('soft, effeminate, unrestrained Muses'—the reference to their femininity adds to the disparaging tone), they will have to take their songs to the authorities to be duly considered. Again a distinction is implied between poets in the traditional sense, that is the sons of the μαλακῶν Μουσῶν, and 'poets' of another sort, that is, philosophers.

This brings me back to the myth of the cicadas in the *Phaedrus* where Plato makes it clear that the true lover of the Muses is the philosopher, not the poet. This explains why it is that earlier on in the dialogue in the scale of lives at 248d3 ff. not only is the *mousikos* ('the musical life') distinguished from the *poietikos* ('the poetic life'), these lives are actually put at different ends of the scale. Socrates there describes the incarnation of the soul in various forms of human life: 'the soul which has seen most on its heavenly journey will be planted in a seed from which will grow a man who will become a lover of wisdom or of beauty, or devoted to the Muses and to love'. The 'musical' man here is none other than the philosopher, the lover of wisdom and beauty. The poet's life, however, comes sixth in the scale of value: 'for the sixth soul the fitting life will be that of a poet or some other life from among those concerned with imitation'. The philosopher is here sharply contrasted with the poet, and the divorce between poetry and the Muses is complete.[31] This divorce is made possible because Plato separates off the technical from the 'musical' aspects of poetry, and appropriates for philosophy the higher functions of poetry which are traditionally associated with the divine. As Curtius (1953) observes apropos the terms *poiesis* and *poietes*: 'The Greek words for poetry and poet have a technical, not a metaphysical, still less a religious, significance. At the same time no people has had a stronger sense of the divine in poetry than the Greeks' (146). It is this divine element, expressed through the figure of the Muse, which Plato incorporates into his conception of philosophy, the pursuit par excellence of the truly 'musical' man.

Plato's Muses are ambivalent figures: as goddesses of poetry they are potentially destructive and harmful, not least because of their association with pleasure, which is so strongly emphasized both in pre-Platonic poetry and in Plato's own dialogues. But whereas the poets regard pleasure as one of the great gifts which the Muses bestow on humankind, in Plato's eyes pleasure is a dangerous thing, which blinds us to the proper goals of life. For Plato the Muses of pleasure, the Muses of poetry, are seductive and dangerous figures like the Sirens: hence they must be expelled from the ideal state, as in the *Republic*, or kept firmly under control by austere lawgivers, as in the *Laws*. On the other hand, the Muses are also symbols of authority, associated with wisdom, knowledge, and truth, and this is the aspect of their traditional function which Plato developed and appropriated for philosophy. The dual aspect of the Muses is well brought out by Boethius, writing in Platonic mode, at the beginning of the *De Consolatione Philosophiae*. He describes how he was trying to banish his sorrows by composing poetry, but whilst he was asleep, the Lady Philosophy seemed to stand above his head. When she saw the Muses of poetry (*poeticas Musas*) helping him to find words for his grief, she cried out with fiercely blazing eyes:

Who let these theatrical tarts (*has scenicas meretriculas*) in with this sick man? Not only have they no cures for his pain, but with their sweet poison (*dulcibus ... venenis*) they make it worse ... Get out, you Sirens, beguiling men straight

---

[31] For discussion of this passage and the difficulty of reconciling it with the picture of the inspired poet at 245a see e.g. Nussbaum (1982); Rowe (1986) ad loc.; Finkelberg (1998) 1–3. On the differentiation between μουσική and ποίησις generally in Plato's work see Dalfen (1974) 295–300.

to their destruction! Leave him to *my* Muses to care for and restore to health (*Sed abite potius Sirenes usque in exitium dulces meisque eum Musis curandum sanandumque relinquite*). (*Consol.* 1. 1, trans. Tester 1973)

E. R. Curtius (1953) long ago drew attention to the vagueness of the image of the Muses in antiquity, pointing out that from earliest times there were conflicting traditions as to their number, lineage, dwelling-place, and function. 'Unlike the Olympians,' he says (229), 'they had no well-marked personalities. They incarnate a purely intellectual principle.' There were indeed very few myths about the Muses, and they were envisaged in different ways in different authors and different periods.[32] But if it is true, as Curtius suggests, that in antiquity the Muses belonged not only to poetry but to all forms of intellectual life besides, this is in no small measure due to Plato. Before Plato the Muses were firmly associated with poetry, but the scope of poetry was very broad, as I have indicated. With the invention of new and competing forms of discourse one might have expected the Muses' influence to diminish. Historians and writers of scientific treatises, after all, do not invoke the Muses. But in appropriating the Muses for prose, and making philosophy the highest form of 'music',[33] Plato paved the way for the extension of the Muses' activities to cover what Curtius calls 'all higher forms of intellectual life' (228). As Cicero put it in *Tusculan Disputations* 5. 66, 'to live with the Muses is to live humanistically' (*cum Musis, id est, cum humanitate et doctrina*).

[32] See also Spentzou in the Introduction, Part I: 'Greek Imprecisions'.

[33] This formulation no doubt owed much to Plato's interest in Pythagoreanism, and, according to a very influential theory first put forward by Wilamowitz (1881) and further developed by Boyancé (1937), Plato set up the Academy as a *thiasos*, a religious corporation dedicated to the worship of the Muses, along lines suggested to him by his contact with the Pythagorean brotherhood in southern Italy. But this thesis should be regarded with caution, as has been shown by the detailed arguments of Lynch (1972) 108–27, and Tecusan (1996), ch. 3 on 'Common meals and the philosophical life'. Nevertheless it is significant that both the Academy and the Lyceum contained *Mouseia*, sanctuaries with statues of the Muses. However we interpret this fact, there clearly is a relationship between the Muses, *mousike*, and philosophy which makes the Muses much more than goddesses of poetry and song. On the subject of *Mouseia* see Hardie (1997).

3

The Envied Muse:
Plato versus Homer

Adriana Cavarero

I

In *Republic* 607a Plato states that there is no place for sweet lyric or the epic Muse in the ideal city. It is philosophical *logos* that must rule in the city, not the passions that poets solicit from their audience. In the *Republic* Plato's famous hostility towards the poets resembles a competition between philosophy and poetry. Plato wants, among other things, to replace Homer as the educator of Greece. The terms of this competition are inscribed in the well-known Platonic distinction between the truth of being and the falseness of appearance. The philosopher has knowledge of 'what is'—the ideas; conversely, the poet is an imitator (*mimetes*), a creator of appearance.

In effect, according to Plato, Homer is only competent in the field of imitation. Presenting himself as omniscient, he speaks about everything but has no knowledge of the things he speaks about. He speaks about war but knows nothing of the art of war; he speaks of medicine but isn't a doctor—he merely imitates doctor's talk (559c). Thus, lacking knowledge of any specific object, which Plato ascribes to the realm of *techne*, Homer 'paints with words and phrases the colours of each of the arts (*technai*) without any knowledge except that of imitation': καὶ τὸν ποιητικὸν φήσομεν χρώματα ἄττα ἑκάστων τῶν τεχνῶν τοῖς ὀνόμασι καὶ ῥήμασιν ἐπιχρωματίζειν αὐτὸν οὐκ ἐπαΐοντα ἀλλ᾽ ἢ μιμεῖσθαι (601a). In so far as he is a creator of simulacra (*eidolon poietes*), Homer knows nothing about reality but only knows appearance (601b).

Imitating the *technai* is, however, only one of Homer's specialities. Still worse is his imitation of the human passions. Through 'a much

varied imitation' (604e) of the irrational parts of the soul, poetic mimesis
τρέφει γὰρ ταῦτα ἄρδουσα, δέον αὐχμεῖν (607e), 'waters and nourishes
them when they ought to be dried up'.[1] The result is that the audience
participates in the irrational flow of poetic song and is carried away by it.
In contrast, the philosopher does exactly the opposite. He educates himself by nourishing the rational part of the soul and, thus, presents himself
as a good educator of his fellow citizens.

In *Republic* 3 Plato ascribes a third type of imitation to Homer. In epic,
simple narrative is mixed with direct speech. There is a specific type
of imitation which consists in the mimesis of the poet who has his
characters speak through direct speech (that is the definition of *mimesis*
which has become a central category in classical literary criticism).
Suffice it to note that in Book 10 the Muse is banished from the ideal city
because of the bad effects of poetry on the audience. Homer solicits the
irrational disorder of the passions in his listeners and, in addition, by pro-
ducing simulacra, false appearances, he tricks them with his talent as a
charlatan-imitator. Plato portrays all of this in the famous cave scene
(*Rep.* 514–17a). Inside the cave we find the bearers of simulacra (*eidola*)
who, like charlatans, cast shadows (*skiai*) on the cave, which acts as a
projection screen. The purpose of the projection is to trick the cave
dwellers, who are tied in such a way that they can only stare at the
screen, into believing that the appearances—the shadows—are the real
world. Even if the overtones of the cave scene verge on the bizarre
and distorting, Plato's message is quite clear: the cave is Athens, the
prisoners are the Athenians, and inside the projection room, next to the
Sophists and the artists in general, is most certainly Homer as well. At
one point in the scene, one of the prisoners manages to untie himself,
turns around, and begins to ascend toward the real world of ideas, which
is outside the cave. He represents the philosopher. Leaving the dark
world of imitations and artifice, he goes to contemplate (*theorein*) the
brightness of being. It is precisely from this contemplation that he
derives the criteria on which to build a city where there is no room for
simulacra and charlatans, or for their games of appearances. This is the
ideal city that banishes the Muse.

---

[1] All translations of ancient Greek texts are mine, unless otherwise specified.

II

Throughout *Republic* 10 Plato often refers to poetry as something which fascinates and enchants. At one point Socrates asks his interlocutor: ἦ γάρ, ὦ φίλε, οὐ κηλῇ ὑπ' αὐτῆς καὶ σύ, καὶ μάλιστα ὅταν δι' Ὁμήρου θεωρῇς αὐτήν; (607d), 'doesn't [poetry] charm you too, especially when you see it through Homer?' It is difficult to resist the great spell cast by metre, rhythm, and harmony (601a). In *Republic* 3 Plato was already concerned with analysing musical instruments, the lyre and the flute, in order to understand and regulate 'the seductive strength of *mousike*'.[2] In epic, the rhythmic modulations of the singing voice and the sound of the lyre intermingle so that the result becomes irresistible. Socrates goes so far as to suggest using philosophical discourses as a magic spell to be used repeatedly as a sort of antidote (608a).

One of the most notable effects of poetry is undoubtedly its power to enchant the audience. The Muse enchants, or better still, she enchains. Plato is well aware of this and, throughout his work, he seems to give it more emphasis than it deserves—at least, more so than Homer, who also analyses the effects of the epic performance.[3] Plato devotes a specific text, the *Ion*, to the enchantment / enchainment produced by the Muse, a text which is replete with accusations of Homer being an imitator and illusionist. However, in contrast to the *Republic*, the central theme in this short text focuses above all on the poet as a performer and enchanter.

The Muse—says Socrates in the most celebrated pages of the *Ion*—is like a magnet that transmits to the things it attracts the power to attract. The magnet 'not only attracts iron rings, but induces in the rings the power to do the same themselves in turn' (533d); likewise, the Muse's divine power, *theia dynamis*, is transferred to the poets, who subsequently pass it on to the rhapsodes. Each ring in the poetic chain hangs one from another by means of an irresistible attraction. However, the *theia dynamis* is not only the power that attracts and binds. It is also, and simultaneously, a condition of *enthusiasm* that is transmitted from one ring to the next. This involves a theme very dear to Plato: the poet's mania. Possessed with divine power, the poet is *en theos*, in-the-god. He is outside his mind; he is in a passive state, empowered to receive and transmit to the rhapsode what the Muse bestows on him. Just as the iron rings that hang from the magnet are magnetized, so the rings of the

---

[2] Barker (1994) 181.   [3] On this, see also Lombardo (1995).

poetic chain that hang from the Muse are deified. The phenomenon of attraction is also a phenomenon of deification.[4] The gift—a divine mania which is different from the pure power to attract—is transmitted from the Muse to the poet, on to the rhapsode, and finally reaches the audience.

The comparison with the magnet holds but only up to a certain point: it holds up to the point where Plato adds a change in the 'scientific' description of magnetism to justify his interest in the strange speciality of Ion, Socrates' interlocutor. Ion is a very successful rhapsode and has just won one of the competitions for rhapsodes held in the Greek cities; but he has one strange quirk. Unlike the other rhapsodes, who have a vast repertoire of different songs, Ion is only able to recite the verses of a single poet: Homer. Homer excites him and brings out the best in him. When he hears people speak of other poets, he gets bored and falls asleep. A special and exclusive attraction binds Ion to Homer.

It has been suggested that the strange case of Ion turns the entire dialogue into an investigation centred on a kind of enigma.[5] This can be exemplified by a series of questions. If it is true, as many interpreters claim, that Plato is attacking the rhapsodes in order to strike at the poets, why choose Ion? Given that a criticism of the poets' illusionism would serve the purpose well enough if Socrates' interlocutor were a 'normal' rhapsode, why choose a rhapsode so peculiar? Perhaps Homer—if this is the point—is not part of the usual repertoire of the rhapsodes?

The answer is, fundamentally, simple. Plato wants Ion precisely because of his specialness. The strange exclusive attraction which binds Ion and Homer serves to illustrate certain very singular aspects of the magnetic chain of which the Muse is the source. The *theia dynamis*, as Socrates insists, is not transmitted to the various rings as a simple and undifferentiated power, as occurs in the natural phenomenon of magnetism. Instead, it is transmitted in the form of a *theia moira*; that is, it is from the outset transmitted in such a way that each ring receives its 'share', *moira*, of *theia dynamis*. The divine power is transmitted from one ring to the next in differentiated portions. The transmission of power throughout the poetic chain is a distribution of different parts. As Socrates explains to Ion, ἅτε οὖν οὐ τέχνῃ ποιοῦντες καὶ πολλὰ λέγοντες καὶ καλὰ περὶ τῶν πραγμάτων, ὥσπερ σὺ περὶ Ὁμήρου ἀλλὰ θείᾳ

---

[4] For a distinctively 'humanized' version of this quasi-erotic bond between Muse and poet, see Sharrock in this volume, and her exploration of Ovid's relationship to his epic Muse.

[5] Nancy (1990), on whose brilliant essay my reading of the *Ion* is largely based.

μοίρᾳ, τοῦτο μόνον οἷός τε ἕκαστος ποιεῖν καλῶς ἐφ᾽ ὃ ἡ Μοῦσα αὐτὸν ὥρμησεν (534c), 'it is not art, but divine dispensation that enables poets to compose poetry and say many fine things about the world as you do about Homer; every individual poet can only compose well what the Muse has set him to do'.

As Socrates further elaborates, the divine dispensation concerns each single poetic genre. One poet may receive dithyrambs, another iambs, and so on. The *moira* which befell Homer was, of course, epic. This explains why Homer sings in hexameters, but not why Ion recites only Homer. The point is that the divine dispensation does involve poetic genres, but it is first directed to each single poet and then to the rhapsodes. Everyone, as a result of this divine partition of poetic material, takes part in and performs his allotted task in the world of poetry. Thus, it is not all that strange that Ion has an exclusive task involving a single poet and that he is divinely adept only with regard to Homer. This exclusive task is precisely his *moira*, his sharing, his part, his lot in the poetic chain. The divine attraction/partition, passing through Homer, is extended to Ion, a rhapsode who is, in fact, so good at his art that he wins all the competitions he participates in.

The *Ion* deals in strangeness beyond this enigma; the short text is also shot through with a strange incoherence. In the space of a few lines, poets are first condemned but then exalted. On the one hand, Socrates presents his usual criticism of incompetence on the part of the poets and their practice of illusionism. On the other hand, however, the exposition of the magnetic chain, discussed above, reflects an open admiration for poets, emphasizes their closeness to the divine, and even extends this privileged position to rhapsodes. An implication of irony is not enough to justify this contradiction. Something in the *Ion* forces Plato toward incoherence. It is as if the philosopher had good reasons to disdain the poetic art of his rival, Homer, but cannot help admiring both the divine mania in which poets, especially Homer, participate and the enchantment effect which, like a contagious delirium, descends from the Muse to the audience.

The Muse's *theia dynamis*, thus, attracts, enchants, and paralyses the audience's attention. 'Doesn't poetry charm you too, especially when you see it through Homer?' (607d), we saw Socrates asking Glaucon in *Republic* 607d. It is a critical commonplace that the Muse's enchanting power poses a problem for Plato to which he is particularly, if not obsessively, sensitive. A justifiable suspicion arises: could the chain which tightly binds the prisoners in the cave and forces them to look at the shadows allude to the Muse's enchanting power? But even if so, there is still one unresolved issue: why do the poet-charlatans in Plato's depiction of the cave scene use artifices involving sight rather than the sweet sound of verses? Can the suggestion that the *Republic* is much concerned with tragedy (whereas the *Ion* is not)[6] be the sole explanation for why they use visual tricks while their speciality is acoustic seduction?

III

Drawing on poetic tradition, Plato in *Ion* 534b suggests that the power that comes from the Muse as a gift consists of honey taken from the divine gardens that the poet transports and transmits by making (*poiein*) verses. This is why he is a poet, *poietes*. In the sweet rhythm of the verses, his voice puts the Muse's honey (*meli*) to words. Playing with the etymology of the word, Socrates suggests here that this applies above all to the lyrical poet, the *melopoios*. However, etymological puns aside, this applies to every sort of poet because poets produce verses. The Muse's gift, the divine nectar, is in the rhythmical sound. The metaphor suggests that the making of poetry has to do with the physicality of a sound which is pleasing to the ear, just as honey delights the taste buds. Imbuing the poets with her gift, the Muse makes them make verses which attract and seduce because of their harmonious tones. Likewise, in *Republic* 601a, Plato affirms that the natural enchantment of poetry lies in its metre, rhythm, and harmony. The metaphor of honey is precise: it is a question of the verses attracting and seducing not only because of their sound, but also through their content. More importantly, this metaphor suggests that the voice, the sweet sound of the voice, passes from the speaker to the listener. Form and content of stories told perfectly coincide in the phonetic stream which delights like honey.

In fact, the original phonetic source corresponds to the Muse's song, in which the narrative and the musicality of the voice are inseparable. The epic Muse represents precisely this indistinguishability between music and word, voice and narration. It is both a narration of stories which is song, and a song which narrates stories. Invoked by the poets, the Muse sings (*aoide*) or tells (*eipe*) a story. However, there is undoubtedly something strange in the sound of this song that only the

---

[6] As Penny Murray has suggested to me *per litteras*, pointing at passages such as 475d–e and 607d. For a fuller examination of this whole problem, see Cavarero (1996).

poet can hear. Simple mortals do not hear the Muse's voice. She is mute to their ears. The audience has access to her song only through the voice of the poet. The divine mute song resounds in the poet's human voice. For the audience, the epic poet is the audible form of that which is inaudible. He is the resounding voice of the mute Muse.

The epic poet has a privileged relationship with the Muse with regard to the physicality and musicality of the voice, in so far as it is the material of narrative communication. The prototype of the storyteller from time immemorial is the poet voicing narration. As others have noted, the question of authorship—and postmodern concerns regarding the 'death of the author'—are issues not by any means central to epic.[7] The central issue of the epic is voice. The poet is not the inventor of the stories; he is the one who gives them a human voice and rephrases the stories through singing.

For this reason, Plato in the *Ion* seems to adhere faithfully to epic's own portrayal. What passes through the first ring of the poetic chain is a divine soundless *logos* that acquires sonorous materiality in the voice of the poet. Socrates' insistence on the passage of the mute voice to the sonorous voice that puts it into audible words is significant. It is the Muse who speaks through the voice of the poets whom she has imbued, ἵνα ἡμεῖς οἱ ἀκούοντες εἰδῶμεν ὅτι οὐχ οὗτοί εἰσιν οἱ ταῦτα λέγοντες οὕτω πολλοῦ ἄχια, οἷς νοῦς μὴ πάρεστιν, ἀλλ' ὁ θεὸς αὐτός ἐστιν ὁ λέγων, διὰ τούτων δὲ φθέγγεται πρὸς ἡμᾶς (534d), 'so that we who hear may realize that it is not these persons, whose reason has left them, who are the speakers of such valuable words, but god who speaks and expresses himself to us through them'. God himself is the speaker. It is through the poets that god makes himself heard, makes a sound that we, the listeners, can hear. In so far as he gives voice to, or rather carries, the mute song of the Muse in his voice, the poet can be defined as god's messenger.

Poets are messengers of the gods (*hermeneis eisin ton theon*), declares Socrates (534e). Most translations would make the poets interpreters of the gods; but the proper meaning of the verb *hermeneuein* is not 'to interpret'. Quoting Heidegger, Nancy emphasizes that the sense is more like 'to announce'.[8] The poet's song is an announcement of that of which he is the messenger. Once again, he is not the author of what he says, but

---

[7] Cf. here Burke (1995) 4–7.

[8] Nancy (1990), 225. For the obvious link between *hermeneuein* and Hermes, the divine messenger, see Plato's *Cratylus* 408a.

rather the messenger. With her divine voice the Muse gives the poet speech that only he can hear, and the poet transmits in an audible voice to human ears the Muse's speech, her song. The concept itself of the message being carried in a voice implies a game of at least three variables: the source, the go-between, and the receiver. In the *Ion* the game has four variables. In epic poetry the rhapsode intervenes between poet and audience. The voice of the voice of the poet, the messenger of the messenger (535a), the rhapsode is, in fact, the second ring in this transmission of soundless material that becomes sonorous material, perceptible song, audible narration. At the beginning is the Muse; at the end, the audience; in the middle, the voices of the poet and rhapsode.

Epic is a matter of musical voices. As is well known, a later tradition, to which Plato also belongs, calls the poet *poietes*. In the Homeric language the poet is a singer (*aoidos*); his song (*aoide*) is his voice (*aude*). Poetry is singing, and singing is voicing.[9] The poet sings songs that enchant the audience (*epaoide*). Without this shift in the name of the poet, from *aoidos* to *poietes*, Plato would not be able to play his games and advance his criticism. In fact, only to the extent that the poet is within the sphere of 'making' (*poiein*) can he be compared to artisans and their art of fabricating (*techne*). But the poet does not 'make'; he sings with a distinctive voice of his own.

As Plato suggests in the *Ion*—a very anomalous Platonic text—the voices that interpret the parts assigned to them by the *theia moira* are always individual and single voices. And it is obviously the Muse herself who speaks through this plurality of single voices. This, according to Nancy, means that the divine is what divides itself in voice,[10] or rather, it is the original *partage des voix* that, even for the Muse, pushes itself outside itself in the single voices of the poet and the rhapsode. Thus, we find yet another explanation for the *Ion*'s puzzling special character. This explanation strongly emphasizes that, even in the most 'repetitive' ring of the poetic chain, that of the rhapsode, the voice is always singular. In other words, by orientating the text around this strange specialness of the rhapsode, the *Ion* tells us that the poetic chain, by means of the *theia moira*, always divides itself into a plurality of single and unique voices. The last ring in the poetic chain consists of the listeners who receive the voiced story through their own ears and undergo the effects of the musical enchantment. In poetry generally, but especially in epic, the poetic mania is essentially a phonetic mania tied to the rhythm of the

[9] Cf. here Ford (1992) 172–97.   [10] Nancy (1990) 237.

song. Voice and sound are at its centre; eyes and sight do not have an important role. Homer is blind.

By contrast, the philosopher, according to Plato, has excellent sight. The myth of the cave recounts the story of the philosophical eye that looks towards ever clearer and brighter objects. The soul's eye is not purely a metaphor; it is at the centre of a philosophy constructed entirely on vision and the terminology of seeing, which determines the philosophical lexicon of Western thought.[11] The prisoner takes his eyes off the shadows on the wall and begins climbing upwards in order to contemplate the splendour of ideas. At the end of this ascent the philosopher contemplates what is brightest (*phanerotaton*) and, thus, truest (*alethestaton*). Philosophy, in so far as it is *theorein*, consists in contemplating the light of truth.

In the competition between Plato and Homer there exists a strong balance between the two candidates in the different skills in which each excels: a sharp eye for the first; a musical voice for the second. The philosopher with a sharp eye challenges the blind poet. As regards the education of the Greeks, the specialist of vision means to replace the specialist of the voice. The theatrical scene of the cave, in which Homer manipulates simulacra and projects shadows, false appearances, and images onto the screen seems therefore ever more bizarre. A blind man controlling the projection of visual tricks. The question is worth repeating. Does Homer not enchain his listeners with the rhythmic sound of his voice rather than visual tricks?

IV

Homer is blind, but the Muse can see well enough.[12] That is why the poet invokes her:

> ἔσπετε νῦν μοι, Μοῦσαι Ὀλύμπια δώματ᾽ ἔχουσαι
> ὑμεῖς γὰρ θεαί ἐστε, πάρεστέ τε, ἴστέ τε πάντα,
> ἡμεῖς δὲ κλέος οἷον ἀκούομεν οὐδέ τι ἴδμεν.
>
> (*Iliad* 2. 484–6)

---

[11] Which, in fact, calls into question Derrida (1981), who famously ascribes to Plato a central role in the history of logocentric metaphysics.

[12] For more on the Muses' capacity to access an absolute narration which cannot be emulated or reproduced by the poet or the rhapsodes, cf. also Laird in this volume, who performs an ontological examination of the Muses' ideological status viewing them as an embodiment of Bakhtin's notion of the 'superaddressee'.

Tell me now Muses, who have your homes on Olympus, for you are goddesses, and are present, and know all, but we hear what is heard and see nothing.[13]

'We see nothing' has a radical meaning in the words of a blind man, but it also applies to the narrators who are not blind. The story always belongs to the past, to that which is no longer visible.[14] The immortal Muse sees because she is present. She sees things happening on the Trojan plain, the deeds of gods and men, the unfolding of events that weave the individual stories and become the story of the *Iliad*. As an eye-witness, she sees with omnipresent sight the events as they happen and, as the daughter of Mnemosyne, she preserves memories of them all. In other words she is the witness and memory of the story. The Muses' omnipresence and perfect memory confer an objective status of reality and truth on the story. The story is true because what happened, happened like this and not in any other way, in the very presence of the Muse, who sees it as it happens and preserves its memory. For the Muse seeing, knowing, and remembering are one. She represents the radical truth and objectivity of the story.

This vision, whose object is 'true' and 'real' things, closely resembles that of the philosopher, as described by Plato in the *Republic* (and else-where). The philosopher sees the ideas that manifest their brightness in his presence, and hence he knows them; he has a true knowledge of *ta onta*, 'the things that really are'. Like the Muse, with whom he shares the reliable power of sight, the philosopher sees and knows. But there is a difference; with her panoramic sight from above, the Muse looks mostly downward at the world of men, and at the contingencies and details of what takes place here. In contrast, the philosopher takes his eyes off the world of human lives and contingencies; he looks upwards to contemplate the fixed sky of ideas. The truth and reality of his visions are not concerned with the world of human stories, but rather with a superior world that is in contrast to the unfolding of stories, in the same way as being is in contrast to appearances, the universal contrasts with the particular, and ideas contrast with the plurality of living things. For example, the Muse sees the individual heroes who carry out courageous deeds; whereas the philosopher contemplates the idea of courage that presents itself, fixed and disembodied, to his vision.

Philosophy is concerned with general and desensitized essences,

---

[13] Contrast here, though, 'Greek Imprecisions' in the Introduction to this volume, which foregrounds the ambiguities inherent in the Homeric Muses' omniscient portrait.

[14] Cf. Arendt (1978) 133.

while epic is concerned with the embodied uniqueness of particular individuals, and celebrates their actions by telling stories.[15] Unlike Plato the philosopher, the Muse does not know Man but rather knows, one by one, all the men and women who act and speak in her presence, distinguishing themselves from one another 'in the unique shape of body and sound of voice'.[16] She knows all the names of those who fought in Troy, knows each thing—facts, actions, words—in detail. Precisely this is the Muse's truth (*aletheia*) mentioned by Hesiod (*Theogony* 27–8): a completeness and inclusion of every relevant detail. In a time-frame expanded to infinity, she could narrate everything to men if such an exhaustive account were humanly audible. But it isn't. An account of this kind, synoptic and detailed, is in fact an *absolute narration* that corresponds perfectly to the radical *objectivity* of the story. In other words, the absolute narration is nothing but the narration of the whole story, of its truth and its reality. Only the poet who is outside himself, *en theos*, can hear the absolute narration and make it into the telling of a story which is necessarily partial and incomplete but humanly audible.

Not all of the story narrated by the Muse therefore passes into the story narrated by the poet. The poet can only sing of some of the more eminent heroes—the more well-known characters—and reduces all the others into a multitude, a general category. As a figure conferring extreme realism on the story, the Muse marks the impossibility of a human narration that could coincide perfectly with the absolute reality of the story it endeavours to narrate. It is, according to Homer, a story about 'The multitude I could not tell nor could I name not if I had ten tongues, and ten mouths, and a voice unbreakable, and a breast of bronze within': πληθὺν δ' οὐκ ἂν ἐγὼ μυθήσομαι οὐδ' ὀνομήνω, | οὐδ' εἴ μοι δέκα μὲν γλῶσσαι, δέκα δὲ στόματ' εἶεν, | φωνὴ δ' ἄρρηκτος, χάλκεον δέ μοι ἦτορ ἐνείη (*Iliad* 2. 488–490).

V

Not even the Muse could make this story into a humanly audible narration. As far as the complete enumeration of details is concerned, the gap between the divine power of perfect sight and the telling of what is seen increases. It is not only a problem arising from the fact that 'sight can represent a complex reality to the mind at once, whereas to tell things

---

[15] On this, see also Arendt (1978) 86–92; (1958) 17–21; 181–96; Cavarero (1997).
[16] Arendt (1958) 179.

requires a sequence, which takes time'.[17] It is rather a question of dealing with the supernatural power of seeing every detail and memorizing it that the Muse seems, curiously, to share with Ireneo Funes, the protagonist of one of Luis Borges's most amazing fictions.[18] Inhuman capacity to grasp global—complete—reality cannot correspond to the narrative performance of human words. In fact, the absolute narration the Muse gives to the poet is inaudible to other mortals.

The Muse is a figure deeply entangled in the intricacies of the narrative. In Homeric poetics she has several fundamental functions. As the eyewitness of the story and source of the tale, the Muse represents above all an indispensable link between the story and the narration, as well as the distinction between them, for the narration is absolute precisely because it corresponds perfectly to the story told but does not coincide with it. Inasmuch as it consists of the interweaving of events that actually happened, the story—which is at the same time history—has no author.[19] The Muse herself is not the author of the story but was merely present as the events happened and now narrates them. Even in the divine horizon, which guarantees the perfect realistic existence of the story and the ideal of absolute narration, the story comes ontologically and logically *before* the narration. With a special ear for the divine voice, the poet does not recount what he saw but that which the Muse told him. The telling of stories in the human world does not consist in communicating what one has seen but in transmitting what one has heard.[20] The 'complete' story the Muse tells the poet alludes to this inscrutable oral source of every tale. It means 'that behind the telling of each story exists one divinely superintended tale, one connected whole that never alters'.[21]

By means of recapitulation: besides representing the musical source of the epic song, the Muse sums up three ideal, but humanly impossible, narrative functions: an infallible eyewitness testimony, a perfect memory, and an absolute tale. There are precise similarities between the narrative functions on both sides—the ideal and the human. The poet's partial tale corresponds to the absolute narration; the mnemonic skills with which the poet controls his memory correspond to the Muse, the daughter of Mnemosyne; the 'sight' of the blind and non-present poet corresponds to the Muse who sees and is present. The initial passage,

[17] Ford (1992) 75.   [18] Borges (1964).
[19] On this, see also Arendt (1958) 184.   [20] Cf. here Deleuze (1998) 76.
[21] Ford (1992) 49–50.

from a visual register to an acoustic one, which in a certain sense takes place in the Muse, is inverted in the poet. The song as voicing retrieves the visual horizon that guarantees the realistic, true, and objective status of the story.

VI

However, this is not an *exclusively* visual horizon. The realistic status of the story is essentially guaranteed by the presence at the events of the Muse, who not only sees but also hears. The story—like any story—is made up of a world of things, faces, names, actions, and speeches. And, it is also made up of sounds and noises, like the clanging of arms and the clip-clop of horses' hooves. The presence of the Muse brings something more than mere sight into play: her eyewitness testimony is also an acoustic testimony. She not only sees the action of those who are in Troy but also hears their words and speeches. By preserving the story in a sort of eternal actuality, Mnemosyne's daughter also preserves the speeches proffered to her presence; in addition, she preserves the sound of the unmistakable tone of the various voices. Her divine memory resounds with individual voices: Zeus, Hera, Athena, Hector, Achilles, Andromache, Helen, and all those who participate in Troy's 'episode', speak through their own individual voice; a voice which is unique—as the shape of each face and body is also unique—and which belongs together with all the other voices to a web of stories in which each character has his or her part. It is this voice which further supports the realistic status of the story and which marks the uniqueness of the part of each character who shares in the events. The story is an interweaving of parts; it is their 'partition'. Its unity is this interweaving of a plurality of uniquenesses made unique through acting and speaking. This is why the Muse knows the story in every single detail and does not generalize. In the original 'partition' of the story, in the divine memory that preserves it, there is no one who does not have his or her part, however small and insignificant. It would be like saying he or she was not there. It would be like not seeing and not remembering their existence. This is forbidden by the realistic status of the story of which the Muse is the foundation and custodian.

If the task of the poet is to voice the absolute narration of the story, the task of the poet is therefore that of further voicing the sonorous universe of the story that the Muse narrates to him: the clanging of arms, the clip-

clop of horses' hooves, but above all the 'partition' of human voices.
Interestingly enough, the poetic duty of narrating the story *kata moiran*,
mentioned in *Odyssey* 8. 496, ends up corresponding to the *theia moira*, as
divine dispensation theorized by Plato. The poet sings and tells a story
about things, actions, and speeches, as well. Confined within his own
vocal specialness, he listens to the Muse's story and represents many
voices with the tone of a unique and different sound of a singular voice—
his own. He reduces the speeches of men and gods to one voice—the so-
called omniscient narrator's voice, which none the less is a single voice.

Discussing epic in *Republic* 3, Plato (like Aristotle) is fully aware of the
issues raised above. But rather than directly addressing the sonorous
physicality of the voice, he chooses to focus on *how* the poet reports the
speeches of the protagonists in the story or recounts their deeds by
means of mimesis or diegesis. Plato's and Aristotle's views on mimesis
and diegesis have become cornerstones in modern narrative studies and
reconstructing them in their totality is outside the scope of this chapter.
In the present context, it is sufficient to be eclectic and explain that in the
case of mimesis, that is the narration in which Homer has his characters
speak in direct speech, the blind poet, according to Plato, pretends to be
someone else and assimilates himself in voice (*phone*) or gesture (*schema*)
to another and so imitates him (393c). The condemnation of the poet as
mimetes is thus reinforced; but this is not the crucial point. To report
words in words and to report actions in words are two different operations. The oral narration of actions displaces the actions themselves,
which are necessarily an object of vision, into another form of existence.
What is visible is different from what is audible and each one addresses
different faculties. For the Greeks, the passage from one to the other is
an interesting problem and worthy of attention. Plato, for his part,
moves almost too easily between the different spheres of the visible and
the audible and appears capable of finding audacious parallelisms
between vision and voice, images and sounds.

The myth of the cave, the scene in which the blind poet manipulates
visual tricks, introduced at the beginning of this chapter, is an excellent
example: in recounting it, Plato is obviously exploiting the transition
from the visual register to the acoustic register which characterizes epic.
However, this is one only of the many nuances of the cave episode: the
rest of this chapter will attempt to explore some more and explain why
it is an episode at the heart of Plato's unsettled relationship with the
figure of the Muse and inspiration.

VII

In *Republic* 10 Plato examines painting, in order to reinforce his condemnation of poetry. Painting is a visual art, and the philosopher feels more
secure on this ground. The dialogue between Socrates and Glaucon
develops a rather imprecise pattern: criticism of painting alternates con-
tinuously with that of poetry. However, the analogy between poetry
and painting is explicit. For Plato, the painter is an imitator because he
creates images and copies of things which, in turn, are copies of the
'forms'. Painting takes advantage of the confusion of the senses caused
by optical illusions, and in this sense, it is not dissimilar to magic,
jugglery, and other such contrivances (602d). In Platonic terms, it means
that painting plays with some natural optical illusions by reproducing
them emphatically. It follows that the painter should be harshly condemned for his artifice; but this is not Plato's true objective. He means to
play on the analogy between painting and poetry in order to transfer the
characteristics of the art which appeals to sight to the art which appeals
to hearing. Later on, Socrates asks his interlocutor if what they have said
about artifice 'applies only to visual imitation or also the auditory—
what we call poetry' (603b). Glaucon responds that it does, and the dialogue continues to reinforce the consequences of the analogy.

This analogical frame does not lack significant details and metaphors.
Metre, rhythm, and harmony of the poetic verse are made to coincide
with words (*onomata*) and phrases (*remata*) with which the poet gives
colour (*chroma*) to the *technai* of which he speaks without being competent in them. The element of colour reinforces the analogy with painting and corresponds significantly to the enchantment effect of poetry.
The suggestion is that just as the painter enchants and tricks with colours
so too does the poet with rhythmic modulations of the voice. Once
again, the focus is on the expressive material rather than the content.
Colour and voice, alongside sight and hearing, are at the heart of the discussion. Nevertheless, the analogy is skewed to the side of painting.
Using terms that undoubtedly belong to the lexicon of visibility,
Socrates accuses Homer of creating images (*eidola*) and appearances
(*phainomena*). We are, once again, encountering the same paradox:
although the blind poet sings with his voice, seemingly Homeric epic
appeals to the eyes instead of the ears, just as the myth of the cave
suggests. Among other things, this myth is valuable in clarifying a crucial
aspect of the paradox. In the cave scene, Homer is not being accused of

exciting the imagination of the listeners or soliciting visions in them, which would thus transform them from listeners into onlookers. He is accused above all of doing exactly what those painters do who, according to the famous example in *Republic* 10, do not know how to look at the 'form' of the bed as the artisan does, but only know how to look at a bed built by an artisan and paint its image. Homer thus looks at the heroes entering battle and, without looking at the idea that inspires the art of warfare, creates an image of the battle. In the *Ion*, Socrates supports this assumption with the illustration of a rhapsode who 'thinks that he is present at the events he is describing, whether they be in Ithaca or Troy or wherever': καὶ παρὰ τοῖς πράγμασιν οἴεταί σου εἶναι ἡ ψυχὴ . . . ἢ ἐν Ἰθάκῃ οὖσιν ἢ ἐν Τροίᾳ ἢ ὅπως ἂν καὶ τὰ ἔπη ἔχῃ (535b); For Plato, Homer is like the painter who looks at a copy and reproduces its image. In other words, the poet, like the painter, makes a copy of a copy of the idea.

Something similar takes place inside the cave: the bearers of simulacra copy the ideas and project shadows, copies of copies, on the screen. The voice does not play an important role; both the bearers and the prisoners speak to one another, but no one tells stories or sings. In the cave 'seeing' and its ingenious imitation reign supreme. The world of the cave is essentially a projection room for captive spectators, who spend all their lives watching shadows which appear on the screen one after another, in a repetitive and monotonous fashion.

It has already been noted[22] that Plato characteristically describes 'the inhabitants of the cave as though they too were only interested in seeing'. The Platonic assumption that what makes men human is 'the urge to see' is what inspires the entire scenography of the myth. The protagonist of the tale is the philosopher who turns away from the shadows and rises upwards in order to contemplate with his acute sight the splendour of ideas. Based on vision, as the guarantee of true knowledge and correct *paideia*, the myth is extremely coherent. The prisoners in the cave are human only in so far as they want to see; they are spectators of shadows as much as the philosopher is a spectator of ideas. What is certain is that the prisoners are spectators whose eyes are chained to a repetitive sequence of images.

We know from the *Ion* that the magnetic chain which descends from the Muse gives similar effects, though in a more pleasant way. As the magnetic power of a ring forms 'a long chain of iron rings suspended

[22] Cf. here Arendt (1993) 114–15.

from one another . . . so too the Muse herself makes people possessed, and from these possessed persons there hangs a chain': ὁρμαθὸς μακρὸς πάνυ σιδηρίων καὶ δακτυλίων ἐξ ἀλλήλων ἤρτηται . . . οὕτω δὲ καὶ ἡ Μοῦσα ἐνθέους μὲν ποιεῖ αὐτή, διὰ δὲ τῶν ἐνθέων τούτων ἄλλων ἐνθουσιαζόντων ὁρμαθὸς ἐξαρτᾶται (533e). And 'the spectator is the last of the rings' of this chain: ὁ θεατὴς τῶν δακτυλίων ὁ ἔσχατος (535e).[23] Homer has the extraordinary power of enchanting the listeners, as if he were tying their ears with the rhythmic string of his voice. The listeners remain seated and immobile, fascinated by the metre, rhythm, and harmony of the verses. They listen, as if they were hypnotized, to Homer's verses always recited afresh by a new rhapsode. The song, in good measure, is an infinite repetition of the same stories in the same sequence with the same words and the same rhythm. Yet, the listeners never tire of listening to it.

So the prisoners of Plato's cave are not so bizarre after all. What is bizarre is the idea of substituting the horizon of listening with that of vision, of transporting a practice of phonetic order into a practice of visual order. The philosopher obviously cannot do otherwise, since contemplation is his speciality. He can only measure the humanity of humans through vision, if not contemplation. However, the thing does not work without artifice. To keep the prisoners immobile, with their eyes fixed on their visions, Plato needs tricks and devices. The magnetic power of the Muse—the source of honey for light and winged songs that enchain the listeners to the tale—must be replaced by an artificial harnessing of the gaze, and this is the very necessary harnessing that the chains, which keep the prisoners tied, and the projectors, which project illusive sights on the wall before them, provide.

As if by some awkward conjuring trick or inescapable ambiguity, these very chains and projectors also diffuse the clarity of a seemingly realistic scene with metaphoric allusions: on one level, the trapped inhabitants of the cave are the audience which listens to the epic songs, the people enchanted by the Muse and caught in the narrative illusion of Homer and in the visions cunningly elicited by means of his tale. On another level, however, these are the chained spectators of Plato alone, who must bind them very tightly so that they keep their gaze fixed on the screen and never turn their heads around or to one side. The paradox

---

[23] It is worth noting that, in an ambiguous fashion which is typical of Plato, the listeners (*hoi akouontes*) will, in the space of a few lines, become the spectators (*hoi theatai*) anticipated at 535b: καὶ ἐκπλήξῃς μάλιστα τοὺς θεωμένους.

of a blind poet who projects images onto a screen—a paradox which is worsened rather than resolved with the analogy between painting and poetry—ultimately finds an explanation. A very able creator of images, Plato is the most blatant of imitators. The cave represents the most spectacular Platonic mimesis of the oral world in which Homer sings and enchants. Plato imitates the fascination effects of the Muse because he envies her.

VIII

As has been famously suggested, the transition from Homer to Plato is a transition from orality to writing: the eye supplants the ear.[24] Indeed, Plato dedicates one of his most intense and anomalous dialogues, the *Phaedrus*, to the theme of writing. In contrast to the spoken *logos* which is alive, writing in the *Phaedrus* is accused of being dead and silent, incapable of responding to questions and incapable of defending itself. In this respect, says Plato, writing is truly analogous to painting: 'the creations of painting are before you as live things, but if you ask them a question they remain in a venerable silence' (275d). As Derrida keenly noted, it is significant how painting (*zoographein*) and writing (*graphein*) have a very close etymological relationship.[25] Writing is the pictorial copy of the living word, the visible sign of the voice, the *eidolon* of living and animated speech (276a). Writing is the visible image of what is audible; it is something that conveys speech from the realm of the ear to that of the eye.

Did not something similar happen on the screen in the cave? Did not the paradoxical figure of the blind poet intent on projecting images suggest a strange passage of the voice to the image, from hearing to vision? Surprisingly, it therefore seems appropriate to put forward another interpretation of the bizarre myth of the cave. In the ambiguous art of Plato the imitator, the inhabitants of the cave, who are only intent on the activity of seeing, are perhaps confined readers. They look at the signs of writing, the obscure traces of speech, the shadow of *logos*. Born from Plato's imagery, the book chains the gaze and perhaps, like the Muse, has the power of enchanting.

With arguments that are reminiscent of the *Ion*, the *Phaedrus* also speaks of poetic delirium. It is a specific kind of madness which, coming from the Muse, 'takes hold of a gentle and pure soul, arouses it and

<hr />

[24] Havelock (1963).   [25] Derrida (1981) 136.

inspires it to songs and other poetry, and thus by adorning countless deeds of the ancients educates later generations': λαβοῦσα ἁπαλὴν καὶ ἄβατον ψυχήν, ἐγείρουσα καὶ ἐκβακχεύουσα κατά τε ᾠδὰς καὶ κατὰ τὴν ἄλλην ποίησιν, μυρία τῶν παλαιῶν ἔργα κοσμοῦσα τοὺς ἐπιγιγνομένους παιδεύει; (245a). The allusion to Homer is perfectly clear. But the poet that sings of the 'countless deeds of the ancients' (*ton palaion erga*) and educates later generations must surely be Homer, first historian and great educator of Greece. What is amazing is that there is no negative tone in the words that Plato puts in the mouth of Socrates. Imbued by the Muse, continues Socrates in the same passage, poets in delirium are the best poets.

Still more amazing is another passage from the *Phaedrus* that ties even philosophers in with the Muse.[26] To illustrate this, Socrates invents the famous myth of the cicadas, which plays a major role in the conceptual framework of the dialogue.[27] As he explains, the family of cicadas came from a certain type of men who lived before the birth of the Muses. When song was invented with the birth of the Muses, these men were so overcome with delight that they sang endlessly, forgetting food and drink, until at last they died unconscious (259b–c). The Muses then transformed these men into cicadas and granted them the privilege of singing their whole lives long without ever needing nourishment and of having access to the Muses in order to report on those humans on earth who honour each of them (259c). It was thus that each Muse came to know and hold dearly those who venerated her own art; for example, the art of dancing for Terpsichore or the songs of love for Erato. The philosophers were even given two Muses: Calliope and Urania, who are most concerned with thought divine and human and whose music is the sweetest (259d).

According to Socrates' tale, therefore, the relationship between the philosophers and the Muse is mediated by the cicadas, and so is the relationship between the Muses and the poets, as well as all those who honour the arts. Even if the delirium is no longer presented as a flow that descends directly from the Muse and invades the soul prompting it to sing, it still pervades the myth. The cicadas are the ambiguous figures of a delirious song and a divine mania which makes one sing. Compared by Socrates with those other irresistible singers, Homer's famous Sirens,

[26] For an extensive presentation on how the Muses came to occupy centre-stage in the Platonic discourse of philosophy, cf. Murray in this volume.

[27] On this cf. also Ferrari (1987).

the cicadas were originally men 'overcome with delight while singing'. In a state of permanent stupor caused by this intense pleasure, the cicadas spend their entire existence without food or drink, singing a stupor-inducing song every day from noontime onwards. The cicadas are also messengers, for the Muses, of the men who dedicate themselves to the song. If not delirium, there lies at the centre of this myth a stupor that enchants, a pleasure that dulls the vital instincts, a song that attracts and kills like that of the Sirens.

Thus, in the *Phaedrus* as well, Plato never tires of concerning himself with the enchanting/enchaining effect that comes from the Muse. Epic as narration concerns Plato on several counts; but epic as a song is his chief preoccupation. Muses and Sirens with a harmonious and irresistible voice, or cicadas with a monotonous and penetrating song, mark most of the Platonic passages devoted to the criticism of poetry with a sort of uncontrollable pathos. The function of these mythical figures is to allude to the sonorous material, that is to say, the pre-discursive element of speech. Their song tells a tale, but it is above all the physical element of the voice, the harmonious sound, that makes them divine singers. Here the visual register no longer matters and the vocal-acoustic register reigns supreme. The voice of these mythical figures is live material, corporeal vibrations that wash over other bodies, in musical modulations, as a gift; a seductive, irresistible, dangerous, and sometimes lethal gift. And they are all female figures.

No doubt, the embodiment of the voice symbolized by the female figure can be easily inscribed into the classic phallogocentric opposition which poses woman as body and man as mind. But there is also another suggestion available to the receptive reader, a rather disconcerting one—which cannot be reduced to the binary economy of the patriarchal canon. Namely the realization that the enchanting musical voice closely resembles the *chora* theorized by Julia Kristeva,[28] and most of all the feminine voice to which Hélène Cixous draws attention:[29] the voice of the mother, 'the voice mixed with milk', whose echo is heard in poetic metre and which gives pleasure with spontaneous generosity. As sweet as honey, suggests Cixous, milk is drunk in rhythmic suction, and its supply will never run dry. Such a female voice could also be an allusion to the rhythmic sound of the heartbeat the baby hears in the mother's womb, or perhaps it even evokes the song the nomadic woman sings to her child as she quickens the heartbeat with the rhythm of her steps

[28] See esp. Kristeva (1984).   [29] See esp. Cixous (1981); (1991).

while giving names to things.[30] The myth from time immemorial repeats, however, the same message: female figures stand at the origin of a song, modulated on pre-discursive assonances, in which voice and story are intermixed and draw the listener towards the pleasure of secret resonances. In the end, such is the very secret of poetry, of Homer's strength, of the magic of epic. Devoted to the *logos* of the father and his disembodied visions—as the philosopher who deals with the transition from the spoken word to the written text—Plato, therefore, faces the problem of giving up metre, rhythm, and harmony without ever losing their secret. The task seems quite impossible, and, wisely, the philosopher turns to Urania and Calliope.

[30] Cf. here Chatwin (1987) 229, 272.

4

Reinscribing the Muse: Greek Drama and the Discourse of Inspired Creativity

Ismene Lada-Richards

What happened to the Muse in the fifth-century Athenian City, when the lone 'inspired' bard gave place to the whole pageant of actors, masks, and costumes captivating the public gaze in the midst of lavish festivals and large-scale, communal celebrations? Did the emergence of dramatic poetry render the functions of the archaic Muse(s) obsolete? This chapter argues that within the context of fifth-century performances the Muse's presence can still be intensely felt, for Drama as a genre has reinscribed and reamalgamated important attributes traditionally attached to her. Much less of a 'real life' entity than her archaic predecessor, the classical Muse operates now on the level of metaphor and figurative discourse, reshaped and reappropriated by the performative frame of fifth-century Athenian culture.

I. MAKING THE HEROES 'PRESENT': MUSES AND DRAMATIC POETS, ARCHAIC BARDS AND CLASSICAL STAGE-ACTORS

In *Odyssey* 8. 487 ff. Odysseus praises Demodocus, the bard in the Phaeacian court:

> Δημόδοκ', ἔξοχα δή σε βροτῶν αἰνίζομ' ἁπάντων
> ἢ σέ γε Μοῦσ' ἐδίδαξε, Διὸς πάϊς, ἢ σέ γ' Ἀπόλλων.
> λίην γὰρ κατὰ κόσμον Ἀχαιῶν οἶτον ἀείδεις,
> ὅσσ' ἔρξαν τ' ἔπαθόν τε καὶ ὅσσ' ἐμόγησαν Ἀχαιοί,
> ὥς τέ που ἢ αὐτὸς παρεὼν ἢ ἄλλου ἀκούσας.

Demodokos, above all mortals beside I prize you. Surely the Muse, Zeus'
daughter or else Apollo has taught you, for all too right following the tale you
sing the Achaians' venture, all they did and had done to them, all the sufferings
of these Achaians, *as if you had been there yourself or heard it from one who was.*

(tr. R. Lattimore; my italics)

The archaic Muse grants to her favoured bard the possibility of a
different vision: the inspired poet enacts a journey to a space beyond
time, where he can have a glimpse of the 'reality that lies beyond the
sensible world' (Thalmann 1984: 147). Like the Platonic Ion, who feels
himself 'transported' among the very events he is narrating (Pl. *Ion* 535c),
the Muse-inspired *aoidos* 'has been' among the heroes themselves and
has acquired 'a direct personal view' (Vernant 1969: 54) of the past.[1] As
Andrew Ford (1992: 120 ff.) has brilliantly discussed, Demodocus' face-
to-face encounter with Odysseus, the very subject of his song, becomes
the symbol of the singer's privileged insight into the heart of ancient
events. It is because his virtual meeting with the heroes has been such an
intense, immediate experience, leading straight into the profundities of
being that he can now, in his turn, evoke them for the sake of the
audience, reinscribe their figure and their presence 'in the here and now
of the performance' (Bakker 1993a: 10). Every time he sings, the epic past
is re-enacted; the barrier between the world of the heroes and his world
collapses—the heroes are 'here'.[2] However, if in the oral tradition it falls
upon the bard to create this immediacy of the heroic presence, in the
realm of Drama this very same task becomes the duty of the actor: it is
the actor who places the characters of legend in the sight of the audience;
it is the actor's body, that irreducible theatrical icon, which becomes the
'site' where past and present meet, and where the abstract reality of
myth can be transformed into a palpable reality of flesh.

But, although the stage-performer and the bard share this role of
'making the past present' to the eyes of the spectators,[3] their mediating
function does not derive from the same source: the vision of the heroes
that the bard acquires directly from the *Muse* the actor can only acquire

---

[1] This paragraph incorporates several *bons mots* of Vernant (1969) 54–8 on poetic memory.

[2] Cf. Bakker's excellent remarks (1993b) 23 on the epic narrator's direct apostrophes to his
heroes at intensely emotional moments of the action.

[3] On 'vividness' (in the 'sense that the past is somehow present before us') as a fundamental
quality of epic performance see Ford's splendid discussion (1992) esp. 54–6; quote from 49. On
the feeling of 'presence' as a constituent element of *enargeia* see the famous characterization of
Lysias' style as turning the reader into an eyewitness who converses with the fictive characters
ὥσπερ παροῦσιν, 'as if they were present' (Dion. Hal. *Lys.* 7); see Zanker (1981).

at one remove, through representations fashioned by the dramatic *poet*. To the face-to-face meeting of the bard and hero in that uncanny 'au-delà' sustained by the Muse corresponds the mediated meeting of the actor with his character through the playwright's script.[4]

The poet is to the actor what the Muse is to the bard: it is only through the Muse that the oral singer can be put in touch with the heroes of the world beyond,[5] just as it is only through the eyes of the poet that the actor can acquire a character with which to merge, a costume and a mask that he must bring to life. It is the poet who makes the heroes or the gods of myth 'accessible' to the performer, by moulding them into personas, 'figures' of human experience to which he, another human, can relate. Searching, then, for incarnations of the Muse in the performative reality of the Athenian theatrical event, we find that her pivotal mediating function has now become amalgamated with the role of the *poeta creator* himself: the dramatist 'plays Muse' to his stage-actor, the professional performer who will bring his own creations into being.

II. TRUTH, LIES, AND TRAGIC *APATE*

ἴδμεν ψεύδεα πολλὰ λέγειν ἐτύμοισιν ὁμοῖα,
ἴδμεν δ' εὖτ' ἐθέλωμεν ἀληθέα γηρύσασθαι.
(Hes. *Theog.* 27–8)

We know how to tell many lies that look like genuine things,
but we also know, when we will, how to proclaim things which are true.

This is undoubtedly one of the most famous utterances of the archaic Muses. However, the privileged control over *aletheia* that Hesiod's Muses claim for themselves should not be readily or exclusively identified with our concept of 'truth' as a faithful, accurate, and all-inclusive representation of reality,[6] that is, to use Dan Sperber's terminology, as 'encyclopaedic' truth containing statements 'about the world' and 'subject to empirical falsification' (see Sperber 1975: 91 ff.). As French scholars and their followers have repeatedly emphasized, archaic 'truth'

---

[4] It is not without significance that the legendary heroes whom Dicaeopolis meets in Euripides' house in Aristophanes' *Acharnians* are costumes, rags in fact, 'wound up to look like scrolls' (Macleod (1974) 221).

[5] On the omnipresence of the Muse, who sees and hears everything 'as it happens and preserves its memory', see Cavarero in this volume.

[6] Although it would be a mistake to believe that such notions do not belong to the semantic field of archaic 'truth'. See Pratt (1993) 21 and cf. Bowie (1993) 17.

(*aletheia*) is primarily the negation of forgetfulness (*lethe*):[7] through the skills of the Muse-inspired *aoidos*, the audience can bring to mind (*mimneskesthai*) the epic heroes with the same immediacy and vividness that Penelope 'brings to mind' (*memnemene*) her absent husband while listening to Phemius' songs (Hom. *Od.* 1. 343–4). The 'truth' created by the bard's performance protects the hero from the danger of becoming *a-mnastos*, without a cause to be remembered, without the privilege of being easily 'accessible'[8] in the community's collective consciousness. The vision of the Muses imparted to the poet has the power to exclude oblivion and death as well as to guarantee the everlasting 'presence' of those mentioned in the song.

And yet, the site par excellence where collective memory becomes a vivid 'presence' is the dramatic genre of the classical Athenian *polis*: the inspired bard's power to create 'vividly', *enargos* (see n. 3 above), has now been inherited by the dramatic players, whose function is not merely to 'sing about' but rather to impersonate the heroes of the past. Merging with their masks and characters the actors now ensure that, for as long as the performance lasts, they *become* the heroes they incarnate: they do not *play at being* Antigone or Oedipus; they *are* Antigone or Oedipus.[9] Their skill in imitation (*mimesis*)[10] *makes* the heroes *present* for the sake of the audience.[11]

Moreover, the song created by the bard blessed with the Muse's truthful vision is 'efficacious' (Detienne 1996: 43) or even 'performative' speech, in J. L. Austin's (1962: 91) sense of the term, whereby some

---

[7] See e.g. Vernant (1969); Detienne (1996) 39 ff.; Nagy (1989) 30–1; cf. Thalmann (1984) 147, following Vernant: 'The "truth" that the Muses can speak . . . has the value accorded memory in mythic thought.'

[8] For this notion see Bakker (1993a) 14 n. 16; cf. 13.

[9] It goes without saying that 'becoming' and 'being' are not to be taken literally here; the actor 'is' Antigone, and not the real-life 5th-cent. Athenian playing the Sophoclean heroine, *only in so far as* his performance encourages the spectator to 'surrender', to lose sight of the process of artistic transformation and to prevent his awareness of the dramatic frame's artificiality from shattering the 'illusion' of the stage-world. See Lada-Richards (1997b).

[10] In this respect the actor is a direct descendant of the Muses, who are mistresses of mimetic disguise (see e.g. the so-called 'Mnesiepes Inscription' (T4 Tarditi), where the three Muses appear to Archilochus as country-women (28–30)) and, in general, 'models of mimesis by way of practicing mimesis' (Nagy (1996a) 73), as, for example, in the ritual persona of the Delian Maidens (see below). And, of course, the concept of imitation is already inherent in Hesiod's claim that the lying statements of the Muses 'look like' the truth (see Pucci (1977) 9).

[11] Cf. Nagy's formulation (1996a) 61 with respect to the rhapsode in the epic tradition: 'when the rhapsode says "tell me, Muses!" . . . this "I" is not a *representation* of Homer; it *is* Homer. My argument is that the rhapsode . . . *is* Homer so long as the mimesis stays in effect, so long as the performance lasts.' Cf. ibid. 86.

utterances do not simply describe, state, or report an action but 'perform' it instead, so that 'to say something may be to do something'. And, if the song of the inspired bard can 'create' reality,[12] in dramatic performance there are times when 'some sequences of words, music and actions could be felt to have exceptional power, something that went beyond the fictive world of the drama and was able to affect the world of the audience for good or ill'.[13] In its most poignant moments, then, Athenian Drama seems to have inherited the efficacy of the archaic Muse's 'truthful' speech. For just as the inspired poet's song 'creates' (cf. *poietes*) the remote world of heroes so vividly that they almost make 'a genuine "breakthrough in the performance"' (Bakker 1993b: 23), many a time the theatrical reality constructed by Drama as a genre appears to defy confinement to the dramatic space and to 'spill over' into the world of the extra-dramatic, real-life *polis*. In this way, the *politai* to whom Aeschylus' *Semnai*, or indeed Aeschylus himself in the concluding scene of Aristophanes' *Frogs*, are expected to bring bless-ings[14] are not only the imaginary inhabitants of the dramatic Athens but, more significantly, the real-life citizens of both the prosperous mid-century Athenian *polis* and the tormented land of 405 BC.

Now, given that the Muses' claim in *Theogony* 27–8, quoted at the beginning of this section, is intricately interlaced with narrative, there is another issue which requires consideration. For *pseudea* which sound 'like true things' (*etymoisin homoia*) may well refer not to 'untrue', that is, inaccurate, representations of the world, but to tales which have an internal logic and coherence, a discursive plausibility which generates *ipso facto* acceptance and persuasion,[15] like Odysseus' lying tales on his return to Ithaca:[16] the stories the disguised king narrated have succeeded in 'enchanting' the faithful Eumaeus (*Od.* 17. 521) not because they were historically accurate, but because they were woven together so artfully

---

[12] In the same way that Silenus, a persona of the inspired bard in Virgil's Sixth *Eclogue*, not only 'sings' (*canebat*, 31; *canit*, 61), but also 'creates' reality through his singing: *circumdat* (62), *erigit* (63).

[13] See Easterling (1988) 109 with special reference to Aeschylus' *Oresteia*; cf. Lada-Richards (1999) 326–9 with respect to *Frogs*.

[14] Cf. *Frogs* 1487: ἐπ' ἀγαθῷ μὲν τοῖς πολίταις.

[15] Cf. the interest in the *internal* plausibility of a fictitious story, something which seems to become a fixture in late literary criticism, as e.g. in Eustathius' *Progymnasmata* 3. 23–6, focusing on τὴν πλάσιν αὐτῶν (sc. τῶν μύθων) καὶ τὴν ἐν αὐτῇ πιθανότητα. See other examples in Meijering (1987) 82.

[16] Tales which attract the poet's comment: ἴσκε ψεύδεα πολλὰ λέγων ἐτύμοισιν ὁμοῖα (*Od.* 19. 203).

as not to leave any narrative gaps, any cause for *aporia* and frustration. Similarly, when Alcinous likens Odysseus to a skilful bard, his praise is based on the shapeliness (*morphe*) of Odysseus' words (*Od.* 11. 367–8), which seem to fit together nicely into a coherent whole. To put it in another way, if in Alcinous' perception Odysseus does not resemble people who wander widely, 'making up lying stories' (ψεύδεά τ' ἀρτύνοντας, 11. 363–6), this is not because the accuracy of his tales has withstood any test, but rather because they form 'an aesthetically convincing truth' (Ford 1992: 124–5).

In archaic poetics, then, 'truth' and 'lies' may well be intrinsic properties of the narrative, not to be measured by their relation to external sources (cf. Dolezel 1980: 24) but rather appreciated as artistic qualities,[17] elements of the bard's 'poetic grammar'.[18] Giving to one's tales *morphe* (*Od.* 11. 367), that is, 'an aesthetically correct "shape" ' (Walsh 1984: 6), as well as speaking *lien . . . kata kosmon* or *kata moiran*,[19] that is, 'very much as it should be' (Bowie 1993: 16), 'fittingly', 'rightly', and in accordance with social propriety,[20] are the sine qua non qualities of a persuasive performance and hence of artistic 'truth'. Yet, it is precisely this ability to construct 'fitting' or 'appropriate' 'characters' (*ethe*) and 'intellects' (*dianoiai*) which lies at the heart of the dramatic poet's art.[21] The dramatist is not concerned with *what has truly happened* (for he is not a historian) but with what *could* have happened[22] and, hence, with plausibility: as Aristotle puts it, 'events which are impossible but plausible should be preferred to those which are possible but implausible'.[23]

Besides, if Hesiod attributes to his Muses the skilled manipulation or even arbitrary (re-)negotiation of the boundaries of *aletheia* and *pseudos*,[24] it is now Tragedy as a genre and the tragic dramatists them-

[17] Cf. Bowie (1993) 17. For a sustained defence of the existence in the ancient world of 'a range of concepts which may usefully be compared to what we call "fiction" ' see Feeney (1993) (quote from 231).

[18] I say 'may' because I *do* take on board Pratt's (1993) 69 very thoughtfully presented warning against assuming that the principle of 'formal coherence' or artistic expertise equals 'truth' is a general credo of archaic or even merely Odyssean poetics.

[19] See Odysseus' praise of Demodocus in *Od.* 8. 487–98.

[20] See on this issue Ford's (1992) 121–5 excellent discussion. Cf. Pratt (1993) esp. 85 and 91.

[21] On *ethos* see Arist. *Poet.* 1454ᵃ30; cf. *Poet.* 1454ᵃ22–4; On *dianoia* see *Poet.* 1450ᵇ5. On the question of propriety (*to prepon*) in literary criticism see Pohlenz (1965).

[22] See Polybius' famous distinction between History and Tragedy (2. 56. 11–12), with Walbank (1985).

[23] Halliwell's (1987) tr. of *Poet.* 1461ᵇ11–12: πρός τε γὰρ τὴν ποίησιν αἰρετώτερον πιθανὸν ἀδύνατον ἢ ἀπίθανον καὶ δυνατόν.

[24] Among the many discussions of the Hesiodic passage see Pucci (1977) 8 ff.; (1980); Bergren

selves who offer to their audience that special kind of *pseudos* and *apate*[25] which results in scenic 'truth'. For tragic 'deception' does not consist in the relaying of falsehoods or the literal cheating of the audience but in drama's psychagogic and illusionist power, its unique ability to bewitch and cast a spell.[26] Just as the *a-letheia* vouchsafed by the archaic Muse co-operates with *lesmosyne*, that is, the forgetting of one's own ills (Hes. *Theog.* 98–103; cf. *Theog.* 55), so that the hero's *kleos* can be kept constantly in mind,[27] the tragic poet relies on his capacity to *apatan* to create a vivid and compelling stage-action. According to Gorgias' famous dictum (B23 DK), 'he who deceives is more just than he who does not deceive, and he who is deceived is wiser than he who is not deceived' (cf. n. 25). And, in any case, tragic *mimesis* wavers constantly between truth and falsehood, for it does not purport to record the *ipsissima verba* of the heroes [28] but only to present what the heroes *could* have said if placed in particular circumstances drawn from the world of myth.[29] Provided the dramatist does not warp beyond recognition the figures he inherits from the legends, it is *expected* that he will create

(1983); Ferrari (1988); Nagy (1992); see esp. Arthur (1983) 106, who understands 'The *logos* which the Muses offer' as 'a self-conscious re-presentation of the ambiguity which constitutes it' and as self-consciously aware 'of its own fictionality'. On the Hesiodic Muses as the 'exclusive subjects . . . of *all* semiosis' see Bal (1983) 127. From the audience's point of view, narrative *aletheia* and *pseudos* are inextricably interwoven with the dialectic of 'belief' and 'disbelief' in such a way that, as Feeney (1993) 240 has expressed it: 'The limits of belief appear to be always implicated in the limits of disbelief—to be, even, defined by them.'

[25] See primarily Gorgias, fr. B23 DK on Tragedy as offering (παρασχοῦσα) τοῖς μύθοις καὶ τοῖς πάθεσιν ἀπάτην, and PKöln VI 242A, line 20: νῦν δ' εἰς ἀπάτας κεκύλισμαι (with Bierl (1990) 385). For tragic fiction understood as *pseudos* cf. Solon's legendary reaction at Thespis' first performance (Plut. *Solon* 29. 4–5) and in a metatheatrical perspective see e.g. Soph. *Phil.* 100; Ar. *Thesm.* 875; PKöln VI 242A, 21 (with Bierl 1990); see Lada-Richards (1998). *Pseudos* is closely linked with *apate* in Polyb. 2. 56. 12.

[26] See in general Lada-Richards (1993); for the debate over the link between Gorgias' *apate* and 'illusionism' see esp. Rosenmeyer (1955); Segal (1962); Pohlenz (1965); Walsh (1984); Verdenius (1981), and, most recently, Bierl (1990).

[27] Cf. Cole's (1983) 12 influential understanding of archaic *aletheia* as embracing the notion of 'not forgetting from one minute to the next what was said a few minutes before, and not letting anything, said or unsaid, slip by without being mindful of its consequences and implications'.

[28] However, as far as epic poetry is concerned see Nagy (1996a) 61: 'What he [the singer of Homeric poetry] then tells his audience is supposed to be exactly what he hears from the Muse or Muses . . . who are conceived as the infallible custodians of the *ipsissima verba* emanating from the Heroic Age.'

[29] Cf. e.g. a very interesting papyrus fragment, where Sophocles (along with Homer) are praised because they attribute to their heroes the kind of words they *could* have said and the manner in which they *would* have spoken: οἷα γὰρ ἂν εἴποι καὶ ὡς . . . (text in Lucas (1968) 159); cf. Feeney (1993) 233.

fictitious, yet plausible, situations,[30] which his actors will be obliged to
sustain throughout the performance, playing at being somebody 'other'
than themselves and pretending to be involved in incidents which never
really happened to them.

III. FROM ALL-KNOWING MUSE TO ALL-ENCOMPASSING *MIMESIS*

One of the ways in which the archaic poet can authenticate his tale is to
present its content as the revelation of the all-knowing Muse(s). It is the
Muses who, planting in his mind 'all paths of song' (οἴμας | παντοίας
Od. 22. 347–8), enable him to roam over a vast poetic space (cf. Ford 1992:
esp. 42–4) and thus to acquire a panoramic vista, a direct and privileged
contact with modes of existence so diverse that no single man would
ever be able to experience except through *kleos*, rumour:[31] gods and
monsters, superhuman heroes and ordinary mortals, kings and swine-
herds, men and women—a limitless repertory of characters and situations. But, if the epic Muse offers to the bard an all-embracing,
all-encompassing survey of cosmic registers, the dramatic Muse never
performs similar services. In fact, in one of the very few glimpses of the
dramatist at work that Greek theatre affords, the poet strives to acquire
the experience that he lacks not through externally received inspiration
but through his own skills in imitation:[32] 'whatever we don't have we
must capture by *mimesis*' (ἃ δ' οὐ κεκτήμεθα, | μίμησις ἤδη ταῦτα
συνθηρεύεται, Ar. *Thesm.* 155–6), reasons Agathon, the tragic poet, in
what may be the earliest (albeit parodic) rendition of the mimetic
theory of art.[33] In the Aristophanic Agathon's perspective, a poet must,

---

[30] This holds true especially in the case of comic poets, who are not bound by mythical plots.
For Tragedy see Feeney (1993) 233: 'Even though Ajax or Achilles may have been thought of as
actual people who had once lived, even receiving hero-cult in historical times, the acts and
speech posited of such characters in epic or tragedy were openly regarded as fictitious . . . it was
taken for granted that there were competing representations of what their deeds *might have
been*' (my italics).

[31] Cf. Hom. *Il.* 2. 485–6, contrasting the Muses' omniscience deriving from their 'present-
ness' to the limitations of the mortal bard, who only works through what he hears (*kleos*). Cf.
Cavarero, IV and V, and Laird, in this volume; contrast Spentzou in the Introduction, 'Greek
Imprecisions', on the limits of the Homeric Muses' omniscience.

[32] Inspiration emanating from 'inside' as well as 'outside' is obviously a main theme of this
volume, which seeks to transcend the traditional images of the Hesiodic Muses: see esp. Fowler
and Sharrock. (Editor's note)

[33] Zeitlin (1981) 177; cf. Cantarella (1970) 325; Sommerstein (1994) ad 156; see contra Muecke
(1982) 54.

like an actor (cf. Halliwell 1986: 114), first 'identify' with his fictitious characters in order to be able to create them (see *Thesm.* 148–50), *mimesis* of costume being a preliminary step inducing assimilation of mood. Thus, the fifth-century audience of *Thesmophoriazusae* witnesses Agathon's spectacular appropriation of female paraphernalia (e.g. saffron robe and breast band) in his attempt to write *gynaikeia . . . dramata* ('plays about women') (151): 'one's body must partake of their habits' ($\mu\epsilon\tau o v\sigma i\alpha\nu$ $\delta\epsilon\hat{\iota}$ $\tau\hat{\omega}\nu$ $\tau\rho\delta\pi\omega\nu$ $\tau\delta$ $\sigma\hat{\omega}\mu$' $\epsilon\chi\epsilon\iota\nu$, 152). In other words, enclosing a character in the dramatic fiction is not a matter of having previously 'seen' or 'met' the character through the eyes of the Muses but rather, as Aristotle would put it, a matter of intelligence, versatility of mind, and imaginative transposition of the 'self' in other situations;[34] to speak the language of eighteenth-century discourse on poetic enthusiasm, it is a matter of 'genius' and 'sensibility'.

However, Aristophanes' Agathon provides a useful link to wider considerations on poetic creativity and gender. For poetry inspired by the Muse cannot escape its gender-specificness. By positing the Muse 'at the beginning' of the activity of poetic composition,[35] oral tradition makes poetry the final product in a *feminine* line of enunciation. The male poet seeks validation of his voice by attributing its origin to a female source, the Muse.[36] Moreover, there is a strong sense in which the archaic figure of the male poet represents a 'totality' of gender experience: appropriating the distinctively female sign of 'weaving' in order to describe his poetic composition, and simulating through his very act of singing the female activity of giving birth,[37] the poet represents, in anthropological terms, human *prima materia*, 'undifferentiated raw material' (Turner 1967: 98).

Now, the dramatic poet has certainly retained a special affinity with the Female through his patron god Dionysus, the *thelymorphos* god (Eur. *Bacch.* 353; Philochorus *FGrHist* 328 F7a), the god who incorporates

---

[34] See Arist. *Poet.* 1455ª32–4, ascribing poetic activity to the $\epsilon\dot{v}\phi v\epsilon\hat{\iota}s$, and positing that such poets are $\epsilon\ddot{v}\pi\lambda\alpha\sigma\tau o\iota$. Cf. ibid. 1455ª23–5.

[35] The bard's song starts when his *thymos*, inspired by the Muse, is stirred to take a particular poetic path (see e.g. *Od.* 8. 44–5).

[36] See the pioneering articles of Bergren (1983) and Arthur (1983).

[37] On weaving see Bergren (1983) 72; Nagy (1996a) 64 ff.; Scheid and Svenbro (1994) esp. 131–63. The analogy between belly / womb and mouth is at work in Hesiod's succession myth; see Arthur (1983) 107, who brings together 'into the same semantic field the acts of ingesting, conceiving, and receiving poetic inspiration, and of vomiting, giving birth, and singing or speaking'.

female nature[38]—after all, it may be no coincidence that Agathon's feminine impersonation in *Thesmophoriazusae* is achieved through Dionysiac self-representation, as a good number of Agathon's parapher- nalia are Dionysiac implements.[39] But, although the experience of the female body offers a primary model for the theatrical representation of male *ponos* (Loraux 1981) and feminine qualities often motivate dramatic plots (Zeitlin 1990), femininity is a dimension that the male poet and his male cast can only build in the course of the performance, create, as it were, 'from the inside'. Rather than being the external authority which inspires and validates poetic speech, femininity in drama is endlessly constructed and *de*-constructed, explored and negotiated as a dangerous alterity with respect to social norms. And it is precisely some thoughts on the relation of poetry to social norm that will conclude this section.

Greek Drama can never fit entirely within the poetic moulds of the pre-classical Muses as creators of *kosmos* and harmony within the universe. For, if the Pindaric Muses 'set in order' the human and divine world,[40] Tragedy par excellence shatters all registers of 'order' and puts society's *kosmos* into question. Yet, there is a strong sense in which the dancers of a tragic Chorus can be themselves perceived as the human equivalents of the Muses[41] through their singing and their dancing, quintessential provinces of the divine inspirers of song.[42] In this respect,

[38] See e.g. Aesch. *Edoni* (fr. 61 Radt) and *Theori* or *Isthmiastae* (fr. 78a, 67–8 Radt). On Dionysus' femininity and its relevance to Greek Drama see Zeitlin (1990; 1st pub. 1985). For Dionysus playing the role of the inspiring Muse in Hellenistic art see e.g. the famous British Museum relief (BM no. 2190; Handley (1973) pl. II) illustrating the widespread theme of 'Dionysus visiting a poet'.

[39] See Lada-Richards (1999) ch. 1 for a full discussion.

[40] See Aelius Aristides' account of Pindar's lost *Hymn to Zeus* (and cf. Murray in this volume ad loc. with n. 19): 'the gods demanded that he [Zeus] create for himself some gods, who, by means of words and music, would set in order [*katakosmesousi*] this great work and his whole creation [of the world]' (ed. Dindorf (1964) ii. 142= Pindar, fr. 31 Snell–Maehler; tr. and defence of *katakosmein* as 'set in order' in Pucci (1980) 164). On the Muses as representing 'a primordial ordering power' in Greek theogonic myth see e.g. Lonsdale (1993) 56.

[41] Needless to say, this analogy should not be taken too literally or too far. On several occasions, conscious of their performative activity in the *orchestra*, the Chorus-dancers under- stand themselves to be in a privileged relation to the Muses as an *independent* entity; see e.g. Eur. *El.* 875, where the girls of the Chorus refer to their dancing as 'dear to the Muses' or Eur. *Her.* 685–6, where the Theban Elders declare themselves unwilling to abandon their bond with the Muses, who roused them to the dance: οὔπω καταπαύσομεν | Μούσας αἵ μ' ἐχόρευσαν. Besides, the Chorus's 'dance-and-song' performance may also become one of the rare metaphors for inspired creativity encoded in the tragic genre (see below, V).

[42] On the Muses' singing-and-dancing *choros* as 'the paradigm image for performance in the Greek *polis*' see Easterling (1997) 157; cf. Easterling (1985) 46: 'The *choros* of Muses is the

even if Tragedy does not inherit the archaic Muses' ability to create and display harmony and social order, the Muses 'written into' the tragic discourse as the dancers/singers of the tragic Chorus safeguard the community's perpetuation through their periodic re-enactment of mythical sequences in strictly patterned performances of dance and song. Like the archaic Muses, who either sing (and sometimes dance) at joyful events[43] or strike up dirges at the funerals of famous heroes (e.g. Achilles), tragic *choreutae* are vital not only in ensuring the unbroken continuity of ritual channels of communication[44] but also in weakening the barrier between stage and auditorium through the integrative force of song and dance.

In Euripides' *Heracles*, for example, in a moment of extreme 'choral self-referentiality' (cf. Henrichs 1995), the Theban Elders very strikingly conceive of themselves and their songs as fulfilling a function parallel to that of the Delian Maidens, those unequalled performers of choral song and dance (cf. Hom. *Hymn Apollo*), the archetypal ritual substitutes for the Olympian Muses (see Nagy 1990: 375–7).

> παιᾶνα μὲν Δηλιάδες
> ⟨ναῶν⟩ ὑμνοῦσ' ἀμφὶ πύλας
> τὸν Λατοῦς εὔπαιδα γόνον,
> εἱλίσσουσαι καλλίχοροι.
> παιᾶνας δ' ἐπὶ σοῖς μελάθροις
> κύκνος ὣς γέρων ἀοιδὸς
> πολιᾶν ἐκ γενύων
> κελαδήσω.   (Eur. *Her.* 687 ff.)

Paeans sing the Delian maidens,
a song for Leto's lovely son,
wheeling at the temple gates
the lovely mazes of the dance.
So paeans at your gate I raise,
pouring like the dying swan,
from hoary throat a song of praise.
                    (tr. Arrowsmith in Grene and Lattimore 1959)

immortal prototype of all human *choroi*.' See also Lonsdale (1993) ch. 2; cf. Nagy (1996a) 57. See Spentzou, IV, in this volume on the gendered aspects of such an assimilation of the Chorus with the Muses.

[43] The Muses dance, e.g. at the marriage of Peleus and Thetis (*LIMC* s.v. 'Mousa, Mousai', nos. 120–2) or Heracles and Hebe (ibid., no. 122 (bis)).

[44] Although drama is certainly distinct from ritual, if one follows Nagy in working with Tambiah's definition of ritual as 'a culturally constructed system of symbolic communications', 'the *performance* of myth as song, poetry, or prose . . . can even be seen as an aspect of ritual': Nagy (1996a) 55; his italics.

Similarly, in the final scene of Euripides' *Hippolytus*, when Artemis decrees that the tragic hero's death will be a 'Muse-fashioned (μουσοποιός) concern of maidens' (1428–9), she not only bestows on the Troezinian *parthenoi* the ritual power to create song commemorative of *pathos*, binding the community together through common grief (*Hipp.* 1462: *koinon . . . achos*), but also ascribes to them a function parallel to that of the archaic Muses who, joining their voice with that of Thetis, lamented Achilles' untimely death[45] and united men and gods in the anguish of mourning.

IV. THE TRAGIC MUSE LEARNS TO FEEL

It is one of the commonest topoi in archaic poetics that the song of the Muse herself or the Muse-inspired bard enchants:[46] it is an instrument of magic, *thelkterion* or *kelethmos*, which can make the listener forget his everyday cares (see esp. Hes. *Theog.* 98–103; cf. *Theog.* 55) or, in Helen's metaphorical description of her magic drug/gift of poetry, 'have no tear roll down his face, not if his mother died and his father died, not if men | murdered a brother or a beloved son in his presence | with the bronze, and he with his own eyes saw it' (*Od.* 4. 222–6).[47] Yet, the primary feeling associated with the response to epic poetry is pleasure, *terpsis* unmitigated by grief.[48] Apart from Penelope, Telemachus, and Odysseus, who suffer by being too closely involved in the events related by the bard,[49] the Homeric 'internal' audiences seem untainted by the paradox of classical theatrical response which centres on pleasure amid tears (Pl. *Phlb.* 48a), the hedonism of 'letting oneself go' which culminates in weeping. Spellbound though they are by the song of Demodocus, the *aoidos* best loved by the Muses (*Od.* 8. 63), the Phaeacians cannot

[45] See primarily Hom. *Od.* 24. 60–4; cf. Quint. Smyrn. *Posthom.* 3. 594 ff., esp. 599–601 and 645–7, where the Muse Calliope promises to Thetis eternal *kleos* for her son through bardic *aoidai*, stemming from her own resolve and the desire of the rest of the Pierian Muses. According to Proclus' *Chrestomatheia* (text in Allen, *Homeri Opera*, v. 106) the *threnos* sung by the Muses over the dead Achilles goes back to the *Aethiopis*. It is also possible (see Garner 1993) that Achilles' funeral had been treated by Stesichorus, although the extant fragments yield no information about the function of the Muses in it.

[46] Cf. e.g. Cavarero's discussion of the Platonic Muse in this volume.

[47] For Helen as a bard in *Od.* 4. 219–64 and for her *pharmakon* as having the characteristics of *logos* and bardic song see primarily Bergren (1981); (1983) 79 ff.; Goldhill (1988) 20; (1991) 62.

[48] See *Od.* 1. 347, 422; 8. 43–5, 91; 9. 3–11; 17. 385; cf. Hes. *Theog.* 36–7; see further Lanata (1963) 8–9.

[49] *Od.* 1. 328–44 (Penelope); 4. 290–5 (Telemachus); 8. 83–92; 521–31 (Odysseus). For stimulating discussions see Nagy (1979) 97–102; Walsh (1984) ch. 1; Goldhill (1991) 58 ff.

participate in the grief of others, for they do not possess the art of projecting themselves imaginatively into the heroic action in such a way as to feel themselves 'into' the consciousness of the heroes celebrated in the embedded *klea andron*.

Now, in the post-archaic world it is first and foremost the Athenian *polis*'s tragic genre which inherits the Muse's power to 'bewitch', to 'captivate', and 'enthrall'—in fourth-century language *psychagogein*.[50] But, more importantly still, the impact that the epic bard could work only on the 'under-distanced' among his audience, that is, the praised hero's close friends or kin, Tragedy can now work upon the whole spectating body. The reaction of Odysseus, who can literally recognize 'himself' in the 'reality' evoked by the Muse-inspired song and weep, is now appropriated by the entire tragic audience, that is, by spectators culturally conditioned in such a way as to recognize in the suffering 'other' the potential mirror of the 'self' (see e.g. Soph. *Aj.* 121–6; *Phil.* 501–6). In fact, the sensibilities of classical audiences are such that a fundamental and successful channel of communication between the author, the performer, and their addressees is sustained through the transfusion of emotion, the identity of shared feelings, which can be so widespread as to transcend the limits of private *penthos* and become a 'common grief for the entire citizen-body' (*koinon . . . achos pasi politais*) (Eur. *Hipp.* 1462–3; see Segal 1988).

In particular, good models for the emotional projection of the 'self' into the condition of the suffering 'other' are offered by the tragic Choruses as well as by stage-characters who, through their relative distance from the hero's plight, are useful analogues for the spectator's own distanced position.[51] For classical spectators of tragedies do not expect the tragic Muse to make them forget all suffering. On the contrary, they expect to be 'invited' to *fuse* and *merge* their own experience with that of the tormented hero (συμπάσχειν),[52] to *appropriate* the grief

[50] On dramatic *psychagogia* see e.g. Pl. *Min.* 321a; Isoc. 9. 10–11; Timocles fr. 6, 5–7 KA; Arist. *Poet.* 1450ᵃ33–5, and cf. schol. Soph. *Aj.* 864 (p. 254 Elmsley, on Timotheus from Zakynthos impersonating Ajax): 'he guided the spectators and beguiled their souls through his delivery' (ἦγε τοὺς θεατάς, καὶ ἐψυχαγώγει τῇ ὑποκρίσει). The broader issues implicated in this section have been discussed at length in Lada-Richards (1993).

[51] On the Chorus and the audience as being on the same level of participation due to their common inability to influence the tragic action and their common status as 'helpless witnesses' cf. Taplin (1996) 194. Audiences 'internal' to the plays often 'cue' the real-life spectators to offer to the hero their compassion (Soph. *Phil.* 507 ff.); see Lada-Richards (1993) 108 ff.; Segal (1996); Easterling (1996).

[52] Cf. Pl. *Rep.* 605d. In an 'internalized' perspective cf. Theseus' response to Heracles' *pathos* in Eur. *Her.* 1202: ἀλλ' εἰ συναλγῶν γ' ἦλθον;

of others (cf. Gorg. *Hel.* 9) staged before their eyes, and weep.[53] In fact, the ps.-Euripidean *Rhesus* goes so far as to bring onto the *skene* as a flesh-and-blood dramatic character a Muse composer of lamenting verse (890 ff.): in clear contrast to the Hesiodic deities with their 'soul free from sorrow' (*Theog.* 61: ἀκηδέα θυμόν) and the epic bard/ *therapon* of the Muses with his grief-allaying song (*Theog.* 98–103), the *pathos*-orientated psychology of the Athenian Drama has fashioned a Muse who not only transmutes her own tormenting affliction into dirges, but, more importantly, appears so broken by her grief that her 'internal' audience, the play's Chorus, feels compelled to identify with her plight:

> ὅσον προσήκει μὴ γένους κοινωνίαν
> ἔχοντι λύπῃ τὸν σὸν οἰκτίρω γόνον   (904–5)

I, too, as much as ever one can grieve who has no kinship with the dead, grieve for your son.   (tr. Lattimore in Grene and Lattimore 1959)

The classical Athenian stage, then, turns the Muse into a tragic character whose *penthos* draws the audience's empathic response. To put it in another way, within the heightened emotionality of the Athenian theatrical context, the archaic Muse has learned to feel.[54]

V. MULTIPLE EXPERIENCES: FURTHER DRAMATIC INCARNATIONS OF THE MUSE

> Tell me now Muses, who have your homes on Olympus—
> For you are goddesses, and are present, and know [*iste*] all,
> but we hear only *kleos* and do not know [*idmen*] anything—
>   (*Iliad* 2. 484–6; tr. Ford 1992: 60)

Omniscient, omnipresent eyewitnesses of the heroic era, the Homeric and Hesiodic Muses seem to have bequeathed their perfect, all-embracing knowledge to both the prologizing deities and the *dei ex machina* of the tragic genre. For, like the archaic inspired poet, such tragic figures possess control over utterances that bridge the gap between the past, the present, and the future. Having devised their own

---

[53] That is, to indulge in the very reaction that the Homeric Helen's drug, κακῶν ἐπίληθον ἁπάντων, had promised to eliminate (*Od.* 4. 220–6). On the tears of tragic audiences see Isocr. 4. 168; Pl. *Rep.* 605d; Plut. *Mor.* 17d; similarly, a successful actor is he who manages πολλοὺς κλαίοντας καθίζειν (see Xen. *Symp.* 3. 11 on Callippides; cf. Plut. *Mor.* 547 f. on Theodorus).

[54] In this respect, the dramatic Muse paves the way for some other striking transformations to be discussed later in this volume: see esp. Spentzou, Janan, Henderson.

plot, divine prologue-speakers appear on the stage to inform the audience they will bring it to completion (e.g. Dionysus in the *Bacchae*; Artemis in the *Hippolytus*),[55] while the gods or goddesses whose sudden entrance steers a play to its conclusion impart to the spectators a vision of the future which exceeds by far the boundaries of the theatrical event itself, the 'here and now' of the performance. Besides, if in the oral tradition the Muses were able to confer everlasting *kleos* (cf. Hes. *Theog.* 32: ἵνα κλείοιμι . . .) through their own song or that of their *therapon* bard,[56] a deus ex machina can safeguard the tragic hero's everlasting *a-letheia* (in the sense of 'memory') through the institution of collective rituals, whose periodic repetition ensures the unbroken continuity of public remembrance.

As for Tragedy's remodelling of the eyewitness function of the archaic Muses, no scene is more revealing than the much discussed 'theatrical' opening of the Sophoclean *Ajax*. Speaking from the height of the *Theologeion*, and therefore overseeing the scenic space (cf. her emphatic καὶ νῦν . . . σε . . . ὁρῶ, *Aj.* 3), Athena is placed in the privileged position of a stage-director,[57] in full control of angles of vision and levels of representation. As the sole contriver and manipulator of an 'enfolded' spectacle (cf. Easterling 1993a: 82) that she can either shroud in darkness or lay bare to the spectator's sight,[58] Athena plays in relation to Odysseus a role analogous to that of the archaic Muse vis-à-vis the inspired bard. Opening up for him the heart of the events themselves, the goddess grants to her favoured mortal the privilege of contemplating what can only be visible through 'borrowed', immortal vision. Moreover, grafting, as it does, upon the tragic genre the dynamics of the interaction between the all-knowing perspective of the Muse and the limited, controlled vision of the bard (cf. *Il.* 2. 485–6 quoted above), the scene between Athena and Odysseus is mirrored, time and again, in the recurrent interplay between the tragic Angelos/Exangelos and the multiple audiences of his performance. An heir to the eyewitness function of the Muse, the Angelos/Exangelos[59] has already seen what is

[55] Cf. Easterling (1993a) 80: 'The gods, one might say, are usually brought on stage to do a job like that of the dramatist himself.' However, as Segal (1992) 88 has put it, in such cases 'we are far from epic clarity. We are left wondering how the divine plan will be realized in the visible, human form of the theater.'

[56] For the notion of the *aoidos* as *therapon* / 'ritual substitute' of the Muses see Nagy (1979) 291–7, 301–8. [57] Cf. Easterling (1993a) 80 and Segal (1995) 19.

[58] Note the contrast between *Aj.* 11–12: καὶ σ' οὐδὲν εἴσω τῆσδε παπταίνειν πύλης | ἔτ' ἔργον ἐστίν and 66: δείξω δὲ καὶ σοὶ τήνδε περιφανῆ νόσον.

[59] Although his mortal vision has severe limitations. The best example is perhaps the

not allowed to take place on the stage, and, through his skills in imitation, he ensures that his spectators (both 'internalized' and theatrical) witness in their turn the deeds accomplished and the *logoi* uttered by invisible dramatic agents, that is, those dramatis personae who advance the plot through their off-stage actions.

Last but not least arises the question of whether Greek Drama has reinscribed in its performative context the very process of inspired creativity per se. However, Tragedy and Comedy need separate consideration at this point.

Tragedians are never visible as stage-characters on the theatrical *skene*, hence tragic poetic composition can only be glimpsed through metaphoric reincarnations of the 'I'/creator of song. I suggest that a mirror-image of poetic creativity in Tragedy can be found in the 'dance-and-song' performance of the Chorus (let us not forget that the archaic Muses not only inspire original poetic creation but are also involved in the [re-]enactment of song). For the members of a tragic Chorus may cast themselves in the role of the Poet by perceiving themselves as the recipients of divine inspiration from the Muses, as happens, for example, in Euripides' *Troades* 511–15: ἀμφί μοι Ἴλιον, ὦ | Μοῦσα, καινῶν ὕμνων | ἄισον σὺν δακρύοις ᾠδὰν ἐπικήδειον. | νῦν γὰρ μέλος ἐς Τροίαν ἰαχήσω, 'Sing, Muse, of Ilium; sing with tears a song of death in strange new strain. For I shall sing an ode for Troy . . .' (tr. Barlow 1986). At other times, a play's imagery may cast its Chorus into the role of a Dionysiac celebrant,[60] as in Sophocles' *Trachiniae* 215–20:

> I am lifted up, nor shall I reject
> the pipe, O master of my mind.
> See, the ivy shakes me up,
> euoi!,
> whirling me round now
> in the Bacchic contest (Βακχίαν . . . ἅμιλλαν).[61]
> (tr. Henrichs 1995: 82–3)

Messenger's report on Oedipus' awesome death at the end of Sophocles' *Oedipus Coloneus*. Not only has he not been allowed to see μόρῳ δ' ὁποίῳ κεῖνος ὤλετ' (1656), but he also knows that even Theseus, the 'privileged spectator' (Easterling 1993b) 199, the sole eyewitness to Oedipus' crossing over to eternity, had to shade his eyes with his hand (1650–2).

[60] See Easterling (1982) ad 218; cf. Henrichs (1995) 81 and 82: 'the *khoreutai* of this particular chorus claim to be wearing ivy while dancing to the pipe, features assimilating them to the dithyrambic chorus as well as the maenadic *thiasos*'.

[61] See Henrichs (1995) 84, who detects in Βακχίαν ἅμιλλαν 'the collective toil of choruses competing with each other in the "Bacchic contest"'.

The young girls' sudden eruption into dancing brings to mind the Platonic fashioning of the inspired poet's contact with the Muse[62]—a special moment of possession and *ekstasis*, when the creative 'I' replicates a Dionysiac maenad's surrendering to frenzy.[63]

As far as Comedy is concerned, we have already seen that it affords good glimpses of the 'inspired' dramatist at work (Euripides in *Acharnians*; Agathon in *Thesmophoriazusae*; see Sect. IV above); I will therefore end this section with the famous Aristophanic portrait of Aeschylus as a poet in the grip of madness.

In an image which could be closely associated with the inspired poet of Democritus and Plato,[64] the artist who creates poetry precisely when 'he becomes possessed and out of his senses and his mind dwells in him no more' (ἔνθεός τε γένηται καὶ ἔκφρων καὶ ὁ νοῦς μηκέτι ἐν αὐτῷ ἐνῇ, *Ion* 534b),[65] the Chorus of Initiates in the *Frogs* predicts that Aeschylus, 'caught in a terrible frenzy (μανίας ὑπὸ δεινῆς), will whirl his eyes this way and that' (816–17). Moreover, just as, in Plato's conception, the poet comes out of his senses when sitting 'on the tripod of the Muses' and 'resembles a fountain giving free course to the upward rush of water' (Pl. *Leg.* 719c), Aristophanes' Aeschylus is about to 'release' his 'fountain', when encouraged to do so by his judge (*Frogs* 1005), thus satisfying in this respect Dionysus' yearning for a *gonimos* (fertile) tragedian. Finally, unlike Euripides, who is charged with having cast away *mousiken* (*Frogs* 1493), Aeschylus seems to conceive his poetic task as culling the 'sacred meadow of the Muses' (*Frogs* 1299–1300).

[62] But also perhaps 'corny' Copa, the dancing and singing 'alternative' muse discussed by Henderson in this volume? (Editor's note)

[63] See especially the much quoted passage in Pl. *Ion* 534a, and cf. Pl. *Phdr.* 245a, where the *mania* of the Muses is working upon the poet's soul ἐγείρουσα καὶ ἐκβακχεύουσα κατά τε ᾠδὰς καὶ κατὰ τὴν ἄλλην ποίησιν.

[64] Democritus frr. B18 and B21 DK, and cf. B17 DK (the Latin tradition of the Democritean theory); for Democritus and the 'inspired poet' see Delatte (1934) 28 ff.; for Plato see e.g. *Phdr.* 245a; *Ion* 533e. Nevertheless, despite the fact that Plato calls it a παλαιὸς μῦθος (*Leg.* 719c), the conception of poetic *furor* may be 'no older than the fifth century B.C.': Murray (1981) 87; contra, Vicaire (1963) 75.

[65] For an opposite conception which, nevertheless, testifies to the diffusion of the poetic *furor*-theory see Arist. *Poet.* 1455ᵃ32–3: διὸ εὐφυοῦς ἡ ποιητική ἐστιν ἢ μανικοῦ, *manikos* being the 'divinely possessed'; Lucas (1968) 178 is willing to accept Aristophanes' depiction of Aeschylus in *Frogs* 816 as an example of such a *manikos*.

VI. CONCLUSION

(a) The 'domesticated' Muse

The previous section ended with the 'inspired' Aeschylus of *Frogs*. I will continue to exploit this same Aristophanic play *both* as a *fin de siècle* product of Athenian culture, where *mousike* carries an exceptionally rich range of semantic possibilities, *and* as an eloquent picture of the special link between inspired creativity, the Muses, and Dionysus, the god of theatre himself. For when the Chorus, in a privileged moment of theatrical self-referentiality, draws attention to the primacy of *mousike* as a lesson to be gained from Aeschylus' victory ('it is therefore a mark of elegance not to sit together with Socrates and chat, having cast away *mousiken* . . .', 1491–3), it would be misleadingly restrictive to translate *mousike*, as Dover (1993: 21) does, merely as 'poetry'. Uttered by the Chorus, a civic community's most treasured medium for the trans-mission of its hallowed song culture, *mousike* must be understood as that special co-ordination of words, melody, and dance which circumscribe the realm of the archaic Muses and lie in the province of the skilled poet. Euripides, on the other hand, pays dearly for his neglect of *mousike*, a fatal oversight whose sinister consequences for the outcome of the poetic contest have already been foreshadowed in Dionysus' wish (872) 'to judge the contest *mousikotata*', that is, 'in a manner most befitting a cultivated critic' (873),[66] and in his prompting of the Chorus to sing a *melos* to the Muses (874; cf. 875 ff.). Besides, even before the poetic com-petition, it was the Muse whom the Chorus of Initiates had summoned to the dance, while the Chorus Leader had banned everyone who 'has neither seen nor danced the secret rites of the noble Muses' (356) (prorrhesis; see below) and extolled those citizens who were brought up 'in poetic-musical education' (ἐν . . . μουσικῇ, 729) (parabasis).

It would therefore seem that by the end of the fifth century BC the Muse has become thoroughly 'domesticated'. With no resemblance to the awesome figure of liminal landscapes who could take offence and mutilate (cf. the legend of Thamyris), the Muse inscribed in the dis-course of dramatic poetry is a figure 'in' and 'of' the City, linked to the communal aspects of artistic creativity. Aristophanes' *Frogs* is an impor-tant text in this respect, for it encodes the Muses as powers inextricably interwoven with the *polis*'s religious and political discourse, in the same

---

[66] See Dover (1993) ad loc. Alternative translations would be 'with exceptional poetic skill', or even 'most harmoniously'.

way that the play in its entirety conceives of drama as an inherent part of civic consciousness (see Lada-Richards 1999: chs. 5–9).

(b) The 'Bacchic Lord', the Muses, and poetic initiation

No discussion of poetic inspiration in Greek Drama could dispense with Dionysus, the divine patron of theatre and poets, a god linked with inspired creativity through his gift of wine which, from a very early date,[67] was considered an important stimulus to the inception of the artist's art.[68] More importantly still, inspired artistic composition can be firmly placed within the wider religious and cultural frame of Dionysianism through the god's direct relation with the Muses, an association amply documented in both literature and cult. To mention only some examples, Aeschylus in his Dionysiac play *Edoni* designated the god as a μουσόμαντις, a 'poet-prophet' (fr. 60 Radt), and Euripides (*Bacch.* 410) included Pieria, the ʿseat of the Muses', among the places which would welcome Bacchic orgies. In Sophocles' account of the fate of Dionysus' enemy Lycurgus, king of the Edonians, the king was punished precisely because he ʿprovoked the flute-loving Muses' (*Ant.* 965), while in Plato the Muses together with Dionysus and Apollo are the 'fellow-celebrants' (συνεορταστάς), whom the gods bestowed on mankind, overcome by pity for the human lot (*Leg.* 653d). In cultic practice, correspondingly, Plutarch (*Mor.* 717a) describes the ritual of the Boeotian Agrionia, where Dionysus is believed to take refuge with the Muses, and Diodorus (4. 4. 3) presents the Muses not merely as followers but also as entertainers of Dionysus. But, once again, the *Frogs* can offer the most fruitful ground for investigation.

Discussing the *poiesis* of his lyric parts, the Chorus designates Aeschylus as 'the Bacchic lord' (τὸν Βακχεῖον ἄνακτα, 1259),[69] a title which may mean the 'master of the Dionysiac art of tragedy' (Sommerstein 1996: ad loc.) but also, given the play's initiatory frame (see Lada-Richards 1999: esp. ch. 2), the poet who is possessed and inspired by Bacchus.[70] And actually, this 'Dionysiac' way of evaluating poetry has

---

[67] Cf. Archilochus fr. 120 West (discussed below in the text).

[68] See Dodds (1951) 101 n. 124; Lucas (1968) 178 on Arist. *Poet.* 1455ᵃ32–4; Bramble (1974) 48–9.

[69] It may be the case that 1257–60 belong to the original production of 405 BC, substituted in 404 with 1252–6, so that the text, as we now have it, is the result of a conflation; see Dover (1993) 343 and Sommerstein (1996) ad 1251–60.

[70] Cf. Eur. *Hec.* 676–7: μῶν τὸ βακχεῖον κάρα | τῆς θεσπιῳδοῦ δεῦρο Κασσάνδρας φέρεις; More significantly still, it is Dionysus himself who is invoked as a *Bakcheios anax* (Orph. *hymn.* 30. 2).

been adequately anticipated by the Bacchic figure of Cratinus, whom the Initiates' prorrhesis had extolled as a poetic prototype. One category of people whom the Chorus Leader bans from the blessed dances of the Mystai (354) includes whosoever has not 'been initiated into the bacchic rites of the tongue of Cratinus, the bull-eating poet' (μηδὲ Κρατίνου τοῦ ταυροφάγου γλώττης Βακχεῖ' ἐτελέσθη, 357). Like the mythical Dionysiac devotee, who participates in the god's essence by devouring his bestial incarnations, Cratinus, the 'bull-eating' poet, is implicitly supposed to derive inspired verbal eloquence from an analogous communion, translated metaphorically into the space of the *polis*.

And I would like to conclude this piece with a very brief discussion of the puzzling choral utterance which excludes from the Initiates' happy company whosoever has 'neither seen nor danced the secret rites of the noble Muses': rather than being treated as yet another literary metaphor, *Frogs* 356 needs to be better understood with respect to its *ritual* dimension. For implicating the Muses in a mystical discourse makes excellent ritual and cultic sense as, from its very first remoulding in the form of a Greek literary text, the contact of the Poet with the Muse complies with well-known patterns of mystic initiatory experience.[71]

The Muses themselves, with their possession of ultimate knowledge and their masterly command over the truth by means of *thea*,[72] can be regarded as initiators, for the transmission of secret knowledge,[73] especially knowledge resulting from the initiate's personal experience of 'blessed sights', lies at the core of mystic initiation rites.[74] Like the

[71] This is not to claim that initiation is the only larger cultural frame within which poetic inspiration scenes can be placed. For a discussion of *Theogony* 22–34 in terms of conventional elements which span various thematic clusters see West (1966) 158–61, who does not, however, consider mystic initiation.

[72] See Hom. *Il.* 2. 484–6 (quoted above, V) with Ford (1992) 61: 'finally they "know" these things, in the special sense compressed in the Greek verb, by having seen them'.

[73] The acquisition of knowledge primarily associated with the transmission of the ritual and verbal secrets of mystic cults is well substantiated in a variety of sources. For example, sacred knowledge which can or cannot be acquired, lies at the core of the Dionysiac mysteries, such as reflected in Euripides' *Bacchae* (see esp. *Bacch.* 73, 472–4), while books seem to play a prominent role in 'private' initiations into orgiastic cults (see e.g. Dem. 18. 259; 19. 199); for books and special knowledge in mystic rites see Burkert (1987) 69–72 (with notes); West (1983) 24–6; and cf. now Obbink's (1997) 39–54 discussion of col. xx of the Derveni papyrus.

[74] Contemplating (*epopteuein*) 'the great, wonderful, most perfect epoptic secret' (Hippolytus, *Refutatio Omnium Haeresium.* 5. 8. 39) means to have achieved the highest possible degree of initiation into the Mysteries of Eleusis, i.e. the grade of the *epoptes*. On the primacy of *thea* in Eleusinian and Bacchic mystic initiation see Lada-Richards (1997a); cf. Lada-Richards (1999) 84 n. 151 on the Eleusinian *epopteia*. It is also significant that mystic *makarismoi* place

uninitiated woman flagellated by a winged figure very probably personi-
fying Agnoia, that is, 'ignorance', in the famous fresco of the Villa dei
Misteri in Pompeii,[75] the uninspired, uninitiated poet hears only *kleos*
and 'knows nothing' (cf. *Il.* 2. 486 quoted above, Sect. V). Like the
initiand who suffers ritual degradation,[76] the poet/initiand of the Muses
is subject to slanderous abuse: 'shepherds dwelling in the fields, base
cowards, mere bellies' (*Theog.* 26). And like the riddling utterances often
used in mystic initiation ritual so as both to confuse and stimulate the
initiand's mind,[77] the Muses' message is a riddle (*Theog.* 27–8), the kind of
riddle that, as Pratt (1993: 112) has put it, one cannot solve unless one
becomes a poet.[78] Moreover, Hesiod's direct, unmediated encounter
with the inspiring divinities on Mount Helicon and his acquisition of the
Muses' staff is a good analogue for that personal, face-to-face contact[79]
which seals the special bond between initiator and neophyte in the
transmission of mystic rites. Thus, while Dionysus, in the guise of a
human *goes*/initiator in the *Bacchae*, claims to have received mystic rites
in intimate communication with Dionysus/the god (see *Bacch.* 465 ff.
and 469–70), Hesiod claims to have received a sceptre and immortal
song during his close encounter with the Muses.[80] Besides, the onset of
poetic inspiration can be alarmingly sudden and profoundly 'trans-
formative', an overwhelming experience comparable with the supreme
ordeal of mystic initiation, the '*pathos* never suffered before', as an

special emphasis on the initiate's visual perception of the rites; see e.g. Pind. fr. 137a Maehler
(ὄλβιος ὅστις ἰδὼν κεῖν' εἶσ' ὑπὸ χθόν'· | οἶδε μὲν βίου τελευτάν, | οἶδεν δὲ διόσδοτον ἀρχάν),
where the semantic fields of vision and knowledge overlap.

[75] It is unlikely that a consensus of opinion will ever be reached concerning the identity of
the winged flagellator.

[76] See sources and discussion in Lada-Richards (1999) 67–8 and 97–8.

[77] See e.g. Demetrius, *On Style* 101; Plut. *Mor.* 388f–389a; cf. Eur. *Bacch.* 470, 474–5, 478–9. See
further Seaford (1981) 254–5 and (1994) 227; Richardson (1974) 22–3, on the Eleusinian password,
synthema, expressed in riddling language; Burkert (1987) 78 ff.

[78] Pratt (1993) notes the initiatory nature of the Muses' insults (108 and 110 n. 16) and riddle
(110). However, beyond the mystic initiatory frame, it should be also noted at this point that a
propensity to riddling expression could be seen as a perfect illustration of poetic temperament
and talent, as can be gauged from passages such as Pl. *Alc.* 2, 147b or *Rep.* 332b–c. Cf. also
Aeschylus' obscure, unintelligible sayings in the *Frogs* (esp. 926–7, 929, 1122), words which,
'unknown to the spectators' (926), are not easy to decipher (929).

[79] Cf. e.g. Lucius' initiatory experience, as related in Apuleius' *Metamorphoses* 11. 23.

[80] *Theog.* 30–2: καί μοι σκῆπτρον ἔδον . . . | . . . ἐνέπνευσαν δέ μοι αὐδὴν | θέσπιν . . .
Didomi in particular is especially relevant to my discussion: not only does it recall an almost
'technical' term in initiation language, the expression *paradosis/paradidonai* of the *telete*,
mysteria, *sacra*, etc. (see Riedweg (1987) 6–7, mainly on Eleusinian initiation), but it also underlines the physical contact between mystes and initiator; cf. again *Bacch.* 470: καὶ δίδωσιν ὄργια,
and *IMagn.* 215a Kern; see Seaford (1996) ad *Bacch.* 470.

inscribed funerary 'gold leaf' from Thurii puts it (tablet A4 Zuntz 1971, lines 3–4).

While Plutarch (fr. 178 Sandbach) compares initiation into great mysteries to the *pathos* of the soul at the threshold of death and speaks of the initiand's 'panic and shivering and sweat and amazement',[81] Archilochus conveys the all-consuming and consecrating nature of his Dionysiac poetic calling with the powerful image of being struck by lightning:

> ὡς Διωνύσοι' ἄνακτος καλὸν ἐξάρχαι μέλος
> οἶδα διθύραμβον οἴνῳ συγκεραυνωθεὶς φρένας
>
> (fr. 120 West = 117 Tarditi)

I know how to lead Lord Dionysus' beautiful song,
the dithyramb, when my wits have been thunderbolted with wine.[82]

As Seaford (1997: 148) has put it, 'Here the singer envisages his own inebriated inspiration as a kind of participation in the blast.' And it is highly significant that this Dionysiac lightning of Archilochus' poetic inspiration finds its closest parallel[83] in the special role played by the thunderbolt in the process of the mystes' disorientation and detachment from his/her previous identity during the liminal phase of mystic initiation rites.[84] Just as Archilochus' wits are utterly combusted by the blast of lightning, Orphic/Bacchic 'gold leaves' from Thurii record the voice of initiates reminding Persephone that they have been fatally struck by the thunderbolt (tablet A1 Zuntz 1971, line 4).

Finally, poetic inspiration, as shaped by the narrative of myth, shares one important element with rites of mystic initiation: in a cluster of symbolic patterns very much akin to the bard's loss of physical eyesight or bodily integrity before acquiring the power of divine song granted by the Muse or Muses,[85] the initiand's 'old' self is 'sacrificed' or subjected to death-like ordeals or even ground down in a process resulting in

[81] Cf. Procl. *Theol. Plat.* 3. 18 (p. 64 Budé); Procl. *In Remp.* ii, p. 108, 21–2 (Kroll); Procl. *In Remp.* ii, p. 181, 5–8 (Kroll); Ael. Arist. 22. 2 (Keil); Plut. *Vit. Ages.* 24. 7; Strabo 10. 3. 7.

[82] See Mendelsohn (1992), esp. 111 with n. 18; cf. Lonsdale (1993) 89.

[83] First noted by Mendelsohn (1992); developed much further by Seaford (1997).

[84] On the role of the thunderbolt in mystic initiation see Seaford (1996) ad 576–641 and Seaford (1997) esp. 147–8.

[85] Demodocus, for example, receives song-craft but also blindness from the Muses (Hom. *Od.* 8. 64), while Thamyris, song-craft and mutilation (Hom. *Il.* 2. 594–600). Cf. Bergren (1983) 93 n. 44. In a more light-hearted version of poetic *Dichterweihe* the poet gains his lyre by losing an emblem of his previous existence and life-style, in Archilochus' case, a cow (see the 'Mnesiepes Inscription', T4, 34–8 Tarditi).

social anonymity and 'structural invisibility', before he/she becomes *re*-fashioned, *re*-moulded, and *re*-born into a new identity.[86]

I round up this brief discussion by harping on its limitations. Rather than *filling* a gap, this chapter has merely *suggested* a re-contextualization of the study of the Muse: there is much to be gained by a more sustained and comprehensive 'reading' of inspired creativity as an *internal* dimension of Greek Drama. At long last, *the Muse must be firmly reinscribed onto the map of Greek theatrical performances.*

[86] On mock sacrifice (qualifying for the initiand's symbolic death) in rites of passage see Seaford (1994) ch. 8; on initiatory ordeals (e.g. mock dismemberment and flagellation) as carrying the symbolism of death see e.g. Eliade (1958) 90–2, 105–6; Brelich (1969) 80 n. 85; Seaford (1994) 294; on the initiand's structural invisibility or 'death' see Turner (1967) 95, 96, 98–9; Turner (1974) 241; for the Greek literary and cultic material see Lada-Richards (1999) esp. 57–60. For initiation as resulting in symbolic rebirth and the initiand's acquisition of a new personality see Lada-Richards (1999) 103–8, with ancient sources and discussion.

5

Stealing Apollo's Lyre: Muses and Poetic ἆθλα in Apollonius' *Argonautica* 3

Efrossini Spentzou

Following more closely the Muses' descent from Helicon, as discussed and assumed in a preliminary way in the Introductory chapter, this essay addresses Medea as a human muse-figure working her way through Book 3 of the *Argonautica*. It thus joins those other contributions to this volume which also have human muses as their subject-matter,[1] in a common attempt to shed light on the complex ways inspiration and creativity can work, once they cease to be expertly administered by divine purveyors and are left in the hands of wandering and erring mortals. In this sense, my approach takes a distinctively different direction from the one taken in a recent article on Medea as a muse figure by Dolores O'Higgins, even though it has found the insight into Medea's 'potential dangerousness' that the latter offers very suggestive. In her essay, O'Higgins also sees Medea, this time in Pindar's *Pythian* 4, as a muse surrogate but her focus is different. Drawing attention to Medea's gradual transformation, in the course of the poem, from powerful divine singer to the passionate woman seduced by Jason, she notices that this transformation is presented as the result of the poet's own poetic charm and may therefore be viewed as reflecting the poet's own relationship with his own muse. Medea is potentially dangerous, but the poet has framed her dangerous voice with his dexterous song.[2]

---

[1] Cf. esp. Fowler, Ancona, Henderson, Janan, Sharrock, Rosati.

[2] O'Higgins (1997) 111–12: 'The Medea of *Pythian* 4 is indeed a diva who had both magical song and drugs at her disposal. She appears near the beginning of the poem as a formidable and divine singer, but later as the passionate Colchian woman . . . the poem contrives that we perceive the transformation as taking place during Pindar's telling of the story. This

Thus, even though O'Higgins does justice to often overlooked signals of Medea's tacit strength, her attention is ultimately absorbed by the male poet. Medea, the muse, acts as a foil for developments in the relationship between the poet and his conventional Muse. And, as she rightly oberves, this relationship represents a winning strategy for the poet, who manages to harness his potentially unruly Muse as he had also managed to harness Medea, the potentially destructive sorceress.

Indeed, the notion of Jason, the winning hero, gently manipulating the efficient but coy young maid, is prevalent amongst recent critics, who have systematically underlined Medea's vulnerability.[3] However, this position hardly tells the whole story. The same critics have expertly noticed the multiple provenance of Medea's character. It is indeed particularly difficult to sum up Medea's character and position in the *Argonautica* exactly because she is at the same time many figures together, most famously Nausikaa, Helen, Calypso, Penelope, Circe.[4] As well as a vulnerable girl, Medea is also a puzzling and complex personality eluding definitive circumscription. Against those who focus on her ultimate desolation, there are those who are instead impressed by her stamina and bold participation in the story. In her work on the women in the Apollonian epos, Stephanie Natzel explores at length Medea's posture throughout Books 3 and 4 and appears determined to overturn previous derogatory appraisals of her character. For her, Medea's falling in love with Jason is not so much a by-product of his own stunning presence as a natural development inherent in her own personality.[5] The full swing of the argument might not be accepted by some, yet Natzel does succeed in turning attention onto Medea herself, her own attitudes, dilemmas, and personal moments through her lengthy discussion of Medea's private moments and emotional soliloquies in the course of Book 3. In fact, the possibility that a reverse appreciation of roles lurks in Book 3 has preoccupied James Clauss in a recent

illusion . . . evokes a sense of Pindar's own magical powers. The apparent metamorphosis undergone by Medea comments on the relationship between the *epinician* poet and *his* Muse, which is a transformation of the traditional relationship between the epic poet and Muse.'

[3] See e.g. Feeney (1991) 82; Hunter (1989) ad 3. 135; Goldhill (1991) 301 ff.; Clauss (1997) 164–73 with further bibliographical references.

[4] Cf. here e.g. Hunter (1993*a*) 12–15, 64, 67, and *passim*; Goldhill (1991) 301–4.

[5] Natzel (1992) 48: 'Apollonios hat die Perspektive radikal umgekehrt. Bei ihm verfällt Medea der Liebe zu Iason nicht aufgrund einer entsprechenden Aktivität des Mannes . . . Die Liebe überkommt Medea weniger als eine dämonische äußere Macht, sondern eher als ein Gefühl, das sich folgerichtig aus ihrer Persönlichkeit und letztlich aus den Gesetzen der menschlichen Seele selbst ergibt.'

article[6] in which he wonders whether Medea's 'compelling' and 'gripping' portrayal throughout Book 3 does not call for a redefinition of the epic hero in this highly anarchic and love-dominated epic.[7] Clauss explores a series of key passages as Jason and Medea cross paths, and discovers a bold and threatening Medea coerced but capable of carrying clear, if latent, overtones of dangerous otherness.[8] And yet, while unearthing such 'pregnant' aspects of the epic, Clauss does not ultimately feel they qualify to reshape the definitions: Medea is not a new hero, but just a helper in Apollonius' epic and Jason's quest of the Golden Fleece.

And yet, Clauss makes sure to leave his readers with a final reminder of Medea's unsettling otherness.[9] It is amidst such an exegetic aporia that Medea, the human and humane muse and not *either* the vulnerable girl, *or* the powerful witch, *or* the agonizing daughter of the king, *or* the threatening foreigner, seems capable of giving momentum to an old, and by now more or less stagnant controversy.

I. GODS, WARRIORS, AND POETIC SURROGATES

But before we turn our attention to Medea's choices and challenges as a muse, it is, I believe, appropriate to give her skill and inspiration a context by exploring at some length the boldly and anarchically metapoetic environment within which the young girl emerges as a muse.

Μῆνιν ἄειδε θεά . . . *Arma virumque cano*: epic poems traditionally focus on battles and boisterous friction. Reckless ventures and figures driven beside themselves through pride and anger jostle for the centre spot of the Muses' epic narrations. Cunning may have countered military prowess with varying degrees of persuasion in the different epics,

---

[6] Clauss (1997).

[7] On which see esp. Beye (1982) esp. 120–42; Pavlock (1990) 19–68 with ample insight into the poet's persistent rejection of traditional patterns of heroism.

[8] Otherness often underlined by means of her very modelling upon previous female figures: 'The systematic imitation of Nausikaa's words and experiences sets Medea's foreignness in relief by placing in the background the icon not merely of a Hellenic woman, but one who was best known for her virtue and restraint' (Clauss (1997) 177).

[9] Clauss (1997) 177: 'Medea, on the other hand, is portrayed by Apollonius as a manipulative, powerful, and threatening foreign woman who, among other things, does not do laundry. . . . Thus, as the passionate and terrifying Medea does things that call Nausikaa to mind, the reader becomes more keenly aware of the "other" that is within Medea.' See also 161: 'The Medean helper-maiden differs markedly from the Nausikaan model in the degree to which she can help. As we shall see, Medea can turn a weak Jason into a powerful Heracles. Moreover, unlike Nausikaa, Medea will not allow the hero she helps to leave without taking her along.'

but it still holds true that the genre self-consciously identifies itself with uproar, with blasts of action. Apollonius Rhodius' epic, however, operates an interesting tour de force on those constituent features of its own making, deriding and at the same time transgressing its own pre-determined boundaries.[10] Jason's notorious unmanly ἀμηχανίη and his strikingly anti-epic composure have already triggered thought-provoking essays.[11] But this chapter is not concerned with the protago-nist's anti-heroic propensity so much as with his liking of words. The snippet that captures this predilection at its best comes early on in Book 3 of the epic: having reached the Colchian land the Argonauts have anchored off-shore in a shaded corner of the river. Once they are gathered in assembly to hear about the deeds and tasks lying ahead, Jason leads the discussion and announces to his comrades that a delega-tion with himself in charge, is about to depart for the palace of Aeetes in order to check out the king's intentions in regard to the Golden Fleece and the Argonauts' claim on it:

> αὐτὰρ ἐγὼν ἐς δώματ' ἐλεύσομαι Αἰήταο,
> υἷας ἑλὼν Φρίξοιο δύω δ' ἐπὶ τοῖσιν ἑταίρους
> πειρήσω δ' ἐπέεσσι παροίτερον ἀντιβολήσας,
> εἴ κ' ἐθέλοι φιλότητι δέρος χρύσειον ὀπάσσαι,
> ἦε καὶ οὔ, πίσυνος δὲ βίῃ μετιόντας ἀτίσσει.
> ὧδε γὰρ ἐξ αὐτοῖο πάρος κακότητα δαέντες
> φρασσόμεθ' εἴτ' ἄρῃ συνοισόμεθ', εἴτε τις ἄλλη
> μῆτις ἐπίρροθος ἔσται ἐεργομένοισιν αὐτῆς.
> μηδ' αὔτως ἀλκῇ, πρὶν ἔπεσσί γε πειρηθῆναι,
> τόνδ' ἀπαμείρωμεν σφέτερον κτέρας. ἀλλὰ πάροιθεν
> λωίτερον μήθῳ μιν ἀρέσσασθαι μετιόντας.
> πολλάκι τοι ῥέα μῦθος, ὅ κεν μόλις ἐξανύσειεν
> ἠνορέη, τόδ' ἔρεξε κατὰ χρέος, ᾗπερ ἐῴκει
> πρηΰνας.
>
> （3. 177–90）

I shall go to Aeetes' palace, together with the sons of Phrixos and two of our comrades as well, and I shall first speak to him to test whether he is willing in friendship to grant us the golden fleece or prefers to refuse and, trusting his might, reject our quest. In this way we shall learn the depth of our plight and

[10] The poem's boasting secondariness and astute self-reflexivity have already attracted the attention of significant criticism in recent years, which has provided a most useful background to the present chapter: cf. e.g. Feeney (1991) 57–98; Goldhill (1991) 284–333; Hunter (1993a); Albis (1996).

[11] See esp. Lawall (1966); Beye (1982) esp. 120–42; Hunter (1988) esp. 436–8, 443, and *passim*; Pavlock (1990) esp. 30–1, 43–4, 66–7.

then be able to decide whether to engage him in war or whether, if we refrain from battle, some other device will help us. Before testing him with words, let us not try simply to deprive him of his possession by force: it is better first to approach him and seek to win him over by arguments. In tight corners arguments have often smoothed the way and achieved what manly strength could hardly accomplish.[12]

Jason is indeed very clear about his priorities. Words and μήτεις (thoughts) come first; it is only after these have failed that might will be resorted to. Of course Odysseus' exemplary cunning immediately springs to mind, with the two heroes' resemblance culminating in Medea's and Jason's furtive tryst in the grove of Hecate to which I will shortly return.[13] And the identification of the poet's own narrative with the *Argo*'s voyage has become a mainstream critical topos by now in a series of subtle metapoetic studies.[14] But Jason's heartily proclaimed preference for words over deeds is another conscious play with generic conventions and a step that even his πολύτροπος Homeric predecessor stopped short of. No doubt Odysseus was an exemplary storyteller, but it is Jason who takes off his heroic hat and tells us that as well as (perhaps even instead of?) a hero, he wants to be a poet and to plot t/his epic as seems best.

A clearer pattern begins to emerge: the myth must be accomplished, the Golden Fleece snatched away from Colchis; and Jason has vested interests that make him eager to bring this mission to a successful completion just as the well-known mythical background of this epos suggests. But, as a poet, the leader of the Argonauts would like to keep his options open: the story is not yet written and the optimal plot is yet to be decided. Jason would like to have the last word in it but (as will be discussed below) this desire means still further struggle, and this time a struggle that could not be resolved on the battlefield. For Jason is not the only aspiring artist in the book: many of its other figures also ambitiously conspire to impose their own version of a plot.

And this is far from being a hidden feature of the book—indeed, Hera and Athena trigger the dance of plotting at the very beginning of it: eager

---

[12] All the translations of Apollonius' text come from Hunter (1993b).

[13] On Apollonius' intriguing use of past examples in general see esp. Pavlock (1990) 1968; Goldhill (1991) 297–300, 313, 319–21, and *passim*.

[14] Cf. esp. Goldhill (1991) esp. 286–300; also more recently Albis (1996) esp. 43–66, who has elaborated on the *Argo*'s metapoetic reflections. Albis's main suggestion though is significantly different: his poets/characters recreate the tasks of a performer rather than a silent, bookish writer, as he contends that Apollonius self-consciously evokes the tradition and social context of archaic performance poetry.

to help the Argonauts through their difficult task, they pull aside from the other gods and try to devise plans to help them out of their impasse (3. 23–35). Athena makes it clear that she has mulled several plans over and over again in her mind. And yet they both admit their inability to come up with a satisfactory plan. It will not be long before they turn to Aphrodite, entrusting her with a plot that they cannot handle on their own. The newly devised plan involves Eros, Aphrodite's son, who would have to be persuaded to charm Aeetes' daughter with love for Jason so that she could grant him her help, and specifically, her mystical knowledge, that would enable the plot to move on unperturbed by the evil guiles of King Aeetes. The episode has already attracted attention for its playful adaptation of Homeric and other earlier precedents and has been expertly discussed as a scene brimming with Alexandrian realism and wit.[15] What concerns us here, however, is Aphrodite's help-lessness. She will accept the mission but not without expressing strong doubts regarding her ability to play her part in this constructive chain, unsure as she feels about her own control over her son (3. 91–9).

This contention and uncertainty underpin the plan of the three goddesses, in spite of its divine authorship, and this is of course closely related to the neoteric doubts cast on divinity not only by Apollonius but also by his equally unsettling and unsettled peers. It comes as no surprise then that the human contestants in this game of plotting appear equally perplexed. King Aeetes himself is a characteristic instance of this generalized confusion that dominates the whole poem, but especially Book 3. Perhaps the most powerful figure in it, he is able to inflict utter despair on the characteristically unepic Jason, as we shall soon see in more detail. His rage and wrathful words in response to the Argonauts' claim on the Golden Fleece deeply disturb Jason's companions (καί ῥ᾽ οἱ μέν ῥα δόμων ἐξήλυθον ἀσχαλόωντες (3. 448), 'Thus they went out of the place deep in depression'). Abandoning his guests in great distress, Aeetes calls a meeting of the general assembly of the Colchians where he announces his own awesome plot, making it widely known that dread-ful deceit is awaiting the troubled guests from Greece (Αἰτίκα δ᾽ Αἰήτης ἀγορὴν ποιήσατο, | . . . | ἀτλήτους Μινύῃσι δόλους καὶ κήδεα τεήχων | (3. 576–8), 'Aietes lost no time in convening an assembly . . . to plan awful treachery and woes for the Minyans').

---

[15] Cf. e.g. Hunter (1989) ad loc. and esp. 43–7, 106–7, 109–10; Lennox (1980) 48–62; Campbell (1983) *passim*. On the Apollonian gods' realism in general, see also Feeney (1991) *passim* and esp. 76 ff., 82 f.

And yet not even his own powerful *doloi* can bring him peace of mind. As he himself admits while addressing the assembly, his own mind is heavy with long-lasting concern over a prophecy of his father Helios, according to which one of his offspring is bound to engage with treacherous plotting and guileful schemes against him (3. 596–600). Hunter notices the riddling language of this prophecy that points at *polytropos* Odysseus, Jason's own counterpart, a riddle easily picked up by a learned reader and yet eluding Aeetes' attention.[16] However, our own interest in the passage lies in the introduction of one more plotting agent. Somebody, and indeed most probably Aeetes' own offspring, is somewhere secretly preparing yet another plot, not clear itself in its details, but threatening to bring down the mighty king.

The haziness and unpredictability of this last (possible) plot make it, in fact, a most appropriate reflection of the programmatic structure of the whole of the *Argonautica*. Suffice it to remember the fundamental discrepancies that lie at the heart of the master-plot sustaining this epic: Pelias may have indeed sent Jason to fetch the Fleece back to Iolkos, but his ultimate plan counts on Jason's failure and subsequent non-return. Furtive plots are thus inscribed 'on the back' of the apparently dominant ones, which have dictated the narration so far.[17] No wonder the persona of the narrator himself reaches a dead end and admits his total dependence on the Muse at the beginning of Book 4: Αὐτὴ νῦν κάματόν γε θεὰ καὶ δήνεα κούρης | Κολχίδος ἔννεπε Μοῦσα (4. 1–2), 'You yourself, Goddess, tell of the suffering and thoughts of the Colchian girl, you Muse, child of Zeus'.[18]

At this point, with this puzzling invocation as well as the impasses reached by the various internal authors in this characteristically unheroic and divinely bereft work in mind, Medea as the doubted, doubting, and humane Muse appears as a most eloquent symbolization

[16] Hunter (1989) ad 597–602.

[17] In his discussion of the gods in Apollonius, Feeney (1991) 59 reads this as a sign of the gods' own reticence and own aporia: 'A homecoming may be the *telos* desired by the gods, but certainly it is the opposite of the plan of Pelias, who is sending Jason on the perilous journey in order to cause his death. Even this early the problem is raised of what the *telos* of the poem will be, and it is linked with the problem of the purpose of god and man.'

[18] Albis (1996) 93–120 provides an interesting insight into the metapoetic qualities of the *Argo*'s long-winded return trip back to Greece. Albis points out the similarity between *oimos*, a frequent metaphor for song, and *oime*, the course of the *Argo*'s trip and thus builds a well-sustained analogy between the Argonauts' journey and the route of Apollonius' song itself. Along these lines, the convolutions and detours of the return journey represent the deviations of the narration, and the doubts of the Argonauts about their ship's path also speak for the poet's anxiety and uncertainty about the competing traditions he has to choose from.

of all the conflicting powers that sway the narration, the narrator, and the ship of the Argonauts herself. In the boldly metapoetic environment of the *Argonautica* just explored above, Jason is the poet and Medea his muse. It is her magical knowledge of the magic herbs and charms which Jason, the poet/hero, needs in order to push his plot forward that makes her his muse. But this is a famously (notoriously) neoteric epic, and Medea is hardly a Hesiodic muse herself. She actually represents everything that the archaic Muses were emphatically and traditionally not: unpredictable, threatened, threatening, unsure, and conscious of her gender. The Introduction to this volume has already paved the ground for such 'fallen' muses.[19] At the time when the Muse has fallen from the Heliconian pedestal, Medea constitutes an intriguing example of the doubted divinity and of the combative muse who may have lost her luxurious rooms in the residence of the gods,[20] but has found, or is struggling to find, her own voice, breaking away from the protective power of Apollo. And yet, at the same time, it is her role as the 'fallen' muse, intricately poised on a blend of power, knowledge, helplessness, and vulnerability typical of post-Hesiodic muses,[21] that sheds light on Medea's paradoxes, her 'ambiguous power' and the 'infamous duplicity' that continue to puzzle the critics.

O'Higgins's discussion of Pindar's *Pythian* 4 mentioned above begins with these very ambiguities: 'One of the paradoxes surrounding the Medea of the famous fifth-century texts—Euripides' play and the great *Pythian* 4 of Pindar . . . is that she appears both exceptional and typical of all females.'[22] O'Higgins then proceeds with an informed exploration of these indecisions in Medea's character. And yet, however subtle, such a description fails to restore another imbalance regarding Medea's character:[23] namely, the persistence of men (be they fellow-protagonists, ancient poets, or modern critics) to heed only her deeds, at the expense of her words, in a way more pertaining to a male character, in the conventional (if not somewhat crude) perceptions of Antiquity on manliness.[24] We are used to dealing with Medea's duplicity, but we are not

---

[19] See esp. Part II: 'Roman Indecisions'.

[20] 'At an angle to the court on both sides stood the taller parts of the palace. The highest of all was occupied by Aeetes and his wife, and another by Aeetes' son Apsyrtos. . . . The other rooms were occupied by servants and by Aeetes' two daughters, Chalkiope and Medea.' *Arg.* 3. 240–8.

[21] Cf. also Introduction, Fowler, Janan, Ancona, Henderson, and esp. Sharrock in this volume.   [22] O'Higgins (1997) 103.

[23] Pointed out to me by Alison Sharrock.

[24] Suffice it perhaps to recall here the heroine's alarming hermetism in Euripides' *Medea* as

used to thinking that her femininity may have been affected as a result of the myth (in)famously attached to her. Medea is positioned on the literary map through her notorious deeds, her words remaining elusive and worryingly inscrutable.[25] We are in need of a text that would give us these words, and of a ploy that would direct the spotlight on Medea. Apollonius' self-conscious epic, dating back to the future, at a time when Medea's notorious deeds have not yet sealed her character and life, is the text. Medea, as the faltering, but intensely self-conscious muse is the— far from gratuitous—ploy which gives credit to her respected, cajoled, derided, and sought-after power.

II. THE MUSE IS TAUGHT TO WRITE

Throughout Book 3 of the *Argonautica*, desire and performance merge in a ceaseless interweaving. It is characteristic that this constant link between Love and Art is emphatically established in the opening lines of Book 3 with the invocation of the poet to Erato (3. 1–5). The significance of the specific choice of Muse for Book 3 should not pass unheeded. As Apollonius keenly stresses, the associations between Erato and Eros,[26] Love and Art are explicitly connected before any further action is triggered. What this opening further adds is a crucial warning about what the whole of Book 3 is about: it does not merely deal with Medea's love for Jason but rather explores the crucial role of Medea's love for Jason's snatching of the Golden Fleece: Εἰ δ' ἄγε νῦν Ἐρατώ, παρ' ἔμ' ἵστασο καί μοι ἔνισπε | ἔνθεν ὅπως ἐς Ἰωλκὸν ἀνήγαγε κῶας Ἰήσων | Μηδείης ὑπ' ἔρωτι, 'Come now, Erato, stand beside me and relate to me how it was that Jason brought the fleece from Colchis to Iolkos through the power of Medea's love'. This meticulous concern with the way matters of love are introduced into the book is far from trivial: viewed through this lens, the whole book identifies itself as the narration of a plot, a μῆτις, which the Argonauts have been asked to accomplish. The existence of such a plot should come as no surprise to us: we already witnessed at some length how this plot, or rather several competing

eloquently portrayed by her Nurse, the Chorus, and other figures time and again throughout the play. Having lost Jason's favour and removed from the conjugal lodgings, the Colchian woman sends waves of disquietude to all around her from the isolation of her new abode, as she refuses to let her thoughts be known. See e.g. *Med.* 26–37, 316–20.

[25] I deal with the silence of Euripides' *Medea* more extensively in an article I am writing on female reticence in general.

[26] 3. 5: 'a lovely name (ἐπήρατον οὔνομα) has been attached to you'.

plots that comprise the book, stumble over overwhelming difficulties. Yet, what this preface further suggests is that a plot will eventually be allowed to flourish but only thanks to Medea's desire for Jason, who thus identifies himself as a potent motivating force, Medea's inspiration or else her own muse.[27]

In fact, the association between the Muse and Eros is marked through a series of sophisticated images: through her specific ability to fill the young girls with cares, Erato will soon be mirrored in the face of Eros, Aphrodite's child, just after he has sent his burning arrows to Medea's heart, according to Hera's and Athena's wishes and his mother's instructions. The descriptions are powerful and eloquent: once the arrows of love are planted inside her, young and innocent Medea is instantly transformed into a labouring old woman unfailingly reminding the learned reader of the toll art takes on the artist (3. 284–98).[28] A flame burns inside, melting her up, and will not abandon her until she turns to action—until she takes up 'writing'.[29] At the sight of Jason, she languishes in a speechless daze, tossed around by the cares that love has stirred up inside her (3. 444–52).[30]

[27] The preface attracts close attention by Clauss (1997) 152, but mainly due to the unconventional and mixed generic signals emitted by it: 'The prologue treats the anxiety of love as a crucial element in the completion of the heroic contest.' Cf. also 152 n. 11 with bibliography on the metaliterary significance of the passage.

[28] The realism and humility of this simile, as well as the intertextual value of the surrounding imagery that likens Medea's love to the flaring up of a fire, have already been discussed by the critics. See esp. Hunter (1989) ad 192–5. But it is the sudden change in Medea's hitherto carefree life that easily leads the reader to acknowledged metaliterary distinctions: toil together with *techne* were famous prerequisites for poetry in the contemporary Callimachean aesthetics. Suffice it to recollect here Theocritus' *Id.* 28 and the much laboured ivory distaff of Theugenis, a succinct testimony of the poetics of toil to which Medea is about to subscribe.

[29] Albis (1996) 67–92 also notices the multiple correspondences between poetry and love, but his conclusions take a different direction. See esp. 70–1: 'Since the divine power depicted as exerting its influence on Medea, Eros, is closely associated with Erato, the deity invoked at the start of the book, one is invited to associate not only these seductive powers themselves but also the objects affected by these powers. Since [Erato] is the deity addressed in a poem's invocation; another obvious recipient of her power is the narrator. . . . Since the poet is in many ways a mouthpiece for the Muse, the ultimate object of Erato's power is the audience; the experience of the audience, as well as that of the poet, is assimilated to the experience of Medea . . . both Medea and the audience are affected by a force that stems at least partly from the Muse Erato.'

[30] This blend of art with care is to find some celebrated expressions in later periods. For example, Catullus' loss of Golden Age innocence is famously connected with the art of ship-making in c. 65; Virgil, *Georgics* 1. 121–5 explicitly suggests that cares and worries are the main presuppositions for sophistication and art, in another typical Golden Age locus—when Zeus decides to insert art in the minds and needs of people, disturbed by the laziness that immediate availability had brought about.

What the above descriptions suggest is that emotional, as well as physical, coercion seems to dominate the proceedings throughout Book 3. Eros, Aphrodite's mischievous offspring, beleaguers the innocent maiden and will not relinquish his grip until she gives in to his power and writes the tricky part of the plot for Jason. And before that, Aphrodite has already been gracefully bullied by Hera and Athena into co-operating with them in a scheme according to which Eros is compelled into filling the girl's heart with desire, so that she can afterwards work out a plot for Jason's safe return to Iolkos.[31]

Indeed, once talked into the scheme with the lure of the golden ball,[32] Eros confidently urges Medea to take action and start 'writing' Jason's part. Even when we tend to forget him, absorbed by the peaks of the love story evolving in the course of the book, the narrative offers subtle yet unambiguous reminders of his unremitting role in it.[33] The young girl is overwhelmed and filled with awe at the task laid before her. But Eros insists and, bending under his pressure, Medea gradually passes from silence to speech, and the text presents this with eloquent, symbolic language. Having been smitten by the arrows of love, tormented by desire to help and fear of punishment, Medea's afflicted mind seeks rest in a deep, but anguished, slumber. Her dreams are destructive and deceitful (ὀλοοί, ἠπεροπῆες ὄνειροι) but stunningly dynamic as well:

> τὸν ξεῖνον δ᾽ ἐδόκησεν ὑφεστάμεναι τὸν ἄεθλον
> οὔτι μάλ᾽ ὁρμαίνοντα δέρος κριοῖο κομίσσαι,
> οὐδέ τι τοῖο ἕκητι μετὰ πτόλιν Αἰήταο
> ἐλθέμεν, ὄφρα δέ μιν σφέτερον δόμον εἰσαγάγοιτο
> κουριδίην παράκοιτιν. ὀίετο δ᾽ ἀμφὶ βόεσσιν
> αὐτὴ ἀεθλεύουσα μάλ᾽ εὐμαρέως πονέεσθαι
>
> (3. 619–24)

She imagined that the stranger undertook the challenge, not at all because he wanted to recover the fleece—it was not for that that he had come to Aeetes' city—but to take her back to his own home as his properly wedded wife. In her dream she herself easily accomplished the challenge of the bulls.

---

[31] See esp. 3. 84–7.

[32] 3. 129–55.

[33] Such reminders are often interlaced in the narrative, as subtle yet unambiguous signals of Eros' unyielding presence. See esp. 3. 927–37: a crow sent by Hera converses with Mopsus the seer and reminds him that Medea has to be left alone to speak the words of love breathed into her by Eros and Cetherea. Hunter (1989) ad loc. cross-refers to his 967–72 n. where the typical image of love as a breath of air is discussed.

The climax of this wondrous and at the same time frightening dream
brings the young maiden into direct conflict with her parents. As she
chooses to align herself with the stranger, 'her parents were seized by
unbearable grief and cried aloud in their anger'. Faced with their rage in
the dream, Medea wakes up with a loud voice (ἀδινήν δ᾽ ἀνενείκατο
φωνήν 3. 635). After that vision, Medea gradually manages to use words
more fluently, always under the unceasing encouragement of bold Eros.
Her encounter with her sister Chalkiope in the wake of dreaming of her
success, expertly illustrates this newly found energy. Medea's urge to
talk to Chalkiope is here marked by a resourceful determination barely
restrained by the girl's natural shame.

> τῆς δ᾽ ἐρύθηνε παρήια, δὴν δέ μιν αἰδώς
> παρθενίη κατέρυκεν, ἀμείψασθαι μεμαυῖαν·
> μῦθος δ᾽ ἄλλοτε μέν οἱ ἐπ᾽ ἀκροτάτης ἀνετελλεν
> γλώσσης, ἄλλοτ᾽ ἔνερθε κατὰ στῆθος πεπότητο·
> πολλάκι δ᾽ ἱμερόεν μὲν ἀνὰ στόμα θυῖεν ἐνισπεῖν,
> φθογγὴ δ᾽ οὐ προύβαινε παροιτέρω. ὀψὲ δ᾽ ἔειπεν
> τοῖα δόλῳ, θρασέες γὰρ ἐπικλονέεσκον ἔρωτες.   (3. 681-7)

Medea's cheeks grew red and for a long time maidenly shame held her back,
though she longed to reply. Words rose to the very tip of her tongue, but then
flew back again deep into her chest; often they rushed up to her lovely mouth to
be uttered, but then went no further and were never spoken. Finally she did
speak, and with cunning, for the bold Loves buffeted hard against her.

Bringing into the discussion a striking intertext, namely Nausikaa's
famous dream of a husband prior to her own meeting with Odysseus in
Odyssey 6. 25–40, Clauss reads this passage as another characteristic
juxtaposition of the heroic and the erotic, in what seems to be a structure
underpinning the *Argonautica* in general, but this book in particular.[34]
Clauss rightly observes the literary subtexts in the background of
this passage as they contribute to the full appreciation of Medea's
personality in Apollonius' epic. However, within the framework of the
present chapter, this specific moment in our text is also a rite of passage
for Medea, the human (and humane) muse.

Tormented by fears but also excited by desire, she longs to help Jason
do his part. The muse-like knowledge that she possesses and which
Jason needs in order to overcome his challenge successfully and write
his own plot, prompts her to plunge into action.[35] But that is quite

---

[34] Clauss (1997) 160. Cf. also Hunter (1989) ad 626–32.
[35] For a different reading of Medea's taking up the role of the poet, cf. Albis (1996) 84–9.

appropriate for the ancient Muses, who were mostly conceived as joint accomplices of the poets in the process of storytelling and poetry-making.[36] But of course Medea is also strikingly dissimilar to those old Muses: her amorous fervour for Jason and overwhelming trepidation before her father is in stark contrast with the carefree nature[37] of her archaic predecessors. Critics' views on the topic of the Muses' sexuality differ,[38] yet it seems fair to suggest that the potential of a gendered relationship is already inscribed in the primordial imagery of the nine Muses in the company of Apollo. And, as I suggest, it is this lurking eroticism and latent sexuality that appears to erupt, as knowledge and inspiration are entrusted to mortals: the Muses' authority can be coveted as well as undermined as the inspired draw nearer. It should be noted that Book 3 of the *Argonautica*, Medea's very book, is marked by this neoteric and unsettling, flirtatious proximity from the very beginning, when the narrator invited the muse Erato to stand by him, and sing together with him the story of Jason and Medea: Εἰ δ' ἄγε νῦν Ἐρατώ, παρ' ἔμ' ἵστασο καί μοι ἔνισπε (3. 1), 'Come now Erato, stand beside me and relate to me'.[39] Erato's close alignment with the poet has an archaic precedent characteristically associated with Medea: in Pindar's *Pythian* 4 the Muse was instructed to stand by the poet and honour Arcesilas, in a poem which subsequently features Medea in a central position as Jason's story evolves in parallel with Arcesilas' own honourable deeds· Σάμερον μὲν χρή σε παρ' ἀνδρὶ φίλῳ | στᾶμεν, εὐίππου βασιλῆϊ Κυράνας, | ὄφρα κωμάζοντι σὺν Ἀρκεσίλᾳ, | Μοῖσα (*Pyth.* 4. 1–4), 'Come Muse, today I bid you stand beside a man well-loved, Cyrene's king, that city of noble steeds, and in his hour of triumph honour Arcesilas.'[40]

To recapitulate and move on. In spite of frequent (neoteric) moments of

---

[36] See e.g. O'Higgins (1997) 108 and 108 n. 15. Cf. also Cavarero, Lada-Richards, Laird in this volume.

[37] See Hesiod, *Theog.* 61 and cf. the Introduction, esp. Part II on the burdened Roman muses of Latin literature.

[38] Contrast e.g. Murray and Sharrock in this volume; see also Doherty (1995) 84.

[39] See here Clauss (1997) 151–2; Campbell (1983) 1–7. For a non-gendered view of the Muses' transformed role in the *Argonautica* in relation to authority, tradition, and 'new strategies of authorisation', cf. Goldhill (1991) 288, 291–4; Feeney (1991) 90–3.

[40] For a different interpretation of the Muses' 'repositioning' see O'Higgins (1997) 112: 'this "relocation" of the Muse from her traditionally remote "otherworld", where she must be sought out by special devotees, to the familiar Greek and civic world of Cyrene parallels Medea's movement within the poem from distant Colchis to Hellas. Hesiod's encounter with the Muses was in the wilderness, a social and sexual no-man's-land where male and female can break out of their traditional roles, and often do.'

doubt and circumspection for which Apollonius' epic has been renowned, the narrative of *Argonautica* 3 also seems to be properly driven to epic resolution by a secure and confident force that appears to counteract and often strangle the ambiguities. Once convinced by his mother in a scene also destined to raise a smile amongst readers, Eros, the assertive and (over?)confident agent, manipulates the plot with remarkable exactitude, and so counteracts much of the authorial retrospection we have witnessed above. Eros is never at a loss, invisibly working on the plot even when the seer Mopsus appears not to know what his position should be,[41] even when the narrator himself appears unsure as to his seer's foreknowledge.[42] It is then little wonder that Medea at first sight appears completely in the grip of his unremitting drive. As her emotionally charged interaction with Chalkiope we discussed above suggests, Medea becomes more and more 'talkative' under the pressure of love. To give it a slightly different angle, Medea, the muse, is introduced to the epic in which her magic knowledge is bound to prove indispensable, already framed and dependent on an external triggering force necessary to motivate her creative urge. Eros insists and, bending under his pressure, Medea passes from silence to speech.

However, as I shall suggest in the rest of this chapter, Medea has not quite spoken her last word. Stepping out of the protected Heliconian grove, the Muse, indeed, loses the privileges of a carefree existence, but as Medea in Apollonius suggests, she gains a powerful character not normally associated with the daughters of Mnemosyne.[43] Love is indeed an extraordinarily resourceful device, and under its cunning pressure Medea learns to write; yet, she also painfully learns to think and agonize over her power and over her fears, in a way the old muses did not, absorbed as they were in 'their single-minded devotion to pleasure'. And this thinking yields dilemmas, agonies, urges, desires, and a spirit which is strikingly gendered, at points that may not have a lasting impact on the epic plot, but are inscribed in it, and available to those who want to heed its voice. And, as we shall now see, this defiant spirit will be Aphrodite's *enfant terrible* with all his mischievous supremacy.

---

[41] Cf. the scene of the crow deriding Mopsus for *not knowing* that he has to stay away as he is escorting Jason to his furtive tryst with Medea (3. 932–5).

[42] See e.g. 3. 926 and Hunter (1989) ad loc.

[43] Contrast here the Introduction, Part I, on the traditional collectivity of the archaic Muses.

III. THE MUSE LEARNS TO THINK

Even though generally dependent on other more powerful motivating forces, as well as a constantly frightened and hesitant figure, Medea becomes a central and crucial factor in the construction of the plot, already from the early stages of the narrative. It is during the meeting of Hera, Athena, and Aphrodite that we get an initial subtle, yet unmistakable, acknowledgement of the maiden's innate powers. While prescribing with assertion and expertise the trick that would outmanoeuvre Medea, Hera cannot help a passing reference to the girl's cunning temperament, as she delivers her instructions to Aphrodite: ἀλλ' αὔτως ἀκέουσα τεῷ ἐπικέκλεο παιδὶ | παρθένον Αἰήτεω θέλξαι ... ἐπεὶ δολόεσσα τέτυκται (3. 85–9), 'Please simply bid your son bewitch the maiden daughter of Aeetes with desire ... If she ... offers him her aid ... he will easily gain the golden fleece ... for she is full of guile'. However, for all of Hera's assured manner, the perceptive reader cannot help the fleeting thought that Hera's plan and Eros' mission cannot be all that *simple*: the maiden may look coy and timid, but she is also full of tricks and guiles, as Hera herself admits in her rather supercilious and condescending manner.

Such references become a regular pattern as the book progresses and Medea gathers character, still retaining her deceiving silence. This acquiescing craftsmanship which lurks inside Medea surfaces again when Argos, Chalkiope's son, introduces the maiden to the Argonauts, who were gathered to make decisions in the face of Aeetes' hard challenge (3. 417–615). Convened with the sole purpose of inventing a way to circumvent the helplessness that afflicted the heroes after Aeetes had laid out his hostile plan, the Argonauts have lost heart, their mood sombre and heavy with worry. The news has cast gloom over the whole group. The journey is imminently threatened by interruption, and so— symbolically—is the poem itself, to use the critics' favourite metapoetic correlation.[44] Overwhelmed by lack of skill and wiles to help him through, a downcast Jason withdraws to one side. When Aeetes had communicated to him the tasks he was expected to get through in order to get the Fleece, he received them in silence with eyes fixed on the ground, at a loss as to how to proceed, and unable to accept the challenge, feeling that this was an all too mighty deed: ἐπεὶ μέγα φαίνετο ἔργον (3. 425).

---

[44] See n. 14 above.

Against this sedated world of suspended ideas, Medea's resourcefulness can hardly pass unheeded, however low-key her introduction. As
Jason the artist finds himself daunted by the task assigned to him, Argos
presents Medea as a possible ally in finding a way out of the trap. Despite
Argos' vague allusion to a previous discussion with Jason about Medea,[45]
this is really the first time that the girl's existence is brought to the
Argonauts' attention, and this is hardly a jubilant entrance: Argos makes
a conscious effort to create a low profile for Medea, mainly to avoid
offending the male pride and sensitivities of the puzzled Argonauts:

> Αἰσονίδη, μῆτιν μὲν ὀνόσσεαι ἥντιν' ἐνίψω,
> πείρης δ' οὐ μάλ' ἔοικε μεθιέμεν ἐν κακότητι.
> κούρην δή τινα πρόσθεν ἐπέκλυες αὐτὸς ἐμεῖο
> φαρμάσσειν Ἑκάτης Περσηίδος ἐννεσίῃσιν·
> τὴν εἴ κεν πεπίθοιμεν, ὀίομαι, οὐκέτι τάρβος
> ἔσσετ' ἀεθλεύοντι δαμήμεναι·   (3. 475–80)

You will not approve, son of Aison, of the plan which I will now propose, but we
can hardly refuse to attempt it in our wretched plight. There is a young girl—
you have already heard me tell you how Hecate, daughter of Perses, inspires her
powers with magic drugs; if we can win her over, I do believe that we need no
longer worry about defeat in the contest.

If the Argonauts' own wishes are anything to go by, Medea can only
become a humble helper in the accomplishment of the voyage and the
poem, and a new hero is unlikely to emerge.[46] Yet, as she acquires
character, Medea's potent side gathers significance and momentum. She
may have just been wedged into the narrative by Argos, and yet his
reluctant introduction directly juxtaposes her cunning to Jason's lack of
inventiveness, as the only possible way out of the dead end. Even if
deliberately undermined, and only indirectly alluded to, Medea nevertheless is already set to gain control over the task—and thus over the
journey and eventually the poem—by means of her knowledge of magic
herbs and therefore her knowledge of the plot, while all the others
flounder in despair and lack of inspiration. Medea the inspired, love-
stricken girl, is at the same time a potent inspirer. She is the only one
who knows how to overcome Aeetes' scheming and carry the
Argonauts' plot through to completion. She has the knowledge famously connected with the Muses.[47] And the Argonauts turn to her, just as a

---

[45] Cf. Hunter (1989) ad 477–8.
[46] Cf. Clauss (1997).
[47] And this is not the only time that a human muse will undertake to rescue the Argonauts

poet would turn to a Muse once his own resourcefulness is exhausted—in fact just as Apollonius himself will do at the beginning of Book 4, smitten by a similar speechlessness to Jason's, and puzzled by fruitless pondering just like him.

> Αὐτὴ νῦν κάματόν γε θεὰ καὶ δήνεα κούρης
> Κολχίδος ἔννεπε Μοῦσα, Διὸς τέκος· ἦ γὰρ ἔμοιγε
> ἀμφασίη νόος ἔνδον ἐλίσσεται·   (4. 1–3)

You yourself, goddess, tell of the suffering and thoughts of the Colchian girl, you Muse, child of Zeus; within me my mind whirls in silent helplessness.[48]

Mirrored in the figure of the supervising Muse of Book 4, when clad in her saviour's garment, Medea's strongest affinities still lie with Erato of Book 3. A connection is established in the very opening of the book. The very moment Erato's bewitching impact over young girls' hearts is invoked (3. 4–5), Medea's (in)famous magic charms spring to the learned reader's mind. But it is Medea's furtive and ill-fated meeting with Jason (3. 956–1147) that will provide the most vivid impersonation of Apollonius' 'relocated' muse of Book 3, as she suffers under the weight of her authority.

With their respective companions duly occupied in other tasks at a safe distance, Jason and Medea meet in the grove of the temple of Hecate, in an encounter set up with unfailing determination by Eros. The meeting has received plenty of attention, in fact it has been thoroughly scrutinized by the critics.[49] Acting against the background of Medea's dumbstruck desire,[50] Jason appears to have the upper hand, as he flirts, flatters, and gently manipulates the dazed and mostly silent maiden. And yet, the same critics who have eloquently indulged in Jason's confident handling of the meeting and the girl, also notice instances in the text that unsettle this complacent balance with subtle

---

(and the plot). In Book 4, Herossae, nymphs of Libya, will also rush to Jason's rescue, saving the men from certain death through their Muse-like knowledge of the plot of the Golden Fleece adventure (4. 1312–31). Cf. Feeney (1991) 91–2, who reads the episode as a characteristic illustration of the fluidity in the muse–poet relation throughout the *Argonautica*.

[48] Cf. here Hunter (1993a) 106 on the significance of the passage for the poet: 'The emphasis on the poet's mental effort, however, as he ponders, ὁρμαίνοντι (4. 3), shows how far we have come from the Homeric conception of inspiration.' Shifting the emphasis to the Muse herself, we could suggest that these lines also point to the poet's diminished understanding of his own Muse, which adds one more interesting twist to the neoteric oscillations in the poet–muse relationship in the *Argonautica*.

[49] See esp. Goldhill (1991) 301–5; Clauss (1997) 164–73, both with extra relevant bibliography.

[50] See, characteristically, 3. 947–53.

innuendoes and other softly uttered, but unmistakable, remarks. Medea's modelling upon Nausikaa easily and predictably underscores the meekness of the Colchian princess, but Apollonius keeps up the tension: as Medea makes her way towards Hecate's grove, he compares her to Artemis. A subtext for this comparison is easily found in the parallel Homeric scene: Nausikaa was also likened to Artemis when playing with her maiden friends.[51] But this time the comparison includes clear hints of Artemis' awesome divine role, and so serves to underline Medea's potentially terrifying power.[52] Even when Medea appears fully tamed by Jason's charm, menacing overtones can still be picked up: she may now seem seduced by Jason's unblinking rhetoric, and yet she will never be like Ariadne (3. 1107–8). If badly provoked and conned, she will not be one to give up without a fight, unlike the Cretan princess. And as the learned reader already knows, back in the future, Medea will indeed be badly provoked with most catastrophic results. As Simon Goldhill aptly puts it on a different occasion: 'Jason is also the dupe, as his language unwittingly reveals him to be the future victim of an attempt to treat Medea like Ariadne. Jason is seducing his way into tragedy.'[53]

If criticism has found such subversive gestures intriguing for their sophisticated treatment of the past, they are also particularly telling for the concerns of the present reading. Let us not lose the thread: Jason may have been the handsome seducer of the unguarded maiden, Medea, who came and threw the girl's hitherto untroubled life into confusion, but he is also the wondering poet in need of a muse's knowledge and guidance through the stagnant moments of the plot. At the moment when the two stand side-by-side on their own by the shrine of Hecate, Medea will stand by her man, like Erato at the beginning of the book,[54] and the two will attempt to sing together:

> τὼ δ' ἄνεῳ καὶ ἄναυδοι ἐφέστασαν ἀλλήλοισιν,
> ἢ δρυσὶν ἢ μακρῇσιν ἐειδόμενοι ἐλάτῃσιν,
> αἵ τε παρᾶσσον ἔκηλοι ἐν οὔρεσιν ἐρρίζωνται
> νηνεμίῃ, μετὰ δ' αὖτις ὑπὸ ῥιπῆς ἀνέμοιο
> κινύμεναι ὁμάδησαν ἀπείριτον·   (3. 967–71)

The pair then faced each other, silent, unable to speak, like oaks or tall firs, which at first when there is no wind stand quiet and firmly rooted on the mountains, but afterwards stir in the wind and rustle together ceaselessly.

[51] Hunter (1989) ad 876–86.
[52] Cf. Clauss (1997) 165–6.
[53] Goldhill (1991) 303.
[54] And like the Muse at the beginnning of Pindar's *Pythian* 4: see II above.

The precedents for the metaphors of people as trees and love as a wind have already been noted.[55] Yet, the symbolic entanglement of the two in silence followed by speech, as Jason and Medea start rustling together, also constitutes a powerful transformation of the archetypal muse imagery. Tied in reciprocity, as they give and take inspiration, Jason and Medea, the poet and his muse 'tried one another with gentle words': ὣς τώγ᾽ ἀλλήλων ἀγανοῖς ἐπὶ τόσσον ἔπεσσιν | πείρηθεν (3. 1146). The constituent features of the new (mortal) poet–muse relationship are expertly summarized in this one, short sentence. Muse and poet, standing by one another, help one another and also try and probe one another. Proximity brings human attraction but it also brings human antagonism. And the subtexts for this meeting also suggest that such antagonism and strife are certainly lurking in the background, despite Jason's self-assured manner: as already noticed, Jason's and Medea's tryst is modelled upon another less furtive but significantly fiercer scene, that of the duel between Hector and Achilles in *Iliad* 22.[56]

IV. TURNING AGAINST APOLLO: MEDEA, THE WOMAN MUSE

In this final section, I would like to trace a little further this rather more unpredictable and less noticeable side of Medea the muse. Far from fulfilling the obedient role of Ariadne, or else the passive inspired pawn in the male-dominated games of inspiration, Medea reverts to her own feminine world and abandons herself to inner struggle, unintelligible to the powerful men that seek to manipulate her life and thoughts. In that world she can cry and formulate her thoughts and decisions, and it is characteristic that only her sister Chalkiope and her handmaids appear to witness her mute suffering.[57] In this women's room, Medea tries to come to terms with the conflicting forces within her, as the human and humane muse proves able and eager to bestow inspiration lavishly, but also proves herself vulnerable to desire and other inspiring forces. Jason's life is in her hands owing to her bewitching spells, her irresistible and indispensable knowledge. She longs to use it and write the story for him. She even dreams of beneficial plots that she would concoct for his sake (3. 616–32), only to wake up steeped in fear and guilt for her emotional (and creative) boldness:

[55] See Hunter (1989) ad 3. 967–72.
[56] See ibid ad 3. 964–5 and cf. Clauss (1997) 167.
[57] See e.g. 3. 665–70.

δειλὴ ἐγών, οἷόν με βαρεῖς ἐφόβησαν ὄνειροι.
δείδια μὴ μέγα δή τι φέρῃ κακὸν ἥδε κέλευθος
ἡρώων· περί μοι ξείνῳ φρένες ἠερέθονται.
μνάσθω ἑὸν κατὰ δῆμον Ἀχαιΐδα τηλόθι κούρην,
ἄμμι δὲ παρθενίη τε μέλοι καὶ δῶμα τοκήων.   (3. 636–40)

Alas, how frightening are these grim dreams! I fear that this expedition of heroes may cause some terrible disaster. How the stranger has set my heart fluttering! Let him woo an Achaean girl far off among his own people: maidenhood and my parents' home should be my concern!

Medea's desire for Jason blocks her plotting urge as well as boosting it. Her love sends her dreams of achievement but she wakes up embarrassed at having written a story for him and upset for her disturbed maiden innocence and independence of mind. The stronger the inspiration she draws from Jason, the more compulsive the need to 'stand by him' grows in her, and then the more out of control of her story she feels, and therefore the more reluctant she becomes to release her knowledge and push the plot forwards. It is the same inhibition that Medea had felt in her very first encounter with the stranger, long before the muse would awake in her (3. 464–70). At the time, letting the stranger know that should death befall him, she would not rejoice in his calamity, was as far as her troubled mind could reach (3. 468–70). But compassion is now hardly a consolation for Medea. It is her own needs that have made her a muse, possessing a knowledge becoming only to muses and available only to them.

Overwhelmed but not defeated by internal strife, Medea will therefore come up with a device worthy of a muse. Eager to save Jason as well as her female pride, she will turn to her sister Chalkiope for help:

ἔμπα γε μὴν θεμένη κύνεον κέαρ, οὐκέτ' ἄνευθεν
αὐτοκασιγνήτης πειρήσομαι εἴ κέ μ' ἀέθλῳ
χραισμεῖν ἀντιάσῃσιν, ἐπὶ σφετέροις ἀχέουσα
παισί· τό κέν μοι λυγρὸν ἐνὶ κραδίῃ σβέσει ἄλγος.   (3. 641–4)

All the same, however, I shall banish shame from my heart and, no longer remaining apart, I shall test my sister to see whether she will beg me to offer help in the contest, panicked as she is for her sons. This will quench the bitter pain in my heart.

Medea's shrewd ploy has been to get round her creative block, by seeking feminine inspiration in the face of her sister Chalkiope. Shame, pride, eagerness, desire grapple with one another inside her and send her back and forth on her way to her (3. 645–64). Eventually a maidservant will notice her grief—as mute and invisible outside the female chambers as the silent sorrow of the young bride mourning her groom to whom Medea is likened (3. 656–63).[58]

With a dexterity developed inside her under the pressure of love, she addresses her sister with cunning and deceptive words, seeking to elicit the latter's own invocation for help and action: 'Chalkiope, my heart is blown around with terrible anxiety for your sons . . .' (3. 688ff.). Chalkiope is only too keen an accomplice. She has been racked by fear over her sons' safety and it is only a matter of time before she conforms to Medea's plan, unwittingly—and yet also most eagerly. The two sisters let their grief pour out freely and then Chalkiope comes up with the crucial request:

> οὐκ ἂν δὴ ξείνῳ τλαίης χατέοντι καὶ αὐτῷ
> ἢ δόλον ἤ τινα μῆτιν ἐπιφράσσασθαι ἀέθλου,
> παίδων εἵνεκ' ἐμεῖο; (3. 719–21)

Could you bring yourself to devise some trick or ruse by which the stranger, who himself also asks for your help, could accomplish the challenge, for my sons' sake?

In spite of her sore troubles, 'Medea's heart leapt for joy, her beautiful face grew flushed, and a mist descended over her in the warmth of her delight' (τῆς δ' ἔντοσθεν ἀνέπτατο χάρματι θυμός, | φοινίχθη δ' ἄμυδις καλὸν χρόα, κὰδ δέ μιν ἀχλὺς | εἷλεν ἰαινομένην 3. 724–6). Medea rejoices in this sisterly request. Even though she cannot efface her desire for Jason for a single moment, fully aware that her creative zest is solely triggered by her desire for him, Chalkiope's begging offers her the perfect opportunity to deny her erotic love as her source of inspiration. Giving up on her one muse, Jason, Medea foregrounds another, just as she promises to make the plot as a sister and as a daughter, as she proclaims with aptly manipulated sisterly fervour:

> Χαλκιόπη, ὡς ὔμμι φίλον τερπνόν τε τέτυκται,
> ὡς ἔρξω. μὴ γάρ μοι ἐν ὀφθαλμοῖσι φαείνοι
> ἠὼς μηδέ με δηρὸν ἔτι ζώουσαν ἴδοιο,
> εἴ γέ τι σῆς ψυχῆς προφερέστερον ἠέ τι παίδων
> σῶν θείην·
>
> .   .   .   .

---

[58] Cf. Pavlock (1990) 54–7, who believes that this scene intimates certain masculine concerns of Medea.

φημὶ κασιγνήτη τε σέθεν κούρη τε πέλεσθαι,
ἴσον ἐπεὶ κείνοις με τεῷ ἐπαείραο μαζῷ
νηπυτίην, ὡς αἰὲν ἐγώ ποτε μητρὸς ἄκουον.
ἀλλ᾽ ἴθι, κεῦθε δ᾽ ἐμὴν σιγῇ χάριν, ὄφρα τοκῆας
λήσομεν ἐντύνουσαι ὑπόσχεσιν· ἦρι δὲ νηόν
εἴσομαι εἰς Ἑκάτης, θελκτήρια φάρμακα ταύρων
οἰσομένη ξείνῳ ὑπὲρ οὗ τόδε νεῖκος ὄρωρεν.   (3. 727–39)

I shall act, Chalkiope, in whatever way you desire and however will please you.
May my eyes not behold the bright dawn and may you not endure the sight of
my life for much longer, if I place anything before the safety of you or your sons
. . . I declare that I am both your sister and your daughter, since your mother
often used to tell me that when I was a baby you took me to your breast just like
your sons. Go then, but shroud my service in silence, so that I may accomplish
my promise without our parents realizing. In the morning I shall go to the
temple of Hecate with drugs to act as charms against the bulls, and I shall give
them to the stranger who is the cause of this strife.[59]

Medea's barely concealed delight at this female support gains
poignancy when juxtaposed to Jason's own irritation at the prospect of
receiving help from a woman:

ὦ πέπον, εἴ νύ τοι αὐτῷ ἐφανδάνει, οὔτι μεγαίρω·
βάσκ᾽ ἴθι καὶ πυκινοῖσι τεὴν παρὰ μητέρα μύθοις
ὄρνυθι λισσόμενος. μελέη γε μὲν ἧμιν ὄρωρεν
ἐλπωρή, ὅτε νόστον ἐπετραπόμεσθα γυναιξίν.   (3. 485–8)

If this seems to you a good plan, then, my friend, I have nothing against it. Be off
and with wise words beg your mother to stir herself to action. Slim indeed are
our hopes, if we must entrust our safe return to women.

While still giving permission to Argos to try and win Chalkiope's and,
ultimately, Medea's alliance, Jason cannot help resenting the need of a
woman's help.[60] Of course, the help is duly sought and accepted in due
course. When Jason affably manipulates Medea's maiden shame and
desire during their secretive rendezvous by the temple of Hecate, he
thinks he is allowed to believe that he has seduced and conquered the
tame girl, as Odysseus had won over Nausikaa in the famous intertext
against which our passage works. However, Jason and his companions

[59] This urge to renounce her overwhelming erotic desire is, in fact, a constant feature of
guilt-ridden Medea throughout Book 3. Cf. also e.g. 3. 778–80, 785–7, when Medea reverts to her
previous doubts while she has just secured a plan of action with Chalkiope.

[60] A lot is indeed at stake here: is this epos a 'properly' heroic, or a love-dominated one?
Consider also Idas, ferociously defending the old-fashioned heroism at 3. 560–63, with Goldhill
(1991) 314 and nn. 70–1 for further bibliography.

(including the seer Mopsus, whose defective foreknowledge keeps fail-
ing him) are totally oblivious to the female bonding latently forming in
the background of this story. Unlike her archaic counterparts, Medea the
muse is conscious woman, when she approaches her poet/man to
bestow her knowledge.

Power, inspiration, knowledge, authority have all played a key role in
this chapter. Once entrusted to mortals, all such notions that may have
seemed capable of providing stability when still in the hands of the gods,
become distinctively unpredictable, unreliable, and fickle. As she
acquires character, the human muse gets desired, cajoled, but also dis-
trusted and even derided. When left in mortal hands, knowledge is at the
same time cherished, scorned, coveted, available, and also elusive.
Medea has it in abundance and yet, as we have seen, there are moments
when she hates it, and sometimes she bends under its weight, overwhelmed by its responsibility. Knowledge is painfully and slowly gained
and when 'asserted', it no longer addresses the community collectively,
as in the old times.[61] This is no longer a trustworthy point of reference
for the community to look up to: its persuasive power is a private affair,
as Jason and Medea's furtive tryst suggests, one in which authority goes
hand in hand with, but also can be prey to, seduction, and vice versa.[62]

Jason has good reason to believe he has tamed the dangerous muse,[63]
as the story of the *Argonautica* progressively brings him nearer to the
successful completion of his own plot. But as Medea the muse steps
down from the residence of the gods, she discovers she has needs,
desires, and her own (independent) thought as well as weaknesses and
shortcomings.[64] And the educated reader knows well that there will
come a time, back in the future, when Medea, the tamed muse, will not
abide by somebody else's demands and preferred plots, but will write
her own version, one that would attempt to speak about her own needs
as a woman, however awesome and destructive it may be. And it is at

[61] On this, contrast Murray and Cavarero, in this volume.

[62] In this sense, Medea's position and authority make her akin to the archaic Sirens. They
would also address individuals and not collectivities in narrations occurring within characteristically non-civic and non-communal environments, with the danger of seduction (in)famously
looming over their audiences. Cf. Doherty (1995) 84–5.

[63] As Pindar (and Arcesilas) felt they had in *Pythian* 4: see II above.

[64] Is it perhaps not coincidental that the harmonious company of the Muses led by their
Musagetes Apollo appears 'already' disturbed in Apollonius' epic? Books 1 and 2 seek inspira-
tion from Apollo, and it is only halfway through the poem (Book 3) that the poet turns to the
Muses.

this point that the educated reader will also remember the ominous lines of the female Chorus in Euripides' *Medea* which in paraphrase run as follows: 'Had Apollo ever allowed the women to take his lyre, they would write very different songs, less tame and more honourable for women' (*Med.* 411 ff.). Aeetes and Jason may not know, but we see that the seeds for such a story to grow were 'already' planted in Apollonius' Book 3, when Chalkiope and Medea conspired in the enclosure of their female rooms to devise a female story wrapped up with a female consciousness, and triggered by a female muse.[65]

[65] This piece is deeply indebted to Don Fowler and his inspirational guidance and support. Alison Sharrock offered valuable criticism through all stages of writing and John Henderson read and very helpfully commented on the final draft. I am grateful to them all.

6

Authority and Ontology of the Muses in Epic Reception

Andrew Laird

While we keep the annual celebration of your giving birth, divine one, advise a poet ignorant of the way and unaccustomed to this labour . . .

Iacopo Sannazaro, *On the Virgin Birth* (1526), I. 31–2

O mysterious apostrophe, teach us to understand your workings! Show us your veiled talents! Such apostrophes may complicate or disrupt the circuit of communication, raising questions about who is the addressee, but above all they are embarrassing: embarrassing to me and embarrassing to you.

Jonathan Culler, *The Pursuit of Signs* (1981), 135

Current accounts of Muses in ancient literature still tend to take their cue from *loci classici* in Homer and Hesiod.[1] The first verse of the *Iliad*, the poet's invocation prior to the catalogue of ships, and the self-characterization of the daughters of Zeus in the *Theogony*, in particular, are used as talismans by classicists in their attempts to understand the role and function of the Muses in ancient literature, Latin as well as Greek.[2] The *Quellenforschung*, in a strong sense, of imagery associated with inspiration and poetics has always led to scrutiny of these early texts. The assumption seems to have been that these Greek poems, if only they could be disengaged from accretions of reception and interlocking literary genealogies, might somehow, by virtue of their archaic

---

[1] For discussion of this scholarship, see the Introduction to this volume, esp. Part I: 'Greek Imprecisions'.

[2] See e.g. Boyancé (1937); Detienne (1960); Russell (1981) 71 f.; Schachter (1986) 147–79; Thalmann (1984) 134–52.

authenticity, reveal the original order of things which became obscured later on.

That assumption may have derived from romantic instincts as much as from an enthusiastic desire for historicity. Homer and Hesiod have themselves performed the very function of Muses for historians of poetic inspiration, by effectively hallowing and legitimizing their endeavours. Of course Homer and Hesiod raise as many questions about the Muses as they do about everything else. Such questions are all too familiar: who is supposed to be ultimately responsible for Hesiodic or Homeric epic—the poet or the Muses? What authority do the Muses hold? How far are they agents in the stories of these poems? Do they occupy the same spatio-temporal realm as the poet or as the characters generated by his narrative? What is the ontological status of the Muses?

Traditional questions like these, which have so often been posed, cannot be answered by reading and rereading the early Greek poets, as numerous existing readings and commentaries already show.[3] There is a lack of information: nothing is really known about the possible influence of earlier Near Eastern epic on the constructions of the Muses, and we can only make conjectures about the function and context of early Greek poetic discourse.[4] We must also remain agnostic about the more immediate traditions and authorities to which such poetry might have been responding. And it should never be forgotten that Homer and Hesiod are opinionated voices, not impartial sources, even though some scholars move from conceptions of the world of the *Iliad* to the 'Homeric world', and thence to 'archaic Greece' with disconcerting ease.[5]

This chapter is concerned with the status of Muses in epic poetry. However, it will eschew positivist inquiries about how powerful or how real Muses were actually supposed to be, for any given poet in any given period of history. Such questions are more aporetic than many seem to realize and their 'answers' can only depend on (and thus reveal something about) the *ideology*—conceptions of power, belief systems,

---

[3] Kirk (1985–93) on the *Iliad*; Heubeck, West, Hainsworth, and Hoekstra (1988–92) on the *Odyssey*; West (1966) on Hesiod, *Theogony*. See also Spentzou in the Introduction, esp. 4–5.

[4] No figures in ancient Near Eastern epic seem to correspond to the Muses in Homer and Hesiod. Whilst there are no specific Muses in Indian epic, contemporary performances are preceded by invocations to gods. See Blackburn, Claus, Flueckiger, and Wadley (1989) 20, and (on specific epics) 79, 198, and 252. Whether, in circumstances like these, such invocations are intra-textual or extra-textual is a moot point.

[5] Griffin (1982), for example, frequently allows this slippage to occur.

and epistemological horizons—of those scholars who provide them. This discussion to follow, conceived principally in terms of reception by current readers and audiences, will suggest that the Muses themselves emblematize the aporias of those very questions about reality and power.

An approach to Muses grounded in current reception may do more than supplement the customary historicist approaches: it could highlight some issues those approaches tend to ignore. The widely accepted distinction between archaic oral epic and epics produced in a culture of writing merits particular attention. That distinction which is based on perceptions of different circumstances of *composition* has extensively influenced *reception* of individual epic poems, according to whether those poems are deemed 'oral' or 'written'.[6] The consequences of this for apprehensions of the Muses are well established: the inspiration provided by Homeric Muses is bound up with, or constituted by, the demands of rhapsodic performance; the highly evolved functions of particular Muses in Hellenistic and Roman poetry, on the other hand, are taken to suggest that the Muses are more like a form of literary adornment, which can be deployed in sophisticated ways.[7] None the less, in spite of this received picture, the degree of community between presentations of the Muses in epic over a long period of time is still remarkable, however much it may be taken for granted.

The first part of the chapter will indicate the nature of that community by considering the Muses in Petrarch's *Africa*—an epic which is neither oral, nor 'ancient', nor even written in a living language spoken by its author. Although the poem's debt to its Roman models is significant, literary genealogy cannot account for all the features Petrarch's epic Muses share with their predecessors. The reception of the *Africa* (in the more general sense) has a part to play, and this bears on its metapoetical features. The importance of the metapoetical status of the Muses in antiquity—particularly Virgil—will be the subject of the next part of the chapter. The third section, which includes comparison of passages from Hesiod and Livy, will examine some further reaching implications of the Muses' metapoetical status for our understanding of the role of ideology

---

[6] For a seminal distinction between primary and secondary epic, see Lewis (1943); Bowra (1972) prescribes approaches to Homer in the wake of such a distinction.

[7] Murray (1981) offers important arguments for a close relationship between the apparatus of inspiration and conditions of performance in early Greece; the account of the Muses' role in the *Fasti* in Barchiesi (1991) shows just how complex such symbolism can be.

in discursive communication. So although this discussion will be principally devoted to epic poetry, it will also show how the Muses allegorize
the configuration of truth and power in other forms of expression.

I

Poetic inspiration and power, both divine and political, are key
categories in the proemic invocations of Italian humanist epic. Neo-
Latin epics can strikingly resemble their 'classical' predecessors in
respect of language, style, amplitude, and theme. The social and literary
contexts for the production of such epics were very different from those
in antiquity, but such epics help point to some of the more enduring
attributes of the Muses. Petrarch's *Africa* (composed between 1338 and
1351) begins by invoking a Muse:

> Et michi conspicuum meritis belloque tremendum,
> Musa, virum referes, Italis cui fracta sub armis
> nobilis eternum prius attulit Africa nomen.
> hunc precor exhausto liceat michi sugere fontem
> ex Elicone sacrum, dulcis mea cura, Sorores,
> si vobis miranda cano. Iam ruris amici
> prata quidem et fontes vacuisque silentia campis
> fluminaque et colles et apricis otia silvis
> restituit Fortuna michi: vos carmina vati
> reddite, vos animos.

(Africa I. 1–10)

Muse, you will recount to me of the man conspicuous for his merits and intimi-
dating in war, on whom noble Africa broken under Italian arms first brought an
eternal name. I beg that it may be granted to me to draw deeply on the holy
spring of Helicon, my sweet care, Sisters, if I sing to you of wondrous things.
Now that Fortune has restored to me the fields of a friendly countryside as well
as the springs, the silence in the empty plains, the rivers, the retreats in dry
glades, give back to the bard his songs and his spirits.[8]

The first three verses establish an interesting connection: Africa brought
(*attulit*) eternal fame to Scipio; the poet here asks the Muse to bring
(*referes*) Scipio to him. And 'Africa', the domain which brought renown
to Scipio, is also the title of the poem now under way: Scipio's glory
should also be the poet's. We shall see that this connection continues to

---

[8]   All translations of Latin and Greek texts are mine, unless otherwise indicated.

be of central importance to the whole conception of Petrarch's poem. In verses 4–6 the poet asks the 'sisters' for permission to drink from the spring of Helicon, provided he sings to them of wondrous things. The single Muse was first beseeched for subject-matter; the plurality of sisters is invoked to assist the poet's faculties. That is made clearer in the next three verses where the sisters, hailed in the second person plural (*vos*), are asked to give back to the poet his songs and spirits. The second mention of springs (*fontes*) in the poet's own country domain could forge a link between the poet's locality and the topography of Helicon.

This is not the end of the invocation, however. There follow appeals to two higher powers, religious and political. First, an apostrophe to Christ as the son of God in the generic form of a prayer:[9]

> Tuque, o certissima mundi
> spes superumque decus, quem secula nostra deorum
> victorem atque Herebi memorant, quem quina videmus
> larga per innocuum retegentem vulnera corpus,
> auxilium fer, summe parens. Tibi multa revertens
> vertice Parnasi referam pia carmina, si te
> carmina delectant

> (*Africa* 1. 10–16)

And You, most certain hope of the world and glory of heaven, whom our own times record as vanquisher of the gods and of Hell, whom we see scarred in his innocent flesh by five gaping wounds, bring help, highest father. I shall return from the peak of Parnassus and bring back to you many pious poems, if poems please you.

These lines suggest rather more about the place of the Muses in the theology of the *Africa*. Here the addressee's position of ultimate *reality* (*certissima . . . spes*, 'most *certain* hope') and ultimate *authority* is emphasized. He is explicitly a 'vanquisher of gods', and this is avowed by contemporary testimony and witness (*secula . . . nostra . . . memorant*, 'our own times record'; *videmus*, 'we see'). The Muses must be among those vanquished gods.[10] As the highest 'father' or 'source' (*summe parens*), the figure the poet addresses is implicitly creator and governor of everything.

That subdued role of the Muses is underlined in verses 15–16, when the

---

[9] On the form of prayers in antiquity, see e.g. Aubriot-Sévin (1992) and Pulleyn (1997) and on invocations in later literature see the discussion of Muses in Curtius (1953) 228–46.

[10] For the topos of rejecting Muses in early Christian literature, see Rosati in this volume, and Curtius (1953) 235–7, although Curtius seems to ignore the prominence they receive in the *Africa* and in Petrarch's work as a whole.

poet offers to bring back poems from the top of Mount Parnassus. As well as the implication that Parnassus is earthly territory which the poet himself can ascend, the use of the word *referam* ('I will bring back') could convey that the poet is rendering to God what is already his.[11] The second-person form of this verb was used earlier in the second verse of the poem, referring to the single Muse (*referes*, 'you will recount'). That repetition could suggest an analogy between the Muse's subordinate position to the poet and the poet's subordination to God. The caution expressed at the end of the prayer ('if poems please you') is also interesting: the 'help' requested in verse 14 may be of a more general kind rather than a specific appeal for inspiration. The overall tenor of my reading— at this point—is that the Muse and sisters of Helicon have a very humble role, although they are not completely eliminated by the Christian theology which has prevailed over paganism.

The poet's invocation of King Robert of Sicily comes next. This is the longest of the three sets of apostrophe in this proem, running on until verse 70, combining an expression of gratitude for support and patronage with *recusatio*: the poet has not yet been able to praise the deeds of the king. Here the portrayal of the Muse is further developed:

> Namque solent, similis quos cura fatigat,
> longuis isse retro: tenet hos millesimus annus
> solicitos; pudet hac alios consistere meta;
> nullus ad etatem propriam respexit, ut erret
> Musa parum notos nullo prohibente per annos
> liberior: Troiamque adeo canit ille ruentem,
> ille refert Thebas iuvenemque occultat Achillem,
> ille autem Emathiam Romanis ossibus implet.
> Ipse ego non nostri referam modo temporis acta,
> Marte sed Ausonio sceleratos funditus Afros
> eruere est animus nimiasque retundere vires.
>
> (*Africa* 1. 45–55)

For poets who are consumed by similar cares are accustomed to go quite a long way back in time: a year a whole millennium away keeps them busy; others feel shamed by stopping even at this measure. None has looked back to his own era, so that the Muse may wander more freely through years that are barely known and no one prohibits this: so one poet sings of Troy falling, another tells of Thebes and hides the youthful Achilles, another fills Emathia with Roman bones. I myself will not recount things just done in our own time—my impulse

---

[11] There are comparable sentiments in Augustine's *Confessions*—a work which profoundly influenced Petrarch. See e.g. *Confessions* 1. 2, discussed in Laird (1999) 23–4.

(*animus*) is to utterly destroy the Africans with Ausonian Mars, and to beat down their excessive might.

Again, as in the very opening of the poem, the Muse is closely associated with subject-matter. The idea of the Muse travelling through space and time has various parallels in Petrarch.[12] However, in a letter to Francesco Bruni, Petrarch conceives reading or writing as a means by which he can *himself* accomplish 'virtual' travel.[13] The idea of poetic travel is sustained. The exemplary poets alluded to here appear to be either Homer or Virgil, followed by Statius, and then Lucan. As the list of Petrarch's epic forerunners goes on, the poets themselves are becoming protagonists in their stories: Statius *himself* hides Achilles, Lucan *himself* fills the Emathian plains with bones; Petrarch then portrays himself as having the impulse to utterly destroy and beat down the Africans. By the end of this passage it seems that an identification is being forged between the poet and his wandering Muse, because the poet's *animus* drives him through space and time to combat the Africans. Consideration of an additional epic predecessor evoked by this passage might reveal more about the function of Petrarch's Muse:

> In nova fert animus mutatas dicere formas
> corpora: di, coeptis (nam vos mutastis et illas)
> adspirate meis primaque ab origineque mundi
> ad mea perpetuum deducite tempora carmen.
>
> (Ovid, *Metamorphoses* 1. 1–4)

My spirit moves me to tell of forms changed into new bodies. Gods, inspire my undertaking—for you yourselves changed those forms—and lead my perpetual song from the origin of the world to my own times.

The principal point of intersection is the word *animus*, which connotes poetic impulse or inspiration. Given its proemic context, Petrarch's *eruere est animus* ('my impulse is to destroy') resonates with *fert animus dicere* ('my spirit moves me to tell').[14] And in common with the passage

---

[12] The *Canzoniere* present a 'mobile Muse'; on Petrarch's translation of Muses and Apollo into the Christian world-view, see M. Boyle (1991) esp. 27–42.

[13] Petrarch, *Senilium rerum libri* 9. 2 to Francesco Bruni in 1368, translated in Bishop (1966) 260: 'So I made up my mind not to visit exotic countries a single time by ship, on horseback or on foot . . . but to make many brief visits with books, maps and imagination. Thus in an hour I could go as often as I liked to those far shores and return safe and sound, unwearied, uninjured.' Cf. Ovid, *Tristia* 4. 2: an account of the poet's mental travel to witness Tiberius' Triumph over the Germans.

[14] This is not to disregard Lucan 1. 67–8: *fert animus causas tantarum expromere rerum* | *inmensumque aperitur opus* . . . ('My *animus* moves me to set out the causes of these great events. A huge task is open before me . . .').

from the *Africa* just quoted, this opening of the *Metamorphoses* is also concerned with temporal movement from the most distant past to the poet's own time.

The *Africa* does more than inherit the Muses as a traditional form of literary decoration. A further passage from Book 9 portrays a relationship between Petrarch and the sisters of Helicon as an actual feature of the story: Ennius recounts to the Younger Scipio how he conversed with Homer in a dream. In the vision which follows, Ennius sees a young man sitting in a secluded valley, pondering something of great importance.[15] Homer explains to Ennius who this person will become:

> Ille diu profugas revocabit carmine Musas
> tempus in extremum, veteresque Elicone Sorores
> restituet, vario quamvis agitante tumultu;
> Francisco cui nomen erit; qui grandia facta,
> vidistique cunta oculis, ceu corpus in unum
> colliget: Hispanas acies Libieque labores
> Scipiadamque tuum: titulus poematis illi
> AFRICA.

(Africa 9. 229–36)

With his poetry he will call back the long-exiled Muses to his distant time, and he will restore the ancient Sisters from Helicon, though disturbed by all kinds of uproar. His name will be Francesco and he will collect all the great deeds you have seen with your own eyes into one volume: the battles in Spain, the trials of Libya and your very own Scipio. The title of his poem will be *Africa*.

So here the poet, through Homer's words embedded in Ennius' account of his vision to Scipio, goes so far as to mention himself and his poem by name. At this point the Sisters of Helicon and the Muses are conjoined as they were in the opening invocation. After the story of the *Africa* ends with an account of Scipio's triumph (9. 324–403), the poet offers an autobiographical farewell to his poem as a conclusion to the narrative (9. 404–84). He explains he used all his strength to imitate the honours of ancient heroes, so as not to allow Homer's prophecies about him to ring hollow: *irrita ne Grai fierent praesagia vatis* (9. 409). At the same time this remark serves to enhance the credibility of the account of Homer's prediction being uttered whether or not it could be fulfilled.

This brief survey of the *Africa* shows that the Muses are given a

---

[15] This episode recalls Ennius' dream of Homer in *Annales* 1. 2–10 (Skutsch), as well as Virgil presenting the ancient poets to Dante in *Inferno* 4. 88. The apparition of a youth still unborn is reminiscent of Marcellus in *Aeneid* 6. 855–86.

considerable amount of prominence. And they are not merely orna-
mental. The character Ennius' avowal that Petrarch will 'restore the
Sisters from Helicon' effectively endows them with an intradiegetic
role—they are also part of the story world of the poem. In the *Africa* the
status of the Muse or Muses shifts considerably. The passages just
reviewed show how on some occasions they can be invoked by a subordinate poet, and how on others they are entirely subject to the poet's
will and may even consist of it.[16] The shifting and unstable status of the
Muses in the *Africa* is not unconnected with the shifts in its presentations
of divine and political power.[17] The divine and political authorities
invoked early in the *Africa* are subject to comparable instabilities: by
the end of the work the poet informs us that King Robert, whom he
exhorted to live a long life in the proem, is actually dead.[18] And the belief
in Christ, which appeared to provide a measure of epistemological and
religious certainty in the proem, merges into the apparatus of pagan
theology later in the story: in Book 7 Jupiter predicts his own incarnation
and death, and unsettles his suppliants, the female deities of Carthage
and Rome, by announcing he is already captive to a virgin whose breasts
soothe him with holy milk.[19]

One might have expected the status of the Muses to be both more
limited and more stable than it actually is in the *Africa*. Given the long-
established topos of rejecting Muses in Christian literature prior to
Petrarch, the particular presentation of the Muses in this poem comes as
something of a surprise.[20] The response that all the characteristics of
this presentation are conflated from the poet's Roman precursors
(notably Ennius, Virgil, Ovid, Statius, and Lucan) may account for the
Muses' appearance in the first place, but not for the complexity of their
portrayal. Overall, Petrarch's *Africa* usefully magnifies two general
attributes of the Muses which are found in ancient epic, and which bear
on the contemporary reception of epic poetry. First, the Muses have a
role which is both intradiegetic and extradiegetic, which inevitably

[16] Comparable complexities in the relationship of the poet with his Muse, are found in
Horace and Ovid, discussed by Ancona and Sharrock, respectively, in this volume.

[17] Compare Rosati's discussion of Statius' Muses in this volume.

[18] *Africa* 9. 423–4: *magnanimum Mors importuna Robertum | intempestive mundo subtraxit
egenti.*

[19] *Africa* 7. 723–4: *Placida sic Virgine captus | iam rapior; sacri sic mulcent ubera lactis!* For a full
study of Petrarch's conflation of paganism and Christianity in his 'theological poetics', see
again M. Boyle (1991).

[20] Esp. to Curtius (1953). See also n. 11 above, and M. Boyle (1991).

provides them with a metapoetical status. Secondly, the presentation of the Muses seems to have something in common with discursive presentations of other forms of authority and power. The significances of each of these attributes—which are in fact connected—will be examined in the next two parts of this chapter.

II

Metapoetical devices can simply be understood as features of self-referral—devices in a poem which call attention to the poem in which they appear.[21] Such devices are clearly conspicuous in the *Africa*, but they are by no means exclusive to this epic. In Homer's *Iliad*, for example, Helen speculates about how the destiny she shares with Hector and Paris will be the subject of songs for future generations.[22] In the *Odyssey* there is a poetic recitation in which the bard Phemius sings of the Achaeans' return from Troy—a subject which again bears on that of Homer's own poem.[23] There are comparable effects in the *Aeneid*: Aeneas' story of his trials in Books 2 and 3 is also, *de facto*, the subject of Virgil's epic.[24] Aeneas' account is marked at its opening:

> infandum, regina, iubes renovare dolorem   (*Aeneid* 2. 3)
>
> Unspeakable, O queen, is the grief you bid me renew

with a verse which recalls the beginning of the *Iliad*:

> Μῆνιν ἄειδε, θεά, Πηληϊάδεω Ἀχιλῆος
> οὐλομένην, ἣ μυρί' Ἀχαιοῖς ἄλγε' ἔθηκε   (*Iliad* 1. 1–2)

Sing of the baneful wrath, goddess, of Achilles son of Peleus, which laid countless woes on the Achaeans.

Regina corresponds to Homer's θεά: Dido is implicitly cast in the role of Muse for the performance of Aeneas' story. It is notable that the invocation to the Muse opening the *Aeneid* itself involves another queen who brings about Aeneas' grief (*dolorem*)—Juno. It is this *dolens regina*, so

---

[21] Colie (1970) pioneered the study of metapoetical features in Anglo-American criticism; Todorov (1973) took this kind of approach further by reading Henry James's stories as thematizing concerns in poetics. The *mise-en-abyme* is also an important dimension of metapoetics. See Dällenbach (1977) and Fowler (2000).

[22] *Il*. 6. 257–8.

[23] *Od*. 1. 325–8. See Macleod (1983c). The impact of Odysseus himself as narrator of a large part of the *Odyssey* on the performance of that poem seems to have been noted by Plato, *Rep*. 393b5.

[24] On a further proemic evocation in *Aeneid* 6. 559–62, see Laird (forthcoming).

often paralleled with Dido, who 'unrolls the book' of misfortunes and toils which are the very programme of Virgil's epic:[25]

> Musa, mihi causas memora, quo numine laeso
> quidve dolens regina deum tot volvere casus
> insignem pietate virum, tot adire labores
> impulerit.
>
> *(Aeneid* 1. 8–11)

Muse, recount to me the reasons why: tell me what offence to her divine power it was, and what grief the queen of the gods suffered to force a man famous for his piety to go through so many misfortunes, to face so many toils.

Lucan's *Pharsalia* provides a more explicit example of self-referral which explicitly involves the Muses:

> o sacer et magnus vatum labor! omnia fato
> eripis et populis donas mortalibus aevum.
> invidia sacrae, Caesar, ne tangere famae;
> nam, si quid Latiis fas est promittere Musis,
> quantum Zmyrnaei durabunt vatis honores,
> venturi me teque legent; Pharsalia nostra
> vivet, et a nullo tenebris damnabimur aevo.
>
> *(Pharsalia* 9. 980–6)

O great and sacred toil of poets! You snatch everything from its natural end and bestow an enduring age on mortal men. You need not be smitten with envy, Caesar, for the glory of consecration. For if it is the divine right of the Muses of Latium to make such pledges, then people to come in the future will read me and read about you, just as long as the fame of the Smyrnaean poet endures; our Pharsalia will live on, and no age will condemn us to the darkness of insignificance.

On neither of the two occasions on which the Muses are mentioned by Lucan are they directly invoked—the other occasion (6. 353) is a purely mythological reference to their blinding of Thamyris by the Pierides. But in the verses quoted here the 'Muses of Latium' do feature—albeit as a metonym for Roman poetry—in relation to the *Pharsalia* itself. Here we see the germ for Petrarch's conceit (*Africa* 1. 50–5 discussed above) of epic poets becoming figured as the protagonists of their own poems: *Pharsalia* in this passage designates Lucan's purported masterpiece as well as the locus of Caesar's achievement. The incidence of the Muses in this metapoetical passage, however tangential their bearing on it

---

[25] Don Fowler's ideas about imagery of the papyrus roll in Roman epic are important here. In addition to forthcoming work, see Fowler (1989) and (1997) 261.

may appear to be, is significant. Coming in an epic in which Muses barely figure at all, this passage hints at the extent to which Muses are generally bound up with metapoetical devices.

In fact invocations of Muses are *always* metapoetical: whenever a poet seeks divine assistance for his poem, the discourse of that poem itself becomes the theme, however briefly or routinely. For example, when the Muses are apostrophized in *Iliad* 2. 484 f., they are described as living on Olympus (Ὀλύμπια δώματ' ἔχουσαι), which is itself the setting for a number of episodes in Homer. Again, the fact that the Muses in Hesiod's *Theogony* are invoked by the poet, as well as heightening the reality effect of their agency and speech later on, brings the poem itself to our attention. The same kinds of effect are to be found in Roman epic (and didactic) invocations. We have already seen that the invocation of the gods at the beginning of Ovid's *Metamorphoses* heralds a poem in which the Olympian deities are the principal agents.

Apostrophe has a dramatic function. It enhances an audience's sense of the 'presence' of those addressed. Epic poets can also directly address the characters in their stories and the audiences themselves, including specific historical individuals, as well as Muses. Modern readers often view apostrophe as an obstacle to realism, although rhapsodes and *recitatores* could use apostrophe to heighten an audience's sense of the 'presence' of Muses and characters alike.[26] The use of apostrophe could thus indicate some kind of parity between the ontological status of characters and the ontological status of Muses in epic narrative. However, an invocation to a Muse or Muses has a distinct effect from that of other species of apostrophe simply because its metapoetical aspects are even more pronounced: when a poet addresses the Muses, the actual discourse of his poem is bound to be foregrounded and actually *thematized*—a foregrounding and thematization which does not necessarily occur to the same degree when the poet addresses other parties.[27]

---

[26] Notwithstanding the legacy of critical opposition to this device—exemplified in Heitland's discussion of apostrophe in Lucan in the Introduction to Haskins (1887) lxxi: 'whatever Romans may have thought of the practice, on us the effect is simply to destroy the illusions of poetry and bring us face to face with an orator'. Culler (1981) 135–54 is now the standard antidote.

[27] Culler (1981) 135 detects self-referral in all forms of apostrophe: 'Apostrophe is different [from other tropes] in that it makes its point by troping not on the meaning of a word but on the circuit of the situation of communication itself'. Perusal of sections 762–5 in Lausberg (1998)

A survey of the occasions in Virgil's *Aeneid* when the Muses are called upon should provide adequate illustration of this. The first of these occasions—*Aeneid* 1. 8–11, from the programmatic proem, considered above—is an obvious example. That proemic invocation is echoed by another 'epic question' in Book 9:

> quis deus, O Musae, tam saeva incendia Teucris
> avertit? tantos ratibus quis depulit ignis?
> dicite
>
> *(Aeneid 9. 77–9)*

Which god, O Muses, turned these fierce fires away from the Trojans? Who drove flames so great as these from the ships? Speak!

The question posed is answered by the narrative which directly follows (9. 79–122). The metapoetic significance of the two remaining instances is equally clear: each of these two invocations thematizes the parts of the poem which respectively succeed them, if only because these invocations both call for the catalogues which then duly follow.

> pandite nunc Helicona, deae, cantusque movete,
> qui bello exciti reges, quae quemque secutae
> complerint campos acies, quibus Itala iam tum
> floruerit terra alma viris, quibus arserit armis;
> et meministis enim, divae, et memorare potestis;
> ad nos vix tenuis famae perlabitur aura.
>
> *(Aeneid 7. 641–6)*

Now lay Helicon open, goddesses, and set the songs in motion: which kings aroused for war, what armies followed them to fill the battlefields, with which men Italy was even then flourishing, and with what arms it was ablaze. For you remember, divine ones, and you can entrust all to memory: the faint breeze of this repute barely reaches us.

The catalogue of Italian heroes referred to here comes immediately in 7. 647–817. Although a passage like 7. 641–6 is unquestionably an instance of self-referral, it seems on the face of it a routine and unspectacular example of metapoetical expression, to say the least. However, the degree of metapoetical reference here is greater than is first apparent. In verse 644, the Muses are specifically asked to set songs (*cantus*) in motion about the 'men' (*viris*) and the 'arms' (*armis*) which were then

indicates ancient theorists (perhaps because their vantage point is primarily rhetorical) do not comment on this reflexive aspect. Perhaps it is more apparent to the critic of literary narrative who is conditioned by silent reading.

prominent in Italy (*Itala . . . terra*). Identification here of an evocation of the opening of the *Aeneid* itself (*Arma virumque cano Troiae qui primus ab oris* | *Italiam fato profugus Laviniaque venit* | *litora, Aeneid* 1. 1–3) would be extravagant, if it were not for the fact that the Muses are also involved in a comparable evocation of the first line of the poem, which is better known:[28]

> amicum Crethea Musis,
> Crethea Musarum comitem, cui carmina semper
> et citharae cordi numerosque intendere nervis,
> semper equos atque arma virum pugnasque canebat.
>
> (*Aeneid* 9. 774–7)

Cretheus friend to the Muses, Cretheus the Muses' companion, to whom songs and the lyre were always dear and who set verses to music, and who was always singing of horses and of the arms of men and battles.

The final example of an invocation in the poem (referring to the catalogue of Etruscan heroes in 10. 166–214) recalls the previous one, specifically repeating 7. 641:[29]

> pandite nunc Helicona, deae, cantusque movete
> quae manus interea Tuscis comitetur ab oris
> Aenean armetque rates pelagoque vehatur.
>
> (*Aeneid* 10. 163–5)

Now lay Helicon open, goddesses, and set the songs in motion: what force meanwhile accompanied Aeneas from the Tuscan shores and armed the ships and sailed across the ocean.

The collocation *Aenean armetque* (following *cantus movete*) again seems to evoke the opening of Virgil's epic—and yet again in a context where Muses are mentioned. And this adds depth to the routine metapoetical function of an invocation which anyway refers to the poetic discourse it heralds.

The convention of the 'messenger scene' may be another metapoetical device which bears on our understanding of Muses. The numerous examples of the convention in epic include Zeus' dictation of messages to Iris in *Iliad* 11. 182–210 and 24. 143–88 and Jupiter's dispatching of Mercury to Aeneas in *Aeneid* 4. 222–78.[30] Scenes of this kind, in

---

[28] Hardie (1994) 239 ad loc.: 'it is difficult not to take this echo of the first two words of the poem as in some sense aligning Cretheus with the epic poet V.' See also Fowler (1997) 267–70 and (2000), on the device in *Aeneid* 9. 176–83 and 1. 565–6.

[29] See Harrison (1991) 111–12 on this passage.

[30] Laird (1999) 300–1 (after a full review of these scenes and their implication); (forthcoming)

which a celestial deity communicates to mortals through a divine messenger or angel, go back to Near Eastern epic, long before the Muses emerged in classical poetry.[31] But such scenes could be a model for the process of epic communication with a correspondence like this:

| God | → | Divine Messenger | → | Mortal Addressee |
| Muses | → | Epic Poet | → | Audience / Reader. |

The epic texts which audiences hear or read could be seen as equivalents to the final speech delivered by the divine messengers in these conventional scenes. Virgil's invocation of the goddesses of Helicon in *Aeneid* 7. 641–6 quoted above suggests this (as well as Homer's celebrated invocation of the Muses prior to the Catalogue of Ships in *Iliad* 2. 484).[32] The poet addresses the Muses as those who remember (*meministis*) and who can entrust what they remember to mortal memory (*memorare potestis*): only the faint breeze of the *fama* ('repute' or *kleos*) of what happened reaches us (*nos*) as humans. Thus the text of the *Aeneid* itself can be conceived as the speech delivered by the poet or *vates* as a kind of divine messenger—with the supposed original discourse of the Muses never being accessible.[33] Incidentally, the parallel proposed here between the messenger scene convention as a metapoetical device and the role of the Muses might connect two exceptional features of Lucan's *Pharsalia*: it is the only epic from Graeco-Roman antiquity to contain no messenger scenes of any kind, and it is also the only epic to eschew invocations to the Muses.

However significant the parallel between Muses and messengers may be, metapoetical devices always bear on issues of reception. The fact that Muses function *extradiegetically* (provided they are actually invoked), as well as intradiegetically, is very important. It means that the role of a Muse in a poem is never a matter which is purely internal to the poem. We cannot ever honestly assess the role of the Muses in a poem without assessing the effect that they have on us as readers or audiences.

on the reflexive significance of Agamemnon's dream in *Iliad* 2. 8–15; Hardie (1999) and his forthcoming study of *Fama*.

[31] See Güterbock (1946) and (1948) on the Hittite translation of the Hurrian *Ullikummi* and J. Greene (1989) on divine messengers in Hebrew scripture and ancient Near Eastern literature.

[32] On *Iliad* 2. 484, see Laird (1999) 301 n. 72.

[33] Cf. Cavarero, V–VI, in this volume; her discussion (III) of Plato *Ion* 534e–535a is in harmony with the parallel I am trying to defend here. At *Ion* 534e Socrates actually says of epic: 'These fine poems are not human, nor the work of humans. They are divine and the work of gods; and the poets are nothing other than interpreters (ἑρμηνῆς) of the gods.' On ἑρμηνῆς, see Murray (1996) 121 ad loc. The messenger Mercury is called *interpres divum* in *Aeneid* 4. 356.

Invocations to Muses have a theatrical and thaumaturgical effect. This is because Muses have a metapoetical status which characters in the story of an epic, by and large, do not possess. Characters can be introduced by purely existential propositions ('Once there was a man called Achilles'). But characters are more often—and more successfully—introduced by more complex second-order statements which presuppose existential propositions ('In the tenth year of the Trojan War Achilles became very angry'). The opening of the *Iliad* ('Sing of the baneful wrath, goddess, of Achilles son of Peleus, which laid countless woes on the Achaeans') is obviously an example of such a second-order statement which has considerable rhetorical power. There is no room here for the 'existence' of Achilles to be questioned because it is not actually asserted—it is presupposed. And once the 'goddess' is beseeched, she is dramatized. Her existence is *outside* the frame of the story. And the story to be told obtains validation by clutching on to the coat-tails of the Muse herself, whose presence is both numinous and dramatic. Thus our possible response to the Muse determines our response to the story.

The epigraph to this chapter from the proem to Sannazaro's *De Partu Virginis* (1526)—a Latin epic recounting Christ's nativity—usefully indicates how wide and how important the range of possible responses can be. This invocation is a prayer to the Virgin Mary, who also has an important intradiegetic role in the poem's narrative. Sannazaro and his audience would have believed in her existence and in her responsiveness to petitionary prayer. The nature of one's belief in the Virgin, in the purpose of such a prayer, and in the efficacy of potential responses to prayer would have had—and indeed still may have—many implications for how one is to interpret the narrative to follow.

Overall, I am maintaining that, simply by virtue of their being subject to invocation, Muses emblematize reception. Their metapoetical status ensures that they work on the level of reception (or performance) of poetry—whether it is orally composed or written. Traditionally, though, the Muses emblematize truth. In slightly different ways Homer, Hesiod, and Virgil present the Muses as symbols (or guardians) of ontological certainty. Though that ontology is inaccessible to us as audiences, its existence must be conceived as representing the common ground which must exist for poetic communication to work, even though shifting conditions of reception seem to determine the ontology of the Muses. If the nature of that 'common ground' which 'must exist' always eludes us, it is because it's really a metaphysical, ideological projection subject to our desire, which we identify and characterize by our own lights.[34] Conceived on these lines, the Muses very neatly embody Bakhtin's notion of the 'superaddressee':[35]

Any utterance always has an addressee (of various sorts, with varying degrees of proximity, concreteness, awareness, and so forth), whose responsive understanding the author of the speech work seeks and surpasses. This is the second party . . . [after the speaker]. But in addition to this addressee (the second party), the author of the utterance, with a greater or lesser awareness, presupposes a higher superaddressee (*third*), whose absolutely just responsive understanding is presumed, either in some metaphysical distance or in distant historical time.

The superaddressee is as much a construction of interpretation as it is of composition.[36] Bakhtin goes on to remark that the superaddressee assumes various ideological expressions: 'God, absolute truth, the court of dispassionate human conscience, the people, the court of history, science, and so forth'. The Muses could fit easily enough into a list like this. Here they represent a particular ideological configuration, rather than the principle of ideology in general.

III

Accounts of the ontological or the hierarchical status of *any* personage or character in a text will depend to some extent on reception—on how the relationship between that text and whoever offers that account is actualized. But the observations in the previous section show that such accounts of the Muses (given their usual metapoetical role) will be even more determined by conditions of reception. The dramatic condition of apostrophic invocation—a condition which is (to use Jonathan Culler's word) *embarrassing*—forces and brings to prominence that relationship between text and readers or audience. So answers readers or audiences may supply to questions about the authority and ontology of the Muses

---

[34] This echoes prevalent views about speech behaviour in analytic philosophy. Davidson (1989) 222 remarks: 'we could not begin to decode a man's sayings if we could not make out his attitudes towards his sentences, such as holding, wishing or wanting them to be true. Beginning from these attitudes, we must work out a theory of what he means, thus simultaneously giving content to his attitudes and to his words. In our need to make him make sense, we will try for a theory that makes him consistent, a believer of truths, and a lover of the good (all by our own lights, it goes without saying).'

[35] Bakhtin (1986) 126.

[36] This is the major respect in which the concept of the 'superaddressee' is something different from the simple addressee of a soliloquy.

will never be neutral. Nor can they be uncomplicatedly informative or factual. Answers to those questions can never be subject to verification or refutation, because issues involving authority and ontology are really ideological. 'Ideology' here can be understood as the range of ways in which notions of truth, and all kinds of other discourses, are connected with power structures or power relations.[37]

That term will be important for what folllows, and merits some discussion because 'ideology' is used as variously in classical studies as it is in other spheres. The word 'ideology' originally denoted a 'science of ideas' which would reveal to people the foundations of their biases and prejudices.[38] Marx and Engels later employed this notion to attack the proposition that ideas are autonomous and the belief that ideas can change or shape reality, and to argue that all ideas are socially determined.[39] But 'ideology' is popularly used in a weaker sense—particularly by historians—to denote a system of thought by which people are mobilized to (political) action, and which can be used both positively and negatively. In cultural theory, ideology has been defined as a scheme social groups use to make the world more intelligible to themselves. This in turn has led to a still more neutral version propounded by Clifford Geertz, who sees ideology as a necessary 'symbolic map' which can replace traditional cultural symbol systems (such as religion or science) which may have broken down.[40] A further development by Michel Foucault has particular significance for this discussion. Foucault unites the stronger and weaker senses of the term: ideology can be regarded as being virtually akin to epistemology—it reflects a desire for an ideal knowledge which would be free of error and illusion.[41]

It might easily be assumed that the Greeks and Romans entertained ideology in the weak sense, but not in the strong one. To ascribe to the ancients anything like our post-Enlightenment science of ideas would seem to be a gross anachronism. One may not want to hold with the contributions to the theory of ideology made by Geertz and Foucault. None the less, their formulations at least show the ever-present potential for slippage between ideas and theories of ideas. Plato's attempts to

---

[37] For an excellent account of recent theories of ideology (minus Foucault), see Thompson (1984). Eagleton (1991) and (1994) offer a broader historical perspective.

[38] The term was coined by the French philosopher Destutt de Tracy in *Éléments d'idéologie* (1801–5).

[39] Marx and Engels (1986).

[40] Geertz (1973) 192–233.

[41] Foucault (1980).

expose the hazards of opinion (*doxa*) as opposed to true knowledge (*episteme*) beg a similar question to those begged by de Tracy and Marx: what is the critical force of calling someone else's position ideological? Theories of ideas end up becoming ideas themselves—just as specific ideas can provide the architecture for grander system-building. The problem of ideology is in fact as old as the hills; Plato's *Republic* is as much a study in the *theory* of ideology as it is a study of epistemology and political philosophy. Earlier sophists and rhetoricians were also concerned with what would now be called the theory of ideology.[42] The issues raised by the doctrine of the *Logos* and sophistic relativism involve language, knowledge, truth, and power in a way that uncannily foreshadows current debates. Indeed reflection on the relation between language, knowledge, truth, and power is even as old as the hills of Helicon:[43]

It was the Muses who taught Hesiod once their beautiful song, as he kept his sheep under hilly Helicon. Yes, me, whom you hear (τόνδε δέ με), the goddesses spoke to unbidden, the Muses of Olympus, the daughters of aegis-bearing Zeus: 'Shepherds dwelling in the fields,' they said, 'living scandals, greedy guts, we know how to tell many lies that resemble the truth, but we know also how to tell the truth when we wish.'

With these words, the eloquent daughters of Zeus plucked and gave me as a staff a splendid branch of growing bay. And they breathed divine song into me that I might tell of the past and of the future, and they commanded me to sing of the race of the immortal, blessed Gods, and always to sing of themselves, both first and last.   (Hesiod, *Theogony* 21–34)

This passage has chiefly been regarded as raising the problem of truth in poetry—it is a customary starting point for a host of discussions about conceptions of fiction and verisimilitude throughout antiquity and into later periods.[44] But here, power, in particular, is profoundly involved in knowledge and the possession of truth: the Muses declare they can choose whether to lie convincingly, or to tell the truth.[45] This account presents a power relation which obtains between the Muses and Hesiod: that much is clear from the fact they address him first, and, after giving him the faculty of poetry, they *command* (ἐκέλονθ') the poet to sing of themselves, 'both first and last'. The efficacy of the command is

---

[42] See e.g. Kerferd (1981) esp. 68–110.

[43] The translation is adapted from Russell and Winterbottom (1972) 3.

[44] See e.g. Nagy (1989) 21–5; Feeney (1991) 13, 18; Gill and Wiseman (1993); Finkelberg (1998) at 58 and 70; Russell (1981) 86–8; Curtius (1953) 229 f.

[45] The discussion of this passage in Pucci (1977) is particularly pertinent here.

demonstrated: the poet's compliance is shown not only by the speech act of narration here at the opening of the poem, but also—according to a received (per)version of the text—by the hymning of the Muses precisely at the end of the *Theogony*.[46]

But Hesiod himself has a degree of power which is conferred on him by the Muses. He is given a staff (σκῆπτρον)—a symbol carried by kings, among others, as a sign of authority for the gods' representatives; he is also endowed with 'divine song'—this too indicates the poet's superiority in relation to other mortals.[47] At the same time, readers or audiences must be aware that it is Hesiod himself who provides this whole account of the Muses and of his relation to them. As first-person *discourse* in Benveniste's sense, this text clearly signals its partiality as a form of utterance.[48] It explicitly belongs to an identifiable (named) 'speaker' who cannot be disinterested and who cannot be impartial. It does not even masquerade as a chronicle or impersonal source. Here it is Hesiod alone who transmits to us what the Muses do, and says what they say. Hesiod is an authority in every sense. How far should he be trusted?[49]

There is always a power relation of some kind between a speaker of a discourse and his addressee, and likewise between a text and its reader.[50] The power relations that obtain between this poem and its audience, however they are configured, will in turn have distinct consequences for the audience's perception of the poet's relation to the Muses, and indeed of the levels of reality and authority the Muses possess. Such a passage could not be more neatly paradigmatic of the problem of ideology:

---

[46] *Theogony* 1021–2; the final two verses, as we have them, are: 'But now sing of the company of women, sweet-voiced Olympian Muses, daughters of aegis-bearing Zeus.' West (1966) 437 ad loc. remarks: 'After 1020 the division was made between the *Theogony* and the *Catalogue* . . . and the addition of 1021–2 in some other MSS is in most cases in a second hand or separated by a space from 1020.'

[47] Again see West (1966) 163–4 on σκῆπτρον; and also Nagy (1990) 258 and 373 n. 185.

[48] Benveniste (1966); Calame (1987). Rudhardt (1996) 28 offers a more finely nuanced reading: 'De la troisième personne des vers 22–3 nous passons brusquement à la première des vers 24 et suivants. Comment comprendre un tel saut? Il me paraît exclu de voir dans les mots τόνδε δέ με . . . le signe du changement du sujet, pour distinguer l'Hésiode le poète qui parle à la première personne. Il en résulterait de manière évidente que l'auteur de la *Théogonie* n'est pas Hésiode. Si le vers 24 avait eu un tel sens aux yeux des Grecs, aucun d'eux n'aurait jamais attribué la *Théogonie* au poète d'Ascra, comme ils le font presque tous.'

[49] It is interesting that even as finely nuanced an examination of this passage as that provided in Pucci (1977) presupposes that Hesiod is at least speaking in good faith, even if he cannot be sure he has access to the truth.

[50] See e.g. Bourdieu (1991). The implications of these issues for interpreting literary texts are discussed at length in Laird (1999) 1–43.

reading it exposes the beams in our eyes when we attempt to view the relation between knowledge, truth, and power in the realm it presents to us. Interpretation of such a passage provides a disquieting, cautionary allegory for the problem of interpretation itself. And yet this passage which so tellingly caricatures our methods of approach, has been, as was remarked at the opening of this chapter, a principal *object* of approach for countless attempts to recover the nature of Muses and their role in ancient poetic theory. The trophy, at the end of this excavation, seems to be a mirror in which we can only see ourselves.

This problem of recursiveness is at work whenever and wherever Muses are found in epic, and in other forms of poetry. Muses can operate on the level of reception itself. Simply by virtue of being subject to invocation, Muses are both evocative and emblematic of poetry as performance—*whatever* its source of composition and provenance. They validate, and are validated by, poetic discourse and—symbolically at least—are involved with its claims to truth and claims to power. By now it should also be evident that Muses, in bearing on the range of intersections between truth, discourse, and power in poetry, are no less emblematic of ideology. In fact, the symbolic figure of the Muse helps us to see the strong community between the theory of ideology and questions of reception. The objects of attention for both fields are neither essential nor fixed. Those objects—ideas or texts respectively— have only a semblance of stability and objectivity. For the theorist of ideology, a given group's conceptions of 'truth', 'power', and 'know-ledge' are not self-standing but consist in their appearance to that group's particular vantage points. And for the critical interpreter, a text is something mutable: its identity is in no small part constituted by what-ever conditions of reception currently prevail.

Problems involving both ideology and reception are naturally involved in the interpretation of all kinds of text. However, the reflexive icon of the Muse is only to be found in certain types of discourse in antiquity and in later periods: notably epic, didactic poetry, elegy, and lyric—and it is by no means always to be found even in these genres. Gods, emperors, patrons, mistresses, received traditions, the judgement of posterity, and metaphysical constructions of transcendent truth can also provide the foci of truth and power for poets, historians, and philosophers who are anxious to secure legitimacy for their discursive production.[51] Yet features which are quite particular to the emblem of

---

[51] Cf. Bakhtin (1986) 126–7: 'The author can never turn over his whole self and his speech

the Muse still find their way into kinds of discourse which neither invoke
nor even mention Muses.

A passage from Livy's history provides a striking example. The
historian is seeking to 'correct' an immediately preceding claim (4. 19. 1)
that Aulus Cornelius Cossus was a military tribune when he won the
spolia opima ('spoils of honour') under command of the dictator
Mamercus Aemilius.[52] Here is part of the 'correction' of that claim:

omnes ante me auctores secutus, A. Cornelium Cossum tribunum militum
secunda spolia opima Iovis Feretri templo intulisse exposui; ceterum,
praeterquam quod ea rite opima spolia habentur quae dux duci detraxit, nec
ducem novimus nisi cuius auspicio bellum geritur, titulus ipse spoliis inscriptus
illos me arguit consulem ea Cossum cepisse. hoc ego cum Augustum Caesarem,
templorum omnium conditorem ac restitutorem, ingressum aedem Feretri
Iovis quam vetustate dilapsam refecit, se ipsum in thorace linteo scriptum
legisse audissem, prope sacrilegium ratus sum Cosso spoliorum suorum
Caesarem, ipsius templi auctorem, subtrahere testem. quis ea in re sit error
quod tam veteres annales quodque magistratuum libri, quos linteos in aede
repositos Monetae Macer Licinio citat identidem auctores, decimo post demum
cum T. Quinctio Poeno A. Cornelium Cossum consulem habeant, existimatio
communis omnibus est.   (Livy, *Ab urbe condita* 4. 20. 5–9)

Following all the authorities [*auctores*] before me, I have stated that A. Cornelius
Cossus bore the second spoils of honour to the temple of Jupiter Feretrius as a
military tribune. But apart from the fact that formally they are called the 'spoils
of honour' which a leader has taken from a leader—and that we only recognise
as a leader one under whose auspices a war is waged, the inscription itself on the
spoils argues against those and me, that Cossus captured them as a consul.
When I had heard that Augustus Caesar, the founder and restorer of all temples,
on entering the shrine of Jupiter Feretrius (which he restored when it had
collapsed from old age), had himself read this very thing written on the linen
breastplate, I thought it almost sacrilege to deprive Cossus of Caesar, the
founder [*auctor*] of the temple itself as a witness to his spoils. What the error in
this matter might be—that such old annals and magistrates' books (the linen
ones that are deposited in the shrine of Moneta, and that Licinius Macer cites

work to the complete and *final* will of addressees who are on hand and nearby (after all, even
the closest descendants can be mistaken), and always presupposes (with a greater or lesser
degree of awareness) some higher instancing of responsive understanding that can distance
itself in various directions. Each dialogue takes place as if against the background of the responsive understanding of an invisible third party who stands above all the participants in the dialogue.'

[52] This whole passage is often deemed a later insertion by Livy, after the original publication
of *Ab urbe condita* 1–5. See Ogilvie (1965) ad loc. I owe much to Miles (1995) 40 f.—a brilliant discussion which supplies further bibliography.

repeatedly as authorities [*auctores*]) do not have A. Cornelius Cossus as consul with T. Quinctius Poenus until ten years later—is anybody's guess.[53]

A passage like this in which the competing claims of written testimonies and spoken sources, memory, political and historical authority all intersect, resists any decisive, positivistic interpretation. Livy tells us that he has followed all the previous authorities in recording that Cossus was only a military tribune, although a written inscription on the spoils themselves (*titulus ipse spoliis inscriptus*), which states that Cossus was consul, contradicts this. However, Livy's access to this inscribed evidence is actually via a testimony he *heard*—that Augustus read this on the linen breastplate (*in thorace linteo scriptum legisse audissem*). The authority of the books (also made of linen) cited by Macer is in tension with Augustus' more general authority as pious founder of the temple itself. The narrator sides with Augustus' authority because he deems not to do so as almost sacrilege (*prope sacrilegium*). But the choice of which version prevails depends, not on weighing up the 'facts' or the 'evidence' presented here, not on what the narrator says, but on how readers or audience actualize their relationship with that narrator in order to negotiate their own position in this competition between piety and a historical tradition.

The quasi-sacred status of Augustus here, in governing and endorsing this historical account is, perhaps disturbingly, rather reminiscent of Hesiod's Muses, who (in *Theogony* 27–8) know how to tell many lies that resemble the truth, but know also how to tell the truth when they wish. And it is notable that, at this point in the work, Livy, like Hesiod at that part of the *Theogony* proem, is writing in a first-person discursive mode. Such a form of expression, as in the *Theogony*, prompts consideration of this text as a reflexive paradigm for the bearing of ideology and performance on interpretation. Preoccupations with truth, knowledge, and power—preoccupations with how what is told can be legitimized—are at the heart of all narrative. It is what can only be called 'desire' for supervalidation from some higher authority which is what drives the production and reception of history, philosophy—and epic.[54] But it is perhaps in epic, which in all its forms is concerned with memory and the

---

[53] Translation from Miles (1995) 40.

[54] The ubiquity of this 'desire' in history is evidenced by any number of prefaces to works of ancient (and for that matter modern) historiography. The diagnoses of Rorty (1979) and (1982) on the aspirations of philosophy to establish truth from some transcendental standpoint are pertinent here. The use of the word 'desire' in contexts like these is not over-dramatizing: cf. the discussion (*inter alia*) of Platonic *eros* and of Hegel in Butler (1995).

past, that this desire is most prominent.[55] This applies to the epics of Homer and Hesiod which constitute myth, to epics which use myth like those of Apollonius, Virgil, or Ovid, as well as to historical epics, like those of Lucan and Petrarch. Above all, the Muses represent the problematic nature of that desire and its object.

It has been a central position in this chapter that the level of authority and the ontological status of the Muses within any particular epic is actually constituted by the relationship between that poem and its audience. This position is perhaps less surprising for the poetry of Homer and Hesiod than it might be for later epic, which often tends to be regarded as more 'closed' and is less often conceived in terms of performance and reception. However, the metapoetical aspects of the *Africa* and the shifting loci of power evident in Petrarch's Renaissance poem, which resist decisive interpretation, can prompt us to discern and 'excavate' similar features in ancient poets like Virgil. There is also a close parallel—which may even be a relation of identity—between questions of reception and the problems of ideology. The Muses provide an effective and coherent allegory, which unifies both sets of concerns. Michel Foucault observed that 'behind the concept of ideology there is a kind of nostalgia for a quasi-transparent form of knowledge, free from all error and illusion'.[56] The Muses are nostalgic symbols for that very nostalgia. To wonder about the status of the Muses, how real they are and how powerful they are, is to wonder about the nature of epic communication, and perhaps the fidelity of discourse in general.[57]

[55] On epic and the past see Bakhtin (1981) 3–40 at 13: 'The epic as a genre in its own right may, for our purposes, be characterized by three constitutive features: (1) a national epic past—in Goethe's and Schiller's terminology "the absolute past"—serves as the subject for the epic; (2) national tradition (and not personal experience and the free thought that grows out of it) serves as the source for the epic; (3) an absolute epic distance separates the epic world from contemporary reality, that is from the time in which the singer (the author and his audience) lives.' This is discussed in Todorov (1984) 88. On Muses, epic, and memory, see (in addition to bibliography in n. 2 above) Murray (1981), Nagy (1989) 30, and for Hesiod, Pucci (1977) 22–7.

[56] See Foucault (1980) *passim*.

[57] I am very grateful both to the British Academy for HRB leave and to the Department of Classics at Princeton University for hospitality during 1998–9. Andrew Ford and Michèle Lowrie read an earlier version of this chapter and made many helpful comments. Andrew Feldherr, Penny Murray, and Maria Vamvouri offered help and bibliography. But this piece owes most to Effie Spentzou for her thoughtful and constructive criticism, and her considerable patience.

7

Masculinity under Threat?
The Poetics and Politics of
Inspiration in Latin Poetry

Don Fowler

At the opening of the *Batrachomyomachia*, the 'Battle of Frogs and Mice', the poet—supposedly Homer—appeals for inspiration:

> Ἀρχόμενος πρώτης σελίδος χορὸν ἐξ Ἑλικῶνος
> ἐλθεῖν εἰς ἐμὸν ἦτορ ἐπεύχομαι εἴνεκ' ἀοιδῆς,
> ἣν νέον ἐν δέλτοισιν ἐμοῖς ἐπὶ γούνασι θῆκα,

Beginning from the first column, the choir from Helicon I pray to come into my heart, because of the song which recently I put in tablets on my knees.

The poet draws attention to two modes of representing his activity. In the one, he is sitting with a wax tablet on his knees composing a new poem beginning at the first column, in an obvious allusion to the opening of Callimachus' *Aetia* (fr. 1. 21–4):

> καὶ γὰρ ὅτε πρώτιστον ἐμοῖς ἐπὶ δέλτον ἔθηκα
> γούνασιν,' Ἀ[πό]λλων εἶπεν ὅ μοι Λήκιος·
> "...]ἀοιδέ, τὸ μὲν θύος ὅττι πάχιστον
> θρέψαι, τὴ]ν Μοῦσαν δ' ὠγαθὲ λεπταλέην·"

For when I first placed my tablet on my knees, Lycian Apollo said to me: . . . singer, rear your sacrifice to the gods as fat as possible, but your Muse, my good man, slender.

The allusion is complicated by the fact that Callimachus lived 500 years later than Homer: this part of the *Batrachomyomachia* is probably post-Callimachean in date, and we are invited to a double reading of the intertextuality, in which we both recontextualize the *Aetia* prologue by 'discovering' the presence in Callimachus of this supposedly archaic precursor and at the same time cheekily recognize the presence in 'Homer' of Callimachus. Either way, the *Batrachomyomachia* poet is revealed as a thoroughly modern and down-to-earth workman crafting his poetry out of paper and ink. But we are also offered a second view of the process out of which the poem springs. The poet prays that the chorus from Helicon will enter his heart and inspire him as he begins his (mock) epic tale. The opening ἀρχόμενος 'Beginning . . .' recalls the canonical meeting with the Muses at the opening of Hesiod's *Theogony*:

> Μουσάων Ἑλικωνιάδων ἀρχώμεθ' ἀείδειν,
> αἵ θ' Ἑλικῶνος ἔχουσιν ὄρος μέγα τε ζάθεόν τε,
> καί τε περὶ κρήνην ἰοειδέα πόσσ' ἁπαλοῖσιν
> ὀρχεῦνται καὶ βωμὸν ἐρισθενέος Κρονίωνος·
> καί τε λοεσσάμεναι τέρενα χρόα Περμησσοῖο
> ἢ Ἵππου κρήνης ἢ Ὀλμειοῦ ζαθέοιο
> ἀκροτάτῳ Ἑλικῶνι χοροὺς ἐνεποιήσαντο,
> καλοὺς ἱμερόεντας, ἐπερρώσαντο δὲ ποσσίν.
> ἔνθεν ἀπορνύμεναι κεκαλυμμέναι ἠέρι πολλῷ
> ἐννύχιαι στεῖχον περικαλλέα ὄσσαν ἱεῖσαι,
> ὑμνεῦσαι Δία τ' αἰγίοχον καὶ πότνιαν Ἥρην

Of the Heliconian Muses let us begin to sing, who possess the great and holy mountain of Helicon, and around the dark spring with tender feet dance, and around the altar of powerful Zeus. Washing their soft skin in Permessus or the Horse's spring or holy Olmeius they set up their dances on the height of Helicon, dances beautiful and lovely, and they nimbly move their feet. Setting off from there, covered in much mist by night they step forth sending forth a voice of surpassing beauty, hymning Zeus of the aegis and Lady Hera.

The juxtaposition of the two modes highlights a gap between reality and poetic pretence, between the perfectly comprehensible picture of the poet and his notebook on the one hand, and the mysterious chorus from Helicon on the other.[1] There is a similar contrast in an epigram of Roman date by the Neronian epigrammatist Lucillius (*AP* 9. 572):

> "Μουσάων Ἑλικωνιάδων ἀρχώμεθ' ἀείδειν,"
> ἔγραφε ποιμαίνων, ὡς λόγος, Ἡσίοδος.
> "Μῆνιν ἄειδε, θεά," καὶ "Ἄνδρα μοι ἔννεπε, Μοῦσα,"
> εἶπεν Ὁμηρείῳ Καλλιόπη στόματι.
> κἀμὲ δὲ δεῖ γράψαι τι προοίμιον. ἀλλὰ τί γράψω

---

[1] For more on the poet's twofold existence as a priest of the Muses and as an independent artist, see also Sharrock in this volume, esp. in connection with the proem to Ovid's *Metamorphoses*.

δεύτερον ἐκδιδόναι βιβλίον ἀρχόμενος;
"Μοῦσαι Ὀλυμπιάδες, κοῦραι Διός, οὐκ ἂν ἐσώθην,
εἰ μή μοι Καῖσαρ χαλκὸν ἔδωκε Νέρων."

'Of the Muses of Helicon, let us begin to sing' wrote, it is said, Hesiod while a shepherd; 'Sing, goddess, of the anger,' and 'Tell me Muse of the man' spoke Calliope in the mouth of Homer. I too must write a proem. But what shall I write beginning to publish my second book? 'Muses of Olympus, daughters of Zeus, I wouldn't be saved unless Nero Caesar gave me money.'

The harsh reality of the market place meets the poetic tradition, as most famously and eloquently stated by the Roman Neronian Persius in the prologue to his satires:[2]

> Nec fonte labra prolui caballino
> nec in bicipiti somniasse Parnaso
> memini, ut repente sic poeta prodirem.
> Heliconidasque pallidamque Pirenen
> illis remitto quorum imagines lambunt
> hederae sequaces; ipse semipaganus
> ad sacra vatum carmen adfero nostrum.
> quis expedivit psittaco suum 'chaere'
> picamque docuit nostra verba conari?
> magister artis ingenique largitor
> venter, negatas artifex sequi voces.
> quod si dolosi spes refulserit nummi,
> corvos poetas et poetridas picas
> cantare credas Pegaseium nectar.

I didn't swill my lips in the nag's fount, nor fall asleep on two-headed Parnasus, so far as I remember, so as to come right out as a poet. The daughters of Helicon, pale Pirene, I leave them to those whose images are licked by twining ivy; as only half a native I bring my song to the poets' ceremonies. Who taught his 'Hello' to the parrot, and instructed the magpie to attempt our words? The master of the art and benefactor of talent is Belly, a craftsman at pursuing forbidden voices. And if the hope of deceptive money has flashed out, you would believe crow poets and magpie poetesses were singing out Pegaseian nectar.

The Hellenistic and later poetics of inspiration should not be simplified: Hesiod is pre-eminently a proto-Callimachean, and the opening of the *Aetia* draws extensively on the poetic geography of the opening of the *Theogony*. In its textual detail Hellenistic poetry constantly

---

[2] Cf. Juvenal, *Sat.* 7. 53–78, and Hardie (1990) esp. 145–6.

deconstructs any opposition between inspired and craftsmanlike poetry, but that opposition underlies its deconstruction. On the one hand, we have a view of poetry as coming from outside the rational self of the individual poet, a 'divine power' as Plato termed it in his classic discussion in the *Ion*:[3]

πάντες γὰρ οἵ τε τῶν ἐπῶν ποιηταὶ οἱ ἀγαθοὶ οὐκ ἐκ τέχνης ἀλλ᾽ ἔνθεοι ὄντες καὶ κατεχόμενοι πάντα ταῦτα τὰ καλὰ λέγουσι ποιήματα, καὶ οἱ μελοποιοὶ οἱ ἀγαθοὶ ὡσαύτως,

For all good poets, epic as well as lyric, compose their beautiful poems not by craft, but because they are inspired and possessed.

On the other hand, we have a view of poetry as craft, in which rational control by the conscious self is paramount, the poetry, we are accustomed to say, of the mind as much as or more than the heart. In the passages of the *Batrachomyomachia*, Lucillius, and Persius, this view of poetry is (with varying degrees of irony, but nevertheless) figured as the reality to which fantasies of divine inspiration are opposed, and we might be tempted to agree with this, at least for later Greek and Latin literature. For the archaic period we might wish to grant greater 'reality' to the Muses, at least within the symbolic discourse of early Greece, to take them more seriously as religious figures, for instance. But that opposition between early 'belief' in the Muses' real role and a later view of them as merely a rhetorical figure is itself suspect. The problems raised by the notion of inspiration go further than facile historicizations. To see the reality of poetic creation as focused in the conscious activity of the individual in contrast to fantasies of control from outside is to endorse a naïve view of authorship which identifies meaning with conscious authorial choice. As modern writers and artists continually stress, literary and other creation *is* a mysterious process which is very much not in the control of the author. Forces pass through the writer just as the chorus from Helicon enter the heart of 'Homer' at the beginning of the *Batrachomyomachia*. What I want to do in this chapter is explore some aspects of the way those forces may be figured by ancients and moderns, in particular in relation to the gendering of poetic creativity. It is a cliché to say that the most important thing about the Muses is their sex, but I believe there is more to be said about the complexities of gender that are generated by the notion of 'inspiration'.[4] And of course

---

[3] 533e: cf. *Phaedrus* 265b and Dodds (1951) 82; 101 n. 26.

[4] Sharrock in this volume also explicitly addresses the gendered workings of inspiration, looking at the Muse as 'goddess and whore'.

I cannot escape the bind that I am in myself as a male writer, albeit of humble Persian academic belly-fodder. I can say whatever I want to say, but what determines those desires?

Persius in the satire mentioned above goes on to describe his belly as *magister artis ingenique largitor*, that is, as providing both native ability, *ingenium*, and technical mastery, *ars*. This Muse has a hand in both of those aspects of the poet's calling, but *ingenium* and *ars* are of course frequently opposed, and the opposition between them lines up with the two images of poetry with which we began. So Horace in the *Ars* describes how Democritus excluded from Helicon those poets who were not mad, because he believed that *ingenium* is better than *ars*.[5] On the one hand is the conception of poetry as a *techne* or *ars*, a rational undertaking: the model is Callimachus, who according to Ovid in *Amores* I. 15. 14, *quamvis ingenio non valet, arte valet*, 'although he was not strong in *ingenium*, he was strong in *ars*'.[6] On the other hand we have the poetry of inspiration, whose champion is Ennius, whom Ovid describes in *Tristia* 2. 424 as *ingenio maximus, arte rudis*, 'greatest in *ingenium*, primitive in *ars*'. Many more oppositions can be mapped onto that contrast. The poetry of *ars* is the poetry of sane, water-drinking,[7] Apollonian, Aristotelian types who write their books without the need of any external stimulus: the poetry of *ingenium* belongs to mad, drunken, Dionysian Platonists who need the incursion of Socrates' 'divine power' (Plato, *Ion* 534 a–c) to be able to sing their songs. The most celebrated version of the contrast is that drawn by [Longinus] *On the Sublime* 33. 4–5:

ἐπείτοιγε καὶ ἄπτωτος ὁ Ἀπολλών⟨ιος ἐν τοῖς⟩ Ἀργοναύταις ποιητής, κἀν τοῖς βουκολικοῖς πλὴν ὀλίγων τῶν ἔξωθεν ὁ Θεόκριτος ἐπιτυχέστατος· ἆρ᾽ οὖν

---

[5] 295–8, *ingenium misera quia fortunatius arte | credit et excludit sanos Helicone poetas | Democritus* . . ., 'Because Democritus believed that native ability was more successful than miserable craft and excluded sane poets from Helicon . . .', with Brink (1971) ad loc. and Pease on Cicero, *De divinatione* I. 80, Democritus B17, 18, 21 DK. Cf. esp. Cicero, *De oratore* 2. 194, *saepe enim audivi poetam bonum neminem—id quod a Democrito et Platone in scriptis relictum esse dicunt—sine inflammatione animorum exsistere posse et sine quodam adflatu quasi furoris*, 'I have often heard that no good poet, as Democritus and Plato say in their writings, can exist without an inflammation of the mind and some inspiration of something like madness.'

[6] Cf. Mckeown ad loc., who notes that on one level there is a 'blatant unfairness' in the criticism, given Apollo's role in the *Aetia* prologue. As I noted above, I am concerned here with the underlying oppositions, not with the complexities of individual texts.

[7] Whether the later (and earlier: cf. Cratinus fr. 199–200, alluded to at Horace, *Epist.* I. 19. 1–2) opposition between water and wine can be traced back to Callimachus has been the subject of much discussion: cf. Knox (1985).

Ὅμηρος ἂν μᾶλλον ἢ Ἀπολλώνιος ἐθέλοις γενέσθαι; τί δέ; Ἐρατοσθένης ἐν τῇ
Ἠριγόνῃ διὰ πάντων γὰρ ἀμώμητον τὸ ποιημάτιον Ἀρχιλόχου πολλὰ
καὶ ἀνοικονόμητα παρασύροντος, κἀκείνης τῆς ἐκβολῆς τοῦ δαιμονίου
πνεύματος ἦν ὑπὸ νόμον τάξαι δύσκολον, ἆρα δὴ μείζων ποιητής; τί δέ;
ἐν μέλεσι μᾶλλον ἂν εἶναι Βακχυλίδης ἕλοιο ἢ Πίνδαρος, καὶ ἐν τραγῳδίᾳ Ἴων
ὁ Χῖος ἢ νὴ Δία Σοφοκλῆς; ἐπειδὴ οἱ μὲν ἀδιάπτωτοι καὶ ἐν τῷ γλαφυρῷ
πάντη κεκαλλιγραφημένοι, ὁ δὲ Πίνδαρος καὶ ὁ Σοφοκλῆς ὁτὲ μὲν οἷον
πάντα ἐπιφλέγουσι τῇ φορᾷ, σβέννυνται δ' ἀλόγως πολλάκις καὶ πίπτουσιν
ἀτυχέστατα.

It is certainly true, moreover, that Apollonius in his *Argonautica* is an impeccable poet, and Theocritus is extremely successful in his bucolics, except for a few faults external to poetics. But would you rather choose to become a Homer or an Apollonius? And again, is Eratosthenes in his *Erigone*, which is an entirely flawless little poem, a greater poet than Archilochus, who sweeps a great mass of matter along without any order, with his outflow of divine inspiration which it is difficult to bring under the control of rules? Furthermore, in lyric poetry, would you rather choose to be Bacchylides or Pindar? And in tragedy, Ion of Chios or (by Zeus!) Sophocles? Bacchylides and Ion are, it is true, impeccable and uniformly elegant in the smooth manner. But Pindar and Sophocles at times as it were burn up everything in their course, though their fire is often unaccountably quenched, and they fall to earth without success.

Of the figures mentioned by Longinus, Pindar plays a particularly important role as the representative of inspired sublimity in Horace, though again he is in fact a major influence on Hellenistic style and imagery, but I linger on Homer and Archilochus. They turn up again, for instance, in a well-known epigram of Antipater of Thessalonica as the antithesis of Callimacheanism:[8]

Φεύγεθ', ὅσοι λόκκας ἢ λοφνίδας ἢ καμασῆνας
  ᾄδετε, ποιητῶν φῦλον ἀκανθολόγων,
οἵ τ' ἐπέων κόσμον λελυγισμένον ἀσκήσαντες
  κρήνης ἐξ ἱερῆς πίνετε λιτὸν ὕδωρ.
σήμερον Ἀρχιλόχοιο καὶ ἄρσενος ἦμαρ Ὁμήρου
  σπένδομεν· ὁ κρητὴρ οὐ δέχεθ' ὑδροπότας.

Get lost all you who sing of *lokkai* (cloaks) or *lophnides* (torches) or *kamasenes* (fish), tribe of thorn-gathering poets who practising twisted word ornaments drink frugal water from a holy spring. Today to Archilochus and manly Homer we make libation: the mixing-bowl does not accept water-drinkers.

---

[8] *AP* 11.20 = xx 185–90 Gow/Page. Cf. *AP* 9. 305 (with a Dionysian rather than Apollonian divine epiphany), 7. 168 on Aristophanes.

The word to which I draw attention there is 'manly' (ἄρσενος). These inspired poets are hairy[9] men with balls, not smooth-skinned wimps of dubious sexual preference, 'uniformly elegant in the smooth manner' as [Longinus] puts it. His word for 'smooth', γλαφυρός, is common as a positive stylistic term,[10] but its potential sexual charge is brought out by [Longinus'] κεκαλλιγραφημένοι, 'beautified'. As has often been observed,[11] the vocabulary of Greek and Latin literary criticism, because moral and aesthetic evaluation is constantly linked, is permeated by sexual metaphor which contrasts the strong and 'manly' with the weak and 'effeminate'. In terms of this opposition, the divine force which produces sublime poetry is figured as a kind of spunk, a force within which overflows and issues into language. [Longinus'] description of Archilochus sweeping a great mass of matter along recalls the Euphrates at the end of Callimachus's *Hymn to Apollo* which τὰ πολλά | λήματα γῆς καὶ πολλὸν ἐφ' ὕδατι συρφετὸν ἕλκει, 'drags along much offscourings of earth and much rubbish on its waters'.[12] But [Longinus] partially reverses the evaluation, admitting the faults that get swept along by Archilochus as he flows but seeing in his flood a masculine power and force which in his view is infinitely preferable to the pouffy little productions of the Hellenistic poets. Archilochus, as the drunken, mad Dionysian poet, is not in control of himself, but possessed by an outburst of divine breath which cannot easily be controlled by law. This comes from within, but from outside the rational part of the soul, and as divine it can also be figured as invasive, as an inspiration from without.[13] As often with descriptions of lost psychological control, the language of internal revolt and external influence easily mingle: a typical example is Lucretius' inspiration in *De rerum natura* 1. 921–7:

> nunc age, quod super est, cognosce et clarius audi.
> nec me animi fallit quam sint obscura; sed acri
> *percussit* thyrso laudis spes magna meum cor
> et simul *incussit* suavem mi in pectus amorem
> Musarum, quo nunc instinctus mente vigenti

[9] Cf. Propertius 4. 1. 61, *Ennius hirsuta cingat sua dicta corona*, 'let Ennius surround his words with a hairy crown'.

[10] Cf. Russell (1964) on [Longinus] 10. 6, 33. 5.

[11] The classic study in English is Bramble (1974).

[12] *Hymn* 2. 108–9. For the exact sense of λύματα and συρφετόν see Williams (1978) ad loc., but [Longinus'] παρασύροντοὶ recalls συρφετόν: note also the common πολλά.

[13] See also Sharrock's discussion in this volume of Ovid's *Met.* 4 and the effeminizing effect of inspiration on manly epic.

avia Pieridum peragro loca nullius ante
trita solo.

Come now, learn what remains and hear it more clearly. Nor does it escape my
mind how dark are these matters: but a great hope of fame has struck my heart
with its thyrsus and at the same time has struck into my breast a sweet love of
the Muses, whereby now inspired with strong mind I traverse the pathless
places of the Pierides, touched before by no man's foot.

The primary imagery here is of the Dionysiac *thiasos* inspiring the poet
to wander like a Bacchant over the wild places of the earth, but we also
have the familiar picture of Cupid's arrows striking their victim (this
time with a love for the Muses) and driving him to wander love-lost over
the landscape. The poet, in Democritean fashion, is on one level inspired
from outside by Dionysus and the Muses, but the *laudis spes*, 'hope of
fame' which strikes the poet is also an internal drive.

These complexities of inside and outside might alert us to another
possible way in which our opposition might be thought to deconstruct.
These descriptions of coming to writing in terms of excess, overflowing
rivers, and an outpouring of emotion inevitably remind the modern
reader of French feminist characterizations of feminine writing, above
all by Cixous,[14] while the Callimachean figure hunched over his tablet
rationally employing his *techne* suggests a masculine poetics of 'orderly,
parsimonious, and obstinate'[15] control. We might want to say that these
images are only of the modern world, and that they should not interfere
with the clear characterization of the 'Bacchic poetics' of epic and
tragedy (to use Alessandro Schiesaro's term) as hypermasculine in the
ancient world, but it is of course precisely the ancient world which laid
so much stress on the self-control of the adult male citizen. This has been
seen as particularly true at Rome, where entry into the Roman elite
involved an unremitting care of the self with regard to every word and
gesture, while emotional outbursts led to disaster.[16] Every detail of com-
portment was relevant: the way you walked, the way you sat, the

[14] Cf. Cixous (1991) e.g. 40: 'Let yourself go! Let go of everything! Lose everything! Take to
the air. Take to the open sea. Take to letters . . .'.

[15] Freud (1989) 294.

[16] Cf. Narducci (1984) 207: 'Si impone una prudenza costante, una precisa ponderazione
di ogni parola e ogni gesto; il dominio di sé, la regolazione della propria emotività, la
consoscenza dei propri simili divengono requisiti indispensabili a condurre con successo la vita
sociale: le esplosioni emotive, le azioni inconsiderate, e non accuratamente programmate,
sono condannate a sicura rovina.' Roman masculinity has received a lot of attention recently:
see esp. Foxhall and Salmon (1998*a*); (1998*b*); C. Williams (1999) 125–59. Cf. also Ancona and
Sharrock, in this volume, who also both engage in discussion of issues of masculine self-control.

expression on your face.[17] Control was all. While the inspired poet therefore may be male in his force and vehemence, his lost control inevitably
places him in the position of the female. Similarly, any characterization
of inspiration as a penetration from outside, as the chorus from Helicon
entering the poet's heart, will lead to a potential ambivalence of gender
in the light of the need for the male to maintain the integrity of his
bodily boundaries, not to 'open up' or be 'taken' by another. Two
familiar scenes of prophetic inspiration, which are clearly also surrogates
for the poetic inspiration of the works in which they occur, show how far
these potentialities may be realized.[18] The Sibyl in Virgil, *Aeneid* 6. 77–80,
like Virgil himself is made to 'sing' by Apollo, but the process is not a
pleasant one:

> at Phoebi nondum patiens immanis in antro
> bacchatur vates, magnum si pectore possit
> excussisse deum; tanto magis ille fatigat
> os rabidum, fera corda domans, fingitque premendo.

But not yet accepting Apollo huge in the cave, the prophetess whirled like a
bacchant, if only she could shake off from her chest the great god: but all the
more he wore out her maddened mouth, taming her savage heart, and shaped
her with his pressing.

Although Austin thought Norden's detection of sexual undertones in
these words 'unnecessary',[19] few would today deny that the Sibyl is seen
as Apollo's sexual victim, just as few would deny that in prophetic scenes
like this the inspired *vates* is a surrogate for the author. These two aspects
of the Sibyl are rarely connected. But if the Sibyl's inspiration is like the
poet's, and inspiration is figured as sexual assault, where does that leave
the creative artist?

The sexual images, and their implications for poetics, are still more
obvious in Lucan's version of the prophetess scene in Book 5 of the
Bellum Civile. After her attempt to fake a prophecy does not work,
Phemonoe is brought to a true orgasmic frenzy (which is so violent that
eventually her life is snuffed out by it):

---

[17] Cf. e.g. Cicero, *De finibus* 5. 57, and Gleason (1995); Edwards (1993).

[18] The stories here offered for Virgil's Sibyl and Lucan's Phemonoe are by no means the only
possible ones about them. Sibyl and Phemonoe have already featured in the Introduction to
this volume, Part II, in a characteristically complementary role as they try to appropriate the
functions of a resisting but also suppressed muse. Such interwoven readings corroborate one of
the main themes of this volume: the protean nature of inspiration where active and passive
blend and overlap in the pursuit of ideas and in the business of writing. For more on the Sibyl
in *Aeneid* 6, cf. also Sharrock in this volume.   [19] Austin (1977) on 6. 77.

spumea tum primum rabies vaesana per ora
effluit et gemitus et anhelo clara meatu
murmura, tum maestus vastis ululatus in antris
extremaeque sonant domita iam virgine voces

(5. 190–3)

Then for the first time the insane madness flowed out of her foaming mouth,
and groans, and from her breathless opening clear murmurs, then a grim shriek-
ing in the vast caverns and final voices sound now the virgin is conquered.

The grim metapoetics of this passage have been well brought out by
Jamie Masters, who connects the specifics of this furious inspiration with
the madness of Lucan's civil war, with Apollo the dark anti-Muse of
Nero.[20] But part of the power of the passage is precisely that it draws on
a more general notion of the *furor* of the inspired poet. Inspiration is an
invasive process, like being the 'passive' and 'penetrated' partner in
intercourse. In the context of the *Bellum Civile*, one might be tempted to
connect this with modern stress on the emperor's sexual dominance, the
sense in which he was the top of tops, the only man in Rome who still
had any balls.[21] But again, too specific a historicization occludes important wider oppositions. Any figuration of poetic creation in terms of an
energizing flow has to deal with the tricky question of where that
energy comes from, within or without, and whether the poet is to be
identified as the powerful source of that energy or as borne along help-
lessly by it.

The imagery which engenders poetic creation is thus inherently ambivalent in a way that transcends more specific contextualizations. It is a
commonplace that one system onto which the opposition between
ingenium and *ars* can be mapped is that of the hierarchy of genres.
Smaller-scale genres like personal lyric or epigram are the sphere of art,
and the province of feminized poets of the small-scale and the domestic:
real men write epic on a grand scale using their native *ingenium*. But the
inspiration which fills these masculine poets simultaneously feminizes
them also, in that they lose control of themselves. One thinks of
Horace's version of Bacchic inspiration in *Odes* 3. 25:

quo me, Bacche, rapis tui
plenum? quae nemora aut quos agor in specus
velox mente nova?

---

[20] Masters (1992) 133–49, who stresses both the similarities and the differences between
Lucan and his surrogate.   [21] Cf. Barton (1993) e.g. 20–3.

To where, Bacchus, are you snatching me full of you? To what meadows, into what caves am I driven swift in my new mind?

Horace later boasts in the poem *nil parvum aut humili modo,* | *nil mortale loquar,* 'I shall speak nothing small or in a low measure, nothing mortal' but in comparing himself to a Bacchant (8–14) he places himself in a role which is notoriously as much driven as driving. The opening lines can be read as figuring him as a rural nymph: he collapses together the typical flight (*velox,* 'swift'), rape[22] (*rapis,* 'carry off'), and insemination (*tui* | *plenum,* 'full of you'), and the meadows and caves are simultaneously the sites of religious and erotic *orgia.* As part of the closing sequence of *Odes* 1–3, the poem can be read both as a gesture towards new projects and a higher generic future (the next poem, 3. 26, has Horace hanging up his tools as a love poet) and as an instance of the higher more inspired poetry that has always been present in the *Odes* alongside the more humble sympotic and love poetry. But even as an inspired poet Horace figures himself as feminized by the process of inspiration. This is important for the political background to Horatian inspiration and its connection with the gendering of inspiration. The influence of a patron or ruler can replace or join with divine inspiration as the motive force behind the poet's coming to writing, filling the poet with awe and inspiring him to celebrate the great deeds of his patron. Horace's praise of Augustus in 3. 25 will be *insigne recens adhuc indictum ore alio,* 'outstanding, new, as yet unsaid by any other's mouth'. By the celebration, the poet in some way comes to share in the magnificence of the ruler, and attains a grandeur and power derived from the deeds that are celebrated. At the same time, however, the reality of power is not obscured. The poet loses control and is feminized before the mighty force of the patron's power. The bacchant model is precise: the god or ruler is both a source of power to the poet and an overbearing master.

The ambiguities of inspiration for the male poet faced with grandeur become even more intense in relation to the iambic and satiric muses, where the forces from within and without are summoned up not by admiration but by disgust. It is a now a commonplace that iambus and satire aspire to a hypermasculine pose of aggression which is constantly undercut by impotence: if the poet could do anything about the object of

---

[22] Cf. Virgil, *Georgics* 3. 290–1, *sed me Parnasi deserta per ardua dulcis* | *raptat amor,* 'but love of sweet Parnasus carries me off through desert heights', immediately after the exposé of the damaging effects of love in 242–83: Virgil depicts himself as in the grip of a passion similar to that of the animals in heat he has just been describing.

his attack, he would not be writing poetry. Horace depicts the polarities at the beginning of his second book of satires (2. 1. 1–4) as extremes that he is avoiding, but they are much more deeply and constantly embedded in the nature of satire:

> Sunt quibus in satura videar nimis acer et ultra
> legem tendere opus; sine nervis altera quidquid
> conposui pars esse putat similisque meorum
> mille die versus deduci posse.

Some people think I am too keen in my satire and strain my work beyond the law: the other half think whatever I have composed is without sinews and that a thousand lines like mine can be spun in a day.

Satire offers a hard-on phallic display but is ultimately flaccid in its inability to do anything about it. So Juvenal in *Satire* 1 denies that anyone can be *iniquae | tam patiens urbis*, 'so passive about the unfair city' (30) as to be able to restrain himself from satire: his liver blazes with anger[23] at what is going on (45 *quanta siccum iecur ardeat ira*), but in the end his *ingenium* cannot rise to the occasion and he can only attack the dead (170–1). The impotence of the poet supposedly faced with a subject-matter that should make him rise to the occasion has been particularly explored in relation to Horace's *Epodes*, where the poet's powerlessness becomes both poetic and political and is intimately connected with his relationship with the dark Muse Canidia.[24] In *Epode* 6, for instance, Horace suggests to an unnamed antagonist that he turn from the inno-cent to Horace, who is liable to bite back. Unlike the enemy, Horace is a proper sheepdog (5–10):

> nam qualis aut Molossus aut fulvus Lacon,
>   amica vis pastoribus,
> agam per altas aure sublata nivis,
>   quaecumque praecedet fera;
> tu, cum timenda voce complesti nemus,
>   proiectum odoraris cibum.

For like a Molossan hound or a tawny Laconian, a friendly force for shepherds, I shall drive on through deep snows with ears pricked up, wherever the wild beast leads: you, when you have filled the grove with a terrifying voice, sniff at the food thrown before you.

The use of *fera*, 'female wild beast', introduces into Horace's pursuit a

---

[23] Cf. Anderson (1982) 278–9; Braund (1988) 1–23.
[24] Cf. Watson (1995) 188 n. 1 with bibliography; Fitzgerald (1988); Oliensis (1991).

sexual element: we are back with the male poet in full cry on the tail of his inspiration. But the image of the hound is ambivalent: dogs pursue, but they are also driven, and though Horace depicts himself as a self-employed sheepdog the hunting imagery inevitably comes in. The inspiration of iambus, like that of satire, is something in the external world which arouses the anger and aggression of the poet and brings him to writing, but the process turns the subject into an object, pursued by the very Muse he pursues.

Satire moves the poet into town,[25] albeit an urban landscape which takes on the wildness of nature in strange and unpredictable ways. Inspired poetry belongs in the trackless wastes, Callimachus' κελεύθους ἀτρίπτους, 'untrodden paths', where the poet can be in touch with the elemental forces of nature.[26] Within Roman culture, part of the force of these expeditions into the wild places comes from their connection with the dynamics of Roman imperial expansion.[27] Just as the true Roman soldier presses on into new territory beyond the Roman domain, so the poet advances into new areas of poetics, and thereby acquires something of the masculine *virtus* or manliness proper to real Roman men. At the opening of the *De rerum natura*, Lucretius famously figures Epicurus in this fashion, and it is an easy trope to see Lucretius' own enterprise as similarly launching itself into the unknown alongside the Master's:[28]

> primum Graius homo mortalis tollere contra
> est oculos ausus primusque obsistere contra;
> quem neque fama deum nec fulmina nec minitanti
> murmure compressit caelum, sed eo magis acrem
> inritat animi virtutem, effringere ut arta
> naturae primus portarum claustra cupiret.
> ergo vivida vis animi pervicit et extra
> processit longe flammantia moenia mundi
> atque omne immensum peragravit mente animoque (1. 66–74)

a Greek man first dared to raise his mortal eyes against [religion] and was the first to set himself against her; a man whom neither the fame of the gods nor the thunderbolts nor heaven with threatening murmur restrained, but all the more

---

[25] Cf. Juvenal, *Sat.* 7. 6–7, *cum desertis Aganippes | vallibus esuriens migraret in atria Clio*, 'when hungry Clio deserted the valleys of Aganippe and moved into urban rooms', with Hardie (1990).

[26] *Aetia* fr. 1. 28: for the green retreats and sacred woods of poetry, see Nisbet and Hubbard (1970) 14.

[27] On boundary-crossing, see Ancona, III, in this volume.

[28] 1. 66–74.

excited his sharp manliness of mind, so that he desired to be the first to break the tight fastenings of nature's gates. Therefore the lively power of his mind conquered and he set out beyond the flaming walls of the world and travelled the whole immensity in his mind and spirit.

The high sublimity of Epicurus and Lucretius goes beyond any military glory, but more lowly poets too can claim their triumphs when they return from the wild places, most notably the elegiac poets, with Propertius 3. 1 the *locus classicus* for the 'triumph theme':[29]

> ah valeat, Phoebum quicumque moratur in armis!
>   exactus tenui pumice versus eat,
> quo me Fama levat terra sublimis, et a me
>   nata coronatis Musa triumphat equis,
> et mecum in curru parvi vectantur Amores,
>   scriptorumque meas turba secuta rotas.
> quid frustra immissis mecum certatis habenis?
>   non datur ad Musas currere lata via.
> multi, Roma, tuas laudes annalibus addent,
>   qui finem imperii Bactra futura canent.
> sed, quod pace legas, opus hoc de monte Sororum
>   detulit intacta pagina nostra via.
> mollia, Pegasides, date vestro serta poetae:
>   non faciet capiti dura corona meo.

Be gone whoever delays Phoebus in arms! Let my verse proceed polished with fine pumice, the verse by which high fame lifts me from the earth and the Muse born of me triumphs with crowned horses, and with me in the chariot ride the little Loves, and the crowd of writers follows my wheels. Why do you contend with me with reins let out? It is not given to run to the Muses by a broad road. Many, Rome, will add your praises to the annals, who will sing of Bactra as to be the end of empire. But to read in peace, my page brings down this work from the mountain of the Sisters by an untouched path. Pegasides, give soft garlands to your poet: a hard crown will not suit my head.

Propertius rejects war, and claims that what he can offer is the fine-spun poetry of achieved victory and peace, the fruits of the victories of others. His head is not suited to a hard crown. At the same time, however, he not only figures the activity of his Muse as that of a victorious general, but he inserts into the picture of the triumphal procession a Homeric chariot race in which rival writers try without success to pass him on the narrow Callimachean untrodden path. His poetic activity acquires the

---

[29] 3. 1. 7–20: cf. Galinsky (1969).

dynamism of epic deeds at the same time as it is disavowing any interest in what makes a Roman a Roman, the expansion of the empire. When his page *detulit* 'brought back' the work from the mountain of the Muses, it functioned like a returning general bringing back spoils and captives, a trope borrowed like much else at the opening of Propertius Book 3 from Horace, *Odes* 3. 30:[30]

> dicar, qua violens obstrepit Aufidus
> et qua pauper aquae Daunus agrestium
> regnavit populorum, ex humili potens
> princeps Aeolium carmen ad Italos
> deduxisse modos. sume superbiam
> quaesitam meritis et mihi Delphica
> lauro cinge volens, Melpomene, comam.

I shall be spoken of where the violent Aufidus roars and where Daunus poor in water ruled his country people, from lowliness powerful, the first to lead down Aeolian song to Italian measures. Take up the pride sought through merit and willingly crown my hair, Melpomene, with the Delphic bay.

Deduxisse, 'brought down', compresses together a complex of metaphors: the bringing back of spoil from foreign wars but also, in an irrigation metaphor, the drawing down of a smaller channel from a larger mass of water. Greece is vanquished, but its superior cultural mass is also acknowledged. Horace will be famous and claim a proud crown worthy of his merits for his conquest of Greece, but at the same time the fame of his *monumentum*, rather than spreading over the whole world, will be modestly limited to his home province of Puglia. He is *ex humili potens*, 'from lowly beginnings powerful' like a growing stream: if this avoids the Callimachean extremes of excess and impoverishment represented by the *violens* river Aufidus and Daunus' parched kingdom, we are also made aware of the origins of true Roman spirit in the violent river and the king who was Turnus' father.

Poets who venture into the wilds are simultaneously assimilating themselves to and differentiating themselves from the Roman general pressing on the expanding frontiers of empire through the arduous paths of glory. They are also, as we have seen, hunters on the trail of their prey in the untrodden thickets of the forest:[31]

---

[30] 3. 30. 10–16. For *deduxisse* cf. Fowler (1993) 310 n. 27.

[31] On the connection between hunting and soldiery, see Nisbet and Hubbard (1970) 12 and note e.g. *Odes* I. 37. 17–21. On poetic composition and hunting, cf. Macleod (1983*a*) 181–2; (1983*b*) 155.

interea Dryadum silvas saltusque sequamur
intactos, tua, Maecenas, haud mollia iussa:
te sine nil altum mens incohat. en age segnis
rumpe moras; vocat ingenti clamore Cithaeron
Taygetique canes domitrixque Epidaurus equorum,
et vox adsensu nemorum ingeminata remugit.

(Virgil, *Georg.* 3. 40–5)

In the meanwhile, let us pursue the woods and untouched thickets of the Dryads, your in no way soft orders, Maecenas: without you my mind begins nothing high. Come now, break slow delays; Cithaeron calls with great clamour, and the hounds of Taygetus, and Epidaurus tamer of horses, and the voice redounds doubled through the echoing of the groves.

Virgil opens Book 3 of the *Georgics* with a *recusatio*, deferring until later the sublime subject of Octavian Caesar's deeds and in the meanwhile dealing with farm animals, especially horses and oxen. But he represents his subject through the wilder pursuit of hunting, and breaks the idle bonds of delay in Lucretian fashion: Cithaeron calls, and the grove resounds with the cries of the hunt. By entering the wilds, the poet acquires the energy to begin the second half of his enterprise and to launch himself on something high and deep: but again, it is left unclear whether Virgil is huntsman or dog when he breaks out of delay. The call of the wild contains its share of ambiguities. Cithaeron is forever associated with Oedipus as well as with Bacchus[32] and to personify Epidaurus as a female *domitrix*, 'tamer', brings to mind the *dominae* and domination of the female figures in elegy whom the poets pursue over their own trackless wastes. The word is rare in Latin, and found first here in Virgil, *domitrix . . . equorum*, 'tamer of horses', forming the equivalent to the Homeric personal epithet Ἱππόδαμος. More significant perhaps is a later use, in the opening invocation of Grattius' hunting poem the *Cynegetica* (16–20):

ascivere tuo comites sub nomine divae
centum: omnes nemorum, umentes de fontibus omnes
Naides, et Latii satyri Faunusque subibant
Maenaliusque puer, domitrixque Idaea leonum
mater, et inculto Silvanus termite gaudens.

The goddesses joined to them a hundred companions under your name: all those of the groves, all the Naiads wet from their fountains, and the Latin satyrs

---

[32] For Bacchus, cf. Mynors (1990) 186, though he denies the relevance: for Oedipus, cf. esp. Sophocles, *Oedipus* 421.

and Fauns were appearing, and the Maenalian boy, and the Idaean mother tamer of lions, and Silvanus rejoicing in the uncultivated bough.

The *domitrix Idaea leonum*, 'Idaean tamer of lions', is Cybele, the Great Mother. A shadowy presence in Virgil's inspiration at the opening of *Georgics* 3 is the most famous of all accounts of a young man's infatuation and pursuit into the wilds of an ideal beyond himself, Catullus' *Attis* poem, with Oedipus' self-mutilation also playing its part.

Catullus 63 recounts how Attis leaves behind his civilized existence to travel to the Phrygian groves of Troy, to revel in devotion to the Great Mother. He castrates himself in her service, but when he wakes from his frenzy bitterly regrets his loss and impotence. Finally driven by Cybele's lions into the *nemora fera*, 'wild groves' (89), he spends his life as an unsexed servant of the goddess, and Catullus closes the poem with a fervent wish to avoid such frenzy himself:

> dea magna, dea Cybebe, dea domina Dindymi,
> procul a mea tuos sit furor omnis, era, domo;
> alios age incitatos, alios age rabidos.   (91–3)

Great goddess, goddess Cybebe, goddess mistress of Dindymus, let all your fury, lady, be far from my house: drive others excited, drive others wild.

Although poem 63 is told exclusively in the third person except for this epilogue, and there are no explicit links between the story of Attis and Catullus' life, the poem is widely read as standing in a figured relationship to the explicitly personal poetry.[33] Catullus too made a journey to Troy, attending as a member of his cohort the praetor Memmius, but his hopes of enrichment came to nothing and he expressed his humiliation in explicitly sexual terms:

> O Memmi, bene me ac diu supinum
> tota ista trabe lentus irrumasti!   (28. 9–10)

O Memmius, you slowly choked me well and long with all that beam of yours!

More significantly, Troy was where his brother died and with it all his joy in life.[34] Both of them went as Roman males to the boundaries of empire but gained nothing from their expeditions. Most commonly, however, poem 63 is read in relation to Catullus' love for Lesbia, in the intensity of the emotional engagement, the abject devotion, and the movement from rapture to disillusion. The love affair, however, is also part of Catullus' poetic project, and it is also easy to read poem 63

---

[33] See esp. Skinner (1997).   [34] See e.g. 64. 91–100, 101.

metapoetically. Inspired by his Muse, the poet is gripped by a *furor* which drives him to brook no delay but to take himself into the wild places of the earth:

> mora tarda mente cedat; simul ite, sequimini
> Phrygiam ad domum Cybebes, Phrygia ad nemora deae,
> ubi cymbalum sonat vox, ubi tympana reboant,
> tibicen ubi canit Phryx curvo grave calamo,
> ubi capita Maenades ui iaciunt hederigerae,
> ubi sacra sancta acutis ululatibus agitant,
> ubi suevit illa divae volitare vaga cohors;
> quo nos decet citatis celerare tripudiis.
>
> (63. 19–26)

Let slow delay leave your mind; go together, follow me to the Phrygian home of Cybebe, to the Phrygian groves of the goddess, where the voice sounds the cymbal, where the tambourines shout back, where the Phrygian pipe sings heavy with its curved reed, where the Maenads clad in ivory forcefully hurl heads, where they pursue the holy rites with sharp cries, where that wandering cohort of the goddess is accustomed to fly around; to where it is fitting we should hurry with swift dances.[35]

The poet receives a new energy for his task in the process (31–4) but eventually sinks exhausted by it and wakes to the full horror of his impotence:

> ego viridis algida Idae nive amicta loca colam?
> ego vitam agam sub altis Phrygiae columinibus,
> ubi cerva silvicultrix, ubi aper nemorivagus?
> iam iam dolet quod egi, iam iamque paenitet.   (63. 70–3)

Am I to dwell in the places of green Ida covered with cold snow? Am I to lead my life under the high columns of Phrygia, where the hind lives in the woods and the boar wanders the groves? Now, now I regret what I did, now, now I repent.

The dynamics of the process of inspiration are here diachronically separated into the rapture and access of energy and the subsequent enervation, but the two poles are always present in that process. The inspired poet is brought to writing and launches his project, but at the moment in which the energy of that project comes to him he is also feminized by that very energy as it turns him from subject to object.

---

[35] Note the Roman terms *cohors* and *tripudium*. The latter was used of the dances of the Salii who were tasked to *per urbem ire canenetes carmina cum tripudiis*, 'go through the city singing songs with dances' (Livy 1. 20. 4). Cf also, however, Accius, *Bacchae*, 249 *laetum in Parnaso inter pinos tripudiantem in circulis*, 'dancing happy on Parnassus between the pines in circles' (after Euripides, *Bacchae* 306).

When poets are inspired, they gain access to something which is both within and without, and which functions as a source of power. They are filled with strength to tackle the most elevated or repugnant of subjects, and that strength is figured as a masculine semen-like force that through the green fuse drives the flower of their verse. At the same time, however, they lose that control of the self which is essential to ancient masculinity and the same empowering flow of force places them in the female subject position, penetrated and overborne. Set free to wander over the untrodden wastes that lesser men avoid, they gain access to the wild power of a satyr, but are simultaneously themselves pursued and enraptured like Bacchants or nymphs. And yet there is a final complication. If we recontextualize this argument in terms of the celebration of lost control (but also the deconstruction of the oppositions which structure our notions of control) by Cixous and French feminism from which we began, then it is possible to flip the power relations once more. The poets claim a power that is illusory within the Roman framework of masculine definition: supposedly wild and free, they are always already topped by the real men who are in control. But suppose that power too is illusory, and the control of the Roman male is bought at too high a price: then the poets, open to penetration by the forces around them, prepared to accept emotion and its consequences, may yet have the last laugh on the grimly smiling statues that fill our museums.

8

The Untouched Self:
Sapphic and Catullan Muses in
Horace, *Odes* 1. 22

Ronnie Ancona

INTRODUCTION

How does Horace negotiate the issues of inspiration, autonomy, self, and desire? How does he simultaneously participate in, reject, and revise generic conventions/expectations? As is apparent in other essays contained in this volume the notion of inspiration is tied to questions of inside/outside, self/other, autonomy/dependence, masculine/feminine. This essay attempts to serve as one more emphatic transgression of the traditional boundaries of the interpretative discourse on the Muses. In what follows I examine not 'the Muse' or 'the Muses' or a particular named Muse, as one could in relation to Horace's *Odes*, but rather some figures who function in a 'muse-like fashion' in one particular ode. I take this less traditional approach to Horace and the Muse in order to show how the figure of 'the muse(s)'—as it/she/he(?)/they appear(s) in this volume of essays—can be utilized as a valuable trope for a nexus of issues involving the poet, the 'untouched self', and erotic/literary transgressions.

This essay will examine the interaction of power, desire, and inspiration in Horace, *Odes* 1. 22 (*Integer vitae*). I will argue that in *Odes* 1. 22 Horace attempts to place himself in and respond to the Sapphic/Catullan tradition of love lyric. I will show that Horace wants both to belong to this tradition and to revise it and that an understanding of his engagement with Sappho and Catullus is essential to our understanding of the ways in which he both adopts and resists the tradition in which he writes. An intertextual reading of the ode will enable us to see that both

Sappho and Catullus function, in a sense, as Horace's 'Muses'. They inspire even as they are resisted and therefore are critical to our understanding of Horace's 'revision of love lyric'.[1] Lalage, the beloved of *Odes* I. 22, can also be regarded as a kind of Muse, for she functions in the poem as 'material' inspiration, both as the substance of the speaker's song—'she IS what he SINGS' (*meam canto Lalagen*, 10)—and as the object of his desire—'she IS what he will LOVE' (*Lalagen amabo*, 23). The paradoxical functioning of Lalage as necessary object 'external' to Horace (otherwise how could she be a love object?) and yet as largely a cipher (who is she apart from her relation to the speaker of the poem?) points to the figure of the Muse as something that challenges the notion of the separation of the world into internal and external realms. (Of course the figures of Sappho and Catullus, as they are both separate from and embedded in Horace's poem, also challenge this notion.)[2] The elusive quality of Lalage (is she beloved? is she poetry? is she self? is she other?) will allow us to see how Horace's manifestation of love lyric in this ode is not separable from issues of power and desire. The speaker's relationship to Lalage will be shown to involve a version of love lyric that attempts to celebrate a kind of mastery within desire which can be seen to be allied with traditional Roman notions about masculinity current in the first century BC that require a man to be an active, unaffected subject.[3] While the ode in a sense champions these traditional Roman notions about masculinity, it contains as well the elements of its own deconstruction, for it makes problematic the position it seems to champion. My argument will be that *Odes* I. 22 should be interpreted in the wider context of Sapphic and Catullan love lyric and that interpretation in such a context will reveal that Horace in this ode is attempting to 'remasculinize' the male lover who has been partially feminized by the problematic masculinity found in Catullus' poems, but that this attempt involves its own frustration and resistance through the intervening and complicating voices of Sappho and Lalage. Through this examination of *Odes* I. 22 we will see that 'muse-like' figures lie at the centre of Horace's struggle with poetic and erotic identities.

---

[1] For discussion of another inspiring, yet resisted Muse, see Spentzou in this volume and her treatment of Apollonius Rhodius' Medea.

[2] Fowler and Sharrock in their contributions to this volume also explore the Muse as a challenge to such simple oppositions as external/internal, male/female, active/passive.

[3] For recent discussions of discourses about masculinity in the 1st cent. BC, see e.g. Edwards (1993) 63–97; Wiseman (1985) 10–14; Skinner (1997); and Richlin (1993).

I. SAPPHIC BACKGROUND

Horace wrote self-consciously as a poet in a lyric tradition as he attempted to bring into Latin the tradition of lyric inherited from the ancient Greeks. In the culminating poem of his collection of odes published as a group in 23 BC (*Odes*, Books 1–3) he sets forth his lyric accomplishment: *Exegi monumentum aere perennius* 'I have built a monument more lasting than bronze' (line 1). He proclaims in lines 13–14 of the same ode that he first adapted Aeolic song to Italian measures (*princeps Aeolium carmen ad Italos* | *deduxisse modos*). The Aeolic song he speaks of is that of the lyric poets, Sappho and Alcaeus, who wrote in the Aeolic dialect of Greek on the island of Lesbos, in Aeolia, the Greek area of Asia Minor, at the close of the seventh century BC. Thus, Horace claims to have first brought to Latin metre the kind of poetry written by these particular Greek lyric predecessors, Sappho and Alcaeus. While Horace's Latin poetic predecessor, Catullus, had used the Sapphic stanza, developed by Sappho, in two of his poems (11 and 51), Horace's claim is justifiable on the basis that his lyric project includes incorporation of both Sappho and Alcaeus, and that his use of Sapphic metre is far greater than Catullus'. (Horace uses the Sapphic metre in twenty-five of his one hundred and three odes, and the Alcaic stanza in thirty-seven.)

It is the 'Lesbian lyre' (*Lesboum . . . barbiton Odes*, 1. 1. 34)—which recalls both Sappho and Alcaeus, through its reference to Lesbos—that Horace claims as the instrument for his poetry in the opening poem of Book 1 of the *Odes*, which introduces his collection of poems. Other references, as well, to Sappho and Alcaeus show that Horace very clearly wants to place himself in their tradition. Horace mentions himself as the first to have brought the Alcaic metre, the lyric metre invented by Alcaeus, to Latin (*Epistles* 1. 19. 32–3: *hunc ego non alio dictum prius ore Latinus* | *vulgavi fidicen*, 'I as a Latin lyricist made him [Alcaeus] known, not spoken earlier by another voice'). (The context makes clear that following Alcaeus' metre is meant.) In the same epistle Horace links himself to both Sappho and Alcaeus by saying that like them, he has utilized Archilochus' metre for his own poems (i.e. the *Epodes*). Warding off the possible charge of timidity for not having changed Archilochus' metre, Horace states that *mascula Sappho* (line 28) and Alcaeus did as he has done. The description of Sappho as *mascula* is meant in the context to suggest, specifically, her poetic 'manly boldness'. However, that Sappho is bolstering Horace's masculinity must be seen as complicated, considering both her female sex and the lesbian or female homoerotic nature of her poetry. This adjective, *mascula*, both links Horace to Sappho while it necessarily opens up their difference.

When Horace mentions the Lesbian or Aeolic tradition we must think of both Sappho and Alcaeus, for both are critical to Horace's self-presentation as a writer composing in their lyric tradition. While Sappho will understandably be more significant than Alcaeus for our discussion of *Odes* 1. 22, since that poem is in part a response, specifically, to Sappho, some further discussion of the influence of both Sappho and Alcaeus seems appropriate in order to address the way in which Horatian critics have often viewed Sappho in relation to Horace.

Critics frequently privilege Alcaeus over Sappho as a model for Horace. For example, R. O. A. M. Lyne wants to see Horace as a Roman Alcaeus who is primarily a public poet, also interested in love and love poetry 'just so long as the love and love poetry did not involve disproportionate or untimely attention'.[4] Yet this seems to involve a prior commitment on the critic's part to a Horace who values the political over the personal, the public over the private, and this Horace seems to me not a product of Horace's poetry, but rather a product of the desire some critics have to undervalue the importance of the erotic element in Horace.[5] While there is, of course, some justification for seeing in Alcaeus a model for Horace, who himself attempted a combination of the political and personal in his own writings, we must not allow ourselves to misread Alcaeus as primarily political nor to allow our perception of the importance to Horace of Alcaeus to eclipse our perception of the importance to him of Sappho.

In *Odes* 1. 32, Horace depicts Alcaeus as a poet who, although political (bold in war), nevertheless wrote amid warfare as well as when at leisure (*ferox bello tamen inter arma*, | *sive iactatam religarat udo* | *litore navim*, 6–8), of wine, poetry, and love. *Liberum et Musas Veneremque et illi* | *semper haerentem puerum canebat*, 'He used to sing of Bacchus and the Muses and Venus and the boy always hanging onto her' (9–10). And like Horace[6] he could write of the beauty of a male beloved: *et Lycum nigris oculis nigroque* | *crine decorum* ('and [he used to sing of] Lycus, beautiful with his black eyes and black hair', 1. 32. 11–12). While there is a political element to what Horace says of Alcaeus that Horace does not connect

---

[4] Lyne (1980) 203.
[5] Ibid. 201–3.
[6] See e.g. Ligurinus in *Odes* 4. 1 and Gyges in *Odes* 2. 5.

with Sappho, the sensuous description of a beloved in Alcaeus may be seen as analogous to Sappho's description of her female beloveds. It is noteworthy that *Odes* 1. 32, so Alcaic in content, is written in Sapphic stanzas.

In *Odes* 2. 13. 25–8 Sappho and Alcaeus both appear singing in the Underworld from which the speaker has narrowly escaped because of a brush with death. In this ode both Sappho and Alcaeus are listened to in the Underworld with awe. Sappho is spoken of as lamenting to the Aeolic lyre about the girls from her homeland of Lesbos (*Aeoliis fidibus querentem* | *Sappho puellis de popularibus*, 24–5), while Alcaeus resounds with the harsh evils of ship, exile, and war (*dura navis,* | *dura fugae mala, dura belli*, 27–8). Yet despite the fact that Alcaeus is depicted as singing more fully or, perhaps, with wider range (*sonantem plenius*, 26), it is surprising that critics see Alcaeus as favoured by Horace,[7] for it is the *vulgus* ('crowd', 32) that prefers Alcaeus when he sings of 'battles and tyrants driven out' (*pugnas et exactos tyrannos*, 31), not the speaker. Considering the primarily negative associations in Horace of the *vulgus* and popular opinion, the preference by the *vulgus* for Alcaeus should not be read as a resounding endorsement of him. (Cf. e.g. *Odes* 1. 1 for Horace's separation of himself from the crowd in his lyric project, as well as the lyric poet's vatic opening of *Odes* 3. 1, *Odi profanum vulgus et arceo*, 'I hate the profane crowd and avoid it'.) A recent argument that the description of the two poets is intentionally 'polarized and reductive' is useful. Gregson Davis argues that Horace's audience would have been aware of the wide range of subject-matter in both Alcaeus' and Sappho's poems and that this reductive polarizing of the lyric tradition is an example of 'the innate rhetoric of polar description: we tend to interpret the two extremes as co-defining a whole'.[8] Sappho and Alcaeus stand here for the 'generic poles available to Horace within the Lesbian tradition—namely, a more public-oriented variety . . . and a more inner-directed, personal one . . .'.[9] Those, like Lyne, who do not see the intentionally reductive nature of the polarity and would privilege a public, Alcaean, Horace seem to me to be both diminishing the importance to Horace of Alcaeus' erotic sensibility (as seen e.g. in *Odes* 1. 32

---

[7] See e.g. Garrison (1991) 278 on line 26 of the poem: 'Unlike Catullus, Horace never tried to imitate Sappho, but he often took Alcaeus as a model.' This article is in part an attempt to counter comments like this one that underestimate Sappho's impact on Horace.

[8] Davis (1991) 85.

[9] Ibid. 85–6.

discussed above) as well as overlooking the importance of Sappho's.[10] So, too, the polarization of Sappho and Alcaeus in *Odes* 4. 9 should be approached with caution. Here the metre is Sapphic (while in *Odes* 2. 13 it was Alcaic) and now Sappho seems to be more prominent.

Sappho and Alcaeus appear in *Odes* 4. 9 among a list of poets whose work partakes of the kind of immortality Horace claims for his own poetic production. In *Odes* 4. 9 Sappho's love is declared to be still alive: *spirat adhuc amor* | *viuntque commissi calores* | *Aeoliae fidibus puellae*, 'her love still breathes and the passions of the Aeolic girl live on entrusted to her lyre' (10–12). This foregrounding of Sappho in regard to love poetry need not deny the erotic side of Alcaeus' writing. Rather we should conclude that while Horace's concern with Alcaeus is undeniable, Sappho appears to hold an equally special place for Horace in regard to writing lyric. What I think we will discover is that the importance of Sappho for Horace's writing of lyric should not be underestimated.

II. CATULLAN BACKGROUND

Although Horace mentions Catullus by name only once in his writings, his influence upon Horace is undeniable.[11] Scholars have noted Horace's use of Catullus in verbal echoing as well as ways in which Horace seems to be interested in separating himself from his Latin predecessor. Catullus wrote Latin poetry in the generation immediately preceding Horace's in the first century BC and used a wide variety of metres including the Sapphic stanza in which *Odes* 1. 22 is written.[12]

Horace mentions Catullus by name only in *Satires* 1. 10. 19, where someone (only referred to as *simius iste*, 'that ape') is criticized for being learned at nothing except reciting/singing/singing the praises of the poets Catullus and Calvus (Catullus' friend and fellow poet): *nil praeter Calvum et doctus cantare Catullum*. Although some have taken this as a negative comment about Catullus,[13] the context makes clear that the problem this 'ape' has is not that he recites 'bad' poets but rather that he does not know the poets of Old Comedy (as opposed to contemporary

[10] For further discussion of Sappho and Alcaeus in *Odes* 2. 13, see Nicoll (1986) with bibliography.

[11] For Catullus' influence on Horace see e.g. M. Lee (1975) and Mendell (1935).

[12] For a discussion of Horace, *Odes* 2. 8, as in part an 'answer' to Catullus, Poem 61, see Ancona (1994) 82–5.

[13] See Morris (1939) 134: 'This is the only allusion to him [Catullus] in Horace, and while the contempt is directed against *simius ipse*, it cannot be denied that the allusion is slighting in tone.'

poets like Calvus and Catullus) whose humour is a valuable ingredient in the writing of satire. This single direct reference to Catullus by name comes some twenty years before the publication of Books 1 to 3 of the *Odes* in 23 BC. As I will show later, *Odes* 1. 22, through its addressee, recalls Horace's earlier writing of satire and therefore it is certainly possible that Horace's use of the verb *cantare* in *Odes* 1. 22 (*dum meam canto Lalagen*) may recall the *cantare* of the Catullan reference in the *Satires*. Just as the reference to Catullus in *Satires* 1. 10 should not be taken as a statement of Horace's evaluation of Catullus, so the possible reference to Catullus, through the verb *canto* in *Odes* 1. 22, should not be taken as signalling either straightforward endorsement or rejection of Catullus. While we have no 'statement' of what Horace thought of Catullus, our discussion of *Odes* 1. 22 will make clear that Horace certainly did not ignore him. Some have thought that Horace must have 'forgotten' about Catullus when he claimed in *Odes* 3. 30 to have 'first' brought the song of Sappho and Alcaeus to Italian measures.[14] However, since Catullus uses the Sapphic metre in his poetry only twice, in Poems 11 and 51, one can argue that Horace was the first to achieve this 'translating' of Greek lyric to Latin lyric in any kind of complete way. In addition, how could Horace possibly 'forget' about Catullus? The fact that he did compose two and only two poems in the Sapphic stanza and the fact that both these poems are central to reading Horace *Odes* 1. 22 suggest that rather than 'forgetting' Catullus, Horace was very self-consciously responding to Catullus' 'intervention' in the poetic line from the Aeolic poet, Sappho, to himself. Catullus chose in Poem 51 (*Ille mi par esse deo videtur*) to write a translation or adaptation of Sappho 31 (φαίνεταί μοι). In *Odes* 1. 22 Horace clearly signals both the 'original' Sappho (ἆδυ φωνεί-|σας ὑπακούει | καὶ γελαίσας ἰμέροεν, 'hears you sweetly speaking and charmingly laughing') and the 'intervening' Catullus (*dulce ridentem*, 5) with the last lines of his poem—*dulce ridentem Lalagen amabo, dulce loquentem* 'I shall love my Lalage sweetly laughing, sweetly talking'. This clear echoing of Catullus and 'restoring' of Sappho suggests that we are meant to read this ode as a self-conscious continuation of a lyric tradition.

[14] See e.g. Bennett (1976 (1901)) 362, on Horace's claim: 'Horace's statement is not strictly accurate.'

III. THE POEMS

In order to see how, in *Odes* 1. 22, Horace is responding to and reworking the love lyric tradition he inherits from Sappho and Catullus, it is necessary for me to discuss Sappho, Poem 31, and Catullus, Poems 51 and 11. These three poems have been the object of a vast amount of critical interest.[15] It is not my intention here to elaborate the scholarly debates concerning these poems, but rather to discuss briefly the poems with regard to one specific issue, namely, the nature of desire. This will provide us with the background we need to see how Horace is handling the tradition that he inherits.

Sappho, Poem 31

φαίνεταί μοι κῆνος ἴσος θέοισιν
ἔμμεν᾽ ὤνηρ, ὄττις ἐνάντιός τοι
ἰσδάνει καὶ πλάσιον ἆδυ φωνείσας ὑπακούει

καὶ γελαίσας ἰμέροεν, τό μ᾽ ἦ μὰν　　　　　　　5
καρδίαν ἐν στήθεσιν ἐπτόαισεν·
ὡς γὰρ ἔς σ᾽ ἴδω βρόχε᾽, ὥς με φώναι-
σ᾽ οὐδ᾽ ἓν ἔτ᾽ εἴκει,

ἀλλ᾽ ἄκαν μὲν γλῶσσα †ἔαγε†, λέπτον
δ᾽ αὔτικα χρῷ πῦρ ὑπαδεδρόμηκεν,　　　　　　10
ὀππάτεσσι δ᾽ οὐδ᾽ ἓν ὄρημμ᾽, ἐπιρρόμ-
βεισι δ᾽ ἄκουαι,

κὰδ δέ μ᾽ ἴδρως ψῦχρος ἔχει, τρόμος δὲ
παῖσαν ἄγρει, χλωροτέρα δὲ ποίας
ἔμμι, τεθνάκην δ᾽ ὀλίγω ᾽πιδεύης　　　　　　15
φαίνομ᾽ ἔμ᾽ αὔτ[ᾳ.

ἀλλὰ πὰν τόλματον, ἐπεὶ †καὶ πένητα†[16]

That man seems to me to be equal to the gods, who sits opposite you and near by hears you sweetly speaking and charmingly laughing, a thing which truly

---

[15] Since my focus is on the way in which these poetic antecedents influence Horace, *Odes* 1. 22, I limit my references to those sources which have clearly influenced the following discussion of Sappho and Catullus in relation to Horace. There are, of course, numerous aspects to these poems that are beyond the scope of this article.

[16] The Greek text of Poem 31 comes from Campbell (1982); see Lidov (1993) for proposed revisions to the text. The Latin texts of Catullus and Horace come from Thomson (1997) and Shackleton Bailey (1985), respectively, except in line 11 of Catullus, Poem 11, where I use the reading *horribilesque* rather than *horribile aequor*.

excites my heart in my breast; for whenever I see you for a moment, then for me to say anything is no longer possible, but my tongue is broken in silence and immediately a thin flame has stolen under my skin, and I see nothing with my eyes, and my ears make a buzzing sound, and cold sweat possesses me, and trembling seizes me completely, and I am greener than grass, and I seem to myself to be lacking little to be dead. But everything must be ventured, since . . . even a needy person . . .[17]

Central to Sappho's famous (and fragmentary) poem is a tension between the self-conscious, integrated, speaking, observing self of the poet and the seeming 'breakdown' of the self which is caused by erotic desire. This poem stands in some sense at the beginning of a tradition of lyric self-consciousness,[18] while ironically constituting that self-consciousness through description of a self undergoing fragmentation. The truly fragmentary state of the poem—we do not know how it ended—makes it impossible to know how the lines we do have would have fitted with the whole, original poem; however the move in line 17, ἀλλὰ πάν τόλματον ('but everything must be ventured . . .'), suggests a bold assertion both of a recaptured sense of self-power and of a commitment to the risks of desire. Rather than describing a complete disintegration of the self through the effects of desire, the speaker gathers her 'self' together for renewed engagement. The tension between the 'integrated' self and the 'disintegrating' self is a product of the speaker's articulate voice and the body of the 'splintered' tongue she describes.[19] Much of the power of the poem comes from the ability of the speaker to speak her own inability to speak. It is that paradox that enables the poem to be, in a sense, a discourse on the ineffable. However, rather than being discontinuous, the integrated and fragmented selves of the poem are symbiotic—the one discoursing and the other becoming renewed through that discourse. Erotic desire is evoked in the poem through its effects upon the body and through the self's 'freshness/greenness' which allows it to pull itself back from the state that seems to it not far from death. The general statement at the poem's beginning about the god-like man who sits and listens to the speaker's object of desire serves as a foil for the speaker's own erotic response and articulated self-reflection.[20] The man gazes with no noted effect. His self-possession

---

[17] All translations of the Greek and Latin texts are mine.

[18] du Bois (1995) 6.

[19] O'Higgins (1996) discusses many of the similarities and differences between Sappho, Poem 31, and Catullus, Poem 51, esp. with regard to speech.

[20] Winkler ((1996) 99 discusses the description of the anonymous man at the poem's

contrasts with the speaker's erotic reactions and self-examination which result from her own gaze, responses not attributed to him.[21] In Sappho, Poem 31, then, we see the power of desire shaping the constitution and articulation of the self.

Catullus, Poem 51

> Ille mi par esse deo videtur,
> ille, si fas est, superare divos,
> qui sedens adversus identidem te
>   spectat et audit
>
> dulce ridentem, misero quod omnis   5
> eripit sensus mihi: nam simul te,
> Lesbia, aspexi, nihil est super mi
>   ⟨vocis in ore⟩
>
> lingua sed torpet, tenuis sub artus
> flamma demanat, sonitu suopte   10
> tintinant aures, gemina teguntur
>   lumina nocte.
>
> otium, Catulle, tibi molestum est;
> otio exsultas nimiumque gestis;
> otium et reges prius et beatas   15
>   perdidit urbes.

That man seems to me to be equal to a god, that man, if it is allowed, seems to surpass the gods, who sitting opposite again and again looks at and hears you sweetly laughing, which steals away all senses from poor me; for as soon as I have seen you, Lesbia, nothing of my voice remains for me in my mouth, but my tongue is numb, a thin flame flows down under my limbs, my ears ring with their own sound, my eyes are covered by twin night. Leisure, Catullus, is troublesome for you; you exult in your leisure and you act without restraint too much; leisure earlier has destroyed both kings and prosperous cities.

Catullus, Poem 51, is Catullus' famous translation or adaptation of Sappho, Poem 31. To the extent that Poem 51 is a translation, the similarities between the poems are obvious. Both are concerned with the effects of desire and with the self. Both begin with a reference to some

---

beginning as a Homeric cliché and as a rhetorical device on the part of the speaker designed to flatter and disarm her addressee. Race (1983) sees the anonymous man as an 'amatory contrast-figure', that is, a figure with whom the speaker contrasts her erotic response. Robbins (1980) focuses on the immortal quality of the god-like man which contrasts with the sense of mortality expressed by the speaker.

[21] On the speaker's disruptive gaze, see Stehle (1996) 220.

'other' whose position with regard to the object of desire differs from that of the speaker. They are written in the same metre. The end of Sappho's poem is lost; the concluding stanza of Catullus' poem supplies a perspective on the previous lines not available to us in the Sappho poem.[22] I am particularly interested, though, in looking at the ways in which the two poems differ, for this will allow us to see Catullus as a mediating voice in the lyric line reaching from Sappho to Horace. I will look primarily at issues of gender, erotic response, constitution of the self, and social context, for these will be significant to my examination of Horace, *Odes* 1. 22.

In his adaptation of Sappho's poem Catullus makes two especially significant, if obvious, changes: the change in the speaker of the poem from female to male and the introduction of a named addressee, specifically, Lesbia. With these changes we are now looking at the desire of a man for a woman, rather than that of a woman for another woman. Yet this seemingly simple switch is complicated by the fact that in the Sappho poem the female speaker is the 'subject' of desire, a role not frequently occupied by a woman in Greek and Roman discourse about desire. Sappho's speaker thus transgresses expected gender roles for 'woman'.[23] The Sapphic speaker's role as *female*/desiring/subject in a sense destabilizes her location in the category of 'woman'. The introduction of 'Lesbia' as addressee in Catullus' poem forces another destabilization of a category, namely, the 'object' of desire. For who is the object of desire in Catullus' poem? As one scholar has recently argued, it is Sappho (the famous woman poet from Lesbos); it is Lesbia, pseudonym for Catullus' beloved; it is Clodia, the woman later identified by Apuleius as the beloved of Catullus.[24] While as translator/speaker Catullus places himself in the same speaking and desiring

---

[22] There is debate among scholars as to whether the last four lines of Catullus, Poem 51, are part of the poem or whether they constitute a separate fragment. For the bibliographical sources on this issue, see the bibliographical section of the commentary on Poem 51 in Thomson (1997).

[23] There is very little preserved from Greek and Roman antiquity that contains women's writing about women's desire. Writings by men on this subject frequently (although certainly not always) present women's desire as dangerous and to be avoided. In Greek archaic poetry, see Semonides 7 for a negative view of women's desire, but contrast e.g. Alcman's *Partheneia* or Maiden Songs for a positive view of women as desirers, specifically, of women. For a negative version of woman as desirer, see Catullus, Poem 11, discussed below. For a similar view in Horace, see e.g. *Odes* 1. 25. Other sources for both Greek and Roman culture, for example legislation on sexual matters, support the generalization stated above.

[24] See Apuleius, *Apology* 10. 'Sapphica Puella: The triple-faceted object of Catullan desire', in Miller (1994) esp. 103, gives an elegant analysis of the function of 'Lesbia' in Poem 51.

position as the speaker in the Sappho poem, to the extent that 'Lesbia' functions as 'Sappho' in Poem 51, Sappho is also Catullus' object of desire. This double positioning of Sappho in the Catullus poem as both subject and object of desire has two significant effects: it introduces a self-consciousness about intertextuality on Catullus' part—he is writing a love poem to his love lyric predecessor, Sappho (is he in love with her? with her work?)—while it simultaneously hints at a self-reflexive, almost masturbatory, version of desire in which Catullus/Sappho is loving Catullus/Sappho. Note the exclusion of the 'other' in Catullus' talk of his ears ringing with *their own* sound (*sonitu suopte*). The reflexive adjective *suopte* has no counterpart in Sappho's poem. There is also greater emphasis in the Catullus poem on the other figure, 'that man'. This is created through the repetition of the word *ille* at the beginning of lines 1 and 2 and the notion that he may even surpass the gods whereas in the Sappho poem he was their equal. This 'outside' figure is also more explicitly connected with the speaker of the poem in Catullus, for both experience the 'sight' of the beloved (*qui . . . spectat*, 'who . . . looks at'; *simul . . . aspexi*, 'as soon as I have seen'). In Sappho only the speaker sees (ὡς γὰρ ἔς σ' ἴδω, 'whenever I see you . . .'). Yet this connection in Catullus between 'that man' and the speaker also introduces a distinction, for the 'other man' participates in a 'repetitive' activity of both seeing and hearing (*identidem*, 'again and again') which is distinct from the experience of the speaker as suggested by the perfect tense of *aspexi*. This repetition from which the Catullan speaker is excluded echoes the experience of the Sapphic speaker (ὡς γὰρ ἔς σ' ἴδω, 'whenever I see you . . .'). This repetition which excludes the Catullan speaker in Poem 51 recurs in Poem 11 to the same effect when Lesbia, rejected by Catullus, 'again and again' (*identidem*) breaks the balls of her adulterous lovers. The 'speaking and laughing' (φωνείσας, γελαίσας) of Sappho's object of desire becomes reduced to only 'laughing' (*ridentem*) in Catullus. This change in the Catullan version eliminates a link between the speaker and the beloved contained in the Sappho poem. In Sappho both speaker and beloved are connected to speaking (or the inability to speak). In Catullus only the speaker is.

Although we have no access to the ultimate conclusion of Sappho's fragment, the little of the conclusion that we do have, 'but everything must be ventured . . .' (ἀλλὰ πὰν τόλματον), is, I think, enough to show a reaffirmation on the speaker's part of the value of the experience she describes in the preceding lines. The 'almost dead self' asserts the necessity of 'venturing', of 'daring'. In Catullus, though, the experience of erotic response is either not commented upon (if one chooses not to see the final four lines as part of Poem 51) and therefore not reaffirmed, or (if one includes the last four lines) is at least on some level rejected through its association with the destructive potential attributed to *otium* or 'leisure'. The word *otium*, the opposite of *negotium* ('business'), places the experience of desire in a social context not explicitly present in the more private poem of Sappho. Specifically, it sets up desire in opposition to the values associated with the publicly committed military or political life of a Roman male citizen.[25]

In Catullus desire provides the occasion for speech about the self but it does not generate a constituting of the self as it does in Sappho. The experience of desire as something to be repeated, something to be reaffirmed, does not occur in Catullus' translation of Sappho. In fact, the word *identidem*, as mentioned above, is specifically associated with the 'other man's' activity, not the speaker's. On the contrary, in Poem 51 the 'near death' experience produced by desire in Sappho becomes a complete negation or loss of the senses (*omnis | eripit sensus*, 'steals away all senses'). The poem either concludes this way or entails a commentary on the destructive power of desire. How, then, does one maintain a Roman masculine sense of power and a sense of self in the face of desire?

Catullus, Poem 11

> Furi et Aureli, comites Catulli,
> sive in extremos penetrabit Indos,
> litus ut longe resonante Eoa
>   tunditur unda,
>
> sive in Hyrcanos Arabasve molles,   5
> seu Sagas sagittiferosve Parthos,
> sive quae septemgeminus colorat
>   aequora Nilus,
>
> sive trans altas gradietur Alpes,
> Caesaris visens monimenta magni,   10
> Gallicum Rhenum horribilesque ulti-
>   mosque Britannos,
>
> omnia haec, quaecumque feret voluntas
> caelitum, temptare simul parati,

[25] See Greene (1999) for further discussion of Catullus' 'translation' of Sappho and pp. 11–15, in particular, on the social and political dimensions of the poem which involve a contrast between the military/political life expected of a Roman male and the life of *otium* ('leisure').

pauca nuntiate meae puellae   15
  non bona dicta.

cum suis vivat valeatque moechis,
quos simul complexa tenet trecentos,
nullum amans vere, sed identidem omnium
  ilia rumpens;   20

nec meum respectet, ut ante, amorem,
qui illius culpa cecedit velut prati
ultimi flos, praetereunte postquam
  tactus aratro est.

Furius and Aurelius, companions of Catullus, whether he will penetrate into the
furthest inhabitants of India, where the shore is beaten by the far resounding
eastern wave, or into the Hyrcani or soft Arabs, or the Sagae and arrow-bearing
Parthians, or the waters which the sevenfold Nile dyes, or he will go across the
tall Alps, visiting the monuments of great Caesar, the Gallic Rhine, and the
terrifying, furthest Britons, prepared together to attempt all these things, whatever the will of the gods will bring, tell a few not nice words to my girlfriend. Let
her live and be well with her adulterers, whom, three hundred, she holds
together having embraced them, loving not one of them truly, but again and
again breaking the balls of all of them; let her not await my love as before, which
through her fault has fallen like a flower of the furthest part of the meadow, after
it has been touched by the plough passing by.

One way to maintain a specifically masculine version of the self is to
reconstitute the self through an attempt at opposition to the feminizing,
weakening impact of desire as seen in Poem 51. Catullus' exclusive use of
the Sapphic metre in Poems 11 and 51 links these two poems as does the
sense of Poem 51 as an introduction to desire for Lesbia and 11 as a
farewell. (Reading 'Lesbia' into *mea puella*, 'my girlfriend', seems justified
considering the links between the two poems and the group of poems in
Catullus that appear to centre on the same figure.) On one level, Poem
11 contains a feminized speaker whose flower-like love has been cut
down by the aggressive, masculine, Lesbian plough. Catullus borrows
his flower image from Sappho's image of the mountain hyacinth
stepped on by shepherds (Fragment 105c). However, it should be noted
that it is the speaker's love and not he, himself, that is cut down by the
passing plough. Thus the poem attempts to split off this destructive feminizing desire in order to allow the speaker to reconstitute (partially) his
self through the incorporation of traditional Roman male values.

The recuperation of the 'masculine self' is attempted through the
assimilation to the erotic images of military conquest and domination.

The journey the speaker says his companions, Furius and Aurelius, are prepared to take with him, is one of wide-ranging travel following the military conquests of Caesar. The language used to describe the journey is distinctly erotic.[26] The words *penetrabit* (he will penetrate) and *tunditur* (it is pounded) introduce into the landscape images of acceptable, active, male sexual behaviour. The (male) speaker will be the 'penetrator' and the landscape is 'pounded'. Rather than places, 'peoples' will be penetrated (e.g. *Indos*, *Hyrcanos*, etc.). The effeminacy of the Arabs (*molles*, 'soft') joined with the phallic description of the Parthians (*sagittiferos*, 'arrow-bearing') suggests a kind of indiscriminacy about the speaker's objects of conquest / desire. What is important for the speaker, and more generally for the Roman male, is playing the role of penetrator.[27] One scholar has suggested that this fictive journey provides a way for the speaker to regain through imaginary conquest some of the power he has lost in his failed relationship to Lesbia.[28] The exterior realm of power, the military, and conquest become eroticized and thus available to the speaker as a kind of substitute power. Another scholar has seen 'rape' as the central image of the poem, with Catullus as rapist switching to Catullus as victim at the poem's conclusion.[29] I would add that the readiness of his male companions to accompany him on his travels suggests a kind of (homo-social) male bonding with regard to sexual / military power, a possibly ironic bonding considering the fact that these same men are the object of abuse elsewhere in Catullus' poems.[30] Indeed, the 'companions' in a sense usurp the speaker's voice, for while he addresses them directly they become the necessary voice mediating the relation between the speaker and Lesbia. They are the ones who are to 'tell a few not nice words' (*pauca nuntiate . . . | non bona dicta*). While vigorously aggressive behaviour is attacked in the poem when it refers to Lesbia (in the images of ball-breaking and ploughing), it also provides

---

[26] See Putnam (1982) 15 and Janan (1994a) 64, for the sexual overtones of the language in this section. 'Pertunda' (which contains the same root as *tunditur*) is the name of the Roman goddess who presides over the penetration of the hymen. For Catullus' humorous and sexual use of this word in Poem 32, cf. Skinner (1980).

[27] Wiseman (1985) 10–14 provides a brief, but useful analysis of the importance in Roman discourse about sexual mores of the polarities of male / active / penetrator and female / passive / penetrated.

[28] See the discussion of this poem in Greene (1998) 26–36.

[29] Forsyth (1991).

[30] See Catullus, Poem 16. 1–2: *Pedicabo ego vos et irrumabo, | Aureli pathice et cinaede Furi* ('I will fuck you in the ass and I will fuck you in the mouth, you queers Aurelius and Furius'). On Furius and Aurelius, see Richardson (1963).

the vehicle for the speaker, even if only through a journey of the mind and through indirect verbal abuse of Lesbia, to regain his sense of a self through aggressive 'masculine' activity.

Horace, Odes 1. 22

> Integer vitae scelerisque purus
> non eget Mauris iaculis neque arcu
> nec venenatis gravida sagittis,
>   Fusce, pharetra,
>
> sive per Syrtis iter aestuosas   5
> sive facturus per inhospitalem
> Caucasum vel quae loca fabulosus
>   lambit Hydaspes.
>
> namque me silva lupus in Sabina,
> dum meam canto Lalagen et ultra   10
> terminum curis vagor expeditis,
>   fugit inermem;
>
> quale portentum neque militaris
> Daunias latis alit aesculetis
> nec Iubae tellus generat, leonum   15
>   arida nutrix.
>
> pone me pigris ubi nulla campis
> arbor aestiva recreatur aura,
> quod latus mundi nebulae malusque
>   Iuppiter urget;   20
>
> pone me sub curru nimium propinqui
> solis in terra domibus negata:
> dulce ridentem Lalagen amabo,
>   dulce loquentem.

The man intact in life and free of wrongdoing does not need Moorish javelins nor bow nor quiver heavy with poison arrows, Fuscus, whether going to travel through the boiling sands of Syrtes or through the inhospitable Caucasus or the places that the legendary river Hydaspes licks. For a wolf in the Sabine forest fled from me unarmed while I was singing of my Lalage and wandering beyond my property line with cares laid aside, the sort of monstrous portent neither warlike Apulia nourishes in its wide oak forests nor the land of Juba bears, dry nurse of lions. Put me in sluggish fields where no tree is refreshed by a summer breeze, the side of the world mists and unfavourable Jupiter press upon; put me beneath the chariot of the sun too near the earth in land denied habitation: I shall love my Lalage sweetly laughing, sweetly speaking.

Although the speaker of Catullus, Poem 11, in the realm of imagination attempts to recapture his 'manhood' through the vicarious 'penetration' of the world, we are left with an image in which 'love' falls like a flower when it has been 'touched' (*tactus*) by the passing plough. I would suggest that the problem posed by Horace in *Odes* 1. 22 is how to love while remaining 'untouched'. While some would see Horace's 'solution' to this problem in a move away from the erotic toward the poetic—a kind of sublimation of desire—thus seeing the ode as a poem about 'love poetry' and not about 'love', such an analysis does not do justice to the erotic content of the poem and its antecedents.[31] In addition it fails to recognize the ways in which Horace is grappling not only with poetic issues, but also with issues of gender, power, and the self. I would argue that in *Odes* 1. 22 Horace wants to explore a version of the erotic that 'allows a man to be a man'. He creates a 'corrective' to the potentially destructive version of desire found in Catullus, and returns in some sense to a potentially more positive version of desire found in Sappho. However, this 'allowing a man to be a man' is accomplished only through the lover becoming the unmoved 'other man' of Catullus, Poem 51, and Sappho, Poem 31. Thus *Odes* 1. 22 collapses the positions distinct in Sappho and Catullus of 'lover' and 'god-like / more than god-like unmoved man'. The problem, then, is one of *integritas*. How does one love 'untouched'? Or, put another way, can one bypass the transgressive nature of desire?[32]

The first word of *Odes* 1. 22 is *integer* and an understanding of that word is essential to an understanding of the ode in its entirety as well as of its relation to its literary antecedents. *Integer*, of course, is derived from the negative *in* 'not' plus the root from the verb *tango, tangere, tetigi, tactum*, 'touch'. Some have seen *integer* and the rest of the beginning of the poem as very distant from its love theme,[33] but *integer* is an important word in Latin erotic vocabulary[34] and Horace uses it elsewhere in the *Odes* in erotic contexts. At *Odes* 3. 7. 22 *integer* is used of a man who is sexually faithful (so far (*adhuc*)) and at *Odes* 2. 4. 22 the speaker praises a sexually attractive woman, while (supposedly) being uninvolved (*integer*).[35]

---

[31] See e.g. Olstein (1984) and McCormick (1973).

[32] For discussion of the transgressive, erotic nature of inspiration and the problems it poses for the male who wants to be in control, see Fowler in this volume.

[33] See Fraenkel (1957) 184–5 on his recollection of the singing of the poem's first four lines at funeral services in German schools.   [34] See Adams (1982) 186–7.

[35] See Ancona (1994) 38–9 on the undercutting of the notion of *integritas* in these two instances in the *Odes*.

Recognizing the erotic meaning of the word *integer* forces us to see the amatory nature of *Odes* 1. 22 starting with its first word. G. L. Hendrickson, in an article from 1910, noted the erotic sense of *integer*, but this sense has been ignored by many later scholars.

In an unpublished paper entitled 'Being "Wholly" Roman', Robert Kaster discusses the nature of *integritas* for the Romans.[36] While Kaster's focus is primarily on the ethical content of *integritas*, his investigation into the semantic range of the word proves very useful for an examination of how the word *integer* is used in *Odes* 1. 22. Kaster argues that *integritas* is not identical with the English 'integrity', with its sense of the self as 'the source of normative principles', but rather, that *integritas* points to a 'wholeness' or 'purity' or 'freshness'. *Integritas*

seems more a negative virtue than a positive virtue—that is, more defensive than assertive, more self-preserving than self-extending: its constitutive personal traits are more the sort that *restrain* the performance of acts thought to be ethically damaging than the sort that urge the performance of acts that are ethically expansive or enlarging . . . *integritas* has about it an air of mistrust, of oneself no less of others: an ethic that invests so much in restraint, fixity, and scrupulousness seems to fear a wild and treacherous caprice lurking close beneath the surface.

On a simple narrative level *Odes* 1. 22 proclaims the speaker's invulnerability and associates that invulnerability with being *integer vitae* ('intact in life') and *scelerisque purus* ('free of wrongdoing') and with singing of and loving Lalage. The poem is composed of three sections, each a sentence long and each occupying eight lines (1–8, 9–16, and 17–24). In each section, the central issue is the speaker's invulnerability, which is supposed to function as a source of immunity from the threats posed by the world. One can see how Kaster's notion of *integritas* as 'defensive' fits well with a figure seeking immunity from the world. As we proceed through the poem we shall see that the ethical will converge with the erotic as we examine what it means to be *integer vitae*.

In the first section (lines 1–8) the speaker proclaims the invulnerability of the one who is *integer vitae scelerisque purus* ('intact in life and free of wrongdoing'). This kind of individual needs no Moorish javelins nor bow nor quiver heavy with poisonous arrows, whether he is about to travel through the regions of the boiling sands of Syrtes or through the

---

[36] This paper was delivered at the Columbia University Seminar in Classical Civilization in 1998. I am grateful to Professor Kaster for his willingness to share a copy of the paper with me and his permission to cite material from it.

inhospitable Caucasus or the lands of the river Hydaspes. Having declared in the first four lines the invulnerable individual's lack of need for weapons, the speaker outlines in the next four lines (5–8) the places through which this individual may travel unharmed. Three places are named: the Syrtes, which refers to the gulf of Sidra or the gulf of Gabes or to the land they touch in northern Africa,[37] the Caucasus, and India. The first two are dangerous and inhospitable to humankind, while the last is described as *fabulosus* (literally, 'full of stories'). The remoteness and the danger of these locations is echoed later in the poem when the poet returns to mentioning places where the invulnerable individual may travel unharmed (lines 17–22).

Horace's initial phrase *integer vitae* would surely have recalled the Roman historian Sallust's description at *Bellum Catilinae* 54. 2 of the anti-Caesarian Stoic, Cato the Younger, who committed suicide rather than surrender to the opposition.[38] Sallust contrasts Cato's virtue with that of Julius Caesar: *Caesar beneficiis ac munificentia magnus habebatur, integritate vitae Cato.* ('Caesar was considered great because of his good deeds and generosity, Cato, *because of his self-contained life*' (emphases mine)). Cicero also uses a form of *integer* to describe Cato at *Pro Murena* 3: *Catoni, gravissimo atque* integerrimo *viro* ('Cato, a very serious and *self-contained* man' (emphasis mine)). Like *integer*, the adjective *purus* ('free of') and the noun *scelus* ('wrongdoing') operate in Latin in the erotic sphere as well as the ethical.[39] Thus through language that operates on both ethical and erotic levels the opening of *Odes* 1. 22 creates a speaker in whom a self-contained life and the life of a lover are joined. If we recall Sappho and Catullus for a moment we can see that the speaker of *Odes* 1. 22 is assuming the 'untouched' behaviour of the man who is equal to or even better than the gods. What follows in the poem is Horace's version of a love whose central feature is its self-containment.

We start with the generalizing statement that the man who is *integer vitae scelerisque purus* ('intact in life and free of wrongdoing') can travel without fear of harm wherever he wishes. The linkage of *integritas* with a kind of boundless travel anticipates the emphasis on boundaries and property which marks the second section of the poem, but here the

---

[37] Nisbet and Hubbard (1970) 265.

[38] The connection between *integer* and Cato has been noted by several scholars including Nisbet and Hubbard (1970) 265–6 and Zumwalt (1975).

[39] Adams (1982) 199 and 202 on *purus* and *scelus* and the *OLD* under *purus* 5. Depending on how one takes *scelus*, the phrase *scelerisque purus*, interestingly, can suggest 'lack of contamination' by '(illicit) sex'.

freedom from limits is addressed solely in terms of the speaker, rather than in terms of the external relation to Lalage, which is developed later in the poem. Note in connection with the notion of *integritas* as a 'negative virtue' that there is an emphasis on negation in this first section of the poem. The figure described as *integer vitae scelerisque purus* does not need such military equipment as javelins, bows, quivers, or poisoned arrows (*non eget*), and his *integritas* is confirmed by his innocence of wrongdoing (*scelerisque purus*). The specific weapons not needed suggest the erotic realm as well as the military, for Cupid, god of love, uses a bow and arrows to bring about love, while the quiver is described as *gravida* ('heavy' or 'pregnant') with its arrows. This description suggests that virtue lies not in explicit exemplary activity but rather in the absence of any activity that would contaminate reputation. At this point in the poem we do not yet know that this generalizing statement will be applied in the second section of the poem to the speaker through the use of an exemplum. As will be the case later in the poem, the world in which the man who is *integer vitae* can freely travel is rather bleakly inhospitable. Thus a tension is produced between the freedom that *integritas* is supposed to give to travel where one wishes, and the absence of any sense of why such travel might be desirable. We can return to the notion of a 'negative virtue' and see that *integritas* seems to allow one freedom 'from' rather than freedom 'for'.

The notion of *integritas* and especially its function as a 'negative virtue' helps to explain the addressee of *Odes* 1. 22 (*Fusce* 4), but let us first look back to the issue of the addressee in Sappho and Catullus. Unlike Sappho, Poem 31, in which the first-person speaker addresses her beloved in the second person but does not name her, Catullus, Poem 51, includes the addressee, Lesbia, which operates, as we have seen, on several levels. In addition, Poem 51, written as well in the first person, shifts to a self-address when the speaker speaks to himself with the vocative, *Catulle*. In Catullus, Poem 11, of course, the addressees are Furius and Aurelius, the speaker's would-be messengers. And the address to them is very long (lines 1–16). Yet here, too, there is a split in the speaker who speaks of himself in the third person (*comites Catulli, penetrabit*) as well as the first (*meae puellae, meum amorem*). Still further, rather than addressing the 'beloved' directly, the speaker refers to her in the third person (*vivat* etc.). Just as the addressee, *Lesbia*, introduces an intertextual element into Catullus, Poem 51, through its recollection of Sappho, so the addressee of *Odes* 1. 22 participates in intertextuality, but this time the intertexts are Horace's own. Gregson Davis has recently argued that *Odes* 1. 22 functions on the generic level as Horace's rejection of the iambic invective of his youth (as represented by the wolf he 'banishes' in the next section of the poem) and his affirmation of his new role as love lyricist in the Lesbian tradition.[40] While Davis opens the door to an interpretation that would include satire as well as iambic verse (the *Epodes*) in the genre rejected by Horace,[41] he focuses primarily on iambic. However, the presence of the addressee, Aristius Fuscus, urges us to look to Horace's satires as well for an understanding of this ode.

We know from commentators on Horace that the Fuscus who is the addressee of *Odes* 1. 22 is also Horace's literary friend of *Satires* 1. 10. 83, the person to whom *Epistles* 1. 10 is addressed, and (most important for our present purposes) the character who refuses to save the speaker of *Satires* 1. 9 from the overly talkative, aggressive social climber with literary pretensions who refuses to leave him alone. In addition, it has been argued recently that Fuscus was a Stoic.[42] The many thematic elements that link *Satires* 1. 9 and *Odes* 1. 22 include speech, song, or writing, and the dangers of the world. The satire contains punning on Fuscus' name ('dark one') and Apollo, associated with the sun through the epithet φοῖβος ('the bright one'), who finally seems to save him.[43] In *Odes* 1. 22 the Moorish javelins (line 2), land too close to the sun (lines 21–2), and Hydaspes (line 8), which Horace had called *fuscus* in *Satires* 2. 8. 14, all recall Aristius Fuscus, now addressee of a poem in which the speaker's invulnerability is the central theme. In *Odes* 1. 22 the Horatian coinage *fabulosus*, 'legendary, storied', used of the river Hydaspes, which is already linked to Aristius Fuscus in *Satires* 2. 8, calls attention to the intertextual and self-referential nature of the ode, for the river becomes 'storied' through Horace's own writings. While Fuscus' presence in the ode seems minimal (the one-word address), he, in fact, anchors the poem to the world, for the speaker needs an audience (in the world) to whom he can proclaim his invulnerability (from the world). This

---

[40] Davis (1999). See p. 60 n. 1 for references to epigrams that include the apotropaic power of sound with which one can compare the speaker's singing during the wolf episode in *Odes* 1. 22.

[41] Ibid. 61.

[42] See Harrison (1992).

[43] Mazurek (1997) argues that the ending of the poem is ironic because by agreeing to serve as a witness the speaker would not have become free of his unwanted companion but rather would have been required to accompany him to court. Apollo's connections with both poetry and justice make this an interesting interpretation.

anticipates and parallels Lalage's function. The repeated imperatives *pone, pone* in the final section of the poem can be seen as expanding the speaker's audience from Fuscus to the reader, who is now included as part of the audience for whom the speaker performs his lack of need. Furthermore, if Aristius Fuscus was a Stoic there is added point to the fact that the speaker, and not the addressee, at the end of the poem becomes associated with (Stoic) *integritas*.

While differing in specific geographical locations, the catalogue of places in the world which appears in this first section of the poem recalls the catalogue of Catullus, Poem 11, through the similarity of its grammatical structure. Both catalogues are built around alternatives linked by the repetition of *sive . . . sive* (whether . . . or). While in Catullus the journey so outlined is one on which Furius and Aurelius were to be prepared to accompany Catullus in 'penetrating' activities mimicking aggressive military campaigns, in Horace the imagined journey focuses on only one individual, the man who is *integer vitae scelerisque purus*. Yet the two catalogues share military and political content. The significance of the places named has been noted by several critics.[44] Cato the Younger (already, as has been argued above, adumbrated by the phrase *integer vitae*) conducted a famous march in 47 BC across the Syrtes.[45] The river Hydaspes is associated with Alexander the Great, who in 326 BC won a great military victory there and sailed down the river.[46] The Caucasus may evoke Pompey the Great, the first Roman general to have reached the area, or perhaps Alexander, who, while not reaching the Caucasus, did reach the Hindu Kush, which was identified with the Caucasus.[47] Thus, all three places are associated with significant military leaders.

In the poem's second section (lines 9–16), the reader learns that the speaker himself is an instantiation of the invulnerable individual described in the first eight lines of the poem, for the speaker adduces an exemplum from his own experience (*namque me*, 9) to prove the notion of invulnerability introduced in the first section of the poem. The proof, which occupies lines 9–12, is signalled by the explanatory *namque*. It consists of the fact that a wolf in the Sabine forest fled from the unarmed

---

[44] Nisbet and Hubbard (1970) 262, 265–7 and Zumwalt (1975) *passim*.

[45] See Nisbet and Hubbard (1970) 265–6 for the ancient sources on Cato the Younger's march. Cf. Catullus, Poem 64. 156, and Virgil, *Aeneid* 1. 111 for the Syrtes as dangerous to ships, and *Aeneid* 7. 302–3 for the linking of Syrtes with Scylla and Charybdis. The word *aestuosas* ('boiling, seething'), used of Syrtes, continues the poem's use of language that has erotic potential.

[46] Nisbet and Hubbard (1970) 267.

[47] Ibid.

speaker while he was singing of his Lalage and wandering beyond his property line with his cares laid aside. The extraordinary quality of this event is underscored by the statement that such an amazing portent is not produced in the wide oak forests of warlike Apulia, Horace's birthplace, or in Africa, the land of Juba, dry nurse of lions (lines 13–16).[48]

The notion of wholeness, of boundaries not transgressed, introduced by *integer*, the poem's first word, clearly continues in this section of the poem in the description of the freedom from the dangerous wolf. The phrase *ultra terminum* makes explicit that the speaker's wandering involves his crossing or transgressing his own property line. Thus, even though the verb *vagor* may include a somewhat aimless idea of travel, *ultra terminum* keeps at the forefront the notion of limits and boundaries. While the speaker is *integer* ('whole, untouched') he freely moves beyond what would be circumscribed as his own space. Moreover, the conditions under which he does this are significant. He wanders while 'singing' of his Lalage (*dum meam canto Lalagen*) and while 'freed from cares' (*curiis*). Unlike the 'speakers' in Sappho, Poem 31, and Catullus, Poem 51, who 'cannot speak' or the 'speaker' in Catullus, Poem 11, who can only speak (to Lesbia) through an intermediary, the speaker in *Odes* 1. 22 not only speaks/sings but his singing (*canto*), which later becomes assimilated to his loving (*amabo*), has a magical effect. Only in *Odes* 1. 22 is the speaker's voice unimpeded by the object of desire.[49] Scholars have noted the motif of the divinely protected lover which may be operating here,[50] but the phrase *curis . . . expeditis* ('freed from *curae*') significantly signals the speaker's desire to *have* Lalage (at least as the object of his song) but also to be *free from* her, for *cura* is a standard word in Latin erotic vocabulary for the 'object' of one's love. (A striking example of this usage is found in Horace, *Odes* 2. 8. 8, where Barine is described as a *publica cura*, or public object of erotic attention.) If one recalls the

[48] The fact that Juba I committed suicide in 46 BC after the battle of Thapsus makes the name Juba relevant to the poem's opening reference to Cato the Younger. His son, Juba II, led in Julius Caesar's triumph and brought up in Italy, was known for his learning and his writing, which included zoological information (about lions, among other things) on Africa. On Juba I and Juba II, see Nisbet and Hubbard (1970) 270–1. Nisbet and Hubbard suggest that Horace and Aristius Fuscus may have known Juba II.

[49] See *Odes* 4. 1. 35–6 for the speaker using speechlessness as an almost stylized sign of desire: *cur facunda parum decoro | inter verba cadit lingua silentio*? ('Why does my eloquent tongue fall amidst my words in a scarcely decorous silence?'). Part of the problem with the erotic is its threat to decorum. Commager (1995 (1962)) 132–3 cites H. J. Munro's connection of *Odes* 1. 22 with Catullus, Poem 45, the Acme and Septimius poem, which also mentions lions and Libya.

[50] See e.g. Tibullus 1. 2. 25–30 and Propertius 3. 16. 11–18 as cited by Commager (1995 (1962)) 134. Commager (130–6) sees the poem as a parody of the elegiac lover.

language of response to the object of desire in Sappho, Poem 31, and
Catullus, Poem 51, one can see that the speaker in *Odes* 1. 22 contrasts
starkly with the speakers in those poems for whom desire necessarily
involves *cura* both in its sense of 'anxiety' or 'care' and in its sense of an
'object of one's anxiety or care'. The erotic dynamic set up in those two
poems involves what happens when one does have *cura*. In contrast, in
the ode of Horace it is the 'other man's' response to the object of desire
that more closely resembles the speaker's response. Unlike the speakers
in Sappho and Catullus whose very selves are affected by their
experience of desire, the Horatian speaker remains unmoved, or at least
'care-free' as the 'other men' appear to be in Sappho and Catullus. What
we must address, then, is what it means to sing about and love Lalage
(*Lalagen amabo*, 23) without being moved. One approach is to argue that
Odes 1. 22 involves a substitution of verbal for sexual activity and that the
poem thus substitutes poetry and its particular procreative powers for
the sexual bond, and that it is Horace whose productivity surpasses the
productivity of the physical world.[51] Compare, for example, *neque . . .
alit* (13–14), *nec . . . generat* (15), *arida nutrix* (16) ('does not nourish', 'does
not bear', 'dry nurse'). While this argument may in part account for the
paradoxical position of the speaker, who seems both to be and to not be
in love, I think it falls short of adequately taking into account the Sapphic
and Catullan backgrounds of the poem in which desire is a central issue.
Given this background, I think the poem must function not (merely) as
a commentary on the power of poetry,[52] but also as a commentary on
the threatening power of love. Although I have argued that there is a
literary self-consciousness in Sappho's articulation of her speechlessness
as well as a highly developed sense of literary intertextuality in Catullus'
addressing 'Lesbia', the one from Lesbos (i.e. Sappho), in Poem 51,
central to both poems is the issue of the effect of desire. In the case of
Horace, then, who was clearly writing with those poems in mind, we
ignore something significant if we see the poem only in terms of poetry
and not in terms of desire. What I think Horace suggests in this poem is
a scenario in which one 'has a Lalage' without the fearful transgression
of the self explicit in the Catullan and Sapphic models of desire. In other
words, in this ode, one loves while staying *integer*. The feasibility of this
scenario (or lack thereof) is to be found in the poem's conclusion.

In the final section of the poem (lines 17–24) the speaker lays down a
challenge: place him anywhere and he will (continue to) love his Lalage.

---

[51] Olstein (1984) 117–19.   [52] As e.g. Olstein (1984).

Place him in cold, lifeless places—in sluggish fields where no tree is refreshed by a summer breeze, the side of the world clouds and unfavourable Jupiter press upon (17–20). Place him in lands too hot— under the chariot of the sun too near the earth in land denied habitation (21–2), he will love his Lalage, sweetly laughing, sweetly speaking (23–4).

The end of the poem returns to the idea of boundless travel intro- duced in the poem's opening section, but now the language of invulnerability which appeared in the third person throughout lines 1–8 (*non eget*, 2: '[he] does not need') has become emphatically first person for the speaker: *pone me . . . pone me* ('put me . . . put me'). In this hypo- thetical journey the speaker's power will come from 'loving Lalage'. Rather than 'penetrating' the world, as the speaker of Catullus 11 would like to do, the Horatian speaker is off on a dizzying trip with Lalage. In the episode with the wolf she seemed to function as a kind of talisman, protecting the speaker from the dangers of the world beyond his borders (*ultra terminum*).[53] It is perhaps tempting to see Lalage as a kind of cipher—merely a symbol of the speaker's own poetic powers. Or one can see her as a physical extension (literally) of the speaker, introducing an almost masturbatory version of love (recalling that same possibility mentioned above in Catullus 51), for she is sung about as his (*meam*) and loved wherever he goes![54] However, Horace's return to Sappho at the poem's conclusion makes Lalage more complicated than that. When Catullus' *dulce ridentem* ('sweetly laughing') becomes Horace's *dulce ridentem . . . dulce loquentem* ('sweetly laughing . . . sweetly speaking') we abandon Catullus and return to Sappho's ἆδυ φωνείσας ('sweetly speak- ing'). Horace's *dulce loquentem*, poised as it is at the end of the poem, is the emblem of Horace's proposed erotics. By returning to Sappho Horace in a sense restores to the beloved the 'voice' she has in Sappho, Poem 31, but not in Catullus, Poem 51. The link between the 'speaker' of the poem and the 'speaking' object of desire is restored. Of course it is not that simple. Lalage still occupies a position unable to be located both outside of and within the speaker of the poem. She is the object of his song and of his love and therefore is 'object' to his 'subject'. She is what

[53] See Davis (1999) 51–2 and 60 n. 1 for λαλάγημα as the name for the instrument used to scare away a beast in Dioscorides (*Palatine Anthology* 6. 220. 15). Davis (52) cites in relation to Lalage's name another Hellenistic source, Moschus 1. 8, for Eros characterized as ἆδυ λάλημα ('sweet talk'). The ἆδυ may be as significant as the λάλημα, for it recalls the ἆδυ φωνείσας ('sweetly speaking') of Sappho 31 which 'returns' in Horace's *dulce loquentem*.

[54] See Sharrock's discussion (esp. n. 14) in this volume of the male poet's (and esp. Ovid's) use of the word *mea* to modify the Muse as part of his male appropriation of her.

protects him from the world, yet she must in some sense be of the world. The poem's first word, *integer*, opens up a vast expanse in which issues of the self, boundaries, transgression, and desire are at stake. While Horace allows the speaker in *Odes* 1. 22 to avoid the overwhelming impact of desire through the exercise of a kind of 'masculine' control over the self, one can argue that Horace's incorporation of Sappho's 'speaking beloved' at the end of the poem potentially shatters that control. For if Lalage 'speaks'—and her name itself is connected with speech (λαλαγεῖν)—there is a 'voice' in the 'object position' that may yet destabilize the *integritas* of the speaker. Muses define and transgress the untouched self.[55]

[55] I would like to thank Don Fowler and Effie Spentzou for inviting me to contribute to this volume. For responding to various portions of this piece in progress, I owe thanks to my Latin Lyric Poetry, Catullus, Horace, and Women and Slaves in Classical Antiquity classes at Hunter College and The Graduate School, The City University of New York. Steven Cole, Ellen Greene, and audiences at conferences of the Pacific Modern Language Association, American Philological Association, Classical Association of the Middle West and South, and Classical Association of the Atlantic States offered useful comments on some early elements of this argument. Effie Spentzou and Ellen Greene also made helpful suggestions upon reading the penultimate draft.

9

The Muse Unruly and Dead: Acanthis in Propertius 4. 5

Micaela Janan

The readings contained in this volume represent a collective effort to listen 'against the grain' for the voice of the alternative, much-doubted Muse that murmurs quietly, though persistently, in ancient literature. Encouraged by this collective ambition, I, too, interest myself in resistant readings of the Muse's representation—the places where she waxes larger than mere "handmaid" to the male poet's work, and becomes his dissentient alter ego. The Augustan elegist Propertius introduces just such an irregular Muse in his fourth book of poems when he brings on-stage in Elegy 4. 5 an old bawd named Acanthis; she counsels his mistress Cynthia to provide against a decrepit old age, and to maximize her youthful economic gain, by strategically cultivating rivalries among wealthy admirers.[1] In the course of her harangue, Acanthis even criticizes the first words Propertius' poetry ever addressed directly to Cynthia. *Quid iuvat ornato procedere, vita, capillo | et tenuis Coa veste movere sinus?* ('What avails it, my life, to go out walking with exquisitely coiffed hair and to create gauzy billows in silky Coan dress?'), she mockingly quotes from the Monobiblos (Prop. 4. 5. 55–6 = 1. 2. 1–2).[2] She reinterprets the distich not as a fine indifference to materialism, but as a poor man's attempt to get something for nothing—to enjoy his mistress's favours without bankrolling her haute couture fashions.[3]

[1] The chief modern discussions of Prop. 4. 5 have been: Celentano (1956) 56–60; Tränkle (1960) 105–8, 175–8; Lefèvre (1966) 100–8; Hallett (1971) 158–63; Hallett (1973); Hubbard (1974) 136–42; Weeber (1977) 114–25; Puccioni (1979); Gutzwiller (1985); Fedeli (1987); Wyke (1987*a*) 165–7.

[2] Some have doubted the authenticity of these lines, convinced by the many arguments of Ulrich Knoche (1936) that they must be an interpolation. However, Reitzenstein (1936) 94–108 cogently refutes Knoche's contentions.

[3] Acanthis enters Propertius' corpus as precisely the type of troublesome Muse that

Acanthis thus reduces to hard economic reality the romantic tug-of-war between mistress and lover regularly engaged in Propertius' earlier books, opposing and displacing the voice of Propertius qua lover-narrator, the voice that had unified the poet's first three volumes of elegies. True, she does not do so uniquely: similar scepticism informs all of Book 4's broad variety of female voices. Where Books 1–3 showcased the lover-narrator's solipsistic male anguish over his affair's difficulties, Book 4's range of female narrators articulate widely various aspects of troubled relations between the sexes in ancient Rome. From faithful wife to patrician mother to Vestal Virgin, each speaker's telling plaint expands the genre's conception of Woman beyond the archetypally coquettish, two-dimensional elegiac mistress. Yet Acanthis' unflinching analysis of what really drives relations between the sexes aptly summarizes the disenchanted, 'feminine' perspective that Book 4 as a whole sets against Propertius' earlier books, and against the masculinist assumptions of the Propertian lover-narrator in the poetic redaction of the Cynthia affair.[4] Though aged, ugly, impoverished, and cynical—a satanic inversion of the typical Muse—Acanthis is Book 4's true Muse in so far as she summarizes its inspiration. Book 4, like the bawd's ironic quote from the Monobiblos, insistently charges its readers to resift Propertius' earlier work from a more disenchanted perspective.

However, these observations on the case to be made for Acanthis'

Sharrock in this volume documents in her analysis of Ovid's *Metamorphoses*, a Muse with whom the poet/lover struggles for dominance. As in Ovid's tale of Salmacis and Hermaphroditus—a tale that Sharrock shrewdly analyses as an allegory of relations between poet and Muse—the poet/lover, Propertius, apparently triumphs over the (rejected) Muse, Acanthis. However, Acanthis enjoys the same kind of victory that Salmacis does, Pyrrhic but significant: though the poet/lover gets the 'last word', the way we read him changes forever after we have heard Acanthis articulate her perspective on what is truly at stake between lover and mistress (just as Hermaphroditus' absorption of Salmacis forever changes him, and his voice:

> ergo ubi se liquidas, quo vir descenderat, undas
> semimarem fecisse videt mollitaque in illis
> membra, manus tendens, sed iam non voce virili
> Hermaphroditus ait . . .

(Ovid, *Met.* 4. 380–3)

[4] By 'feminine', I refer not only to the prominence of women narrators in Book 4, but to its articulation of punctual disruptions in the rule-based systems of language and culture. These poems are also 'feminine' in the sense that postmodern theorists like Jacques Lacan lend that term; I shall be drawing upon Lacan in particular for this essay.

Lacan's most extended meditation on the concept of the feminine can be found in his twentieth *Séminaire*, entitled 'Encore!' (Lacan (1975)). It has now been fully translated into English (Lacan (1998)). Mitchell and Rose (1985) provide a useful basic guide to this difficult work, Copjec (1994) 201–36 and Zizek (1994) more advanced elucidations of its implications.

scepticism broach very little that is new—Kathryn Gutzwiller covered virtually the same deconstructionist and feminist territory in her *Ramus* article more than a decade ago.[5] None the less, I wish to push Gutzwiller's analysis further, and to ask: granted that Acanthis strategically calls Propertius' bluff, why does he need her to do so? Fewer than a hundred lines later in Book 4, he imagines the recently deceased Cynthia returned from the dead, her body charred by the funeral pyre, her lips scoured by Lethe, her bones rattling. The ghostly Cynthia wastes no time in telling her lover off: her picture of their affair and its aftermath radically conflicts with the way Propertius has depicted their relations in his previous three poetry books. She was the faithful one, not he, she says (4. 7. 53; cf. 4. 7. 13, 21, 49, 72, 93), she the one who ran risks to meet him secretly in the Subura (4. 7. 15–18). All that her loyalty and courage earned her was his indifference to her death, and a tawdry, cheap funeral (4. 7. 23–33). Cynthia commands him to burn all the poetry he wrote about her, and to remove from her tomb the symbol of his inspiration, the ivy of Bacchus (4. 7. 77–80).[6] If, in 4. 7, Propertius goes to the trouble of hauling Cynthia out of the Underworld in order to have her call him a liar to his face, can Acanthis possibly trump that? Further, even if we assume the poet's grim delight in representing himself as pilloried by women (a pleasure so keen that he must sample it *twice* in Book 4), does he really need such an elaborately detailed old woman as Acanthis just to tell him that he talks trash? Loving strokes are lavished on this verse portrait of a beggared procuress: is that gratuitous? Just what does the portrait of the messenger add to the message?

I shall argue that Acanthis' significance, like the ghostly Cynthia's, revolves around being a messenger who is female and dead, but that Propertius' virulent loathing for Acanthis is also crucially important. *Communis opinio* on this poem sees his hatred as unproblematic: Propertius has exposed the venality of an old flesh-pedlar in all its ugliness (so the common reading runs), and asks but simple justice when he wishes upon her the miserable death and afterlife that he has the good fortune to see fulfilled (4. 5. 1–4, 63–78).[7] I, on the other hand, am troubled by the fact that he continues to hate Acanthis long after she has

---

[5] Gutzwiller (1985).

[6] On Bacchus as Propertius' poetic inspiration, see e.g. 2. 5. 26, 2. 30. 39, 4. 1. 62. Richardson (1977) ad 4. 7. 80 makes the point in his sensitive commentary on Cynthia's injunction.

[7] The scholars whose published opinions I list in n. 1 all side with 4. 5's lover-narrator, where they see fit to hazard an opinion on the merits of the case; Gutzwiller stands alone in taking up the cudgels on Acanthis' behalf.

any power to harm him—even after she is dead—just as he continues to be fascinated by Cynthia even when she returns to him as a scorched and macabre spectre in 4. 7. Both his hatred and his love turn on the same irrational fantasy of an ineffable 'core' in the two women that inspires his emotions toward them; his devotion and despite are structurally indistinguishable. Of that imagined core I shall have more to say presently, but I must first account for the theme of the living dead that both elegies share, in order to found further discussion of Propertius' relation to these women.

I. THE RETURN OF THE LIVING DEAD

A certain fascination with the living dead traverses Book 4: halfway through the book, Cynthia returns from the grave (4. 7) and at the end of it, so does the Roman matron Cornelia (4. 11)—each to defend her life before the quick and the dead. Acanthis is the third of these illustrious revenants; although Propertius does not explicitly sketch Acanthis as one of the undead, he wavers uneasily between past and present tenses when speaking of the old woman, as if unable to be sure she has really died. For example, after he has roundly cursed her sepulchre and shade, he none the less describes her putative magical powers as though she yet lived to wield them. *Illa velit, poterit magnes non ducere ferrum | et volucris nidis esse noverca suis* ('should she will it so, the magnet will not draw iron and the bird will be a stepmother to its own nest', 4. 5. 9–10). These lines' sudden shift in temporal perspective implies that Acanthis lives on in some form after her physical death. She still possesses power from beyond the grave in her hold on the lover's imagination—his vivid record of her advice to Cynthia, and his reaction to it, attest as much. As the prelude to 4. 7's reproachful courtesan and 4. 11's embittered matron, the 'revenant' Acanthis offers a disenchanted view of the mores governing Roman women's behaviour, and she foreshadows Cynthia's and Cornelia's fierce intransigence when she argues her case. Propertius allots that candour and fury exclusively to women claimed by death's domain: the 'return of the dead' in Book 4 marks the uncanny appearance of truths about women that challenge received wisdom. The ghosts of 4. 5, 4. 7, and 4. 11 figure crucially in the interpretation of a book focused on Woman as *the* icon that locates the failings of cultural symbolization systems. Yet Acanthis' cool impeachment establishes the fundamental terms of that plaint.

II. A PORTRAIT IN PERSUASION

The poem opens with Propertius cursing Acanthis' grave (1–4) and cataloguing her powers as a witch; his description implies his rage, but 4. 5
none the less courts belief.[8] The catalogue of Acanthis' abilities and practices falls within generic lines mapped out by other Roman poets'
descriptions of witches' powers, such as those of the sorceress who Dido
claims will rid her of unrequited love, and the one Tibullus employs to
cozen a too-vigilant husband.[9] Indeed, Acanthis rather pales next to the
horrors Horace imagines of Canidia: she certainly does not practise
human sacrifice.[10] Propertius unsettles the reader's expectations, not
when he describes Acanthis, but when she herself speaks. Gutzwiller
compares the elegy to *Amores* I. 8, Ovid's portrait of the *lena* Dipsas, and
notes that, surprisingly, Acanthis' counsel evidences neither venality
nor self-interest (as Dipsas' advice clearly does).[11] Acanthis speaks eloquently and learnedly, ornamenting her argument with mythological
allusions and intricate rhetorical figures, and rising to pathos when she
evocatively describes the rose gardens at Paestum suddenly blighted by
a summer sirocco (61–2). She can be accused, at worst, of hard-headed
realism in her advice to Cynthia, advising the younger woman to put
long-term economic self-interest ahead of the *beau geste* her lover urges
upon her, fidelity to a gifted pauper. The details of Acanthis' speech,
Gutzwiller concludes, reveal the old woman's unexpected depth and
humanity.[12] Yet the wealth of fine detail with which the elegy draws
Acanthis' portrait, from her motley eloquence to her disenchanted perspectives on youth and love, also figures crucially in rethinking the
sources of antagonism between the sexes.

One mannerism that Gutzwiller overlooks, for example, is Acanthis'
doggedness.[13] The old woman returns again and again, both in eloquent

---

[8] Hermann Tränkle (1960) 107 comments on the lover's rage, comparing this passage to its
closest analogue, Ovid's sketch of the *lena* Dipsas (*Am.* I. 8. 5–20): 'Aus allen diesen Beispielen
[von 4. 5] spüren wir den Ingrimm des Dichters über die Macht der lena, während bei Ovid nur
scheues Staunen hier und dort anklingt, im übrigen aber der äussere Vorgang geschildert wird'.

[9] *Aeneid* 4. 487–91, Tibullus I. 2. 43–52.

[10] Cf. Hor. *Epist.* 5.

[11] Gutzwiller (1985) 107.

[12] See ibid. esp. 108–9; 111–12.

[13] A feature that has even struck Propertius' textual critics and informs their sober work of
emendation. For example: emendations offered for the problematic distich 19–20 frequently
work toward a comparison between Acanthis' speech and the effect of some persistent force
(water, a mole) working its way through stone, the parallel resting upon the idea of wearing

and vulgar turns of phrase, to the chief gravamen of her advice: 'look to the cash!' (*aurum spectato*, 4. 5. 53).[14] But why need she repeat herself so insistently? Admittedly her advisee, on the evidence of Propertius' other three books, is no simple mercenary: Cynthia displays altruism alongside venality in her long career as mistress and might at moments be inclined to fall in with her lover's idealism.[15] Still, after assimilating the other books, the reader can hardly imagine a Cynthia who would need this much persuasion, even as a novice, ultimately to favour her own interests. The old woman observes that Cynthia already has expensive tastes (21–6) and presumably also the will to fulfil them. Where Ovid's Corinna blushes modestly at Dipsas' suggestion that a man might wish to purchase her favours (*Am.* 1. 8. 35), Cynthia evidences no such demur at Acanthis' advice. Why, then, does Propertius represent Acanthis as reiterating her message so persistently, when her own shrewd analysis of Cynthia's predilections indicates that the old woman preaches, if not exactly to the converted, then to the easily convertible? Is Acanthis simply plagued by an old woman's garrulity, or is her repetitiveness significant?

III. REREADING THE PAST

Acanthis' persistence mirrors the melancholy tenacity of the undead, the inert stubbornness with which they haunt the living. The poem as a whole shapes Acanthis' death and afterlife, like her speech, into an 'eternal return': Propertius strews evidence for the posthumous repetition of her will throughout her speech. The old woman's various devices for cajoling money out of the lover and increasing the mistress's hold over him can be matched by scenes from Propertius' other three books: Cynthia pleading the rites of Isis as a reason for sexual abstinence, or exploding with anger at his peccadilloes, or arousing his suspicion and jealousy because her crowded house reminds him of the courtesan Thais' establishment.[16] 4. 5 rereads Propertius' 'woman trouble' as

away resistance through slow but constant application. Also, Richardson (1977) ad 58 urges the reading *sine aere* over *sine arte* in 58 guided by repetition: 'though this is repetitious [after the twice-iterated *aurum* in 53], it is in character with Acanthis'.

[14] Cf. Richardson (1977) ad 4. 5. 45–6.

[15] To name but one of several examples: 1. 3. 41–6 finds her waiting with Lucretia-like modesty and wifely devotion for Propertius' return from revelry. Cf. also her description of her own exemplary faithfulness in 4. 7. 51–4, and her residence among the Good Beauties of the Underworld (4. 7. 63–70).   [16] Cf. Weeber (1977) 116–17.

Acanthis' 'eternal return'; the elegy gathers together the disparate threads of Cynthia's recorded behaviour and reduces them to order as the posthumous unfolding of the *lena*'s demand that economic self-interest come first, well before altruism.

Yet the poet's insistence on this reinterpretation should give us pause, given that it jars with what his previous poems had told us of Cynthia's conduct of her sexual affairs. Scholars have often noted how ill Acanthis fits the chronicle of Propertius' affair with Cynthia set down in Books 1–3. However Cynthia's always-ambiguous status may be conceived, either as *matrona* gone wrong or *demi-mondaine*, she has no connection with any bawd outside this single poem; she transacts her business with her clients quite independently.[17] Acanthis' late entrance into the 'Cynthia Wars' implausibly blames the liaison's difficulties on a third party. Acanthis' eleventh-hour appearance urges us to ask: why remember the old woman only now?

Because she ultimately exonerates Cynthia: though Acanthis infuriates Propertius, the elegy offers her advice to the younger woman as the source that conveniently 'explains' his mistress's irritating actions. According to this revision, the dead Acanthis poisoned the affair between Propertius and Cynthia implicitly from the beginning of its history in the Monobiblos. He thus retrospectively reconstrues the previous corpus as a record of failure for which Acanthis, rather than Cynthia, bears the blame; the love affair's vicissitudes evidence a 'return of the dead' in the form of Acanthis' continuing influence over his mistress.

Yet second thoughts do not accrue entirely to the credit of the lover's case: where 4. 5 urges rereading upon us most insistently, with Acanthis quoting the Monobiblos' scorn for fashionable dress (55–6), her reading of the line as swindle rather than asceticism (54) makes the lover look mean and sly. Given the *amica*'s general economic vulnerability, depending as she does on the generosity of her lover(s), Acanthis' point tells; rereading cuts both ways in this poem.

IV. THE OBSCURE OBJECT OF DESPITE . . .

Given the weakness of Propertius' case against her, precisely what *is* it about Acanthis that so inflames his ire? Scholars usually point to her counsel of economic self-interest before all other considerations as the

---

[17] Weeber (1977) 114; Wyke (1987a) 165–6.

reason,[18] especially given that her tenets directly oppose his doctrine of placing love above all material, social, or political considerations.[19] The logical consequences of Acanthis' beliefs lead her to balk the lovers' affair, allegedly by magic as well as dissuasion. Yet the old woman's money worries are not for herself: she frets for Cynthia, acknowledging her protégée's taste for luxury and advising the younger woman how to satisfy her own predilection, without any expectation that Acanthis herself will benefit. Predictably, Propertius sophistically twists her concern for another's welfare into an accusation of 'greed'.

Propertius' hatred of the old woman verges on unreason in its dogged single-mindedness. He traces a path from the apex of her alleged power (puissant magic) to its nadir (solitary and impoverished death). Yet the 'fall' he so records raises fewer questions about Acanthis than about himself. According to his own testimony, the *lena*, as object of his hatred, changes completely within the course of the poem. Once powerful even over the elements of nature, she becomes physically weak and socially downtrodden; once Cynthia's confidante and mentor, she later wastes away as an isolated outcast; once able to borrow the shape and vigour of animals, she deteriorates into mortal illness. Whatever erstwhile opposition she presented to Propertius has vanished, and *yet he continues to hate her*. A puzzle: when every one of Acanthis' objective properties has changed to its opposite, what remains to hate in her?

Propertius' illogically persistent thirst for vengeance, continuing even after her death, points to an irreducible kernel round which his aversion to the *lena* coalesces, something that cannot be articulated as a logical proposition along the lines of 'I hate her because she is (terrifyingly powerful, a jinx to love relationships, a threat to my vitality, an interfering busybody . . .).' His antagonism operates as if above and beyond all Acanthis' putative loathsome properties existed some mysterious '*x* factor' that inspired hatred even when all such features have vanished. He fastens upon the paltry details of her squalor to justify his malice

[18] 'Ein Hetärenkatechismus, eingekleidet in die Form eines Nachrufes für eine vor kurzem verstorbene Kupplerin, die durch die schlimmen Lehren, die sie der Geliebten des Dichters gegeben hat, ihn unglücklich gemacht und sich seinen bitteren Haß zugezogen hat': Rothstein (1966) 260; 'Propertius curses an old procuress named Acanthis, now dead, for thwarting his love by corrupting the mind of his mistress': Butler and Barber (1933) 350; 'Such is the retribution merited by an individual with Acanthis' values, proof of how debased the attitudes which Propertius condemns in Rome's public policies are when applied to private affairs': Hallett (1971) 163; '[Acanthis] made [Propertius'] life hell by urging his mistress, her pupil, to faithlessness and almost daily demands of presents and cash': Richardson (1977) 441.

[19] Cf. e.g. 1. 8; 1. 14; 2. 1; 2. 7; 2. 14; 2. 16; 3. 5; 3. 7; 3. 11.

when Acanthis lies sick and dying, gleefully pointing to a foul, stolen headband (71–2) as evidence of the old woman's avarice. Yet the absurdity of his proofs shows that he cannot in fact pinpoint exactly what he despises about her; no matter the intellectual resources mustered for the problem, the ultimate object of his animosity remains ineffable. The fact that this mysterious x cannot find expression, and yet forms the putative core of Acanthis' personality so strongly sketched within the elegy, indicates an encounter with that which ineluctably evades symbolization, the category of phenomena Lacan labelled the Real.

The Lacanian Real differs from 'reality' in so far as it includes phenomena that most of us would consider unreal (dreams and hallucinations, for example); these phenomena none the less impinge on our lives, often with dramatic results. Face to face with the Real, 'the mind makes contact with the limits of its power, with that which its structure cannot structure'.[20] The Real evidences itself, for example, in the clumsy paradoxes of racial hatred. Racists formulate a plethora of logically contradictory accusations about the Other to justify their hatred (that other races are, for example, shiftless and lazy, but at the same time compulsive workers who steal employment from 'legitimate citizens'—i.e. members of the dominant group).[21] These self-contradicting reproaches indicate that a fantasized 'kernel of being' organizes the racist's conception of the Other, something over and above any nameable, immanent, symbolizable properties the despised group possesses (such as being hardworking or indolent). This kernel makes a member of the group the Other (in the eyes of the dominant group), and hence makes him objectionable. Lacan calls this 'x factor' enfolded by fantasies of identity *objet a* (shorthand for *objet autre*). *Objet a* is a little piece of the Real that eludes all attempts to reduce it to symbolization and that persists as an inert remainder. In the Acanthis poem, Propertius has once again stumbled upon the 'little piece of the Real' that organizes subjectivity.

V. . . . AND DESIRE

I say 'once again' because his sketch of Acanthis and his hatred for her structurally reiterate, point for point, his portrayal of, and his passionate love for, Cynthia: he moulds his mistress around an equally inarticulable

---

[20] M. Bowie (1991) 105.   [21] Zizek (1993) 200–37, esp. 203.

core. In 2. 3, for example, Propertius praises his mistress as a Muse of supreme power, capable of inspiring modern artists to surpass the achievements of prior ages (2. 3. 41–2); in the course of contemplating her power, he wonders about the source of her sway over himself. Propertius considers a number of possible objective catalysts for his love (Cynthia's beautiful face, her lovely voice, her skilful lyre-playing); yet he discards each one by saying, 'no, it cannot be that, either'.[22] He finally despairs of putting his finger on the exact feature that inspires his love, contenting himself with general hyperbolic praise of her power to fascinate. None the less, he returns to this puzzle from a different angle when he bitterly dismisses Cynthia at last in 3. 24, telling her that his praises for her beauty were all false:

> mixtam te varia laudavi saepe figura,
>   ut, quod non esses, esse putaret amor;
> et color est totiens roseo collatus Eoo,
>   cum tibi quaesitus candor in ore foret
>
> (3. 24. 5–8)

I have often praised you as a composite of various kinds of beauty so that love might think you what you were not. And your complexion, how often it was compared to the rosy Dawn, when the alabaster in your cheeks was make-up!

His dismissal does not imply that Cynthia was actually plain: *candor* (8), 'shining fairness', simply denotes a different kind of beauty from the rosy blush he attributed to her. He substituted what he wished her to be for the way she represented herself, without ever being able to grasp the essence of her attraction for him. Even the moment of disillusionment reveals nothing essential about her: when he finally observes Cynthia's pallor, he still only sees make-up (quaesitus *candor*, 8), another version of 'what she is not'. From the peak of his fascination to the nadir of his disgust, the core object of his passions ultimately eludes him.

Something about Acanthis and Cynthia escapes Propertius' grasp and constitutes a source of fascination for him even after the objective properties of these women have either changed or been dismissed as the object-causes of his reactions. Not by accident, then, does 4. 5 link the careers of *lena* and mistress, though the connection jars his previous history of the affair. Propertius' indignation at Acanthis' stolen headband is symptomatic: he reacts to this petty larceny as though it epitomized all Acanthis' wrong to him—and so it does. Acanthis, the thief of

---

[22] Christopher Spelman (1994) has well analysed the workings of *objet a* in 2. 3, and my use of that poem depends upon his ground-breaking work.

baubles, appears more damningly in this poem as a 'thief of enjoyment', having 'stolen' Propertius' enjoyment of Cynthia the 'way it might have been' without the old woman's intervention.

Yet his rage at her 'theft' conceals the embarrassing secret that he never possessed what was allegedly taken from him: Cynthia-as-object lies forever beyond his—or anyone else's—grasp. Jacques-Alain Miller has expressed this inescapable human impasse as follows:

We know, of course, that the fundamental status of the object is to be always already snatched away by the Other. It is precisely this theft of enjoyment that we write down in shorthand as minus phi, the matheme of castration. The problem is apparently unsolvable as the Other is the Other in my interior.[23]

Miller's statement that the theft precedes any (external) thief turns upon Lacan's model of the subject as constructed around a fundamental lack imposed by language, by the ineluctable gap between the 'I' who speaks and the 'I' represented in speech.[24] Lacan illustrates this gap with his ingenious dismissal of the famous Liar's Paradox: the statement 'I am lying' is only a paradox, he remarks, if one does not realize that two 'I's are involved—the one who speaks, and the one represented by that speech—and only one of these is lying.[25] This gap or lack inevitably returns in human symbolization systems represented as some essential part of the subject, his most precious possession, alienated from him, rendering him metaphorically 'castrated'. Desire resulting from this aboriginal lack motivates a futile search for the object as if it were a missing part of the subject: desire turns ultimately upon a search for identity, for 'what is missing from *me*'.[26] In particular, Man's commerce with

---

[23] Jacques-Alain Miller, *Extimité*, unpub. lecture, Paris, 17 Nov. 1985; quoted in Zizek (1993) 203. Zizek quotes from one of the lectures in the course on *Extimité* that Miller gave over the course of the academic year 1985–6 in the Department of Psychoanalysis at the University of Paris VIII. The extremely condensed version of that course now translated into English (Miller 1988) does not contain the remarks quoted by Zizek.

[24] Lacan (1966) 691/(1977*b*) 286–7; Lacan (1973) 127/(1981) 139.

[25] Lacan (1973) 127–30/(1981) 138–42.

[26] Zizek (1993) 205 deftly illustrates the operation of this notion at the level of the polity as a whole with his remarks upon America's attitude toward Vietnam POWs (he credits William Warner's paper, 'Spectacular Action: Rambo, Reaganism, and the Cultural Articulation of the Hero', as his inspiration):

How the 'theft of enjoyment' (or, to use a Lacanian technical term, imaginary castration) functions as an extremely useful tool for analyzing today's ideological processes can be further exemplified by a feature of American ideology of the eighties: the obsessive idea that there might still be some American POWs alive in Vietnam, leading a miserable existence, forgotten by their own country. This obsession articulated itself in a series of macho-adventures in which a hero undertakes a solitary rescue mission (*Rambo II, Missing*

Woman as object of desire seeks to ground the identity 'Man' by construing Woman as His complement, His 'other half', as if the positions Man and Woman were interlocking identities founded on essence rather than mere signifiers defined only by difference.[27]

This search for complementarity ultimately bears upon the production of meaning per se, in so far as the signifiers Man and Woman represent in exemplary fashion the way language, like all symbolization systems (systems that Lacan collectively designates 'the Symbolic'), produces meaning through binary opposition. The way that the conceptualization of gender slips and slides, unable to ground the primary binary 'Man/Woman' in any pre-symbolic reality, epitomizes the inadequacy of the Symbolic as a whole: the Symbolic lacks the capacity to ground itself in a signifier that has an unassailable ontological status and is not defined purely through difference. Lacan's infamous aphorism 'the sexual relation does not exist' summarizes just this lack of any complementarity that would support essential identities, not only for Man and Woman, but for *any* signifier. Commerce between the sexes in particular rests, in Lacan's view, on dissimulating the lack of an essence to gender; hence he punningly equates the term *jouissance* ('enjoyment', but also 'orgasm') with 'non-meaning as such'.[28]

in Action). The underlying fantasy-scenario is far more interesting. It is as if down there, far away in the Vietnam jungle, America had lost a precious part of itself, had been deprived of an essential part of its very life substance, the essence of its potency; and because this loss became the ultimate cause of America's decline and impotence in the post-Vietnam Carter years, recapturing this stolen, forgotten part became an element of the Reaganesque reaffirmation of a strong America.

[27] The concept of *objet a* corresponds broadly to the contradictory logic that both Fowler and Ancona in this volume see as governing the poet/lover's relation to the Muse/beloved. Fowler and Ancona rightly perceive the Muse/beloved occupying a position both outside the poet/lover (as his desired object/*materia*) and inside him (she has no existence apart from his desire/his poetry). The Muse/beloved thus perfectly epitomizes the object that is a precious piece of the self and yet has been inexplicably stolen away by the Other. According to Ancona's reading of *Odes* 1. 22, Horace raises this view of love/poetry only in order to rewrite it along lines that assert the poet's integrity; Fowler's broader analysis of Latin Muses in general (and their Greek antecedents) marks Horace's efforts as both anomalous and a species of wishful thinking.

[28] On *jouissance* as non-meaning, see Lacan (1975), esp. the passages in which Lacan sets *jouissance* at odds with significance, the suspect representation of Woman, and experience for which there is no account ('Il y a une jouissance à elle, à cette *elle* qui n'existe pas et ne signifie rien. Il y a une jouissance à elle dont peut-être elle-même ne sait rien, sinon qu'elle l'éprouve—ça, elle le sait. Elle le sait, bien sûr, quand ça arrive', 69/74; 'Et de quoi jouit-elle [Sainte Thérèse]? Il est clair que le témoignage essentiel des mystiques, c'est justement de dire qu'ils l'éprouvent, mais qu'ils n'en savent rien', 70–1/76; 'Là où ça parle, ça jouit, et ça sait rien', 95/104). Illuminating discussions of *Séminaire XX*'s connections among *jouissance*, that which

Lacan's model of the subject of desire fits Propertius' self-construction as the perpetually frustrated lover-poet, who has always lost to another something essential to himself—his woman, his patrimony, his chance to be an epic poet.[29] More particularly, though, Lacan's sketch of the sexual non-relation as a grappling with non-meaning illuminates Propertius' repeated moments of impasse. Wherever he strives to grasp the nature of his relation to Cynthia, whether he stalks the source of its enchantment (2. 3) or its disappointment (3. 24), he grapples in vain to articulate something upon which signification cannot find a foothold, that 'falls outside of' the Symbolic. The impasse reduces him to saying, 'it is not that, nor yet that, nor that either . . .'.[30]

VI. THINGS FALL APART

None the less, Propertius avails himself of the only graceful way out of the dilemma created by the sexual non-relation when he reconfigures the impossibility of enjoyment—an impossibility founded on the fundamental status of the subject—as a prohibition. A third party (Acanthis) blocks his access to Cynthia: she sets the watchdog on him (73–4), advises his mistress against unprofitable liaisons (47–8, 54, 57–8), and urges the young woman to find wealthy lovers in order to coin her beauty into gain (49–53). Yet his portrait of the *lena* symptomatically conjures up the very essence of the impasse Acanthis glosses: the Symbolic can find no purchase on her as a phenomenon. We have already seen how Propertius' description of her wavers between extremes of power and weakness; he even seems uncertain whether she lives or has died. His record of her speech, too, sways giddily between high-style poetic

escapes significance, and non-knowledge may be found in Lee (1990) 171–99, and Copjec (1994) 201–36.

[29] As a representative sample of poems that detail losing his love to a rival, consider: 1. 8 (almost—Cynthia relents at the last moment), 2. 9, 2. 16, 4. 8. Propertius only explicitly mentions his patrimony's partial confiscation late in his work (4. 1. 126–30); however, his claims to poetic 'poverty' as a foil to Cynthia's 'greed' form a consistent thread throughout the corpus, especially as a combination that tempts his mistress toward a rival's riches (witness e.g. 1. 8, 2. 16, 2. 24, 3. 5, 3. 7, 3. 13). As for poetic talent, Propertius generally sketches himself (whether ironically or not) falling short of his more illustrious and ambitious epic predecessors and contemporaries, such as Ennius and Virgil (witness e.g. 2. 1, 2. 34, 3. 3, 3. 9, 4. 1). Elegy 3. 3 constructs the comparison explicitly as an opportunity taken from him, albeit gently: Apollo and Calliope combine forces to redirect his ambition to follow in Ennius' footsteps and shepherd him back to erotic elegy.

[30] Cf. Spelman (1994).

expression, learned allusions to mythology, and pungent vulgarities borrowed from comedy, mime, and everyday idiom.[31] Representations of Acanthis slide as if unanchored between the antitheses that found meaning (weakness/power; death/life; high style/low style), attesting that another logic impossible to capture in binary opposition governs her portrait: she exceeds the Symbolic as governed by 'reason' and its stepchild, 'common sense'. Around Acanthis, all attempts at symbolization fail; she figures the intrusion of another order into the Symbolic— the intrusion of the Real as that for which the Symbolic cannot account.

Propertius sketches the effects of this intrusion on quotidian expectations of cause and effect, the laws assumed to underpin the Symbolic, when he describes Acanthis' powers as a witch. For the most part, his material touches upon generic commonplaces—drawing down the moon, shape–changing, deceiving the wary—but includes a power puzzling in its vagueness, and precisely as such, appropriate to the Real-as-ineffable. *Quippe et, Collinas ad fossam moverit herbas,* | *stantia currenti diluerentur aqua* ('in fact, if she should toss herbs collected near the Colline gate into a ditch, things solidly fixed would dissolve in running water', 11–12). Camps and Richardson find this expression so enigmatic that they gloss it as power over green crops (*herbas*) and crops standing in the fields (*stantia*). However—as Camps scrupulously notes even while defending his reading—such a use of *stantia* has no parallel in extant Latin literature. The unease of two such sensitive readers should none the less give us pause; it indicates the disturbing implications of the distich's imprecision. *Stantia* embraces any solid, upright object whatsoever, a term all the more menacing for its lack of specificity. Propertius sketches a moment in which all the world's organization as conferred by the Symbolic melts away, leaving only the chaos of the Real. Matter forgets itself and the laws that govern it, as the permanent foundation of the world we know trickles through our fingers.[32]

---

[31] As commentators at least since Tränkle have remarked; Tränkle's is still the definitive analysis of the elegy's breathtaking amalgam of styles and diction, but Giulio Puccioni offers some further refinements (though his overall assessment of the poem is unfavourable and, to my mind, quite unjust). See Tränkle (1960) 68, 81, 105–8, 110–14, 117, 123, 127, 129–32, 140–1, 175–8; Puccioni (1979) 614–23.

[32] Propertius' picture has certain affinities with Lucretius' portrait of the world as it would be, were matter not made up of indestructible atoms: things could be destroyed by insubstantial forces, in the wink of an eye, without the relation of magnitude and appropriateness between cause and effect ordinarily observable in the world (*De rerum natura*, 1. 217–24, 238–49). The powers imputed to Acanthis realize this absurd state of affairs, in that Propertius alleges her magic to prevail against everything solid, without exception or discrimination.

Acanthis' 'hetaira-catechism' reproduces this fundamental derail-ment, in so far as it destroys any sense that Woman possesses a substan-tial core, something irreducible to be loved (or hated) *behind* all the observable features. Acanthis teaches her disciple various poses to grieve the lover, and a few gestures to enchant him as well; her counsel implies that neither coldness nor amiability from the beloved has any intrinsic basis whatsoever—the mistress merely performs whatever role momentarily advantages her. Acanthis thus reduces Woman to a series of strategically devised veils ultimately hiding . . . nothing. The old woman radically undermines the lover's fantasy of an inexpressibly precious substance hidden within the beloved that fascinates him, but that escapes causal explanation—the fantasy Propertius pursues so energetically in elegy 2. 3 and that underwrites the power of *objet a*. In so far as Acanthis shows the beloved to be devoid of substance, an image strategically composed to irritate or please, she threatens the *lover's* stable sense of self, too. His mistress can hardly be his complement if composed of airy nothings;[33] she cannot ground his identity either as lover, or as poet of her charms and irritations.[34] No wonder, then, that Propertius depicts Acanthis as a witch able to subvert nature and undo matter itself, so that the world dissolves in the face of her power. His extravagant claims have a personal application: the old woman under-mines *the* crucial *objet a*—the enchanting quiddity he imagines at the centre of his mistress' being—that justifies his poems and confirms his identity as poet, lover, and Man.

Acanthis' implied portrait of the 'ideal' hetaira has other unsettling implications that also draw a significant response from Propertius. Woman seen as a series of masks donned to complement Man reveals Her inadequate definition within the Symbolic: She emerges only through antithesis, as merely 'not-Man'. *Objet a* springs from this con-ceptual deficiency within the Symbolic, both marking and dissimulating whatever cannot be thought or spoken within the limits defined by the binary 'Man/Not-Man'. (This excess gives rise, for example, to the

---

[33] 'The *object small a* designates precisely the endeavour to procure for the subject a positive support of his being beyond the signifying representation; by way of the fantasy relation to *a*, the [divided and decentred] subject ($) acquires an imaginary sense of his "fullness of being", of what he "truly" is independently of what he is for others, i.e., notwithstanding his place in the intersubjective symbolic network': Zizek (1993) 266 n. 15. ('$' is the Lacanian grapheme for the divided subject.)

[34] Which is—as Maria Wyke (1989) 34 points out—her central function in elegiac discourse: 'The female is employed in the [elegiac] text only as a means to defining the male'.

question, What is Cynthia apart from her lover's constructions of her?—
an enigma that 3. 24's petulant retraction of his flatteries engages, but
signally fails to solve.) *Objet a* provides a 'screen' for fantasy that sets
symbolization in motion, as when the lover justifies his attachment by
imagining an ineffable siren's core to his beloved. But while Acanthis
insists on Woman as insubstantial fantasy, eluding reification,
Propertius' tenacious hatred of the *lena* denies the dilemma in which her
revelation places him. He disavows her construction of Cynthia as
cipher by attributing to Acanthis *herself* an *objet a*: his hatred insists that
there *is* 'something' in Woman, an essential kernel that can provoke
his loathing even when (as we have seen) every one of Her objective
properties that irritated him has disappeared.

   Yet the structure of the poem itself reveals the logical weakness of this
attempt to find a tangible enemy. Even Acanthis cannot bear the entire
burden of Propertius' resentment; he must construct a further despoiler,
in the form of the putative 'rich rival lover'. Though proffered as the
principal thief of enjoyment within the poem, Acanthis has remarkably
ascetic tastes. Even in her heyday as Cynthia's welcome confidante,
Acanthis' tepid attitude towards riches reveals her *contemptus mundi*.
While haranguing Cynthia to secure all possible luxuries, she herself
scorns antique paintings as mere 'rotting pictures' (*putria signa*, 24). By
contrast, the rich rival to Propertius she urges Cynthia to cultivate fully
embodies the blissful enjoyment the old woman supposedly bars; the
rival supplements Acanthis' role as prohibiter. As in previous poems
devoted to the subject of Cynthia's wealthy admirers, 4. 5 erects the rival
as a figure of excess. He, unique among subjects, really *does* have access
to bliss: his money will buy him anything, most particularly the heaven
that Cynthia's favours constitute in Propertius' eyes. In 4. 5, the rival's
excess even manifests itself in marks of violence his mistress bears;
Acanthis advises:

> semper habe morsus circa tua colla recentis
> litibus alterius [alternis *Barber*] quos putet esse datos.
>
> (39–40)

always have fresh lovebites around your neck; let him think these inflicted by
disputes with another man!

Yet notwithstanding these physical signs of the rival's existence, the *lena*
speaks of him chiefly as an effect of perspective. Propertius' three earlier
books treated Cynthia's other admirers as solid facts discovered through

his jealous watchfulness. By contrast, Acanthis emphasizes playing up to erotic jealousy with bruises that may be thought (*putet*) to be from a rival's violent attentions. The old woman's advice reduces the rival to a clever stratagem; she forces a rereading of his assumed presence in the previous books. Now the rival appears to be a mere sign, an *objet a* in his own right whose features the fantasies of others will fill out. Not only will Propertius as jealous suitor obligingly lend the rival materiality, but so shall we, the readers who have eavesdropped on the imagined affair between Propertius and Cynthia during the course of three books. Ironically, the rival proves a perversely fecund source of imagination to poet-lover and reader alike—a diabolic 'Muse' in his own right!

VII. LOVE BEFORE THE BAR

Yet Acanthis' curious terminology in sketching the rival as putative source of the mistress's bruises emphasizes his status as a schematically necessary, but empty, place-holder in an erotic triangle. Acanthis describes a quarrel with such a lover as a *lis* ('dispute') where one would expect the more usual term *rixa* ('brawl'). As Camps and Richardson both note, *lis* does not point to physical struggle, so would be unlikely to cause the bruises that must appear about Cynthia's neck.[35] *Lis* at root means 'lawsuit'; it differs from *rixa* not only in abjuring physical violence, but in being a contention enacted for the eyes of a third party— the judge or jury appointed to hear the trial. A *lis* deduced from the marks of the putative wealthy rival sketches the triangular frame assumed by the sexual non-relation even in the absence of a tangible other.

Invoking the idea of a lawsuit in this context points to Law's surprising imbrication with the realm of erotic license figured by the rival. Law springs from construing enjoyment not as impossible, but as laid under prohibition: Freud outlined as much in *Totem and Taboo*, an essay that traces Law to the (primordial) Father as agent of prohibition, a role familiar from Freud's earlier writings on the Oedipus complex. His mythical history sketches a tribe's powerful leader and father who, by keeping all the women of the tribe to himself, inspires resentment in his

---

[35] L. Richardson (1977) ad 4. 5. 40; Camps (1965) ad 39–40. Yardley (1976) argues convincingly that *lis* must be taken here as a quarrel, as against Fedeli's (1965, ad 40) and Camps's interpretation of the word as rough sexual play. Yardley does not, however, smooth the difficulty of linking *lis* to physical force.

follower-sons. The sons eventually rebel and murder him, but remorse leads them to renounce the reward their deed has gained—the women; hence the inception of Law as the incest taboo.[36]

The dubious historicity of Freud's account does not concern us, only its structure as a necessary supplement to his earlier formulation of the Oedipus complex. Freud's essay shows how Law summarizes the sexual non-relation as Man's and Woman's relation, not to each other (that would be the 'sexual relation' that does not exist), but of each to a third term, to the murdered 'Father of Enjoyment', the *one* being imagined as 'having had everything'. The Father's murder conveniently relegates him to the realm of absence, while the sons' renunciation of the women their patricide won them reconstrues enjoyment—the fantasized, impossible excess the greedy tyrant embodied—as something voluntarily renounced. Killing the Father thereby conveniently transforms impossibility into prohibition. Read according to the same logic, the rival's punctual, self-satisfied appearance signals hope for Propertius, as the obverse of the poet-lover's fantasy. The other man's wildly passionate enjoyment of Cynthia, fierce enough to leave her bruised, paints that bliss as only circumstantially beyond Propertius' reach—just a matter of finances and luck, really—not as intrinsically unobtainable. The rival's imagined transports also beguile Propertius with fantasies of Cynthia as the nonpareil mistress and Muse, the woman who will underwrite his identity as lover and poet—as if Woman really *did* exist as something solider than just 'not-Man'.

Rewriting relations between the sexes as a lawsuit instead of a brawl underlines the degree to which the assumed binary, complementary relationship between Man and Woman is aboriginally sundered by a third term. The party occupying that third place can be wealthy rival, hostile procuress, or whoever. He or she only marks the place of the Other in the affair—ultimately, the place of the Symbolic and the limitations it imposes on relations between subjects. Like the formalities of some interminable trial, the Other promises but prevents a 'resolution' of the impasse between Man and Woman. Such a resolution is impossible, because it would depend upon abolishing the lack that produces the alternately poisonous and beguiling fantasies that frustrate relations between the sexes; that very lack defines the subject, so resolution would mean destroying the subject. The Acanthis elegy records some of the feints and stratagems organized about this impasse.

---

[36] Freud (1953–73) 13: 1–162, esp. 140–61.

VIII. OWED TO WOMAN

The tenacious undead mark the failure of such stratagems—and Acanthis as 'sister' to the restless ghosts of Cynthia and Cornelia prompts another word about the Return of the Dead here. As the foundational revenant elegy in Book 4, 4. 5 provokes a simple, even naïve, question: why *do* the dead return? Lacan has put this query to ancient texts (such as the *Antigone*) and elicited a deceptively simple answer: because they were not properly buried—something went wrong with their obsequies.[37] Zizek aptly summarizes Lacan's meditations on the phenomenon: 'the return of the dead is a sign of a disturbance in the symbolic rite, in the process of symbolization; the dead return as collectors of some unpaid symbolic debt'.[38] Propertius wishes just such a symbolic omission on Acanthis when he hopes that her grave will be adorned with a broken-necked wine-jar (*sit tumulus lenae curto vetus amphora collo*, 75)—a vessel incompletely destroyed, as opposed to the more thoroughgoing breakage required by funeral rites. Breaking a vessel associated with the dead person symbolically releases her or his spirit from its earthly abode, by getting rid of familiar objects that might otherwise entice the shade to linger among the living. By contrast, the wine-jar Acanthis' grave will sport still retains its essential integrity and usefulness—its symbolic efficacy is reversed.[39] Marked by this sign, her posthumous existence winds around a repetitive, futile attachment to a world Acanthis cannot leave behind: the incompletely broken wine-jar summarizes the sins of omission Acanthis' advice to Cynthia unveils. The conceptual lacunae she counters, that would rarefy the elegiac mistress into pure self-denial, all ultimately revolve around the lack of any signifier for Woman's desire in a system implicitly centred on the signifier 'Man'; that omission returns as 'unpaid debt', haunting elegy with its shadowy, but persistent, complaint.

This fundamental omission in Woman's representation renders

[37] Lacan had already articulated this point clearly in analysing *Hamlet* during the course of *Séminaire VI*, 'Désir et ses Interprétations', the year before he addressed *Antigone* (Lacan (1981–3), 30–1/(1977a), 37–9), but he returned to and expanded his ideas in the later seminar (Lacan (1986) 324–5, 329/(1992) 278–9, 283).

[38] Zizek (1991) 23.

[39] For the breaking of vessels as a rite to ensure the dead person's release from her or his earthly haunts, see Fedeli (1987), esp. 118–20. See also Lombardi Satriani and Meligrana (1982) esp. 172–5. On the broken-necked wine-jar as a useful object—worth making to order, in fact—see Cato, *Agr.* 88.

legible the fact that 4. 5, like 4. 7 and 4. 11, turns upon Law, support and subset of the Symbolic, in its specific manifestation as the ethical judgement of Woman. While Cynthia in 4. 7 brands as pure slander Propertius' poetry about her as unfaithful whore, and paints an Underworld that eschews any simplistic distinction between so-called Good and Evil women, Cornelia in 4. 11 justifies her life in a way that calls into question the very ethical codes imposed upon her as a *matrona*. Acanthis in 4. 5 anticipates both scepticisms, casting doubt equally on the criteria that putatively condemn and ennoble Woman, when she rejects as just a poor man's scam the *beau idéal* of impoverished fidelity that Propertius manufactures for Cynthia; the *lena* shrewdly turns his own lines against him when she quotes the Monobiblos. Acanthis, like Cynthia and Cornelia, stages the place of the Law as radically empty and aligns herself instead with the Real: she refuses the customary graceful dissimulations of Woman's inadequate representation and insists instead upon the 'inconvenient' ruptures in that fiction. If the Symbolic cannot adequately account for Woman, her poem implies, it can hardly judge Her. Acanthis 'returns' from the dead as the Muse who insists that her poet tell the *whole* story.[40]

[40] A different and more detailed version of this essay appears as ch. 5 in my book *The Politics of Desire: Propertius IV*; the shared material is reprinted here by kind permission of the University of California Press.

An A-musing Tale: Gender, Genre, and Ovid's Battles with Inspiration in the *Metamorphoses*

Alison Sharrock

Poetry about inspiration is self-referential, even self-performative: how can you deny, or claim, or even invoke inspiration, without irony? The claim in such denial might be for 'originality'—that the poetry comes 'from inside' not from something 'out there', but it is a claim which the text itself figures as self-refuting. The language of inspiration is part of a traditional discursive nexus through which poets play out the tensions involved in the poetic process as both creative and derivative. This essay is particularly concerned with inspiration as relationship. That may sound very friendly, liberal, and positive, but relationships can of course be sites of battle as well as co-operation, and a notion of inspiration as struggle also underpins this paper. The *Metamorphoses* is a story about stories, patterns, paradigms, which are themselves constantly metamorphic. There are many possible manifestations of the relationship between poet and muse: identity, desire, hatred, struggle, which itself works at least two ways, for the poet may struggle to achieve inspiration, or he may struggle for independence—or even both at once. Much of this chapter sees inspiration in violent, forceful images, appropriately for epic, the forceful genre: for I suggest that the role of the Muse is inseparable from the challenge of genre.[1] Ovid is constantly tempting us into denying the epicness of his poem, while at the same time refusing our possibility of doing so, and the Muse contributes to this battle. On the one hand, her normal epic power and function is denied, but, on the

---

[1] See Laird, Ancona, and Rosati, in this volume for the entanglement of the Muse with questions of genre.

other hand, Ovid needs 'inspiration', needs a Muse-figure, in order to achieve the poetic and specifically epic status for which he bids. He is struggling both ways.

The classic way to figure inspiration is in the form of a divine Muse— or rather nine Muses. The nine daughters of Mnemosyne and Zeus have been inspiring poets at least since Hesiod met them wandering on Mount Helicon.[2] In the archaic Greek world, the activity of the Muses in poetic creation is an expression of the mythic world-view, through which states and events are 'explained' as cosmic as well as human, just as the path of a spear is both cosmically and humanly directed.[3] Is this 'just a poetic conceit' for moderns like Ovid? I think not.[4] If we consider what is at stake for a sophisticated poet in calling on a muse, I suggest it would go something like this: (1) since the poet is necessarily 'quoting' earlier invocations, it serves to place him in a long tradition of using this kind of vocabulary for talking about inspiration, and indeed it actually *performs* the inspiration, in the sense that it is precisely through such intertextual activity that poetry comes into being;[5] (2) that tradition allows the text to claim a cosmic authority which may be based as much in intertextuality as it is in religion; (3) a point not always mentioned but to my mind particularly important—it enacts the fetishizing and objectification of 'poetry' as 'woman' (goddess and whore) which is subliminal in so much of the discourse of poetics.[6] Our questions for the *Metamorphoses*, then, go something like this: Does Ovid call on divine

[2] On this founding moment see also Spentzou in the Introduction to this volume.

[3] By 'explanation' here I do not mean anything which literal-minded moderns would want to call explanation, but rather a vocabulary for talking about the world, in the manner of the Homeric 'double motivation', by which actions are explained both as the will of the gods and as the responsibility of the human agent. See Taplin (1992) 99–100; 104–5; 207–8. He is particularly concerned with the question of blame, which is not relevant to our case. The point is that such kinds of explanation make perfectly good sense to the archaic mind. On this, see also Thalmann (1984), esp. 139–40.

[4] Several contributors to this volume see the Roman Muses as functioning primarily in the manner of a 'poetic conceit'. I would suggest that the activity of the Muses, even in the sophisticated world of the Augustan and imperial poets, raises the same questions about 'belief' and multiplicity of level as are raised more generally by Roman religion. On the question of belief and fictionality in contemporary attitudes to epic see Feeney (1991) 5–56 and (1998) 22–5. Questions of belief and fictionality are discussed in the Introduction to this volume, too; they are also central for Fowler's gendered approach, in this volume.

[5] See Cavarero in this volume; also Fowler, Ancona, and Rosati touch, in passing, upon performed nature of inspiration. As Gianpiero Rosati has pointed out (in conversation), the Statian phrase *longa retro series* (*Theb.* 1. 7) is particularly expressive of this point.

[6] The function of the Muse, and indeed of poetry generally, in this way, as goddess and whore, is crucial to Henderson's contribution to this volume.

inspiration for his epic? Does his song come from the Muse? On what authority does he speak? Who or what gives him the right? These questions imply the level at which the poem presents itself as an epic. Underlying this level (and perhaps subverting its epic pretensions) is a question of power: Who controls? Who makes meaning? The epic pose gives authority to the Muse, and therefore denies room for the reader or even the poet to contribute to the production of meaning.[7] Ways in which Ovid uses the Muses for the epic pose, and also distances himself from them partially to undermine that pose, will be considered below.[8] When Ovid disclaims divine inspiration, he seems to claim authority for himself; but in the midst of his bid for independence, he also opens the possibility of its undoing, because if he is not 'divine' then we can challenge him, and the reader gets a say. The very claim to personal, rather than external, authority, then, may at some level be self-refuting, because it allows for the contesting of that authority.

Let us look for a moment at the Muse as goddess and whore. Her relationship with the poet is sometimes overtly, more often covertly, shot through with erotic undertones. She includes hints of the 'goddess courting a mortal man' (a situation which often uses rhetoric similar to that of an older man courting a younger one[9]), and also elements of the passive desired object, as I will discuss further below. This is especially clear in the exile poetry, where the Muse is both loved and hated. Even when not eroticized, the relationship between poet and 'Muse' is a gendered one. Poets are practically all men, and the 'poet's voice' is a male voice: Muses are all women. In this regard, the ancient and modern practice of calling Sappho 'the tenth Muse' should be deeply troubling. This practice is something which, with no doubt the best of intentions, has been perpetrated on women writers from Sappho's day to our own. Why it should trouble us, I suggest, is because it has the effect, albeit subliminal, of crossing out or undermining the active creative function of women poets.[10] It is only a small step from calling a woman poet 'a Muse' to constructing her as 'poetry' rather than 'poet', as the 'blank

[7] The issues of truth, authority, and the potential instability of knowledge are crucial to the concerns of this volume: see Spentzou's Introduction, esp. Part I.

[8] On the general point of 'disclaiming divine inspiration in Ovid' see La Penna (1979) and Miller (1986).

[9] Dover (1978) 172.

[10] Williamson (1995) 15 notes the way that calling Sappho the 'tenth muse' 'may also indicate a difficulty in thinking of real women as poets'. Calling all later female poets (particularly classical and 'classical' ones) 'a second Sappho' also—it is part of the same thing—contributes to the tendency to see women as all the same. See also Williamson (1995) 22–3; Greer (1995).

page' who 'is a poem' rather than being someone who writes a poem.[11] The classic example of this tendency is the epigram of Antipater of Thessalonica, in which nine women poets are 'celebrated' as the nine Muses. Ovid's (if so it be) strange last single *Heroid* letter, from Sappho to Phaon, is symptomatic of a similar inability to see a women poet as creative agent rather than created object.[12] Roman elegy, with its beloved as Muse and poetry, and its one woman poet, Sulpicia, is particularly prone to this way of thinking.[13] The desire and the power games between poet and poetry expressed in the obsession with 'my Muse' (which we will see particularly in Ovid's exile poetry) are not just an inert metaphor or a religious experience, but rather dramatize (perhaps unintentionally) the attitude of the male poet towards his creative source—as something sexualized and objectifying, a fetishization of 'poetry'.[14]

The desire which the poet feels for his inspiring deity might seem easily to contribute to the construction of his masculine authority as a

[11] Gubar (1982).

[12] Rosati's (1996) reading of this poem, which leads in the direction of authenticity, argues that Ovid (the ventriloquist) constructs the voice of this poem as elegiac and female, as a comment on the inherently feminine nature of the elegiac voice. But, as he rightly points out, the femininity of the elegiac voice is a masculine construction. The feminization or otherwise of the speaker's voice is a big question for the *Heroides*, in which the work of Effie Spentzou and (differently) Rosati (1992) needs to be considered.

[13] Holzberg (1999) argues that Sulpicia is a fiction. The whole of [Tib]. 3 is written by (one?) Pseudo-Tibullus, and purports to be the pre-history to the real works of Tibullus. Most modern readers respond to at least some of the poems as 'authentically female'. See Flaschenriem (1999) for a typical recuperative reading of Sulpicia. On the more general issue of the elegiac beloved as 'muse', particularly in the sense of being an embodiment of poetry, see Wyke (1987b) and (1989). The idea that the beloved-muse is internal to the poet, as well as being at another level external, is examined in this volume by Ancona, Fowler, and Rosati.

[14] The common form of book title as something like *The Mannered* (or *Maculate*) *Muse* has tendencies in this direction: not that I am suggesting that such titles should be avoided, just asking for awareness of their potential. It is true, of course, that not all inspiring deities are Muses, and not all are female. There is Apollo, who often accompanies the Muses; there is Bacchus; and there is Augustus. In these cases, however, the kind of inspiration they give the poet, and the poet's attitude to them, is quite different. It is, for instance, much more specific. Poets, particularly Ovid, frequently talk about 'my muse' as if it were something not wholly separate from themselves. Prop. 2. 1. 35, 2. 10. 10, 2. 12. 22. This clearly links closely with *mea Cynthia* and *mea puella*, especially in the phrase *quando scripta puella mea est* (2. 10. 8), on which see Wyke (1987b). They can even do so when using a personal name of a muse, for example *Thalia mea* (Ov. *Trist.* 4. 10. 56, 5. 9. 31), *mea Calliope* (*Trist.* 2. 568). But I don't think a poet ever talked about 'my Apollo', or envisaged his Augustan poetry as 'my Augustus'. Men, whether divine or imperial or otherwise, are not subject to appropriation in such a way. Ovid does describe Apollo as *noster* at *Rem.* 251, but this is significantly lacking in the appropriative ring of *meus*, and refers to Apollo's role as healer in the *Remedia Amoris* as well as god of poetry. Stories like the invention of the pan-pipes in *Met.* 1. 689–712 are indicative of the same tendency.

speaker and creator of meaning (performative desiring being figured as male). The gendering of the Muse is, I think, crucial to our understanding of Ovid's battles with inspiration in the *Metamorphoses* (and throughout his corpus), but it is not a straightforward gendering, for although the Muse is whore she is also goddess, with power to speak and to undermine the masculinity of the epic poet. It is crucial in the persona of the epic poet that he is figured as a receptacle for the divine song which comes from the Muses. He himself is a channel, a mouthpiece, self-effacing, invisible, a voice speaking another's story in another's words.[15] This construction of the epic poet as 'mouthpiece' for another's song seems to hint at an inversion of the normal gendered relation (and power-relation) between man and woman, poet and Muse. If the singer is the channel of the Muses, then the masculinity of his poetic voice is undermined, feminized by its depowerment. The bard is not a powerful agent who stamps his control on the meaning of his material, but rather the purpose of the epic voice is to speak for someone else: it is all concentrated on the mouth, and the one who controls what goes into and comes out of the mouth has power. Epic poets have presented themselves as 'mouths' since Homer expressed the need for ten mouths and tongues to recite the ships before Troy (*Il.* 2. 489–90).[16] Virgil moved up by an order of magnitude, requiring a hundred mouths (*Georg.* 2. 43) to sing the praises of Octavian. The Sibyl's hundred-mouthed cave in *Aen.* 6 must be a continuation of Virgil's earlier self-construction as mouth. While performative political speaking is a 'male' thing, the mouth is often seen as a 'female' thing.[17] So if the epic poet loses control of his mouth to another, he loses something of manly autarky.

Before we look at this gendered relationship more closely in Ovid, it might be useful to consider an extreme version of the pattern in that particularly strong intertext, Virgil's *Aeneid*.[18] With the genders tellingly

[15] Or rather, it is part of the epic persona to play that role. The fact that the epic poet also has a role as speaking voice and weaver of his own song does not undermine this point.

[16] Strictly speaking, Homer says that without the aid of the Muses he could not do it even *if* he had ten mouths and a tireless voice and a heart of bronze. See Minton (1960) and (1962), and Fowler in this volume.

[17] See Fitzgerald (1995) for an excellent discussion of how mouths function in poetic and sexual discourse, and how the mouth may be a site for conflict over gender and control. I said that 'speaking is male': this should be nuanced by noting that it is speaking in the public world, speaking with a purpose, which is 'male'. 'Talking', or still more 'chatting', is generally presented as female (a female vice). Remember that history and oratory are the really manly genres.

[18] On the issues of masculinity and autarky, and the explicit connection with the Sibyl and Virgil, see Fowler and his brilliant closing paragraph.

inverted, such is the pattern produced by Virgil's *vates* at Cumae. The various prophets in the *Aeneid*, mouths of the gods as they are, are all symbols or substitutes for the poet himself, but the Sibyl, whose poetic prophecy consumes her and flows through her without her control but to her great pain, images Virgil in a particularly close way.[19] When the poet plays 'sibyl', then, he becomes a woman, a tortured, agonized woman who speaks the words of Apollo (playing 'muse') because she must, when she is forced by a kind of prophetic rape to accept the god's domination and to open her mouth and the hundred mouths of her cave (6. 76–82) to allow his words to pass.[20]

Such a powerful presentation of the poet's subjugation to his inspiration might seem to have little resonance in the *Metamorphoses*. It is, after all, in large part the eliding and denial of the Muse which makes Ovid's poem a-musing, or is it a-mused?—as I shall discuss further below. But there is one tale in which the epic force of the 'Muse' is triumphant, her will is imposed on the depowered and emasculated poet, and her desire for him is fulfilled. His desire for her, on the other hand, against which he struggles, is fulfilled in the final subjugation of her personality—and her desire—into his. In this case, we have not literal muse and poet, but mythic material with poetic symbolism: the story of Salmacis and Hermaphroditus.[21]

The story is one of those told by the Minyeides. As ever, the frame and the framing narrator of this metamorphic story contribute to its

---

[19] Ovid's Sibyl, in his 'little *Aeneid*', is a classic Ovidian storyteller telling her tales to lighten their journey, and finally ending up as just a voice herself. Paschalis (1997) 209–10 brings out the connections between mouths, penetration, prophecy, and the deliverance of Aeneas, but passes over the violence and pain involved in this process.

[20] See Fowler in this volume, and cf. Spentzou in the Introduction, II, where she makes the exciting suggestion that if the Sibyl had been allowed to speak her own words, we might have had a very different *Aeneid*. Our readings have different emphases: I am looking at the feminizing of the bardic persona through the Sibyl's subjection to Apollo, while Spentzou is concerned to express the awakening of the 'Muse's' female consciousness which brings her to clash with Apollo. These complementary readings show the blend of active and passive in the business of inspiration and writing.

[21] See Labate's (1993) excellent discussion of this surprisingly neglected story, and in particular his emphasis on the capacity of Ovidian language to slip between the literal and the metaphorical. On this story more generally, in particular its afterlife in the Renaissance, see also the discussion of Bate (1993). The reading I shall offer is a metapoetic one. Lepick (1981) reads the story of Hermaphroditus as a story of castration—men will be semi-men, more than they are half-man and half-woman. The parody of the story, especially in Renaissance English texts, is itself also an act of castration—because the loss of bits involved in parody is itself a figure of castration. See also Nugent's (1990) telling analysis of gendered aspects of the tale.

meaning,[22] for these spinning and weaving storytellers create a locus in which poetry and its relationship with poetic authority is foregrounded, and an atmosphere in which a poetic element in their stories might be expected. While everyone else is celebrating the godhead of Bacchus, the daughters of Minyas refuse to acknowledge his divinity.[23] Primly ignoring the wild festivities outside, they concentrate on their work as weavers. Although this wool-working, of itself, signifies appropriately modest feminine behaviour, the wild, transgressive, erotic nature of the tales which the women tell to lighten the work raises problems and contradictions in their self-presentation as too respectable for Bacchic inspiration. Moreover, their 'work of Minerva' is presented in language which is redolent with the vocabulary of Augustan poetics.[24]

> aut ducunt lanas aut stamina pollice versant
> aut haerent telae famulasque laboribus urgent.
> e quibus una levi deducens pollice filum . . .

> (*Met.* 4. 34–6)

Either they draw forth the wool or they turn the threads with the thumb, or they stick at the loom and urge the slave-girls to their tasks. One of them, spinning out the thread with light thumb . . .

It is hard to resist the poetic significance of a speaker 'drawing out the thread with light thumb' as she begins her tale.[25] That sister kicks off with the story of Pyramus and Thisbe, which she chooses as being not *vulgaris* ('commonly known').[26] Since she speaks *lana sua fila sequente*

---

[22] It is essential, and also impossible, to look at the frame when reading any story in the *Metamorphoses*. The decision as to where to place the frame, which could be anywhere from just the story itself (if one can identify that) to the whole fifteen books, or even beyond on to a vast range of *Metamorphic* intertexts, is an act of reading. I try to consider this kind of intra-textual strategy in *Intratextuality*: Sharrock and Morales (2000).

[23] We should, of course, muse on the significance of a set of sisters telling stories. These sisters are themselves 'muses', of a sort, who tell stories about 'muses' (again, of a sort). This is because singing/creating is a Bacchic trap, whether it is 'for' or 'against' the god. On the weaving and spinning of these sisters see Rosati (1999a).

[24] It is thus redolent, of course, because the language of Augustan poetics has appropriated the language of weaving, rather than the other way round. On the Minyeides as narrators see Janan (1994b), who argues that the Minyeides do not resist desire so much as pose the question of a gendered desire. They are singers of transgressive tales, in contrast to their apparent respectability. Janan sees as specifically 'feminine' the way in which the Minyeides transmute not only these tales but even public values into private pleasure. The tales are too delicate to be called either straightforwardly prudish or prurient, but the women 'transcend the conditions of their bondage—such as Woman's imposed duty to weave—for private pleasure' (437).

[25] For *deducere* as a programmatic term, see Hinds (1987a) 18–21.

[26] This is probably not an Ovidian joke. It is *vulgaris* to us, because Shakespeare took it from Ovid and spread it around.

('with the wool following its threads', 4. 54) it is hard not to think of the narrative thread with which the reader constantly battles in this poem. The last sister to speak, Alcithoe, is the one who concerns us, however, and she also makes a claim for originality in her tale. Like the first, the last casts about among the possibilities (metamorphic and transgressive stories) before choosing a tale marked out *dulci ... novitate* ('by sweet novelty', 4. 284). These women know a lot of wild tales, and demand the right to make their own choices and to sing with 'sweet novelty'.[27] But the god of wild inspiration is not going to let them get away with it: after Alcithoe's performance, the women and their looms are entwined in ivy and vines, the house is thrown into confusion, and finally the Minyeides become bats.[28]

Alcithoe tells the story of the son of Hermes and Aphrodite, who acquired a dual gender when he was raped by the nymph Salmacis, in a sexual encounter which achieved the performatively self-destructive goal of total union, as Labate (1993) and differently Bate (1993) discuss.[29] When the story begins, Hermaphroditus is clearly on a Quest, with all the initiatory implications of that. He is filled with desire to see unknown places, unknown rivers:

> ignotis errare locis, ignota videre
> flumina gaudebat studio minuente laborem
>
> (*Met.* 4. 294–5)

He rejoiced to wander in unknown lands, to see unknown rivers, his eagerness lessening the effort.

A clear pool offers itself to him, full of vibrant creativity and erotic promise. The nymph of the place, no follower of virgin Diana but an experienced, forceful, and many-wiled woman, desires Hermaphroditus as he desires her pool, and addresses him in unmistakably epic terms. She plays out the role of Odysseus, almost quoting his meeting with Nausicaa on the shore of Scheria (*Od.* 6. 149–57):[30]

> tum sic orsa loqui 'puer o dignissime credi
> esse deus, seu tu deus es, potes esse Cupido;

---

[27] See Spentzou in this volume on the Muses' own needs and desires.

[28] Would it be fanciful to note that bats are about as far away from a poetic animal as you can get?

[29] On this story, and Renaissance readings and renditions of it, as encapsulating an image of the marriage union of spiritual equals, 'how sex should be' and even sexual equality within a patriarchal structure, see Bate (1993) 61–5. The violence of the rape and the subjugation of each member by the other, seem played down by the Renaissance readers.

[30] This point is noticed also by Labate (1993).

> sive es mortalis, qui te genuere, beati,
> et frater felix, et fortunata profecto
> si qua tibi soror est, et, quae dedit ubera, nutrix.
> Sed longe cunctis longeque beatior illa,
> si qua tibi sponsa est, si quam dignabere taeda!
>
> (*Met.* 4. 320–6)

She thus rising to speak, 'oh boy worthy to be believed a god, if you are a god, you could be Cupid; or if you are mortal, blessed are those who bore you, and happy is your brother, and certainly fortunate your sister if you have one, and the nurse who gave you suck. But far more blessed that all these is she, if there is any, who is engaged to you, if you deem any worthy of your marriage-torch!'

When her attentions are rebuffed, Salmacis pretends to leave. Hermaphroditus, overcome with desire for the pool, leaps in; Salmacis, overcome with desire for Hermaphroditus, leaps in after him, and locks him in her embrace. A struggle ensues. Finally, the two bodies become one, and the duality of identity which Hermaphroditus had inherited from his parents is fulfilled.

I suggest this as one pattern for the relationship of Muse and poet. The setting is almost overdetermined with poetic connotations: the clear pool, surrounded by 'living' turf, the chance meeting of wandering mortal and goddess,[31] while the well-known scene of poetic initiation in such a landscape is not hard to see figured also as sexual initiation.

> videt hic stagnum lucentis ad imum
> usque solum lymphae. non illic canna palustris
> nec steriles ulvae nec acuta cuspide iunci:
> perspicuus liquor est; stagni tamen ultima vivo
> caespite cinguntur semperque virentibus herbis
>
> (*Met.* 4. 297–301)

He sees a pool of water clear to the very bottom. There no marshy reed grows nor sterile sedge nor rushes with sharp thorn. The water is completely see-through; but the edges of the pool are ringed with living turf and ever-green grass.

---

[31] For water, e.g. Prop. 3. 1; for meeting the Muses, see Hes. *Theog.* 22–5; Prop. 3. 3; Gallus in Virg. *Ecl.* 6 and 10 and cf. Ross (1975) 119–22. For *caespite vivo* see Hor. *Carm.* 3. 8. 4, where it is the setting for his own learned musings. The *locus amoenus*, as is well known, sets the scene for poetic inspiration. See e.g. Hinds (1987a) 33–5 (and *passim*). One non-Hippocrenic connection between Muses, inspiration, and water comes at Hor. *Carm.* 4. 3. 10–12: *sed quae Tibur aquae fertile praefluunt | et spissae nemorum comae | fingent Aeolio carmine nobilem*. The poem is a hymn to Melpomene.

The clarity of the pool expresses its untouched state and is heavily charged with sexual promise. If a poetic reading is entertained, it is also suggestive of the 'pure fountain' from which the good poet drinks in order to gain his inspiration and write his poetry (Callim. *Hymn* 2, to Apollo, Prop. 3. 1, etc.). We might then remember that Hermaphroditus (like Alcithoe) was seeking novelty. He finds it in this *fons et origo*[32] of poetic creativity, and yet what he finds is 'poetic' precisely because it is not 'original'. The 'pure fountain' can only inspire because it has inspired poets before, just as Propertius wants to drink from the unsullied waters from which Callimachus and Philetas had drunk. The contradiction between originality and tradition is inherent in the whole notion of inspiration. For Hermaphroditus, however, the tension rises still further, for this 'sweet novelty' will take him straight back to the *fons et origo* of all literature—Homer. If there is one unmistakable allusion in this passage it is that to Odysseus and Nausicaa. The allusion takes him also specifically to epic, despite the light 'Callimachean' tone of the Minyeides' song and this meeting.[33] With this in mind, we might look back to the beginning of Alcithoe's song, which she introduces as an *aetion* to explain the enervating force of Salmacis' water:[34]

> unde sit infamis, quare male fortibus undis
> Salmacis enervet tactosque remolliat artus,
> discite! Causa latet, vis est notissima fontis
>
> (*Met.* 4. 285–7)

How it came to be infamous, why Salmacis enervates and softens limbs that are touched by her harmfully strong waters, learn! The cause lies hid, but the power of the spring is well known.

Salmacis' waves (I presume *unda* really just means water here) are *fortes* and have *vis*, both big strong words which convey a sense of her epic power. It is a paradoxical power, however, because of the effect it has on anyone who comes into contact with her: they are *male fort[es]* waves, 'badly strong', and she *remolliat*, softens and emasculates, the limbs of those who touch her. The argument I hope to derive from this font is similar to that from Virgil's Sibyl, that the bardic persona of the epic poet

---

[32] See Hinds (1987a) 6 for the programmatic force of these terms.

[33] Cameron's important book (1995) stresses the need for nuance in our distinctions between the categories of 'epic' and 'Callimachean', but that does not stop Ovid's generic games, as Hinds pointed out some years ago (1987a).

[34] For the story as an *aetion* see Myers (1994) 79–80.

is emasculated through his connection with the overpowering Muse of epic.

There is something rather unusual about Salmacis' story, however. What we see here which is not otherwise part of our experience of these things is the *Muse*'s desire. This perhaps is the 'sweet novelty' of the story. We normally see the Muse only in the second person, only in so far as she relates to the poet, and from his point of view. Here, however, she speaks her own desire.[35] That desire will overwhelm any man, who will leave her pool with his masculinity subverted. Let this be a warning to you: writing epic may be emasculating. Her triumph is short-lived, however, and this is part of what it is to be a Muse, for in the moment of possession she is subsumed into the personality of her poet. The two become one, *nec duo sunt, sed forma duplex* ('and they are not two, but a double form', 4. 378), but the 'one' which they become is Hermaphroditus. It is finally he who speaks, changed by her presence certainly, and unable to throw off her influence, but none the less directing our point of view through his, and speaking his story.[36]

What's so a-musing about that? I shall return later to the gendered relationship of poet and Muse, but first I want to look at how Ovid does and does not use real Muses in the *Metamorphoses*. The act of invoking the Muse is not only representative of epic, but actually constitutive.[37] From the beginning of time, epic poems have opened by calling on divine aid from the Muse:

Μῆνιν ἄειδε θεά. . . (Hom. *Il.* 1. 1)

Sing, goddess, the wrath . . .

ἄνδρα μοι ἔννεπε, μοῦσα, πολύτροπον. . . (Hom. *Od.* 1. 1)

Speak to me, Muse, of the versatile man . . .

musa mihi causas memora . . . (Virg. *Aen.* 1. 8)

Muse, commemorate the causes for me . . .

We could add to this list the opening of Lucretius' didactic epos on the universe:

---

[35] The presentation of women, especially Muses, as desiring subjects is, to say the least, rare in antiquity. See Spentzou and, more tangentially, Ancona in this volume. There is an excellent discussion of subject position, as regards Sulpicia, in Keith (1997). From a theoretical point of view, it is particularly telling that Keith uses Dido and Sulpicia to illuminate each other.

[36] Nugent (1990).

[37] On aspects of performance and the epicizing of the Muse, see Laird in this volume. See also Minchin (1995), Minton (1960) and (1962). As an opening gambit, esp. Minchin (1995) 27.

Aeneadum genetrix . . .

Mother of the people of Aeneas . . .

The invocation comes 25 lines later, but it is unmistakably an epic invocation of Venus as Muse.[38] Ovid's proem presents a proper epic opening
proclaiming divine inspiration, or rather playing with the pose of proclaiming divine inspiration, in which the metamorphosis of verse form,
subject-matter, and genre all self-referentially signify the poem itself:[39]

> In nova fert animus mutatas dicere formas
> corpora: di, coeptis—nam vos mutastis et illa[40]
> adspirate meis primaque ab origine mundi
> ad mea perpetuum deducite tempora carmen.
>
> (*Met.* I. I–4)

The mind brings me to tell of forms changed into new bodies: gods, inspire my
efforts—for you change them also—and from the first beginnings of the world
lead down to my own time a perpetual song.

The invocation of the generalized (and male-centred, although not
necessarily exclusively male) *di*, however, rather than some form of
Musa, must be some kind of a playful refusal, as well as an allusion to the
overwhelming epic intertexts and their invocations of the Muse.
Moreover, there is a tension here between poet as priest of the Muses
and poet as independent artist. Ovid has an idea, but he does not say
explicitly whether the *animus* comes from the gods or himself. Within
the expectations raised by the epic medium, we read *animus* as coming
from the gods: within the knowledge we are encouraged to think we
have of Ovid the poet, inclined as he is to disclaim divine inspiration, we
think it comes from himself. To translate: on the one hand, 'the spirit
moves me to speak of forms changed into new bodies'; but on the other
hand, 'I think I'll tell some stories of metamorphosis'. He calls on the
gods to inspire him in language which at one level is *more* overtly
hymnic than in the standard epic formula. In the canonical three (*Iliad,*

---

[38] An interesting variant is Apollonius Rhodius, who opens his *Argonautica* with Phoebus
(Apollo). The Muses are brought in as well, at I. 22, although with an optative rather than an
imperative. The use of the third-person optative rather than a second-person imperative
distances the speaker from the Muses, by comparison with a more direct mode of address in the
canonical examples. This manner of invocation is both an allusion to Homeric precedent and
also a refusal to follow it. On Apollonius' Muses see also Spentzou, and Fowler quoting
[Longinus], in this volume. On the role of the Muse in epic poetics see Nuttall (1992) 3–4.

[39] Hinds (1987a) 19–22, 121, 132.

[40] Or *illas*?

Odyssey, and *Aeneid*), the invocation is lightly done. They are simply asked, in a single word, to 'sing' or 'tell', but Ovid's gods get the ritual-formulaic construction with *nam*, which reminds the gods of their benefits to mankind, which might especially incline them to fulfil the prayer, and they are asked to direct not just the beginning (the *causae*) but the whole story *ab origine ad mea tempora*.[41] And yet battling against this pose of religious ecstasy is the implication that this is really all Ovid's idea—the poem is his *coeptum*. The gods can come into the poem and help him build up his epic voice, but it is towards *his* times that the poem is heading.[42]

Throughout the poem there is a tension between these two elements: independence from the Muse (and the intertextual tradition) and desire for the Muse and the epic grandeur she can bestow. The Muse is a necessary part of Ovid's generic pretensions and games, as we can see in two passages of overt invocation together with generic ambiguity.

The one time when Ovid seems to work himself fully into the persona of priest of the Muses is almost at the end of the poem. This ending has been brilliantly discussed by Barchiesi (1997) and Hardie (1997). The mite I would add has to do with the Muse:

> pandite nunc, Musae, praesentia numina vatum—
> scitis enim, nec vos fallit spatiosa vetustas . . .
>
> (*Met.* 15. 622–3)

Open now, Muses, godheads present to aid bards—for you have knowledge, and the long age does not deceive you,

a proper invocation to the Muses, a proper sense of the poet's humility before the goddesses whose mouthpiece he must become in order to speak epic truths. It is a near-quotation of a Virgilian invocation, the more so because Virgil quotes himself with this phrase. Virgil calls on the Muses to help him relate the roll-call of warriors at the start of the war in Italy:[43]

[41] Lucretius' 25-line opening hymn is a still more extreme version of this prayer-formula.

[42] See Holzberg (1998) 90. For *animus* as signifying the power of poetic possession, see Paschalis (1997) 209. It is important—though odd—to remember that Ovid is echoing himself here, for he has used the phrase *fert animus* previously at *Ars* 3. 467. It looks like the other way round. For the ambiguous possibilities of internal and external inspiration in this context see also Fowler with his discussion of the Hesiodic Muses and their reception by Lucillius, in this volume. For the force of an invocation which is also a refusal of epic inspiration, see Rosati in this volume. The way in which the Muse gives Statius an excuse to defer Domitianic epic through a discourse of power and inspiration owes something to Ovid's negotiations of the minefield of power and politics in the *Metamorphoses*.

[43] Jenkyns (1998) 472 expresses the contrast between the Homeric and the Virgilian

> pandite nunc Helicona, deae, cantusque movete,
> qui bello exciti reges, quae quemque secutae
> complerint campos acies, quibus Itala iam tum
> floruerit terra alma viris, quibus arserit armis;
> et meministis enim, divae, et memorare potestis;
> ad nos vix tenuis famae perlabitur aura.
>
> (*Aen* 7. 641–6)

Open now Helicon, goddesses, and move the song: which kings were roused to war, which troops, and following whom, filled the fields, with which men the kindly Italian land even then flourished, with which arms she burned; for you both remember these things, goddesses, and you can commemorate them; hardly does the slender breeze of rumour slip through to us.

He reiterates the invocation for a similar purpose in Book 10:

> pandite nunc Helicona, deae, cantusque movete,
> quae manus interea Tuscis comitetur ab oris
> Aenean armetque rates pelagoque vehatur.
>
> (*Aen.* 10. 163–5)

Now open Helicon, goddesses, and move the song: what band at this time accompanied Aeneas from the Tuscan shores and readied the ships and sailed over the sea.

Given its position in the final book, Ovid's invocation must also recall that passage at *Aen.* 12. 500 when Virgil calls on the gods to help him relate the great climax of his work (the various acts of slaughter which will culminate in the death of Turnus), although this time it is not an address to the Muse but in the form of a question:[44]

> quis mihi nunc tot acerba deus, quis carmine caedes
> diversas obitumque ducum, quos aequore toto
> inque vicem nunc Turnus agit, nunc Troius heros,
> expediat?
>
> (*Aen.* 12. 500–3)

What god will now open in song for me so many bitter things, the diverse slaughters and the death of the leaders, whom now Turnus, now the Trojan hero, in turn drives over the plains?

invocations: 'Homer is lucid, factual and absolute: the goddesses are present and know everything; men know nothing. Virgil softens the distinction between omniscience and ignorance. His Muses remember and recollect; for them, as for us, these events are way back in the past.' His reading is determined by the thesis of his book, which is to study the Virgilian poems as 'experience', but the point about the sameness and difference of epic Muses is still useful.

[44] Invocations in the *Aeneid* are not all that common. Indeed, it is famously the case that authorial intrusions of any sort are rare, and emphatic, in the epic. For this reason, the Ovidian allusions seem particularly strong.

Each of Virgil's invocations heralds something big. When Ovid uses this striking authorial pose of invocation, then, we expect that the pose and the reference to Virgil will herald some sort of great climax (however ironic) like the apotheosis of Augustus we know we should expect. The divine presence in Virgil's poem authenticates and sanctions its Augustan story as cosmically ordained: you need an inspiring god to celebrate Augustus. What we get from Ovid, however, is the story of the reception into early Rome (in 293 BC) of the cult of the healing god Aesculapius[45]—a bit of an anticlimax after such a pose, although I accept that there is some Augustan nuance. I would suggest that the entry of the Muses here refuses to build up to the climax, refuses to contribute to the cosmic teleology of epic, precisely by denying the full force of the Virgilian allusion on which it depends. Let us look briefly at the 'climax'. After *Aesculapius* the narrative undergoes a huge temporal jump of several centuries and an outrageously bumpy transition, before we reach the story of the death and deification of Julius Caesar, oddly, perhaps parodically, stressing the biologicality of Caesar's 'fathering' of Augustus. Then, after over 100 lines of Julius Caesar, we get, with typical Ovidian ill proportion, just 20 on Augustus, where Caesar's fatherhood still features rather heavily. It ends with a prayer that Augustus will remain long on earth and only late return to the gods in order to become a divine protector to the Romans in his absence. But the poem ends not with the final word on Augustus (*absens*) but the metamorphosis of the poet himself, and the final word on Ovid (*vivam*). The supposedly encomiastic ending is a climax which refuses to offer a proper epic climax—teleological, linear, and unified—and the Muses are made to contribute to that denial of the epic telos.[46] Ovid's Muses are invited into the poem, but then denied their proper role as the inspiration for Augustan celebration.

A similar negotiation of power and genre happens in connection with another self-displaying epic story in the *Metamorphoses*: the Calydonian boar hunt in Book 8. This narrative, overdetermined with epic

[45] He is called *salutifer* for the *urbs*, which may have Augustan connotations. Barchiesi (1997) takes a slightly different line on this passage, stressing the various closural strategies at work in Book 15. I would not really dispute his argument, since the strategies at work need to be—indeed—closural for the *denial* of Virgilian teleology (which is what I am suggesting) to be able to work. Book 15, of course, only plays with denying its expected ending. In some ways, it is far more massively end-stopped than any previous epic.

[46] See Hardie's sophisticated reading (1997) of the power-games involved in this final book. I think, however, that he is over-zealous in denying the potential for political subversion in Ovid's non-encomium.

features and a sense of its own importance, is told without any external authority. It does, however, evoke a moment which might cause us to expect divine intervention. The reason for the boar's behaviour is to exact vengeance on behalf of Diana for the Calydonian farmers' failure to pay her due honour, for, the poet tells us, *tangit et ira deos* ('anger touches even the gods', 8. 279). The statement answers the question for which the Muses were first invoked in the *Aeneid*—*tantaene animis caelestibus irae?* ('Is there such anger in heavenly hearts?', *Aen.* 1. 11). The *lecta manus iuvenum* ('picked band of young men'), rolled out by name, who accompany Meleager against the boar are clearly constructed in the tradition of epic confrontations.[47]

It is not in this great epic narrative but in the little tale tagged onto the end that epic invocation occurs—or rather fails to occur:

> non mihi si centum deus ora sonantia linguis
> ingeniumque capax totumque Helicona dedisset,
> tristia persequerer miserarum fata sororum.
>
> (*Met.* 8. 533–5)

Not if a god gave me a hundred mouths resounding with a hundred tongues, a genius big enough and the whole of Helicon, c/would I relate right through the sad fates of his sisters.

The hundred mouths and tongues, the entire power of Helicon, are insufficient for Ovid to tell the grief of Meleager's sisters at their brother's death. The intertextual antecedents (*Iliad* 2. 489–90, *Georgics* 2. 43–4) for the hundred-tongued (or ten-tongued) speaker of epic are obvious, again, almost overdetermined. The invocation is as epic as can be, but for the least epic and smallest part of this great epic tale. Through this invocation, the Muses' epic power is both invoked and denied.

Ovid needs the Muse, then, because without one you can't write epic. The Muse, as embodiment of epicness, is throughout the *Metamorphoses* both desired and resisted. When Muses enter poems, it is almost always in the second person (it may be some kind of imperative)—'come, enter, inspire, speak to me'. In the *Metamorphoses*, however, Muses play a larger role than in any other epic, for they themselves tell and partake in stories in Book 5. A number of excellent studies have shown how the presence of the Muses here is active in the construction of Ovidian art

---

[47] See Hollis (1970) ad loc., esp. 62–8 and 73–4, for the epicness of the boar hunt: 'perhaps the most strictly epic passage in all the *Metamorphoses*' (68). Keith (1999) is an important study of masculinity and genre in the *Metamorphoses*, in which the boar hunt features as an extreme site of epic masculinity.

which is displayed by the poem.[48] I do not mean to question or undermine any of that in noting how when the Muses become subject-matter,
rather than omnipotent authorities, the power-relations must be
changed. Instead of inspiring from the outside, Muses actually become
part of the story; they enter by the third person, and use the first person.
They tell subjective stories of themselves, not truths about the world
through the mouth of the poet.[49] In doing so, they become subordinate
to the poet, for they are given no greater authority for their speech than
any other narrator. Where the second person gives them power (power
to inspire), the third person subjects them to the poet's power. It is
particularly worth noting that the Muses in Book 6 are given no privileged access to the Ovidian authority. Of variant narrators it is only
Pythagoras who is aware that he is telling a story of metamorphosis—
that he is working in a poem called the *Metamorphoses*—and he is shored
up by the authority of his own inquiry, and a deep intertextual background.[50] The Muses, like everyone else, think they are just telling a
story which happens to include transformation, not being storytellers of
metamorphosis.

If we are following a reading in which the Muses' entry into the
subject-matter of the poem subordinates them to the poet, we might
look at how they came there.[51] They arrive by means of Perseus, whose
behaviour with the Gorgon's head makes statues of all his opponents.
This violent metamorphosis apes Ovid's own narrative activity.
Perseus' last act in the poem is to turn the doubting Polydectes to stone,
and then suddenly Athene is visiting the Muses and asking about their
stream, which sprang from the foot-stroke of Pegasus. The winged
horse's relationship with the stream of poetic inspiration is almost completely elided. All we hear is Athene's elliptical statement that *vidi ipsum
materno sanguine nasci* ('I saw him born from his mother's blood', 5. 259),
and that the stream, according to rumour, has been created by *Medusaei
. . . praepetis ungula* ('the hoof of the flying offspring of Medusa', 5. 257).
The abruptness of the transition is likely to nudge us into looking for

[48] Hinds (1987a), Leach (1974a), Lateiner (1984). Most critics are inclined to see the role of the
Muses as participants in the poem as an expression of their own power. While agreeing that this
is a possible reading, I offer here an alternative. See also Spentzou's Introduction to this
volume for a powerful reading of the workings of the Ovidian metamorphic Muses.

[49] Lada-Richards, Fowler, and Spentzou, in this volume, are also particularly concerned
with this subjectivity of the Muses they explore.

[50] See Hardie (1995) on the intertextual background to Pythagoras' speech. He argues for the
importance of Empedocles as well as Lucretius and Ennius in the background here.

[51] The same cautions apply, of course, as I mention à propos Salmacis and Hermaphroditus.

connections. Hinds's detailed analysis of this passage (1987: 3–24) brings out the programmatic force of the winged horse's hoof-beat. In this regard, we might note not only the Aratean intertexts for the origin of the Hippocrene,[52] but also the Callimachean, since the myth is clearly alluded to in the fragmentary but programmatically crucial meeting of Hesiod with the Muses in *Aetia* fr. 2. I would suggest, moreover, that the poetics can be taken a stage further back. The result is a little less comfortable, but then Ovid is not a well-behaved poet. Would it be fanciful, I wonder, to consider that Perseus is a kind of Ovid-figure, and he is somehow responsible for the Muses? They enter the poem on his terms, through his creation. Perseus the violent epic hero shakes the castrated head of the monster-woman and produces an *aetion* for poetry. Ovid the violent epic poet (sort of) kicks poetry into gear by shaking the head of Callimachus.[53] Moreover, when the Muses start talking about themselves, the first story they tell is of how they were deceived, captured, and pursued by the mortal Pyreneus. Their tale is one of poetic success: they escape by flying away (flying being a common metaphor for writing poetry), while the mortal, who is trying to enclose and occlude their poetic activity, falls to his death when he thinks he can fly after them.[54] Pyreneus must stand for the failed poet, who thinks he can succeed by raping the Muses. But on another level, their story also tells of virginal fears and vulnerability (*et nondum tota me mente recepi*, 'and even now I have not quite recovered myself', 5. 275). These Muses are like any other lovely maiden (except that they just might fly away from one who desires them).

In the last paragraph I have argued that the Muses' entry into the poem as subject-matter undermines their authoritative function as purveyors of poetic truth. But one might say that the Muses who tell their own stories and the stories of others in the *Metamorphoses* are being allowed a greater activity as agents of poetic creation than those who only inspire. If the Muse is to assist the poet (the second-person address), then her construction as 'powerful to aid' involves also the compression of her active personality into the services of the poet, as happened to Salmacis. If she speaks for herself she is writing poetry, not being a poem.[55] Moreover, although I have stressed the vulnerability and

---

[52] This is fully discussed by Hinds (1987a) 3–24.

[53] Cf. here Fowler in this volume, on the complexities of Callimachus' role in the ancestry of poetic inspiration.

[54] On artistic failure in the *Metamorphoses* see esp. Leach (1974a).

[55] Can a woman's voice shine through the male author? See Spentzou (forthcoming).

createdness of the Muses in Book 5, it is also true that they are clever singers making sophisticated generic statements.[56] It seems to me that both these readings are possible in the *Metamorphoses*, just as the Muse is both desired and denied.

This ambivalent relationship between poet and Muse is especially significant in the *Metamorphoses* because of that poem's complex inter-textual relationship with the traditions of epic and the stable categories of genre. I should like now to take a little further what I said above about the way in which the Muse is inseparable from the challenge of genre. It seems to me that in the interaction between epic and elegy, the two main genres of Ovidian poetry, we have a conflict of gendered identity, in which the Muse plays a crucial role. Muses look different in different genres, and the way in which they are different itself performs the difference of genre, and it is partly a gendered difference. The sexy Muse of elegy helps to make elegy a 'female' genre with a 'male' speaker, while the goddess-Muse of epic (even if she has a hint of the whore about her as well) contributes to making epic a 'male' genre with a feminized, depowered speaker.[57]

To consider this question further, it will be useful to look briefly at the Muse in various generic guises, for Ovid's relationship with the purveyors of inspiration has always been complex. In the amatory poetry, the Muse is a sexy and passive elegiac *puella*, who is courted, desired, fought, rejected. As regards direct reference, the Muse does not appear much in the *Amores*, but it would be difficult to separate the personified 'Elegy' in poems such as *Am.* 3.1 or the generalized *puella* in poems like *Am.* 2.18[58] from the Muse. Since in these poems loving and writing poetry are so intimately entwined, the object of desire neces-

---

[56] The most extensive discussion of the Muses' role here is Hinds (1987a), chs. 1 and 2.

[57] I have made a slippage here between depowerment and feminization, a slippage which may itself enact the depowerment of women that it seeks to expose. This is an inevitable problem, but in these circumstances it is, I think, at least valid to point out the connection between loss of power and feminization. On this subject, see Ancona in this volume, and also Fowler, esp. where he discusses Horace. I have argued that the traditional Muse is an 'epic' feature. Various less traditional Muses can play with genre in other ways: see e.g. Henderson in this volume for Copa as an anti-epic Muse.

[58] The poet addresses an epic colleague on the subject of his own attempts to stop writing elegy. Whenever he tried to tell his *puella* to go away, however, she caressed and wheedled him into continuing with elegy. This surely is the Muse. The connection is made explicit by Statius, when he presents Elegy, as a typical elegiac woman, trying to be the 'tenth Muse' (*Silv.* 1. 2. 7–10). I am grateful to Gianpiero Rosati for drawing my attention to this passage. See Rosati (1999b) on this.

sarily becomes the lover-poet's Muse.[59] In the didactic poetry again the figures of inspiration serve Ovid's generic purpose, when he claims authority for himself by 'disclaiming divine inspiration'.[60] In the exile poetry, Ovid becomes obsessed with his Muse, both as an extension of himself and as a mobile advocate in Rome for his constrained and distanced voice. The Muse's exilic roles are multiple: often connected with *crimen*, she is blamed for Ovid's exile, and even hated, for example, when he tells the story of his attempt to burn the unfinished *Metamorphoses*, in a clear statement of its epicness and relationship with Virgil. On the other hand (or is it?), she is also a sexy woman, the *Musa iocosa*, who once figured in his boyish sexual fantasies (4. 10. 20) and who is his one solace on the journey and in exile. The *Musa iocosa*, however, is *not real*—it's all made up, imaginary, has no authority. Indeed, much of the *Tristia* is concerned with a paradoxical denial of authority to Ovid's poetry—in poetry—and the Muse contributes to that. She is employed to deny her own power. But at the same time, she is a dangerous and harmful object of desire, whose power is all too great and too real. In the *Fasti*, which may be a schizophrenic work, the Muse is both the interlocuting god with privileged knowledge who tells Ovid how it is, and also the embodiment of the exiled poet's grief.[61]

In the change from elegy to epic, the balance of power shifts in the poet–muse relationship in a way which is programmatic for and perhaps essential to the genre itself. The elegiac persona is male, albeit problematically so;[62] the genre is problematically female, as is clear not only from the appearance of Elegia in *Am.* 3. 1, but also from the metre itself. The elegiac couplet is, as is well known, the epic hexameter manqué, weakened, lessened, emasculated.[63] Epic, by contrast, is a male genre, using

---

[59] Ovid refuses to follow Propertius by starting with Cynthia. Propertius' opening statement *Cynthia prima suis miserum me cepit ocellis* presents himself and his poetry as in thrall to the beloved, and perhaps acts like the epic invocation of the Muse. Ovid, as is well known, subverts the Propertian opening passion with an intertextual game and an attempt to claim total ownership of his poetry. A failed attempt, of course.

[60] Miller (1986); La Penna (1979). And also here the figures of inspiration serve Ovid's *intertextual* purpose: see Casali (1995). I leave aside the horribly complicated question of the *Heroides*, which has been discussed by Barchiesi (1991) and Spentzou (forthcoming), among others.

[61] Homesickness, and the wrong genre, break out at 4. 82–4: *me miserum, Scythico quam procul illa solo est! | ergo ego tam longe–sed supprime, Musa, querellas: | non tibi sunt maesta sacra canenda lyra.* Newlands (1995) 84: 'The disagreement of the Muses and the three goddesses is part of a larger epistemological crisis in the latter part of the extant poem in which the narrator's relationship with his topic and with his guiding authorities comes under severe strain.'

[62] See Wyke (1995) and Sharrock (1995).

[63] Kennedy (1993) 57–63, Wyke (1995), Sharrock (1995).

only that manly metre and talking of manly things. The speaker of epic is necessarily male, in sociological reality and in some element of the persona, while the subject-matter is—at least 'officially'—quintessentially male, being war and politics; yet the images of the bardic persona are feminized in two directions—by relation to the powerful Muses, on the one hand, and the epic subject-matter, the hero, on the other. The elegiac poet is one who loves, but the epic poet is generally *not* one who fights. 'Blind Homer' and Demodocus are archetypal examples of this.[64] So I suggest that while elegy shows us a (problematically) male speaker in a feminized genre, epic gives us a feminized/weakened speaker in a male genre. The depowerment of the speaker as active agent of meaning is brought about by his subjection to the voice of the powerful female speaker, the Muse.[65] But then Ovid refuses the passivity and feminization of inspiration, and does indeed seek to stamp his control on the meaning of his material. His material, of course, fights back, because it is in the nature of metamorphosis to slip about in meaning.

CODA

Behind this discussion of the relationship between the poet and the Muse has hidden the figure of Augustus, the source and inspiration of all Augustan poetry.[66] I find it hard to separate Ovid's claims for independence from the Muse, from similar attempts throughout his poetic corpus to make himself independent of Augustus. I think this is not just an act of political protest, but an attempt to renegotiate the position of the poet and ultimately even the self in a changed world.[67] In Ovid's final statement of his independence as an epic poet, in the 'epilogue', the Muse has been completely elided by the more powerful god—'Jove', who must be Augustus. Ovid makes a claim for self-direction and for a self-centred fame, but in a passage so overdetermined with Ennian and Horatian intertextuality as to acknowledge—perhaps even despite himself—that ideas do not spring *ex nihilo*, that the poet does not have individual control, and that inspiration is always part of a relationship. The same, of course, goes for criticism.[68]

[64] Mario Labate has pointed out to me the odd case of Ennius going to war and writing the *Annals*. Poets in the *Aeneid*, as Sergio Casali has pointed out, just die.

[65] See Cavarero in this volume.

[66] For the emperor as Muse, see Rosati in this volume.

[67] Hardie (1997), Barchiesi (1997). See also Segal (1969).

[68] On which note, I thank many friends and several audiences who have contributed to my thinking about this chapter. Special mention is due to Sergio Casali, Gianpiero Rosati, and above all Effie Spentzou.

Muse and Power in the
Poetry of Statius

Gianpiero Rosati

I. NEGOTIATING WITH THE MUSES

Lassata . . . totiens mihi numina, Musas: 'the heavenly Muses, so often wearied by my prayer'[1]—thus Statius (*Silv.* 1. 5. 2) defines his relationship with the Muses. Compared with the practice of post-Ovidian poets, the particular emphasis Statius assigns to the Muses, and more generally to the theme of poetic inspiration, is striking. Perhaps this is less surprising in a 'professional' poet such as Statius, a poet, that is to say, who repeatedly inquires into his condition as a poet, and into the nature and the instruments of his work. The Muses and the divinities that tradition-ally share with them the function of inspiring poets (Apollo, Bacchus, Mercury, etc.) are in effect symbols, or figures, of a self-reflecting dis-course about the creation of poetry, metonymies of literary discourse.[2]

Furthermore, such frequent reference to inspiration also marks out a borderline, a distinction (already fixed by Plato, *Ion* 533e) between poetry that is inspired and poetry that is not. Inspiration becomes a proud affirmation of a criterion of quality, even a claim to a condition of privilege. As we shall see in the first passage analysed below, Statius does not invoke the Muse's inspiration, but rather says that he is *already inspired*; he is already endowed with a superior gift, of divine origin. Lastly, there is the fact that in the case of Statius (unlike e.g. Lucan, Valerius, or Silius) we possess both his epic production and the 'lighter' variety of the *Silvae*. The presence of the Muses is no less constant in these differing works, which reveals that Statius' discourse on the theme of inspiration and on his composition of poetry is more complex,

---

[1] Translations of *Silvae* come intact or adapted from Mozley (1928).
[2] For an elegant demonstration of this, with specific reference to Ovid, see Barchiesi (1991).

and is inflected differently, depending on the genre within which it is developed.[3]

Let me start, then, from what seems to me to be the most significant passage in Statius' discourse: the proem of the *Thebais*.

> Fraternas acies alternaque regna profanis
> decertata odiis sontesque evolvere Thebas
> *Pierius menti calor incidit. Unde iubetis*
> *ire, deae?* gentisne canam primordia dirae,
> Sidonios raptus et inexorabile pactum
> legis Agenoreae scrutantemque aequora Cadmum?
> *longa retro series,* trepidum *si* Martis operti
> agricolam infandis condentem proelia sulcis
> *expediam penitusque sequar,* quo carmine muris
> iusserit . . .   (1. 1–10)

The strife of brothers and alternate reigns fought for in impious hatred and the guilt of tragic Thebes, these themes *the Muses' fire has kindled in my heart. Whence, Heavenly Ones, am I to take the road?* Shall I relate the origins of that disastrous race, Europa's rape, Agenor's ordinance inexorable, Cadmus' searching quest across the sea? *Far back the chain would reach, should I recount* the trembling husbandman of hidden warfare and the battles sown in fiendish furrows, *should my verse pursue* what song . . .[4]

Unlike the traditional invocation addressed by the poet to the Muse to beseech her to assist and inform him about the contents of his poem (Homer, Hesiod, Virgil, etc.), Statius says that already—at the moment when the poem begins—he is under the inspirational influence of the *Pierius calor* of the Muses, who are guiding him to sing of *fraternas acies alternaque regna*, that is to say, a precise subject that they have chosen and practically imposed on the poet.[5] *Incidit* underlines the external origin of the impulse and the passive nature of the poet. The inspiration is something that has 'happened' to him, something unexpected (the verb is commonly used for illnesses),[6] and above all, unrequested.[7] After the *propositio* of the first two lines synthetically expounding the theme of the

---

[3] On the importance of literary genre in determining the features and functions of the Muse, see the observations of Ancona and Sharrock, in this volume.

[4] Translations of the *Thebaid* come from Melville (1992).

[5] I would not say, therefore, that 'the Muses sent him inspiration without direction': Ahl (1986) 2817.

[6] Cf. *TLL* s.v. 898,36 ff.; 903,21 ff.; 904,69 ff.

[7] Also the conclusion of the poem (12. 208 f.) 'is in many ways imposed upon, rather than by, the poet': Hershkowitz (1998) 270, who suggests that the poetics of the *Thebais* is a 'poetics of madness' (268 ff.; 63 f.).

work (described in greater detail in the following lines: 9–14), the poet immediately implores the same Muses that have 'inspired' him to show him the *unde*, a beginning for his narration, the particular starting point of that narrative segment of the endless saga of Thebes which is to be the subject of Statius' epos.

In other words, Statius thematizes the problem of how to begin: what should he choose as his starting point? It is especially difficult picking a place to begin an epic poem on the Theban saga like the *Thebais*, not only because of the abundance and complexity of the narrative subject, but also because there are numerous texts which have already narrated those stories (and likewise invoked the Muses). The words *longa retro series* are in effect an admission that the poet is facing a problem. Inspiration is also a question of intertextuality; poems do not leap out of a vacuum. Writing a new work, especially on a topic so often treated before, amounts to positioning oneself within a network of other texts, a grafting of the new poem onto that poetic *longa series* and a negotiation of one's own space within that tradition.

It is curious, however, that, at the moment when he asks the Muses to indicate the starting point for the story that they are also 'ordering' him to narrate, the poet begins stubbornly to delineate the limits of his task (ll. 7–9), pointing out the need for a selection of the narrative material:

> atque adeo iam nunc gemitus et prospera Cadmi
> *praeteriisse sinam: limes mihi carminis esto*
> Oedipodae confusa domus, quando Itala nondum
> signa nec Arctoos ausim spirare triumphos
> bisque iugo Rhenum, bis adactum legibus Histrum
> et coniurato deiectos vertice Dacos
> aut defensa prius vix pubescentibus annis
> bella Iovis   (1. 15–22)

rather at present *I'll permit* the joys and agonies of Cadmus *to have passed*. The troubled house of Oedipus *shall set the limit of my lay*, since I'll not dare as yet to hymn the standards of Italy, the triumphs in the North, the Rhine reduced twice to our yoke, the Danube twice beneath our jurisdiction, Dacians hurled down from rebel peaks, Jove saved from war's assault when boy had scarce reached man.

Thus the poet follows up his recognition of his subordination and submission to the Muses' will with an affirmation of autonomy and freedom of choice; and in the end he is the one that personally decides, with the peremptory tone of a future imperative, the limits of his *carmen* (16).

The passivity of the poet 'inspired' by the *calor*, the 'enthusiasm', of the Muses, is redeemed by his autonomous choice of imposing precise limits for the work that he is beginning.[8] At the beginning of the *Aeneid* Virgil famously asked the Muse to enlighten him about the *causae* of the events to be narrated (1. 8: *Musa, mihi causas memora*, 'Recount to me, O Muse, the causes') and—in the second proem—to give him the necessary information about the origins of the war against the Latins (7. 37: *nunc age, qui reges, Erato, quae tempora . . .* 'Now lead me forwards, Muse Erato: who were the kings, what were the early events . . .'; 41: *tu vatem, tu, diva, mone*, 'You, goddess, you advise your bard'). Instead, Statius uses his long preterition to reveal a complete mastery of the enormous amount of narrative material offered to him by tradition (4–17 and 33–40). He limits himself to asking the Muse simply about the *ordo* of the narration, about how to start it off (as he repeats in his appeal to Clio at the end of the long proem:[9] *quem prius heroum, Clio, dabis?* 'which of the heroes, Clio, shall rank first?', 41).

The poet–Muse relationship—which is to say, the problem of inspiration—is shown to be from the start one of conflict. It is a field of potential tensions between different forces (the poet's own artistic intentions, the literary tradition, the material circumstances conditioning the poet's work, etc.). All these exert a conditioning influence on the process of artistic creation. The figure of the Muse ends up by subsuming in itself everything that opposes a fully rational mastering of that process by the poet.

Thus Statius recognizes in the poetic act an external influence, the inspiration of the Muses, which guides him to sing of a precise subject; but he does not expect to receive any information from this external, supernatural agent about the contents of his song, which are already clear in his mind (even if occasionally, at the canonical points—particularly before catalogues or battle scenes—he appeals to the Muses for help: cf. *Theb.* 4. 32 ff.; 649 ff.; 6. 296 ff.; 7. 628 ff.; 8. 373 ff.; 9. 315 ff.; 10. 628 ff.; 827 ff.). *Doctrina* is no longer the preserve of the Muses, but a responsibility that the poet claims for himself. Statius is not only a *poeta*

---

[8] Cf. also, here, the conclusion of the poem and Malamud (1995) 23 (who sets other correspondences between the proem and the epilogue of the work).

[9] For another apostrophe to Clio, the Muse of history, see 10. 630. As regards the individual identity of the various Muses and their respective functions, cf. Coleman (1988) 198 f.; Barchiesi (1991) 11. For the figure of Clio, cf. Georgacopoulou (1996). On the single Muses invoked by Statius, see Georgacopoulou (forthcoming) esp. ch. 5 (which I have been able to consult by the kind permission of the author) and Steiniger (1998).

doctus; he also makes this almost anxious condition the subject of his discourse.[10] The appeal to the *deae* is not, therefore, from the formal point of view, a real *invocatio*, but merely a request for illumination on a point which is actually a mere detail of narrative economy. By putting on the conventional figures, the Muses, the poet is actually sketching a discourse about the organization of the poem (structure and selection of the narrative material)[11] and his own literary choices (essentially his relationship with Antimachus).[12]

There is another aspect of the proem, and of the discourse on the inspiration, which deserves attention here. Whilst imposing his decision on the Muses, and demonstrating his 'bargaining power' in front of the authority of literary tradition,[13] Statius passes brusquely—with a break in the logical reasoning which has raised the suspicion of a textual corruption[14]—to another subject, something that shows no apparent link with the previous discourse. The poet will speak of Oedipus' *domus confusa, because* he is not sufficiently inspired to sing of the achievements of Domitian (while, as suggested by the development of reasoning, the reader is rather led to expect a determination of the limits of his story with respect to other elements of the Theban saga).[15]

In other words, what we find here, quite unexpectedly, is a veritable *recusatio-excusatio*, in which the poet justifies his choice of a mythological epic and his refusal, or rather deferment, of a historical one. Unlike the kind of *recusatio* common among Augustan poets, it does not serve to justify the refusal of epic poetry in favour of a lighter kind of poetry, but rather the preference for a particular kind of epic, that is to say, the mythological epic. However, the refusal is not total: the poet— again revealing an attitude unlike the Augustan poets—does not declare his inability to deal with higher themes of the historical-celebratory kind of epic (much less does he manifest a prejudicial hostility to this genre). The situation is similar to that of Ovid before him, a poet who had

---

[10] Feeney (1991) 340 ff. For fine observations on Statius' awareness of the 'secondariness' of his discourse, see Hinds (1998) 92 ff.

[11] A problem analogous to the one that Statius raises, in a context that does not require the pretence of the relationship with the Muse, can be located in *Silv.* 1. 3. 34 (*quid primum mediumve canam, quo fine quiescam?*, 'what shall be my first, what my middle theme, whereon shall I conclude?').

[12] Cf. e.g. Carrara (1986).

[13] 'Le narrateur prend ses distances même envers les Muses. Il ne place pas son sujet sous l'égide des *deae*': Georgacopoulou (1996) 181 n. 45.

[14] Cf. esp. Kytzler (1960) with the effective answer of Schetter (1962) 208 ff.

[15] Also Caviglia (1973) 12 speaks of 'innegabile sfasatura logica'.

shown a more flexible and 'professional' attitude than the Augustan *recusationes* by not declaring himself incapable of composing any poetic genre. Ovid had asked for a pause before dedicating himself to higher poetry (*Am.* 3. 1. 67, 70). Similarly, Statius does not respond with an absolute refusal of all generic expectations, but he motivates his momentary *recusatio-excusatio*[16] by saying that he 'does not dare yet' (17 f.) to measure his ability with the achievements of the emperor, and he puts the task off to an indefinite future, when he may feel 'more inspired' to celebrate them:

> tempus erit, cum Pierio tua fortior oestro
> facta canam: nunc tendo chelyn satis arma referre
> Aonia et geminis sceptrum exitiale tyrannis . . .   (32–4)

a time shall come when I shall hymn your deeds emboldened by the Muses' spur; but now it is enough to tune my lyre to tell of Theban arms and of the throne that doomed the tyrant pair . . .

Singing of Domitian requires a higher inspiration, a more energetic impulse of 'frenzy' (*oestro*) from the Muses.[17] The implicit comparison between the mythological epic (*arma Aonia*), to which the poet limits himself for the present, and the celebration of the achievements of Domitian (the *Itala signa* of 17 f.) is again found at the beginning of his second epos, the *Achilleis*, where Statius once again justifies further post-ponement of his promise to the emperor; and once again the refusal is counterbalanced by an encomiastic hyperbole:

> at tu, quem longe primum stupet Itala virtus
> Graiaque, cui geminae florent vatumque ducumque
> certatim laurus—olim dolet altera vinci—,
> da veniam ac trepidum patere hoc sudare parumper
> pulvere. te longo necdum fidente paratu
> molimur magnusque tibi praeludit Achilles
>   (*Achil.* 1. 14–19)

But you whom far before all others the pride of Italy and Greece regards with reverent awe, for whom the two laurels of poet and warrior-chief flourish in mutual rivalry—already one of them grieves to be surpassed—grant pardon and allow me anxiously to toil in this dust for a while. Yours is the theme at which

---

[16] As regards Statius' *recusationes*, cf. Coleman (1988) 156, 198.

[17] A motivation which can give rise to ambiguity: the poet of the *Thebais* also invokes a *maior amentia* ('finer frenzy') instilled into him by the Muses in order to sing of the deeds of Capaneus (10. 830). For a possible double interpretation of the 'exceptionality' of the deeds of Domitian, cf. Ahl (1986) 2821.

with long and not yet confident preparation I am labouring, and great Achilles plays the prelude unto you.[18]

Here too Statius motivates his momentary postponement (*parumper*) by recognizing his still insufficient confidence in his own capacities. In *Silvae* (4. 4. 94 ff.) continuing to put off a task that he considers to be inevitable makes the poet feel deeply embarrassed:

> Troia quidem magnusque mihi temptatur Achilles,
> sed vocat arcitenens alio pater armaque monstrat
> Ausonii maiora ducis.[19] trahit impetus illo
> iam pridem retrahitque timor. stabuntne sub illa
> mole umeri an magno vincetur pondere cervix?
> dic, Marcelle, feram? fluctus an sueta minores
> nosse ratis nondum Ioniis credenda periclis?
>
> (4. 4. 94–100)

It is Troy I am attempting and great Achilles, but the Sire that wields the bow calls me elsewhere and points me to mightier arms of the Ausonian chief. Long since has impulse urged me thither, but fear holds me back. Will my shoulders sustain so great a burden, or will my neck yield under the weight? Tell me, Marcellus, shall I essay the task? or must my bark that knows but lesser seas not yet be trusted to Ionian perils?

There is, however, a significant difference in these verses compared with the two epic proems, in particular with that of the *Thebais*. Here Statius declares that he is not up to the task of describing the emperor's achievements, but at the same time he says that he is 'carried away' by a desire to celebrate them; on the one hand, he is restrained by his *timor*; on the other, he is urged on by his *impetus*. The poet recognizes here that he had already felt for some time (*iam pridem*) the inspiration which in the proem to the *Thebais* he expected to receive *in the future* from the Muses; and this inspiration has been at work thanks to Apollo, the god who traditionally accompanies the Muses in their function (even if, in the tradition of *recusationes*, Apollo does not usually urge the poet on, but rather *dissuades* him from singing of certain subjects which are not suitable for his capacities).[20]

The inspiration to celebrate Domitian in an epic work, which Statius

---

[18] Adapted from Mozley (1928).

[19] The definition of Apollo as *arcitenens*, 'the Sire that wields the bow', followed by the mention of the arms of Domitian, sets up a comparison for the latter not only with Achilles but also with the god himself.

[20] Hardie (1983) 167. The archetype is, of course, Callim. *Aet.* fr. 1. 22 ff.: for the Latin tradition, cf. Wimmel (1960) 135–42; Coleman (1988) 198.

claims in the *Silvae* to have taken possession of him, is in this case excluded from the poet's panorama at the most delicate moment: in the presentation of the poet's most ambitious work, the *Thebais*—and even *De bello Germanico* must have been no more than a sample of the poem so often promised.[21] His Muses order him to compose something else, a different kind of epic, a mythological epic. We get a clear impression of an embarrassment, of a lack of rigour in his process of reasoning: if it is the Muses that inspire a subject already chosen by them, then how can the poet promise that 'one day' he will sing of the achievements of Domitian? Clearly the discourse about the Muses and inspiration implies, or better masks, a discourse about the relationship of the poet with power, and about the conflict between the liberty of the poet and the conditioning brought to bear upon him by those who possess political power.[22]

And yet, things are far from settled: for all his urge to negotiate poetry and politics, in key points in his work, as, for example, in the proem to the *Thebaid*, Statius does not oblige the emperor nearly as enthusiastically as we would expect, especially from a post-Lucan work. After the proem to the *Pharsalia* with the famous eulogy of Nero (it is irrelevant for our purposes whether it is interpreted as being ironic or serious) and the emphatic refusal of the traditional divinities which of course include the Muses and which are substituted by the *deus in terra* Nero, what strikes us in Statius is the wide-scale reuse of those Muses and, conversely, the absence of the figure of the emperor as the source of inspiration.[23] It is true that the emperor is mentioned, but instead of carrying out the inspirational function (as e.g. in Valerius: 1. 11 f.; 20 f.) he here assumes the role of determining the production of the poet, controlling and directing it (the role that had become familiar to readers of Latin poetry through the *recusationes* of the Augustan age).

But, of course, Statius' elaborate relationship with the Muses is itself far from smooth and equal. It is, in fact, the very figure of the Muse, as an agent that is external to the poet and yet necessary to him for his creative activity, that implied a problem of dependence of the poet.[24] Involving the Muse in the discourse means raising the problem of the determina-

[21] Cf. Lotito (1974) 40 ff.

[22] After the proem, the new mention of Domitian at the end of the *Thebais* is significant (12. 814; Dominik (1994) 167) as it suggests a continual presence, controlling the entire work.

[23] Cf. Caviglia (1973) 93.

[24] A similar opposition between 'within' and 'without' is also important for Fowler in this volume.

tion that shapes the poet's creative process. In other words, the problem of inspiration is, in itself, a problem of authority; and the relationship of the poet with the goddess-Muse, the symbol of his dependence on an external agent who determines his choices and his creative activity, may be seen as a version of the relationship with literary authority, of inspiration as a problem of intertextuality but also as a 'figure' of the relationship of the poet with another authority, the political one. The immediate passage, in the proem to the *Thebais* (ll. 16–17), from the direct negotiation with the Muses to the implicit negotiation with the emperor is the most striking confirmation of the fact that the negotiation is one and the same, and so is the discourse (as we shall see further on). The claim to a full mastery over the contents of the poem, and the right to select them in accordance with one's own logic of poetic economy goes hand in hand with the poet's wish to escape from the pressures of political power—a wish cunningly hidden behind the encomiastic excuse of an inspiration that is still inadequate for the greatness of the achievements to be celebrated.

So it is then that behind the literary pretence of the Muses, Statius carries out his skirmishing with his real interlocutor. He negotiates his own autonomy with the real, political authority which determines his creative activity. It is indeed likely that real political pressures were exerted on the poet by the Imperial authorities, not to mention the keen co-operation of the poet himself who, for his part, is very well aware of all hopes and expectations pinned on him. When a poet openly declares that the Princeps has high expectations of him, he is also implementing an operation of self-promotion. While flaunting his freely chosen association with the powers-that-be, he is also showing that his poetry is held in great esteem in high places.

Clearly, straightforwardness and coherence cannot be expected as Statius deliberately mixes the literary and the political in his poetry under the tag of inspiration. But if motives and motivations are intricately interwoven in Statius' work, an exploration of the related tradition, and especially the proem literary tradition, may result in a better understanding of the intricate bonds that hold these motives together. This is the task of the following, middle section of the chapter.

II. THE EMPEROR-MUSE, OR THE INSPIRATION
OF POWER

It is a well-known fact in Latin poetry that, starting from the Augustan age, the traditional relationship of the poet with the Muse, 'the fount of knowledge and inspiration', is integrated with—or even at times substituted by—the relationship with the emperor, who is assigned an identical inspirational function. Clearly, it is the 'divine' nature of the emperor, the new *deus in terra*, that facilitates this homology of functions. In fact, the phenomenon is nothing more than the consequence, on the level of literary forms, of the different politico-institutional situation, and the new conditions in which poets and men of letters found themselves in the exercise of their creative activity. The increasingly invasive presence, in the various fields of social life, of the figure of the emperor and the most influential members of his court also results in a reformulation of the language and the ways in which a poet speaks of his own poetry and addresses the source of his inspiration. In parallel with the progressive development of a language expressing the attitude of homage and flattering deference typical of a client, there is an increasing tendency to involve, together with, or in the place of, the inspiration of Muse, that of the emperor himself. The imperial quasi-Muse is the very symbol of the control exercised by political power over literary activity and the pressures that it brings to bear, more or less openly, in order to orientate it towards an obliging attitude of appreciation and praise of the regime.

The assumption of the emperor as the source of inspiration in the place of the traditional mythological figures (an assumption which is a realistic recognition of the poet's new condition as a client) also partly derives from the development of a poetry self-styled as linked to everyday life. This is something which had become common in Rome particularly in the more explicitly 'realistic' genres, and which is crystallized in the motif of the 'refusal of the Muse'.[25] This motif is implicit in the parody of the *invocatio* that we read, for example, in Horace's Brundisian satire (1. 5. 51–3) and becomes common in the elegy, which declares itself to be linked to *usus* and *puella* (Prop. 2. 1. 3 f.; Ov. *Ars* 1. 25 ff.). The refusal of mythological pretence, also motivated by the need for an ethical revolt, was to find its most drastic expression in Persius' *Choliambi*,[26] and

---

[25] Precedents can also be found in the Greek comic tradition: cf. Aristophanes, fr. 348 KA (Häußler (1973) 122 n. 25).

[26] For more on that aspect of Persius, cf. also Fowler in this volume.

was to become widespread, more famously, in Christian poetry which invokes Christ or the Holy Spirit instead of the pagan Muse.[27]

But there is another element of the poetic discourse which acts as a significant indication of the increasing importance of the presence of the emperor in the space of the proem as the destination of the homage or the invocation of the poet. This may be summed up in the standard ancient phrase for beginnings, *ab Iove principium*, which in Latin poetry is re-employed in an explicitly encomiastic tone, that is to say as an apology for the *Juppiter in terra*. Hesiod, in his opening invocation to the Muses, had already exhorted them to celebrate their father Zeus (*Works* 1 ff.); and Pindar tells us expressly how ancient and widespread the habit was of 'beginning from Jupiter' (*Nem.* 2. 1 ff.: 'Just as the sons of Homer, those singers of verses stitched together, most often begin with a prelude to Zeus . . .').[28] This habit obviously implies the idea that the *arche*, the beginning of the poem, belongs to Zeus rather than to any other god, because Zeus is the origin of everything, and his primacy applies to poetry just as it does to every other aspect of reality. There is nothing strange, then, in a 'monarchical' social structure, if the primacy of the emperor is assimilated to that of Zeus, recognizing for him the same pre-eminence as the father of the gods—again, in poetry as in reality. And it is in the Hellenistic age, in the court poetry, that this standard phrase, which was to become extremely common in Latin poetry, particularly following the model of Aratus,[29] assumes an openly encomiastic function. At the beginning of Theocritus' encomium for Ptolemy, the function becomes explicit, and is openly declared: 'From Zeus let us begin, and with Zeus in our poems, Muses, let us make end, for of immortals he is the best; but of men let Ptolemy be named, first, last, and in the midst, for of the men he is most excellent'[30] (17. 1–4). Thus the way is open for a political use of the standard phrase, and consequently, for the assumption of the figure of the emperor in the space of the proem, together with, or even instead of, the figures who traditionally occupy this space (the Muse and the divinities associated with her), and whose help and protection the poet invokes.[31]

[27] Cf. Curtius (1948) 241 f. For more on the Christian conceptions of the Muse, see also Laird, I, in this volume.

[28] Translations of Pindar come from Race (1997).

[29] For a list of the occurrences see Bömer (1958) on Ov. *Fast.* 5. 111.

[30] Translation from Gow (1950).

[31] Aratus himself, in his proem (15–18), associated Zeus (in his divine form, without likening him to powerful mortals) with the Muses, invoking him together with them as a guide for his work.

Furthermore, the close association between Zeus, the Muses, kings, and poets is one of the theoretical foundations of the relationship between poetry and political power. This is based on a famous section of the proem to Hesiod's *Theogony* (ll. 68–103), which is widely echoed in the encomiastic literature of the Hellenistic age.[32] Though performing different functions, these four are linked as depositaries of an authority, of power and / or of the word, that they reciprocally negotiate according to circumstances. It is clear that for all their differences, politico-institutional orders like Hellenistic monarchies and the principate, and later the empire, show close analogies in the relationships of single poets with their patrons or political interlocutors, determining analogous responses in the literary form expressing the attitude of the various poets to an absolute power. The fact is that the presence of the figure of the emperor (as dedicatee of a gesture of homage, or invoked as the poet's inspiration) is a constant in Latin poetry (and particularly in epic and didactic poetry) starting from the Augustan age.[33] Accordingly, the assimilation of the emperor to the divinity means that the appeal addressed to him is expressed in forms that closely repeat those of religious language, often actually in hymn-forms.[34]

In the Augustan age, the first poet to assign this inspirational role to a political personality (be this the *princeps* himself or one of his closest advisers) was Virgil in the *Georgics*. Indeed, while it is true that the help and protection he prays to receive from the gods of nature and Octavian (*da facilem cursum atque audacibus adnue coeptis*, 'grant me a calm voyage, favour my daring enterprise', 1. 40) is not technically the 'inspiration' traditionally invoked by poets, the words with which, in his 'proem in the middle', Virgil addresses Maecenas come very close to this: *te sine nil altum mens incohat* ('without you my mind can begin no lofty theme', 3. 42). Similarly the invocation by Tibullus of his powerful friend Messalla also recalls the traditional request for inspiration (2. 1. 35: *huc ades adspiraque mihi*, 'hither come and breathe upon me your inspiration').[35] But it is in the proem to Ovid's *Fasti* that we read an explicit assimilation of the dedicatee, Germanicus, to the role of an inspiring divinity:[36]

---

[32] Cf. Hunter (1996) 81 f. and n. 17.

[33] A list of passages can be found in Häußler (1973) 127 n. 42.

[34] For Theocritus and Hellenistic Greek poetry cf. Hunter (1996) 46 ff. and 79 ff.

[35] Cf. also Prop. 3. 9. 49 and 52 (to Maecenas).

[36] See the detailed analysis of Fantham (1985) esp. 248 f.; in her opinion, the Ovidian proem is modelled not only on that of Virgil's *Georgics* 1, but it also alludes to, and pays homage (as to his Octavian) to the proem of Germanicus' own *Phaenomena* (254–6).

> excipe pacato, Caesar Germanice, voltu
>   hoc opus et timidae derige navis iter,
> officioque, levem non aversatus honorem,
>   en tibi devoto numine dexter ades.   (1. 3–6)

Caesar Germanicus, accept with serene brow this work and steer the passage of my timid bark. Do not spurn the slight honour, but come propitious as a god to take the homage vowed to you.[37]

His approval will offer support and will be a stimulus for the poet and for his creative faculties:

> adnue conanti per laudes ire tuorum
>   deque meo pavidos excute corde metus.
> da mihi te placidum, *dederis in carmina vires*:
>   ingenium voltu statque caditque tuo.
> pagina iudicii docti subitura movetur
>   principis, ut Clario missa legenda deo   (15–20)

Approve my effort to rehearse the praises of the kin, and cast out quaking terrors from my heart. Show yourself mild to me; *thus you will have lent vigour to my song*; at your gaze my Muse must stand or fall. Submitted to the judgement of a learned prince my page does shiver, as if sent to the Clarian god to read.

The formulation of the invocation is undoubtedly influenced by the fact that the dedicatee-*princeps* is also a poet, and a poet who sings of the heavenly world in particular (25: *vates rege vatis habenas*, 'yourself a poet, guide a poet's reins'). Germanicus is thus likened to Apollo, a god, or rather, *the* god of poetry (while a more generic appeal to *Caesar*, that is to say, to Augustus, the old dedicatee, follows in the proem to the second book: *ergo ades et placido paulum mea munera voltu* | *respice, pacando siquid ab hoste vacat*, 'come, then, and if the conquest of the foe leaves you a vacant hour, cast a kindly glance upon my gift', 17 f.).

However, this circumstance is not decisive. The presence of the *princeps* in the proemial space, together with the Muse, or in her place, has become by now effectively compulsory. This is shown by the example of Marcus Manilius, who lived in Rome during the reigns of Augustus and Tiberius. In the first proem of his *Astronomica*, Manilius does not invoke the Muse or any other supernatural agent, but recognizes his sovereign god—and consequently *the emperor as such*, as guarantor of that peace which makes it possible to devote oneself to the study of the heavenly world—the merit of giving him the *animus* and the strength for such an ambitious task:

[37] Translations of *Fasti* are adapted from Frazer/Goold (1989).

> hunc mihi tu, Caesar, patriae principesque paterque,
> qui regis augustis parentem legibus orbem
> concessumque patri mundum deus ipse mereris,
> *das animum viresque facis ad tanta canenda.*   (I. 7–10)

You, Caesar, First Citizen and Father of your Country, who rule a world obedient to your august laws and merit the heaven granted to your sire, yourself a god, are the one who inspires this purpose and *gives me strength for such lofty themes.*[38]

There is no mention of the Muse. The only function of the divinity, who is addressed further on, is to 'tune' the song of the poet as he illustrates his material (*in numerum Phoebo modulante referre*, 'to tell thereof in verse with Apollo tuning my song', 19), and not to supply him with any kind of information or inspiration.

It would be difficult—and purposeless—to try and assign a firm timeline for the developments in the Muses' tradition and presence in Roman poetry: literary traditions evolve subtly and slowly. But, by the early first century AD, the Muse's time-honoured authority appears significantly eroded and ousted by the need to pay homage to the political power. It is no coincidence that the voice that most openly and assertively stands as a testament to the newly won primacy of political authority, while also making explicit the link between the poet and the figure of Jupiter (*Juppiter in terra*), is that of a poet-politician, a figure thus more directly involved in the dialectics of the relationship between political power and literary production. I am talking about the poet-prince Germanicus, and it may have been his formulation[39] that influenced the many comparable invocations to be found in the proemia of other contemporary poets:

> Ab Iove principium magno deducit Aratus.
> *carminis at nobis*, genitor, *tu maximus auctor*,
> te veneror tibi sacra fero doctique laboris
> primitias. probat ipse deum rectorque satorque
> *(Phaen.* 1–4)

Aratus began with mighty Jupiter. *My poem, however, claims you*, father, *greatest of all, as its inspirer.* It is you that I revere; it is to you that I am offering sacred gifts, the first fruits of my literary efforts. The ruler and begetter of the gods himself approves.[40]

---

[38] Translation from Goold (1977).

[39] If the suggestion of Fantham (1985) 255 f. is correct, who also places the proem of Germanicus prior to that of the *Fasti*. The chronological relationship between the work of Germanicus and that of Manilius is notoriously controversial.

[40] Translation adapted from Gain (1976).

The substitution of the traditional divinity of the proem, Jupiter, with his earthly homologue, the *princeps* (in this specific case Tiberius, or less probably Augustus), is expressly declared and justified here. The peace that the emperor guarantees for the world (5 ff.) is the necessary condition for literary activity; and the poet asks the emperor, as the *carminis . . . maximus auctor*, for his protection and *numen*, or inspiration, for his poetry:

> haec ego dum Latiis conor praedicere Musis,
> pax tua tuque adsis nato numenque secundes   (15–16)

May your presence and the peace you have won aid your son; grant your divine power, to favour me as I attempt to tell of this in Latin verse.

Not only has the old inspirational function of the Muses for the poet disappeared, but the roles have been literally overturned: now it is the poet who assigns himself the task of *praedicere* to the Muses, who consequently assume the passive role of reception, which in previous times had been the role of the poet.[41]

This gradual metamorphosis of the array of inspirational figures, whereby the ruler takes over from the Muse and assumes her one-time prerogatives and functions, takes place, as we saw, especially in the context of the didactic genre, where realistic motivations (the general aspiration for peace, the poet's need for protection and freedom from economic preoccupations, etc.) are visibly exhibited as important factors. It appears, however, as a more radical innovation in the epic genre, where the Muse was traditionally the dispenser and guardian of memory, and therefore the retainer of that peculiar type of knowledge ascribed to the poet. The first poet to introduce this element of novelty in Latin epics is Lucan, and this is one of the reasons why his proem marks out a major break with the epic tradition.[42] Lucan too does not limit himself to renouncing the authority of the traditional epic Muse, but substitutes her with another source of inspiration, another *numen*:

> sed *mihi iam numen*; nec, si te pectore vates
> accipio, Cirrhaea velim secreta moventem
> sollicitare deum Bacchumque avertere Nysa:
> *tu satis ad vires Romana in carmina dandas.*
> fert animus causas[43] tantarum expromere rerum . . .   (1. 63–7)

[41] Cf. Murray (1981) 96 f.

[42] Cf. e.g. Feeney (1991) 274 ff.

[43] I am obliged to Alison Sharrock for the observation that this line seems to combine two distinct allusions to the proem of Ovid's *Metamorphoses* and to the *Aeneid*. Is this a way to deconstruct the role of inspiring figure ostensibly just assigned to Nero, while on the other hand reasserting the dominant role of intertextuality and poetic tradition?

But *already to me you are deity*, and if I as bard receive you in my breast, no wish have I to trouble the god who has control of Cirrha's secrets or to distract Bacchus from Nysa: *you are enough to give me strength for Roman song*. My spirit leads me to reveal the causes of such great events.[44]

It is Nero that Lucan salutes as his inspirational divinity; thanks to him, he will not have to *sollicitare* Apollo or Bacchus, the gods who habitually assist the Muse. The source of inspiration of the poem about the triumph of tyrannical power will not be one of the divinities of the epic tradition (Apollo, Bacchus, the Muse), but—very suitably, as has been observed[45]—Nero himself.

And the motif of the emperor as the alternative, political muse, keeps transforming ever so slightly. In the case of Calpurnius Siculus, a bucolic poet of the age of Nero, the standard incipit *ab Iove principium* is re-employed in an encomiastic key (following the model of Germanicus):

> ab Iove principium, si quis canit aethera, sumat,
> si quis Atlantiaci pondus molitur Olympi.
> at mihi, qui nostras praesenti numine terras
> perpetuamque regit iuvenili robore pacem,
> laetus et augusto felix arrideat ore.   (4. 82–6)

From Jove let every bard begin, who so sings of the sky, who so essays to describe the Olympian burden which Atlas bears. For myself, may I win a glad propitious smile from the imperial lips of him whose incarnate godhead rules our lands and whose youthful prowess rules the eternal peace.[46]

The contrast between the *numen praesens* of Nero and the faraway heavenly Jupiter reflects not only an opposition of literary genres: *aether* indicates Aratus (to whom the phrase is closely linked) and astrological poetry, but also the idea of an abstract power, which is realistically subjected to a far more concrete and influential authority, that of the earthly Jupiter, Nero. But the awareness of the relationship of economic dependence of the man of letters on a patron, or a political protector, is expressed most clearly, with sarcastic disenchantment, in the epigram of a Greek poet, Lucillius, likewise living at Rome during the reign of Nero (*AP* 9. 572):

> 'Let us begin our song from the Heliconian Muses'; so
> Hesiod wrote, they say, while he kept his sheep. 'Sing, O

---

[44] Translation from Braund (1992).
[45] Ahl (1976) 48; Johnson (1987) 122; Feeney (1991) 276 ff.
[46] Translation from Duff and Duff (1934).

goddess, the wrath,' and 'Tell me, Muse, the man,' said
Calliope by the mouth of Homer. Now I have got to write a
proem of some sort. But what shall I write now I am
beginning to publish this second book? 'Olympian Muses,
daughters of Zeus, I should not have been saved unless
Nero Caesar had given me money.'[47]

Let us now return to Statius' proems, and attempt a reappraisal of his
tussles with his Muse(s), in the light of our recent exploration. Roman
Augustan, and mainly post-Augustan, literature seems to have interlaced the discourse on imperial political power with major topoi from
the Muses' literary tradition and Statius embraces it with ingenuity. The
'refusal of the Muse' seems to come more easily and naturally in the
'lighter' poetry of the *Silvae*, a kind of poetry for which, unlike the epic,
no divine inspiration is needed: for instance, in the poem illustrating the
baths of Claudius Etruscus, where, in order to 'frolic' (*lascivire*) with a
friend, Statius does not need the Muses, Apollo, or Mercury:

> Non Helicona gravi pulsat chelys enthea plectro,
> nec lassata voco totiens mihi numina, Musas;
> et te, Phoebe, choris et te dimittimus, Euhan;
> tu quoque muta ferae, volucer Tegeaee, sonorae
> terga premas: alios poscunt mea carmina coetus   (1. 5. 1–5)

My harp does not resound at Helicon's gates in fierce, ecstatic melody, and I do
not call on the heavenly Muses, so often wearied by my prayer; you, Phoebus,
and you, Euhan, are released from my choral song, and you, swift Tegean, keep
in mute silence your tuneful tortoise-shell: my song demands other choirs.

But the Naiads are sufficient (1. 5. 6–8), as is also shown in 2. 3. 6 f. (*quid
Phoebum tam parva rogem? vos dicite causas,* | *Naides*, 'why ask so slight a
tale of Phoebus? you, O Naiads, relate the cause').[48] But the refusal of the
solemn mythological figures may serve, also, to emphasize, with an
obsequious gesture (analogous to the elegiac *Werbung*, or rather to
Lucan's homage to Nero), the preference that the poet gives to a powerful friend as the source of his inspiration; this is the case, for example,
when he addresses the politician and orator Rutilius Gallus in order to
celebrate his recovery:

---

[47] Translation from Paton (1917). On this 'gap between reality and poetic pretence' (seen
especially in the context of Persius' *Satires*) cf. Fowler, in this volume.

[48] The same refusal can be found in 1. 6. 1 ff. As regards variations in Statius' way of invoking
the divinity in a manner congruous to the nature of his single compositions, cf. van Dam (1984)
290.

> ast ego nec Phoebum, quamquam mihi surda sine illo
> plectra, nec Aonias decima cum Pallade divas
> aut mitem Tegeae Dircesve hortabor alumnum
>
> (I. 4. 19–21)

But I will call neither on Phoebus, although my quill is mute without him, nor on the Aonian goddesses with Pallas the tenth Muse, nor on the gentle sons of Tegea and of Dirce.

On the other hand, *ipse veni viresque novas animumque ministra* | *qui caneris* . . . ('come yourself and bring new strength and spirit, you who are my theme', 22 f.) is the apostrophe to the dedicatee, whose protection and 'inspiration' Statius invokes, almost likening him to Virgil's Juno (*Aen.* 9. 764: *Iuno viris animumque ministrat,* 'Juno supplies strength and courage').[49]

Likewise, the figure of the emperor, present throughout Statius' work (a rather cumbersome, obsessive presence), gets specifically mentioned every time that the poet discusses his own literary choices, and consequently his own social role. One example of this is a passage of the *Silvae* whose literary referent has not been adequately appreciated. *Silvae* 5. 1 is an epicedium in honour of Priscilla, the wife of Abascanthus, a freedman of Domitian, and a friend of Claudia, the wife of Statius himself; the composition opens with some considerations about how figurative art, and sculpture in particular, tries to confer a glory that lasts beyond death:

> Si manus aut similes docilis mihi fingere ceras
> aut ebur impressis aurumve animare figuris,
> hinc, Priscilla, tuo solacia grata marito
> conciperem. namque egregia pietate meretur
> ut vel Apelleo vultus signata colore
> Phidiaca vel nata manu reddare dolenti:
> sic auferre rogis umbram conatur, et ingens
> certamen cum Morte gerit, curasque fatigat
> artificum inque omni te quaerit amare metallo.   (1–9)

Had I but skill of hand to mould likeness in wax or to leave a living impress upon gold or ivory, thence would I imagine, Priscilla, a grateful solace for your husband. For his conspicuous devotion merits that you yourself, whether painted by Apelles' brush or given life by Phidian art, should be brought back to calm his grief; so valiantly strives he to rescue your ghost from the pyre, and

---

[49] 'It is apparent that traditional imagery connecting creativity with superhuman intervention has been redeployed to interpret the influence of powerful but human friends': White (1993) 20.

wages a mighty struggle with Death, and exhausts the cunning of the craftsmen, and in every metal would seek to show his love of you.

The efforts of Abascanthus to obtain the artistic immortality of his wife are, however, destined to be frustrated. The only art that can really guarantee the immortality of its subject is poetry:

> sed *mortalis honos, agilis quem dextra laborat.*
> *nos* tibi, laudati iuvenis rarissima coniunx,
> *longa nec obscurum finem latura perenni*
> *temptamus dare iusta lyra*, modo dexter Apollo
> quique venit iuncto mihi semper Apolline Caesar
> annuat: haut alio melius condere sepulcro.   (10–15)

But *mortal is the honour that toil of clever hands can pay: it is the poet's endeavour to bring you*, peerless consort of a youth renowned, *an enduring tribute that will not suffer oblivion in the end, the due offering of eternal song*, provided that Apollo is propitious, and Caesar, who ever in Apollo's company aids me, gives assent; no other nobler sepulchre will you find.

A comparison between sculpture and poetry, followed by a proud affirmation of the superiority of the word over the figurative image, also opened the fifth *Nemea* by Pindar ('I am not a sculptor, so as to fashion stationary statues that stand on their same base. Rather, on board every ship and in every boat, sweet song, go forth from Aigina and spread the news . . .')—one of the strongest declarations of an artist's awareness of his own power,[50] and of his determination to negotiate it. The use of the Pindaric model is the mark of a fundamental analogy between the 'professionality' of ancient Greek choral lyric poetry (Simonides, Pindar, Bacchylides), already revived by the encomiastic poetry of the Hellenistic age, and that of Statius, who cleverly exploits the social prestige poetry had acquired amongst the new imperial élite, of which the patrons who commission his occasional poetry are members.[51]

By alluding to Pindar, Statius underlines the importance of his own role vis-à-vis the specific patron who had commissioned the work, Abascanthus, the official at the court of Domitian, but also vis-à-vis the emperor himself. It is enough to read the words with which Statius accompanies his task. He guarantees the success of his poetry (which is to say, lasting glory for the subject of his work) on one condition: that he does not lose the favour of Apollo, or that of Caesar, the earthly

---

[50] Cf. Gentili (1984) 214 ff. with abundant material on the developments of the motif of competition between the word and marble; Svenbro (1984) esp. 151 ff.

[51] See also here Hardie (1983); Citroni (1992) esp. 453 ff.

power, which for him is always linked to the former. By declaring that the inspiration of *Caesar* is inseparable from divine inspiration, Statius is actually negotiating his power as a poet with the emperor's protection, solicited through Abascanthus. But at the same time, this is also an implicit admission of weakness, a recognition of the difficulty of his role on the part of a poet in need of protection and help, and therefore attentive to acquire favours both directly from the god-emperor and through his 'ministers' (*Praef.* 8 ff.: *praeterea latus omne divinae domus semper demereri pro mea mediocritate conitor. nam qui bona fide deos colit, amat et sacerdotes*, 'Further, I always strive, insignificant as I am, to deserve well of all adherents of the Sacred Palace. For he who in good faith worships the gods, loves their priests too').

In the proem to the *Thebais* it is the *recusatio*, the form that had given voice to the discomfort of poets before the pressures of power, that acts as an indication of this experimental, and at times uneasy, blend of the political and the literary. Really, therefore, *ab Iove principium*, the ancient poetic formula, now reveals all its authentic political value, of a compulsory homage to *Iuppiter in terra*. This phrase is the very symbol of the control of political power over the poet's activity, as Statius himself suggests in the *praefatio* to the first book of the *Silvae*. In quoting several witnesses of the speed with which he has composed the various poems, he starts with Domitian, to whom the first composition of the book is dedicated: *Primus libellus sacrosanctum habet testem: sumendum enim erat 'a Iove principium'* ('The first piece can appeal to a witness of inviolable sanctity: for "from Jove must I begin"'). The affirmation that it was necessary to start from Jupiter-Domitian[52] sounds ambiguous: it was a necessary homage to a traditional principle of poetics, but it was also necessary because that ritual literary topos had by now become a carefully calculated gesture of political prudence.[53]

But it is the *praefatio* to *Silvae* 4 which eloquently confirms how compulsory this homage actually was: immediately after dedicating the new *liber* to his friend Vitorius Marcellus, Statius feels the need to justify himself for a beginning that does not include the ritual invocation to the emperor. It is the first time that he has broken this rule (2 f.: *reor equidem aliter quam invocato numine maximi imperatoris nullum opusculum meum coepisse*, 'I believe that no work of mine has opened without an invoca-

---

[52] The controversially extreme interpretation of Dominik (1994) 161 ff. insists on the likening of Domitian to Jupiter in the poetry of Statius.

[53] On the ambiguity of this prefatorial letter cf. also Ahl (1984) 91.

tion of the godhead of our mighty Prince'), and he feels the need to make up for this lack of an initial homage by dedicating the first three *Silvae* to the emperor. This is the same emperor to whom the poet had submitted most of his compositions for approval (in order to defend himself from expected attacks against his light poetry): *multa ex illis iam domino Caesari dederam, et quanto hoc plus est quam edere!* ('I had already presented many of them to our Imperial Master, compared with which publication is a trivial affair', 28 f.). The 'control' of the emperor is thus also a literary test and legitimation, an *imprimatur* guaranteed by the highest authority. The poet makes use of his dependence on power, and his condition of weakness, as instruments for his professional promotion, cleverly exploiting the act of homage to his own advantage. To negotiate with the prince the terms of one's engagement is also an indirect way to declare one's personal reluctance to write propagandistic poetry, as well as to exhibit one's credentials to the readers.

III. AN INSPIRATION THAT NEVER ARRIVES

Let us now close by attempting yet one more evaluation of Statius' ambiguous relationship with inspiration. Together with the invocation to the Muse (in the two epic proems), we have seen in Statius the explicit, disenchanted refusal of this ancient convention (e.g. in *Silv.* 1. 5. 1 ff.). And yet it would be a mistake to assert that the function of the traditional system is irrelevant.[54] To suggest this is to miss the meaning that can be conveyed through this topos, and how it may differ depending on the contexts in which it is set (it is significant, for example, that the role of the Muse is maintained in the higher genre, the epic).

It seems possible to deduce that Statius was probably atypical in this regard, and that his revival of the Muses was seen by his contemporaries (or at least by his enemies) as an antiquated attitude. We might look, for instance, to the parody of the *invocatio* to Calliope and the Muses that Juvenal includes in his fourth satire, before the description of the gigantic turbot that has been caught and presented to Domitian:

> incipe, Calliope. Licet et considere: non est
> cantandum, res vera agitur. narrate, puellae
> Pierides, prosit mihi vos dixisse puellas   (34–6)

---

[54] Thus Schetter (1960) 20, who suggests that these are 'Requisiten, die man nach Belieben weglegen und wieder hervornehmen kann'.

Begin, Calliope—and so sit down, it isn't a matter for singing; the theme is a true event; recount it, you maidens of Pieria—and may I win some credit for calling you maidens.[55]

The sarcasm of the incongruity between the solemn tone of the *invocatio* and the low character of the subject to be described probably has Statius himself as its target, seeing that a few lines later (71 ff.) the description of the emperor's 'Cabinet' (which has met to discuss the lack of a pan big enough to cook the turbot) is the parody of Statius' description of the Cabinet in *De bello Germanico* (the work he produced at the Alba competition in AD 90), where there was probably another *invocatio* to the Muses.[56] Statius is considered as a late singer of the Muses, a follower of the most conservative poetic tradition.

In actual fact, the use of the traditional 'Musean' instruments seems to be far more skilful and anything but naïve or repetitive. In his relationship with the Muse, Statius discusses problems of inspiration, tradition, and authority, which are the various forms of conditioning perceived by the poet in the exercise of his creative activity. While we see in Virgil's epos the 'partnership of poet and Muse, the asserted harmony between tradition and authority in the poet's own voice',[57] in Statius the relationship between the poet and the Muse seems to be less harmonious, and more problematic. The poet receives from the Muses an impulse to sing of that precise subject, but he does not need to invoke their help as informers, nor does he let himself be conditioned in organizing his work. Lucan had claimed for himself (1. 67: *fert animus*) the responsibility for the choice of the topic to be dealt with, trusting in the inspiration of Nero. Valerius Flaccus, who, it is true, appeals to the help of Apollo (1. 5: *Phoebe, mone*)—if for no other reason, in view of his position as *quindecimvir sacris faciundis*—none the less fixes his subject himself (1. 1: *Prima deum magnis canimus freta pervia natis*, 'I sing of the waters first crossed by the mighty sons of gods'), just as Silius does (1. 1: *Ordior arma*, 'I begin the war'). Statius also exhibits his own personal autonomy in his decisions. And yet at the same time, he attributes to an external impulse (*Theb.* 1. 3: *Pierius menti calor incidit*) his poetic inspiration and the choice of the topic to be dealt with. These tactics, as is obvious, offer him an excellent excuse in the face of the pressures that he feels in his poetic choices, seeing that they allow him to deny responsibility for his choice. It is not the

---

[55] Translation from Rudd (1991).

[56] Cf. Braund (1996) ad loc.

[57] Feeney (1991) 186. On the comparison between the two proems cf. also Ahl (1986) 2817 f.

poet himself who personally decides the subject of his work, but it is his inspiration—an external agent, of divine origin—that makes the decision. And as this inspiration is not yet powerful enough to allow him to devote himself to a historical epos (17–18: *Itala nondum | signa . . . ausim spirare*), that is to say, to celebrate the achievements of Domitian, he can only compose a mythological epos, a great subject, but inferior to the warlike achievements of the emperor; he will be able to devote himself to these only when, one day, the inspiration of the Muses enables him to face such a weighty task (32).

Thus we find in Statius a significant phenomenon in the context of the Latin epic tradition: on the one hand, he brings to completion the process of gradual emancipation of the poet from his divine sources,[58] and from the external authority which traditionally validated his work (that is to say, unlike Homer and Virgil, he has no 'subjects' about which he needs to be informed by a superhuman guarantor). On the other, moving in a direction that is only apparently the opposite one, he revives and emphasizes the intervention of a supernatural agent, as the source of inspiration for the poet (a step backwards, that is, compared with Lucan and didactic poetry, which had 'transferred to the earth' that abstract authority, recognizing it in the *princeps*). At the end of the long struggle that has set them one against the other, the poet has taken away from the Muse that authority that used to be a prerogative of hers. The poet has thus emancipated himself from the Muse's guardianship. But he now uses his newly conquered authority to smuggle back in again, to his advantage, the pretence, the ghost of the Muse. Because although he tells us that the Muse is, in fact, a figure of power, of the control exercised by political authority over the free creative spirit of the artist, it may be useful for him to make her appear to be a higher entity, who escapes from his control, and thus to make use of this highly suitable instrument for his '*nondum* strategy', the deferment *sine die* of a more direct political involvement, which Statius pursues to the end. Thanks to the Muse, and to her useful function of a protective screen, Statius will be able to avoid beginning the work which power desired to impose upon him.

[58] A process that started decidedly in the Hellenistic age: cf. Paduano (1970) and Pretagostini (1995) 170.

12

Corny Copa, the Motel Muse

John Henderson

I. WELCOME TO THE DIVE . . . COME ALIVE, COME ALIVE (DOWN IN DEVIL GATE DRIVE)

> Leave your troubles outside! So—life is disappointing?
> Forget it! In here life is beautiful—the girls are
> beautiful—even the orchestra is beautiful!

> Willkommen, Bienvenue, Welcome
> Im Cabaret, Au Cabaret, To Cabaret!
>   (The emcee's δεῦρ' ἴθι, seguing into F. Ebb's lyric 'Will-
> kommen')[1]

'Dance is a space where desire manifests itself.'[2] A neatly self-contained—'one-page'[3]—elegiac poem hitches a ride to eternity on the back of the *Appendix Vergiliana*, known as the *Copa* for both first word and starlet of the opening two couplets:[4]

> Copa Syrisca caput Graeca redimita mitella,
>   crispum sub crotalo docta movere latus,
> ebria fumosa saltat lasciva taberna
>   ad cubitum raucos excutiens calamos.

©orny Copa

[1] One of his songs (music by J. Kander) for J. Masteroff's stage and film musical *Cabaret* (1966 > 1967, New York), out of C. Isherwood's short story 'Sally Bowles' in *Goodbye to Berlin* (1939), as reread in J. Van Druten's Broadway then film script *I am a Camera* (1951 > 1955, New York); before B. Fosse's Hollywood Liza Minnelli musical *Cabaret* (1970–2): Mizejewski (1992) esp. 162 n. 5. Divine decadence, darling.

[2] Sumic-Riha (1997) 231.

[3] The thirty-eight verses of elegies such as Propertius 1, 1 suggest formating along with a suprascript title, in a sealed package of one or two columns: Henderson (1982) 142 on Ps.-Alcuin, *O mea cella*.

[4] Not much wrong with Kenney's OCT in Clausen etc. (1966): I pour out breathless commas, jazz up other punctuation marks, and remove daggers; prefer *huc* to *huic* at v. 25 and back Clausen's *formosa et* for the paradosis *formosus* at v. 33. (I have not seen Alessandro (1988).)

quid iuvat aestivo defessum pulvere abisse 5
    quam potius bibulo decubuisse toro?
sunt topia et calybae, cyathi, rosa, tibia, chordae,
    et triclia umbrosis frigida harundinibus,
en et Maenalio quae garrit dulce sub antro
    rustica pastoris fistula more sonat, 10
est et vappa cado nuper defusa picato,
    est crepitans rauco murmure rivus aquae,
sunt etiam croceo violae de flore corollae
    sertaque purpurea lutea mixta rosa
et quae virgineo libata Achelois ab amne 15
    lilia vimineis attulit in calathis,
sunt et caseoli, quos iuncea fiscina siccat,
    sunt autumnali cerea pruna die
castaneaeque nuces et suave rubentia mala,
    est hic munda Ceres, est Amor, est Bromiùs, 20
sunt et mora cruenta et lentis uva racemis,
    et pendet iunco caeruleus cucumis,
est tuguri custos armatus falce saligna,
    sed non et vasto est inguine terribilis.
huc calybita veni; lassus iam sudat asellus: 25
    parce illi, Vestae delicium est asinus.
nunc cantu crebro rumpunt arbusta cicadae,
    nunc varia in gelida sede lacerta latet:
si sapis, aestivo recubans nunc prolue vitro,
    seu vis crystalli ferre novos calices. 30
hic age pampinea fessus requiesce sub umbra
    et gravidum roseo necte caput strophio,
formosa et tenerae decerpens ora puellae—
    a pereat cui sunt prisca supercilia!
quid cineri ingrato servas bene olentia serta? 35
    anne coronato vis lapide ossa tegi?
pone merum et talos: pereat qui crastina curat.
    Mors aurem vellens 'vivite' ait, 'venio'. 38

Copa shakes a swish tail-feather in the Stuart interregnum, as Thomas
Stanley's 'Hostesse':[5]

[5] 'The Hostesse', from *Poems from the Excitations*', in *Poems, 1651*, Poole and Maule (1995) 498.
Royalist, translator, and poet Stanley (1625–78: pupil of William Fairfax, Greek Scholar,
Pembroke Hall 1639, FRS 1663) was in post-regicide retirement. He would expatiate on the
History of Philosophy, and brave editing Aeschylus under the Restoration (Crump (1962)
xxi–xxxiv).

Stanley, I presume, despairs at v. 25; he goes puritan dry, for an instant, by cutting vv. 29 f.
(for that couplet, see Wilkinson's version below).

The Syrian Hostesse, with a Greek Wreath crown'd,
Shaking her wither'd side to th'Bagpipes sound,
Drunk, 'fore the Tavern a loose Measure leads,
And with her elbow blows the squeaking Reeds.
   Who would the Summers dusty labours ply,   5
That might on a soft Couch carowsing ly?
Here's Musick, Wine, Cups, and an Arbour made
Of cooling flags, that casts a grateful shade:
A Pipe whereon a Shepherd gently playes,
Whilst the Mœnalian Cave resounds his layes: 10
A Hogshead of brisk wine new pierc'd: a Spring
Of pleasant Water ever murmuring:
Wreaths twisted with the purple Violet;
White Garlands with the blushing Rose beset;
And Osier Baskets with fair Lilies fraught   15
From the Bank-side by Achelois brought:
Fresh Cheese in Rushy Cradles layd to dry:
Soft Plums, by Autumn ripened leisurely:
Chessenuts, and Apples sweetly streakt with red;
Neat *Ceres* by young Love and *Bacchus* led: 20
Black Mulberries, an overcharged Vine;
Green Cowcumbers, that on their stalks decline:
The Gardens Guardian, with no dreadful look,
Nor other weapon than a pruning-hook.
Tabor and Pipe come hither: see, alasse,
Thy tir'd Beast sweats; spare him; our wel-lov'd Asse.   (25)
The Grassehopper chirps on her green seat,
The Lizard peeps out of his cold retreat;   (28)
Come, in this shade thy weary Limbs repose,   (31)
And crown thy drowsie Temples with the Rose.
A Maids Lip safely maist thou rifle here;
Away with such whose Foreheads are severe.
Flowers why reserv'st thou for unthankful Dust?   (35)
To thy cold Tomb wilt Thou these Garlands trust?

    The bizarre 'bag-pipe' visualization of v. 4 skirls on: cf. Goodyear (1977) 121 f., Tarrant (1992) 336–8, Drabkin (1930) 96 f. Ferniqué (1887) shows an arsenal of clappers and slap-sticks, with one puzzling panoply fastened to palm, neck, and . . . elbow (fig. 2079). John Crook gets *my* plaudit: 'shaking to and fro the noisy castanets in time with (the rhythmic motions of) her elbow(s)' (cited by Goodyear (1977) 122)—except that my *Copa* would do this by banging her bamboo eurhythmically *on* her forearm, or elbow: Skiera (1985) describes assorted *Castañuelas* and *Palillos* ('little sticks'), some 'made out of split bamboo', and explains the wondrous potentialities of their intricate counterplay with foot-stamping, finger-snapping, hand-clapping—Olé, olé. (I have not seen the definitive history: E. Skiera, *Kastagnettenschule/ Method for Castanets* (Berlin, n.d.).)

Bring Wine and Dice; hang them the morrow weigh:
Death warns, *I come* (saith he) *live while you may.*

Private dancer at a Roman Blue Angel, *Copa* makes Latin music, dresses the part, and figures poetry as rhythmic seduction. She is an invitation to join an elaborately itemized social scene. Here, old chum, is Roman desire à la carte, an aid to pleasure for tired businessmen and academics slumming it. Traditionally, both sets of clients have had their minds on only one thing—on *dating Copa*, while chortling on the side at each 'ludicrously inept use of language' from 'our unfortunate poet', whose every 'gaffe betrays ignorance of Latin idiom'.[6] Gents and toffs drop by this Kopy Kat Klub floor-show to jeer at the inept secondariness, *folies* down the road apiece; but it's the phoney imitativeness they have come to leer at, attracted by the turns that link, even as they divide, act, and punter.[7] Suckers for 'satire (if) scarcely of a serious kind':

Surisca's tavern, a low and tawdry place, parades before its lower-class clientele second-hand and second-rate attractions, which the poet presents with an amused contempt but also some lively interest.[8]

Yes: Men cluster round like moths round a flame, | and if they burn, she aint to blame. Fresh out of that Weimar wine-bar, Long Tall (Aunt) Sally Bowles is the draw—as in John Betjeman's not-so-swinging sixties tribute, all piled cans of mock-Tudor soup, alliteration-tic and hyphenitis:

---

[6] 'On dating the *Copa*': Westendorp Boerma (1958). Quotes from Tarrant (1992) 340 (on v. 11), 'resisting the remarkable affection felt for the poem by earlier generations of scholars' (331), and dating *Copa* as Flavian, and past it.

   To show off *my* 'amused contempt but also some lively interest', here is Goodyear (1977) in his element: 'Or perhaps he is simply incompetent. . . . Subtlety was usually beyond his powers, and he perhaps attempted more than he could execute. . . . But should we just take this couplet as a fumbling imitation and leave the matter there? Anyone who has perused the *Culex* will hesitate to set limits to the absurdities Latin poetasters can commit when pillaging the works of their betters. But absurdities may sometimes be calculated. . . . There is no clearer case of unhappy adaptation in this poem. . . . The two passages became confused in his mind. . . . Shameless pilfering from Vergil. . . . Propertius, whom our poet is freely pillaging . . . This line is a patchwork, but a happy one. . . . Wilamowitz believes that the poet has simply got himself into a hopeless muddle. . . . I do not believe he was as incompetent as that. (Incompetent adaptation): I know that a line is hard to draw in this area, but I will draw one here' (120–31).

[7] In the dim nooks of this lap-dancer's paradise, you can make out their silhouettes, a galaxy of special ghosts—Wilamowitz, Leo, Housman, Clausen, Courtney, Goodyear, Kenney, quite an apparatus: *inepta est Vergilii imitatio*, they mutter, *frustra sollicitaverunt interpretes*, just won't play ball (OCT *ad* vv. 15–16, 17–22).

[8] Goodyear (1977) 120.

Margery, mine hostess at Ye Olde Tudor Tavern,
   Waggling her seductive hips outside upon the grass,
Dressed like Mistress Quickly in *The Merry Wives of Windsor*,
   Saucily solicits the tourists as they pass.

'What's the good of plodding on, perspiring in the sunshine?   5
   Why not put your feet up here and have a drink? We've got
Hedges clipped in fancy shapes, a summer-house with thatch on,
   Pergolas and inglenooks and warming-pans—the lot;
Madrigals on disks we have; and hear that background-music?—
   Someone playing the flute in Walter Raleigh's Bower.   10
Try our Merrydown in cask—it's only just been opened.
   Sit and listen to the stream. And what about a flower?
We've got knots of violets to stick into your hair-do.
   Crimson roses woven in with yellow ones; and look!
Such a lovely basketful of pure-white waterlilies!   15
   Tamesis our river-sprite has skimmed them from the brook.
Here are creamy cheeses just drying in their strainers,
   Plums that ripen smooth as wax this sunny autumn morn,
Chestnuts by the dozen and sweetly blushing apples.
   Valentine's our patron-saint, and old John Barleycorn.   20
Taste those blood-red mulberries, those grapes in luscious bunches,
   Try that dark-green cucumber that's hanging from its stem.
See our wooden statue too, the watchman with his halberd
   (Never mind his codpiece, dear: the Tudors all had them).
You, sir, leave your Vespa there: your engine's overheated;   25
   Spare a little thought for it; you're tempting Providence.
Bumble-bees incessantly are droning round the garden;
   Even puss is lurking in the shadow of the fence.
If you're wise, you'll take a seat and drain a pint of pewter;
   Or if you prefer it, we have brand-new crystal-ware.   30
Come along. You're tired out. Lie down beneath this pear-tree.
   Here's a drop of lavender to sprinkle on your hair.
Choose a girl with cherry lips and don't be shy of kissing.
   Eye-brow-raising puritans can chase themselves, I say.
What's the point of keeping flowers to put on thankless tombstones?   35
   You won't want them on your grave when you have had your day.'

'Draw a pint. Get out the darts. Who cares about tomorrow?'

   Death is whispering in your ear, 'Live now. I'm on my way.'
               (Words for muzak by L. P. Wilkinson, 1965)

Pull her leg, boys, put *Copa* down. Put *Copa* in its place, dons, down
town. But, for all the catachresis, acknowledge the power of the Muse:

bound to her role as the other, fixed in representation by her abject costume and objectified body parts, her shimmy vibrates with homo-sociality. Here in the ballroom of (all-male) life, the go-go girl clicks her castanets for two couplets to hang a sign, fix an emblem, for the pulse of elegiac energy: 'Let me entertain you, | You'll have a real good time'.

This neon 'Salome Dancing' advertises The Dance, of poetry:

Amid the heady odour of these perfumes, in the over-heated atmosphere of the basilica, Salome slowly glides forward on the points of her toes, her left arm stretched in a commanding gesture, her right bent back and holding a great lotus-blossom beside her face, while a woman squatting on the floor strums the strings of a guitar.

With a withdrawn, solemn, almost august expression on her face, she begins the lascivious dance . . .[9]

Once we give up trying to direct *Copa*, by specifying a voice or voices for a mime,[10] the dancer's dance will figure the writing ahead. It puts move-ment into calm, action into stare, body into desire, life into inertness. 'She's a mover', doing it for 'our' selves: *saltat* (v. 3) pivots between her past and present participles, trailing an emphatic nominative to shimmer in the afterglow, *excutiens* (v. 4; *redimita . . . docta*, 1–2). The (rest of the) tavern teems with the dummy copula verbs of expository deixis: *sunt . . . en . . . est . . . est . . . sunt etiam . . . sunt . . . sunt . . . est . . . est . . . est . . . sunt . . . pendet . . . est . . . huc . . . veni . . . nunc . . . nunc . . . nunc . . . hic . . . pone*, and rolls out plentiful participles of its own (past×5; present×6), showcasing a suite of resonant present nominatives: *crepitans . . . recubans . . . decerpens . . . vellens* (vv. 12, 29, 33, 38).[11] Non-stop *Copa* 'dances sexy' (*saltat lasciva*, v. 3), topicalizing 'pleasure—more, not less' (*iuvat . . . quam potius*, vv. 5 f. ~ *ingrato*, 35), the pleasure of the moment (~~erastina~~ *curat*, v. 37), as the clientele of *Amor* (v. 20) is likened to a goddess's 'sex-toy' (*delicium*, v. 26). 'Glass or crystal—take your pick' (*seu vis*, vv. 29 f.); 'funny hats now—or at your wake, which is it?' (*anne . . . vis*, vv. 35 f.). *La-la-la* murmurs LaBelle, 'mmm', all labials (*redimita*

---

[9] J. Floressas Des Esseintes describes Gustave Moreau's painting *Salome Dancing*, itself inspired by Flaubert's *Salammbô* and inspiring his *Hérodias*, in Huysmans (1903 = 1959: trans. R. Baldick) 64, see Meltzer (1987) 19 f.: 'The verbs are overwhelmingly of motion. . . . The play of light . . . the immediacy . . . the cataloguing in the passage is almost vertiginous: Huysmans uses verb after verb, adjective after adjective . . . repeated use of anaphora . . . a barrage of synonyms . . . by their very accumulation and repetition evoke in the reader the heady odor of perfumes, the overheated atmosphere of the basilica . . . *ecphrasis*'.

[10] Cf. Goodyear (1977) 118 f., Cutolo (1990) 118 n. 6. Contrast esp. the elaborate montage of Wilkinson (1965), cf. 38.

[11] Past: vv. 11, 14, 15, 23, 36; present: add *rubentia, olentia* (19, 35).

mitella, latus, lasciva, vv. 1–3). Get in the mood with 'curvaceous' Margery (*crispum . . . latus*, v. 2)—'no call for terrorism with that unholy bazooka down your trousers' (*armatus . . . sed non et vasto est inguine terribilis*, vv. 23 f.), go grab a 'juicy girl's lovely lips' (*formosa . . . tenerae . . . ora puellae*, v. 33).

Copa Syrisca is a heady exotic import to Italy, and to Latin; to party, this chick wears Hellenic chic, and so does every horizontal dancer hanging out (*caput Graeca redimita mitella*, v. 1 ~ *roseo necte caput strophio*, 32).[12] Everybody gets into uniform, trussed for a tryst: 'garlands in a mingle . . . lilies fetched together in wickerwork baskets . . . cheeses oozing through their rushy containers' (vv. 14–17). 'Legless' Copa (*ebria*, v. 3) flashes thighs in the 'smokey' bar, the dimmed lights of underworld thrills, the demon drink, steamy windows and grimy walls running from the hot food cooking at the servery (*fumosa . . . taberna*, v. 3): guests get 'soaked where they lie back . . . in the cool of the shade, ladling down killer punch, in the caveman depths under Mount Madness' (*bibulo . . . toro*,[13] *cyathi, umbrosis . . . harundinibus, . . . Maenalio . . . sub antro*, vv. 6–9);[14] downing 'the new vintage, just uncorked', with 'baking to go with the alcoholic buzz' (*vappa . . . nuper defusa, Ceres . . . Bromius*, vv. 11, 20).[15] A bite and a cuppa: only mention 'Vesta's poor donkey' (v. 26) and you'll smell, not sex but the mill, and home-made bread from the oven, to help the 'vino' on its way, a 'dousing, by the glassful . . . down in the shady pergola' (*prolue, calices, pampinea . . . sub umbra*, vv. 29–31). In the end we all get 'smoke-grilled'—so fill that nose with 'strong flowers', take a chance, and have the 'booze neat' (*cineri, bene olentia, merum*, vv. 35–7). Get your ya-yas out, y'hear. For Lady Marmalade.

She dances *hot*: we skulk out of 'baking summer dust', swapping it for 'bumper summer goblets' (*aestivo . . . pulvere, aestivo . . . vitro*, vv. 5, 29). 'Chick-a-dees' like her 'bust a gut chirping' (*rumpunt*, v. 27), while lounge-'lizards chill out under cover' (*frigida, in gelida sede . . . latet*, vv. 8, 28), and, well—'lounge' (*decubuisse, recubans*, vv. 6, 29). *She* sweats, we don't (*sudat*, v. 25). She's busy—working up a storm; so *we* can have time off, for bad behaviour (*requiesce*, v. 31). The beat goes on, the bump and grind never slackens—her job is catering for working men 'worn out' with tramping and grinding (*defessum, lassus, fessus*, vv. 5, 25, 31). Of

---

[12] Cf. *corollae sertaque, serta . . . coronato*, vv. 13 f., 35 f. Greece: esp. *Maenalio, Achelois, Bromius*, vv. 9, 15, 20.

[13] *bibulo . . . toro* recently defended (from R. F. Thomas): Kershaw (1992).

[14] *Maenalus* < μαίνομαι: O'Hara (1996) 249, 252, 254 on Virg. *Ecl.* 8. 21, 10. 55, *Georg.* 1. 17.

[15] *Bromius* at Ov. *Met.* 4. 11 (a solitary in Augustan poetry).

course she can cope: this is 'her poem' (*docta*, v. 2). She makes her own music (samba, tarantella, bee-dance, belly-dance, salsa?). Dancing like the clappers in her far-out cutesy headgear (v. 1), she clicks castanets above her quivering quim (v. 2), banging melody from reeds bashed against her forearm (elbow? v. 4). This is *body-talk* (*caput . . . latus . . . cubitum*). Sex-show. Sex in public. Sex-mime. Sex with(out) sex. Priapus without his chopper. A donkey for Vesta (vv. 23–6). Feels like we're *almost* making love.[16]

Percussive polyrhythms pound in the ear, from first to last: *Copa Syrisca caput Graeca, redimita mitella, crispum* sub *crotalo docta, cubitum* raucos *ex-cutiens calamos*, vv. 1–4 ~ *defessum . . . abisse, bibulo decubuisse*, vv. 5 f., *garrit dulce* sub *antro, rustica pastoris fistula . . . sonat*, 9 f.; *crepitans* rauco *murmure rivus aquae . . . croceo . . . corollae . . . purpurea lutea*, 12 ff.; *iunco caeruleus cucumis*, v. 22; *lassus . . . asellus*, v. 25; *cantu crebro . . . cicadae, . . . lacerta latet*, vv. 27 f.; *crystalli . . . calices*, v. 30; *coronato . . . crastina curat*, vv. 36 f.; *aurem vellens 'vivit*[ ]*' ait, 'venio'*, v. 38.[17] Poetry in motion (*movere*) tumbles out prostheses for pleasure, through a blur of party-pack jumble: *sunt topia et calybae-cyathi-rosa-tibia-chordae,* | *et triclia . . .* (vv. 7 f.), to a seriously committed ostension of heaven as slap-bang shop:

- rustic pipe (one couplet);
- plonk and babbling brook (one couplet);
- flower-garlands and trugs (two couplets);
- fruits and nibbles, nuts and crisps (three couplets: vv. 9 f., 11 f.; 13–16; 17–22).[18]

Then *Copa* just finds time to cash in the catalogue twice (*huc . . . veni . . .* | *parce*, vv. 25 f. ~ *hic age . . . requiesce . . . necte*, 31 f.), before the lights go out, when the finale interrupts that kiss—[19]

As we inventory the dance, the sensuous body of writing shimmers— with *figurality*: it is not that the dancer presences her routine with prelusory promise of performative improvisation; her faceless preface figures the Image as the dance of writing, the erotics of metaphor. She is

---

[16] Onomatopoeic and onomatopic *crotala* (< κροτέω) clatter, for instance, on coins of *Croton*: Ferniqué (1887) 1572.

[17] *crispare* of sexy undulation: Adams (1982) 137; *movere* of copulation / dance: ibid. 194 f.

[18] *sunt topia* (v. 7) to start the *demonstratio* just *has* to be a witticism concretizing / abusing the formula *est locus*. Roman topiary: Grimal (1984) 99.

[19] -*ogram* (v. 33). In accepting Clausen's *formosa et* I envisage dwelling on 'canoodling' drool—safely rifling a Maids Lip (Stanley: *decerpens*, v. 33)—as exactly the moment to interrupt, with a curse for spoilsports in (evocative?) anacolouthon—

a men-u, for sexuality diffused through the fantasy furniture of instant idyll; in a word, the promise, for what we are about to receive, of *copia* (abundant plenitude).[20] The spice girl of (vicarious) life on the page: *vivite* (v. 38). Shake, rattle, and roll:

> . . . at the still point, there the dance is,
> . . . Except for the point, the still point,
> There would be no dance, and there is only the dance.
> (Eliot (1943) 'Burnt Norton' ii. 17–21)[21]

II. HAVE YOU EVER BEEN TO ELECTRIC LADYLAND?

A savoir que la danseuse *n'est pas une femme qui danse,* pour ces motifs juxtaposés, qu'*elle n'est pas une femme,* mais une métaphore résumant un des aspects élémentaires de notre forme, glaive, coupe, fleur, etc., et qu'*elle ne danse pas,* suggérant, par le prodige de raccourcis ou d'élans, avec une écriture corporelle ce qu'il faudrait des paragraphes en prose dialoguée autant que descriptive, pour exprimer, dans la rédaction: poème dégagé de tout appareil du scribe.

> (Mallarmé (1945) 304)[22]

'Muse moderne de l'Impuissance', Margery is a sexual-textual operator, not a person.[23] Her music marks off her poem as a special space with palpable boundaries, her dance patterns a habitus—conjuring kinesic, scopic, aural dynamics into place for her assembled admirers.[24] This communal *domina* runs the joint, we are admitted on her terms. She is the threshold, these premises are hers, we get to share her, in every

---

[20] See Cave (1979) 3–34 on the copious image-repertoire of *copia* (*verborum*). The mock self-deleting ~~urbanity~~ of a listing of comestibles at dinner: Gowers (1993) 277, on Pliny, *Letters* i. 15. 2.

[21] See Ellmann (1987) 118 for all that jive.

[22] 'Let it be known that the [Dancing Queen] *is not a woman dancing*; that, within those juxtaposed motifs, *she is not a woman,* but a metaphor that summarizes one of the elemental aspects of our form, sword, goblet, flower, etc., and that *she is not dancing,* suggesting, by the wonder of ellipses or bounds, with a corporeal writing, that which would take entire paragraphs of dialogued as well as descriptive prose to express in written composition: a poem detached from all instruments of the scribe' (tr. Meltzer (1987) 45). 'This is Mallarmé's accurate prediction of Yeats's poem', Kermode (1971) 100 (62–106, 'The Dancer'): see below.

[23] G. Mallarmé, 'Symphonie Littéraire', discussed by B. Johnson (1985) 274: Ms Impotence (the woman's body as fantasmic textuality, denied interiority and subjectivity, cf. Sumic-Riha (1997) 231 f.) can make potent creators of her poets—turning, *through* despair, to rereading.

[24] Copa 'is' the flutegirl, the siren, the cicada, seduction of all that figures unPlatonic (unruly, unauthorized, unclassical) desire—she is the 'being' of desire, even the desire for truth, order, hierarchy: cf. Murray in this volume. She is not apostrophized; but (unforgivably) her present indicatives (vv. 1–4) pose her in a presence as timeless as Being.

petal, swig, kiss—figure for our lack, she posits and supplies our need. Common as muck, she defers death. What she gives is 'life', life in our 'death'—the deathliness of our life, deadly dull lives. Staying alive, staying alive: 'Mort: me met hors'.[25]

In the perfect closural gesture, *vivit*[ ] . . . *venio, Copa* brings us (exactly) the kiss—of death, that ultimate vulgarity: always room, room for all, at this inn.[26] The shimmy drums a death-rattle on our ears, so we can dance with Mr D—and deliver the mythological claptrap of the Horatian 'spring' lyric to burlesque (*Odes* 1. 4):

> The dancing feet of the spring Graces may never be the same again. Horace has made us hear the foot of Death among them.[27]

> The contrast between the alternating feet of the dance of the Graces (*alterno . . . pede*, 7) and the single, levelling foot of death (*aequo . . . pede*, 13) is a verbal icon of the different kinds of time. The dance . . . is subject to iteration in a way that death for any individual is not.[28]

Dance keeps death at bay. So history, politics, bosses, patrons, dates, and other shifts at authorization are banned. Welcome to the cult of the milli-second, here the attention-span lasts a page, a day, a boogie—less than can be. Having a real good time eludes great emperors, displaces eternal Rome, kissing—a curse at all their 'tomorrows'.[29] Inelegantly, deafinitely maybe, *Copa* turns on epic as the house of death, warden of 'Deathstiny', *fatum* as the stamp of death's foot imprinted on futurity. These elegiacs stigmatize *Aeneid* 6 as the enemy within, by displayed quotation from the burial of Virgil's horn-player, Misenus, figure for the amplified voicing of militarist glory in heroic poetry. Paroxysms of warrior commemoration make *this* the house of ill-repute (vv. 212 f.):

> . . . Misenum . . .
> flebant et *cineri ingrato* suprema ferebant

> They were giving their tears to Misenus,
> They were paying their last respects to joyless ashes.

If you're not against all this, you're for it—or you might as well be.

---

[25] M. Leiris: Picard (1995) 26.

[26] Death as πανδοκεύς: Lycophron, *Alex.* 655, cf. Artemid. *Dreambook* 3. 5, Borghini (1987).

[27] Lyne (1995) 65–7: 'An example. *Ode* 1. 4: "find the unity".'

[28] Lowrie (1997) 52; cf. Nisbet and Hubbard (1970) 65 ad loc.: 'Dancing in the ancient world . . . was not effete gliding, but vigorous and noisy exercise'.

[29] *pereat . . . crastina*, v. 37: Horace, *Odes* 4. 7. 17, *crastina* (hapax in Horace), Boscoreale cup 'A', ζῶν μετάλαβε. τὸ γὰρ αὔριον ἄδηλόν ἐστι (Dunbabin (1986) 194). Tomorrow belongs to Them. Tomorrow never knows—

'Hatred' on behalf of common humanity clings to these vocables, at the heart(lessness) of the deadly Epic Muse.[30] *Copa* inoculates its devotees by rubbing in one of Virgil's most relentless images of militarist totalitarianism, Hector-as-trumpeter, the Gungha Din who lived and died for music. In his case, precisely, for *arma viro* (v. 233):

> quid *cineri ingrato* servas bene olentia serta?   (v. 35)[31]

Copa pirouettes away from the grandiosities that acclaim threatens for Elegy.[32] For ambience, hum-drum *Copa* knows enough (*docta*, v. 2) to ditch the city's 'kings and battles' and ape the classic Callimachean gesture (Virg. *Ecl.* 6. 3 f.):

> . . . Cynthius *aurem*
> *vellit et* admonu*it*
>
> . . . Poetry—Apollo—in my ear
> gave a tweak, set me straight.

Young Virgil could have been proud, after all, of this Death's head Poesie. Get on down, with the 'slender Muse' of a Callimachean *deductum . . . carmen* ('song spun fine'):

> Mors *aurem vellens . . . ait.*   (v. 38)

So 'Death' plays 'Apollo', after all? *Bidding* the 'inn' of our lives to echo with the dancing Muse; speaking of life as intruder, from the outside—closure.

Between them, poetic text, or *pas de de*—ath: our *carpe diem, Copa* spells death, too, all the same. For she bids us live (it up), by surrendering to *her* hypnotic dance, and obeying her command to take our rest, lie down in the shadows, and be still (vv. 5, 6, 25, 31: *defessum, decubuisse toro, lassus, fessus requiesce sub umbra*). The *performance* of her mime of life mimics our wake, with flowers, garlands, libations of wine, and a bier for the deceased (vv. 6, 13–14, 29, 32, 35, 36: *toro, corollae . . . sertaque, prolue,*

---

[30] *Misenus* μῖσος: Paschalis (1997) 218 n. 31. *Copa* is an 'alternative' Muse, resistance to deadly Epic C[alli]opa, cf. Janan in this volume.

[31] Austin (1977) 102 ad loc., 'The cremation is anticipated. The phrase recurs in *Copa* 35; it is very striking: Servius glosses *ingrato* by "tristi", adding "alii *ingrato* dicunt gratiam non sentienti", certainly the true meaning.' A classic example of the recently incinerated short way with language long fetishized by Latinists. Was Virgil messing with elegy—Calvus as re-echoed by Catullus 96. 1: *si quicquam mutis gratum acceptumue sepulcris | accidere a nostro, Calve, dolore potest*? (Ibid.: 'far less explicit than Virgil'.)

[32] Muses dramatize generic friction and schism, cf. esp. Ancona, Lada-Richards, Rosati, Sharrock in this volume.

necte, serta, coronato . . . lapide . . . tegi). *Copa* dances, not on our grave, but the *memento mori*—woman's work, for Death's hired mourner.

For the finale, it seems, Apollo takes the lead; to reclaim the power of *Copa* for Death[less Poetry]: she did her own thing, but lured *us* to treat living as already the dance of the Other. They are in it together—this underworld, undercover, underhand pair plot our demise: in undecidable equivalence / polarity, they set living to the past *against* living to the future, but at the same time they show how living is *both* living like the dead *and* not living now, not living yet (vv. 34, 37: *pereat cui sunt prisca supercilia, pereat qui crastina curat*). We are stuck with no place to stay but the excluded middle, no time to be in which we can heed the call; mesmerized in performative contradiction, deafening music on stopped ears. Or, at elegiac best, life as unepic pledge of irrationalism: 'To Hell with it—play on' (if 6 was 9).[33]

III. LIKE WE DID LAST SUMMER

> Souls of Poets dead and gone,
> What Elysium have ye known,
> Happy field or mossy cavern,
> Choicer than the Mermaid Tavern?
> Have ye tippled drink more fine
> Than mine host's Canary wine?
> Or are fruits of Paradise
> Sweeter than those dainty pies
> of venison? O generous food!
> Drest as though bold Robin Hood   10
> Would, with his maid Marian,
> Sup and bowse from horn and can.
>   (Keats (1994) 242, 'Lines on the Mermaid Tavern')[34]

But *Copa* is a 'trained musician' (*docta*, v. 2). As this chapter will now explore, only snobbery can deny her at least as deafinite 'tendentiousness' in 'allusive practice' at her literary diner as any of the big names on the canon.[35] Her creativity turned back to Virgil's 'earliest work—and

---

[33] On the teasing song-and-dance, the power-relation dynamics, between (male-god) Apollo / author and (female-slave-working woman-goddess) Muse / textuality, cf. Cavarero, Sharrock, Spentzou in this volume.

[34] Cheapside; written *c*.3 Feb. 1818, copied to seven friends, published 1820: reputedly the local of Shakespeare and Ben Jonson, of Beaumont 'n' Fletcher, as a call to revive stout Elizabethan poetics.

[35] Hinds (1998) esp. 99 f.: 'Treat[ ] poetic tendentiousness . . . as . . . constitutive of allusive

the *Second Eclogue* may be his earliest published work',[36] to find a voice to vindicate the self from scorn, and celebrate the multiple urbanities of self-promotion. In Corydon's serenade to stuck-up Alexis, *Eclogue* 2, *Copa* found inspiration from lines that rank 'among the most poignant and haunting in all Latin literature' (vv. 8–13):[37]

> *nunc* etiam pecudes umbras et frigora captant,
> *nunc* viridis etiam occultant spineta *lacertos,*
> Thestylis et rapido *fessis* messoribus *aestu*
> alia serpyllumque herbas contundit olentis.
> at mecum *raucis* . . .
> sole sub ardenti resonant *arbusta cicadis.*

> Now even the animals grab shade and cool,
> now even lizards hide their green under cover of thorn-bushes,
> and Thestylis ready for harvesters exhausted by racing summer-heat
> bruises garlic, thyme, smelly herbs.
> But along with me loud . . .
> cicadas under a blazing sun make the groves resound.

Where love-sickness sang these summertime blues 'from death's door' (*mori me denique cogis?*, v. 7), The Tavern says 'Wise up', sit out the heat, let the songstress do the chirping (vv. 27–31):

> *nunc* cantu crebro rumpunt *arbusta cicadae,*
> *nunc* varia in gelida sede *lacerta* latet:
> si sapis, *aestivo* recubans nunc prolue vitro
> .   .   .   .
> hic age pampinea *fessus* requiesce sub umbra.

Copa heard Virgil's 'echoing' cicadas (ar*denti* resonant ar*busta*) re-echo, only less empathetically, in the surreal midday sun of *Georgics* 3 (327 f., 331):

> inde ubi quarta sitim caeli collegerit hora
> et *cantu* querulae *rumpunt arbusta cicadae*
> .   .   .   .
> *aestibus* at mediis umbrosam exquirere vallem,[38]

writing and of the alluding poet's emplotment of his work in literary tradition'. Add to this: '*cultural* tradition'. The spurious supplementarity of ascription to ~~Virgil~~, the *biggest* name in Latin literature, puts *any* reading of *Copa*'s 'pilfering' automatically ~~in denial~~.

[36] Clausen (1994) 61 f. From the horse's mouth: Wishart (1995) 247.

[37] Kenney (1983) 49–52 at 51, eloquently celebrating the elegiac blend of pathos with pastoral humour.

[38] *umbrosas* ~ umbrosis *frigida harundinibus,* v. 8.

Next when the day's fourth hour concentrates thirst
and cicadas make the groves burst with their insistent noise

. . . .

But in midday heat, search valley's shade out.

From *Eclogue* 2, our poet caught the sound for *Copa*'s racket and for back-
ground-water-music (*raucis*, v. 12 ~ *raucos, rauco, Copa* 4, 12);[39] and he
returned to Virgil's first bars of verse, *patulae* recubans sub *tegmine fagi*
(*Ecl.* 1. 1: 'reclining under cover of the spreading beech')[40]—to mix a
come-on cocktail of idyllic setting with a twist of summery love-song
(*Ecl.* 7. 9–11, 57–8):

> *huc* ades, O Meliboee, . . .
> et si quid cessare potes, *requiesce sub umbra.*
> *huc* . . . venient . . . iuvenci
>
> . . . .
>
> Aret ager, vitio moriens sitit aeris herba,
> Liber *pampineas* invidit collibus *umbras.*

Come over here, Meliboeus, do . . .
and if you may take a break, rest in the shade.
Over here, the bullocks will arrive

. . . .

Parched is the land, from bad in the air the grass is dying of thirst,
Bacchus has begrudged the hills shade from the vines.

Copa's 'Come hither' bait, however, is decked out with the profusion of
countrified love-gifts catalogued, in increasingly amplified copiousness
by Virgil's poor/humiliated, humble/proud, Corydon, bidding to outdo
his rival, the Theocritean Cyclops of *Idyll* 11, in 'this most elegiac of
pastorals'[41] (*Ecl.* 2. 44–53, 56):[42]

---

[39] This brook saved parched crops from summery death in *Georgics* I: *cum exustus ager
morientibus* aestuat *herbis,* | . . . *undam* | *elicit. illa cadens* raucum *per levia* murmur | *saxa ciet* (vv.
107–10). *raucus* (= ἠχήεις) as aesthetically neutral, open to context and taste: Servius on *Aen.* 9.
458, Moore-Blunt (1977) 38. The brook 'channels water' from *Ecl.* 8. 87, *aquae rivum*, where love-
sick Daphnis throws himself down in exhaustion (*fessa*, v. 85): Virgil's stream flows on in Tib. 1.
1. 27 f., aestivos *ortus vitare* sub umbra | *arboris ad* rivos *praetereuntis* aquae, cf. Cairns (1979) 105
(Ov. *Rem.* 194, *Met.* 8. 334).

[40] Displayed quotation at Prop. 3. 3. 1, *Visus eram molli* recubans *Heliconis in* umbra, dreaming
of Virgil's Callimachean Apollo recalling him from epic kings and battles to his proper habitat
in Arcadia, elegiac-pastoral style (Fedeli (1984) 146: Hesiod–Callimachus–Ennius–Gallus–
Virgil).

[41] Coleman (1977) 108. Cf. the unpoetic topology at Ov. *Tristia* 3. 10. 71–3: *non hic* pampinea
dulcis latet uva sub umbra . . .

[42] Corydon's pipe in four verses (36–9), kids in five (40–4), flora in eleven (45–55: flowers×6,
fruits×3, garland×2, for closure): Du Quesnay (1979) 55 f. *Suave rubens, suave rubenti, Ecl.* 3. 63,

> . . . quoniam sordent tibi munera nostra.
> *huc* ades, o formose puer: tibi *lilia* plenis   45
> ecce *ferunt* Nymphae *calathis*, tibi candida Nais,
> pallentis *violas* et summa papavera carpens,
> narcissum et *florem* iungit *bene olentis* anethi,
> tum casia atque aliis intexens suavibus herbis
> mollia *luteola* pingit vaccinia caltha.   50
> ipse ego cana legam tenera lanugine *mala*
> *castaneasque nuces* . . .
> addam *cerea pruna* . . .
>   .   .   .   .
> rusticus es, Corydon, nec munera *curat* Alexis.

>   as my presents for you are such trash.
> Come here, lovely boy, do: for you lilies in full
> baskets—just look!—are fetched by Nymphs, by dazzling Naiad, for you
> the shrinking violets and poppy-heads she's picking,
> as she bunches narcissus with anise bloom smelling so fine,
> with cassia and the rest of the spice herbs she's entwining,
> as she daubs saffronish marigolds on pastel bilberries.
> As for myself, I shall gather quinces white with their juicy down
> and chestnuts . . .
> throw in glossy plums . . .
>   .   .   .   .
> A hick you are, Corydon—Alexis don't care for the presents.

Just here, where Virgil's swain quits his model, modulating into floral gifts and then unconventional fruit-and-nut delights, *Copa* rushes in, to emulate the questionable (hick) tone:

His attempts at elegance are interspersed with lapses into homely rusticity. The addition of nuts and plums turns the traditional flower-garland into a kind of living-room decorator's piece.[43]

The same thought must draw an ~~epic~~ Ovid like flies: when his Cyclops production produces produce to beggar any Virgilian product (*Met.* 13. 810–37):

---

4. 43 ~ *suave rubentia*, v. 19; cf. Ciris 96–8, *suave rubens narcissus . . . lilia*. Is *Copa*'s hapax *caseoli*, v. 17, a half-echo of Virgil's rarity *capreoli*, v. 41?

[43] Leach (1974b) 149; cf. Moore-Blunt (1977) 32 f. Nymphs fetched flowers (for Medea's wedding-bouquet) at Apollonius 4. 1143–5, ἄνθεα . . . νύμφαι . . . ἐσφόρεον (but in their *sinus*, not baskets . . .).

Some may regard the rhetoric of the soliloquy as overdone, others . . . find it an effective demonstration of Ovid's immense fertility and *copia verborum*.[44]

Where young Virgil strained, and laureate Ovid waltzed his way into the record books, these couplets of ours swoon (vv. 13–19):

> sunt etiam croceo *violae* de *flore* corollae
> sertaque purpurea *lutea* mixta rosa
> et quae virgineo libata Achelo*is* ab amne   15
> *lilia* vimineis *attulit* in *calathis*,
> sunt et caseoli, quos iuncea fiscina siccat,
> sunt autumnali *cerea pruna* die
> castaneaeque nuces et suave rubentia *mala*.[45]

Further rem(a)inders of rustic Virgil link *Copa*'s two main twirls of pastiche (vv. 13–19; 27–31):

- the *sanguineis . . . moris* of Silenus sleeping it off at *Ecl.* 6. 22 ('blood-red mulberries') ~ *mora cruenta*, v. 21;
- *fert uva racemos/*, *Georg.* 2. 60, 'the vine bears bunches' ~ v. 21;
- *iunco*, *Ecl.* 1. 48 ~ v. 22;
- *cucumis*, *Georg.* 4. 122 ~ v. 22.
- Then the vignette for Priapus the garden gnome parades its fresh dash of vintage early Virgil (*Ecl.* 7. 33 f.):

> . . . *Priape* . . .
> . . . *custos* es pauperis horti

> Priapus, you're the humble garden's warden.

A gnome soon promoted to Superintendent of Flowers, in the *Georgics* 4 *praeteritio* (vv. 109–11):

> invitent croceis halantes floribus *horti*
> et *custos* furum atque avium cum *falce saligna*
> . . . tutela *Priapi*.

> Feel the lure of gardens breathing the saffron blooms,
> and warden against thieves and birds, with willow sickle,
> . . . security from Priapus.

---

[44] A. Griffin (1983) 193: Cyclops' thirty comparisons outdo Virgil's seven (*Met.* 13. 787–807 ~ *Eclogues* 7. 37–45: Corydon Corydon again, churning out more on Galatea—with Thyrsis his pale echo). In Ovid's fruit-and-flower show: *sunt . . . antra . . . sunt . . . sunt . . . sunt . . . sunt . . . sunt . . . sub umbra . . . autumnalia . . . prunaque . . . nouasque imitantia ceras . . . nec . . . castaneae . . . deerunt . . . sunt . . . sunt* (vv. 810–28; Griffin (1983) 194). Ovid reaches back to Theocritus: *pace* Drew (1923, 1925), *Copa* does not.

[45] Add: *huc . . . veni*, *bene olentia*, *curat*, vv. 25, 35, 37. Apples, plums, nuts with pederastic innuendoes: Du Quesnay (1979) 40. Tutti frutti, All rootie.

Now he takes another bow for *Copa* (v. 23) :

est tuguri *custos* armatus *falce saligna.*[46]

At this point we are sliding toward elegy. And not for the first time in the poem. *Copa* announced early on the intent to echo the joy of Virgilian 'pastoral' (*pastoris . . . more*, v. 10), chattering *Maenalio . . . sub antro* (v. 9, 'in a grot à la Arcadia'), where the pipe of *Eclogue* 8 intones its manic mantra of *Maenalios . . . versus* (v. 21, etc.: *Maenalus*' shrill forest and gossiping pines, vv. 22–4; *audit amores*, v. 23 ~ *garrit dulce*, v. 9). This (self-enacting) bucolic 'twiddling' (*rustica . . . fistula . . . sonat*, v. 10) teams up here with the 'vinous haze' of elegiac nostalgia which is promised in the slangy next couplet (*vappa . . . nuper defusa*, vv. 11–12). As we shall see, Virgil's scarecrow Priapus is to pair off with an elegiac Vesta (vv. 23–6). Above all, those re-cycled highlights of *Eclogue* 2 are intertwined with snippets from elegy and from one flowery purple Propertian passage in particular that is anthologized so that its evocative emulation of Virgil's Corydon may be plainly appreciated.

Late Virgil is (we saw) *persona ingrata* for *Copa*'s geisha. There is room for just a coolant hint of pre-Roman Tiber's 'thatched garland' (*et crinis umbrosa tegebat harundo*, *Aen.* 8. 34) in the Mermaid's 'thatched nooks' (*umbrosis frigida harundinibus*, v. 8): stranger Aeneas is accosted by this dream-ticket of an usher, told by Tiber, in no uncertain terms, to make himself at home in Club Italia—float upstream: *hic tibi certa domus, certi (ne absiste) penates, . . . hic locus urbis erit, requies ea certa laborum,* |, *hic mihi magna domus* (*Aen.* 8. 36–65: 39, 46, 65).[47] And the poet finds congenial intertextuality in the oeuvres of the great *elegists*, too, in just such back-waters of the world state. Thus there is room at the inn for those patches of throwback rusticity that vie for Propertius' affections as he fights him-self in a bid to monumentalize elegy without writing grossness on Rome.

[46] *tuguri* < *Ecl.* 1. 68. From Virgil's (cut) ~~nursery catalogue~~: *cucumis, pruna* (vv. 121 f., 145). The ~~Virgilian~~ *Priapeum* 3 shares several features with *Copa*: *vimine iunceo, tuguri, corolla, luteae violae . . . cucurbitae et suave olentia mala,* | *uva pampinea rubens educata sub umbra*, Priapo (vv. 2, 5, 10, 12–14, 17; Drabkin (1930) 67 n. 140: same author?). So does the cosmopolitan *Carmina Priapea* 27: *Deliciae populi, magno notissima circo* | *Quintia, vibratas docta movere nates,* | *cymbala cum crotalis, pruriginis arma*, Priapo | *ponit et adducta tympana pulsa manu . . .* (vv. 1–4; Tarrant (1992) 335: 'almost certainly related').

[47] Tiber's words here, underwriting Helenus' prophecy, return in Ovidian Hercules' annunciation of Pythagorean Croton, counter-point to the finality of Rome (*Met.* 15. 16–18, *requie longum relevasse laborem . . .* | *hic locus urbis erit . . .* ; see P. Hardie (1997) 196 and n. 45). So, now, if you're looking to escape umpteen labours, persecution by epic torment, Rome, here's your moment, pick this spot, for *the topos* of all *topoi*—why not try the *Copa* instead?

One glimpse concerns Book 3. Venereal girls always were venal, but now the stakes have gone through the Augustan roof: once upon a time (13. 29–30, 33–4):

> nunc *violas* tondere manu, nunc *mixta* referre
> *lilia* virgineos lucida per *calathos*
> . . . furtiva per antra *puellae*
> *oscula* . . . . dedere.

Now their hands snipped violets, now they fetched back blended
lilies gleaming in the girly baskets
. . . in grottoes girls stole
kisses to pay.

This is where *Copa* culled its floral decoration and kisses (vv. 13–16, 33):

> . . . *violae* . . .
> sertaque . . .   *mixta* . . .
> et quae . . . libata virgineo Achelois . . .
> *lilia* vimineis attulit in *calathis*.
> . . . *ora puellae*.[48]

But it is the equivocal project of Book 4 (Propertius' grandstand finish to his writing Rome)[49] that gets *Copa really* mellow. 'Dig' (*if* you can dig it: *si sapis*, 29)—you borrow from Propertius, or else you leave literature behind, and swallow 'crystal' in your cups (*novos calices*, vv. 29 f.).

- Propertius partied in style, that summer, with Two Ladies, booze, castanets, and bongos (4. 8. 37–42):

> Lygdamus ad cyathos *vitrique aestiva* supellex
> et Methymnaei Graeca saliva meri;
> Nile, tuus tibicen erat, crotalistria 'Phyllis',
> . . . .
> Magnus et ipse . . .
> iactabat truncas ad cava buxa manus.

Lygdamus at the jug, glass to serve up summer,
plus the Greek bite to retsina from Drunkston on Lesbos;
Up the Nile—the piper's down to you, so's Ms dancing girl with castanets!
. . . .

---

[48] *vimineis* cf. Ovid, *Fasti* 4. 435 (Proserpine's pals pick posies), *lento calathos e vimine nexos*; but against rewriting Propertius' *virgineos*: Baker (1974). *lilia . . . attulit ~ saepe* tulit *blandis argentea* lilia *Nymphis*, Prop. 4. 4. 25 (love-sick Tarpeia, in the thick of it).

[49] Edwards (1996) 52–7, esp. 55.

And Little John himself . . .
  was beating stubby arms on boxwood hand-drums.

Whence *Copa*'s (swish ? outlandish?) *aestivo . . . vitro*, v. 29.[50]

- More importantly, 'Vesta's pet donkey' (*Copa* 25 f.) is down to a
  laconic motif early in Propertius' introductory orientation for his
  tourist-readers (4. 1. 21):

    Vesta coronatis pauper gaudebat *asellis*.
    Far from loaded Vesta used to take pleasure in garlanded asses.

This olde worlde / folksy version of Augustan sanctity / sanctimony set
Ovid off on a fast-and-loose adventure (*Fasti* 6. 311):

    ecce *coronatis* panis dependet *asellis*.
    Hey presto! Buns dangle from garlanded asses.

Copa got its teaming of Vesta with Priapus (vv. 23–6) from sassy Ovid's
inventive tribute to my (daughter's) birthday, as he assesses why the ass
is honoured at the Vestalia, asserts that bakers decorate mill-stones and
their donkeys with garlands (vv. 311–18), and then invests in telling how
one ass saved Vesta from assault by Priapus (347 f.). In both Ovid and
Propertius, this was certainly 'part of a wider conflict between elegy's
new nationalistic subject and its amatory roots'.[51]

Now the geniuses of elegy come on down to the Mermaid Café—have
fun tonight. Heading *Copa*'s elegiac intertexts is Propertius' talking
statue, the emotive Vertumnus: *caput . . . redimita mitella*, v. 1 ~ *cinge
caput mitra, speciem furabor Iacchi* (4. 2. 31, 'wind my head in a turban and
I'll steal the look of Bacchus'); encored, as we shall see, in Ovid's
Vertumnus: *picta redimitus tempora mitra* (*Met.* 14. 654, 'temples bound
in a technicolour turban'). This most mobile of marbles figures the
metamorphic poetics of Book 4, slipping and a-sliding his way out of
Augustan Rome back to the days when Italians owned the place, and
country ways built Rome (4. 2).[52] Here

Propertius produces, perhaps for the first time in aetiological elegy, that kind of
literary rusticism pioneered in Latin verse by Vergil.[53]

---

[50] On this *descriptio loci*: Dee (1978) 47, 'intensifying the atmosphere of decadence and
shallow revelry'. Cf. crotalo, ad *cubitum . . . excutiens calamos*, cyathi, *Copa* vv. 2, 4, 7.

[51] Newlands (1995) 130, cf. esp. 133; G. Williams (1991) 196–200.

[52] P. Hardie (1992) esp. 75, 'The long catalogue of metamorphoses has been uttered by a
motionless statue: the principle of mutability frozen in the perfection of a work of art'.

[53] Dee (1974) 46. *Eclogue* 2 ~ Prop. 4, elegy 2 (cf. Hor. *Epode* 2).

All fruit-'n'-veg. and where'd-'e-go?, Vertumnus-Propertius pitches his stall for another Hellenistic tour de force of 'personal monologue',[54] this time set in downtown Rome (vv. 13–16):

> prima mihi variat *liventibus uva racemis*
>   et coma lactenti spicea fruge tumet;
> hic dulcis cerasos, hic *autumnalia pruna*
>   cernis et aestivo mora rubere die.

> For me the first grapes are a palette of bunches turning black
>   and bearded heads of corn swell with milky grain;
> here tasty cherries, here autumn plums
>   meet your eyes, and mulberries going red in a summer day.

Suburbanized by *Copa* (vv. 18–22):

> sunt *autumnali* cerea *pruna die*
> castaneaeque nuces et suave rubentia mala,
>   est hic munda Ceres, est Amor, est Bromius,   20
> sunt et mora cruenta et *lentis uva racemis*,
>   et pendet iunco caeruleus cucumis,

and simultaneously stereographed in with Vertumnus' 'all-time greatest hit', divertingly presented by the garrulous godlet as an 'irrelevant digression',[55] namely *his* reprise of Virgil's maiden *pastor* Corydon (a slight return: Prop. 4. 2. 39–46):

> pastor me ad baculum possum curvare, vel idem
>   sirpiculis medio pulvere ferre rosam.
> nam quid ego adiciam, de quo mihi maxima fama est,
>   hortorum in manibus dona probata meis?
> *caeruleus cucumis* tumidoque cucurbita ventre
>   me notat et *iunco* brassica vincta levi,
> nec flos ullus hiat pratis, quin ille decenter
>   impositus fronti langueat ante meae.

> To go pastoral: I can bow myself over a crook, or go
>   fetch roses in bulrush ties through the thick of the dust.
> Why would I add what gives me my greatest fame:
>   that quality garden gifts lie in my hands?
> The blue-green cucumber and gourd with swelling belly
>   are my insignia, and cabbage bundled with light rush.
> Not a bloom opens wide in the meadows without it nicely
>   drooping down in front when it's set on my forehead.

---

[54] Theocritean 'personal monologue' as inspiration for Latin erotic writing, the Polyphemous poetics of macrology and repetitiveness: Cairns (1979) 133–43.

[55] Mader (1991) 146: *quid ego adiciam . . .?*

So *Copa*'s 'blue cowcumber dangling from a rush' (v. 22) depends on 'one of the most deliciously alliterative lines in Latin poetry, capped by the amusing and surely unparalleled double "cucu"' (Dee (1974) 47), Propertius' v. 43, parading the 'pregnant' conceit conceived in the horticultural *praeteritio*, *Georg.* 4. 121 f.: *tortusque per herbam* | *cresceret in ventrem cucumis* ('twining through the grass, | cucumber would grow to a belly'. So too both ~~Virgil~~'s *Moretum* 75 f.: *crescit . . .* | *gravis in latum demissa cucurbita ventrem*, 'there grows . . . | the gourd sinking to a belly filling out to term', and the acolyte Columella 10. 380, 385, 391: *cucumis praegnansque cucurbita serpit, ventre, ventre*, 'cucumber, and pregnant gourd creeps on . . . belly . . . belly').[56]

Similarly, *Copa*'s Priapus the Not-So-Terrible (v. 24) wags a 'willowy sickle' from Virgil's garden (as we saw),[57] but his vast bulge below the belt borrows (refuses to borrow) from the last *amor* in Ovid's mighty epic, where Mr Metamorphosis Vertumnus (in Propertian Vertumnus' headdress, remember)[58] thinks of picking chérie Pomona's cherries,[59] after the rest of the boys with bulges have failed before him: Satyrs, Pans, Silenus—and Priapus (*Met.* 14. 640):

> quique deus fures vel *falce* vel *inguine terret*.

> and the god that scares thieves with either his sickle or his bulge.

In *Metamorphoses*, all Vertumnus' shifts fail to shape up Pomona— including his impersonation of the old witch/procuress who on the Vestalia once told Ovid in *Fasti* 6 all about Vertumnus' patch in Rome[60]—until he drops Ovidian *artes amatoriae* altogether, only to find that his Maid Marian is his, and that he's made—once he's in his own shape, because 'sexcess lies in reciprocity': *mutua vulnera* (v. 771).

This moment climaxes the whole epic's Not-So-Brief History of Time for lovers of poetry who can do without 'kings and battles'. The moment dwarfs the seriously *unsexy* earnestnesses of Aeneas' and

---

[56] Cf. n. 46 on *cucumis*, *pruna* in *Georg.* 4. *Aestivo*, *pulvere*, Prop. vv. 16, 40 > *aestivo . . . pulvere*, *Copa* v. 5; *uva racemos*, | Prop. v. 13 < *Georg.* 2. 60, *uva racemos* | (> Ov. *Met.* 3. 484, *Trist.* 4. 6. 9, Petron. 135 v. 14). Elegiac pastoral strains cheese: Tib. 2. 3. 15, *fiscella . . . vimine iunci*.

[57] Longing for Virgilian country pursuits, Tibullus' steamy elegiac dream-world pivots around *pomosis . . . custos . . . ponatur in hortis* | *terreat ut saeva* falce Priapus *aves* (1. 1. 17 f.). Thus, *Priape*, . . . armatus *curva . . . falce*, 1. 4. 1, 8 > *Copa* v. 23 (Tib. 1. 4. 1, 6, *umbrosa . . . tecta*, *aestivi . . . Canis ~ Copa* vv. 8, 5).

[58] Propertius' Vertumnus > Ovid's: Myers (1994) 119.

[59] *Met.* 14. 649 f., *vitisque putator* | *. . . lecturum poma putares*: Tissol (1997) 25. Erotic 'reading' 'picks' the Elegiac Woman, still—Epic or no. In *this* (s)exchange, Vertumnus sports Priapus' 'sickle': but so does Ms Cherry Bomb Pom(on)a! (vv. 649 ~ 628).

[60] 6. 395–416: Barchiesi (1994) 175–8.

Romulus' one-way transformations in apotheosis which Ovid's long trek has just reached in his journey toward the eventual closure of Augustus' and his own ~~deaths~~.[61] *Copa* caters for those (like Virgil?) who wish poetry, and life, could keep *arma virumque* for later, another day, death in life. Our Hostesse (with the Mostest) runs a members-only Dead Poets Society pledged to steer metropolitan Elegy away from Empire. To *Robin Hood*, and 'Get Back' rustic Callimacheanism.

In this design for life, we *are* flowers: that's why we need flowers—brought by a fetching water-nymph (*Achelois*, v. 15: not Corydon's Theocritean *Nais*) from Ovid's epic store, but Ovid the master of flower-picking erotics, not Ovid the servant of cosmos-licking Rome (*Met.* 5. 552–5):

> vobis, *Acheloides*, unde
> pluma pedesque avium, cum virginis ora geratis?
> an quia, cum legeret vernos Proserpina flores,
> in comitum numero, doctae Sirenes, eratis?

> Acheloids, where do your
> bird feathers and claws come from, when you wear a girl's face?
> It's not, is it, because, when Proserpine was picking spring blooms,
> you were in the catalogue of chums, Sirens in on the scholarship?

The same set of moves, but in hexameter mode, are made by Columella, out to plug the *Fourth Georgic*'s gap in the garden-fence, with the *Second Eclogue* (10. 298–300),

> et tu, ne Corydonis opes despernat Alexis,
> formoso Nais puero formosior ipsa,
> fer calathis violam . . .

> and you, too, so Alexis doesn't scorn Corydon's riches,
> Naiad lovelier yourself than that lovely boy,
> fetch the violet in your basket . . .

and with a chorus line of ~~epic~~ escorts and bucolic Sirens, after Ovid and Virgil (vv. 263 f.),

> nunc vos Pegasidum comites *Acheloidas* oro
> *Maenaliosque* choros Dryadum . . . [62]

---

[61] Littlefield (1965) 470; cf. Myers (1994) 113–32, 'Pomona and Vertumnus'. The parity of simultaneous climax for man and woman in penetrative sex is the scandalous grail of Ovid's *Ars Amatoria* (2. 727 f.: his, all generosity ~ hers: 3. 800 — faked, if necessary).

[62] We already mentioned Columella's 'pregnant cowcumber' < *Georgics*/Propertius. His Ovidian Priapus: *Priapi* | terribilis *membri, medio qui semper in horto* | *inguinibus puero, praedoni*

> Now my prayer calls upon the Acheloids, chums of the Muses,
> and the dancing Dryads on Arcadian Maenalus.

But our elegy jumps, through Propertius and Ovid, over the *Eclogues'* hedge, to join Virgil's Tityrus, Corydon, and the boys. Actress *Copa* and princess *Achelois* both make sexy Sirens, suburban catachresis for the Muse. This click-clacking Madame George supplies all you can want from the moment. So rock on, ancient queen:

> O body swayed to music, O brightening glance,
> How can we know the dancer from the dance?
> (Yeats (1965) 130, 'Among schoolchildren VIII')[63]

IV. DO THE HIP SHAKE THING/
SHAKE YOUR HIP THING

> I could be the dancer of your dreams
> I can turn all your music on
> I can make you feel alive . . .
> (Nicks (1983), 'Nothing ever changes')[64]

The 'not-Virgil' tag has made *Copa* a case of (necessarily inferior) literariness, and the dance a *textual* figure. But Dance is a *cultural* operator, articulated within a specific historicity,[65] and the poem is ideologically emplotted along particular trajectories. This one-woman band performance (= 'dance'?) is marked 'Just Entertainment' by milieu, wordlessness, castanets, and wiggle wiggle wiggle (till you raise the dead).[66] Most dancing we know is communal because 'everyone' joins in

falce *minetur* (10. 32–4): *Copa* vv. 23 f., falce . . . inguine <u>terribilis</u>. (I see these 'terrorist' scarecrows as *independently* inflated from Ovid's *terret*, cf. Hor. *Serm.* 1. 8. 7, *terret*, Tibullus' *terreat*, n. 57 above.)

[63] Published 1919: Kermode (1971) 101. De Man (1979) 130–2 famously nags us to ask (how rhetorically?) *how* rhetorical is Yeats's question? Try asking 'How *can* we, since we must?' Sign and referent, erotic desire and musical form, converge in the *power* of dance: performance can/must animate any text (Grigely (1995) 113).

[64] 'The Dance': this wrinkly essay *was* written to Fleetwood Mac (1997).

[65] Not a 'self-evident universal category': Cowan (1990) 17–21, 'Conceptualizing the Dance'.

[66] Dancing while making music (among child novelty acts at the symposium): Xen. *Symposium* 2. 1. Solo dancing as crazy (Socrates working out—with a wooden chair): ibid. 2. 19. Pantomimic male soloist (orchestra backing and mythic score): Jory (1996). Roman *un*males dance (invective): Corbeill (1996) 136 f., 167 f. Castanets and clappers, women only: West (1992) 123.

Be told: 'The flamenco dancer is not Rosie la Derriere, bumping and grinding herself to a burlesque climax. . . . The use of castanets is an excellent way to destroy the *jondo* effect of a dance. . . . Castanets, not traditionally used in flamenco, beside being unsightly and distracting, the patterns customized by their group; our dancing generally encodes an 'emancipatory imperative' for the individual, through (stylized) bodily abandon, teaching techniques of erotic release and turn-on with or without intimacy.[67] But *Copa* music generates pleasure vicariously, with 'frenetic, constant motion' signifying the fantasy of 'The "That's Supposed to Enjoy" ', a simulated 'body-enjoyment' wired through the audience to provoke, feed, and satisfy surplus stimulation.[68] Not to beat about the bush, *Copa*'s shimmy was a candid pornotopia, a desire machine overtly designed as pricktease for a full house of erections:[69] a lascivious herd of Priapuses all after Vesta's ass, kept safe by her very own sweetie-pie donkey . . .

Between Little Queenie in her smokey cabaret and the affluent furnishings of 'high mimetic' discourse—the mythic-idyllic topiary of Arcadian décor, *Maenalus*, the powers that between them personify 'Hellenism', *Ceres-Amor-Bromius*, and (if that don't beat all) the nobs' nymphette *Achelois*, *Copa* constructs a social space, the space for 'socializing', a 'protopolitical centre', where customers purchase the sensation of being (made) real through leisure.[70] The exchange lets free adult male egos buy massage by women and other servants put at their disposal. The hard graft of delivering the full range of amenities to make an oasis away from the exhausting heat, dust, and sweat of brute mundane labour, is dissimulated in this factory of sensuality, as the woman works her butt off to mime 'I-need-a-Man' lust. This urban microcosm affords and markets its clientele conspicuous consumption. Here alcohol and gambling rule the roost, for real men, wined and dined, pampered with petals and tit-bits: that risquée show-girl humps air to cap the repertoire of excitement. Saucy? She's got it.[71]

disturb natural fluidity and beauty of the hands and fingers' (Pohren (1984) 63 and plate 2 caption).

   [67] Dancing à deux as erotic coupling is constantly reinvented by modernity, as in the tango-mania of 1911–14 (no, *not* from *tangere*), where the anti-traditional cabaret jive of Buenos Aires was reprogrammed by Parisian stage gauchos and re-exported to Argentina, Hispanicized and Arabicized: the 'political economy of passion': Matsuda (1996), Savigliano (1995).

   [68] Quotes and theory: Sumic-Riha (1997) 227, 230, 233. Lost together in music, to feel sexy: Frith (1996) 142; to feel 'ambivalent pleasures: dance as a problem for women': Cowan (1990) 188–225. Dance scholarship confined to collective ritual, to the socio-political: e.g. Spencer (1985), Washabaugh (1996 and 1998); but cf. Thomas (1990 and 1995).

   [69] Explicit e.g. Mart. 6. 71, *Priapea* 19, 27; cf. Richlin (1983) 54, Toner (1995) 67 f., 107, Edwards (1997).

   [70] 'High mimetic' as operator of mastery: Fitzgerald (1996) 404 f., on *Moretum*. 'Protopolitics' of leisure: Toner (1995) 76.

   [71] Social capital and identity-formation in the tavern: Toner (1995) esp. 77, 81, 90 f.; compila-

Copa is herself leisure ware. 'Dancing girls' came from Syria or Cadiz.[72] Which means, this titillation is *exotic*. *Copa Syrisca* is, then, precisely *not a woman dancing; she is not a woman,* and *she is not dancing.* Rather, this is a cultural package that works with the woman's body, clothes her with a role as Muse, one man's magic drama of *Duende,* another male's 'sex act' Babe.[73] The routine pins on her the name of the defamiliarized and mystified 'Other', whether Orientalized or Occidentalized—far out. The Roman Empire has fetched the delights of a planet for the pleasure of the master-race. Wherever Margery was raised, however she got into this line of work, a summer season as the latest 'Queen of Sheba', she sexes the *imperium,* concretizing in her 'wild', yet 'decadent', fandango all the bottomless excess of Lust Beyond Words.

The writhing, undulating, incessant gyrations of a Salomé spell the tantalizing unseizability of the exotic[74]—and stand in for the tavern's cornucopia of good-time goodies. Like Carthage in Flaubert's *Salammbô,* *Copa*'s Syro-Grecian convolutions epitomize sheer abundance, beyond calculation, language, comprehension:

Beyond the copiousness of this description, there are things that cannot even be described: *they don't even have names.* Copia merged with the unavailability or straining of language produces the ungraspable quality of things exotic.[75]

AMusements, literary or otherwise, must always be explored as locations in culture, social scenarios, sites of power and desire. Thus at least one ancient scholar (word-tinker?) decided that

caupona *taberna a* copiis *dicta.*[76]

'*Caupona*': tavern, so called from 'copiousness'.

---

tion of evidence: Kleberg (1957), Jashemski (1963–4). Threat to society, linkage with prostitution: Toner (1995) 67 f., 107, Robinson (1992) 135–8, 'Bars, eating-houses, and inns'.

[72] Fear (1996). *Gaditanae* shimmied, too, both in cabarets and for 'dinner theater': e.g. Mart. 5. 78. 26–8, *de Gadibus . . . vibrabunt sine fine prurientes* | lascivos docili *tremore lumbos,* Jones (1991) 193 f.

[73] Cf. Roland Barthes on striptease: Célestin (1996) 145.

[74] Webb (1997), cf. Apter (1995) 168 on Flaubert's *Hérodias.* ' "Aphrodite danced in a totally lascivious, vulgar way [*hidhea*]." . . . In 1976, while researching the *tsifte teli* in Athens, I found that many Greeks . . . often tend to dismiss the dance as "Gypsy" or "Turkish"—in other words, as "Other"—and "not really Greek" ': Cowan (1990) 217 n., 216, 'Follow-up to Aphrodite's party'.

[75] Célestin (1996) 131 f.

[76] Paulus in Festus p. 40 Mueller. *caupo/na* and *copo/na* are alternative spellings.

And an ancient grammarian (word-pedlar?) tells us that

caupona ... *significat tam ipsam* tabernam *quam* mulierem, *'hic tamen una Syra'.*[77]
'Caupona' . . . refers equally to tavern and to woman: 'Here, mind, a Syrian female'.

The sex-text-ual signifier *Copa = caupona* accordingly condenses within her copious capacity *both* those hapaxes in her poem, the 'dens' and the 'denizens': *calybae* and *calybitae*, vv. 7, 25.[78] Corny or not, *all* the persons and *all* the places strewn through the motel/poem combine to figure *Copa* as *Cabaña*, *Cabaña* as *Copa*. The Café à Go-Go. Live Music.

'All that interests the French about the Empire', lamented Prime Minister Jules Ferry, 'is the belly dance.'[79]

---

[77] Priscian in *Corpus Glossariorum Latinorum* ii. 209. 6 Keil, quoting a scrap of Lucilius (123 Warmington).

[78] *Copa* is extant only at *Copa* 1, Suet. *Nero* 27. 3, conjectured at Plin. *Natural History* 34. 90, and garbled as Virgil's poem *'Cupa'* by Charisius (*Corpus Glossariorum Latinorum* i. 63. 11 Keil: a vatic 'Vat', then). Could Cupid lurk in these parts?

[79] Garelick (1995) 295.

References

ADAMS, J. N. (1982) *The Latin Sexual Vocabulary*, Baltimore.

AHL, F. M. (1976) *Lucan: An Introduction*, Ithaca and London.

—— (1984) 'The Rider and the Horse: Politics and Power in Roman Poetry from Horace to Statius', *ANRW* 2. 32. 1: 40–110.

—— (1986) 'Statius' Thebaid: A Reconsideration', *ANRW* 2. 32. 5: 2803–912.

ALBIS, R. V. (1996) *Poet and Audience in the Argonautica of Apollonius*, Lanham and London.

ANCONA, R. (1994) *Time and the Erotic in Horace's Odes*, Durham, NC, and London.

ANDERSON, W. S. (1982) *Essays on Roman Satire*, Princeton.

—— (1997) *Ovid's Metamorphoses, Books I–V, edited with Introduction and Commentary*, Norman and London.

—— (1999) (ed.) *Why Horace?*, Wauconda, Ill.

APTER, E. (1995) '*Figura Serpentinata*: Visual Seduction and the Colonial Gaze', in Cohen and Prendergast (1995) 163–78.

ARENDT, H. (1958) *The Human Condition*, Chicago.

—— (1978) *The Life of the Mind*, New York.

—— (1993) 'What is Authority', in *Between Past and Future*, New York.

ARTHUR, M. B. (1983) 'The Dream of a World Without Women: Poetics and the Circles of Order in the *Theogony* Prooemium', *Arethusa*, 16: 97–116.

AUBRIOT-SÉVIN, D. (1992) *Prière et conceptions religieuses en Grèce ancienne jusqu'à la fin du Ve siècle av. J-C*, Lyons.

AUSTIN, J. L. (1962) *How to Do Things with Words*, Oxford.

AUSTIN, R. G. (1977) *P. Vergili Maronis, Aeneidos Liber Sextus*, with a Commentary, Oxford.

BACON, H. (1990) 'The Poetry of *Phaedo*', in M. Griffith and D. J. Mastronarde (eds.) *The Cabinet of the Muses: Essays on Classical and Comparative Literature in Honor of Thomas Rosenmeyer*, Atlanta: 147–62.

—— (1995) 'The Chorus in Greek Life and Drama', *Arion*, 3rd ser. 3/1: 6–24.

BAKER, R. J. (1974) 'Propertius III 13–30: whose baskets?', *Mnemosyne*, 27: 53–8.

BAKHTIN, M. M. (1981) *The Dialogic Imagination*, ed. and tr. C. Emerson and M. Holquist, Austin.

—— (1986) 'The Problem of the Text', tr. V. McGee, in *Speech Genres and Other Late Essays*, Austin: 103–31.

BAKKER, E. J. (1993a) 'Activation and Preservation: The Interdependence of Text and Performance in an Oral Tradition', *Oral Tradition*, 8/1: 5–20.

BAKKER, E. J. (1993b) 'Discourse and Performance: Involvement, Visualization and "Presence" in Homeric Poetry', *Classical Antiquity*, 12/1: 1–29.

BAL, M. (1983) 'Sexuality, Semiosis and Binarism: A Narratological Comment on Bergren and Arthur', *Arethusa*, 16: 117–35.

BARCHIESI, A. (1991) 'Discordant Muses', *Proceedings of the Cambridge Philological Society*, 37: 1–21.

——(1994) *Il Poeta e il Principe. Ovidio e il Discorso Augusteo*, Bari.

——(1997) 'Endgames: Ovid's *Metamorphoses* 15 and *Fasti* 6', in D. H. Roberts, F. M. Dunn, and D. P. Fowler (eds.) *Classical Closure: Reading the End in Greek and Latin Literature*, Princeton: 181–208.

BARKER, A. (1994) 'The Daughters of Memory', *Musica e storia*, 2: 31–54.

BARLOW, S. A. (1986) *Euripides, Trojan Women, with an Introduction, Translation and Commentary*, Warminster.

BARMEYER, E. (1968) *Die Musen: ein Beitrag zur Inspirationstheorie*, Munich.

BARTON, C. (1993) *The Sorrows of the Ancient Romans*, Princeton.

BATE, J. (1993) *Shakespeare and Ovid*, Oxford.

BELFIORE, E. (1980) 'Elenchus, Epode and Magic: Socrates and Silenus', *Phoenix*, 34: 128–37.

BENNETT, C. E. (1976) *Horace: Odes and Epodes*, New Rochelle, NY (orig. pub. 1901).

BENVENISTE, E. (1966) *Problèmes de linguistique générale*, Paris.

——(1971) *Problems in General Linguistics*, tr. Mary E. Meek, Coral Gables, Fla.

BERGIN, T., and WILSON, A. (1977) (tr.) *Petrarch's Africa*, New Haven and London.

BERGREN, A. L. T. (1981) ' "Helen's Good Drug": *Odyssey* IV 1–305', in S. Kresic (ed.) *Contemporary Literary Hermeneutics and the Interpretation of Classical Texts*, Ottawa: 517–30.

——(1983) 'Language and the Female in Early Greek Thought', *Arethusa*, 16: 69–95.

BEYE, C. R. (1969) 'Jason as Love-hero in Apollonius' *Argonautica*', *Greek, Roman and Byzantine Studies*, 10: 31–55.

——(1982) *Epic and Romance in the Argonautica of Apollonius: Literary Structures*, Carbondale, Ill.

BIERL, A. F. (1990) 'Dionysus, Wine, and Tragic Poetry: A Metatheatrical Reading of *P. Köln* VI 242 A = *TrGF* II F 646a', *Greek, Roman and Byzantine Studies*, 31: 353–91.

BING, P. (1988) *The Well-Read Muse. Present and Past in Callimachus and the Hellenistic Poets*, Göttingen.

BISHOP, M. (1966) *Letters from Petrarch*, Bloomington and London.

BLACKBURN, S., CLAUS, P., FLUECKIGER, J., and WADLEY, S. (1989) (eds.) *Oral Epics in India*, Berkeley.

BLAISE, F., JUDET DE LA COMBE, P., and ROUSSEAU, P. (1996) *Le Métier du mythe: Lectures d'Hésiode*, Lille.

Bömer, F. (1958) *P. Ovidius Naso. Die Fasten. B. II Kommentar*, Heidelberg.

——(1976) *P. Ovidius Naso: Metamorphosen IV*, Heidelberg.

Borges, J. L. (1964) 'Funes the Memorious', in *Labyrinths*, New York.

Borghini, A. (1987) 'La taverna, il letame ed altro: Percorsi simbolici della morte', in R. Raffaelli (ed.) *Rappresentazioni della Morte*, Urbino: 131–223.

Bourdieu, P. (1991) *Language and Symbolic Power*, Cambridge.

Bowie, E. L. (1993) 'Lies, Fiction and Slander in Early Greek Poetry', in Gill and Wiseman (1993) 1–37.

Bowie, Malcolm (1991) *Lacan*, Cambridge, Mass.

Bowra, C. M. (1972) *Homer*, New York.

Boyancé, P. (1937) *Le Culte des Muses chez les philosophes grecs*, Paris.

Boyle, A. J. (1987) (ed.) *The Imperial Muse*, Victoria, Australia.

——(1993) (ed.) *Roman Epic*, London.

Boyle, M. O'Rourke (1991) *Petrarch's Genius: Pentimento and Prophecy*, Berkeley, Los Angeles, and London.

Boys-Stones, G. (forthcoming) (ed.) *Metaphor and Allegory in Ancient Thought*, Oxford.

Bramble, J. C. (1974) *Persius and the Programmatic Satire: A Study in Form and Imagery*, Cambridge.

Braund, S. H. (1988) *Beyond Anger*, Cambridge.

——(1992) *Lucan. The Civil War*, Oxford.

——(1996) *Juvenal. Satires Book I*, Cambridge.

Brelich, A. (1969) *Paides e Parthenoi*, Rome.

Brink, C. O. (1971) *Horace on Poetry: The 'Ars Poetica'*, Cambridge.

Bronfen, E. (1992) *Over her Dead Body: Death, Femininity, and the Aesthetic*, New York.

Burckhardt, J. (1998) *The Greeks and Greek Civilization*, tr. S. Stern, ed. with Introduction by O. Murray, London.

Burke, S. (1995) *Authorship: From Plato to the Postmodern*, Edinburgh.

Burkert, W. (1987) *Ancient Mystery Cults*, Cambridge, Mass., and London.

Burnet, J. (1911) *Plato's Phaedo*, Oxford.

Butler, H. E., and Barber, E. A. (1933) (eds.) *The Elegies of Propertius*, Oxford.

Butler, J. (1995) 'Desire', in F. Lentricchia and T. McLaughlin (eds.) *Critical Terms for Literary Study*, Chicago: 369–86.

Cahoon, L. (1990) 'Let the Muse Sing On: Poetry, Criticism, Feminism and the Case of Ovid', *Helios*, 17: 197–211.

——(1996) 'Calliope's Song: Shifting Narrators in Ovid *Met.* 5', *Helios*, 23: 43–66.

Cairns, F. (1979) *Tibullus. A Hellenistic Poet at Rome*, Cambridge.

Calame, C. (1987) *Le Récit en Grèce ancienne: Énonciation et représentation des poètes*, Paris.

——(1995) *The Craft of Poetic Speech in Ancient Greece*, tr. J. Orion, Ithaca and London (1st pub. as *Le Récit en Grèce ancienne*, 1987).

CAMERON, A. (1995) *Callimachus and his Critics*, Princeton.

CAMILLONI, M. T. (1998) *Le Muse*, Rome.

CAMPBELL, D. (1982) *Greek Lyric Poetry*, Bristol.

CAMPBELL, M. (1983) *Studies in the Third Book of Apollonius Rhodius' Argonautica*, Hildesheim.

CAMPS, W. A. (1965) *Propertius: Elegies, Book IV*, Cambridge.

CANTARELLA, R. (1970) 'Agatone e il Prologo delle '"Tesmoforiazusae" ', in *Scritti Minori sul Teatro Greco*, Brescia: 325–33.

CARRARA, P. (1986) 'Stazio e i primordia di Tebe. Poetica e polemica nel prologo della Tebaide', *Prometheus*, 12: 146–58.

CASALI, S. (1995) 'Altre voci nell'*Eneide* di Ovidio', *Materiali e discussioni per l'analisi dei testi classici*, 35: 59–76.

CAVARERO, A. (1996) 'Regarding the Cave', *Qui parle*, 10: 1–20.

—— (1997) *Tu che mi guardi tu che mi racconti*, Milan.

CAVE, T. (1979) *The Cornucopian Text. Problems of Writing in the French Renaissance*, Oxford.

CAVIGLIA, F. (1973) *P. Papinio Stazio. La Tebaide—Libro I*, Rome.

CELENTANO, L. (1956) 'Significato e Valore del IV Libro di Properzio', *Annali della Facoltà di Lettere e Filosofia dell'Università di Napoli*, 6: 33–68.

CÉLESTIN, R. (1996) *From Cannibals to Radicals. Figures and Limits of Exoticism*, Minneapolis.

CHATWIN, B. (1987) *The Songlines*, London.

CITRONI, M. (1992) 'Produzione letteraria e forme del potere', in E. Gabba and A. Schiavone (eds.) *Storia di Roma*, 2/3, Turin: 383–490.

CIXOUS, H. (1981) 'The Laugh of the Medusa', in S. de Courtivron and E. Marks (eds.) *New French Feminism*, Minneapolis.

—— (1991) *Coming to Writing and Other Essays*, ed. D. Jenson, Cambridge, Mass., and London.

CLAUSEN, W. (1994) *Virgil Eclogues, edited with an Introduction and Commentary*, Oxford.

—— GOODYEAR, F. R. D., KENNEY, E. J., and RICHMOND, J. A. (1966) (eds.) *Appendix Vergiliana*, Oxford (*Copa*, ed. E.J.K: 79–82).

CLAUSS, J. J. (1997) 'Conquest of the Mephistophelian Nausika: Medea's Role in Apollonius' Refinition of the Epic Hero', in Clauss and Johnston (1997) 149–77.

—— and JOHNSTON, S. I. (1997) (eds.) *Medea: Essays on Medea in Myth, Literature, Philosophy, and Art*, Princeton.

COHEN, M., and PRENDERGAST, C. (1995) (eds.) *Spectacles of Realism: Gender, Body, Genre*, Minneapolis.

COLE, T. (1983) 'Archaic Truth', *Quaderni urbinati di cultura classica*, NS 13: 7–28.

COLEMAN, K. M. (1988) *Statius, Silvae IV*, Oxford.

COLEMAN, R. (1977) *Vergil, Eclogues, edited*, Cambridge.

COLIE, R. L. (1970) *'My Ecchoing Song': Andrew Marvell's Poetry of Criticism*, Princeton.

COLLINS, D. (1999) 'Hesiod and the Divine Voice of the Muses', *Arethusa*, 32: 241–62.

COMMAGER, S. (1962) *The Odes of Horace*, New Haven and London.

COPJEC, J. (1994) *Read My Desire: Lacan Against the Historicists*, Cambridge, Mass.

CORBEILL, A. (1996) *Controlling Laughter. Political Humor in the Late Roman Republic*, New Jersey.

COWAN, J. K. (1990) *Dance and the Body Politic in Northern Greece*, New Jersey.

CRUMP, G. M. (1962) *The Poems and Translations of Thomas Stanley*, Oxford.

CULLER, J. (1981) *The Pursuit of Signs: Semiotics, Literature, Deconstruction*, London.

CURTIUS, E. R. (1948) *Europäische Literatur und Lateinisches Mittelalter*, Bern.

——(1953) *European Literature and the Latin Middle Ages*, tr. W. R. Trask, Princeton.

CUTOLO, P. (1990) 'The Genre of the *Copa*', *Papers of the Leeds Latin Seminar*, 6: 115–19.

DALFEN, J. (1974) *Polis und Poiesis. Die Auseinandersetzung mit der Dichtung bei Platon und seinen Zeitgenossen*, Munich.

DÄLLENBACH, L. (1977) *Le Récit spéculaire*, Paris.

DAVIDSON, D. (1989) *Essays on Actions and Events*, Oxford.

DAVIS, G. (1991) *Polyhymnia: The Rhetoric of Horatian Lyric Discourse*, Berkeley and Los Angeles.

——(1999) '*Carminá Iambi*: The Literary-Generic Dimension of Horace's *Integer Vitae* (C. 1,22)', in Anderson (1999) 51–62 (orig. pub. in *Quaderni Urbinati di Cultura Classica*, 27 (1987) 67–78).

DE MAN, P. (1979) 'Semiology and Rhetoric', in J. V. Harari (ed.) *Textual Strategies: Perspectives in Post-Structuralist Criticism*, New York: 121–40.

DE VRIES, G. J. (1969) *A Commentary on the Phaedrus of Plato*, Amsterdam.

DEE, J. H. (1974) 'Propertius 4.2: Callimachus Romanus at Work', *American Journal of Philology*, 95: 43–55.

——(1978) 'Elegy 4.8: A Propertian Comedy', *Transactions of the American Philological Association*, 108: 41–53.

DELATTE, A. (1934) 'Les Conceptions de l'enthousiasme chez les philosophes présocratiques', *L'Antiquité classique*, 3: 5–79.

DELEUZE, G. (1998) *A Thousand Plateaux*, Minneapolis.

DERRIDA, J. (1981) 'Plato's Pharmacy', in *Dissemination*, Chicago.

DETIENNE, M. (1960) *Les Muses d'Homère et d'Hésiode*, Paris.

——(1996) *Masters of Truth in Archaic Greece*, tr. J. Lloyd, New York (orig. pub. as *Maîtres de vérité dans la Grèce archaïque*, Paris, 1967).

DEVEREUX, G. (1987) 'Thamyris and the Muses', *American Journal of Philology*, 108: 199–201.

DINDORF, G. (1964) (ed.) *Aelius Aristides*, vol. 3 (Hildesheim).

DODDS, E. R. (1950) (1951) *The Greeks and the Irrational*, Berkeley and Los Angeles.

—— (1959) *Plato: Gorgias, a revised text with commentary*, Oxford.

DOHERTY, L. E. (1995) 'Sirens, Muses and Female Narrators in the *Odyssey*, in B. Cohen (ed.) *The Distaff Side: Representing the Female in Homer's Odyssey*, New York and Oxford: 81–92.

DOLEZEL, L. (1980) 'Truth and Authenticity in Narrative', *Poetics Today*, 1/3: 7–25.

DOMINIK, W. J. (1994) *The Mythic Voice of Statius: Power & Politics in the Thebaid*, Leiden, New York, and Cologne.

DOVER, K. J. (1978) *Greek Homosexuality*, London.

—— (1980) *Plato: Symposium*, Cambridge.

—— (1993) *Aristophanes: Frogs*, Oxford.

DRABKIN, I. E. (1930) *The Copa: An Investigation of the Problem of Date and Authorship*, Geneva.

DREW, D. L. (1923) 'The *Copa*', *Classical Quarterly*, 17: 73–81.

—— (1925) 'The *Copa—II*', *Classical Quarterly*, 19: 37–42.

DU QUESNAY, I. LE M. (1979) 'From Polyphemus to Corydon. Virgil, *Eclogue* 2 and the *Idylls* of Theocritus', in D. West and T. Woodman (1979) (eds.) *Creative Imitation and Latin Literature*, Cambridge: 35–69.

DUBOIS, P. (1995) *Sappho is Burning*, Chicago.

DUFF, J. W., and DUFF, A. M. (1934) (tr.) *Calpurnius Siculus*, Cambridge, Mass., and London.

DUNBABIN, K. M. D. (1986) '*Sic erimus cuncti*. The skeleton in Graeco-Roman Art', *Jahrbuch des Deutschen Archäologischen Instituts*, 101: 185–255.

EAGLETON, T. (1991) *Ideology*, London.

—— (1994) (ed.) *Ideology*, London.

EASTERLING, P. E. (1982) *Sophocles:* Trachiniae, Cambridge.

—— (1985) 'Greek Poetry and Greek Religion', in P. E. Easterling and J. V. Muir (eds.) *Greek Religion and Society*, Cambridge: 34–49.

—— (1988) 'Tragedy and Ritual: "Cry 'Woe, woe', but May the Good Prevail"', *Métis*, 3: 87–109.

—— (1993a) 'Gods on Stage in Greek Tragedy', in J. Dalfen, G. Petersmann, and F. F. Schwarz (eds.) *Religio Graeco-Romana: Festschrift für Walter Pötscher*, Graz and Horn: 77–86.

—— (1993b) 'Oedipe à Colone: Personnages et "réception"', in A. Machin and L. Pernée (eds.) *Sophocle: Le Texte, les personnages*, Aix-en-Provence: 191–200.

—— (1996) 'Weeping, Witnessing, and the Tragic Audience: Response to Segal', in Silk (1996) 173–81.

—— (1997) 'Form and Performance', in P. E. Easterling (ed.) *The Cambridge Companion to Greek Tragedy*, Cambridge: 151–77.

EDWARDS, C. (1993) *The Politics of Immorality in Ancient Rome*, Cambridge.

—— (1996) *Writing Rome. Textual Approaches to the City*, Cambridge.

—— (1997) 'Unspeakable Professions: Public Performance and Prostitution in Ancient Rome', in Hallett and Skinner (1997) 66–95.

ELIADE, M. (1958) *Birth and Rebirth: The Religious Meanings of Initiation in Human Culture*, tr. W. R. Trask, New York.

ELIOT, T. S. (1943) *Four Quartets*, London.

ELLIS, J. M. (1989) *Against Deconstruction*, Princeton.

ELLMANN, M. (1987) *The Poetics of Impersonality. T. S. Eliot and Ezra Pound*, Brighton.

FANTAZZI, C., and PEROSA, A. (1988) *Iacopo Sannazaro: De Partu Virginis*, Florence.

FANTHAM, R. E. (1985) 'Ovid, Germanicus and the Composition of the Fasti', *Proceedings of the Leeds Latin Seminar*, 5: 243–81.

FEAR, A. T. (1996) 'The Dancing Girls of Cadiz', in I. McAuslan, I. and P. Walcot (eds.) *Women in Antiquity*, Oxford: 177–81.

FEDELI, P. (1965) *Properzio: Elegie, Libro IV*, Bari.

—— (1984) 'Simbolo, metafora, ambiguità. Properzio 3, 3 e le smanie epiche del poeta elegiaco', *Grazer Beiträge*, 11: 141–63.

—— (1987) 'Acanthis e la sete dei morti', in R. Raffaelli (ed.) *Rappresentazioni della Morte*, Urbino: 93–129.

FEENEY, D. C. (1991) *The Gods in Epic*, Oxford.

—— (1993) 'Towards an Account of the Ancient World's Concepts of Fictive Belief', in Gill and Wiseman (1993) 230–44.

—— (1998) *Literature and Religion at Rome: Cultures, Contexts, Beliefs*, Cambridge.

FERNIQUÉ, E. (1887) '*crotalum*', in C. Darembourg and E. Saglio (eds.) *Dictionnaire des Antiquités Grecques et Romaines*, Paris: i. 2. 1571–2.

FERRARI, G. R. F. (1987). *Listening to the Cicadas*, Cambridge.

—— (1988) 'Hesiod's Mimetic Muses and the Strategies of Deconstruction', in A. Benjamin (ed.) *Post-Structuralist Classics*, London and New York: 45–78.

FESTA, N. (1926) (ed.) *Francesco Petrarca: Africa*, Florence.

FINKELBERG, M. (1990) 'A Creative Oral Poet and the Muse', *American Journal of Philology*, 111: 293–303.

—— (1998) *The Birth of Literary Fiction in Ancient Greece*, Oxford.

FITZGERALD, W. (1988) 'Power and Impotence in Horace's *Epodes*', *Ramus*, 17: 176–91.

—— (1995) *Catullan Provocations: Lyric Poetry and the Drama of Position*, Berkeley, Los Angeles, and London.

—— (1996) 'Labor and Laborer in Latin Poetry', *Arethusa*, 29: 389–418.

FLASCHENRIEM, B. L. (1999) 'Sulpicia and the Rhetoric of Disclosure', *Classical Philology*, 94: 36–54.

FLASHAR, H. (1958) *Der Dialog Ion als Zeugnis platonischer Philosophie*, Berlin.

FLEETWOOD MAC (1997) *The Dance*, Reprise Records.

FORD, A. (1992) *Homer: The Poetry of the Past*, Ithaca.

FORSYTH, P. YOUNG, (1991) 'The Thematic Unity of Catullus 11', *Classical World*, 84: 457–64.

FOUCAULT, M. (1980) *Power/Knowledge: Selected Interviews and Other Writings 1972–7*, New York.

FOWLER, D. P. (1989) 'First Thoughts on Closure: Problems and Prospects', *Materiali e discussioni per l'analisi dei testi classici*, 22: 75–122.

——(1993) 'Images of Horace in Twentieth-Century Scholarship', in C. Martindale and D. Hopkins (eds.) *Horace Made New*, Cambridge: 268–76, 308–12.

——(1997) 'Virgilian Narrative: Story-Telling', in Martindale (1997) 259–70.

——(1998) 'On the Shoulders of Giants: Intertextuality and Classical Studies', *Materiali e discussioni per l'analisi dei testi classici*, 39: 1–34.

——(2000) 'Epic in the Middle of the Wood: *mise en abyme* in the Nisus and Euryalus episode', in Sharrock and Morales (2000) 89–113.

FOXHALL, L., and SALMON, J. B. (1998a) (eds.) *Thinking Men: Masculinity and its Self-Representation in the Classical Tradition*, London.

————(1998b) *When Men were Men: Masculinity, Power and Identity in Classical Antiquity*, London.

FRAENKEL, E. (1957) *Horace*, Oxford.

FRANZOI, A. (1988) *L'Ostessa, Poemetto Pseudovirgiliano, Introduzione, Testo, Commentario*, Venice.

FRAZER, J. C. (1989) (tr.) *Ovid, Fasti*, 2nd edn., rev. G. P. Goold, Cambridge, Mass., and London.

FREUD, S. (1953–73) *The Standard Edition of the Complete Psychological Works of Sigmund Freud*, ed. J. Strachey, 24 vols., London.

——(1989) 'Character and Anal Erotism', in *The Freud Reader*, ed. P. Gay, London: 293–7.

FRITH, S. (1996) *Performing Rites: On the Value of Popular Music*, Cambridge, Mass.

GAIN, D. B. (1976) (tr.) *The Aratus ascribed to Germanicus Caesar*, London.

GALINSKY, G. K. (1969) 'The Triumph Theme in the Augustan Elegy', *Wiener Studien*, 82: 80–91.

GARELICK, R. (1995) '*Bayadères, Stéréorama*, and Vahat-Loukoum: Technological Realism in the Age of Empire', in Cohen and Prendergast (1995) 294–319.

GARNER, R. (1993) 'Achilles in Locri: *P. Oxy.* 3876. frr. 37–77', *Zeitschrift für Papyrologie und Epigraphik*, 96: 153–65.

GARRISON, D. H. (1991) *Horace: Epodes and Odes*, Norman and London.

GEERTZ, C. (1973) *The Interpretation of Cultures*, New York.

GENTILI, B. (1984) *Poesia e pubblico nella Grecia antica*, Rome and Bari.

GEORGACOPOULOU, S. (1996) 'Clio dans la Thébaïde de Stace: à la recherche du kléos perdu', *Materiali e discussioni per l'analisi dei testi classici*, 37: 167–91.

——(forthcoming) *Technique narrative et voix du narrateur: l'apostrophe dans la Thébaide de Stace*.

GILL, C., and WISEMAN, T. P. (1993) (eds.) *Lies and Fiction in the Ancient World*, Exeter.

GLEASON, M. (1995) *Making Men: Sophists and Self-Presentation in Ancient Rome*, Princeton.

GOLDHILL, S. (1988) 'Reading Differences: The *Odyssey* and Juxtaposition', *Ramus*, 17 / 1: 1–31.

——(1991) *The Poet's Voice: Essays on Poetics and Greek Literature*, Cambridge.

——and OSBORNE, R. (1999) (eds.) *Performance Culture and Athenian Democracy*, Cambridge.

GOODYEAR, F. R. D. (1977) 'The *Copa*: A Text and Commentary', *Bulletin of the Institute of Classical Studies*, 24: 117–31.

GOOLD, G. P. (1977) (tr.) *Manilius*, Cambridge, Mass., and London.

GOW, A. S. F. (1950) (tr.) *Theocritus*, Cambridge.

GOWERS, E. (1993) *The Loaded Table. Representations of Food in Roman Literature*, Oxford.

GREENE, E. (1996a) (ed.) *Reading Sappho: Contemporary Approaches*, Berkeley, Los Angeles, and London.

——(1996b) (ed.) *Re-Reading Sappho: Reception and Transmission*, Berkeley, Los Angeles, and London.

——(1998) *The Erotics of Domination: Male Desire and the Mistress in Latin Love Poetry*, Baltimore and London.

——(1999) 'Re-Figuring the Feminine Voice: Catullus Translating Sappho', *Arethusa*, 32: 1–18.

GREENE, J. T. (1989) *The Role of the Messenger and Message in the Ancient Near East*, Atlanta.

GREER, G. (1995) *Slipshod Sibyls: Recognition, Rejection, and the Woman Poet*, London.

GRENE, D., and LATTIMORE, R. (1959) (eds.) *The Complete Greek Tragedies*, vols. 1–4, Chicago and London.

GRESSETH, G. (1970) 'The Homeric Sirens', *Transaction and Proceedings of the American Philological Association*, 101: 203–18.

GRIFFIN, A. (1983) 'Unrequited Love: Polyphemus and Galatea in Ovid's *Metamorphoses*', *Greece and Rome*, 30: 190–7.

GRIFFIN, J. (1982) *Homer on Life and Death*, Oxford.

GRIFFITH, M. (1990) 'Contest and Contradiction in Early Greek Poetry', in M. Griffith and D. J. Mastronarde (eds.) *The Cabinet of the Muses: Essays on Classical and Comparative Literature in Honor of Thomas Rosenmeyer*, Atlanta: 185–207.

GRIGELY, J. (1995) *Textualterity. Art, Theory, and Textual Criticism*, Ann Arbor.

GRIMAL, P. (1984³) *Les Jardins romains*, Paris.

GRUBE, G. M. A. (1965) *The Greek and Roman Critics*, London.

GUBAR, S. (1982) 'The Blank Page and Female Creativity,' in E. Abel (ed.) *Writing and Sexual Difference*, Brighton: 73–93.

GÜTERBOCK, H. (1946) *Kumarbi. Mythen vom churritischen Kronos, aus den hethitischen Fragmenten zusammengestellt, übersetzt und erklärt*, Istanbuler Schriften 16, Zurich and New York.

——(1948) 'The Hittite Version of the Hurrian Kumarbi Myths: Oriental Forerunners of Hesiod', *American Journal of Archaeology*, 2nd ser. 52: 123–34.

GUTZWILLER, K. (1985) 'The Lover and the Lena: Propertius 4.5', *Ramus*, 14/2: 105–15.

HALL, E. (1999) 'Actor's Song in Tragedy', in Goldhill and Osborne (1999) 96–122.

HALLETT, J. (1971) *Book IV: Propertius' Recusatio to Augustus and Augustan Ideals*, diss. Harvard.

——(1973) 'The Role of Women in Roman Elegy', *Arethusa*, 6: 103–24. Repr. in John Peradotto and J. P. Sullivan (1984) (eds.) *Women in the Ancient World*, Albany, NY: 241–62.

——and SKINNER, M. B. (1997) (eds.) *Roman Sexualities*, Princeton.

HALLIWELL, S. (1984) 'Plato and Aristotle on the Denial of Tragedy', *Proceedings of the Cambridge Philological Society*, NS 30: 49–71.

——(1986) *Aristotle's Poetics*, London.

——(1987) *The Poetics of Aristotle: Translation and Commentary*, London.

HANDLEY, E. W. (1973) 'The Poet Inspired?', *Journal of Hellenic Studies*, 93: 104–8.

HARDIE, A. (1983) *Statius and the 'Silvae'. Poets, Patrons and Epideixis in the Graeco-Roman World*, Liverpool.

——(1990). 'Juvenal and the Condition of Letters: The Seventh Satire', *Papers of the Leeds Latin Seminar*, 6: 145–209.

——(1997) 'Philetas and the Plane Tree', *Zeitschrift für Papyrologie und Epigraphik*, 119: 21–36.

HARDIE, P. R. (1992) 'Augustan Poets and the Mutability of Rome', in A. Powell (ed.) *Roman Poetry and Propaganda in the Age of Augustus*, Bristol: 59–82.

——(1994) *Virgil Aeneid 9*, Cambridge.

——(1995) 'The Speech of Pythagoras in Ovid *Metamorphoses* 15: Empedoclean Epos', *Classical Quarterly*, 45: 204–14.

——(1997) 'Questions of Authority: The Invention of Tradition in Ovid *Metamorphoses* 15', in T. Habinek and A. Schiesaro (eds.) *The Roman Cultural Revolution*, Cambridge: 182–98.

——(1999) 'Metamorphosis, Metaphor and Allegory in Latin Epic', in M. Beissinger, J. Tylus, and S. Wofford (eds.) *Epic Traditions in the Contemporary World: The Poetics of Community*, Berkeley, Los Angeles, and London: 96–100.

HARRISON, S. J. (1991) *Vergil Aeneid 10*, Oxford.

——(1992) 'Fuscus the Stoic: Horace *Odes* 1. 22 and *Epistles* 1.10', *Classical Quarterly*, NS 42: 543–7.

HASKINS, C. E. (1887) *Lucani Pharsalia*, London.

HÄUSSLER, R. (1973) 'Der Tod der Musen', *Antike und Abendland*, 19: 117–45.

HAVELOCK, E. A. (1963). *Preface to Plato*, Cambridge, Mass.

HENDERSON, J. (1982) 'A Room (–) with a View', *Liverpool Classical Monthly*, 7: 142–5.

HENDRICKSON, G. L. (1910) 'Integer Vitae', *Classical Journal*, 5: 250–58.

HENRICHS, A. (1995) ' "Why Should I Dance?": Choral Self-Referentiality in Greek Tragedy', *Arion*, 3rd ser. 3/1: 56–111.

HERSHBELL, J. (1970) 'Hesiod and Empedocles', *Classical Journal*, 65: 145–61.

HERSHKOWITZ, D. (1998) *The Madness of Epic*, Oxford.

HEUBECK, A., WEST, S., HAINSWORTH, J., and HOEKSTRA, A. (1988–92) *A Commentary on Homer's Odyssey*, 3 vols., Oxford.

HINDS, S. (1987a) *The Metamorphosis of Persephone: Ovid and the Self-Conscious Muse*, Cambridge.

——(1987b) 'Generalizing about Ovid', in Boyle (1987) 4–31.

——(1998) *Allusion and Intertext: Dynamics of Appropriation in Roman Poetry*, Cambridge.

HOLLIS, A. S. (1970) *Ovid Metamorphoses Book VIII*, Oxford.

HOLZBERG, N. (1998) '*Ter quinque volumina* as *carmen perpetuum*: the division into books in Ovid's *Metamorphoses*', *Materiali e discussioni per l'analisi dei testi classici*, 40: 77–98.

——(1999) 'Four Poets and a Poetess or a Portrait of the Poet as a Young Man? Thoughts on Book 3 of the *Corpus Tibullianum*', *Classical Journal*, 94/2: 169–91.

HUBBARD, M. (1974) *Propertius*, London.

HUNTER, R. L. (1988). ' "Short on Heroics": Jason in the *Argonautica Book III*', *Classical Quarterly*, 38: 436–53.

——(1989) *Apollonius of Rhodes, Argonautica Book III*, Cambridge.

——(1993a) *The Argonautica of Apollonius: Literary Studies*, Cambridge.

——(1993b) *Apollonius of Rhodies. Jason and the Golden Fleece: A New Translation*, Oxford.

——(1996) *Theocritus and the Archaeology of Greek Poetry*, Cambridge.

HUYSMANS, J.-K. (1959) *Against Nature*, tr. R. Baldick, Harmondsworth.

JANAN, M. (1994a) '*When the Lamp is Shattered*': Desire and Narrative in Catullus, Carbondale and Edwardsville.

——(1994b) ' "There beneath the Roman ruin where the purple flowers grow": Ovid's Minyeides and the Feminine Imagination', *American Journal of Philology*, 115/3: 427–48.

JASHEMSKI, W. F. (1963–4) 'A Pompeian Copa', *Classical Journal*, 59: 337–49.

JENKYNS, R. (1998) *Virgil's Experience. Nature and History: Times, Names, and Places*, Oxford.

JOHNSON, B. (1985) 'Les Fleurs du mal armé: Some reflections on Intertextuality', in C. Hosek and P. Parker (eds.) *Lyric Poetry. Beyond New Criticism*, Ithaca: 264–80.

JOHNSON, W. R. (1987) *Momentary Monsters: Lucan and his Heroes*, Ithaca and London.

JONES, C. P. (1991) 'Dinner Theater', in W. J. Slater (ed.) *Dining in a Classical Context*, Ann Arbor: 185–98.

JORY, E. J. (1996) 'The Drama of the Dances: Prolegomena to an Iconography of Imperial Pantomime', in W. J. Slater (ed) *Roman Theater and Society* (E. Togo Salmon Papers I), Ann Arbor: 1–27.

KASTER, R. A. 'Being "Wholly" Roman', unpublished paper.

KEATS, J. (1994) *The Works of John Keats*, Ware.

KEITH, A. (1997) '*Tandem venit amor*: A Roman Woman Speaks of Love', in Hallett and Skinner (1997) 295–310.

—— (1999) 'Versions of Epic Masculinity in Ovid's *Metamorphoses*', in P. Hardie, A. Barchiesi, and S. Hinds (eds.) *Ovidian Transformations: Essays on the Metamorphoses and its Reception*, Cambridge (*Camb. Philol. Soc. Suppl.* 23): 216–41.

—— (2000) *Engendering Rome: Women in Latin Epic*, Cambridge.

KENNEDY, D. F. (1993) *The Arts of Love: Five Studies in the Discourse of Roman Love Elegy*, Cambridge.

KENNEY, E. J. (1983) 'Virgil and the Elegiac Sensibility', *Illinois Classical Studies*, 8: 44–64.

KERFERD, G. B. (1981) *The Sophistic Movement*, Manchester.

KERMODE, F. (1971) *Romantic Image*, Glasgow.

KERSHAW, A. (1992) '*Copa* 5–6 once more', *Classical Philology*, 87: 240–1.

KIRK, G. S., JANKO, R., HAINSWORTH, J. B., and RICHARDSON, N. (1985–93) *The Iliad: A Commentary*, Cambridge.

KLEBERG, T. (1957) *Hôtels, restaurants et cabarets dans l'antiquité romaine. Études historiques et philologiques*, Uppsala.

KNOCHE, U. (1936) 'Zur Frage der Properzinterpolation', *Rheinisches Museum*, 85: 8–63.

KNOX, P. E. (1985) 'Wine, Water, and Callimachean Poetics', *Harvard Studies in Classical Philology*, 79: 107–19.

KRISTEVA, J. (1984) 'The Semiotic Chora Ordering and Drives', in *Revolution in Poetic Language*, New York.

KYTZLER, B. (1960) 'Bemerkungen zum Prooemium der Thebais', *Hermes*, 88: 331–54.

LA FONTAINE (1966) *Fables*, Paris.

LA PENNA, A. (1979) 'L'*usus* contro Apollo e le Muse: Nota a Ovidio *Ars Am.* 1.25–30', *Annali Scuola Normale Superiore Pisa*, 3: 385–97.

LABATE, M. (1993) 'Storie di instabilità: l'episodio di Ermafrodito nelle *Metamorfosi* di Ovidio', *Materiali e discussioni per l'analisi dei testi classici*, 30: 49–62.

LACAN, J. (1966) *Écrits*, Paris.

—— (1973) *Séminaire XI: Les Quatre Concepts fondamentaux de psychanalyse*, Paris.

—— (1975) *Séminaire XX: Encore, 1972–73*, Paris.

—— (1977a) 'Desire and the Interpretation of Desire in *Hamlet*', in *Literature and Psychoanalysis: The Question of Reading: Otherwise*, tr. J. Hulbert, *Yale French Studies*, 55/56: 11–52.

—— (1977b) *Écrits: A Selection*, tr. Alan Sheridan, New York.

—— (1981) *The Four Fundamental Concepts of Psychoanalysis*, tr. Alan Sheridan, New York.

—— (1981–3) 'Hamlet', in *Ornicar?* 24: 7–31; 25: 13–36; 26/27: 7–44.

—— (1986) *Le Séminaire de Jacques Lacan, Livre VII: L'Éthique de la psychanalyse, 1959–1960*, Paris.

—— (1992) *The Seminar of Jacques Lacan, Book VII: The Ethics of Psychoanalysis, 1959–1960*, tr. D. Porter, New York.

—— (1998) *The Seminar of Jacques Lacan, Book XX: On Feminine Sexuality, the Limits of Love and Knowledge (Encore!), 1972–1973*, tr. B. Fink, New York.

LADA-RICHARDS, I. (1993) 'Empathic Understanding: Emotion and Cognition in Classical Dramatic Audience Response', *Proceedings of the Cambridge Philological Society*, 39: 94–140.

—— (1997a) 'Neoptolemus and the Bow: Ritual *Thea* and Theatrical Vision in Sophocles' *Philoctetes*', *Journal of Hellenic Studies*, 117: 179–83.

—— (1997b) ' "Estrangement or "Reincarnation"? Performers and Performance on the Classical Athenian Stage', *Arion*, 5/ 2: 66–107.

—— (1998) 'Staging the *Ephebeia*: Theatrical Role-Playing and Ritual Transition in Sophocles' *Philoctetes*', *Ramus*, 27/1: 1–26.

—— (1999) *Initiating Dionysus: Ritual and Theatre in Aristophanes' Frogs*, Oxford.

LAIRD, A. (1999) *Powers of Expression, Expressions of Power: Speech Presentation and Latin Literature*, Oxford.

—— (forthcoming) 'Figures of Allegory from Homer to Latin Epic', in Boys-Stones (forthcoming).

LANATA, G. (1963) *Poetica Pre-Platonica*, Florence.

LATEINER, D. (1984) 'Mythic and Non-Mythic Artists in Ovid's *Metamorphoses*', *Ramus*, 13: 1–30.

LAUSBERG, H. (1998) *Handbook of Literary Rhetoric*, ed. D. E. Orton and R. D. Anderson, Leiden, Boston, and Cologne.

LAWALL, G. (1966) 'Apollonius' *Argonautica*: Jason as Anti-Hero', *Yale Classical Studies*, 19: 119–69.

LEACH, E. W. (1974a) 'Ekphrasis and the Theme of Artistic Failure in Ovid's *Metamorphoses*', *Ramus*, 3: 102–42.

—— (1974b) *Vergil's Eclogues: Landscapes of Experience*, Ithaca.

LEE, J. S. (1990) *Jacques Lacan*, Amherst, Mass.

LEE, M. O. (1975) 'Catullus in the Odes of Horace', *Ramus*, 4: 33–48.

LEFÈVRE, E. (1966) *Propertius Ludibundus*, Heidelberg.

LENNOX, P. G. (1980) 'Apollonius. Argonautic 3.1 ff and Homer', *Hermes*, 108: 45–73.

LEPICK, J. A. (1981) 'The Castrated Text: the Hermaphrodite as Model of Parody in Ovid and Beamont', *Helios*, 8/1: 71–85.

LEWIS, C. S. (1943) *A Preface to Paradise Lost*, London.

LIDOV, J. B. (1993) 'The Second Stanza of Sappho 31: Another Look', *American Journal of Philology*, 114: 503–35.

LITTLEFIELD, R. J. (1965) 'Pomona and Vertumnus: A Fruition of History in Ovid's *Metamorphoses*', *Arion*, 4: 465–73.

LOMBARDI SATRIANI, L. M., and MELIGRANA, M. (1982) *Il Ponte di San Giacomo: L'ideologia della morte nella società contadina del Sud*, Milan.

LOMBARDO, G. (1995) 'Paleoestetica della ricezione', *Aesthetica*, 45: 5–66.

LONSDALE, S. H. (1993) *Dance and Ritual Play in Greek Religion*, Baltimore and London.

——(1995) '*Homeric Hymn to Apollo*: Prototype and Paradigm of Choral Performance', *Arion*, 3rd ser. 3/1: 25–40.

LORAUX, N. (1981) 'Le Lit, la guerre', *L' Homme*, 21/1: 37–67.

LOTITO, G. (1974) 'In margine alla nuova edizione Teubneriana delle Silvae di Stazio', *Atene e Roma*, 19: 26–48.

LOWRIE, M. (1997) *Horace's Narrative Odes*, Oxford.

LUCAS, D. W. (1968) *Aristotle: Poetics*, Oxford.

LYNCH, J. (1972) *Aristotle's School: A Study of a Greek Educational Institution*, Berkeley.

LYNE, R.O.A.M. (1980) *The Latin Love Poets: From Catullus to Horace*, Oxford.

——(1995) *Horace: Behind the Public Poetry*, New Haven.

McCORMICK, J. (1973) 'Horace's *Integer Vitae*', *Classical World*, 67: 28–33.

MCKEOWN, J. (1989) *A Commentary on Book One of the Amores*, Leeds.

MACLEOD, C. W. (1974) 'Euripides' Rags', *Zeitschrift für Papyrologie und Epigraphik*, 15: 221–2.

—— (1983a) 'Catullus 116', in *Collected Essays*, Oxford: 181–6.

——(1983b) 'Callimachus, Virgil, Propertius, and Lollius', in *Collected Essays*, Oxford: 154–6.

——(1983c) 'Homer on Poetry and the Poetry of Homer', in *Collected Essays*, Oxford: 1–16.

MADER, G. (1991) 'Changing Forms: An Addendum to Propertius 4, 2, 21–48', *Wiener Studien*, 104: 131–47.

MALAMUD, M. A. (1995) 'Happy Birthday, Dead Lucan: (P)raising the Dead in Silvae 2. 7', *Ramus*, 24: 1–30.

MALLARMÉ, G. (1945) *Œuvres Complètes*, Paris.

MARTI, B. (1945) 'The Meaning of the Pharsalia', *American Journal of Philology*, 66: 352–76.

MARTINDALE, C. (1997) (ed.) *The Cambridge Companion to Virgil*, Cambridge.

Marx, K., and Engels, F. (1986) *The German Ideology*, New York (orig. pub. 1845–6).

Masters, J. (1992) *Poetry and Civil War in Lucan's Bellum Civile*, Cambridge.

Matsuda, M. K. (1996) 'Desires: Last Tango at the *Académie*', in *The Memory of the Modern*, Oxford: 185–203.

Mazurek, T. (1997) 'Self-Parody and the Law in Horace's *Satires* 1.9', *Classical Journal*, 93: 1–17.

Meijering, R. (1987) *Literary and Rhetorical Theories in Greek Scholia*, Groningen.

Meltzer, J. (1987) *Salome and the Dance of Writing. Portraits of Mimesis in Literature*, Chicago.

Melville, A. D. (1986) *Ovid, Metamorphoses*, Oxford.

——(1992) *Statius, Thebaid*, tr. with an Introduction and Notes by D. W. T. Vessey, Oxford.

Mendell, C. (1935) 'Catullan Echoes in the Odes of Horace', *Classical Philology*, 30: 289–301.

Mendelsohn, D. (1992) 'συγκεραυνόω: Dithyrambic Language and Dionysiac Cult', *Classical Journal*, 87: 105–24.

Miles, G. (1995) *Livy: Reconstructing Early Rome*, Ithaca.

Miller, J.-A. (1988) 'Extimité', *Prose Studies*, 11: 121–31.

Miller, J. F. (1986) 'Disclaiming Divine Inspiration: A Programmatic Pattern', *Wiener Studien*, 20: 151–64.

Miller, P. Allen (1994) *Lyric Texts and Lyric Consciousness: The Birth of a Genre from Archaic Greece to Augustan Rome*, London and New York.

Minchin, E. (1995) 'The Poet Appeals to his Muse: Homeric Invocations in the Context of Epic Performance', *Classical Journal*, 91/1: 25–33.

Minton, W. W. (1960) 'Homer's Invocations of the Muses: Traditional Patterns', *Transactions and Proceedings of the American Philological Association*, 91: 292–309.

——(1962) 'Invocation and Catalogue in Hesiod and Homer', *Transactions and Proceedings of the American Philological Association*, 93: 188–212.

Mitchell, J., and Rose, J. (1985) *Feminine Sexuality: Jacques Lacan and the école freudienne*, New York (1st edn. 1982).

Mizejewski, L. (1992) *Divine Decadence: Fascism, Female Spectacle, and the Making of Sally Bowles*, New Jersey.

Moore-Blunt, J. (1977) '*Eclogue* 2: Virgil's Utilisation of Theocritean Motifs', *Eranos*, 75: 23–42.

Morris, E. P. (1939) *Horace: Satires and Epistles*, Norman.

Mozley, J. H. (1928) (tr.) *Statius: Thebaid, Achilleid and Silvae*, vol. 2, Cambridge, Mass., and London.

——(1934) (tr.) *Valerius Flaccus*, Cambridge, Mass., and London.

Muecke, F. (1982) 'A Portrait of the Artist as a Young Woman', *Classical Quarterly*, 32: 41–55.

MURRAY, P. (1981) 'Poetic Inspiration in Early Greece', *Journal of Hellenic Studies*, 101: 87–100.

——(1996) *Plato on Poetry*, Cambridge.

——(1999) 'What is a *muthos* for Plato?', in R. Buxton (ed.), *From Myth to Reason? Studies in the Development of Greek Thought*, Oxford: 251–62.

MYERHOFF, B. G. (1982) 'Rites of Passage: Process and Paradox', in V. Turner (ed.) *Celebration: Studies in Festivity and Ritual*, Washington, DC: 109–35.

MYERS, K. S. (1994) *Ovid's Causes. Cosmogony and Aetiology in the Metamorphoses*, Ann Arbor.

MYNORS, R. A. B. (1990) *Virgil, Georgics*, Oxford.

NAGY, G. (1979) *The Best of the Achaeans: Concepts of the Hero in Archaic Greek Poetry*, Baltimore and London.

——(1989) 'Early Greek Views of Poets and Poetry', in G. A. Kennedy (ed.) *The Cambridge History of Literary Criticism*, 1: *Classical Criticism*, Cambridge: 1–77.

——(1990) *Pindar's Homer: The Lyric Possession of an Epic Past*, Baltimore and London.

——(1992) 'Authorisation and Authorship in the Hesiodic *Theogony*', *Ramus*, 21: 119–30.

——(1996a) *Poetry as Performance: Homer and Beyond*, Cambridge.

——(1996b) *Homeric Questions*, Austin.

——(1996c) 'Autorité et auteur dans la *Théogonie* hésiodique', in Blaise, Judet de la Combe, and Rousseau (1996) 41–52.

NANCY, J.-L. (1990) 'Sharing Voices', in G. L. Ormiston and A. D. Schrift (eds.) *Transforming the Hermeneutic Context. From Nietzsche to Nancy*, New York: 211–59.

——(1996) *The Muses*, tr. P. Kamuf, Stanford: California.

NARDUCCI, E. (1984) 'Il comportamento in pubblico (Cicerone, de officiis I. 126–149)', *Maia*, 36: 203–29.

NATZEL, S. (1992) Κλέα γυναικῶν, *Frauen in den Argonautica des Apollonios Rhodios*, Bochum.

NEWLANDS, C. E. (1995) *Playing with Time. Ovid and the Fasti*, Ithaca and London.

NICKS, S. (1983) *The Wild Heart*, Modern Records.

NICOLL, W. S. M. (1986) 'Horace's Judgement on Sappho and Alcaeus', *Latomus*, 45: 603–8.

NIETZSCHE, F. (1993) *The Birth of Tragedy*, tr. S. Whiteside, Harmondsworth.

NIGHTINGALE, A. W. (1995) *Genres in Dialogue: Plato and the Construct of Philosophy*, Cambridge.

NISBET, R. G. M., and HUBBARD, M. (1970) (eds.) *A Commentary on Horace: Odes Book 1*, Oxford.

NUGENT, G. (1990) 'The Sex Which Is Not One: De-constructing Ovid's Hermaphrodite', *Differences*, 2/1: 160–85.

NUSSBAUM, M. (1982) ' "This Story isn't True": Poetry, Goodness and Understanding in Plato's *Phaedrus*', in J. Moravcsik and P. Temko (eds.) *Plato on Beauty, Wisdom and the Arts*, Totowa, NJ: 79–124.

——(1986) *The Fragility of Goodness: Luck and Ethics in Greek Tragedy and Philosophy*, Cambridge.

NUTTALL, A. D. (1992) *Openings: Narrative Beginnings from the Epic to the Novel*, Oxford.

OBBINK, D. (1997) 'Cosmology as Initiation vs. the Critique of Orphic Mysteries', in A. Laks and G. W. Most (eds.) *Studies on the Derveni Papyrus*, Oxford: 39–54.

OGILVIE, R. (1965) *A Commentary on Livy 1–5*, Oxford.

O'HARA, J. (1996) *True Names: Vergil and the Alexandrian Tradition of Etymological Wordplay*, Ann Arbor.

O'HIGGINS, D. (1996) 'Sappho's Splintered Tongue: Silence in Sappho 31 and Catullus 51,' in Greene (1996b) 68–78 (orig. pub. in *American Journal of Philology*, III (1990) 156–67).

——(1997) 'Medea as Muse: Pindar's *Pythian 4*', in Clauss and Johnston (1997) 103–26.

OLIENSIS, E. (1991) 'Canidia, Canicula, and the Decorum of Horace's Epodes', *Arethusa*, 24: 107–38.

OLSTEIN, K. (1984) 'Horace's Integritas and the Geography of Carm. I.22', *Grazer Beiträge*, 113–20.

OTTO, W. (1956) *Die Musen und der göttliche Ursprung des Singens and Sagens*, Düsseldorf.

PADUANO, F. L. (1970) 'L'inversione del rapporto poeta-musa nella cultura ellenistica', *Annali della Scuola Normale Superiore di Pisa*, 2nd ser. 39: 377–86.

PASCHALIS, M. (1997) *Vergil's Aeneid. Semantic Relations and Proper Names*, Oxford.

PATON, W. R. (1917) (tr.) *The Greek Anthology*, Cambridge, Mass., and London.

PAVLOCK, B. (1990) *Eros, Imitation, and the Epic Tradition*, Ithaca.

PICARD, M. (1995) *La Littérature et la mort*, Paris.

POHLENZ, M. (1965) '*Τό πρέπον*. Ein Beitrag zur Geschichte des griechischen Geistes', in *Kleine Schriften*, ed. H. Dörrie, Hildesheim.

POHREN, D. E. (1984) *The Art of Flamenco*, 4th edn., Shaftesbury, Dorset.

POLLARD, J. (1965) *Seers, Shrines and Sirens*, South Brunswick, NJ.

POOLE, A., and MAULE, J. (1995) (eds.) *The Oxford Book of Classical Verse in Translation*, Oxford.

PRATT, L. H. (1993) *Lying and Poetry from Homer to Pindar: Falsehood and Deception in Archaic Greek Poetics*, Ann Arbor.

PRETAGOSTINI, R. (1995) 'L'incontro con le Muse sull'Elicona in Esiodo e in Callimaco: modificazioni di un modello', *Lexis*, 13: 157–72.

PUCCI, P. (1977) *Hesiod and the Language of Poetry*, Baltimore and London.

——(1980) 'The Language of the Muses', in W. M. Aycock and T. Klein (eds.) *Classical Mythology in 20th century Thought and Literature*, Lubock, Tex.: 163–86.

PUCCI, P. (1987) *Odysseus Polutropos: Intertextual Readings in the Odyssey and the Iliad*, Ithaca and London.

PUCCIONI, G. (1979) 'L'elegia IV 5 di Properzio', in *Studi di Poesia Latina in Onore di Antonio Traglia*, Rome: 609–23.

PULLEYN, S. (1997) *Prayer in Greek Religion*, Oxford.

PUTNAM, M. C. J. (1982) 'Catullus 11: The Ironies of Integrity', in *Essays on Latin Lyric, Elegy, and Epic*, Princeton: 13–29 (orig. pub. in *Ramus*, 3 (1974) 70–86).

RACE, W. H. (1983) ' "That Man" in Sappho fr. 31 L-P', *Classical Antiquity*, 2: 92–101.

——(1997) (tr.) *Pindar: Nemean Odes, Isthmian Odes, Fragments*, Cambridge, Mass., and London.

REITZENSTEIN, E. (1936) *Wirklichkeitsbild und Gefühlsentwicklung bei Properz*, Leipzig.

RICHARDSON, L., Jr. (1963) 'Furi et Aureli, Comites Catulli', *Classical Philology*, 58: 93–106.

——(1977) *Propertius: Elegies I–IV*, Norman.

RICHARDSON, L. (1992) *A New Topographical Dictionary of Ancient Rome*, Baltimore and London.

RICHARDSON, N. J. (1974) *The Homeric Hymn to Demeter*, Oxford.

RICHLIN, A. (1983) *The Garden of Priapus. Sexuality and Aggression in Roman Humor*, New Haven.

——(1993) 'Not Before Homosexuality: The Materiality of the *Cinaedus* and the Roman Law against Love between Men', *Journal of the History of Sexuality*, 3: 523–73.

RIEDWEG, C. (1987) *Mysterienterminologie bei Platon, Philon und Klemens von Alexandrien*, Berlin and New York.

ROBBINS, E. (1980) ' "Every Time I Look at You . . .": Sappho Thirty-One', *Transactions and Proceedings of the American Philological Association*, 110: 255–61.

ROBINSON, O. F. (1992) *Ancient Rome. City Planning and Administration*, London.

RORTY, R. (1979) *Philosophy and the Mirror of Nature*, London.

——(1982) *The Consequences of Pragmatism*, Minneapolis.

ROSATI, G. (1992) 'L'elegia al femminile: le Heroides di Ovidio (e altre Heroides)', *Materiali e discussioni per l'analisi dei testi classici*, 29: 71–94.

——(1996) 'Sabinus, the *Heroides* and the Poet-Nightingale. Some Observations on the Authenticity of the *Epistula Sapphus*', *Classical Quarterly*, 46: 207–16.

——(1999a) 'Form in Motion: Weaving the Text in the *Metamorphoses*', in P. Hardie, A. Barchiesi, and S. Hinds (eds.) *Ovidian Transformations: Essays on the Metamorphoses and its Reception*, Cambridge (*Camb. Philol. Soc. Suppl.* 23): 241–55.

——(1999b) 'La Boiterie de Mademoiselle Élégie: un pied volé et ensuite retrouvé (aventures d'un genre littéraire entre les Augustéens et Stace)', in J. Fabre-Serris and A. Deremetz (eds.) *Élégie et épopée dans la poésie ovidienne*

(Héroïdes et Amours). En hommage à Simone Viarre, Lille: 147–63.

ROSENMEYER, T. G. (1955) 'Gorgias, Aeschylus and *Apate*', *American Journal of Philology*, 76: 225–60.

ROSS, D. O. (1975) *Backgrounds to Augustan Poetry: Gallus, Elegy, and Rome*, Cambridge.

ROTHSTEIN, M. (1966) *Propertius Sextus Elegien*, 2 vols., Dublin (1st edn. 1898).

ROWE, C. J. (1986) *Plato: Phaedrus*, Warminster.

—— (1993) *Plato: Phaedo*, Cambridge.

RUDD, N. (1991) (tr.) *Juvenal, The Satires*, Oxford.

RUDHARDT, J. (1996) 'Le Préambule de la *Théogonie*. La vocation du poète. Le langage des Muses', in Blaise, Judet de la Combe, and Rousseau (1996) 25–39.

RUSSELL, D. A. (1964) '*Longinus*', *on the Sublime*, ed. with Introduction and Commentary, Oxford.

—— (1981) *Criticism in Antiquity*, London.

—— and WINTERBOTTOM, M. (1972) (eds.) *Ancient Literary Criticism*, Oxford.

RUTHERFORD, R. (1995) *The Art of Plato*, London.

SAUNDERS, T. (1972) 'Notes on the *Laws* of Plato', *Bulletin of the Institute of Classical Studies*, suppl. 28.

SAVIGLIANO, M. E. (1995) *Tango and the Political Economy of Passion*, Boulder.

SCHACHTER, A. (1986) *Cults of Boiotia*, vol. 2, London.

SCHEFER, C. (1996) *Platon und Apollon: von Logos zurück zum Mythos*, Sankt Augustin.

SCHEID, J., and SVENBRO, J. (1994) *Le Métier de Zeus: Mythe du tissage et du tissu dans le monde gréco-romain*, Paris.

SCHETTER, W. (1960) *Untersuchungen zur epischen Kunst des Statius*, Wiesbaden.

—— (1962) 'Die Einheit des Proemium zur Thebais des Statius', *Museum Helveticum*, 19: 204–17.

SCHIESARO, A. (1997) 'L'intertestualità e i suoi disagi', *Materiali e discussioni per l'analisi dei testi classici*, 39: 75–109.

SCHREINER, C. (1985) (ed.) *Flamenco. Gypsy Dance and Music from Andalusia*, Portland, Ore.

SEAFORD, R. (1981) 'Dionysiac Drama and the Dionysiac Mysteries', *Classical Quarterly*, 31: 252–75.

—— (1994) *Reciprocity and Ritual: Homer and Tragedy in the Developing City-State*, Oxford.

—— (1996) *Euripides Bacchae, with an Introduction, Translation and Commentary*, Warminster.

—— (1997) 'Thunder, Lightning and Earthquake in the *Bacchae* and the Acts of the Apostles', in A. B. Lloyd (ed.) *What is a God? Studies in the Nature of Greek Divinity*, London: 139–51.

SEGAL, C. P. (1962) 'Gorgias and the Psychology of the Logos', *Harvard Studies in Classical Philology*, 66: 99–155.

SEGAL, C. P. (1969) 'Myth and Philosophy in the *Metamorphoses*: Ovid's Augustanism and the Augustan Conclusion of Book 15', *American Journal of Philology*, 90: 257–92.

—— (1983) 'Kleos and its Ironies in the *Odyssey*', *L'Antiquité Classique*, 52: 22–47.

—— (1988) 'Theatre, Ritual and Commemoration in Euripides' *Hippolytus*', *Ramus*, 17: 52–74.

—— (1992) 'Tragic Beginnings: Narration, Voice, and Authority in the Prologues of Greek Drama', *Yale Classical Studies*, 29: 85–112.

—— (1994) 'Female Mourning and Dionysiac Lament in Euripides' *Bacchae*', in A. H. F. Bierl and P. von Möllendorff (eds.) *Orchestra: Drama, Mythos, Bühne: Festschrift für Helmut Flashar*, Leipzig: 12–18.

—— (1995) *Sophocles' Tragic World: Divinity, Nature, Society*, Cambridge, Mass.

—— (1996) 'Catharsis, Audience, and Closure in Greek Tragedy', in Silk (1996) 149–72.

SHACKLETON BAILEY, D. R. (1985) *Q. Horati Flacci Opera*, Stuttgart.

SHARROCK, A. R. (1995) 'The Drooping Rose: Elegiac Failure in *Amores* 3. 7', *Ramus*, 24: 152–80.

—— and MORALES, H. L. (2000) (eds.) *Intratextuality: Essays on Greek and Roman Textual Relations*, Oxford.

SILK, M. S. (1996) (ed.) *Tragedy and the Tragic: Greek Theatre and Beyond*, Oxford.

SKIERA, E, (1985) 'Castanets and Other Rhythmic and Percussive Elements', in Schreiner (1985) 147–52.

SKINNER, M. B. (1980) 'Pertundo tunicamque palliumque', *Classical World*, 73: 306–7.

—— (1997) '*Ego mulier*: The Construction of Male Sexuality in Catullus', in Hallett and Skinner (1997) 129–50 (revision of longer article orig. pub. in *Helios*, 20 (1993) 107–30).

SKUTSCH, O. (1985) *The Annals of Q. Ennius*, Oxford.

SNELL, B. (1953) *The Discovery of the Mind: The Greek Origins of European Thought*, tr. T. G. Rosenmeyer, Cambridge, Mass.

SOLMSEN, F. (1954) 'The "Gift" of Speech in Homer and Hesiod', *Transactions and Proceedings of the American Philological Association*, 85: 1–15.

SOMMERSTEIN, A. H. (1994) *The Comedies of Aristophanes*, viii: *Thesmophoriazusae*, ed. with Translation and Notes, Warminster.

—— (1996) *The Comedies of Aristophanes*, ix: *Frogs*, ed. with Translation and Notes, Warminster.

SPELMAN, C. (1994) 'Propertius 2.3: The Disgusting Subject of Desire', paper read at the Classical Association of the Atlantic States Annual Conference, Carlisle, Pa., April 1994.

SPENCER, P. (1985) (ed.) *Society and the Dance. The Social Anthropology of Process and Performance*, Cambridge.

SPENTZOU, E. (forthcoming) *Reading Characters Read: Transgressions of Gender and Genre in Ovid's Heroides*, Oxford.

SPERBER, D. (1975) *Rethinking Symbolism*, tr. A. L. Morton, Cambridge.

STALLEY, R. (1983) *An Introduction to Plato's Laws*, Oxford.

STEHLE, EVA (1996) 'Sappho's Gaze: Fantasies of a Goddess and Young Man', in Greene (1996a) 193–225 (orig. pub. in a slightly different form in *differences*, 2 (1990) 88–125).

——(1997) *Performance and Gender in Ancient Greece*, Princeton.

STEINIGER, J. (1998) ' "Saecula te quoniam penes et digesta vetustas": die Musenanrufungen in der *Thebais* des Statius', *Hermes*, 126: 221–37.

SUERBAUM, W. (1987) 'Muse', in *Enciclopedia Virgiliana*, vol. iii, Rome: 625–41.

SUMIC-RIHA, J. (1997) 'The Diasporic Dance of Body-Enjoyment: Slain Flesh / Metamorphosing Body', in S. Golding (ed.) *The Eight Technologies of Otherness*, London: 225–35.

SVENBRO, J. (1984) *La parola e il marmo. Alle origini della poetica greca*, Turin.

TAPLIN, O. (1992) *Homeric Soundings: The Shaping of the Iliad*, Oxford.

——(1996) 'Comedy and the Tragic', in Silk (1996) 188–202.

TARRANT, R. J. (1992) 'Nights at the *Copa*: Observations on Language and Date', *Harvard Studies in Classical Philology*, 94: 331–47.

TECUSAN, M. (1996) 'Symposion and Philosophy', unpub. D.Phil. thesis, Oxford.

TESTER, S. (1973) *Boethius: De Consolatione Philosophiae*, Cambridge, Mass.

THALMANN, W. G. (1984) *Conventions of Form and Thought in Early Greek Poetry*, Baltimore and London.

THOMAS, H. (1990) (ed.) *Dance, Gender and Culture*, London.

——(1995) *Dance, Modernity and Culture: Explorations in the Sociology of Dance*, Basingstoke.

THOMPSON, J. B. (1984) *Studies in the Theory of Ideology*, Berkeley and Los Angeles.

THOMSON, D. F. S. (1997) *Catullus*, Toronto, Buffalo, and London.

TISSOL, G. (1997) *The Face of Nature. Wit, Narrative, and Cosmic Origins in Ovid's Metamorphoses*, New Jersey.

TODOROV, T. (1973) 'The Structural Analysis of Literature; The Tales of Henry James', in D. Robey (ed.) *Structuralism: An Introduction*, Oxford: 73–103.

——(1984) *Mikhail Bakhtin: The Dialogical Principle*, Manchester.

TONER, J. P. (1995) *Leisure and Ancient Rome*, Cambridge.

TRÄNKLE, H. (1960) *Die Sprachkunst des Properz und die Tradition der lateinischen Dichtersprache*, Wiesbaden.

TRIMPI, W. (1983) *Muses of One Mind: The Literary Analysis of Experience and its Continuity*, Princeton.

TURNER, V. (1967) *The Forest of Symbols: Aspects of Ndembu Ritual*, Ithaca and London.

——(1974) *Dramas, Fields, and Metaphors: Symbolic Action in Human Society*, Ithaca and London.

VAN DAM, H. J. (1984) *P. Papinius Statius. Silvae Book II. A Commentary*, Leiden.

VERDENIUS, W. J. (1981) 'Gorgias' Doctrine of Deception', in G. B. Kerferd (ed.) *The Sophists and their Legacy*, Wiesbaden: 116–28.

VERNANT, J.-P. (1969) 'Aspects mythiques de la mémoire', in *Mythe et pensée chez les Grecs*, 2nd edn., Paris: 51–78 (1st pub. in *Journal de Psychologie* (1959) 1–29).

VICAIRE, P. (1963) 'Les Grecs et le mystère de l'inspiration poétique', *Bulletin de l'Association Guillaume Budé*, 4th ser. 1: 68–85.

WALBANK, F. W. (1985) 'History and Tragedy,' in *Selected Papers: Studies in Greek and Roman History and Historiography*, Cambridge: 224–41 (1st pub. in *Historia*, 9 (1960) 216–34).

WALSH, G. B. (1984) *The Varieties of Enchantment: Early Greek Views of the Nature and Function of Poetry*, Chapel Hill and London.

WASHABAUGH, W. (1996) *Flamenco: Passion, Politics and Popular Culture*, Oxford.

——(1998) (ed.) *The Passion of Music and Dance. Body, Gender and Sexuality*, Oxford.

WATSON, L. C. (1995) 'Horace's *Epodes*: The Impotence of *Iambos*', in S. J. Harrison (ed.) *Homage to Horace, A Bimillenary Celebration*, Oxford: 188–202.

WEBB, R. (1997) 'Salome's Sisters: The Rhetoric and Realities of Dance in Late Antiquity and Byzantium', in L. James (ed.) *Women, Men, and Eunuchs in Byzantium*, London: 119–48.

WEEBER, K.-W. (1977) *Das 4. Properz-Buch: Interpretationen zu seiner Eigenart und seiner Stellung im Gesamtwerk*, Inaugural-Dissertation zur Erlangung des Grades eines Doktor der Philosophie in der Abteilung für Philologie der Ruhr-Universität, Bochum.

WEST, D. (1990) *The Aeneid: A New Prose Translation*, London and New York.

WEST, M. L. (1966) (ed.) *Hesiod, Theogony*, Oxford.

——(1983) *The Orphic Poems*, Oxford.

——(1988) *Hesiod, Theogony and Works and Days*, tr. with an Introduction and Notes, Oxford.

——(1992) *Ancient Greek Music*, Oxford.

WESTENDORP BOERMA, R. E. H. (1958) 'On dating the *Copa*', *Mnemosyne*, 11: 331–8.

WHITE, P. (1993) *Promised Verse. Poets in the Society of Augustan Rome*, Cambridge, Mass., and London.

WILAMOWITZ, U. (1881) *Antigonos von Karystos*, Berlin.

WILKINSON, L. P. (1965) '*Copa* Today', *Greece and Rome*, 12: 38–41.

WILLIAMS, C. (1999) *Roman Homosexuality*, New York and Oxford.

WILLIAMS, F. (1978) *Callimachus, Hymn to Apollo: A Commentary*, Oxford.

WILLIAMS, G. (1991) 'Vocal Variations and Narrative Complexity in Ovid's *Vestalia: Fasti* 6. 249–468', *Ramus*, 20: 183–204.

WILLIAMSON, M. (1995) *Sappho's Immortal Daughters*, Cambridge, Mass.

WILSON, P. (1999) 'The *aulos* in Athens', in Goldhill and Osborne (1999) 58–95.

WIMMEL, W. (1960) *Kallimachos in Rom. Die Nachfolge seines apologetischen*

Dichtens in der Augusteerzeit, Wiesbaden.

WINKLER, JACK (1996) 'Gardens of Nymphs: Public and Private in Sappho's Lyrics', in Greene (1996a) 89–109 (orig. pub. in slightly different form in H. P. Foley (ed.) *Reflections of Women in Antiquity*, New York, 1981: 63–90).

——and ZEITLIN, F. I. (1990) (eds.) *Nothing to Do with Dionysos? Athenian Drama in Its Social Context*, Princeton.

WISEMAN, T. P. (1985) *Catullus and his World: A Reappraisal*, Cambridge.

WISHART, D. (1995) *I, Virgil*, London.

WYKE, M. (1987a) 'The Elegiac Woman at Rome', *Proceedings of the Cambridge Philological Society*, NS 33: 153–78.

——(1987b) 'Written Women: Propertius' *scripta puella*', *Journal of Roman Studies*, 77: 47–61.

——(1989) 'Mistress and Metaphor in Augustan Elegy', *Helios*, 16: 25–47.

——(1995) 'Taking the Woman's Part: Engendering Roman Elegy', in A. J. Boyle (ed.) *Ramus Essays in Honour of J. P. Sullivan*, Bentleigh, Vic.: 110–28.

YARDLEY, J. C. (1976) 'Lovers' Quarrels: Horace Odes 1,13,11 and Propertius 4,5,40', *Hermes*, 104: 124–8.

YEATS, W. B. (1965) *Selected Poetry*, London.

ZANKER, G. (1981) '*Enargeia* in the Ancient Criticism of Poetry', *Rheinisches Museum*, 124: 297–311.

ZANKER, P. (1995) *The Mask of Socrates: The Image of the Intellectual in Antiquity*, tr. A. Shapiro, Berkeley and Los Angeles.

ZEITLIN, F. I. (1981) 'Travesties of Gender and Genre in Aristophanes' *Thesmophoriazusae*', in H. Foley (ed.) *Reflections of Women in Antiquity*, New York: 169–217.

——(1990) 'Playing the Other: Theater, Theatricality, and the Feminine in Greek Drama', in Winkler and Zeitlin (1990) 63–96.

ZIZEK, S. (1991) *Looking Awry: An Introduction to Jacques Lacan through Popular Culture*, Cambridge, Mass.

——(1993) *Tarrying with the Negative: Kant, Hegel, and the Critique of Ideology*, Durham, NC.

——(1994) *The Metastases of Enjoyment: Six Essays on Woman and Causality*, London.

ZUMWALT, N. K. (1975) 'Horace, *C.* 1. 22: Poetic and Political Integrity', *Transactions and Proceedings of the American Philological Association*, 105: 113–20.

ZUNTZ, G. (1963) 'Once More: The So-Called "Edict of Philopator on the Dionysiac Mysteries" (BGU 1211)', *Hermes*, 91: 228–39.

——(1971) *Persephone: Three Essays on Religion and Thought in Magna Graecia*, Oxford.

Index Locorum

General Index

The Spiritual Legacy
OF
JOHN FOSTER DULLES

The
Spiritual Legacy

OF

JOHN FOSTER

DULLES

SELECTIONS
FROM HIS ARTICLES AND ADDRESSES

❖❖❖❖

Edited with an Introduction by
HENRY P. VAN DUSEN

❖❖❖❖

Essay Index Reprint Series

 BOOKS FOR LIBRARIES PRESS
FREEPORT, NEW YORK

Library of Congress Cataloging in Publication Data

Dulles, John Foster, 1888-1959.
    The spiritual legacy of John Foster Dulles.

    (Essay index reprint series)
    1. Christianity and international affairs--
Addresses, essays, lectures. 2. United States--
Religion--Addresses, essays, lectures. I. Title.
[BR115.I7D8 1972]   261   72-3360
ISBN 0-8369-2899-7

PRINTED IN THE UNITED STATES OF AMERICA

Contents

The President's Tribute

JOHN FOSTER DULLES is dead. A lifetime of labor for world peace has ended. His countrymen and all who believe in justice and the rule of law grieve at the passing from the earthly scene of one of the truly great men of our time.

Throughout his life, and particularly during his eventful six years as Secretary of State, his courage, his wisdom, and his friendly understanding were devoted to bettering relations among nations. He was a foe only to tyranny.

Because he believed in the dignity of men and in their brotherhood under God, he was an ardent supporter of their deepest hopes and aspirations. From his life and work, humanity will, in the years to come, gain renewed inspiration to work ever harder for the attainment of the goal of peace with justice. In the pursuit of that goal, he ignored every personal cost and sacrifice, however great.

We who were privileged to work with him have lost a dear and close friend as all Americans have lost a champion of freedom.

DWIGHT D. EISENHOWER

Gettysburg, Pa.
May 24, 1959

Preface

WHEN THIS VOLUME was first projected, it was expected that ten or a dozen items might be discovered that would merit inclusion. However, an examination of John Foster Dulles' files disclosed more than fifty addresses and articles concerned primarily with the moral and spiritual foundations of world order, the significance of religion, and the role of the churches. From these, the present selection has been made.

In speaking or writing on the same or closely related themes on different occasions and to different audiences over a period of twenty years, it was inevitable that Mr. Dulles should make some reiteration of emphases and even repetition of certain phrases, sentences, and quotations. In some instances, these have been omitted from the later sources, as have sections of material dealing with then current but now past issues. But for the most part, the articles and addresses stand as originally prepared.

Thanks are gratefully acknowledged to Mrs. Dulles and to Mr. Allen Dulles for fullest collaboration and assistance in the preparation of the collection, and also to Mr. Dulles' former secretary at the State Department, Miss Phyllis Bernau. Miss Barbara Griffis, librarian of the William Adams Brown

Ecumenical Library in Union Theological Seminary, has rendered invaluable help in tracking down sources and gathering items for inclusion. I am also indebted to the several publishers for permission freely given to reprint copyrighted materials.

H.P.V.D.

Union Theological Seminary
New York
February 12, 1960

Man of Faith

THE DEATH of John Foster Dulles on May 24, 1959, was the occasion of an outpouring of acclaim without precedent in our day unless for royalty or a chief of state. Not only throughout the length and breadth of his own country but across the world, tributes of admiration, of gratitude, almost of reverence, welled up from persons in every rank and station of life and of every outlook and allegiance. Veteran Washington taxi drivers declared that they could not recall crowds in such density as the tens of thousands who lined the route of his funeral cortege from the Episcopal Cathedral on Mount Saint Albans to Arlington Cemetery. Heads of Governments and of political parties who had often been his sharpest critics and most unyielding opponents vied with close associates and lifelong friends in the warmth and sincerity of their eulogies. It was universally recognized that his nation and the community of nations had lost one of the most gifted, dedicated, and influential statesmen of this century. No less frequent was the recognition that from history had passed a man of most unusual character.

Time and again, the question has been asked, not in idle curiosity but in eager desire to understand the secret of his greatness: What manner of man was he? How are we to interpret, if not explain, this remarkable person?

From time to time, columnists and correspondents who had had the opportunity of being much associated with Mr. Dulles have spoken of the human being they had discovered: a combination of qualities so contrasted as to seem almost contradictory—formidable yet touchingly gentle, aloof yet engagingly friendly, stern yet delightfully playful, solemn and yet heartily savoring authentic wit and humor.

His gifts of intellect were evident to all. As an undergraduate of Princeton University, they had placed him at the head of the graduating class. In middle life, they had brought him to pre-eminence in his chosen profession of the law. As Secretary of State, they won the respect of statesmen on both sides of every issue. No less obvious was an iron discipline of mind and habit and unyielding fixity of purpose. But behind both intellect and will was a profounder center and source of strength.

No one who had the privilege of Mr. Dulles' intimate confidence could for one moment be in doubt as to the key to the person who harbored such contrasting qualities, as to the deeper springs of his character, or as to the secret of its strength and its endurance. "Man of faith," he has often been called. But "faith" is a weather-worn word of a hundred variant meanings, and for many, rather hackneyed and uncongenial associations.

"Man of Christian faith"—there is the bedrock without which everything else that might be said about him is incomplete, indeed inexplicable.

It was formed—that character—in a Presbyterian manse in Watertown, New York, in attendance four times each Sunday at church worship and Sabbath school, and around the family piano through the singing of hymns that, as many would testify, can form the substratum of personality almost as decisively as overt instruction or formal worship. The imprint of those early associations was deeply implanted upon his convictions and his character, as he himself repeatedly bore witness in later years. It was no accident that, in his last days when suffering sharpened and the inescapable end threatened, he longed to hear again the hymns that had nourished his spirit in youth and across the years—not sentimental modern hymns but the grand old affirmations of faith: "The Spacious Firmament on High"; "When Morning Gilds the Skies"; "God of Our Life, Through All the Circling Years"; "Work, for the Night Is Coming"; All Praise to Thee, My God, This Night"; and especially the hymn beginning, "Through the night of doubt and sorrow onward goes the pilgrim band," for this last was, not only by expressed preference but also by inherent sympathy, John Foster Dulles' favorite hymn. And so a recording of these hymns was made and, night by night, the waning spirit was rekindled by the great hymns of Christian faith.

A dozen years ago, returning from a conference of the Churches' Commission to Study the Bases of a Just and Durable Peace over which Mr. Dulles had presided and to which he had lured some of his skeptical colleagues from the world of affairs, one of these close friends turned to him and chided playfully: "Foster, your mother must have been terribly disappointed when you didn't become a minister." The stern jaw stiffened, and that familiar granite voice blurted sharply, almost rudely: "Nearly broke her heart."

As a matter of fact, his mother rejoiced in his achievements as lawyer and statesman. In any event, the maternal hope was not defeated. He who might have been a powerful preacher of the Christian gospel became a pre-eminent pioneer in a Christian vocation, rarer and perhaps far more needful than professional clergy—the lay ministry, fulfilling one of the central and greatly neglected ideals of the Calvinist tradition in which Mr. Dulles had been reared: "Every profession, a sacred calling; every Christian, a minister of Christ."

Plato defined the ideal state—when "statesmen should be philosophers" and "philosophers, statesmen." Christianity envisions a loftier and more demanding conception of public leadership: the minister of state—a minister of Christ in his sacred calling. It is difficult to name anyone in our day who has more fully discharged that high vocation.

How firmly the truths of Christian faith had established themselves within Mr. Dulles' securest certainties was disclosed by the words to which he habitually had recourse, especially in moments of special intensity, in speech of climactic importance.

A study of John Foster Dulles' vocabulary, particularly at those times when he was speaking from central conviction and to the crucial point, discovers a single phrase occurring over and over again like a reiterated refrain: "a *righteous* and *dynamic faith*." Each of the three words was carefully chosen; each is essential to the whole.

"*Righteous*." A passion for justice, for righteousness impregnating the affairs of men, the affairs of state. "Too much these days," he declared, "we forget that men's ability to control the physical depends upon the moral. Nothing that statesmen can contrive will work if it does not reflect the moral conscience of the time. Whenever that limitation is ignored, failure ensues." Moralism, he was sometimes ac-

cused of; so far as I know, he never denied the charge. To
have done so would have been to repudiate a basic certitude:
the moral order, a divine order, the will of God—by which
the decisions of statesmen must ultimately be judged, into
conformity with which the relations of peoples, as of persons,
must finally be brought.

"Dynamic." Another of his great, recurring words, demanding a "dynamic peace," in the conviction of the living,
moving, ever-changing character of the divine order for
human life with its openness to change, its hopefulness toward a better ordering of society. Dynamic—the very temper
of the pilgrim.

"Faith." "Righteous" and "dynamic"—these are the adjectives. But "faith" is the noun, which the adjectives identify
and which alone can translate them into reality. To this we
shall return.

The springs of character are revealed, not only in the words
to which men habitually have recourse, but—far more—in
their spontaneous *actions,* sometimes trivial as the world
measures importance.

One such incident, doubtless representative of many, may
now be disclosed. A very minor official in our foreign service
was threatened with dishonorable dismissal and disgrace on
charges of subversion, one of many victims of the witch
hunt directed by Senator McCarthy and his lieutenants. The
man laid his case before a friend of Mr. Dulles', who became
convinced of his innocence and brought the matter to Mr.
Dulles' attention.

The young man had already been condemned, deprived of
appointment and salary, and his appeal had been denied by
a loyalty board and the Undersecretary. Only direct interven-

tion by the Secretary of State could save him. At the time, Mr. Dulles was in the midst of pressing affairs—journeying to Europe, to Asia, to South America. But he personally reviewed the voluminous record, overrode the loyalty board and his Undersecretary, ordered exoneration and honorable restitution leading to appointment to a much more responsible post. Reporting his decision to the friend who had ventured to trouble him with so small a matter, he wrote:

"The final papers in D——'s case have now come before me. I know that you will be pleased to learn that on the basis of convincing evidence I have given him a full and complete clearance.

"Thank you again for writing me about this matter."

The career of a minor subordinate was salvaged, his honor vindicated. This was the concrete action of a man of faith— "righteous and dynamic faith."

From his own clear view of the practical and active faith demanded of Christians sprang his impatience with the churches that caused him to hold somewhat aloof from them in middle life. He was alienated by what he considered their disregard of, and disloyalty to, the mind of Christ. In 1937 he wrote:

"I am a layman, of Christian upbringing. Despite the fact that my beliefs are somewhat diluted, I have always assumed, as a matter of course, that it was the Christian churches which could be looked to, to lift mankind from those morasses of which the underlying cause is usually moral decay. But recently, I had begun to doubt. The churches had lost those qualities which in the past had made them formidable. . . . The church, it seemed, had become 'soft.' . . . Church membership had ceased to be synonymous with dangerous and difficult living for a high ideal. . . . The church as institutionalized by man . . . had too much devoted itself to vain repetitions and too little to doing the Father's will."

However, when World War II lowered and then broke, and Mr. Dulles' abilities and energies were given almost wholly to the furtherance of a "just and durable peace," he found himself drawn into a new appreciation of the churches as effective allies through their generation of a righteous and dynamic faith. He declared:

"The churches are peculiarly qualified to promote a solution of the kind of problems which today vex mankind. . . . The Christian churches are powerful for good in so far as they propagate spiritual truth. . . . They are unique in their combined qualifications. . . . Only through an approach of such universality is there any promise of a solution."

It was in this conviction that he consented, somewhat reluctantly, to serve on the Board of Directors of Union Theological Seminary, and did so from 1945 until he left for Washington in 1953. His only query was, "What do you want me to do?" For he disdained nominal memberships; he was impatient with perfunctory meetings or inactive service. He felt that time was too precious, the issues of our day too urgent, to permit anything less than vigorous and sustained effort in behalf of whatever responsibility one accepted.

It was as a convinced and active churchman, more particularly as Chairman of the Commission to Study the Bases of a Just and Durable Peace, that Mr. Dulles was led to re-examine and rethink his own convictions on the nature and content of Christian faith, especially in their bearing upon the issues of peace and world order, which were his central concern. It was in that context that he formulated and gave expression to the great bulk of writings and utterances that constitute the substance of this collection, whether they were addressed to church groups or to a great variety of secular audiences—the readers of *Life* magazine, the Missouri Bar Association, the graduates of the War College, many national radio audiences.

It is not difficult to identify the structure of Christian conviction that determined his own attitude toward public affairs, which though Christian in origin he felt to be of universal authority, which he believed to be of the essence of the American tradition, and which he sought to have laid as the foundation principles of world order. Those convictions ring, like a determinative motif, through all his speeches and writings:

1. *The reality and regnancy of moral law, of moral principle and moral structure undergirding and ultimately conforming the affairs of nations, the relations of peoples no less than of persons.* "The moral law, happily, is a universal law. It is reflected by many great religions. . . . That fact is of immense value. It is why, even today, moral concepts can have world-wide influence."

2. *The divine endowment of human beings as children of God, made in his image and endowed by him with certain inalienable rights.* "Since those rights are given by God, no men,

however powerful or however numerous, can rightfully take them away from other men, even though those others be only weak or few."

3. *The authority and practicability of the teachings of Jesus.* He spoke often of the ethical precepts of Jesus. He regarded them, not as counsels of perfection with authority solely upon religious devotees or as specifications for some transworldly Kingdom, but as guiding principles for daily life and practice here and now, not only of individuals, but also of communities and the world community. He believed that Christ gives and expects, in particular, four indispensable qualities: vision, compassion, clarity of mind, action.

"Christ wanted men to see, to see far and to see truly. To get that kind of vision, he pointed out, requires avoidance of hypocrisies and group prejudices, which distort the vision and make men imagine they see what is not really there.

"Christ wanted men to have hearts that comprehend the human significance of what is seen. That kind of heart requires, he pointed out, avoidance of material self-seeking, which makes men hard and indifferent to all that cannot serve their selfish ends.

"Christ wanted men to reason clearly and serenely. That requires, he pointed out, avoidance of evil emotions, such as hatred and vengefulness, which enflame men's minds and distract them from the real problems that confront them.

"Christ wanted men to act."

4. *The obligation to action.* "Finally, we must act. Christ did not teach a purely contemplative religion. 'Go' and 'do' were his constant injunction. 'Let your light so shine before men that they may see your good works.' "

5. *The necessity of faith.* One cannot fail to be struck by the fact that, taken together, these five convictions embody the very heart of the Judaeo-Christian faith, from the teaching regarding man's creation in Genesis, through the insistence upon the divine ordering of society in the great prophets, and the pivotal authority of the mind of Christ and his reiterated emphasis upon deeds no less than belief, to the climactic stress upon faith in Paul and the author of The Letter to the Hebrews, although there is no evidence that Mr. Dulles himself was aware of the comprehensiveness of his interpretation of Christian certitude.

The final emphasis falls on *faith,* and returns us to the note with which we began.

However, we have said, "faith" is a weather-worn word with countless meanings, and for many, vague and somewhat hackneyed associations. One always recalls the lad who replied to his Sunday school questionnaire, What is faith? with "Faith is believing what you know ain't true!" Despite its manifold uses, in Christian understanding faith always carries a twofold connotation: It speaks of convictions believed to be true but never fully proved true—"certainty of things not seen." But, in another and less recognized sense, faith denotes *action;* it is life devotion to ends, to ideals that are held to be sound and realizable but are never wholly realized—"assurance of things hoped for." So, in the classic exposition of Christian faith in the eleventh chapter of The Letter to the Hebrews, to which Mr. Dulles himself reverted over and over again—the catalog of the figures of faith, the chronicle of the pilgrims of faith—the emphasis throughout is upon action: "Abraham, when he was called, went, not knowing whither." . . . "Noah built." . . . Others "conquered kingdoms, enforced justice,

won strength out of weakness." Yes, and "these all died in
faith, not having received the promises, but having seen them
afar off."

If it be asked, How is such faith with its practical fruit in
action born and nurtured and sustained within the human
spirit?, this is the answer: It has its basis in that other side of
faith which we more familiarly associate with the word. Faith
is devotion to ends believed to be achievable but never fully
achieved. Such life devotion is possible because faith is also
and more fundamentally trust in certainties felt to be true but
never wholly proved true: certainty that truth alone permanently prevails, that right does ultimately triumph, certainty
of God.

If one were to associate a single Biblical passage with
Mr. Dulles' life, there could be little hesitancy in its choice—
Heb., ch. 11, his own most-quoted chapter of Scripture. And,
from the literature of Christianity down through the centuries
might be chosen those words in *The Pilgrim's Progress* describing the journey of Valiant-for-truth which were so appropriately spoken at his funeral.

In that catalog of the pioneers of faith, John Foster Dulles
takes his rightful place; in that chronicle his struggles for a
better world, for a just and lasting peace, are to be entered:
man of faith, man of Christian faith—a righteous and dynamic faith.

So it was altogether in character that toward the last his
spirit should turn to "Through the Night of Doubt and
Sorrow" and that as his mortal body was borne up the slopes
of Arlington Cemetery to its last resting place the strains that
greeted his funeral cortege should have been those of the triumphant words of his best-loved hymn:

"Through the night of doubt and sorrow
 Onward goes the pilgrim band,
Singing songs of expectation,
 Marching to the promised land.
One the object of our journey,
 One the faith which never tires,
One the earnest looking forward,
 One the hope our God inspires."

I

The Faith of a Statesman

At the time of John Foster Dulles' birth on February 25, 1888, his family were making their home in Watertown, New York, where his father, Rev. Allen Macy Dulles, had been called the previous year to the pastorate of the First Presbyterian Church. There they lived until 1904, the year in which Foster left home to enter Princeton University and Dr. Dulles became Professor of Theism and Apologetics in Auburn Theological Seminary, Auburn, New York. It was in Watertown and its environs, near the southern shore of Lake Ontario, in the church of which his father was minister and the home over which he presided, that the years of infancy, boyhood, and youth were spent. It was during those years that the physique, the mental outlook, and the spirit were molded by forces of whose formative influence upon him Foster was deeply conscious. It was on a small island off the southern shore of Lake Ontario not far from Watertown that he and his wife built the roughhewn camp where they sought retreat from the pressures of public life and found physical and spiritual reinvigoration.

Twice during the last decade of his life, Foster Dulles returned to the church of his childhood to speak from the pulpit where his father had preached throughout his boyhood. The first of these addresses is perhaps the most frankly autobiographical and revealing self-disclosure that he ever uttered. In it are summarized many of the convictions that infused all he said and did. The second address in the Watertown church, one of his last public statements on religion and morals, concludes this volume.

Mr. Dulles referred frequently to the Conference on "Church, Community, and State" at Oxford in July, 1937, which he attended as one of the American delegates. It was there that he first became convinced of the potential influence of the churches as effective forces for the advance of peace and peaceful change—a reversal of his previous attitude that may, not unfairly, be described as a "conversion," an about-face. The second paper in this section is an interpretation of that conference; the third reiterates its profound effect upon him.

It was in his negotiation of the peace treaty with Japan in 1951 that Mr. Dulles felt that he had the most significant opportunity actually to test in practice the moral principles for international order to which he was committed. This attempt is set forth in personal terms in the fourth selection.

John Foster Dulles was born in the home in Washington, D.C., of the grandfather whose name he was to bear, John W. Foster, Secretary of State in the Benjamin Harrison administration. In June, 1955, he was invited to give the baccalaureate address and receive an honorary degree from Indiana University on the one hundredth anniversary of his grandfather's graduation and the fiftieth anniversary of his honorary degree from his Alma Mater. This was the occasion for another declaration of Foster Dulles' personal faith, this time with special emphasis upon the American tradition. It supplies an appropriate transition to the next section of selections on "The American Heritage."

1

Faith of Our Fathers

To you who listen, this is just another Sunday. To me, it is an eventful day. This is the pulpit from which my father preached for many years, and from which he radiated an influence that is still felt here and elsewhere. Before me is the pew where I sat as a boy, little dreaming that this day would come when I would be speaking from his pulpit.

Those were times when Sunday was really set apart as God's day. There were then three church services — morning, afternoon, and evening — and Sunday school besides. The minister's family regularly attended all four services. Also, on each Sunday, we memorized about ten verses from The Psalms or the New Testament and in addition two verses of a hymn. Sunday then was a holy day, but hardly one of rest.

I cannot say that my mind never wandered during the church services. During the morning service there was the distracting prospect of licking the dasher with which I was to freeze the Sunday dinner ice cream. And during the afternoon service my thoughts returned to the woods and fields which I had roamed while bird-watching the Saturday before. But by the time I left Watertown in my seventeenth

Address at the First Presbyterian Church, Watertown, New York, Sunday, August 28, 1949.

year I had accumulated a considerable knowledge of the Bible and of Christian writings.

During the same time, I had developed a great interest in international affairs. That came from my grandfather, John W. Foster, who used to spend his summers in these parts and with whom I used to fish regularly at Henderson Harbor. As we sat together in a fishing skiff he would tell me of his diplomatic experiences in Mexico, Russia, Spain, and China. Also, he told of his experiences as a soldier in the Civil War — experiences that made him hate war and devote himself to the cause of peace. It became my ambition to go forward in that way.

I started as law clerk in an international law firm and came to work on many international problems and to attend many international conferences. During that period it did not seem to me that what I had learned here in church had much to do with the practical problems of war and peace. That was indeed my state of mind for thirty years, from 1907 when I attended with my grandfather the Second Hague Peace Conference, until 1937. In that year I presided at an international conference held at Paris under the auspices of the League of Nations, and then went on to attend the Oxford Conference on Church and State. That was a great Christian conference, with representatives of almost all the nations and all the races of the world. We discussed there the same critical problems that diplomats were discussing futilely at the League of Nations. But at Oxford we approached those problems with the guidance of a common standard — the moral law as revealed by Jesus Christ; and we dealt with each other as brothers, irrespective of national or racial differences. Under those conditions we could see how to solve problems that could not be solved in the distrustful atmosphere of national competition.

Then I began to understand the profound significance of the spiritual values that my father and mother had taught, and by which they had lived, here at Watertown. From then on I began to work closely with religious groups — Protestant, Catholic, and Jewish — for I had come to believe that, of all groups, they could make the greatest contribution to world order. Most of all I worked with the Commission on a Just and Durable Peace of the Federal Council of the Churches of Christ in America. During these same years I helped organize the United Nations and attended its meetings and those of the Council of Foreign Ministers. Serving at the same time in both religious and political groups made ever clearer the relationship between the two. I saw that there could be no just and durable peace except as men held in common certain simple and elementary religious beliefs: belief that there is a God, that he is the author of a moral law which they can know, and that he imparts to each human being a spiritual dignity and worth which all others should respect. Wherever these elementary truths are widely rejected, there is both spiritual and social disorder.

That fact is illustrated by fascism and communism. These are, in the main, atheistic and antireligious creeds. Orthodox Communists believe that there is neither God nor moral law, that there is no such thing as universal and equal justice, and that human beings are without soul or sacred personality. They are free of the moral restraints and compulsions which prevail in a religious society, and they think it quite right to use force and violence to make their way prevail.

In Russia, Communists have designed a form of society which they call "the dictatorship of the proletariat." They believe that their mission is to press all mankind into that precise mold and to do so by any and all means available.

Communists are, of course, entitled to have their own belief as to what is best for men, and they are entitled to try peacefully to bring their ideals into reality. That is the privilege of every human being. But since there is a God, since there is a moral law, since human personality is sacred, no human rulers can rightly use ruthless and violent methods and pitilessly crush all within their power who do not conform to their particular dictation.

At the first session of the United Nations Assembly at London, Mr. Vishinsky spoke about refugees — poor, wretched creatures who had fled Russia to escape liquidation. In words that were powered with deep hatred, and that struck like bullets from a machine gun, Mr. Vishinsky proclaimed the resolve of the Soviet Government to scour the face of the earth to find these refugees, to seize them and bring them back.

It was a cruel and frightening speech. It typified the fanaticism of Soviet Communism and its total denial of tolerance toward any who disagreed. Terrorism, which breaks men's spirits, is, to Communists, a normal way to make their creed prevail, and to them it seems legitimate because they do not think of human beings as being brothers through the Fatherhood of God.

If communism and fascism are hateful because of the consequences of their godlessness, it is equally true that they can be successfully resisted only by societies imbued with strong spiritual convictions. In Washington these days Congress is working on great plans to halt Communism by giving economic and military aid to those who, we hope, will resist. It is, however, perfectly clear that these plans will not succeed if they merely put material things into the hands of men who do not have a spiritual faith and who do not feel a sense of human brotherhood and of social responsibility. . . .

◇◇◇◇

[Here Mr. Dulles dealt in some detail with specific issues that at that time were to the fore.]

◇◇◇◇

Napoleon said that in time of war the moral is to the material as three is to one. I suppose that, in waging peace, the ratio is at least as high. We are apt to forget that and to think that the struggle in which we are now engaged can be won by material things alone. That is totally wrong. Wherever one looks around the world, one sees disorder that can be cured only by drawing on sources of moral power.

The Western democracies have had great prestige and authority in the world. That is because their practices developed under the dominating influence of religious beliefs. Their laws came, more and more, to protect the individual and to provide more equal justice. They found ways for bringing about social improvements peacefully, without class wars or the crushing of the weaker by the stronger. They encouraged men to develop their individual talents and to experiment along diverse and competitive lines of their own choosing. Under those stimulating conditions there developed material, intellectual, and spiritual richness; and to some degree at least that richness was shared with other peoples of the world. For one thousand years Western civilization grew in power and influence and was not seriously challenged. There was such a challenge by Islam one thousand years ago, and now we have the challenge of Soviet Communism. Whether or not we peacefully surmount the present challenge depends on basic things and most of all on whether our people love the Lord their God and their neighbors, and act accordingly.

The hope of America and the hope of the world does not lie

in our economic and military might. We have a duty to be materially strong and to share that strength with others who are in peril. But that is only a defensive, holding operation. The role of material power, as Admiral Mahan said, is to give moral ideals the opportunity to take root. Our basic strength is our capacity to propagate these moral ideals which must prevail if there is to be peace and justice in the world.

I am not, of course, suggesting that men and women should become Christians because that is the way for them to get peace. Such an argument would reverse the proper order of values. What I do say is that those who are Christians should see more clearly the possibilities that reside in the life and work of the churches.

There are millions in the world who want to do something for peace. They know the indescribable horror that another war would be, and they are eager to dedicate themselves to the preservation, in peace, of the freedoms that are our heritage. They are quite willing to give time and money to attain those ends. Many of them feel frustrated because they cannot find a channel through which to work. I suppose that, in sum total, thousands have asked me personally to suggest what they might do to help the cause of peace. Many in their worthy zeal become faddists, joining organizations that would stop war by paper slogans. After the First World War many of our finest people sought to end war by working for a treaty that would, as they put it, "outlaw war." They got what they asked for in the form of the Kellogg-Briand Pact, but it did not stop World War II by a single day. Many today are engaged in similar futilities. It is tragic that so much good intention goes for naught.

Men and women who have spiritual faith and who want also to do something practical to preserve peace and to meet the challenge of communism have, in their local church, the most effective medium that exists. It is the churches that dependably keep alive and pass on, from generation to generation, belief in God, in moral law, and in the spiritual nature of man. It is the churches that provide recruitment for the ministry. It is the churches that have missionary affiliations that spread great spiritual truths throughout the world. They have central agencies . . . that provide studies of world problems by qualified Christian statesmen. These, if used, can create an enlightened public opinion that will directly influence the acts of government and of the United Nations. That has been proved. Yet, today, such studies barely trickle into local congregations.

Many who are zealous for peace seem to feel that all this is remote from reality. They want a more direct and obvious role.

That mood will never bring lasting peace. Peace is won, as victory is won, by cumulative efforts, no one of which alone is decisive. In time of war men and women labor in munition plants and feel that they are contributing to victory; and so they are, although no single effort appreciably affects the outcome. But the outcome would be defeat if no one worked unless he was confident that the bullet he made would kill an enemy general.

The struggle for peace will never be won without the cumulative efforts of millions of individuals working in ways that develop moral power and organize it as mobile force. If believers would direct their zeal for peace more into church and missionary channels, the prospect of war would steadily recede.

Today our nation is relying greatly on material and military might. That is dangerous. A nation that possesses a great military establishment is apt to be influenced by the counsel

of persons who believe in the inevitability of war or who believe that good ends can be gained by violent means. Our present course skirts, dangerously, the road to war. Our leaders
take that risk because they feel that there is no adequate alternative. Policy makers work with the tools that, it seems, can
be made available. Economic and military power can be developed under the spur of laws and appropriations. But moral
power does not derive from any act of Congress. It depends
on the relations of a people to their God. It is the churches to
which we must look to develop the resources for the great
moral offensive that is required to make human rights secure
and to win a just and lasting peace.

Nearly two thousand years ago Christ said, "The truth shall
make you free." Every one of the intervening years sustains
that utterance. We meet here beneath a spire that points upward. That is symbolic. It points to the power above us from
which we derive our spiritual strength, and it marks this
building as the place where men can gather and draw that
strength which alone enables those on earth to have the power
to be free.

2

As Seen by a Layman

Large conferences are usually to be avoided. Intellectual advancement is apt to be in inverse ratio to the number of those participating therein. And while the massing of human beings facilitates the generation of emotion, that is a quality with which we are today surfeited. Nevertheless, I attended the Oxford Conference because it seemed to me that I might there find the answer to certain questions which perplexed me.

I am a layman, of Christian upbringing. Despite the fact that my beliefs are somewhat diluted, I have always assumed, as a matter of course, that it was the Christian churches which could be looked to, to lift mankind from those morasses of which the underlying cause is usually moral decay. But recently I had begun to doubt.

At few times in history have human needs been so great as during recent years. The world war had destroyed material and spiritual values to a degree which has only gradually been appreciated. Every country faced a long period of readjustment which tried the souls of men. It was obvious

An interpretation of the Oxford Conference on "Church, Community, and State," July 12–26, 1937. *Religion in Life,* Winter, 1938. Copyright, 1937, by Abingdon Press.

that the situation called for some constructive and directive force, based upon recognition of a common need rather than merely that of self or community or even nation. Instead of this, in international affairs those nations which were dominant sought to perpetuate for themselves a monopoly of the advantages which they had derived from the successful prosecution of power politics. Those nations which felt themselves wrongfully disadvantaged sought to redress the balance at the expense of others still weaker. Within the state, class warfare was waged in the effort of some to obtain, and of others, to retain, such relatively small amounts of accumulated wealth as existed in transferable form. All of this occurred in states which were nominally Christian and where public opinion was dominated, and public leadership exercised, by those who were members of Christian churches.

Deep troubles usually produce a new order of thinking. Thus, in certain areas there emerged new political and spiritual conceptions. The "state" was personified, even deified, as the sole source of human salvation. To the state's chosen objectives all else was to be subordinated, including the privilege of individual judgment and action. The state not only claimed complete allegiance but demanded of its followers those Spartan qualities necessary to make them most useful in the state's scheme of things.

These new creeds promptly came into conflict with the church. In retrospect we can see that this was inevitable. Nevertheless, at the time the conflict took us rather by surprise. We could look back over a record of centuries throughout which the church had successfully maintained its right to teach allegiance to Christ as superior to any secular loyalty. At many times the struggle had been bitter and had entailed heavy sacrifice. But the church had historically shown such vitality in defense of this principle that it came to be assumed that politicians would never again find it expedient to challenge the church upon this issue.

However, as is usually the case, it is when we feel most secure that the greatest danger is present. It had doubtless become apparent to any astute observer that the churches had lost those qualities which in the past had made them formidable. No religion can survive which does not demand and receive sacrifice from its adherents. Sacrifice is not only the measure of loyalty but itself induces loyalty. We believe intensely only in those causes to which we have contributed of ourselves. But the churches, it seemed, had become "soft." It had become conventional and even socially and materially advantageous to become an enrolled Christian. No risk and no sacrifice were involved. Church membership had ceased to be synonymous with dangerous and difficult living for a high ideal. This inspiring concept had been dropped by the wayside for others to take up and incorporate in their own authoritarian programs. Christianity was thus fought with weapons abandoned by it from its own armory. In the resultant struggle, the churches in many countries were pushed aside with surprising ease.

In the face of such occurrences it is not, I think, surprising that many should have lost confidence in the church as institutionalized by man. Its weakness and ineffectiveness seemed to prove that it had too much devoted itself to vain repetitions and too little to doing the Father's will. . . .

◇◇◇◇

It was under such circumstances that the Oxford Conference was held. It was attended by delegates from practically all of the Christian churches except the Roman Catholic Church, but including the Greek Orthodox Church. The delegates, numbering some four hundred, were drawn from virtually every land and race and represented all shades of political opinion.

It is not my purpose here to summarize or to review the reports themselves. To some extent, as was inevitable, the reports are platitudinous; to some extent there were concessions to expediency in that words were chosen with a view to covering up differences which developed. To a considerable extent the reports devote themselves to condemning admitted evils. In this respect they are without particular value. It is easy to wax eloquent in denunciation of war and social injustice. But the danger of pursuing this course is that too often those who denounce feel that they have thereby fully discharged their duty.

But if the reports show evidence of human frailties, they are nonetheless documents of profound significance. Each of them contains an analysis, which is both intelligent and realistic, of great problems which today face the world. Each suggests, in relation thereto, a concrete and constructive approach which, if sincerely adopted by Christians, would go far to make possible a solution.

I illustrate by reference to the report of the Fifth Section dealing with international relations. The report goes deeper than a facile denunciation of war and eulogy of peace. It develops the fact that where, within a country, domestic tranquillity is on a firm basis, this is only because of the existence of a superior force — government — which is able and disposed, by new legislation, to adapt from time to time the social structure to changing social needs. In the world of nations no superior political agency exists. This means that change, which is always inevitable, can occur only through force or the voluntary action of the nations. "It therefore particularly devolves upon Christians to devote themselves to securing by voluntary action of their nations such changes in the international order as are from time to time required to avoid injustice and to permit equality of opportunity for individuals throughout the world. . . . The unequal distribution of natural advantages is one of the causes of war, if control is used to create a monopoly of national advantage. Christian people should move their governments to abstain from such policies and to provide a reasonable equality of economic opportunity."

"Christian influence," it is noted, "cannot be made effective without adequate factual knowledge. To meet this initial need, Christians should take measures to obtain information on world conditions more adequate and reliable than that now furnished by secular and nationalistic agencies, which are too prone to ignore or belittle the needs of alien people, or to express those needs in terms of sacrifice to be made by nations other than their own. Once the need of change is apprehended, its accomplishment depends upon governmental action. This will require of statesmen and politicians a broader vision than now exists of the true welfare of their nation. The heads of states, under whatever form of government, are ultimately dependent upon the support of their people, who must make it clear that they are prepared to accept temporary sacrifices in order that a greater good may ultimately emerge.". . .

◇◇◇◇

From the nature of the reports and the unanimity with which they were adopted, I draw certain conclusions:

1. Christianity as exemplified by the church leadership represented at Oxford is still vital. The reports deal realistically and deeply with highly controversial problems. They were drafted by men differing in nationality, race, culture,

creed, social position, and political affiliation. It would have been utterly impossible to secure agreement had there not been some controlling common denominator. That common denominator was found to be present. It was a genuine belief in Christ's life and teachings as the guide to human conduct.

I can emphasize this point by reference to another conference. Immediately preceding the Oxford Conference, I had attended at Paris the biennial meeting of the International Studies Conference. The topic of study was "Peaceful Change," the same topic as that dealt with by that portion of the Oxford report from which I quoted above. The Paris Conference was made up of students and men experienced in public affairs drawn from substantially the same nations as were represented at Oxford and selected to represent the best contribution which each country could make to an unofficial, dispassionate, and scholarly study of the chosen problem. No attempt was made to arrive at any agreed report. It was, however, apparent from the discussions which took place that it would have been impossible to agree either as to the nature and scope of the problem itself or the proper approach to its solution. Certainly not more than a small fraction of the delegates would have been willing to subscribe to such a statement as that which emanated from Oxford.

Each of the differing national viewpoints represented at Paris was also represented at Oxford. Only a powerful influence could have obliterated those differences. That this obliteration occurred at Oxford is clear evidence that the Christianity of those present was more than a name—it was a vital force.

2. A second conclusion which I draw from Oxford is that the churches are peculiarly qualified to promote a solution of the kind of problems which today vex mankind. These problems are not, like mathematical problems, susceptible of

an abstract, static solution. They require a dynamic solution, involving transition from one condition of affairs to another. If there be agreement upon the ultimate goal, then the way of solution becomes revealed. In this regard the churches have a great opportunity. They represent an important cross section of all mankind which, in theory at least, has a single, permanent and all-embracing objective: that human affairs be so ordered that "Thy will be done, on earth as it is in heaven."

The ineffectiveness of political agencies derives largely from the concept of "corporate responsibility." For example, directors of companies cannot, as a matter of existing law, indulge in generosities or largesses except as they believe that the stockholders whom they represent will gain a material advantage therefrom in the form of enhanced company profits.

Whatever the proper view may be as to so-called "corporate responsibility," and as to this the Oxford Conference made no pronouncement, the fact is that this concept is deeply rooted. This is serious when problems are so vast as not to be solvable by those who feel that they owe a duty of allegiance to certain groups alone. But in the eyes of God, all men are equal and their welfare is of equal moment. This is distinctively the Christian approach, and it is only through an approach of such universality that there is any promise of a solution. This, I think, was made apparent by the Oxford reports. It was not that the Oxford Conference discovered any new and clever formulas for the quick solution of stubborn problems. But it went far in showing that problems which otherwise seem unsolvable become susceptible of solution if approached from the standpoint of the universal brotherhood of man.

I do not mean to suggest that organized Christianity is the only instrument through which our problems may be solved, or, as a corollary, that it is futile to seek to eliminate wars and social unrest and injustice until the whole world has first become Christianized. There was no disposition at Oxford to contend for such a proposition, or to deny the contribution which other religions and philosophies and social agencies can make toward a solution of our human problems. The Christian churches are powerful for good in so far as they propagate spiritual truths. It is the truths which are important, not the name, and those truths often appear under alien guise. As such they should be recognized and welcomed and co-operated with. But the Christian churches are unique in their combined qualifications. Not only are they founded upon a concept of universality, but they have in fact attained this to a degree permitting them to approach every problem with understanding of the diverse underlying national and social conditions.

3. If the Oxford Conference showed the unique potentialities of the Christian churches, it also exemplified the restraints necessary to prevent the churches becoming enmeshed in partisan politics. The Conference did not claim for its reports the imprimatur of divine, or even ecclesiastical, authority. The reports themselves were, in the main, limited to analyzing problems to a point which made evident the spiritual failures which caused them. There was no advocacy of particular political solutions. This was sound, for specific measures will almost always involve matters of close judgment and of expediency and will seldom be such an embodiment of Christ's teaching that the church can permit the two to be equated. Christ, for example, told a certain rich young man to give all he had to the poor. But this gives us no clue to how far the state should go in taxing those who have for the benefit of those who have not. Normally, the state should not attempt

this to such a degree as to impair the functioning of the economic mechanism and thereby increase the net amount of need. But at this point we are involved in economics, not religion, and, as said in the Oxford Conference report on the Church and the Economic Order, "every tendency to identify the Kingdom of God with a particular structure of society or economic mechanism must result in moral confusion for those who maintain the system and a disillusionment for those who suffer from its limitations." This, however, does not mean that the church and state live in separate compartments. There must be communication. Normally this will be through the churches' so impressing spiritually upon the individual that his secular life will be affected thereby. It is notably in this respect that the churches have failed, and their first task is to make good this failure. Secondarily, and under special circumstance, the churches can accelerate and orient the reaction of the spiritual upon the secular by analyzing human problems so that the individual can more readily apply a spiritual test to political measures. But this must be attempted with caution. The Oxford Conference was so constituted as to make such an attempt permissible. There was present a wealth of knowledge and experience drawn from every nation, race, and social order. This was made available and utilized in a spirit of profound consecration. Such a combination of secular knowledge and spiritual consecration is indispensable if the churches are to attempt even an analysis of political and economic problems. Too often spiritual and secular motives become unconsciously mixed, and it requires unusual practical experience to detect the pitfalls which the worldly constantly prepare to secure for themselves the appearance of church benediction.

4. I have already referred to the extent to which the differences represented at the Conference were submerged by a

vital common denominator. This occurrence was indicative not merely of vitality, but it also demonstrated an amazing unity of thought and interpretation on the part of the different Christian denominations. There persisted, of course, the well-recognized differences of approach and emphasis which flowed from different ecclesiastical views and different conceptions of worship. No attempt was made to deal with or to eradicate such differences. Indeed, I think the generally prevalent view was that such differences were healthy and useful to preserve. Men worship God in different ways and interpret revelation in terms that vary according to education, race, and culture. But there emerged a unity in defense against pagan beliefs and a unity in offense against the problems which, if left unsolved, will inevitably destroy the Christian churches and prove that their name is a misnomer. . . .

◇◇◇◇

I had prepared for the Oxford Conference a paper entitled "The Problem of Peace in a Dynamic World." In concluding that paper I said that the major obstacles were created by pride and selfishness and that these could be got rid of "only by replacing them by some sentiment more dominant and gripping and which would contain in it the elements of universality as against particularity." I asked: "What of the democratic nations? What of the so-called Christian nations? They boast of high ideals, but have they the spiritual fire with which to drive out the petty instincts which bind them to a system which spells their doom?"

Since having attended the Oxford Conference, I think it possible that this question can be answered in the affirmative. It requires, however, that the spirit of Oxford should not die down but be projected through the membership — particularly the lay membership — of all our churches.

3

The Churches and World Order

You ARE going out into the world at one of the critical periods of human history. It will be the period when victory is consummated and when the task of preserving civilization will pass from the military to the civilian. The decade following this war will determine whether the nations will move toward another great war, or whether they will move toward peaceful solutions of the future differences which inevitably will arise.

During this critical period, you will often ask yourselves, and you will often be asked, What can the churches do to influence the pattern of the future?

My judgment is that their influence can be decisive.

That judgment is very different from that with which I started a career of international activity. For many years it never occurred to me that the Christian gospel had any practical bearing on the solution of international problems. I came to my present view only after thirty years of experience with futility.

At the Second Hague Peace Conference in 1907, I saw the

Address delivered to the graduating class of Princeton Theological Seminary on May 16, 1944, published in *Theology Today*, October, 1944.

delegates of each nation, in the name of peace and humanity, maneuver for rules of war that would give their nation some advantage in the next war.

In Central America, I saw differences settled by the coercive use of our economic power.

At the Paris Peace Conference, I saw national rivalries so disunite the principal Allies that neither Wilson's program for a League of Nations, nor Clemenceau's program for a permanently weakened Germany, ever emerged from treaty words into living realities.

In 1923, during the French occupation of the Ruhr, I saw balance of power politics wreck a program substantially worked out between the German, French, and Belgian Governments whereby Germany would voluntarily cease passive resistance and resume reparation deliveries.

As counsel in relation to many postwar stabilization and rehabilitation loans, I saw their purpose frustrated. Borrowers used the proceeds to build up military establishments and lenders demanded the letter of their bond, while their nations refused to accept the goods and services through which alone repayment could be made.

At the German debt conferences which immediately followed Hitler's becoming chancellor, I saw Germany's policy poised between pursuit of international trade and pursuit of autarchy. I saw that policy swing to autarchy when the United States, for reasons of domestic policy, wrecked the contemporaneous London Economic Conference of 1933. Subsequently, in Germany, I saw the Nazi Party, by new scientific techniques for arousing mass emotion, instill in the German people a perverse belief in a "new order" to be achieved by force and administered by a German *Herrenvolk*.

At the 1937 Paris session of the Institute of Intellectual

Co-operation, held under the auspices of the League of Nations, I saw the impossibility of bringing the delegates present even to discuss the agreed topic of "peaceful change," lest it might be inferred that their own nation admitted the possibility of change to its disadvantage.

In China and Japan in 1938, I saw a Japanese military clique, which controlled the emperor, bend the Japanese people to their will by teaching that wherever the divine emperor led, there the people must fanatically follow.

In all of these matters, in which I played some part, I earnestly sought to promote peace and decent national relationships. Yet when a new and greater world war became certain, I saw that my record was one of complete futility. That personal failure was, of course, unimportant to anyone but myself. What was important was that I was not an isolated case. All of the good intentions of public officials and of private groups had been useless. So I took time out to analyze the record and to seek the cause of failure.

In that effort I obtained great enlightenment from one international event that, to me, stands out above all the others. That was the 1937 Oxford Conference on Church and State. It was made up of men and women who, like those who gathered at Pentecost, came "from every nation under heaven." There was but one bond of unity — that was faith in God as revealed by Jesus Christ. As at Pentecost, that bond of unity enabled us to understand each other. We discussed matters which, before, I had seen always give rise to violent dispute. We found intelligent, practical agreement as to how such matters should be dealt with. We did not find any formulas of quick and easy solution. But we did find that the toughest problems could be tackled in ways which, instead of creating discord, drew men together in fellowship.

How did that come about? What was the explanation of the amazing contrast between discussions which occurred in a Christian atmosphere and those which occurred in the conventional atmosphere of diplomacy?

When I analyzed the failures which I could judge of my personal knowledge, I found the causes.

There was idolatry. The national representatives who conducted foreign relations did more than seek the long-range welfare of their people. That would have been their duty. But they often personified their state as quasi-god. To enhance its power and prestige became their great objective. To that they subordinated the true welfare of the human beings who composed the nation.

There was hypocrisy. Each national representative usually considered that his own national group was predominantly endowed with virtue and all others with vice.

There was blindness. Men seldom saw beyond what served their nation's short-range material interest. With so limited a vision, the full elements of the problem were not grasped.

There was much evil emotion. Men readily became suspicious and resentful and angry. They had frequent rushes of blood to the head, which prevented their minds from working as keen tools to dissect the problem and resourcefully find ways for its solution.

There was little good emotion. Few were inspired to combat evil and to promote righteousness. They saw their tasks as isolated events in a materialistic world rather than as elements in some great progression toward human betterment. They were ineffective because they lacked the faith that is requisite for great deeds.

These causes of failure, I saw, were precisely those that Christ had sought to eradicate. He did not attempt to give ready-made solutions of the problems of world order and of social welfare. What he did was to tell men what were the qualities they needed to solve those probems for themselves.

He told men to give their spiritual allegiance only to God and to look upon human beings, rather than some personified state, as the highest earthly unit of value.

He inveighed against hypocrisy and taught men to concern themselves first with the evil in themselves.

He wanted men to see — to see far and to see truly. Blind men, following blind leaders, he pointed out, will always end up together in the pit.

He taught men to avoid the evil emotions of hatred and blind vengefulness which so drive them to wreak destruction that they cannot plan intelligently for construction.

He showed men a great vision and sought to implant in them a sense of great purpose in life. He taught not a purely contemplative religion but a dynamic faith which would make men strong and powerful in action.

Now, of course, it was nothing new to me that Christ had taught these things. I had learned that as a boy. What was new was the realization that the qualities Christ taught were the qualities that men needed in order to deal realistically with practical problems. That lesson seems to me of the utmost importance, and that is my excuse for telling you of it in the way which may be the most graphic—namely, in terms of my own experience. That lesson suggests, I think, the way in which the churches and Christian ministers like yourselves can decisively aid the cause of world order.

Some of you may have sufficient technical knowledge to enable you to espouse concrete solutions of specific problems. If you have that knowledge, it is of course your duty to put it to work, for you are not only ministers of the gospel but citizens of your nation. But by and large, your greatest contribution will be to implant the qualities of soul and mind that Christ taught and then to get those qualities into actual use. It may be that you will have personal contact with those who implement national policy. You will find that such persons, even though avowed Christians, seldom use the Christian qualities I have referred to. That is the kind of omission which, if opportunity offers, you must seek to correct. Whether or not you have personal contact with public leaders, you will surely have contact with those who, as citizens, basically determine our national policies and choose our political leadership. The voters of this nation need to realize that leadership can safely be entrusted only to those who possess and will exercise, not only in word but in competent deed, the qualities taught by the great religions. Democracies always face great peril because the evil qualities I have mentioned seem, peculiarly, to have a mass appeal. Human beings in the mass find it pleasant to deify their corporate group; they like to be told that they are pre-eminently endowed with virtues; they get a pleasurable thrill by being stirred to passionate hate; and they often choose for themselves political leaders who pander to those trends. That happened, to an extreme degree, in Germany. There Hitler came to power through the constitutional processes of democracy. The German churches had failed to make the people Christian in the sense that, as citizens, they would reject leadership which exemplified qualities which Christ most strongly condemned. That same sort of thing happens to a degree everywhere. So, I say, your greatest contribution toward world order will be to bring Christian citizens to realize that their political leadership will be futile and end only in disaster unless it is the leadership of men who have and will use qualities of the kind Christ taught. . . . .

◇◇◇◇

I think the vision Christ taught was total vision, which sees all the facts. Like Pilgrim, we must move forward through obstacles; we do not soar above them. Unless we see those obstacles, we shall stumble and get nowhere.

One reality we need to see is that the society of nations is in a most primitive stage of development. We have, in essence, a society of some sixty members who have never even established a common meeting place. There is little community sentiment. Each member goes his own way, and power, whether or not actually used, primarily determines whether one or another nation gets what it wants or keeps what it wants. As Lord Lothian constantly emphasized, the society of nations is in a state of anarchy.

No society moves at a single bound from the primitive stage of anarchy to a highly developed order. That comes through gradual stages.

The first stage is psychological. There must be an intellectual and emotional conviction that the existing system is so bad that it must be changed, even though that means, for some, forgoing advantages that they have the power to grasp. It takes hard and cruel experience to get a primitive group into that frame of mind. Those who think they have the power, or can get the power, to do what they want, usually prefer a power system.

Two world wars may have brought the nations really to want to organize their society so that principles, rather than relative power, settle conflicts of desire. However, we must not take that for granted. Such a sentiment is the usual accompaniment of a hard war. But when victory comes, nations which emerge with great power, or which want to develop power in order to reverse the verdict of a lost war, are apt to conclude that, after all, a power system is the best.

If that happens after this war, we will again fail to have the state of mind which must precede any genuine progress toward world order. To prevent that psychological relapse must be the concern of those, like yourselves, who aspire to moral leadership. . . .

◇◇◇◇

I am told nowadays that there is much discouragement among our people. That is largely due to increasing realization that permanent peace cannot be easily and quickly assured by military victory or by some treaty formula. That cause of discouragement is to me a most encouraging fact. All great wars give rise to visionary hopes that victory itself will assure lasting peace. Usually the treaty of victory has proclaimed permanent peace, and that has satisfied the popular demand. Men have not seen how superficial that was until a new war was actually in the making. Now we know, in time, that to win a victory and to proclaim a peace does not suffice. To know that is the beginning of wisdom.

To achieve world order is a long, hard task. It will only have begun when the fighting stops. It is not a task for those who are weary or of faint heart. It calls for men who are clear of vision, strong of faith, and competent in deed. Fortunately, there is a goodly number of those men among our leaders and among the rank and file of our people. How much they can achieve, and how quickly, depends on whether their ranks are steadily augmented. We need many more who possess and will use the qualities Christ taught. To assure that is your task.

4

A Diplomat and His Faith

IN SEPTEMBER, 1951, the President asked me to undertake the diplomatic negotiation of a Japanese peace treaty. I was given broad discretionary authority, subject only to certain security requirements stipulated for by the Department of Defense. The responsibility was a heavy one. There was urgent need for action, for already the occupation was ending its fifth year and further inaction would breed disastrous bitterness and resentment against us in Japan. On the other hand, there were some fifty Allied nations which had declared war against Japan, and they differed much among themselves. It had been possible to achieve unity for war against Japan, but how could we achieve unity for peace with Japan?

As I pondered the problem, my thoughts went back ten years to the time when the Federal Council of Churches had organized its Commission on a Just and Durable Peace and I had become chairman of that Commission. I recalled the Statement of Guiding Principles, which had been adopted at Delaware, Ohio, in 1942, with its triumphant proclamation of the supremacy of moral law and of the special responsibility

First in a series of articles on "How My Faith Helped in a Decisive Hour," *The Christian Century,* March 19, 1952.

which devolved upon the United States to bring international relations into conformity with that moral law. Such pronouncements are often made in religious circles by those who have no actual responsibility for the conduct of affairs. But would it be prudent and possible, now that I had a national responsibility, actually to practice what we had preached?

As I reviewed the international scene, I saw powerful influences which seemed not to accord with the moral law of which we had spoken.

In the countries which had been invaded by Japan, such as the Philippines, Indo-China, and Indonesia, there was much hatred and vengefulness. In this country we had not forgotten Pearl Harbor, Bataan, and the "March of Death." In countries not actually invaded but threatened with invasion, such as Australia and New Zealand, there was widespread fear and a desire that the treaty should seek to make Japan permanently weak and unarmed. Among those who had experienced prewar commercial competition from Japan, there was a widespread desire for a treaty which would cripple Japan commercially so that in shipbuilding, ship operations, textiles, fishing, and so on, she could never again be a serious competitor. In Asian countries, peoples who hated and feared Western colonialism wanted a treaty which would totally eradicate Western influence from Japan. Some, who saw the international problem as primarily a military one, wanted to make Japan into a great military bastion against Soviet Russia. Others wanted a treaty which would compel Japan, by discriminatory provisions, to become the proving ground for an experiment in disarmament which their own countries rejected.

These were the sentiments that were most vocal, and at first glance it seemed that the peace would have to draw on some such sentiments for its support. However, I was not hopeful that it would be possible in this way to get a just and durable peace. It might perhaps be possible to get a piece of paper labeled "Peace." But as one who had had close contact with the making, and then the unmaking, of the Treaty of Versailles, I realized how undependable was a peace treaty that was discriminatory, that had to be forcibly imposed, and that gave expression to the evil passions which war leaves as its aftermath. Such a treaty almost inevitably creates a new series of evil passions and thus perpetuates a cycle of recurrent war.

It seemed to me that here, if ever, was the occasion to try to make a peace which would invoke the principles of the moral law. The opportunity was the greater because General MacArthur was prepared to put all of his great prestige behind the invoking of a new concept in international relations. So we drafted a treaty which invoked the spirit of forgiveness to overcome the spirit of vengefulness; the spirit of magnanimity to overcome the spirit of hatred; the spirit of humanity and fair play to overcome the spirit of competitive greed; the spirit of fellowship to overcome the spirit of arrogance and discrimination; and the spirit of trust to overcome the spirit of fear.

The territorial terms of peace had already been determined at Potsdam over five years before and had actually been put into effect through the elimination of Japanese jurisdiction over Korea, Formosa, South Sakhalin, and the Kurile, Ryukyu, and Bonin Islands. To the extent that those decisions were debatable on their merits, we planned to keep open the possibility of future adjustments.

As far as reparations were concerned, the principle of reparations would be affirmed, as a matter of simple justice. However, justice would be tempered with mercy by provisions which would assure that reparations could not be exacted which would impair Japan's viable economy or would throw foreign-exchange burdens upon Japan. In substance, reparations would be in terms of the creditor nations' availing of the assets which Japan had in surplus, namely, a surplus trained population and surplus industrial facilities. These could be put to use for account of the reparation creditors, provided they supplied the raw materials. Thus the arrangement would not be a burden upon Japan's ability to buy abroad the goods and raw materials that she needs to maintain a decent standard of living.

Subject to these provisions, the treaty would restore Japan to complete and equal fellowship in the community of free nations. Japan would not be subjected to commercial or political discriminations which, however well intentioned, the Allied powers were unwilling to accept for themselves. As to armament, that would be left to Japan's own decision. The treaty would not compel armament, nor would it require disarmament. The ugly past would be merged into an act of reconciliation by a treaty which placed trust in the desire of the Japanese people themselves to become self-respecting and honored members of the world community.

We contemplated also procedures which would be those of reconciliation. I recalled vividly how, at the end of World War I, the German peace delegation was put into a barbed-wire enclosure at Versailles, exposed to the populace as animals in a zoo and denied any personal contact with Allied delegates. That procedure in itself had gone far to ensure that the peace treaty, even though it had been meritorious in substance, would be deeply resented.

We proposed in this case to consult fully with the Japanese, who by their loyal compliance with the surrender terms had won the right to be fully heard. Indeed, after the basic principles had been discussed with the principally concerned Allied powers, the Japanese were the first to be consulted with respect to the detailed application of these principles.

The success of the program which I have sketched depended upon there being within the Allied countries, including the United States, a majority who both believed in moral principles and were willing to make their beliefs effectively felt as a political force. We went about the world trying to find out whether that was the case. Greatly to our satisfaction, and I must admit somewhat to our surprise, we found that when the issues were clearly presented, there was little doubt as to where the balance of power lay. It lay in favor of the principles of the moral law. Even in countries where there was understandably great bitterness and great fear, the majority were for reconciliation and for trust.

After a year of negotiation, a period which seemed long at the time but which was short considering the complexities of the task, there assembled at San Francisco the delegates of fifty-two nations. Of these, three were from the Soviet Communist bloc and came with the announced intention of attempting to block the treaty. The other forty-nine, constituting all but two of the fifty-one non-Communist countries which had been invited, came to sign the treaty and to express their nations' support in words which showed, unmistakably and eloquently, the tremendous appeal of the moral principles which the draft treaty had invoked.

The prime minister of Japan, speaking from a platform where the flag of Japan would soon stand with the flags of the Allied countries, said: "It is not a treaty of vengeance, but an instrument of reconciliation. The Japanese delegation gladly accepts this fair and generous treaty." And the chairman of the conference, Dean Acheson, concluded it with a benediction never before pronounced at such a gathering but which had been made appropriate by all that had gone before: "I close this conference with words which in many languages, in many forms, in many religions, have brought comfort and strength: 'May the peace of God, which passeth all understanding, be amongst us and remain with us always.'"

In a paper which I wrote in 1942 for the Federal Council's Commission on a Just and Durable Peace, I said that communism had moved into a spiritual vacuum which had resulted from the loss elsewhere of a dynamic faith. At San Francisco there was no spiritual vacuum. The atmosphere was charged with the power of the moral law, and those who denied moral law were ignominiously put to rout.

I do not exaggerate the importance of that moment. It does not mean that we made a perfect treaty. Indeed, the delegates constantly disclaimed perfection. It does not mean that the peace will necessarily be durable. That will depend upon the future. The treaty, while it did not express hatred, jealousy, or vengefulness, did not and could not obliterate these sentiments from the world. They persist and might again take control and, through irresponsible national action, inflict the discriminations which the treaty itself rejected. Evil ambition might be reborn in Japan.

On the other hand, if we do not exaggerate, also we need not belittle. What was done showed that moral principles are not something to be relegated to Sunday services in our churches. They can be brought boldly and unashamedly into the arena of world affairs. There *is* a moral law which, no less than physical law, undergirds our world. It *is* relevant to the corporate life of men and the ordering of human society. It *can* be drawn upon — indeed, it *must* be drawn upon — if mankind is to escape chaos and recurrent war.

5

Patriotism and the American Tradition

IT IS indeed a great privilege for me to be here and to have the opportunity of talking with you on an occasion which for me is full of sentiment. It was just one hundred years ago that my grandfather, John W. Foster, was graduated from this university. It was just fifty years ago that he received from this university the honorary degree which, I understand, the university plans to confer upon me tomorrow. My grandfather, whose name I bear, exerted a great influence over my life, and he had ideals and purposes which I have tried to make my own.

He was a deeply patriotic American. He belonged to the period which saw this country rapidly developing from a small Atlantic Coast group into a nation that spread across the continent. He fought to preserve the Union; and then, on diplomatic missions and as Secretary of State, he helped to spread the influence of this nation throughout the world both in Europe and in Asia.

He deeply revered his forebears, who had been pioneers in settling this part of our nation. He wrote a private booklet inscribed "Don't Let the Little Ones Forget," in which he

Baccalaureate address at Indiana University, June 12, 1955.

told for his descendants the story of his own forebears: his grandfather (my great-great-grandfather) on whose grave I laid a wreath today, and his father.

To me that story has symbolized the spirit of our nation. I vividly recall being told of how my great-grandfather, as a young boy of seventeen, had struck out into the West to get away from what seemed to him the overpopulated East. After a foot voyage of exploration, he had fixed upon a forest tract in southern Indiana as a future homestead. He then brought his aged parents — his father was then seventy-nine years old — from the East to settle here and gained a livelihood by hunting and by cutting hickory for hogshead hoops and floating them on a raft down the Ohio and Mississippi Rivers to New Orleans, where hogsheads were needed for molasses. Then he would walk back through the twelve hundred miles of dangerous trails from New Orleans to his log-cabin home here in Indiana. Finally he become a farmer, a merchant, and then a judge in the growing community he had helped to create.

That spirit of enterprise, that vision, that industry, and that rugged independence have been characteristic of our nation. There are indeed few Americans who cannot find in their family history similar stories of those who risked much and endured much to bring a dream into reality. It is those qualities which, within the short span of one hundred and fifty years, have brought our people from national infancy into forming the greatest nation on earth.

In some quarters there has developed a tendency to scorn patriotism. Indeed, there are a few who find patriotism unfashionable and who go so far as to assume that institutions and ideas are better if only they bear a foreign label. Also there is a theory that this mood is necessary if we are to develop international institutions and maintain international peace.

It seems to me that love of country is one of the great and indispensable virtues. No community is weaker because the members of the families which make it up — the mother, the father, the sons, the daughters, the brothers and sisters — are bound together by distinctive ties of love, respect, and admiration. So I am convinced that the family of nations will not be the poorer or the more fragile because the peoples who form the different nations have a special affection and pride for their own people and for the nation they form.

I recall that St. Paul took great pride, which he did not attempt to conceal, in the achievements of his own people. To me, one of the most inspiring chapters in the Bible is the eleventh chapter of Hebrews, where St. Paul recalls, in epic words, the great deeds which had been wrought through faith by national heroes, men and women.

Recently I was asked to open an exhibit of the oldest-known print of the Bible, in the Aramaic language, and in that connection to select one of my favorite verses. I selected that portion of The Epistle to the Hebrews where St. Paul, after the historical recital to which I allude, concludes by saying, "Seeing that we are compassed about by so great a cloud of witnesses, let us run with endurance the race that is set before us."

If it was appropriate for St. Paul to entertain those sentiments, I think it is equally appropriate for us. We too of our nation can look back with pride to the great figures which our nation has produced, who through faith wrought much.

Surely we too can feel "that we are compassed about by a great cloud of witnesses" who are observing our conduct and who by their spirit seek to inspire us to carry forward the great national and international tasks to which they dedicated their lives and to which they committed our nation by their strivings and by their faith.

Our national course has to a unique degree been shaped by religious beliefs. Our people have in the main been God-fearing people. They believed in moral principles derived from a Source above us. They were dedicated to human liberty because they believed that men had been endowed by their Creator with inalienable rights. So they provided that those rights must at all times be respected, assuring the sovereignty of the individual against the dictatorship of the state. They were confident that the human liberty they thus assured would not be exercised recklessly and in disregard of fellow men, because they were confident that our citizens would obey the moral law which prescribes the Ten Commandments of the Old Testament and the two great commandments of the New Testament, "Thou shalt love thy neighbor as thyself" and "Whatsoever ye would that men should do to you, do ye even so to them."

As George Washington pointed out in his Farewell Address, religion and morality are the two indispensable supports of a free society. "In vain," he said, "would that man claim the tribute of patriotism who should labor to subvert these great pillars of human happiness, these firmest props of the duties of men and citizens." Indeed, a society which is not religious cannot tolerate much freedom. It is dangerous to give freedom to those who do not feel under moral compulsion to exercise self-control and who are unwilling to make sacrifices for the good of others.

It results that true patriotism, which vitalizes liberty and freedom for ourselves, can never be a purely selfish force. That has been ever evident so far as our nation was concerned. Our people have always been endowed with a sense of mission in the world. They have believed that it was their duty to help men everywhere to get the opportunity to be and to do what God designed. They saw a great prospect and were filled with a great purpose. As said in the opening paragraph of *The Federalist* papers, "It seems to have been reserved to the people of this country, by their conduct and example, to decide whether societies of men are capable of establishing good government." "Failure on their part," it continues, would be "the general misfortune of mankind."

Under the impulsion of that faith there developed here an area of spiritual, intellectual, and economic vigor the like of which the world had never seen. It was no exclusive preserve; indeed, sharing was the central theme. Millions were welcomed here from other lands, all to share equally the opportunities of the founders and their heirs. Through missionary activities and the establishment of schools and colleges abroad, American ideals were carried throughout the world. Our Government gave aid and comfort to those elsewhere who sought to increase human freedom.

These have been the characteristics of our nation since its foundation, and those characteristics have persisted. They today make our nation the leader in the struggle to maintain liberty in the world. I believe we can say that in these times, when despotism menaces as never before, our nation is playing a part worthy of our forebears and is imbued with the spirit of those who founded our republic. We have availed of every opportunity, whether it be through the United Nations or through mutual security associations with other free nations, to make our influence felt in support of freedom. We have, as a matter of enlightened self-interest, contributed largely out of our vast productivity to others who, if left alone, could not sustain the freedom and independence for which they yearn.

All of that is in the American tradition. We can be happy that that tradition thrives and is vigorous, and we can take pride in the fact that, inspired by our founders who saw a great vision, we are indeed with steadfastness pursuing the course upon which they embarked us.

There come times in the life of peoples when their work of creation ends. It is easy to diagnose the symptoms of that national decadence. It is seen when a people lose their sense of mission in the world, when they think only of themselves, when they forget the Biblical injunction that, although we have different offices, we are all members one of another and that those who are strong ought to bear the infirmities of the weak. No one, be he individual or nation, is truly great who does not have the will and the capacity to help others or who is without a sense of mission.

We can take pride in our nation because since the day of its creation, and with but few lapses, our purposes have been large and their goals have been humane. We can rejoice that that spirit animates our nation today and makes us still young, still vital, and still capable of great endeavor. Our youth, such as you who now enter into the larger world, are spirited, not selfish nor fearful. Our religious heritage and our national traditions are not forgotten. As we are faithful to their guidance, we can have the satisfaction which comes to those who, in fellowship, are embarked on the great adventure of building peacefully a nation and a world of human liberty and justice.

II

The American Heritage

John Foster Dulles was not only a convinced Christian. He was a loyal American, proud of his nation's history and traditions, persuaded that an intelligent understanding of that heritage was essential equipment for citizens who would serve their country effectively.

But he believed profoundly that "something has gone wrong with our nation," that what was wrong was a loss of vision and of courage, that what was required was the recovery of "a righteous and dynamic faith."

This is the burden of the writings and speeches that follow. They were prepared for the most diverse publics, from the readers of Life magazine to the graduating class at the National War College.

It was a steadily deepening emphasis with him. It was anticipated in his first book, War, Peace and Change, written in 1938; but there it holds a subordinate place. That book speaks of "the decline of religion as a vital influence" (p. 115). In the successor volume, however, War or Peace, published in 1950, the penultimate chapter, which immediately precedes a summarizing "Conclusion," is devoted to "Our Spiritual Need," where both his disquiet over the loss of national vision and his own prescription for remedy are set forth in the bluntest and most forceful terms.

6

A Righteous Faith

ALL GREAT wars bring with them some sort of spiritual revival. For when we are at war material things must be sacrificed. Money, goods, life itself, are poured into the fiery furnace. Men then grope for spiritual things as the only available alternative.

Too often, however, the spiritual revival of war is but shallow emotionalism. Men fill their souls with hatred and vengefulness and they deify their nation. When the war is over, these passions quickly subside and materialism again becomes rampant.

If this occurs in the United States it will be a serious matter, for already before this war our great weakness was lack of that faith that makes men strong. If we now merely win military victory, that will not make us safe unless we also win back faith such as sustained us when we were yet small and materially weak.

If we look back over the last two hundred years, that will make plain what I mean. Until the time of the First World War three peoples held undisputed leadership in the world. These three were the British, the French, and ourselves. We three were not great because of our numbers, for no one of us constituted 10 per cent of the world's population. We were not great because of our natural wealth, for Great Britain and France are poor countries and, during most of this period, the resources of the United States were undeveloped. We were great because our three peoples were imbued with and radiated great faiths. These were not perfect faiths, but they incorporated the Christian idea that man owes a duty to fellow man. We sought our own advantage, but we sought it in ways that would also advantage others. Our spirit was one of mission in the world. Often we were hypocrites, but even that showed that we felt under a moral compulsion to justify what we did as being for the welfare of others.

The French toward the end of the eighteenth century had exploded upon a world of despotism the revolutionary slogan of human "Liberty, Equality, and Fraternity." Their belief in the rights of the individual partook of a religious fervor, and so contagious was their faith that it changed the face of the Western world and broke the political chains that were fastened upon the people.

In England, inventive genius showed how man's labor could be made infinitely more productive by using mechanical power and machinery. Thereby raw materials could quickly and cheaply be turned into finished goods and standards of living greatly raised. The possibilities thus opened up were carried by England into the uttermost parts of the earth and were given moral sanction as a carrying of the "white man's burden." Today we laugh at that phrase, but under its influence hundreds of thousands of Britain's best youth went forth to do what they believed to be in the general welfare. Britain gained, but in the process more was done to improve the general lot of mankind than ever before in any comparable period of time.

◇◇

We in the United States became conscious of a "manifest destiny" and "American dream." We visioned here a vast continent to be opened up to the repressed and oppressed of other lands. We saw that we might fashion here a state of ordered freedom that would be a beacon in the world. We went far toward making that dream come true. Millions came to us from other lands and found here the material opportunities and the spiritual freedoms which they had vainly sought for themselves and their children.

All that we did, at home or abroad, was profoundly influenced by our Christian faith. As Dean Weigle shows us, our domestic political evolution was determined by men's conception of their duty as sons of God. And abroad, wherever trading posts sprang up, there, too, a mission post was planted.

Thus each of our three peoples had hold of something bigger than ourselves, something that forced us into a kind of partnership sharing with the rest of the world. It was that that made us great and strong. It was that that made us safe and free.

The beginning of this century showed a steady exhaustion of our spiritual springs. Woodrow Wilson, it is true, inspired a wartime idealism that did much to bring us victory. But that was a flare-up that quickly subsided. We emerged from that war — the French, the British, and ourselves — as burnt-out peoples. We no longer felt a sense of mission in the world. We had nothing so big that it had to be shared. Indeed, we had so lost faith in our own institutions that we felt it necessary to shelter them from contact with the outer world. We sought only to be left alone, and in our isolated and, as we thought, "matured" economies, we found little to do except to squabble over the partition of the material wealth we had theretofore created. Upon the world there descended a spirit of disillusionment and discouragement. The youth were without opportunity or hope, the workers were without employment, and the aged were without security. All were without faith. Even in church circles where the word "faith" was still used, it had lost any real significance.

It is impossible to perpetuate a spiritual vacuum. So, inevitably, it came about that here and there, throughout the world, new faiths were born. In Russia, out of the collapse of 1917, there had arisen a militant faith in Marxian communism. Like all great faiths, it could not be confined. It sought world-wide realization through world revolution. Next Italy seemed, momentarily, to recapture the tradition that was Rome's, and, under that pagan impulse, sought glory in Africa. In Germany arose a militant faith in a "new order" under which the national barriers of Europe would be torn down and each non-German given an allotted task to be performed under the dominance of a German *Herrenvolk*. Japan had meanwhile come under the control of a military clique who fanatically sought a "co-prosperity sphere," which would give Japan in the Orient that which Germany sought in the Western world.

These faiths were largely repugnant to us. In the case of Germany, Italy, and Japan they were evil faiths that led to war — and will lead to frustration — because they asserted racial supremacy and exalted force and violence as the means of achieving it. But, good or bad, they were faiths that, while they lasted, made men strong. We have been startled by what those nations have performed. We were stupefied when Germany, enfeebled, disarmed, and dismembered by the Treaty of Versailles, grew into a blazing volcano that erupted over all Europe. We were aghast when Japan in a few months took under her military sway the vast areas of the Indies, Malaya, and Burma. We were wholly taken by surprise by the valor and tenacity of Russia's resistance and forced to a total revaluation of things Russian.

If history teaches anything, it is that no nation is great and no nation is strong unless its people are imbued with a faith. It also shows that no nation can be *permanently* great or *permanently* strong unless that faith be a *righteous* faith that is compatible with the welfare and the dignity of others. Unless during this war we regain that kind of faith, then military victory will serve no permanent good. For again new faiths will arise to attack us and in the long run we will succumb. The impact of the dynamic upon the static — while it may be resisted in detail — will ultimately destroy that which it attacks. The First World War, this World War, and the next world war may go down in history as a series of rear-guard actions by disillusioned peoples who, equipped only with the material products of past greatness, sought valiantly but vainly to resist the penetration of alien faiths.

The Protestant churches of America are awake to the spiritual need that faces our nation. They are determined to do all that lies in their power to assure that out of this war will be born, not just ephemeral passions, but a faith that will endure and that will project us into the world as a great force for righteousness. As Professor Hocking puts it, the church must seek "to discern 'the mind of Christ' and to announce concretely the divine attitude which man in wartime may strive toward." . . .

◇◇◇◇

We know that if the principles we have proclaimed become mandatory in the consciousness of American people, they will know in what direction to move and they will move in that direction and they will thereby assure that our nation will again become a dynamic moral force in the world.

What is the great obstacle we encounter? It is not opposition to our ends. Almost everybody would agree that it would be a nice thing if the American people were again united and enthused by a great dynamic faith. The difficulty we encounter is that men are skeptical of the way we propose to get that faith. Christ said, "I am the way." But most people have ceased to believe it. They have come to look upon Jesus as an impractical idealist, and they consider that those of us who urge men to follow his way are uttering a counsel of perfection that is unrelated to the practical needs of the times. For that attitude the church leaders of the past have a heavy responsibility. They have often made Christ seem to be wholly different from what he really was. Some have made it appear that Christ taught an "idealism" that was wholly unrelated to worldly problems and that served men only when they died. Others, going to the opposite extreme, have sought to put Christ's authority behind specifics that practical men could see were of dubious worth. The truth is that Christ was neither impractical nor was he specific. He told men, not *what* to do, but how to acquire the qualities of soul and of mind that would enable *them* to know what to do.

I recall that Christ ministered at a time when international and social problems existed in aggravated form. Much of the world was under the heel of a military dictator and labor was largely slavery. Tiberius had achieved for Rome what Hitler has sought for Germany. Yet Christ advocated no specific revolts and sponsored no specific reforms. This cannot be because he was indifferent to the human misery that surrounded him. Rather, he sought to do something bigger and more enduring than to cure the particular evils of his day. He sought to show men how, throughout the ages, they might find the way to surmount evil that would constantly be reappearing in ever-changing form. That way, he taught, was for men to act out of visions that would see clear, minds that would think straight, and hearts that would comprehend the essential unity and equal worthiness of all human beings. He inveighed against hatred and vengefulness, self-conceit and deification of one's particular nation, race, or class. He did so not only because such emotions are repugnant to God's will for man, but also because they always make men incompetent to deal with human problems. They create those blind masses and those blind leaders who, he pointed out, end up together in the pit.

Jesus was, as Dr. Fosdick tells us, "everlastingly right." "He was the 'truth' — the realistic, factual revelation of what life actually means." Until we believe that and act accordingly, we are the ones who are impractical. Surely the catastrophes that inevitably overtake those who operate on anti-Christian principles powerfully argue that it is those principles that are not true.

What, then, shall we do to equip ourselves to deal with the problem of our time? The answer is eternally the same: we must develop those qualities of vision, of soul, and of mind that Christ taught and then act under the directive of those qualities. Let us glimpse at what that means.

If we have vision, what is it we shall see? We shall, like Christ, see a multitude who hunger. That multitude is all about us — some near, some afar. They hunger not only for things material but for things spiritual. We would not be seeing truly if we saw only material wants. Such needs exist and they are great. But the greatest need is not for things. Men hunger for sympathy and fellowship that will lift them out of their physical environment. They crave the vibrant thrill that comes from creative effort. They need a religious faith that will carry them through tribulations which no material wealth can prevent.

Christ saw, and if we have vision we too will see, that material things serve chiefly as instruments for bringing into being those nonmaterial values that men need most. When he told the rich young man to give all to the poor, he saw not so much the material advantage for the poor as the value of the spiritual outlook that would prompt such an act. By similar standards he appraised the widow's gift of her mites and Mary's sacrifice of her precious ointment. So it is that as our eyes are opened we will see material needs, but we will see them in subordinate relationship to spiritual needs.

If we have hearts that are comprehending, we shall, like Christ, be moved with compassion. We shall hear the cry of the masses that a way be found to save them and their children from the death, the misery, the starvation of body and soul which recurrent war and economic disorder now wreak upon man. We shall be so moved by that cry that we shall resolutely dedicate ourselves to the achievement of a better order. We shall find, in that dedication, something that will make our own lives worth living and our own nation worth preserving.

If, in addition to acquiring vision and human understanding, we free our minds from warping emotions — like hate and prejudice — then we can think straight and approach with competence the technical problems of our time. The broad principles that should govern our international conduct are not obscure. . . . The overwhelming majority of Christians would surely agree with them. So, too, for that matter, would those of other great faiths. But that is not enough. We need men who, as citizens, will think out the application of those principles to the daily life of our nation. That is something that everyone must do for himself. The church cannot and should not try to do that for him. If the church follows Christ's example, it will proclaim eternal verities in terms such that their practical significance is made plain, but it will avoid sponsoring specifics that necessarily must be compromises compounded out of worldly knowledge. That is what the citizen must do, and he can do it competently if he equips himself with the qualities of vision, of soul, and of mind that Christ taught.

Finally, we must act. Christ did not teach a purely contemplative religion. "Let your light so shine before men, that they may see your good works." We must not be paralyzed by fear lest what we do may not be perfect. Neither must we wait until someone develops a spectacular plan for achieving at once all that we desire. Action is a thing that, itself, is good. It is out of action that there is born a sense of creative power and purpose. Every individual, every nation, must make an effort to find opportunities where faith can be converted into action. Those opportunities are always available. It is unimportant if initially our acts, as individuals or as a nation, are unspectacular. For if what we do is prompted by clear vision, human comprehension, and clear thinking, we will be surprised at the fruitful consequence of what we do. Inspired and urged on by those consequences, we will steadily move forward, enlarging the practical expression of our faith and developing for it a defined and expanding pattern. As our national faith is made manifest by works, and grows under that stimulus, its influence will be contagious throughout the world. As the evil faiths that combat us collapse, leaving death and ruin as their fruit, the faith that makes us strong will encompass the earth.

It will unite men, as never before, in common and constructive purpose.

I am full of hope. On every side there is evidence that a new faith is emerging and that this faith will be born out of the gospel of Jesus Christ. I am told that there is one book that cannot be kept in adequate supply at our Army camps. That book is the New Testament. Throughout the land, church meetings and study groups are seeing, with Christian vision, the opportunities that open before us. I believe that the spiritual rebirth we are witnessing will not be spurious, but that it will give us an abiding faith. That faith, now in its formative stage, we must constantly nurture, and we must constantly test it by the mind of Christ. Above all, we need to have it shared by the many millions who, at this Christmas time, celebrate the birth of our Lord, but who otherwise live their lives without regard for the fact that he *is* the way, the truth, and the life.

7

The American Vision

THIS meeting opens the churches' National Mission on World Order. By that mission we seek to revive in our people a sense of destiny in the performance of a great work of creation. Upon the success of our effort, with parallel efforts by others, depends the future of our nation. For we are at one of those critical periods that can readily mark the end of our greatness.

We have been a people of vision and self-confidence. Our founders, though a mere handful of colonists, from the start conceived of their task as of world-wide import. They saw a great prospect, and were filled with a great purpose. The opening paragraph of *The Federalist* papers reads: "It seems to have been reserved to the people of this country, by their conduct and example, to decide whether societies of men are capable of establishing good government." Failure on their part, it continues, would be "the general misfortune of mankind." Moreover, they did not see their experiment as something to be conducted under the conditions of a laboratory. That would have meant little to others than themselves. They

Address at the opening of the churches' National Mission on World Order, Cathedral of St. John the Divine, New York City, October 28, 1943.

had the courage to launch their principles into the world. The thirteen colonies did not form themselves into a closed political unit. They adopted a constitution which was an "open-end" instrument, designed to bring more areas and more people into federal union. By the operation of this provision the original states and their citizens quickly became a minority. They had disdained subtle formulas for perpetuating their own control, and fearlessly entrusted their destiny to the inherent soundness of the structure they had conceived.

Not only was their society designed boldly to expand into the world but it was designed to absorb from the rest of the world. Millions were welcomed here from other lands, to share equally the opportunities of the founders and their heirs.

Under the impulsion of that creative and courageous spirit, the original vision assumed reality. Within a few generations there existed here an area of spiritual, intellectual, and economic vigor the like of which the world had never seen. Americans had, I know, their share of human defects. But their dominant qualities were creative.

The best proof of that is the judgment of others. Throughout the nineteenth century the American accomplishment was everywhere recognized as outstanding, and no land is without institutions inspired by our example.

Another objective test of our achievement is the security we enjoyed. We had no army and only a small navy. We were the least militarized of any Western nation. Yet for a century we were not endangered. No foreign people sought to destroy the great American experiment which they admired and in the fruits of which they shared.

Then something happened. We lost our vision. We no longer conceived that we were creating for the benefit of mankind. We lost our courage. We doubted that we could any longer endow our society with the capacity to expand and to absorb. We closed, *de facto*, our political orbit. This was not because we had achieved a higher order of morality which judged the growth of federal union to be evil. It was because we were afraid. We dared not allow more resources and more people to come into equal sharing with us. "America for the Americans" became our slogan. To keep what we had became our basis for action. On all fronts we began to build barriers — higher tariffs, severe restraints on immigration, and increasing exclusion of foreign capital.

When we had to decide whether to join the League of Nations, we refused. Some good reasons could be found for that action. But the reason that was decisive was a bad reason: it was fear.

I know that there are always prophets of evil and that to them the past always seems glorious and the present pallid. But sometimes they are right. The fact of our fallen estate can be proved by the same objective tests that proved our greatness. Half of the population of the world — one billion people — will face tomorrow the task of rebuilding their economic, social, and political order. All their established institutions will have been swept away. Where will they turn for guidance, example, and inspiration? One hundred years ago, fifty years ago, they surely would have turned to us. But they will not do so as we are today, for we present the spectacle of a people who have lost confidence in themselves.

A further proof of our changed condition is to be found in the dangers from without we have had to meet. It is no mere accident that we have now had to fight two great wars in quick succession — wars to parry the first real menaces to our national life. We had become rich and materially powerful, but we were no longer a life-giving society. Daring nothing, we endangered all.

What has happened is grave. It means that our children and grandchildren will not breathe an air suffused with the elixir of creative effort. They will grow up in a sordid atmosphere of quarreling about the division of what former generations created. The shadow of danger will be upon them. It will be a danger that neither armament nor alliances can avert, for such externals never compensate for lack of spiritual power.

There comes a time in the life of every great people when its work of creation ends. Perhaps that hour has struck for us. But it need not be so. Essentially we are still vital and capable of great endeavor. Our youth are not soft or fearful of peril; they crave adventure. Our tradition and our heritage are not forgotten. No forces that we cannot master compel our national decadence. If, however, we are to avoid that fate and recapture the spirit that made us great, we must first diagnose and then cure the malady that attacks us. Something has happened. What is it that has happened and why?

We have had to meet the severest test that can come to a people, that is, the test of prosperity. We have failed to meet that test successfully.

It was said by Christ that material things would be added unto those who seek first the Kingdom of God and his righteousness. But when that happens, then comes the great trial. For, as Christ warned, those material things can readily become the rust that corrodes men's souls.

Thus there often occurs a typical cycle. Men who feel a sense of duty to some higher Being strive here to do his will. Because of their faith, they have power and virtue and simple wisdom. They build not only for the day but for the morrow;

not merely for themselves but for mankind. A society so founded will, when nature favors, produce wealth and luxury for many. When those by-products come, they seem so good that they become promoted to be the all-sufficient end. Men are drawn away from long-range creative effort. They struggle to get and to hold material things.

When that happens in a national group that nation loses its soul. That is what has happened to us, and today we face the problem of how to regain that soul.

For guidance let us turn to Jesus Christ, who revealed to men not only the way of spiritual salvation but how to create a fellowship on earth. For that he sought for men four simple and very practical qualities: to see, to understand, to reason, and then to act.

Christ wanted men to see, to see far and to see truly. To get that kind of vision, he pointed out, requires avoidance of hypocrisies and group prejudices, which distort the vision and make men imagine they see what is not really there.

Christ wanted men to have hearts that comprehend the human significance of what is seen. That kind of heart requires, he pointed out, avoidance of material self-seeking which makes men hard and indifferent to all that cannot serve their selfish ends.

Christ wanted men to reason clearly and serenely. That requires, he pointed out, avoidance of evil emotions such as hatred and vengefulness, which enflame men's minds and distract them from the real problems that confront them.

Christ wanted men to act. He did not teach a purely contemplative religion. "Go" and "do" were his constant injunctions. "Let your light so shine before men, that they may see your good works."

If individuals today will follow these four simple precepts, then they will have found a way to lift themselves out of the state to which they have fallen. He who sees clearly, in whatever be his environment, who comprehends the human significance of what he sees, who thinks serenely what to do about it, and then does it, will find his action fruitful, probably far beyond his expectation. He will sense the power of creation and a satisfaction which far surpasses that of possession. He will become a person of righteous and creative faith.

If that happens, in sufficient numbers, then and only then can we as a nation resume a creative role in world affairs. Without that we are doomed. For the harmonious association of men is not achieved by treaties, or councils, or armies. These things may help. But the essential is that people find the way to do together works of creation. That way can never be found and followed by a nation unless it has first become the way of the individuals who make that nation's policy. There is no national being apart from you and me who can dream and hope and aspire. That is for men and women and children possessed of qualities unique to those whom God created to be but little lower than the angels. So if we would be a nation of creative faith, we must be individuals of creative faith.

Thus there devolves on every citizen a personal responsibility to develop in himself the qualities which we want to be characteristic of our nation.

When that has happened, our nation will again be a nation of vision. With that vision, we shall see a world in which most of humanity has been torn away from all established institutions. Almost everywhere a new society must be built. This is not only a calamity, it is an opportunity, the like of which men never saw before. So, if we see, we shall see the greatest challenge of all time.

We shall, as a nation, be comprehending. We shall hear the cry of multitudes that a way be found to save them and their children from the death, the misery, the starvation of body and soul which recurrent war and economic disorder now wreak upon man. We shall be so moved by that cry that we shall resolutely dedicate ourselves to find that way.

We shall, as a nation, think out the way to advance our purpose. The broad principles which need to be incorporated into the new world are not obscure. They involve practices which are widely followed as between men who live in personal contact with each other. Such practices now need world-wide application, because the world has grown so small. . . . To devise political machinery to implement these principles presents no insoluble problem. It needs only that we give our best thinking to that instead of to making some passing gain or satisfying some hate or prejudice.

Finally, we will act. We will not merely see the challenge, feel the sympathy, think out the way. We will act. We will embark, in company with others, on the next great adventure, that of building a fellowship that is world-wide in scope. Out of the perils, the difficulties, the accomplishments of that task, will come again the joy that is reserved to those who seek here to create in God's image.

8

Our Spiritual Heritage

THE PEOPLE of the United States have a great heritage. We are vaguely aware of it, but we are confused about its nature. To some it seems a material heritage. To others it seems a political heritage. It is, in its essentials, a religious heritage.

The founders of this nation were consciously launching a great experiment. It became widely known as an experiment in human freedom. So it was. But the experiment took that form because those who sponsored it were, for the most part, persons of deep religious faith. They were seeking to translate, into living reality, their spiritual convictions.

One of those convictions was that human beings are the children of God and as such endowed by him with certain inalienable rights. Since those rights are given by God, no men, however powerful or however numerous, can rightfully take them away from other men, even though those others be only weak or few.

Another of their basic convictions was that there are eternal principles of truth and righteousness which are reflected in a moral law. That law is one which all men can apprehend

Address at *New York Herald Tribune* Forum, October 21, 1947.

through their consciences, and it is a law which most men freely recognize as an obligation. It establishes a duty and a code of conduct so that the freedoms to which men are entitled will not be abused as license but will be used with respect for the general welfare.

A third basic conviction was that those who found a good way of life had a duty to help others to find the same way. The American experiment was never a purely selfish effort to get something exclusive for the American people. Our founders were imbued with a deep sense of mission. Their Declaration of Independence, as President Lincoln pointed out, was not a mere matter of the separation of the colonies from the motherland, but something "giving liberty, not alone to the people of this country, but hope for the world for all future time — it was that which gave promise that in due time the weights should be lifted from the shoulders of all men and that all should have an equal chance."

So it is that when today we ask ourselves what religion can contribute to man, we find some of the answers plainly written in our historical experience. As spiritual convictions have found vital expression, our nation has shown true greatness. As spiritual convictions have been feeble, we have lost in internal health and unity and our external prestige has declined. It is sure that if ever the unhappy day came when spiritual convictions were generally abandoned, then our great experiment in human freedom would ingloriously collapse.

The sovereignty of man rests upon a religious estimate of his nature. Without that estimate he tends to slavery.

A society of freedom cannot exist for long except on a foundation of belief that man is a child of God. If every human being does not contain within himself a spark of the Divine and a right to self-development in accordance with the dictates of his own conscience and of his own mind, then a society which dignifies the individual is purely a matter of expediency. It may be argued that a free society is the most expedient society because it is the most productive society. Certainly societies of freedom have, through their inventiveness, resourcefulness, and industriousness, developed a productivity never equaled by any society of dictatorship or despotism. But it is not possible to prove, merely on the basis of expediency, that a free society will for all time be the most productive society. Marxists concede the immense and superior productivity which the American system has achieved. But they contend that is merely a phase, of history. They say that different forms of society are adapted to different times; that there was a time when slavery was the preferred form of society; then came serfdom; then came capitalism; now comes dictatorship of the proletariat as the next phase in a great historical progression.

There is no factual way to prove or disprove estimates of the future. But the Marxist thesis must be totally rejected if one accepts the religious view of the nature of man. Under that view, slavery, however expedient, was never right. Under that view, the despotism of a police state can never be right. It might be that a time would come when men would be more productive and more secure if they were treated as domesticated animals and driven to pasture and back to shelter under the direction of some superior human will. It is unnecessary to argue that point if one accepts, as did our forebears, the Christian view that man is destined to be more than a material producer and that his chief end is something more than physical security. The religious conception of the nature of man is the premise and the only premise from which political freedom surely follows.

But, also, freedom is indefensible if it stands alone. Freedom must be coupled with recognition of the moral law and of the fact that men's rights carry with them duties to fellow men. This nation was launched with emphasis upon individualism because the original environment was one which called for personal resourcefulness and pioneering. The satisfaction which comes from a sense of being creative then depended more on individual than on collective effort. But extreme individualism is no integral part of our religious heritage. The Jewish and Christian faiths have at all times emphasized the duty of man to his fellows, and that duty is a fundamental of our Christian faith. The moral law is sublimely reflected by the Ten Commandments and by the injunctions: "Thou shalt love the Lord thy God with all thy heart, and with all thy soul, and with all thy mind" and "Thou shalt love thy neighbor as thyself." Christ particularly emphasized these two commandments. Upon them, he said, "hang all the law and the prophets."

As any society matures and as its population becomes more dense and its economy more complex, love of neighbor is of increasing social significance. Then individual acts sharply affect others, and it is essential that, with respect to those acts, there should be a large measure of self-control and self-discipline and a sense of being a part of a combined effort to meet a common need. The joy of creation has to be derived more from joint efforts than from efforts which are isolated. Freedom becomes increasingly an opportunity for fellowship rather than an opportunity for private indulgence. If personal freedom is exercised without regard to the fate of others, then it becomes socially intolerable and, in fact, it will disappear. Broadly speaking, it can be said that unless a society is religious, it cannot be free. Without the disciplines of the moral law, freedom becomes chaotic and men accept the order of slavery.

A sense of mission is also needed if a society is to become and remain free. A people without a dynamic faith are constantly on the defensive, and that is a losing posture. But it is not enough to have a faith that is dynamic; that faith must be a righteous faith. Otherwise, it will break itself against the moral law. That law is no less a reality than is physical law, and its operation, though not always immediate, is inexorable.

Today some are frightened at the prospect of a world of strongly conflicting faiths. They fear that the consequence will be world turmoil, if not world war. Strident voices say that, for us, supineness is the recipe for peace.

There is indeed danger when men seek to make their faith prevail by methods of violence, coercion, and deceit. But these are not the methods of the Christian faith. Christ said: "Go ye into all the world, and preach the gospel to every creature" and "Let your light so shine before men, that they see your good works." A righteous faith prevails by appeal to the conscience and reason of men and by showing good fruits. Christians have learned, sometimes by their own bitter experience, that however good a faith may be, its proponents produce only ugly and evil things if they seek to promote their faith by methods of intolerance. That truth is a precious part of our spiritual and political heritage.

The American people must be resolved, and I am confident that they are resolved, to maintain that heritage. It makes senseless the fear, being recklessly spread, that for us to be strong in faith and works is to endanger the peace.

Freedom cannot be bought and peace cannot be had at the price of abandoning all faith that is dynamic. Those who preach that are either knaves or fools. What is essential is that men's faith should be a righteous faith, both in its substance and also in its means. Our society of freedom would quickly succumb to the overlordship of others if we renounced a sense of mission in the world. We would encounter unconquerable opposition if we sought to make our way prevail by might and not by merit. The need is for purposeful action inspired, in every aspect, by the ideals of the moral law.

Two thousand years ago Christ said: "The truth shall make you free" and "I am the way, the truth, and the life." Every one of those two thousand years sustains that utterance. The church spires which silhouette the skyline of America symbolize acceptance of his way. They point to a power above us from which derives our freedom.

9

Our Spiritual Need

Something has gone wrong with our nation, or we should not be in our present plight and mood. It is not like us to be on the defensive and to be fearful. That is new in our history.

The trouble is not material. We are establishing an all-time world record in the production of material things. What we lack is a righteous and dynamic faith. Without it, all else avails us little. The lack cannot be compensated for by politicians, however able; or by diplomats, however astute; or by scientists, however inventive; or by bombs, however powerful.

Once a people comes to feel dependent on material things, unfortunate consequences are inevitable.

At home, our institutions do not attract the spiritual loyalties needed for their defense. There is confusion in men's minds and corrosion of their souls. That makes our nation vulnerable to such hostile penetration as is illustrated by the spy activities so far revealed. No FBI, however efficient, can protect us under those circumstances.

Abroad, our foreign policies can be implemented only by

Chapter Twenty-one in John Foster Dulles, *War or Peace*. The Macmillan Company, 1950. Copyright, 1950, by John Foster Dulles.

money and goods. These are limited; and because they are limited, our policies are limited. Limited policies inevitably are defensive policies, and defensive policies inevitably are losing policies.

Today our military leaders define what they conceive to be strategic areas for military defense — perhaps the "North Atlantic area" as set forth in the North Atlantic Treaty. We draw a line which, like the Maginot Line, we then fortify as our defense.

Economists and budgetary experts, department heads and the Congress, calculate how much we can afford to give away in economic subsidies. The result may be, for example, $5,000,-000,000. Then we study to see where it can be spent to the best advantage, and, generally speaking, we spend it within the strategic area which the military have defined.

The result of this planning in military and economic terms is the staking out of a citadel, which we try to fortify and to provision. We have no affirmative policies beyond, for we cannot go farther with material things. Already we are straining our material resources to the limit, and we cannot greatly expand the scope of our policies if that means expanding our material expenditures. Regional policies, as expressed in the Rio Pact, the North Atlantic Pact, and the Truman Doctrine for Greece and Turkey, suggest that the Americas, Western Europe, and the Mediterranean mark the limits of our concern because they mark the limits of our immediate military and economic interests. We seem to have lost the spirit which animated Lincoln when he said of our Declaration of Independence that it gave "liberty, not alone to the people of this country, but hope for the world for all future time. It was that which gave promise that in due time the weights should be lifted from the shoulders of all men."

Up to the present, the American people have always had those qualities of the spirit that can be projected far beyond the limited reach of our material grasp. Those are the qualities that have made us great.

Our nation was founded as an experiment in human liberty. Its institutions reflected the belief of our founders that men had their origin and destiny in God; that they were endowed by him with inalienable rights and had duties prescribed by moral law, and that human institutions ought primarily to help men develop their God-given possibilities. We believed that if we built on that spiritual foundation, we should be showing men everywhere the way to a better and more abundant life.

We realized that vision. There developed here an area of spiritual, intellectual, and economic vigor the like of which the world had never seen. It was no exclusive preserve; indeed, world mission was a central theme. Millions were welcomed from other lands, to share equally the opportunities of the founders and their heirs. We put our experiment on public exhibition so that all might see and follow if they would. Through missionary activities and the establishment of schools and colleges, American ideals were carried throughout the world. We gave aid and comfort to those elsewhere who sought to follow in our way and to develop societies of greater human freedom.

That made it easy to conduct the foreign policy of the United States. In those days influence and opportunity abroad and security at home came naturally as by-products of what our people stood for in the world. Americans were welcomed everywhere because, it was judged, they were working in a common human cause. Our economic opportunities were not circumscribed by fears and jealousies such as penned in many others. We were the least militarized of any Western nation, yet, for a century, we were not endangered. No foreign ruler could have brought his people to try to destroy the "great American experiment" which they admired and the spiritual fruits of which they shared.

These conditions prevailed for one hundred years and more. Then, as our material power waxed, our spiritual power seemed to wane. We appeared to be less concerned with conducting a great experiment for the benefit of mankind and to be more concerned with piling up for ourselves material advantages. Our vision seemed to contract, and our sense of mission to lessen. Others began to think of us more as a possible source of money and material things and less as a source of inspiration and of guidance.

We have had to meet the severest test that can come to a people, the test of prosperity.

It was said by Jesus that material things will be added unto those who seek first the Kingdom of God and his righteousness. But when that happens, then comes the great trial. For, as Jesus warned, those material things can readily become the rust that corrodes men's souls.

Thus there is a familiar pattern. Men who feel a sense of duty to some higher Being strive here to do his will. Because of their faith, they have power and virtue and simple wisdom. They build not only for the day, but for the morrow; not merely for themselves, but for mankind. A society so founded will, when nature favors, produce wealth and luxury for many. When those by-products come, they seem so good that they become promoted to be the all-sufficient end. Men are drawn away from long-range creative effort. They struggle to get and to hold material things.

With that change comes ever growing danger. Americans

had security in the only way in which security can be assured, namely, as a by-product of great endeavor. When our endeavor lagged and we began to seek security as an end in itself, it more and more eluded us. It will always be that way. However rich we are, security cannot be bought at any money price. Five billions, or fifty billions, is not enough. Security and peace are not purchasable commodities. The Roman emperors in their declining days tried to buy peace, and the effort only whetted the appetites of those who sought to destroy them.

While our influence and security have been declining, those of Soviet Communism have been rising. That is not primarily due to the fact that Russia as a nation has great power, although the Red Army is a background threat. It is rather due to the fact that Soviet Communism has a creed, a creed of world-wide import. It is a creed in which the hard core of Party members believe fanatically, and which they are spreading with missionary zeal throughout the world.

There is no nook or cranny in all the world into which Communist influence does not penetrate. When the Politburo is making policies it does not say that there is no use having a policy for Guatemala or the Union of South Africa or the United States of Indonesia because they are too far away and cannot be reached either by the Red Army or by economic subsidy. Neither of these devices is the primary reliance of Soviet Communists in policy-making. They can and do implement policies with the portrayal of a "great Soviet Communist experiment" with which, during this century, they are catching the imagination of the people of the world, just as we did in the nineteenth century with our "great American experiment."

We know that that Communistic portrayal is a fraud and

a delusion. We know that Soviet Communists will not open their experiment at home to the test of free and impartial inspection. We know that those who are finally caught by the false lure of that portrayal quickly learn how different is the reality. The spider spins a beautiful web which shimmers in the sunlight, and he invites the fly into his parlor. Communist propaganda, like the spider's web, does attract. Once it has caught the people, despotism sucks them spiritually dry. But, as a prospect, Communism does have an appeal to the masses everywhere in Asia, in the islands of the Pacific, in South America, in Africa, and even in Western Europe.

The prestige of Soviet Communism in the world has been greatly increased by the fact that even in the West the Governments have adopted what, at first glance, seem to be basic parts of Soviet Communist doctrine.

Stalin said, "The strength and vitality of Marxism-Leninism lies in the fact that it does base its practical activity on the needs of the development of the material life of society."

Many non-Communist countries of the world, including indeed many "Christian" nations of the West, now seem to put primary emphasis upon developing "the material life of society" and to subordinate the spiritual development of the individual. The Communists cite that to prove that even the Western societies have had to adopt the materialistic thesis of Communism. The leaders in the West do not make any convincing denials, and the prestige of Soviet Communism in the world is greatly increased.

The difficulty is that we, ourselves, are unclear as to our faith and the relationship of that faith to our practices.

We can talk eloquently about liberty and freedom, and about human rights and fundamental freedoms, and about the dignity and worth of the human personality; but most of our vocabulary derives from a period when our own society was individualistic. Consequently, it has little meaning to those who live under conditions where individualism means premature death.

Also, we can talk eloquently about the material successes we have achieved, about the marvels of mass production, and about the number of automobiles, radios, and telephones owned by our people. That materialistic emphasis makes some feel that we are spiritually bankrupt. It makes others envious and more disposed to accept Communist glorification of "mass" effort to "develop the material life of society."

We are in a dilemma, and it is a grave dilemma. Because we have not resolved it, our spiritual influence in the world has waned, and we are tied down to the area that we can reach and influence by material things — guns and goods. That is why it is possible for our encirclement to proceed apace.

We cannot successfully combat Soviet Communism in the world and frustrate its methods of fraud, terrorism, and violence unless we have a faith with spiritual appeal that translates itself into practices which, in our modern, complex society, get rid of the sordid, degrading conditions of life in which the spirit cannot grow.

We are still unsure in our own minds where to look for solid ground between individualism and materialism. Our faith lacks the power and clear definition that would make it contagious in the world.

The religious faith of our founders emphasized individualism because the original environment called for personal resourcefulness and pioneering. Individual effort was the best way to get the satisfaction which comes from a sense of being creative. Also, individual creativeness was usually the means whereby society as a whole was most enriched.

But extreme individualism is no integral part of our religious heritage. The Jewish and Christian faiths have at all times emphasized the duty of man to his fellows; and that duty is fundamental in our religious faith. The moral law, the law of the prophets, is sublimely compressed into the two injunctions "Thou shalt love the Lord thy God" and "Thou shalt love thy neighbor as thyself."

There is an essential difference between a spiritual society and a materialistic society. The difference is not that the spiritual society is purely individualistic while the materialistic society is purely collectivist. It is not that the free society ignores material welfare while the materialistic society makes material welfare primary. The difference is that the spiritual society seeks material welfare by relying on and developing the individual's sense of duty to his fellow man and his willingness to exercise self-control and self-restraint in the discharge of that duty. The materialistic, irreligious society, which denies the existence of God or of a moral law, cannot depend upon love of God and love of neighbor. It must depend on governmental compulsion rather than on voluntary controls.

We have failed lamentably to see that we can get social justice without practicing atheism and materialism. It depends upon the willingness of the individual voluntarily to accept and discharge social obligations to his fellow man.

Because we have not seen that, many of our people have lost faith in a society of freedom. As a nation, although still religious, we have lost the connection between our religious faith and our practices. We keep religion and practices in separate compartments. We no longer see that our faith is relevant to modern conditions.

Once the connection between faith and works is broken, we can no longer generate a spiritual power that will flow throughout the world. The "conduct and example" of which our founders wrote are no longer a beacon light to those who live in the deep shadows cast by a mighty despotism. We have no message to send to the captive peoples to keep their hope and faith alive.

We must change all that. We can, and must, reject totally the Marxian thesis that material things are primary and spiritual things only secondary. Slavery and despotism, even if they seem expedient, can never be right. We must not be afraid to recapture faith in the primacy of human liberty and freedom, and to hold to the religious view that man is destined by God to be more than a material producer, and that his chief end is something more than physical security. We must believe that men everywhere ought to be released from the spiritual, intellectual, economic, and political strait jackets into which they are increasingly being put on the theory that this will improve the material welfare of the social group to which they belong.

Equally, we must clearly see that a society of freedom is not a society of un-co-ordinated self-seeking individuals. It is a society that is co-ordinated. But the bonds are primarily the bonds of fellowship which derive from belief that men are destined to be brothers through the Fatherhood of God, that each man is his brother's keeper, and that we should love our neighbors as ourselves.

That belief translates itself into a society of individuals who love God and their fellow man, and who fear only God and not any man; who work hard as a matter of duty and self-satisfaction, not compulsion; who gain personal and family security primarily through ability and willingness voluntarily to earn and save; who are self-reliant, resourceful, and adaptable to changing conditions, and for whom life is not merely physical growth and enjoyment, but intellectual and spiritual development. It also translates itself into public organizations, through which men willingly co-operate, at national and local levels, to do what they cannot well do otherwise.

But governmental authority at all times and places is limited by the principle that governmental action expresses, but does not replace, voluntary acceptance of social responsibility. Government action must stop short of seeming to shift social responsibility from the individual to the government.

That limitation on governmental power makes some imperfections inevitable. The existence of imperfections does not prove that the system is wrong, and it need not make us feel ashamed or defeated. In a sense, the existence of flaws proves that the system is right. Human nature at best is imperfect, and any system which is based on human nature is bound to have defects. The only system that is theoretically flawless is one of absolute despotism, "unlimited power, based on force and not on law" (Stalin). Then, in theory, all disharmonies, all imperfections can be removed, all grit can quickly be cleaned out, and perfect mechanical harmony can result. However, the attempt to do that creates moral enormities. That is always the case when men indulge in the conceit that they can do better than God.

Our greatest need is to regain confidence in our spiritual heritage. Religious belief in the moral nature and possibilities of man is, and must be, relevant to every kind of society, throughout the ages past and those to come. It is relevant to the complex conditions of modern society. We need to see that, if we are to combat successfully the methods and practices of a materialistic belief.

There is no use having more and louder Voices of America unless we have something to say that is more persuasive than anything that has yet been said.

To find that message is, above all, a task for the spiritual leaders of our nation. In finding it they can contribute, and contribute decisively, to the peaceful frustration of the evil methods and designs of Soviet Communism.

Many preachers and educators bemoan the fact that scientific knowledge has greatly advanced man's capacity to do harm. We must not believe that new knowledge is, of itself, something to be shunned. Great material power is dangerous in an age of materialism. It is not dangerous in an age of spiritualism. New scientific knowledge is dangerous today because it comes at a time when spiritual leadership has failed to make clear the connection between belief and practice. It is more important to advance the spiritual clock than to try to stop or set back the scientific clock.

President Wilson, in an article written a few weeks before he died, reviewed the threat of the revolutionary doctrines and practices of Communism. He concluded: "The sum of the whole matter is this, that our civilization cannot survive materially unless it be redeemed spiritually. . . . Here is the final challenge to our churches, to our political organizations, and to our capitalists — to everyone who fears God or loves his country."

10

Morals and Power

S INCE I have been Secretary of State, I have been to Europe, the Near East, and South Asia. Before that, in connection with negotiating the Japanese peace treaty, I had an excellent chance to get a firsthand look at our foreign representatives in Japan, Korea, and other parts of the Far East.

One of the things that most impressed me in these areas was the down-to-earth co-operation which existed between our civilian and military officials. . . .

◇◇◇◇

It is teamwork between the military and civilian which has given us the necessary strength whenever and wherever we have needed it.

I should like to talk for a few minutes about power in a material sense, such as is represented by our splendid military establishment. What is the purpose of this power? Admiral Mahan is credited with one of the best answers to this question. It is that the role of power is to give moral ideas the time to take root. Where moral ideas already are well rooted, there is little occasion for much military or police force. We see that

Address at the graduation exercises of the National War College, June 16, 1953.

illustrated in our own communities. Where the people accept the moral law and its great commandments, where they exercise self-control and self-discipline, then there is very little need for police power. Under these circumstances, it is sufficient to have a very modest force to take care of the small minority, always found in every community, which disregards the precepts of the moral law.

Where, however, there are many who do not accept moral principles, then that creates the need of force to protect those who do. That, unfortunately, is the case in the world community of today.

At the present time, there is no moral code which has worldwide acceptance. The principles upon which our society is based — the principles which we believe to be both humanitarian and just — are not accepted by governments which dominate more than one third of mankind.

The result is that we have a world which is, for the most part, split between two huge combinations. On the one hand, there is the United States and its free-world associates. This is a voluntary alliance of free peoples working together in the recognition that without unity there could be catastrophe.

On the other hand, there is the totalitarian bloc led by the Soviet Union — an artificial, imposed unity which cannot be called an alliance in the sense that we use the word.

These huge concentrations are in conflict because each reflects differing aims, aspirations, and social, political, and economic philosophies. We must assume that they will continue to remain in basic conflict, in one way or another, until such time as the Communists so change their nature as to admit that those who wish to live by the moral law are free to do so without coercion by those who believe in enforced conformity to a materialistic standard.

This is one of the hard facts of international existence which we must accept. We cannot close our eyes to it. It will not go away simply because we hope that it will do so.

We must plan accordingly. . . .

◇◇◇◇

What makes the Soviet Union — the fountain-head of world communism — act as it does? Why do the Soviets seek power and more power?

These complex questions are not simply answered. There are many forces which motivate the Soviet drive for power. Among those forces are these which I should like to mention: ideology, the historic imperialistic urge, and the chronic insecurity complex which besets those who rule by force.

◇◇◇◇

This picture which I have given of the international situation is not a pleasing one. It does not hold out the prospect of any quick change for the better or any early elimination of our need for power in order to permit moral principles to take root rather than be uprooted.

However, if we do maintain power, and if we do subject it to moral law and use it truly to enable moral principles to survive, and thrive, and spread in the world, we can have hope in the future. For we know that in the long run the fruits of a spiritual faith prevail over the fruits of materialism.

The great weakness of Soviet Communist doctrine is that it denies morality. That is its Achilles heel, of which we must take advantage. We can take advantage of it if — but only if — we ourselves accept the supremacy of moral law.

Our nation was founded by men who believed that there was a divine Creator who endowed men with inalienable rights. They believed, as George Washington put it in his Farewell Address, that religion and morality are the great pillars of human happiness and that morality cannot prevail in exclusion of religious principles.

Our Federal and State Constitutions, our laws and practices, reflect the belief that there is a Being superior to ourselves who has established his own laws which can be comprehended by all human beings and that human practices should seek conformity with those laws.

Seeking first the Kingdom of God and his righteousness, many material things were added to us. We developed here an area of spiritual, intellectual, and material richness, the like of which the world has never seen. What we did caught the imagination of men everywhere and became known everywhere as the "great American experiment." Our free society became a menace to every despot because we showed how to meet the hunger of the people for greater opportunity and for greater dignity. The tide of despotism, which at that time ran high, was rolled back and we ourselves enjoyed security.

We need to recapture that mood.

Today some seem to feel that Americanism means being tough and "hard-boiled," doing nothing unless we are quite sure that it is to our immediate short-term advantage, boasting of our own merit and seeing in others only demerit.

That is a caricature of America. Our people have always been generous to help, out of their abundance, those who are the victims of misfortune. Our forebears have traditionally had what the Declaration of Independence refers to as a decent respect for the opinion of mankind. They sought to practice the golden rule by doing to others as they would have others do unto them. Their conduct and example made our nation one that was respected and admired throughout the world.

So, in conclusion, I say to you who graduate from the National War College: Be proud of your association with U.S.

power, which is indispensable in the world today; but remember that that power is worthy only as it is the shield behind which moral values are invigorated and spread their influence; and accept, as citizens, the obligation to preserve and enhance those moral values. They are the rich heritage that has been bequeathed us. It must be our ambition that future generations shall look back upon us, as we look back upon those who preceded us, with gratitude for the gift to our republic of the qualities that make it noble, so that men call it blessed.

III

The Spiritual Foundations
of World Order

As we have noted, at the Oxford Conference on "Church, Community, and State" in July, 1937, Mr. Dulles' estimate of the influence that the churches might exert in the furtherance of peace and world order underwent a radical reversal. His previous attitude of skepticism and aloofness gave way to admiration and hopefulness. From then on, he joined actively in Christian concern with international issues.

He participated in an International Conference of Lay Experts and Ecumenical Leaders convened by the Provisional Committee of the World Council of Churches in Geneva in August, 1939, on the very eve of World War II. His mind and pen are evident in its notable Memorandum, which sought less to forestall a conflict that, by then, was clearly inescapable than to define the relations that should be maintained between Christians in nations at war and to outline some of the principles that should determine the eventual peace.

When war finally broke, he gave prodigally of time and energy to attempt to stir and inform the consciences of churchmen and, through them, of the American people on the character of the peace that should follow. In 1940, a Commission to Study the Bases of a Just and Durable Peace was formed under Mr. Dulles' chairmanship. Its purposes were set forth in his Foreword to one of its earliest publications:

"The American people face grave alternatives. Shall we continue to be a people without a faith, contenting ourselves with ceaseless and exhausting combat against alien faiths? Or will we develop a faith of our own? If so, *will that faith be a righteous faith or an evil faith?*

"Upon the answers to these questions will depend the kind of world in which we and our children will live.

"This book has been written as part of the effort of our Commission to assure a faith that will be righteous and that, because it is righteous, can be shared by other peoples and lead to just and durable peace.

"We realize that to achieve a righteous faith calls for spiritual leadership of increased intensity. It is our hope that some of the thoughts here expressed will produce that leadership. None are too humble to achieve it. That is one of our objectives. Our other purpose is to assure a general level of thinking that will make easier the task of Christian leadership and which will make it impossible for evil faiths to take root among us. That calls for education. All who take part in it will help to shape our destiny."

From that time until he was called to Washington as adviser to President Roosevelt's Administration in 1945, a very considerable proportion of Mr. Dulles' effort was channeled through this Commission. Under his guidance, it issued a series of documents and proposals that received wide attention and exerted marked influence. It sponsored and organized consultations and conferences, in which he was often a leader. Although its statements seldom bore his name, his was always the major hand in their authorship, and, since they were commended by him as Chairman, they may be recognized as expressing his views. One is included in this collection of his writings. His own extensive speaking, whether before church or secular gatherings, reiterated his convictions on the moral and spiritual prerequisites for world order.

After 1945 he was able to give less constant attention to the Commission's work, but he continued to maintain close contact. In the summer of 1947 he went to Cambridge, England, to preside over the international meeting that created the Commission of the Churches on International Affairs, of which he was Vice-Chairman. In the postwar period, he continued to set forth substantially the same principles essential to a "just and durable peace."

11

The Need for a Righteous Faith

THIS paper forms part of an effort by the churches to assure peace which will be just and durable. Many question the timing of our effort. They urge that our thoughts should be of nothing beyond military victory and our emotions only those hot ones which, they conceive, best feed the flames of war.

The challenge is one that must be met. I do not doubt that it can be met, for what we seek for the American people is nothing that will prove a weakness. Rather, we seek that strength which is to be found only in the propulsion of a deep faith and sense of high mission in the world. I assert that:

1. It is our lack of impelling faith that has weakened us and encouraged the development elsewhere of the evils which now imperil us;

2. The primitive emotions, such as anger, hatred, and vengefulness, are no substitutes for the faith that makes men strong. Such emotions are false stimulants which weaken men by burning out their moral fiber;

3. The goals which can inspire us to great endeavor are to

Opening chapter in the pamphlet *A Righteous Faith for a Just and Durable Peace,* published by the Commission of the Churches on a Just and Durable Peace, October, 1942.

be found by having and using the qualities which Christ taught. We need visions that see clear, minds that think straight, and hearts that are comprehending. If, then, we act under such directives, there will be rekindled in us a sense of creative purpose that will make us strong.

During the period of one hundred and twenty-five years which preceded the First World War, the French, the British, and the American nations were imbued with and radiated great faiths. These were partly good and partly bad, but at least they served to make these nations the three great powers of the world. The spirit of the French Revolution, with its slogan of "Liberty, Equality, and Fraternity," changed the face of the Western world. It inspired the birth of democratic processes and it created widespread admiration and sympathy for France. In England, the Industrial Revolution opened up a new economic era. Its consequences were carried into the uttermost parts of the earth through an imperial policy sought to be given moral sanction as a carrying of the "white man's burden." Hundreds of millions of people became politically and economically related to Britain, and, by and large, their material and social status was thereby greatly improved. We, in the United States, became conscious of a "manifest destiny" under the impulse of which we opened up a vast continent. We, too, sometimes used reprehensible methods, but we fashioned here a new freedom for millions of repressed persons from other lands. Another faith which burned bright in Britain and the United States was a religious faith. It found expression in missionary efforts which profoundly influenced the moral fabric of much of the world. Wherever trading posts sprang up, there, too, was a mission post. Thus we balanced the materialistic motives which dominated much of economic penetration.

The close of the First World War seems to have marked an exhaustion of our spiritual springs. The French, the British, and ourselves emerged as burnt-out peoples. In the United States, there was a quick descent from the lofty motives that had made so notable a contribution to victory. In all three countries postwar efforts were concentrated upon searching for "security." We had nothing to give. We had no fire to impart. Those few in Germany and Japan who sought after the war to carry there the torch of democracy received no help from us. We wanted merely to be left alone, and in our isolated and, as we thought, "matured" economies, we found little to do except to squabble over the partition of the material wealth we had theretofore created. Upon the world there descended a spirit of disillusionment and discouragement. The youth were without opportunity or hope, the workers were without employment, and the aged were without security. All were without faith.

It is, of course, impossible to perpetuate a spiritual vacuum. So it inevitably came about that here and there, throughout the world, new faiths were born. . . . These faiths were largely repugnant to us. . . . But, good or bad, they were faiths for which men were eager to sacrifice and, if need be, die. We have been startled by what those nations have performed.

From all this I deduce that we, too, need a faith, a faith that will make us strong, a faith so profound that we, too, will feel that we have a mission to spread it through the world. Today we have it not. The American people believe in nothing with conviction. We are cynical and disillusioned. Even our war effort we look upon primarily as one of resistance, not of accomplishment; and victory as being that which will assure our being left alone.

Such a spiritual state is conducive neither to a military victory nor, when victory is won, to subsequent peace. For again new faiths will arise to attack us, and in the long run we will succumb. The impact of the dynamic upon the static — while it may be resisted in detail — will ultimately destroy that which it attacks. The First World War, this World War, and the next world war will go down in history as a series of rear-guard actions by disillusioned peoples who, equipped only with the material products of past greatness, sought valiantly but vainly to resist the penetration of alien faiths.

At this critical period in our national life we are told that we should not waste time in seeking to arouse in the American people a sense of great purpose in the world. It is best, they say, that we think only of military victory and that we seek to promote it by generating anger, hatred, vengefulness, and self-righteousness.

There are, of course, those who must concentrate upon the immediate prosecution of the war. That is peculiarly true of our combat and production task forces. But the vast remainder of us are, too, a task force, our task being to dedicate our nation to long-range purposes of human welfare. Thereby alone can we compensate the sacrifices that war will exact. Thereby alone can we give the youth who must die the sense of accomplishing more than the gallant performance of cold duty. Thereby alone can we assure that out of this war will be born an impetus that will carry through victory into an era of creative peace.

Christians, if they be true, must seek to discharge this task, whatever the world may say. For Christ's whole ministry taught the subordinate role of immediate material objectives. He sought to inculcate in men a spiritual power which would turn earthly events, whether labeled "victory" or "defeat," into an increased doing of God's will on earth.

I recall that Christ ministered at a time when international and social problems existed in aggravated form. The relations of the nations were determined by force, and much of the world lived under the heel of a military dictator. Slavery was a generally accepted institution. In the face of that situation Christ did not devote himself to achieving specific reforms. The reason surely was not indifference to the evils and human misery that surrounded him. Must it not have been that to have effected such reforms in the social structure of his time would have been of but passing value? He sought rather to show men how, throughout the ages, they might find the way to surmount evil, which could constantly be reappearing in ever-changing form. That way, he taught, was for men to act out of visions that would see clear, minds that would think straight, and hearts that would comprehend the essential unity and equal worthiness of all human beings. He inveighed against hatred and vengefulness, self-conceit and deification of one's particular nation, race, or class. He did so not only because such emotions are repugnant to God's will for man, but also because they always make men incompetent to deal with human problems. They create those blind masses and those blind leaders who, he pointed out, end up together in the pit.

Because many are afraid to trust Christ, I cite the example of temporal leaders acting in their political capacities.

Of what did the greatness of Lincoln consist? It was that he rejected hatred and vengefulness as the stimulant of war effort. He pleaded that there be malice toward none, and found in great moral and political truths the armor of righteousness. I cite, also, the contemporary example of Mr. Roosevelt and Mr. Churchill. When they met on the Atlantic they sought to use that dramatic occasion to advance to the utmost the cause to which their nations were committed. What was the way they elected? It was to compose and to proclaim the Atlantic Charter. Thereby they sought to achieve that moral leadership which they recognized as an essential ingredient of victory.

The Atlantic Charter was no hysterical call for victory as an end in itself. There is not in it a word which evokes hatred, vengefulness, and the deification of our own nations. It portrays, calmly, the better world we seek. And that world is one of greater opportunity for all men everywhere, victor and vanquished alike.

I cite, finally, the example of the Axis Powers. To the extent that they were propelled by a sense of constructive achievement, their peoples were unified and made strong. But because their faiths were shot through with evil, evil men readily came to leadership, and these have increasingly invoked hatred, vengefulness, cruelty, and lust. Thereby the moral strength of their peoples has deteriorated, resistance has constantly mounted, their victories have proved illusory, and ultimate failure is inevitable.

We can, therefore, be confident that in following Christ we are not jeopardizing the welfare of our nation. The stimulation that comes from hatred and vengefulness is like the stimulation produced by drugs and alcohol. There is created, to be sure, a sense of fervor. But that sense is false. Actually such emotions make neither for competence nor for sustained power. They confuse the thinking, blur the vision, and burn out the souls of those who rely upon them. They arouse, in others, a resistance which makes victory more difficult to achieve, and renders it illusory if, finally, it be achieved. Such emotions are no substitute, either in war or peace, for a sense of identification with some great creative purpose.

How are we to achieve a sense of mission and of great purpose? Our answer is: by action based upon seeing, understanding, and thinking. We urge that men clarify their vision so that they may see truly the world in which they live; that they purify their spirits so that they may be comprehending; that they free their minds of paralyzing emotions so that they may be competent. We then ask for action. Out of action directed by such qualities of vision, of soul, of mind, will be born the faith that will make us strong.

1. If we have vision, what is it we shall see? We shall, like Christ, see a multitude who hunger. That multitude is all about us — some near, some afar. They hunger not only for things material but for things spiritual. We would not be seeing truly if we saw only material wants. Such needs exist and they are great. But the greatest need is not for things. Men hunger for sympathy and fellowship and hope. They want education and the possibility of mental pursuits which will lift them out of their physical environment. They crave the vibrant thrill which comes from creative effort. They need a religious faith which will carry them through tribulations which no material wealth can prevent.

Christ saw and taught that material things served chiefly as vehicles for bringing into being those nonmaterial values that men need most. When he told the rich young man to give all to the poor, he saw, not so much the material advantage for the poor as the value of the spiritual outlook that would prompt such an act. By similar standards he appraised the widow's gift of her mites and Mary's sacrifice of her precious ointment.

So it is that as our eyes are opened we will see material

needs, but we will see them in subordinate relationship to
spiritual needs.

2. If we have hearts that are comprehending, we shall,
like Christ, be moved with compassion. We shall hear the
cry of the masses that a way be found to save them and their
children from the death, the misery, the starvation of body
and soul which recurrent war and economic disorder now
wreak upon man. We shall be so moved by that cry that we
shall resolutely dedicate ourselves to the achievement of a
better order. We shall find, in that dedication, something that
will make our own lives worth living and our own nation
worth preserving.

3. If we have minds that function, we shall find ways to
advance our purpose and to assure that we, and others, may
have life and have it more abundantly. The broad principles
that should govern our international conduct are not obscure.
They grow out of the practice by the nations of the simple
things Christ taught. . . . Such principles mark the channels
into which our minds must direct our international acts if
they are to be productive of permanent good.

We have already, in politics, learned much of how to organize large units of society so that those within them will
live at peace with each other. We have not thought out, however, how to carry such principles forward into the international field. We have already, in economics, learned how to
create tools and harness natural forces, so that today the effort
of a human being can be multiplied one hundredfold. There
is no lack of the natural bounty with which God endowed
the earth. There is no technical or material obstacle to achieving a constantly expanding measure of both production and
consumption. We still have not learned, however, how to
construct an economic machine which will not blight those

spiritual values which man needs most.

To create political organs of international operation, to make economics our servant, not our master, calls for minds that function free of the paralyzing emotions that Christ condemned.

4. Finally, we must act. Christ did not teach a purely contemplative religion — "Let your light so shine before men, that they may see your good works." We must not feel impotent until there has been developed some great and all-inclusive pattern of a perfected world order. The essential is to develop in ourselves a sense of creative power and purpose. That can be achieved out of a series of acts which, of themselves, may be nonspectacular. If such acts are born out of clear vision, human comprehension, and intelligence, we will be surprised by the fruitful consequences of what we thus do. Inspired and propelled by those consequences, we will steadily move forward, enlarging the practical expression of our faith and developing for it a defined and expanding pattern. The Delaware Conference noted, as illustrating the type of international action which should even now be begun, certain proposals of our Government designed to effectuate the "good neighbor" policy and to work out the obligations of allied nations under "lend lease." Those pronouncements, if translated into reality, seemed to us to be national acts of enlightened self-interest of the kind that might start us in ways of creative purpose. Even in the midst of war there exist ample opportunities for action which will rekindle a sense of power to accomplish a great mission in the world. As our national faith thus grows and is made manifest by works, its influence will be contagious throughout the world. As the evil faiths that combat us collapse, leaving death and ruin as their fruit, the faith that makes us strong will encompass the earth. It will unite men, as

never before, in common and constructive purpose.

This war is often called a war of survival. We must make it more than that, for survival, of itself, is a barren thing. Let us conceive of this war as a war for opportunity, for the chance to become a positive force for human betterment. Only thus will we be infused with spiritual power that will make us strong, whether for victory or for peace. It is that strength — not a weakness — that we seek.

12

Moral and Spiritual Bases for a Just and Lasting Peace

As MEMBERS of the Christian church, we seek to view all problems of world order in the light of the truth concerning God, man, and God's purpose for the world made known in Jesus Christ. We believe that the eternal God revealed in Christ is the Ruler of men and of nations and that his purpose in history will be realized. For us he is the source of moral law and the power to make it effective.

From this faith Christians derive the ethical principles upon which world order must be based. These principles, however, seem to us to be among those which men of good will everywhere may be expected to recognize as part of the moral law. In this we rejoice. For peace will require the co-operation of men of all nations, races, and creeds. We have therefore first set out (Points 1 to 9) those guiding principles which, it seems to us, Christians and non-Christians alike can accept.

We believe that a special responsibility rests upon the people of the United States. We accordingly (Point 10) express our thoughts in that regard.

Above all, we are impressed by the supreme responsibility

Adopted by the Federal Council of the Churches of Christ in America, December, 1942.

which rests upon Christians. Moral law may point the way
to peace, but Christ, we believe, showed that way with greatest
clarity. We therefore, in conclusion (Points 11 and 12), address ourselves to Christians.

GUIDING PRINCIPLES

1

WE BELIEVE that moral law, no less than physical law, undergirds our world. There is a moral order which is fundamental and eternal, and which is relevant to the corporate
life of men and the ordering of human society. If mankind
is to escape chaos and recurrent war, social and political
institutions must be brought into conformity with this
moral order.

2

WE BELIEVE that the sickness and suffering which afflict our
present society are proof of indifference to, as well as direct
violation of, the moral law. All share in responsibility for
the present evils. There is none who does not need forgiveness. A mood of genuine penitence is therefore demanded of us — individuals and nations alike.

3

WE BELIEVE that it is contrary to the moral order that nations
in their dealings with one another should be motivated by
a spirit of revenge and retaliation. Such attitudes will lead,
as they always have led, to renewed conflict.

4

WE BELIEVE that the principle of co-operation and mutual
concern, implicit in the moral order and essential to a just
and durable peace, calls for a true community of nations.
The interdependent life of nations must be ordered by
agencies having the duty and the power to promote and

safeguard the general welfare of all peoples. Only thus can wrongs be righted and justice and security be achieved. A world of irresponsible, competing, and unrestrained national sovereignties, whether acting alone or in alliance or in coalition, is a world of international anarchy. It must make place for a higher and more inclusive authority.

5

WE BELIEVE that economic security is no less essential than political security to a just and durable peace. Such security nationally and internationally involves among other things the use of material resources and the tools of production to raise the general standard of living. Nations are not economically self-sufficient, and the natural wealth of the world is not evenly distributed. Accordingly, the possession of such natural resources should not be looked upon as an opportunity to promote national advantage or to enhance the prosperity of some at the expense of others. Rather, such possession is a trust to be discharged in the general interest. This calls for more than an offer to sell to all on equal terms. Such an offer may be a futile gesture unless those in need can, through the selling of their own goods and services, acquire the means of buying. The solution of this problem, doubtless involving some international organization, must be accepted as a responsibility by those who possess natural resources needed by others.

6

WE BELIEVE that international machinery is required to facilitate the easing of such economic and political tensions as are inevitably recurrent in a world which is living and therefore changing. Any attempt to freeze an order of society by inflexible treaty specifications is bound, in the long run, to jeopardize the peace of mankind. Nor must it be forgotten that refusal to assent to needed change may be as immoral as the attempt by violent means to force such change.

7

WE BELIEVE that that government which derives its just powers from the consent of the governed is the truest expression of the rights and dignity of man. This requires that we seek autonomy for all subject and colonial peoples. Until that shall be realized, the task of colonial government is no longer one of exclusive national concern. It must be recognized as a common responsibility of mankind, to be carried out in the interests of the colonial peoples by the most appropriate form of organization. This would, in many cases, make colonial government a task of international collaboration for the benefit of colonial peoples who would, themselves, have a voice in their government. As the agencies for the promotion of world-wide and economic security become effective, the moral, social and material welfare of colonial populations can be more fully realized.

8

WE BELIEVE that military establishments should be internationally controlled and be made subject to law under the community of nations. For one or more nations to be forcibly deprived of their arms while other nations retain the right of maintaining or expanding their military establishments can only produce an uneasy peace for a limited period. Any initial arrangement which falls short of this must therefore be looked upon as temporary and provisional.

9

WE BELIEVE that the right of all men to pursue work of their own choosing and to enjoy security from want and oppression is not limited by race, color, or creed. The rights and liberties of racial and religious minorities in all lands should be recognized and safeguarded. Freedom of religious worship, of speech and assembly, of the press, and of scientific inquiry and teaching are fundamental to human development and in keeping with the moral order.

10

WE BELIEVE that, in bringing international relations into conformity with the moral law, a very heavy responsibility devolves upon the United States. For at least a generation we have held preponderant economic power in the world, and with it the capacity to influence decisively the shaping of world events. It should be a matter of shame and humiliation to us that actually the influences shaping the world have largely been irresponsible forces. Our own positive influence has been impaired because of concentration on self and on our short-range material gains. Many of the major preconditions of a just and durable peace require changes of national policy on the part of the United States. Among such may be mentioned: equal access to natural resources, economic collaboration, equitable treatment of racial minorities, international control of tariffs, limitation of armaments, participation in world government. We must be ready to subordinate immediate and particular national interests to the welfare of all. If the future is to be other than a repetition of the past, the United States must accept the responsibility for constructive action commensurate with its power and opportunity.

11

WE BELIEVE that, as Christian citizens, we must seek to translate our beliefs into practical realities and to create a public opinion which will insure that the United States shall play its full and essential part in the creation of a moral way of international living. We must strive within the life of our own nation for change which will result in the more adequate application here of the principles above enumerated as the basis for a just and durable world order.

12

WE BELIEVE that a supreme responsibility rests with the church. The church, being a creation of God in Jesus Christ, is called to proclaim to all men everywhere the way of life. Moreover, the church, which is now in reality a world community, may be used of God to develop his spirit of righteousness and love in every race and nation and thus to make possible a just and durable peace. For this service Christians must now dedicate themselves, seeking forgiveness for their sins and the constant guidance and help of God, upheld by faith that the kingdoms of this world shall become the Kingdom of Christ and that he shall reign forever and ever.

STATEMENT OF POLITICAL PROPOSITIONS

Introductory Statement by the Commission

It seems to have been reserved to the people of this country, by their conduct and example, to decide whether societies of men are really capable or not of establishing good government from reflection and choice, or whether they are forever destined to depend for their political constitutions on accident and force. The crisis at which we are arrived may be regarded as the era in which that decision is to be made, and a wrong election of the part we shall act may deserve to be considered as the general misfortune of mankind.
                                        —THE FEDERALIST, 1787.

The American people again find themselves in an era of critical decision. It must now be determined, this time in world-wide terms, whether men are capable of establishing good government from reflection and choice, or whether they will continue to be buffeted about by force and by accident. Now, as before, it is reserved to the people of this country to play a decisive role. Now, more than ever, a wrong choice of the part we shall act will involve us in the general misfortune of mankind.

In anticipation of this critical period, the Federal Council of Churches, over two years ago, set up this Commission to Study the Bases of a Just and Durable Peace. We have diligently pursued that study. We have seen and said that the ills which afflict our society are fundamentally due to nonconformity with a moral order, the laws of which are as imperative

---

Issued by the Commission to Study the Bases of a Just and Durable Peace, March, 1943.

and as inexorable as are those that order our physical world. Indifference to and violation of these moral laws always bring such sickness and suffering as today afflict mankind. We have, in a Statement of Guiding Principles, set down certain principles of that moral order as being particularly relevant to our times and to our national responsibility and opportunity. That Statement has been officially endorsed by the Federal Council of Churches, and the widespread response which it has evoked from Christian people makes it clear that they predominantly hold the beliefs therein set forth.

Many now ask, What shall we do?

The first and paramount task of the Christian churches remains that of bringing more persons to subject their lives to the will of God as revealed in Jesus Christ. For us he is the source of the moral law of which we speak. He is the source of moral judgments on the issues of this war upon which the Federal Council of Churches has also spoken. Only if the Christian churches of this land build a spiritual foundation that is broad and deep, will this nation pursue righteous policies. Only if spiritual revelation strike from our eyes the scales of hatred, hypocrisy, intolerance, and greed, will we be competent to cope with the immensely difficult problems that confront us.

But there is a secondary task to which our Commission can now properly address itself. That is to point out that the Guiding Principles we have proclaimed compel certain broad political conclusions. We do that now because the course of events is such that a time for action is at hand.

Military peril has dramatized, for all to see, the need for international co-operation. But as military victory becomes more certain and draws more near, that need will be less obvious. As we come to grips with the appalling moral, social, and material aftermaths of Axis rule, transitory issues will arise to perplex and divide the United Nations. These may loom large and obscure the fundamentals and incline us to relapse into reliance only upon our own strength. Thus, if our nation does not make the right choice soon, it may never be made in our time.

We have, accordingly, now formulated and we present herewith a Statement of Political Propositions that flow from the moral principles we have heretofore enunciated.

We have stated our Propositions in simple and minimum terms. We recognize that as so stated there is much latitude as to their form and detailed content and as to the timing of their full realization. These matters are important, and their determination will involve much honest difference of opinion which, ultimately, must be reconciled. But the Propositions, as stated by us, serve to force the initial and vital decision on the direction in which this nation will move. They force that decision in relation to six major areas within which the factual interdependence of the world has become such as to require political mechanism for co-operative action. If the six Propositions we enunciate become an official program of this nation, we will be committed to move, by definite steps, to bring ourselves into an ordered relationship with others. Only if the nations join to do this, can we escape chaos and recurrent war. Only if the United States assumes a leadership, can it be done now. For we, more than any other nation, have the capacity to influence decisively the shaping of world events. . . .

◇◇◇◇

The many who believe the things we believe and who desire, as citizens, to do something about it, have here a field for action.

—John Foster Dulles, *Chairman*

POLITICAL PROPOSITIONS

I

The peace must provide the political framework for a continuing collaboration of the United Nations and, in due course, of neutral and enemy nations.

II

The peace must make provision for bringing within the scope of international agreement those economic and financial acts of national governments which have widespread international repercussions.

III

The peace must make provision for an organization to adapt the treaty structure of the world to changing underlying conditions.

IV

The peace must proclaim the goal of autonomy for subject peoples, and it must establish international organization to assure and to supervise the realization of that end.

V

The peace must establish procedures for controlling military establishments everywhere.

VI

The peace must establish in principle, and seek to achieve in practice, the right of individuals everywhere to religious and intellectual liberty.

13

World Brotherhood Through the State

Iᴛ ɪs not easy these days to talk about the brotherhood of nations. It would have been easier a year or two ago. Then there was a brotherhood in arms. Now that brotherhood has given way to strain and tension.

War coalitions usually fall apart when they have destroyed the common peril. This time, however, what is happening is more than that. We seem to be witnessing a challenge to established civilization — the kind of thing which occurs only once in centuries.

In the tenth century after Christ the so-called Christian world was challenged by an alien faith. The tide of Islam flowed from Arabia and swept over much of Christendom. It was not primarily a military thrust. Rather, it was a social challenge. H. G. Wells said of it: "Islam prevailed because it was the best social and political order the times could offer. It prevailed because everywhere it found politically apathetic peoples and selfish and unsound governments, out of touch with any people at all. . . . It offered better terms than any other to the mass of mankind."

Address under the auspices of The Brotherhood of St. Andrew, Convention Hall, Philadelphia, Sunday, September 8, 1946.

Now another ten centuries have rolled by, and the accumulated civilization of those centuries is faced with another challenge. This time the challenger is Soviet Communism.

The faith and institutions of Soviet Communism differ vastly from those of the Western democracies. The official creed of the Party is an abstruse materialism. The form of government is dictatorship. The economic life is an extreme form of state socialism. The official methods are ruthless and intolerant. The spirit is revolutionary. The scope of its effort is universal.

Soviet leaders consider, as Islam considered, that the Governments of the outer world are selfish and unsound and out of touch with the people. They believe that they can offer better terms than any others to the mass of mankind. They proclaim to seven hundred and fifty million dependent people their right to be independent, and publicly and secretly they encourage revolutionary efforts to throw off the yoke of what they call Western imperialism. By intensive Spanish and Portuguese language propaganda in Latin America they prod the peoples there, upwards of one hundred million, to arise from political apathy and to take power — as Communists. Through Chinese Communists they hold out to four hundred million Chinese the promise of change from corruption and incompetence which have become traditional in some circles of Chinese officialdom. To the three hundred and fifty million of Continental Europeans, economically wrecked by two world wars, they offer a plan which, they promise, will sustain productivity more surely than an individualistic economy.

Thus the Soviet Communist Party challenges the supremacy of the so-called Christian world. Controlling at home 10 per cent of the human race, it offers leadership to a further 75 per cent, constituting the overwhelming majority of Europe,

Asia, Africa, and South America. That challenge has had an initial success. In every part of the world there are influential groups which accept leadership from Moscow.

To many, this is dismaying. It ought to dismay us to discover that the Western democracies, after ten centuries of unchallenged economic and military supremacy in the world, have so slight a spiritual hold on the masses of mankind that they eagerly listen to those who have not even shown that they can establish a good society at home. What is happening is not a measure of Soviet Communist capacity. That is still an unproved factor. What is happening is a measure of Western inadequacy. We no longer inspire confidence because we have not done that of which we are capable.

What is happening now could not have happened during the nineteenth century. Then the British Industrial Revolution, the French Revolution, with its concept of "Liberty, Equality and Fraternity," the "great American experiment" in political freedom, had created world-wide confidence in the dynamic and life-giving quality of our institutions. Now, within a few decades, that confidence is gone and our prestige is everywhere in jeopardy. The Western democracies risk being surrounded and isolated, if not overrun, by an alien faith.

What has happened is not without cause. The Western democracies have been guilty of grave lapses. As colonial powers, they should have advanced more rapidly the self-government of dependent peoples. In the American hemisphere, the United States should have been more concerned with being a good neighbor to peoples and not merely to Governments. In China, the Western democracies should have had a deeper concern than that the Chinese Government should be merely acceptable to Treaty Port traders. American industrial and labor leaders ought to have found a way so that, in the prewar depression, our economy would not have been a dead weight on the world, unable to translate idle men and idle machines into productivity.

Of course, it is easier to say that those things should have been done than to have done them. Each was a task calling for a high order of ability and statesmanship. Nevertheless, we could have done much more than we did. Some Christians saw that, but their exhortations carried little weight. So long as no foreign nation was exploiting our inadequacy it seemed safe and easier to drift along. Now that our failures are seen to be jeopardizing our society of freedom, our people may arouse themselves to remedial action. In that sense the prospect is far from dismaying.

The most important task which faces the American people is that of mental adjustment to a dynamic peace. Most of us would like a peace which is a condition of tranquillity. We would like all threat and challenge to be removed and to feel that we can safely relax. We are inclined to believe that unless we get that kind of peace, we have not peace at all. That is a dangerous mental condition. It can readily lead to a mood of frustration, for we are not likely, this time, to get a peace of tranquillity. We may, however, get something much better. Peace ought to be a condition of vigorous effort to redress wrongs and to advance the .general welfare of mankind. That kind of peace is available to us. It requires no prior agreements or settlements. No nation can close to another that door of opportunity.

It is, of course, of immense importance to the life of Europe and Asia that the victors quickly agree on the terms of peace. The Conference now going on in Paris warrants the attention and effort it is receiving. On the other hand, there is no warrant for feeling that until everything is settled between the victors, nothing worth-while can be done. We should see the future in truer perspective. We should not permit ourselves to despair because of disagreements, obstacles, and delays which are now almost inevitable and which, probably for a long time, will prevent a conventional form of peace.

After long exertion the principal victors may agree on what shall be the future territorial, economic, and political status of Germans, Japanese, and Italians. However, by that time a new group of unsettlements will doubtless have risen to plague us. That will go on until a new equilibrium is established in the world as between the faith and institutions of Soviet Communism and the faith and institutions of the Western world. That equilibrium will never be achieved by paper agreements or compromises or surrenders. It will be established by the weight of facts. It must first be determined how much constructive influence each society can exert in the world. That will take time.

Such a period of unsettlement is not a disaster. It has its disadvantages and its risks. But a settled peace has, too, its risks. It is apt to generate an atmosphere of stagnation within which forces of evil readily breed. That was shown by the aftermath of World War I.

The "Big Three" of the victory of 1918 — Great Britain, France, and the United States — were all satisfied nations. Their peoples had similar beliefs and institutions. None challenged the other. All three had already achieved for themselves an advantageous position in the world. Their idea of peace was, consequently, to buttress that existing position and then to relax from the great effort of war. So they disarmed Germany and dismembered the German Empire. They broke up the Austro-Hungarian monarchy. They made the Covenant of the League and the Kellogg-Briand Pact whereby they ruled that there should be no more war. Then they went their several ways of self-enjoyment, feeling that this was safe because, internationally, everything had been settled.

For a time that peace seemed good. If this meeting were being held in the atmosphere which for a few years followed 1920, it would be easier to talk about the brotherhood of nations.

Actually, that postwar condition was unhealthy and treacherous. The Treaties of Versailles and of Trianon were not bad treaties as treaties go. The Covenant of the League and the Kellogg-Briand Pact were good as such things go. What was wrong was the spirit which dominated the principal victors. They abandoned initiative and sense of mission. That role was left to be taken over by evil spirits who brought the peace to a quick and ignominious end. The impression of the victors that all was settled proved their undoing.

History teaches that a static peace is a dangerous peace. Christ taught that same truth. Christ did not preach peace as a condition of tranquillity. Surely it was a static peace that Christ had in mind when he said, "Think not that I am come to send peace on earth: I came not to send peace, but a sword."

Christ's gospel was evolutionary, in some respects revolutionary. It taught men constantly to struggle against the imperfections of world order. So Christians want a peace that does not stifle but encourages efforts to promote human welfare.

In recent years we have been coasting on the waning momentum of the past. Now our people are beginning to see that they must choose between contributing to the world and being isolated, crowded, and jolted by the world. Once that alternative is clearly understood, there is little doubt as to what our choice will be. We shall prove again, as we have proved before, that our society of freedom can gloriously serve mankind.

Of course, a dynamic peace has its risks. It will, under present conditions, involve competition between great powers. There is always danger in such a competition. It may become so keen that the competitors will use unscrupulous methods. Each may exasperate the other to a point where ill will is great and peace can be jeopardized by minor incidents. That appears to be the greatest present danger.

Communist leaders have always professed to believe that capitalism uses war in order to keep itself going. They also profess to believe that the capitalistic nations will engage in armed conflict against Soviet Communism as the only way to overcome it. It is understandable that some phases of our nation's armament and strategic defense policies may, to Soviet leaders, seem threatening.

On the other hand, Soviet leaders themselves have never believed in tolerant methods. They have, at home, regularly employed coercion, purge, and propaganda unrelated to objective truth. They employ these same methods in aid of their foreign policy. They seem to believe that the ends which they seek justify any means.

We know, from our own political system, that it is possible to have a society which, on the one hand, is peaceful and, on the other hand, contains many different beliefs, each with devoted adherents who seek competitively to propagate their faith. However, that is possible only under a system where no one is allowed to propagate his faith by coercion, intimidation, purge, or fraud. We need, internationally, the same restraint on intolerant methods. The big question is, Will we get it?

It is possible that we can. Powerful aids are at hand to prevent the competition of great powers becoming unbridled and unscrupulous and dangerous to peace. There is no warrant whatsoever for concluding that a peace which is dynamic, competitive, and vigorous must, for that reason, culminate in violence.

First of all, none of the competitors wants war. None would willingly provoke it. Each may strain the patience of the other, but none will deliberately do what it thinks will lead to major war. The danger that exists is more a danger of miscalculation than a danger from actual malevolence. That risk of miscalculation can be reduced if the nations deal with each other in terms of candor. The cause of world peace is not really served by giving Soviet leaders the impression that the Western peoples are indifferent and complaisant toward Soviet methods of intolerance.

In the second place, we have the United Nations. Public attention focuses upon its Security Council. Actually, other aspects of the life of the United Nations may, for the present, be more important. A major purpose of the United Nations is "to be a center for harmonizing the actions of nations" in regard to economic, social, and humanitarian matters. If any member state wants to see undernourished people get more food, idle workers get more employment, ignorant people get more education, impoverished people get more economic development, dependent people get more self-government, there is an organ of the United Nations through which it can prosecute its desire.

These activities of the United Nations are already getting under way. At the first meeting of the Assembly in London, all but one of the nations holding colonial mandates expressed the intention to accept United Nations trusteeship. Great Britain is showing in India that it respects its undertaking under Chapter XI of the Charter. It is performing there a historic task of great delicacy by the use of statesmanship of a high order. The Dutch Government is promoting autonomy in the Netherlands East Indies. The United States has proposed that atomic energy should be developed by the United Nations so that there will not be competition along national lines. There already exist organs or specialized agencies to deal with food, health, economic development of backward areas, and monetary stability.

That illustrates how the United Nations can effectively serve as a harmonizing center. If the members of the United Nations will vigorously develop its humanitarian activities, that will do much to prevent human misery and discontent being exploited by particular groups for ulterior purposes. Indeed, the gain can be more than negative. The United Nations, by developing common peacetime goals, may revive the spirit of brotherhood which existed when the United Nations were fighting for common wartime goals.

Finally, there is the moral law. That is not something which only preachers talk about on Sunday. It is something that the most realistic politicians take into account. Today all national leaders talk in terms of the moral law. No doubt that reflects some hypocrisy. But the very fact that it seems necessary to present a moral façade is proof that the moral law is a recognized power.

Moral law is variously expressed and understood. Its implications do not seem to all to be the same. It needs to be translated into codified world law. But even today moral law can serve mightily to direct the conduct of nations into ways consonant with peace.

Last month the representatives of non-Roman Christian churches from fifteen lands met at Cambridge, England, to discuss the part which the churches might take in world affairs. It was unanimously agreed that "the judgment and guidance of the Christian conscience upon international problems must be clearer and more decisive than hitherto." To that end we established a permanent Commission of the Churches on International Affairs. It can be expected that that Commission will recognize that peace requires the co-operation of men of all nations, races, and creeds and that the principles upon which world order depends are those which men of good will throughout the ages have accepted as part of the moral law. A great body of Christian churches, representing many denominations and many races, is committed, as never before, to subject the conduct of nations to moral law.

Nothing that we have said affords a basis for easy optimism. We would only delude ourselves if we did not look on the future as one of peril. That, however, is no reason for pessimism. The future has always been a future of peril. Often the perils have been hidden, so that there has been no defense against them. Also, those perils brought with them no opportunity comparable to the risk. This time the perils are seen; possible defenses are at hand, and the vigorous and dynamic spirit which produces the peril can also produce an era of unprecedented progress. Thus we have great opportunity at the price of measurable risk. More than this, men should not ask.

14

Principle Versus Expediency in Foreign Policy

S HOULD our foreign policy reflect or disregard moral principles? That may sound like an academic question, but it
is one of the most practical problems of our time. I chose it
as my topic tonight because lawyers are a principal custodian
of the belief that human conduct should conform to law and
that law in turn should conform to justice. Lawyers would
generally agree with Chief Justice Marshall's statement that
"there are principles of abstract justice which the Creator of
all things has impressed on the mind of his creature man and
which are admitted to regulate, in a great degree, the rights
of civilized nations."

Until recently, this point of view has dominated American
foreign policy and American diplomacy.

Our Declaration of Independence was based upon an appeal
to "the Laws of Nature and of Nature's God."

Our first great foreign policy, the Monroe Doctrine, was
stated in terms of "asserting, as a principle" the right of the
American republics to be free.

Our next great foreign policy was in relation to the Far

Address to the Missouri Bar Association, St. Louis, September 26, 1952.

East and asserted the principle of equality called "the open door."

When President Wilson called upon Congress to enter the First World War, he said "our motive" will be "only a vindication of human right," and will "prefer the interests of mankind to any narrow interest of their [our] own."

When we entered the Second World War, our purposes were set out in the Atlantic Charter. It affirmed "the right of all peoples to choose the form of government under which they will live" and "no territorial changes that do not accord with the freely expressed wishes of the peoples concerned," and it called for "the restoration of sovereign rights and self-government to those who have been forcibly deprived of them."

Of course, moral principles do not alone provide all the practical answers that men need. And no doubt, at times, our nation has strained morality to make it coincide with national self-interest. But few would doubt that the past dynamism of our nation has genuinely stemmed from a profound popular faith in such concepts as justice and righteousness and from the sense that our nation had a mission to promote these ideals by every peaceful means.

Soviet Communism reflects a view totally different from the U.S. historic view. Its creed is materialistic and atheistic. It does not admit of any moral law. Stalin mocks at the concept of eternal justice. Under the Soviet Communist system "law" is defined as the means whereby those in power impose their will on their class enemies. . . .

This creed and practice are repellent to us. Yet, within our own nation, the idea is gaining ground that our traditional American viewpoint is wrong and that, like the Russian rulers, we should discard concepts of morality, righteousness, and justice from our foreign policy-making.

Toward the close of World War II, when Soviet Russia was our cobelligerent in Europe, our Government made private agreements with Stalin which clearly violated the Atlantic Charter and the principles of international morality which it proclaimed.

It is said that we got advantages out of these agreements and that Russia would in any event have taken what she took. Probably this is so. But the significance of our action lies in the fact that our Government was willing to violate principle in order to gain what it thought were immediate practical advantages. That was nonmoral diplomacy. Of course, it was practiced in wartime, when nonmoral, short-range expediency has its maximum justification. But the same practice is being carried into some areas of our foreign policy even though that war is over. . . .

◇◇◇◇

U.S. policy toward the United Nations further illustrates the encroachment of the nonmoral approach. That story goes back to 1944, when our Government agreed with the Soviet Union on the so-called Dumbarton Oaks draft of Charter. It reflected the Soviet Communist philosophy by omitting all mention of law or justice. Primary reliance was placed on the possibility of practical deals within a Security Council dominated by the five great powers, with each having a right of veto so that it could not be bound against its will.

That plan was radically altered at the San Francisco Conference of 1945, primarily under the impact of Senator Vandenberg, whom I strongly supported in this respect. The Charter was made to provide for the development of international law, and the "principles of justice and international law" were prescribed as the guide for the settlement of disputes. The powers of the General Assembly were greatly enlarged to make it what Senator Vandenberg called "the town meeting of the world," where world opinion could be mobilized to exert an influence upon the conduct of the nations. . . .

◇◇◇◇

The American people are today disappointed in the United Nations. They made a big investment in it, an investment not only of money but, even more, of faith. The investment has not paid the expected dividends. One reason is that the United Nations is not designed to use physical force, as in Korea, and our present foreign policies are largely under the influence of those who do not believe in moral force upon which the United Nations must primarily rely. So, the United Nations has not been given a chance to work seriously on the great problems of our time.

The growing tendency toward nonmoral diplomacy is not healthy. I could give you many reasons, but I shall develop only two.

First, it inevitably makes for a break between our Government and our people. Whether we like it or not — and I like it — our people are predominantly a moral people, who believe that our nation has a great spiritual heritage to be preserved. We do not feel happy to be identified with foreign policies which run counter to what we have been taught in our churches and synagogues and in our classes on American history.

Proof of what I say is to be found in the popular reaction to the foreign policies which I have discussed.

The American people as a whole are embarrassed and

ashamed at the secret wartime agreements which we made at the expense of our friends and allies. Some honestly feel that what we did can be defended on the ground that in war all moral principles go by the board. But there is little doubt but what most of the American people feel that these agreements are a weight upon their conscience. . . .

◇◇◇◇

As regards the United Nations, there is great popular disappointment that it has not more largely fulfilled its purpose of promoting international law and justice, and that our policy makers are increasingly bypassing the United Nations and its open processes, as though our policies cannot stand the light of day.

Of course, private diplomacy is necessary to pave the way to the final formulation of foreign policies. But the American people have always believed that their foreign policies should show "a decent respect to the opinions of mankind," and they believed that the United Nations Assembly, as the "town meeting of the world," would assure that.

A dictatorship can, within limits, make its foreign policy without regard to public opinion. Perhaps a more accurate way to put it is that totalitarian dictatorships can largely create their own domestic public opinion. Surely, however, a government like ours, which depends upon popular processes, should conform its foreign policy in its broad outlines to what our people can understand and approve in the light of what they believe to be right.

A second reason against divorcing diplomacy from morality is that this strikes at the heart of free-world unity. Today, the United States has an inescapable responsibility for leadership. Only leadership that inspires confidence will prevent the free world from falling apart and being picked up, piece by piece, by Soviet Communism. United States foreign policies today represent the core of potential unity, and that core is rotten unless it is a core of moral principle. Other countries will feel, and justifiably feel, that they cannot depend upon our policies if they avowedly reflect only shifting expediencies.

Throughout the ages men have experimented with artificial means for binding nations into common action for a common cause. They have experimented with military alliances, with subsidies, with coercion. None of these methods has stood the stress and strain of fluctuating danger.

The only tie which dependably unites free peoples is awareness of common dedication to moral principles.

I have given examples of the operation of nonmoral diplomacy. There are, happily, many cases where our diplomacy has reflected moral principles. One of these, and the one with which I am most familiar, is that of the Japanese peace. There, United States initiative drew the free nations together by appealing to moral principles. Our Government invoked the spirit of forgiveness to overcome vengefulness, the spirit of magnanimity to overcome hatred, the spirit of humanity and fair play to overcome greed, the spirit of fellowship to overcome arrogance, the spirit of trust to overcome fear. The free Allied nations responded. The peace treaty became a treaty of reconciliation and liberation, and forty-nine free nations joined to sign it in a drama of peace-making unity such as the world has never seen before.

As the closing speaker in the Conference which preceded the signing, I spoke of the unity which had drawn the free nations together. I said, "What are the ties that create this unity? . . . There is a common faith, a common belief in certain great principles. . . . There can be and there will be and there is unity as between those peoples from all corners of the earth, from every creed, from every civilization, who do have that common faith in great moral principles, who believe in the worth and dignity of the human individual and who believe in justice and who believe in mercy. That is why," I said, "we are able to agree."

Many things have changed since President Washington delivered to the nation his Farewell Address. But we can still usefully ponder these words: "Of all the dispositions and habits which lead to political prosperity, religion and morality are indispensable supports. In vain would that man claim the tribute of patriotism who should labor to subvert these great pillars of human happiness."

Those sentiments were uttered with primary reference to domestic tranquillity at a time when we were but a young and feeble nation without world-wide responsibilities. However, what General Washington said assumes continuing and added significance in the world of today.

There is no doubt but what our nation has quickly moved from what seemed to be supreme security won in World War II into what is now great danger. . . .

Some conclude that because of this peril we should cut loose from the great principles which have historically animated our people and enabled them to guide our nation through past perils. That is a counsel of panic. This is above all the time to adhere loyally to those enduring principles upon which our nation was founded. This is a time, not to change our faith, but to renew it.

15

The Moral Foundation
of the United Nations

T HIS "Festival of Faith" is held here today because ten
years ago the United Nations was created in this city.
Also, we are assembled here because the religious people of the
world contributed largely to that great act of creation, and
they have ever since been steadfast in their support of the
United Nations. Thus, it is particularly appropriate that those
of many faiths should gather here to renew publicly their
dedication to the purposes and principles of the United
Nations.

There are many who share credit for the great accomplishment that the United Nations represents. But we can usefully
recall that moral concepts largely prompted the political decisions that, ten years ago, were recorded here.

When the Atlantic Charter was drawn up in August, 1941,
to define the hopes for a better world, it was decided to omit
reference to the creation of a world organization. It was
judged that our people did not want to repeat the League of
Nations experiment. That point of view was carried forward
into the United Nations Declaration of January 1, 1942. The

Address at the "Festival of Faith" of the San Francisco Council of Churches,
San Francisco, June 19, 1955.

religious people then came to see their responsibility and opportunity. In this country they organized and campaigned widely to develop a public opinion favorable to world organization. The political leaders quickly responded on a bipartisan basis.

I recall that history in order to remind ourselves that under a representative system of government it is private persons and organizations that must themselves make it possible to move ahead to develop great new institutions.

Our religious people also exerted a profound influence upon the form and character which the world organization would take. As originally projected at Dumbarton Oaks, the organization was primarily a political device whereby the so-called great powers were to rule the world. The projected charter did not attempt to bind the organization to standards of justice or of law, and the General Assembly was cast for a subordinate role. A Security Council, dominated by five nations, each of which had veto power, was designed to be the mainspring of the organization.

It was the religious people who took the lead in seeking that the organization should be dedicated not merely to a peaceful order but to a just order. It was they who sought that reliance should be placed upon moral forces which could be reflected in the General Assembly, the Social and Economic Council, and the Trusteeship Council, rather than upon the power of a few militarily strong nations operating in the Security Council without commitment to any standards of law and justice.

The great debates of the San Francisco Conference of 1945 centered on these issues. In the end the Charter was written so as to require the organization to conform to principles of justice and international law. Also, the powers of the General Assembly were enlarged so that the influence of world opinion could be effectively brought to bear upon the conduct of the nations.

As we can now see, looking back, these changes were of profound significance. Indeed, without them the United Nations might not have survived these early, difficult years.

The Security Council has grievously disappointed those who believed that the great powers would act in concert to maintain world order. Not once during the ten years of its life has the UN Security Council taken direct action under the provisions of the Charter. It could not do so because the UN contingents of land, sea, and air power contemplated by the Charter have never been brought into being. Whatever the Security Council has done, as in the case of Korea, has been in the form of a recommendation, a request, or a plea — never a command. And even the scope of its recommending has been gravely limited by abuses of the so-called veto power. The political vitality of the organization has been found principally in the General Assembly and its right to recommend, a right which carries great authority because its recommendations reflect the judgment of sixty nations, representing many races, creeds, and areas.

Significant achievements have been recorded by other organs of the United Nations which are not dominated by the so-called great powers and where no veto power exists. That is particularly true of the Economic and Social Council and the Trusteeship Council. By the Declaration of Human Rights the United Nations has raised a standard which will exert a profound influence throughout the world for all future time.

So, as this past decade has unrolled, it has revealed that the power of the organization was primarily a moral power, derived from the judgment of the participating nations and their peoples as to what was right and what was wrong.

The successes of the United Nations have been largely due to those throughout the world who believe that there is a God, a divine Creator of us all; that he has prescribed moral principles which undergird this world with an ultimate authority equal to that of physical law; that this moral law is one which every man can know if only he opens his heart to what God has revealed; that these moral principles enjoin not merely love and respect of the Creator but also love and respect for fellow man, because each individual embodies some element of the Divine; and that moral principles should also govern the conduct of the nations.

It is a most encouraging fact that all governments, even including those who deny the existence of moral law, feel it necessary to try to defend their conduct, if it is challenged, in terms of moral principles. This is particularly the case when the challenge occurs, and when defense must take place, within the General Assembly. This is a testimonial to the power of moral law.

Thus, as we gather here as representatives of many faiths held throughout the world, we can find much ground for satisfaction. It has been demonstrated that the religious people of the world can generate the motive power required to vitalize a world organization by providing it with principles which are guiding not merely in theory but in fact.

We must, however, also recognize that, while the history of the United Nations shows what the religious people of the world can do, it equally discloses that they do not always do it. Sometimes they seem weak, so that moral principles do not make themselves felt. Sometimes they are confused and divided. Sometimes, also, they are intolerant and impractical, demanding solutions which do not take account of the fact that until individual human beings in sufficient numbers are themselves dedicated to high moral principles, the moral solutions which may be devised by political authorities have little effect.

To recognize these facts is to accept a challenge for the future. The first ten years of the United Nations teaches a clear lesson. The lesson is that the people of the world who are committed to the moral law have a great responsibility to assure the continued vitality of the United Nations and its capacity to influence the course of international conduct.

If the world organization were primarily operated by military power, those of us who are here would have little to do. If it were primarily operated by the self-interest of a few great powers, those of us here would have little to do. Since, however, the United Nations, as now constituted, derives its authority primarily from the moral forces generated by our respective faiths, then those who participate in this "Festival of Faith" have much to do. Indeed, we and our fellows throughout the world carry a primary responsibility.

A prophet of one of the faiths represented here said, "Not by might, nor by power, but by my Spirit, saith the Lord of hosts." That sentiment is common to all of our faiths. It can well guide us as we look to a future which contains greater hazard than any future men have ever faced, but which also contains greater opportunity. That opportunity can be grasped with confident hope if men and women of faith throughout the world develop and mobilize moral strength so that moral standards will increasingly prevail in the United Nations. •

IV

The Role and Responsibility of the Churches

Much of Mr. Dulles' thought on the issues of world order was formulated in connection with his chairmanship of the Commission of the Churches on a Just and Durable Peace, and many of his most important utterances were made to Christian audiences. But both the formal declarations and his exposition of them had in view the wider audience beyond the churches. It was the outlook and the policies of the American nation that he sought to reach and influence.

In this section are included articles and speeches in which Mr. Dulles addressed himself directly to the churches and their members and leaders, but his wider audience should not be forgotten.

It must be recalled that Mr. Dulles' activities and his leadership were not confined to the American scene. Throughout this period he was one of the most trusted and influential guides of the churches of the world, especially as they joined together in the newly formed World Council of Churches. He had presided over the meeting in Cambridge, England, in the summer of 1947, which brought into being the Commission of the Churches on International Affairs, in many respects the counterpart at the world level of the American Commission on a Just and Durable Peace; and he continued in active relationship to it as its Vice-Chairman. The following summer, in August 1948, he interrupted especially demanding public responsibilities to fly to Amsterdam to address the First Assembly of the World Council. The paper that he prepared in anticipation of the Amsterdam Assembly is perhaps the fullest exposition of the underlying presuppositions and guiding principles of all he *had to say on the Christian approach to international issues, as well as a discussion of some of the most vexing problems that were then pressing.*

From 1945 until he went to Washington as Secretary of State in 1953, Mr. Dulles was a member of the Board of Directors of Union Theological Seminary. He was one of the speakers at the inauguration of a new president of the seminary in November, 1945. In May, 1958, just a year before his death, he returned to the seminary for the graduation of his daughter. The address delivered on those two occasions concludes this section of selections.

16

The Church's Contribution
Toward a Warless World

FOR UPWARD of thirty years I have devoted myself to inter-national problems. Throughout most of this time I have believed that the attainment of a peaceful world órder was exclusively a political problem. As I have studied more deeply I have come to realize that this is not the case. Of course proper political devices are indispensable. But such devices will not be adopted or, if adopted, will not work so long as millions of people look upon state, rather than God, as their supreme ideal.

In order to understand the reasoning which leads to my conclusion, it is necessary first to see the problem as it is presented for political solution.

I start with the very simple and fundamental premise, pointed out by Alexander Hamilton in one of his *Federalist* papers, that in every community there are men who are ambitious, fanatical, and disposed to violence. Further, as Hamilton points out, it is utopian to make political plans on the assumption that it will ever be otherwise. Given this premise,

Article in *Religion in Life,* Winter, 1940. Copyright, 1939, by Abingdon Press.

the political problem is to organize society so that such men will not dominate a community and lead it into violent and destructive ways. Fortunately, most people are normally pacific and desire to live at peace with their neighbors. The few who, out of love for adventure or lust for power or predatory instincts, tend toward violence are usually a small minority. As such, they can readily be controlled. But at times great sections of a community may come to feel that they are repressed and subjected to injustices. If so, and if they are virile and dynamic people, they then accept a leadership which offers, through force, to break through the restraints and to abolish the injustices. When this happens we have revolution. If the blame for restraint and injustice is placed upon one's own Government, we have civil war. If the responsibility is attributed to other nations, then we have international war.

Now, society has found political devices which measurably serve to protect itself from developments of this character. We set up a sort of arbiter, called government, which has a dual mandate. On the one hand, it is expected through police power to repress individual and sporadic acts of violence. On the other hand, it is expected to keep this problem within controllable limits by maintaining social conditions such that there will not develop great areas where discontent is rife and a sense of injustice is acute. This is achieved in the main by laws which are constantly being made and frequently being changed so as to provide an equality of opportunity. Even theoretical equality before the law is not sufficient. Ability is very unequal, and opportunity is largely fortuitous. It is necessary that both be controlled by law or it would lead to extreme inequalities. Thus we have laws to prevent monopoly, and laws which regulate the exploitation of property which is devoted to public service, such as railroads, utilities, etc. When there are many who are in dire need it may become necessary by taxes on income or estates to take away from some for the benefit of others. This procedure is accepted by the taxpayer, who realizes that it is better to be able to enjoy peacefully a part of what he has than to face the violent attack which would be inevitable if his Government did not function to alleviate conditions of widespread discontent.

Governments which are even moderately wise and reasonably impartial can maintain domestic order. Of course they do not always do so. We had in France, during the monarchy, and in Russia, under the czars, governments which denied the principle of equality of opportunity and which drove millions into feeling that the government functioned for the benefit of a few and without any sense of responsibility to the many who were subject to its power. The masses became so aroused as to follow leadership which was violent and ruthless, and which led them into bloody revolt. While these revolts were in sway, the outside communities were shocked and repelled at the horrors and cruelty which were incidents thereof. Today we recognize that the cause lay in the failure of political mechanism to work. It was that failure which created mass discontent which, whenever it exists, gives violent, ambitious, and unscrupulous men the opportunity to become formidable.

Through such experiences as the French and Russian Revolutions we have learned the imperative necessity of political devices which assure equality of opportunity and which constantly are at work to prevent conditions becoming rigid and fixed to the advantage of one class and to the detriment of another.

We have failed, however, to give universal application to our political knowledge. As between national groups, there exist no political mechanisms comparable to those which serve to maintain domestic tranquillity. Each state is sovereign. There is no superior arbiter to regulate the use of its powers. The rulers of each state seek primarily the advantage of their own people. This is so even though some of their powers directly and seriously affect outsiders. Toward them no responsibility is felt. For example, when the United States raises its tariff, we legislate not only upon those within the country but upon those without, who may suffer widespread distress due to the dislocation of their industries. When we prohibit or severely restrict immigration, we are not only legislating for those within the country but equally putting restraints and inhibitions upon those without. When we put difficulties in the way of foreigners investing here, we prevent them from sharing in our economic opportunities. When we arbitrarily raise the price of silver, we are not merely legislating for the benefit of silver-mine owners in the West. We are legislating a distribution of the fiscal regimes of such countries as China, which use silver for their currency. When we decide to devalue the dollar, we are legislating not only for our own people but we are breaking up currency relationships upon which depend the industry and commerce of a large part of the world.

I could continue indefinitely to illustrate how the sovereignty system violates fundamental political precepts. As we have seen, power *should* be exercised with regard for all who are subject to that power. Actually, the power of sovereignty is exercised to the end of creating for some a monopoly of advantage. No responsibility is assumed toward multitudes who are affected. Inevitably, there result areas of disaffection, which give men of violence the opportunity to make themselves formidable.

Japan, Germany, and Italy furnish modern illustrations of

the consequences of such a system.

The Japanese people are people of energy, industry, and ambition. Constituting a large population, they inhabit a small area meager in natural resources. They keenly feel the need for raw materials and for markets. But they have persistently encountered a resistance predicated largely upon the white man's conception of Japanese racial inferiority. Even in China, the Japanese found their trade blocked. England had control of the principal ports and railroads, control of the currency, and administration of the tariffs, so that from the standpoint of Japanese economic expansion in China the scale was heavily weighted against her. For many years the leadership of Japan was moderate and liberal. Under this leadership, Japan sought economic and social equality in the world. As this was denied and as the economic position in Japan became progressively more desperate, liberal leadership was ousted in favor of the army war lords who proclaimed that, by force, they would break through the restraints which the Japanese people felt had been thrown around them.

Take Italy. When World War I closed, those in Paris, like myself, who had had some occasion to study the economic and financial position of Italy, could not see how Italy would find it possible to survive. Like all the belligerents, she carried heavy burdens from the war, but unlike England, France, and the United States, she lacked the sources of food and raw materials apparently necessary to support her debt-ridden and impoverished population. It was, therefore, no surprise when grave social disturbances quickly occurred. Her liberal leaders were discarded and communism and fascism struggled for the ascendancy. Fascism won, and the Italian people followed a militant leadership which offered to make Italy powerful and to force France and England to accord Italy that share in the rich areas of North Africa which the Italian people thought had been promised them as a reward for their participation in the war.

Take Germany. It is unnecessary here to detail the severity of the treaty terms and their many departures from the pre-Armistice agreement, in reliance on which Germany had laid down her arms. Secretary of State Lansing, on the day following the delivery of the Conditions of Peace to Germany, wrote: "Resentment and bitterness, if not desperation, are bound to be the consequences of such provisions." This forecast, shared by many at the time, was quickly realized. Yet for fifteen years following the Armistice the German people followed liberal leadership under democratic institutions. But the burden continued heavy, and the sense of inequality and injustice was rendered more poignant by the economic collapse of 1930. Already then the people were beginning to listen to radical leadership which offered again to make Germany strong and to break the bounds which denied her equality of opportunity. Brüning, the last and perhaps the greatest of a series of liberal German chancellors, pleaded for treaty changes which would alleviate the condition of the German people and prevent their falling under the radical leadership of Hitler and the Nazi Party. His pleadings were in vain, and the German people finally accepted the leadership and control of the proponents of force.

I do not recite the history of Japan, Italy, and Germany with a view to placing personal blame on the leaders of England, France, or the United States. They had a power, in respect of such matters as trade, control of raw materials, markets, and money, which vitally affected the peoples of Japan, Italy, and Germany. They exercised that power without responsibility for the welfare of these other peoples. In so doing, they lived up to the dictates of the sovereignty system.

But if I do not blame these rulers, neither do I place blame upon the Japanese, German, and Italian people. They are in the main orderly and peace-loving, quite the equals in this respect of the Americans, English, and French. But like any dynamic and virile people, when they fall into economic distress, they rebel against restraints and humiliations ascribable to other states and, like all revolutionists, they then follow leadership which extols violence.

The fault is that of the system. That which has occurred was bound to have occurred. And such occurrences are bound to repeat themselves under any international system which ignores this political axiom: there are always, in every country and at every time, those who are eager to lead the masses in ways of violence. They can be rendered innocuous only by preventing the many from feeling that they are subject to power which is exercised without regard for their welfare and which condemns them to inequalities and indignities.

Now, the failure to apply in the international field the lessons we have learned in the national field is not because the problem is essentially different or inherently unsolvable. Various solutions are known which offer good chance of success. These solutions generally assume one of two forms, which may conveniently be described as the "league" formula and the "federal" formula. The League of Nations is, of course, the outstanding example of an attempted solution of the first type. Under the League Covenant, the nations bound themselves to two essential principles. Article 19 of the League Covenant empowered the Assembly of the League from time to time to "advise the reconsideration by Members of the League of treaties which have become inapplicable and the consideration of international conditions whose continuance might endanger the peace of the world." Article 16 provided that in the event that any member resorted to war without first submitting the dispute to arbitration or the Council it would be subject to nonintercourse measures applied by the other League members. There was thus present in the League, in theory at least, the two elements indispensable to the preservation of peace. There was, first, the obligation to make changes from time to time necessary to prevent that mass discontent which always turns to dynamic leadership and makes it formidable. Second, there was provided collective power sufficient to repress violence which, so long as it is not backed by a great popular movement, is sporadic and controllable.

Actually, the League failed because at no time were the dominant members of the League ever ready to give vitality to Article 19, and to revise treaties or to alleviate conditions which obviously threatened the peace of the world. But in principle the conception was sound.

There are, of course, many possible variations of the political formula represented by the League, notably those which call for regional leagues which bind together those states whose powers are particularly apt to be overlapping in their scope.

The second line of political approach is that represented by the federal system. The federal system recognizes that sovereignty is a bundle of powers which do not necessarily all have to be vested in the same entity or exercised with regard for the same group of people. Certain powers, for example those relating to trade, immigration, and money, operate upon a far wider circle of persons than do those relating to sanitation, education, etc. It, therefore, vests the first set of powers in a body having responsibility toward a large group of people, while it leaves the second group of powers in bodies responsible only to smaller groups of persons. Our own Constitution is, of course, the best-known example of the federal system, but the federal principle is subject to indefinite expansion and has many possible variations. For instance, any number of states might agree that the matter of trade between them was a matter of common concern and, therefore, that authority over trade between these nations should be vested in a body which derived its authority from and had responsibility toward all the peoples concerned. In this way power and responsibility tend to become coextensive, and we do away with a condition whereby certain persons are restrained and restricted by power exercised without regard for their welfare.

I have no intention here to advocate any particular political formula. I merely want to make clear that there *are* possible solutions and that there is no reason why we cannot find, for the international field, political devices comparable to those which serve in the national field to prevent that mass discontent which makes quick transition to mass violence.

At the Conference at Geneva, which I attended last summer on the initiative of the World Council of Churches, there were formulated certain principles which, it was said, "stand out as clear applications of the Christian message." The first of these was that political power and responsibility should be coextensive. The second was that power should be exercised in accordance with the principle that all human beings are of equal worth in the eyes of God and should be so treated in the political sphere. A third principle was that it is as necessary to effect changes in the interest of justice as to secure the protection of the *status quo*.

These are not merely Christian principles. They are the principles which must be applied within any society which effectively maintains domestic tranquillity. They are principles which can be extended into the international field through mechanisms such as those I have mentioned. But, and this is of the essence, *any* such formula involves some dilution of sovereignty. For example, under the league system a member state may be called upon to contribute to change conditions elsewhere, the continuance of which might endanger the peace of the world. If, for instance, the League had functioned and the United States were a member thereof, we might have been called upon to take a different attitude toward Japanese immigration and toward Japanese goods from that which, purely in our own interests, we had decided to take. It might have been felt that thereby mass discontent within Japan might have been alleviated, moderate leadership preserved, and explosion into China prevented. Now, any nation which honestly agrees, in advance, to contribute to changes deemed necessary to preserve the peace elsewhere has deprived itself of some of the panoply of full sovereignty. Similarly, under the federal system, power is divided up as between different bodies having different jurisdictions. There is no single entity which has the majesty of full power. Thus the establishment of a common money might be vested in a body created by and responsible to the English, French, German, and American people. This would deprive our own Government of exclusive control over a national money and we could not, for example, repeat our 1933 attempt to cure our depression by devaluing our particular money. Any peoples which participate in a league system or a federal system inevitably deprive their national government of certain attributes of power.

It is at this point that we encounter the serious and presently insuperable obstacle. It is an obstacle for which the church must accept large responsibility. It is an obstacle which, perhaps, the church alone can dispel. It is this: to great masses of mankind their personified state is, in effect, their god; it represents the supreme object of their devotion; its power and dominion are, to them, sacred, and to subtract therefrom is akin to sacrilege.

It is apparent that so long as this sentiment prevails it is impossible for a sound international order to be established, for any such order requires a dilution of sovereignty as now practiced.

One hundred and thirty-five years ago, in New England, a group of Christians comprising the Massachusetts Peace Society appointed a committee to study the causes and results of war. They found among other causes what they referred to as an "infatuation" and "delusion" by which individuals identify themselves with the nation to which they belong and invest this personified entity with godlike attributes such that its majesty becomes of primary importance. With respect to this cause of war they said: "Should the increase of moral light in the ages to come be in the ratio of that in the past, we predict that this sentiment will be regarded by posterity as one of the most childish and absurd of the present age."

Unhappily, it would appear that moral light has not increased in the ratio expected by the Massachusetts Peace Society. A delusion which they expected would be quickly dissipated has on the contrary grown until today it is the most powerful and dangerous force in the world. It is today the formidable obstacle which makes it impossible to apply in the international field those political solutions which work within the domestic field.

How do we account for the fact that this delusion has engrafted itself so firmly upon us? The explanation, I think, lies in the failure of the churches to provide mankind with a loftier means of satisfying its spiritual cravings. Most men are aware of their own finite character and their own inadequacies. They seek to identify themselves with some external being which appears more noble and more enduring than are they themselves. Most men are not purely selfish. They are attracted to a cause which is so sure of itself that it dares to call for sacrifice. Mankind demands a creed through which to achieve spiritual exaltation. This creed *should* be a religious one. But it is not. Our religious leaders have seemed unable to make vital and gripping the concept of God as revealed by Christ. Has the church, in recent years, called for sacrifices even remotely approaching those called for in the name of patriotism? Religion does not become more vital as it becomes softer and easier. On the contrary, the people lose confidence in a creed, the exponents of which dare not call for sacrifice on its behalf.

It is because of this failure that the false gods of nationalism have been imagined to fill the spiritual need which most men feel.

The present situation is a cause of deep concern to those who genuinely seek a system of world order. Many political leaders, it is true, give only lip service to this concept. To most of them it is a smug formula for advancing the national interest. But there exists in every country an influential group of men who understand the political problem and earnestly and intelligently seek its solution. But, under present conditions, they are impotent. Any sound world order can be achieved only by a major operation upon sovereignty. But you cannot operate upon an entity which is popularly deified.

I have been deeply impressed by the fact that when, as at Oxford three years ago and in Geneva this year, there met to-

gether Christians of conflicting nationalities none of the difficulties between their nations seemed insuperable. They quickly fell into the category of those matters which are calmly discussed and peacefully settled. This is because under such circumstances the problems are discussed purely from the standpoint of the welfare of the human beings involved. What
aggravates such problems beyond the possibility of solution is
their presentation, not in terms of the welfare of human
beings, but in terms of the relative powers and prerogatives of
personified nations each of which, by its own people, is looked
upon as quasi god.

Can the church repair its failure? That I do not know. I am
discouraged when I see Christian leaders, in countries which
include our own, seeking to identify righteousness with one or
another national cause. In many churches the national flag
and national anthem today replace the Christian symbols.
This seems the easy way. Thereby an anemic church draws
vitality from the coursing blood of nationalism. But this not
merely aggravates the problem we are seeking to solve. It also
exposes a dependence of the churches upon the human rather
than the divine. Political leaders are not slow to draw the obvious inference. The church becomes to them a human institution upon which they can stamp whenever it serves their
purpose. This today is occurring in not a few of the so-called
Christian countries.

The other way is the evangelical way. It requires that we
vitalize belief in a God who is the Father of us all, a God so
universal that belief in him cannot be reconciled with the
deification of nation. This seems a hard, slow way. But it is
the way Christ showed. He did not engage in political controversy and had little to say about the functioning of state
or even of war and peace. He issued one solemn guide and

warning, namely, that we should not render unto Caesar that which is God's. We have come to our present pass because that warning has gone unheeded. All that is best and noblest in mankind has been put at the service of a political mechanism which is human and fallible and which, in its international operation, violates every Christian precept. We have been rendering unto Caesar a spiritual devotion and a sacrifice which belong only unto God. Thereby we have encompassed our own destruction.

There can be no salvation until we have set right the fundamentals. The urgent task of the church is to restore God as the object of human veneration and to recreate in man a sense of duty to fellow man. National governments must be seen to be what they are — pieces of political mechanism which involve no sanctity and which must be constantly remolded and adapted to meet the needs of a world which is a living, and therefore a changing, organism.

I know that it is difficult to transfer devotion to that which is abstract and universal. I know that it is difficult to enlist sacrifice except by invoking the ideology of combat and of hate. But I also know that mankind is paying a fearful price for its worship of false gods and that never before did the world so need a vital belief in a universal God. That need is the measure of our opportunity and it must equally be the measure of our works and of our faith.

17

Christian Responsibility for Peace

THE CHRISTIAN churches of this country bear a heavy responsibility for peace. If there should be war between the United States and Russia, it might be due to circumstances beyond our control. More probably, the war would be one which the churches could have prevented. If we should fail in that prevention, it would not be through lack of desire, for the churches' desire for peace is immense; it would not be for lack of power, for if the churches work zealously and in unison, their power too is immense. If there is failure, it would be because our churches do not have the know-how. That is the elusive, often lacking, quality.

I doubt that the churches can prevent war merely by preaching the evil of war. Also, I doubt that the churches can prevent war by attempting to prescribe in detail the conduct of foreign affairs. I do think it likely that war can be prevented if our churches assure that our people will not, in the words of the psalmist, "rage and imagine vain things." In other words, if our people are free of hatred and anger

---

Address at the General Conference of The Methodist Church, Boston, May 4, 1948.

so that they think straight and see truly, war probably will be avoided.

There is, as I say, a chance that war might come about through Russian action which we could not prevent. But the available evidence and the logic of the situation strongly indicate that Russian leaders do not now want war and would not initiate war unless they genuinely felt that war was our intention. The Russian nation has already achieved its traditional ambitions in the Far East and in the West. Only toward the Middle East are there unsatisfied national ambitions which war might realize.

On the other hand, Russia suffered horribly from the last war. Because she emerged victorious and because her leaders now adopt a hard attitude, we forget how deeply she was wounded. Scarcely a beginning has yet been made in healing those wounds, and the Russian people who survived the last war profoundly dread any repetition.

So, while there is a risk of war on Russian initiative, which our national policy must take into account, it seems that that risk is small if we conduct ourselves properly.

From the standpoint of the United States, there is no reason whatever for war against Russia. We have no quarrel with the Russian nation, which has nothing that we want, and there is a tradition of unbroken friendship between our peoples.

The danger of war comes from the fact that the Soviet Communist Party is attacking free institutions by methods of penetration, propaganda, and terrorism which the American people deeply resent and which create in them a disposition to strike back. That frame of mind leads to thoughts of war because the world has for centuries been highly organized on a national basis; international controversies have been those of state against state, and war has been the accepted instrument of solution. Also, the conventional defense against aggression is military defense and deeply rooted habits of thought and action lead our people now to turn to that. Also, there is a vested interest in that type of defense, in building it up and, perhaps, in using it.

The instinctive reaction of our people, while understandable, is unfortunate because it does not fit the present case. We are not witnessing a conventional type of effort by one state to take something away from another state. It is not a state, but it is a party, which originates that which arouses our people. It is not operating against us as a nation but against our institutions. What is happening is novel, the like of which men have not seen since, one thousand years ago, the new and dynamic Moslem faith struck out against the established institutions of Christendom. Islam, however, invoked military effort to make its faith prevail, and there is little evidence that the Soviet Communist Party now has that intention. It does believe in violence, coercion, and terrorism, but as weapons against individuals. War is not its preferred method. Also, war is not an appropriate countermeasure to the Communist Party attack. In fact, instead of defending our free institutions, war would weaken them, and in the long run probably inure greatly to the benefit of the Communist Party. That party's first great opportunity came out of World War I. Its second great opportunity came out of World War II, and a third world war might well make the Communist Party supreme in the world.

It is possible to pile argument upon argument to show that war is unnecessary and could not serve its intended purpose. The problem of preserving peace is, however, not at the moment a problem of marshaling arguments. It is a problem of finding minds that are receptive to reason. We are seeing in this country a natural tendency to rush to arms in time of peril. That tendency is accentuated by a mood of hatred, which makes some want to lash out blindly. Many also feel that war is inevitable and that it is better to get it over with, particularly when we still have atomic bombs and the Russians do not. Also, the thought of war no longer evokes the horror which prevailed when atomic bombs ended World War II. The result is an inflammable situation which could be exploded by even a minor incident.

The immediate task is to create an atmosphere such that the future will be determined by reason, not by accident.

That is a task which peculiarly falls within the province of our churches. We have free institutions because our founders took a Christian view of the nature of man. They believed that men were endowed by their Creator with certain inalienable rights and also that men had a duty to God and fellow man which would induce the self-control needed to make freedom socially tolerable. Those two interdependent religious conceptions are the foundation of our free society.

There is no doubt that a free society has its dangers. There is always danger that the people will be swept by mass emotionalism into doing reckless and unreasonable things. That risk is one which Soviet leaders constantly harp upon to justify their system of dictatorship and their control of press and speech. A free society justifies itself only if its members exercise self-control. If our churches will see to that, they will make a great contribution to peace. . . .

◇◇◇◇

It would be much more exciting if church leaders could invent some dramatic, specific formula which of itself would resolve the tensions which now exist. Perhaps that can happen. I hope so. But peace is more apt to come about through a gradual day-to-day improvement of the situation. If the churches will realize this, they will, I am sure, exert their influence in favor of the myriad of little acts which, in the aggregate, exert a tremendous influence. Little things multiplied many times become great things. If the American people will individually exercise the self-control and self-restraint which is the duty of members of a free society, then the situation will instantly improve because then reason and calm counsel can prevail. There are plenty of reasons available, and there is plenty of calm leadership. But, in times of crisis, reason and calm leadership become impotent unless the people themselves exercise self-control. To assure that is the first and imminent task. If the churches will do it, they will have made an indispensable contribution to peace.

To restore clear vision and calm thinking will not, of itself, produce peace, but only the conditions that make peace possible. Some think that peace can be assured if we see only the good that is in others and the evil that is in ourselves. I believe that that involves blurred vision rather than clear vision, and that peace requires our seeing clearly what there is of righteousness in our institutions and then defending that, not with arms, but with faith. War is always likely when a people largely endowed with worldly goods do not have faith in their institutions and practices. That situation invites attack, and those who are not armed with faith are apt to be quick on the trigger.

Arnold Toynbee in his volume *Civilization on Trial* refers to the fact that Western civilization has "been living on spiritual capital, I mean clinging to Christian practice without possessing the Christian belief – and practice unsupported by belief is a wasting asset, as we have suddenly discovered, to our dismay, in this generation."

Our people still have Christian faith to a degree equal to the past; at least that is indicated by statistics. Our national practices still produce bountifully. But the connection between faith and practice seems broken, and that is a source of weakness and danger. It is time either to get new institutions in which we can place confidence and take pride or to recapture our faith in our existing institutions.

Our churches have, perhaps, contributed to breaking the connection between our faith and our practices by emphasizing the imperfection of what is. What is, is always imperfect, and it is clearly the duty of the churches to point that out and to urge Christian citizens to seek constant improvement. It would be morally indefensible and practically disastrous to identify what is with perfection and to attempt to sustain it unchanged. But that attitude does not involve discrediting what is the essence of our political institutions — that is the procedure by which change is made.

The quality in our institutions which justifies our confidence is that they make possible change which is peaceful and which accords with the view of the majority without doing violence to the minority. In that respect our institutions reflect a Christian concept of the nature of man and of the dignity and worth of the human personality. It is, above all, that method of change which distinguishes our society from many others, notably that of Soviet Communism. . . .

◇◇◇◇

Soviet professions attract great attention and a considerable following for the very reason that the Soviet Party is dedicated to carrying them out by methods of violence. When people are so sure they are right that they are willing to die and kill for their views, that seems to carry great conviction. Fanaticism gives an impression of zeal which is lacking when people seek their goals by peaceful means. But Christians, just as they reject war as a method of achieving international goals, must equally reject coercion and violence against the individual as a method of achieving social goals. Such methods are unchristian, and whenever they are invoked — even in support of Christianity, as has happened — the result is an evil and ugly thing.

I believe that Christians can proudly recognize the worth of institutions which, because they reflect a Christian conception of the nature of man, provide for change in ways that respect the dignity and worth of the human person. Certainly our institutions are not perfect. But it is undeniable that they have been the means whereby there has been steady progress toward Christian goals. Those goals are not nearly achieved. There is much to be done, particularly in terms of broad social welfare. The churches ought never to relax their pressure for constant improvement, and Christians ought always to be humble in the face of present inadequacies. But by demonstrating their capacity for peaceful change, our free institutions have, I submit, earned the faith and confidence of our people.

Let us not fear that faith. It will not lead to war, either a national war or a "holy war." Faith in things, interest that is vested — that is what is dangerous and stultifying. But faith in institutions which on the one hand facilitate change and on the other hand assure that it will occur peacefully, without violating human personalities — that is something very different. Such a faith, if coupled with works, is the best possible insurance against assault from without. Also, that faith will assure against our own resort to arms. We shall have new confidence in the rightness and in the efficacy of peaceful ways. As we believe in them nationally, so, internationally, we shall seek peaceful processes and those habits of tolerance which permit different faiths to subsist peacefully side by side.

That is our goal; may God guide us to it.

18

The Christian Citizen
in a Changing World

THIS PAPER is written by a layman who has been active in the field of international affairs. It is primarily an action paper, not a theological paper. It accepts, explicitly or implicitly, basic Christian beliefs and suggests how, in the actual situation, they may impose on Christian citizens a duty of practical conduct.

There is no thought that the church should endorse the conclusions reached or the lines of action suggested. The writer is, indeed, one who believes that the church ought not to make authoritative pronouncements with respect to detailed action in political, economic, or social fields. Practical political action is not often a subject for authoritative moral judgments of universal scope. Those who act in the political field must deal with the possible, not with the ideal; they must try to get the relatively good, the lesser evil; they cannot, without frustration, reject whatever is not wholly good; they cannot be satisfied with proclaimed ends, but must deal with actual means. Those necessities prevail conspicuously in the

A paper written as part of the preparation for the First Assembly of the World Council of Churches, Amsterdam, August, 1948. Printed in full in *The Church and the International Disorder* (Harper & Brothers, 1948).

international field where tradition, national interest and group loyalty have accumulated to an unusual degree. They place limits on what is practically possible; they introduce error into every human judgment; they increase the ever-present risk that men will see as "right" that which is self-serving.

Facts such as those mentioned require that the churches should exercise great caution in dealing with international political matters. They should not seem to put the seal of God's approval upon that which at best may be expedient, but which cannot wholly reflect God's will.

It does not, however, follow that Christian faith and Christian political action are unrelated. All citizens have to act in relation to political matters — inaction being only a form of action, a clearing of the way for others who do act. Also, Christian citizens, when they act, will try to be guided by Christian insight and Christian inspiration. Political institutions molded by those who take a Christian view of the nature of man will be different from those molded by atheists. What the churches elect to say will have political consequences. What they elect to keep silent about will also have political consequences. So the churches, too, have a relationship to practical politics that is inescapable.

Since that is so, it seems that the churches ought to know what are the problems which Christian citizens face. "Thy word is a lamp unto my feet, and a light unto my path." But the churches cannot throw light of the Word upon the Christians' paths unless they know where those paths lie and what are the obstacles that need to be illumined lest the Christian pilgrim stumble and fall. It is useful, no doubt, for Christian citizens to be inspired by the vision of a distant, heavenly scene. But also it is useful to have light upon the way.

Obviously, Christian citizens throughout the world do not

all face identical problems or have identical duties. No single presentation can adequately inform the churches. There are, in the world, many paths for Christians, all leading toward a central point, the doing of God's will on earth. Some paths lead from the East, some from the West, some from the North, some from the South. Each of these paths has obstacles of its own. In turn, these obstacles constantly shift. What is described now may be irrelevant by tomorrow. Despite the fact that the scene is world-wide and shifting, the churches should seek to keep informed. Otherwise, they cannot keep each way illuminated with shafts of the divine light.

This paper seeks to show in relation to international affairs, what is the political path which some Christians have to tread, what they see as the obstacles ahead, and how they think they can, perhaps, overcome these obstacles and wrest the initiative from forces of evil, ignorance, and despair, which exist in every land and which seem to be conspiring to overwhelm mankind with awful disaster.

The writer recognizes, quite frankly, that the path he describes is a path which leads from the West. He knows full well that that way differs from other ways. These, too, should be known, for the church concedes no priority or privilege to any nation, race, or class.

As the churches come to know better the practical problems which Christian citizens have to face and the lines of action in which they may become engaged, the churches in turn will be better able to minister to the actual needs. They will be better able to show, to each and to all, that Christ is indeed the Way, the Truth, and the Life. As Christ is so revealed, he will draw all men unto him, and that supreme loyalty will provide the unifying force which otherwise men seek in vain.

THE INEVITABILITY OF CHANGE

The basic political and social fact that citizens must face up to is the fact of change. Life and change are inseparable. Human beings constantly change. So, too, do human societies. There are always some who unthinkingly wish that they could stop change and freeze a moment into eternity. That cannot be and, indeed, we should not want it to be. If it happened, it would mean an end and the replacement of life with death.

Christians do not regret the inevitability of change. Rather, they see in it a cause for rejoicing. Some religions see man as bound to a wheel which turns and on the turning of which he can exert no influence. As a result of that assumption it follows, for them, that the ideal mental state is one of indifference and renunciation of hopes and efforts which can end only in frustration. The Christian believes that he can do something about change to determine its character and, accordingly, he looks upon the inevitability of change as something that provides opportunity. That opportunity has a dual aspect. Outwardly, there is the opportunity to make the world more nearly one in which God's will is done on earth as it is in heaven. Inwardly, there is the opportunity for personal growth and development which comes out of grappling with situations and trying to mold them.

When there is change, something that *is* disappears and something that *was not* appears. Also, whenever there is change there is a means, a force, that brings change to pass. The Christian seeks the disappearance of that which he deems imperfect. But the disappearance of something imperfect is not, of itself, sufficient to make change good. If that were so, all change by whatever means would be good, for everything is to some extent imperfect, and there cannot be change without the disappearance of some imperfection. The Christian tries to appraise change not merely in terms of what disappears but also in terms of what replaces that which disappears. This appraisal involves an appraisal of means as well as ends, for the means by which change is accomplished makes an indelible impression upon the result and becomes, indeed, a part of the result.

For Christians, the great social task is to deal with the forces that make *some* change imperative so that (a) these forces will make their principal impact on what can be and will be replaced by something better; (b) the forces for change will leave relatively immune what at the moment cannot be replaced by something better; and (c) the forces for change will not themselves be evil and unchristian in character.

THERE IS NEED THAT CHANGE BE INSTITUTIONALIZED

Political leaders who have or want power usually talk much alike as to the social ends they seek. They all propose to increase the sum total of human happiness. The manifestos of communism, nazism, and democracy have much in common. Many people pick their leaders simply on the basis of their promises and on the basis of the zeal which they seem to manifest. Sometimes the very violence with which leaders would seek their ends seems a recommendation, as being a proof of zeal.

The Christian citizens will consider not only the social ends which are professed in words but also those elements which, we have seen, make up the nature of change. They will inquire into whether the changes proposed will replace something imperfect by something better, will leave immune what cannot be improved, and will avoid means which are evil. They have learned that the actual result will probably be determined more by the means than by the professions of long-range ends. Also, they know that a choice of violent means may not indicate honest zeal but a lust for the increased power which comes to political leaders whenever violent means are sanctioned.

Difference of opinion about means is often the critical difference. Christians prefer means of the kind which, they believe, Christ taught. They are not inclined to look with approval upon means of violence and coercion. They have seen that over the ages war, revolution, and terrorism have been repeatedly invoked for noble ends. But change brought about in that way is hurried and it usually gets out of control. It crushes blindly what happens to lie in its path. At times it inspires fine and sacrificial qualities, but also it develops in men hatred of fellow man, vengefulness, hypocrisy, cruelty, and disregard of truth. History seems to show that, when these evil qualities are invoked to produce good ends, in fact they vitiate or postpone the professed ends. Change sought by methods of force, violence, and coercion seldom produces lasting, good results.

The Oxford Conference of 1937 said:

"Wars, the occasions of war, and all situations which conceal the fact of conflict under the guise of outward peace, are marks of a world' to which the church is charged to proclaim the gospel of redemption. War involves compulsory enmity, diabolical outrage against human personality, and a wanton distortion of the truth. War is a particular demonstration of the power of sin in this world and a defiance of the righteousness of God as revealed in Jesus Christ and him crucified. No justification of war must be allowed to conceal or minimize this fact."

Some Christians believe that the use of violence is of itself so unchristian that it should never under any circumstances be resorted to. Most Christian citizens, it seems, do not accept that view. The vast majority appear to believe that, while they ought not themselves to initiate the use of force as a means, once force is invoked by others to do injustice, and to impose conditions violative of the moral law and of the Christian conception of the nature of man, then to use force to prevent those results may be the lesser of two evils. Christians would generally agree that methods of change other than violence are to be preferred because violence, unless it be the dispassionate force of police power under law, almost always generates unchristian qualities which cancel out, or at least greatly dilute, the value of the changes which violence brings about.

If force is discarded as the accepted means of change, then there have to be established procedures and political organizations for the purpose of making peaceful change. Such procedures have to a considerable extent been established within states, but they are lacking in the international field. There, as elsewhere, history teaches the inevitability of change. If one examines a historical atlas and looks at the political arrangement of the world one hundred years ago, two hundred years ago, and so forth, one cannot but be impressed by the magnitude of the changes that have occurred. Most of these changes have been effected by war or the threat of war. Each war brought about the disappearance of something that was imperfect. Often it involved the doing away of power in some men and nations which had become disproportionate to their ability or readiness to use that power for the general welfare.

In that sense, the change was good. But, also, the method of violence has done terrible things to the hearts of men. It has not brought individuals to greater love of God and neighbor in accordance with the great commandments. Indeed, the result has been, on the whole, quite the contrary. The prestige of Christianity in the world has been gravely impaired by the frequency with which the so-called Christian nations have used violence as a method of international change. Furthermore, the hatred, falsification, cruelty, and injustice incident to each war have, we can see in retrospect, done much to provoke new war and all the evil that that entails.

INSTITUTIONS FOR CHANGE REQUIRE DECIDING WHO CONTROLS

Christian citizens can readily conclude, as a generalization, that there ought to be political institutions which will enable international change to take place in a peaceful way. But that conclusion is not, of itself, very significant. It cannot have any practical consequence unless also there is another decision, namely, whose judgment will determine the timing and the nature of peaceful change. Change *ought* to be based upon reflection and deliberate choice, not upon accident and force. Of course. But *whose* reflection and choice are to be controlling? That is a hard question. Within nations there is no uniform answer. In the international field few have attempted seriously to answer it, and those few are not in agreement. Uncertainty, disagreement, and competition about that largely explain why, in the international field, change has so far been left mostly to accident and violence.

It used to be widely held that political decisions should be made by rulers who were not responsible to their people.

Today, it is generally agreed, at least in theory, that it is better that men should be self-governing through some representative process which they control. But that theory is seldom carried out in practice, even within nations. In many countries of the world, power is exercised by dictators. Of these, there are many types. Some are men who, loving power, have taken it and make no attempt to rationalize their action. Often, by written constitution, their government is a "republic" or "democracy." Some dictators are benevolent, taking power only to tide over a real or imagined crisis. Some exercise dictatorial power in order, professedly, to train the masses and discipline them into a common mold which, it is thought, ought to precede self-government. Such purposeful dictatorships are often termed "totalitarian."

There are other countries where the peoples do in fact, through representative processes, exercise a very large measure of influence upon the choices that are made as to change. These societies customarily describe themselves as "free societies." Some call them "responsible societies" or "self-disciplined societies." We use the phrase "free societies" because it has wider popular use, although we recognize and hereafter emphasize that there is interdependence between freedom and self-discipline and sense of responsibility. We also recognize that even in the so-called free societies there are usually some who are, in fact, excluded from equal opportunity to participate in the deliberative process which determines when and how change shall be effected.

In no country is there a pure democracy in the sense that all of the people have equal and direct participation in all of the deliberations which determine change. Also, in no country are dictatorships so absolute that those who possess the governmental power wholly disregard what they sense to be the wishes of the people. Even so, the organization of the different nations shows that there are great and momentous differences, both in theory and in practice, as to whose choice should determine change. These differences are a great obstacle to institutionalizing change at the international level. Therefore, the matter deserves further consideration.

FORMS OF GOVERNMENT
COMPATIBLE WITH CHRISTIAN IDEALS

Christians tend to favor the free society of self-discipline. That is probably because Christians think of man primarily in terms of the individual and his relations to God and to fellow man. It is only individuals who have souls to be saved, and God, it seems, is not concerned with nations, races, and classes, *as such*. He is concerned with individual human beings. Christians, who believe that, want a political society which, recognizing the value and the sacredness of individual personality, gives the individual the opportunity to develop in accordance with the dictates of his own conscience and reason, and also puts on him a responsibility to exercise freedom with regard for the welfare of fellow men.

Christians believe that for one man to possess arbitrary power over his fellow men is an unchristian relationship. It usually corrupts him who rules and it tends to debase those who are ruled, if in fact they acquiesce in being ruled.

Furthermore, Christians believe that civil laws made by men should, so far as possible, reflect the moral law. We believe that there is implanted in every individual a potential awareness of right and wrong and that under favoring conditions the composite of such individual judgments will reflect the moral law better than the judgments of absolute and self-perpetuating rulers. Also, as a practical matter, unless laws reflect and codify the moral judgments of those subject to them, they are not apt for long to be enforceable.

For such reasons, Christians tend to prefer the free society. But also they recognize that peaceful and selective change is not assured merely by giving people a right of suffrage. The voice of the people is not always the voice of God. It is easy to arouse masses for destruction without regard to the problem of replacement. Mob psychology is seldom conducive to selective change, and it does not in fact represent individual reflection and choice.

A free society, if it is to effect peaceful and selective change, must be a society where in addition to the right to vote the people possess and use personal freedoms and access to information and the opportunity to exchange and propagate thoughts and beliefs so that there is, on an individual basis, genuine reflection and sober choice of minds and spirits which are both free and developed by use and self-discipline. There is also need of tolerance, particularly in the sense that political power may not be used to promote any particular creed.

The free society may at times of emergency, such as the emergency created by war, grant one man or a few men very extraordinary, even dictatorial, powers. But the people will reserve effectively the opportunity to end these powers when the occasion for them has passed.

Economically, a free society does not have to be a laissez-faire society. There are some who profess to believe that only a laissez-faire society adequately encourages individual development. There are, however, few who today would put that belief wholly into practice. In all states, even those most dedicated to free enterprise, there is governmental control of at least some of the tools of production, such as railroads and public utilities, which are endowed with a special public interest. In most countries, there are important collective and co-operative enterprises. It would seem that there is no inherent incompatibility between the Christian view of the nature of man and the practice of economic communism or state socialism. Communism in the sense of "from each according to his abilities, to each according to his needs," was early Christian practice.

In the modern world, particularly where there is industrialization, there is much interdependence and necessity for co-operation. In part, this necessity can be met by individual knowledge of how, in a complicated society, individual acts affect others. To that knowledge there needs to be added self-control and sense of duty to fellow man so that individuals will voluntarily refrain from acts which they see have injurious consequences more than offsetting the benefits to self. But even where the people are possessed of much self-control and sense of duty there may have to be added public controls and centralized direction to promote the equitable distribution of goods in short supply and to ensure co-operative and co-ordinated action on a scale adequate to the needs of our complicated economics.

One may have different judgments as to what economic structure is best adapted to modern conditions and as to the kind of incentive which is required to insure needed productivity. There are times and conditions when the most effective appeal is to self-interest. There are other times and conditions when the greatest appeal may be to men's sacrificial spirit. The Christian church seeks constantly to make men's motives more lofty and to invoke concern for others rather than for self. Christians believe that those that are strong ought to bear the infirmities of the weak, and not to please themselves. But there are few who fully heed that injunction. Christian citizens in seeking to organize society have to take account of what men *are,* not what the church thinks they ought to be.

From the Christian viewpoint, the essential is political and economic conditions which will help, and not stifle, growth by the individual in wisdom and stature and in favor with God and man. We want conditions which in so far as practical will, in fact, exalt the dignity of man. The essential in this respect is the content, not the form. The conditions which best assure that will doubtless vary from time to time and from place to place.

It is not possible to attach the Christian label to any particular political or economic organization or system to the exclusion of all others. It is not possible to say that free enterprise is Christian and socialism unchristian — or vice versa. It is not possible to say that a popular representative system of government is Christian, or temporary dictatorship inherently unchristian. It is, however, possible to condemn as unchristian societies which are organized in disregard of the Christian view of the nature of man. This would include those which are totalitarian in the sense that they recognize the right of some men to seek to bring the thoughts, beliefs, and practices of others into conformity with their will, by processes of coercion.

It could be argued that if Christians really believe that the truth is uniquely revealed by God through Jesus Christ, they ought to seek an organization of the state which would make it possible to use every power, including police power, to compel acceptance of that truth and the liquidation of heretics and nonconformers.

There have been times when that viewpoint prevailed.

Christianity over its two thousand years has had many experiences and has learned much. It has learned that when Christians use political power, or any coercive or artificial means, to give special advantage to their distinctive sect, the outcome is apt to be an ugly thing. We reject methods which, history seems to teach, pervert Christianity. If we reject totalitarianism for ourselves, we a fortiori reject it for others. Believing that our own faith cannot remain pure when coupled with methods of intolerance, we also believe that no faith can enter into that partnership without corruption.

PEACEFUL CHANGE IS POSSIBLE

Practical experience seems to show that where the people have a considerable degree of self-discipline, where they recognize duty to fellow men and where they have considerable education, then they can operate political processes which make for change which is peaceful and selective. In the Western democracies, the political institutions have to a great extent been influenced by Christianity. (By Christianity we do not mean clericalism which may be an impediment to peaceful and selective change.) In these countries, conditions approximating those of a free society have on the whole existed for one hundred and fifty years or more. During that period, social and economic change has been so immense that conditions in any one of these countries today would completely bewilder those who lived there one hundred or fifty years ago.

The changes have, in the main, been peaceful changes. There has been little coercion, terrorism, or civil war. The conspicuous apparent exception is the United States war of eighty-five years ago, called in the North the War of the

Rebellion, but in the South the War Between the States. It was, in essence, more international than civil war. The basic issue was whether certain sovereign states had, by prior compact of union, given up the right to resume full sovereignty.

The social changes effected by free political processes have in the main tended to increase the opportunity of the individual to develop according to the dictates of his conscience and reason. Slavery has been abolished. There has been a definite trend away from treating laborers as animals or machines are treated. Women have been freed from grave disabilities. Economically, individual initiative, experimental and competitive, has produced great richness. The Industrial Revolution, while it has brought evils, has shown men how, with less physical effort, they can produce much more. Infant mortality has been greatly reduced, health generally improved, and the span of life lengthened. Education is general, and the development of spiritual life has been kept free of political inhibitions. Graduated income taxes and death duties effect a considerable distribution of production in accordance with need.

To say these things is not to be self-righteous or complacent. There are many great blots and many deficiencies. One notable blot is the persistence in the United States of a considerable, though diminishing, measure of race discrimination. There persist inequities of many kinds, economic, social, and political. There is no assurance that ways have been found to prevent the cyclical breakdown of production process and the vast misery consequent thereon. By no means is God's will done as it is in heaven. To be satisfied would be unchristian.

But it is not unchristian to point out that where political institutions show evidence of Christian influence, the result is good fruit. If that were not so, one could doubt that Christianity did in fact reflect God's ultimate revelation to man. Christ said, "By their fruits ye shall know them." (Matt. 7:20.)

It seems, both on the basis of theoretical reasoning and on the basis of practical experience, that peaceful and selective change can be assured under the conditions of a free society of self-discipline. There is no comparable evidence to show that under a despotic or totalitarian form of society there can be sustained change that is peaceful and selective and which progressively increases the opportunities for individual growth.

WORLD SHORTAGE OF FREE SOCIETIES WITH TESTED POLITICAL INSTITUTIONS

There are not in the world many societies which have tested political mechanisms whereby decisions reflect the choice and reflection of the people as a whole. That, in the main, is not because such institutions are not wanted but because various conditions have militated against their realization. Many peoples have been long in colonial dependency. Some, like the peoples of India and Pakistan and certain Arab states, are only now moving from dependency to full independence. Some, like the peoples of China and Indonesia, are in chaos and strife. Some, like the Germans, Japanese, and Italians, are still under, or just emerging from, the military control of the victors. Some live under constitutions which in words vest sovereignty in the people, but they are, in fact, ruled by a small group which perpetuates itself in power by force, subject to change by periodic revolution. Some live under "dictatorships of the proletariat."

These facts are significant because they affect the practicability of developing internationally processes of change which will be peaceful and selective. It means that there do not exist, on a world-wide scale, tested institutions of political liberty and that there is an absence of the foundation needed for building a world structure which has political power to legislate change. The creation of a world state involves a mechanism of power and the selection of individuals to direct it. If the power is to be sufficient to make possible change which is adequate to replace violent change, there must, somewhere, be large discretionary authority. But it would not be possible today to assure that the discretion would come from peoples who were free, and morally and intellectually trained for the use of political freedom.

Theoretically, it is possible to devise a world representative system so weighted in favor of the societies of tested freedom that their representatives would have the preponderant voice. The others, who are the majority, would never consent to those few societies being accorded world supremacy. They would, in a sense, be justified. For while the free societies have shown good capacity to govern themselves, they have not shown the same good capacity to govern others of different races and cultures. It would not advance us to recreate and extend the colonial system under the guise of world government.

Today any world-wide system for institutionalizing change would inevitably be despotic. Either it would vest arbitrary power in the persons of a few individual officials, or it would vest great power in the small fraction of the human race who have tested political processes for reflecting the individual choice.

The great majority of the world's population will not, and should not, agree to be ruled by the free societies. The free societies will not, and should not, go back under despotism.

This impasse is a source of great peril. It leaves international change to be effected largely by force and coercion. It does so at a time when the means for corrupting men's souls and destroying their bodies have grown far beyond anything that the world has ever known. Thus, Christian citizens can feel that each, according to his means, has a duty to act to increase the possibility of world political unity and processes for peaceful change. That does not mean that Christian citizens will treat unity as the all-sufficient end, to which they should sacrifice what to them seem justice, righteousness, and human dignity. They will seek the conditions for unity with the urgency of those who know that great disaster impends and with the practicability of those who know that such disasters cannot be averted merely by the incantation of fine words.

THE DEVELOPMENT
OF FREE SOCIETIES

If peaceful change requires deciding whose judgment is to prevail, and if the judgment of a free, disciplined society is the only reliable and generally acceptable judgment, then the extension of free societies throughout the world is prerequisite to a world-wide institutionalizing of change. Many Christian citizens see that as the great long-range political task. Its accomplishment would make it possible to set up and operate in a nondespotic way international mechanisms for peaceful change. That task has two aspects:

a. It is first necessary to preserve and improve free societies where they now exist. Free societies are delicate plants. To grow them is a long, hard task and, once they are grown, they are in constant danger of withering away. The postwar climate has been particularly hard on free societies. The cumulative result of two world wars is grave economic distress coupled with great human weariness and disillusionment. Under these conditions, men have a longing to be taken care of. Also, the economic margin for survival has been reduced to a point where centralized planning has seemed necessary. To men who are preoccupied with the struggle for the basic, material needs of life for their families, bread may be of more compelling and immediate importance than civil rights and freedom. Such conditions lead to giving great power to a few men.

Delegation of power does not, of itself, necessarily mean an abandonment of freedom. It may be an exercise of freedom to meet an emergency, and the people may retain both the legal right and the practical political mechanisms for ending the delegation when the emergency has passed. As we have noted, free societies usually give dictatorial powers in time of great emergency, such as war, and it has been shown that they can withstand temporary dictatorship of this kind. Nevertheless, there is always grave risk in conferring dictatorial power because such power can readily become self-perpetuating.

To preserve the characteristics of a free society within the areas where it now measurably prevails will itself be a difficult task. It will require vigilance and dedication by Christians as citizens. That dedication should not be merely in the interest of *preservation*, but of *improvement*. Only effort motivated by the creative urge can generate the needed energy and enthusiasm. Struggles are seldom won merely by a defensive strategy.

b. New free societies must be developed, and this can be done and should be done rapidly wherever the necessary human foundation exists. Fortunately, much has been done through varied channels to create those foundations. The Christian churches have played, in this, a great part. The Christian missionary movement has had a great world-wide influence in developing in men a sense of duty to fellow man. Also, Christian schools and colleges have stimulated education throughout the world. On the moral and educational foundations developed over past generations, much is now being done to erect free political institutions.

Until recently, nearly one third of the world's population were the subject peoples of the free societies. Within the last three years free institutions have been set up in India, Pakistan, Burma, Ceylon, the Philippine Islands, and certain of the Arab states. A large measure of autonomy is envisaged for Indonesia. The total number of peoples thus acquiring political freedom represents about one quarter of the population of the world and could more than double the total population of the free societies. That is an amazing and encouraging occurrence which should confound the pessimists and inspirit the disillusioned.

Of course, it is not certain that all of these new political entities will, in fact, maintain societies of freedom in the full sense. In part the present development represents a great experiment. In many of the areas momentous and difficult decisions remain to be made, and there is not yet the kind and degree of individual moral and intellectual development which would easily assure a peaceful outcome. There will be need of sympathetic understanding, material aid, and scientific and technical assistance from the older societies of freedom.

There remain dependent colonial areas which can be developed toward self-government and free institutions. The colonial powers, by the United Nations Charter, have pledged themselves to seek that development, and to aid in attaining the result, there has been created the Trusteeship Council.

It should be remembered in this connection that political wisdom generally comes only with practical experience. If people are to be held in guardianship until they have fully developed all the qualities desired, there will be an indefinite prolongation of guardianship. It is better to err on the side of giving freedom prematurely than to withhold it until there is demonstrated proof of ability to use it wisely. To learn by self-experience is apt to involve much suffering. But few learn adequately from the experience of others.

There is in China nearly one fifth of the human race. Some Chinese leaders have, in recent years, sought to replace despotism with free political institutions. But progress has been slow. The people are materially impoverished, and only a few have book-learning. They have had to undergo a war and occupation longer than that of the European Continental Allies. Individualism, in terms of the family, is perhaps excessive, and a sense of community too restricted. But the people still possess richly the qualities which will enable them to make a great addition to the foundations of political liberty.

During the last century there developed a sense of fellowship between the Chinese people and the peoples of the West, largely because of the activities of Christian missionaries, educators, and doctors. Now, more than ever, such activities need to be continued and, indeed, intensified.

There is a great responsibility toward the vanquished peoples of Germany, Japan, and Italy. The victors have made themselves the Government of Germany; they, in fact, direct the Government of Japan and will largely influence the postwar development of Italy. The peoples of these countries have education and personal morality in large measure. It ought to be possible for them to develop into free societies. That is a task of great difficulty because of the evil war has bred. But it is a task of unique importance.

A survey of the globe shows that it is possible for upwards of three quarters of the human race to develop peacefully and quickly — say, within one or two generations — the use of free political institutions. No doubt there would be many inadequacies, as indeed there always are. But it is possible to foresee conditions under which there would be obtainable, from most of the peoples of the earth, judgments which reflect the thinking, on an individual basis, of minds and spirits which are free and developed by political experience and self-discipline. On that foundation it would be possible to establish, internationally, procedures for peaceful change which would not be despotic but which would reflect that moral sense which, we believe, is potential in every human being.

The program suggested has a particular appeal to Christians because it is a peaceful program to which the Christian churches can make a great contribution. There can be parallel effort by the churches and Christian citizens.

The free society cannot be equated with a Christian society, and it is possible to have free societies whose institutions are predominantly influenced by non-Christian religions. But the Christian faith especially emphasizes those qualities of self-control and love of neighbor which are needed for the good operation of a free society. So, Christian citizens could feel that to extend free societies was a great long-range effort to which they could worthily dedicate themselves and seek to dedicate their nations. Thereby they would be laying the indispensable foundation for world institutions for peaceful and selective change. Those engaged in that effort could feel that they were making the world more nearly one where God's will would be done, and they would be responsive to the appeal of the masses that a way be found to save them and their children from the death, the misery, the starvation of body and soul which recurrent violence now wreaks upon man.

◇◇◇◇

[*Here followed a discussion in some detail of the then prevailing problems posed by the policies of the Soviet Union.*]

◇◇◇◇

PEACEFUL RECONCILIATION OF PROGRAM WITH SOVIET PROGRAM

The Soviet reliance on change by force and violence constitutes a serious obstacle athwart our suggested program. Soviet influence is considerable, and it is now favored by external conditions. World War II created a vacuum of power in many areas. Of the eight so-called great powers, three — Italy, Germany, and Japan — have been engulfed by the disaster of defeat. Three —United Kingdom, France, and China — have been enfeebled by the struggle for victory. Therefore, there is about the Soviet Union a power vacuum into which it has already moved to bring some three hundred million people, representing about fifteen nationalities, under the dominant influence of dictatorship of the proletariat and its revolutionary theories and practices.

Even more important than this fact of political vacuum is the fact that there has developed in the world much of a moral vacuum. The so-called Western or Christian civilization has long accepted most of the social ends now professed by the Soviet Communist Party and, indeed, its goals have been even more advanced. But of recent years it has seemed to be halfhearted and lacking in fervor or sense of urgency. The result has been that many people have unthinkingly compared the idealized purposes and theories of the Soviet program with the worst practices of Western nations. Others, eager for quick results, uncritical of means, have been attracted to the Soviet program by the very violence of its means, which have seemed a proof of zeal. The fact that Christian citizens tend to favor nonviolent means is taken as proof that they lack zeal. The consequent degree of following attracted by the Soviet dynamic program has encouraged Soviet leaders to entertain great expectations of realizing their particular "one world." Their ambitions have mounted so that there is indeed grave danger of that "series of frightful collisions between the Soviet Republic and the bourgeois states" which Lenin and Stalin have forecast as inevitable.

Christians must dedicate themselves to prevent such developments. There are in the main two ways of doing so.

First, Christians must reject, and see to it that their nations reject, the Soviet thesis of the inevitability of violent conflict, and they must not imitate Soviet leadership by placing reliance on violent means.

Secondly, Christians must see to it that their nations demonstrate that peaceful methods can realize the goals which we all espouse.

There is disturbing evidence that the so-called free societies are themselves tending to adopt those features of Soviet procedure which Christians particularly condemn. In the United States great emphasis is being placed upon achieving military supremacy, and military counsels are more influential than has normally been the case in that republic. Some portions of the American press are stirring up emotional hatred against the Soviet Union, and there is some distortion of truth, principally through the exaggeration of what is true but of minor importance. . . .

◇◇◇◇

The most important response to the Soviet challenge will be in effecting peacefully the reforms which Soviet leaders contend can only be effected by violent means. We must by actual demonstration disprove Stalin's dictum that "one must be a revolutionary, not a reformist."

The Western democracies won their prestige in the world through their great peaceful accomplishments. The Industrial Revolution, the concept of "liberty, equality, and fraternity," and the experiments in political freedom created world-wide confidence in the dynamic and life-giving quality of their institutions. But for long now these democracies have faced no serious competition. The quality of their effort has deteriorated, and they have, to a considerable extent, been coasting with a momentum that is waning. Many do not like it that a challenge has now arisen. Many would prefer peace which is a condition of tranquillity or stagnation, where all threat and challenge are removed and where men can feel that they can safely relax. Some are inclined to the view that unless we get that kind of peace, we do not have peace at all, and an irresponsible few talk of using force to crush the challenger. That is folly. Those of us who are of the Western peoples face the task of mental adjustment to a dynamic peace where there is competition. We need to make it clear to ourselves and we need to make it clear to proponents of other systems that we welcome a world in which there is peaceful competition. Above all, we need to make it clear that we can peacefully, through reform, bring about results which all men want, and which they will be apt to seek by the violent methods which the Soviet sponsors, unless we can prove that they can be achieved by peaceful means.

Whenever a system is challenged, there is a tendency to rally to support the system as is. The world becomes divided between those who would maintain the *status quo* and those who would change the *status quo*. As we have seen, those who would sustain the *status quo* inevitably are defeated. And almost inevitably the issue is resolved by violence. The result may not be the particular changes desired by the dynamic powers, but equally, it does not maintain the status which their opponents sought to preserve. So it is that in the face of Soviet challenge we must not rally to the defense of our institutions just as they are, but we must seek even more ardently to make them better than what they now are.

In fact, much progress has been made along this line. We have already referred to the action of Great Britain in bringing about five hundred millions of colonial dependent peoples peacefully to self-government. That has been the most effective way to demonstrate that the achievement of self-government by dependent peoples was not dependent upon a Soviet "revolutionary alliance," and that it is possible to achieve by peaceful means results which the Soviet leaders profess to want but which they have said could only be achieved by violent means.

The free societies have also made considerable progress in achieving an economy whereby production is on the basis of ability and distribution on the basis of need. The steeply graduated income and estate taxes which now prevail generally in capitalistic countries take largely from those who have ability to accumulate, and to an increasing extent this is being distributed to those in need in the form of Social Security programs. These countries are in fact much closer to the so-called higher phase of communism than is the Soviet Union itself.

Socially, the great blot on the escutcheon of the democracies is the discrimination against colored persons practiced by much of the white population of the United States. Here, however, the problem is recognized, and great efforts are being made to deal with it. It is not possible by legislative fiat to eradicate social prejudices, the origins of which go back hundreds of years. There is, however, a vast change which is in peaceful process.

The danger is that those who face the Soviet challenge will feel they must defend themselves on every count. There is some evidence that the Soviet challenge is, to an extent, having that natural result. Christians must stand strong against that, recognizing the imperfection of every system and of every nation, not identifying righteousness with anything that is, but constantly striving to prove that the evils that exist can be eradicated by peaceful means. . . .

◇◇◇◇

The years between the Soviet Revolution and World War II involved a very large exposure of practical bankruptcy on the part of non-Communist nations. During that period the free societies, at least, were not at their best. Soviet leaders have encountered weaknesses which have afforded them great opportunities and given them great encouragement. Within recent years that situation has begun to change. There have been some great constructive developments. To some of these we have alluded. It is possible to push forward along these lines and it is imperative that this should be done. . . .

◇◇◇◇

The Soviet challenge loses its potency once the free societies show a capacity for constructive action. As we have said, the challenge in its present phase seems not a militaristic challenge, like that of Hitler, Mussolini, and the Japanese war lords. It is a call to revolution. If the non-Communist societies, faced by that challenge, stand still and do nothing, for fear of offending Soviet leadership, they are lost. If they quietly move ahead, showing a practical capacity to achieve peacefully the things which Soviet leaders say can come only after an "entire historical era" of violence, then those talkers will quickly be rated as "incorrigible windbags" — to use Stalin's expression.

It is important that there be these peaceful developments both domestically and internationally. We have already outlined what might be the grand, over-all, international program. But such a long-range program is not enough to meet the present need because it does not contain enough possibility to register quickly decisive results and thus to create general recognition of the capacity of the free societies. Intermediate programs are needed, where successes can be registered, prestige gained, and momentum acquired. We shall go on to consider what might be some of these intermediate programs.

INTERMEDIATE STEPS PRESENTLY PRACTICABLE

It is not necessary to stand still and do nothing internationally until there has been laid the world-wide foundation for a free world society. There is much which can be done, today and tomorrow. There are already two great assets with which to work. One is the great and all-pervading force of the moral law. A second is the existence of an organization — the United Nations — which brings together in public association most of the nations of the world. On the basis of these two facts, many intermediate successes can be achieved.

The moral law has universal influence. There are some who deny its existence and who try to educate men to ignore it. It is never immediately and universally effective. But still there is general, world-wide agreement about right and wrong in their broad outlines. That fact is of immense importance, for it makes it possible to use moral force for peace and justice at a time when there cannot yet be an adequate political mechanism.

Moral power can be a powerful force in the world. That is not a mere pious hope. It is the judgment of every realist throughout history. It was Napoleon who said that "in war, moral considerations make up three fourths of the game." It was Admiral Mahan who said that physical force was useful only "to give moral ideals time to take root."

Allied leaders during both the First and Second World Wars did much to consolidate and marshal world sentiment to insure Germany's defeat. They did that through great statements of aims, such as the Fourteen Points and the Atlantic Charter, which appealed to the moral conscience of the world. It is possible also to frame issues and organize moral power in the interest of peace.

The United Nations is a political machine which even now can be used to make moral power work during peace to preserve peace. That is largely due to Christian influence.

Many thought that world organization should be primarily a military organization to carry out the will of the great powers. That was, indeed, the conception which dominated the representatives of the Soviet Union, Great Britain, and the United States when they met at Dumbarton Oaks in the summer of 1944 to make a first draft of the Charter. But our church people did not think much of an organization which would be primarily military and which would depend chiefly on physical force. So they worked hard to make their point of view prevail. It did largely prevail at the San Francisco Conference of 1945, thanks in great part to the small nations, which did not want to be placed permanently under the military dictatorship of the three big powers.

So the San Francisco Conference radically changed the plan of Dumbarton Oaks. It emphasized the United Nations General Assembly as a place where the representatives of all states, big and little, would meet and discuss any problems of international relations, and where even the great nations could be required to subject their conduct to the judgment of world opinion.

The United Nations has now been functioning for over two years. Many are disappointed with the results. They would like the United Nations to be able to dictate and enforce the particular results which they want. As we have seen, the United Nations cannot now be that kind of an organization. However, it has revealed great possibilities. Of course it has not settled everything. Indeed, the international situation is gravely troubled. But the United Nations has shown that it need not be a mere spectator. It can do something. It can call every nation's international acts to the bar of public opinion, with confidence that that will have healthy practical consequences.

We have seen how, in time of war, the public verdict of right and wrong exercises a powerful effect. The United Nations has begun to show how, in time of peace, public opinion can exercise a powerful effect. At the San Francisco Conference and at the subsequent Assemblies of the United Nations, political leaders from many lands have presented views on many matters. Always the speakers were obviously conscious of the fact that their audience included the representatives of many million people who possessed great power and who were primarily swayed by moral considerations. Every speaker presented his case with regard to what he thought was world opinion, and he tried to get its backing. Almost always the different Governments presented their positions otherwise than they would have done had they been meeting in secret and not subject to informed world opinion. That is a fact of great moment. It does not make future war impossible. It can make war less likely. . . .

◇◇◇◇

So, while the United Nations cannot today be converted into a mechanism directed by a few persons having power to rule the nations, it can be used to subject national acts to the test of moral judgment. Moral power arises from the most humble to reach the most mighty. It works inexorably, even though slowly. It will not suit the impatient. But it can achieve solid results. The important thing is that the United Nations be used for purposes for which it is adapted and not be discredited by attempted use for purposes for which it is ill adapted. . . .

◇◇◇◇

[*Here followed a series of specific suggestions for the more effective functioning of the United Nations.*]

◇◇◇◇

We could go on indefinitely in this vein. We have, however, said enough to indicate that, with a moral law of universal scope and with the United Nations as a place to bring together national acts and world-wide judgments, important intermediate results can be achieved. There is much to be done on a less than universal basis, within the framework of the Charter. Nations and peoples can do much to help each other. Such efforts do not take the place of our long-range program because they do not constitute a conscious, planned effort to create, on a world-wide basis, the conditions prerequisite to a general institutionalizing of change. But interim measures can gain the time and the prestige needed for successful development of a long-range program.

What seems urgent — and possible — is to revive in men a sense of moving peacefully toward a state of greater perfection. Many have been beaten and broken in spirit by the violence of the forces that have been loose in the world for now upward of a decade. They temporarily placed hope — perhaps undue hope — in the United Nations. But that hope has largely gone, and there is despairing acceptance of the idea that continuing violence is inevitable for an entire historical era.

That is a dangerous mood. It can, perhaps, be broken by acts which, even in a small way, show the possibility of peaceful change. Let us, therefore, not despise what is presently possible, knowing that out of small things can come a rebirth of faith and hope, and that out of faith and hope can come great things, far beyond any that are here portrayed.

CONCLUSION
The Role of the Christian Church

Many will feel that the programs here outlined are quite inadequate; and those who feel that way may be quite right. . . . We have tried to write under a self-imposed ordinance, namely, to propose only what we felt might *practically* be achieved by *peaceful* means and without the sacrifice of hard-won human rights. No doubt, even within this limitation, there are better prospects than are here portrayed. But no program which is both practical and peaceful will seem as exciting and dramatic as a program which is purely imaginative or violent. . . .

◇◇◇◇

We are fully conscious of the fact that peaceful and practical programs will seem to many to evidence a lack of zeal and to conceal a desire selfishly to preserve the evils of the *status quo*. That appraisal, in our opinion, can be and should be changed. Christians should, we believe, appraise more highly than they seem to do the self-control, the self-discipline, and the respect for human dignity required to make change peaceful. The Christian churches could, we think, find the way to make peaceful efforts seem more inspirational and be more sacrificial. It is a tragedy that inspiration and sacrifice in large volume seem to be evoked only by ways of violence. If the Christian churches could change that, then, indeed, they would help the Christian citizen along his way.

We have not outlined tasks which could be participated in only by Christians because we believe that if Christians advance a political program which only Christians can support, they logically must contemplate a monopoly of power and privilege on behalf of their particular sect. That, we have made clear, would in our opinion vitiate the program. But the task which we have outlined is a task which should arouse the Christian churches to a sense of special responsibility.

What is the need? The need is for men and women who can see what now is and what can be. Christ put particular emphasis on vision and light. He taught men to see truly and to avoid the hatred, hypocrisy, and selfishness which blind men or warp their visions. If Christian churches do not produce the needed vision, what can we expect but that mankind will stumble?

The need is for men who have the peacefulness which comes to those who are possessed by the Christian spirit of love, who have the power which comes to those who pray, repent, and are transformed, and who have the dedication of those who leave all to follow Him.

The need is for more effective political use of moral power. The moral law, happily, is a universal law. But Christians believe that, through Christ, the moral law has been revealed with unique clarity. The Christian churches ought, therefore, to be especially qualified to help men to form moral judgments which are discerning and to focus them at the time and place where they can be effective.

The need is for full use of the present great possibilities of the United Nations. It was Christians most of all who wanted a world organization which would depend primarily on moral, rather than physical, power. They have it. Now it is up to the churches to generate the moral power required to make the organization work.

The need is to build the foundation for a more adequate world organization. A world of free societies could be that foundation, and free society depends in turn on individuals who exemplify Christian qualities of self-control and of human brotherhood, and who treat freedom, not as license, but as occasion for voluntary co-operation for the common good. So, again, the Christian churches have the great responsibility.

The need is for effort on a world-wide scale. The Christian church is a world-wide institution. Consequently, the individual Christian may exert his influence not only as a citizen but also as member of a church which in its corporate life has a contribution to make. The church demonstrates in its own life the achievement of community out of various races, nationalities, and communions. It develops a common ethos. Its missionary movement constantly extends the fellowship of those who share the same loyalties and purposes. Its ecumenical movement deepens and consolidates that fellowship.

Its program of relief and reconstruction restores hope to the despairing and reconciles those who have been enemies. The Commission of the Churches on International Affairs is beginning to give stimulus and leadership to the more direct impact of the churches on the current problems of relations between the nations. Thus the churches themselves in many ways can help build the bases for world order.

So it is that, as we analyze the need, Christian responsibility emerges as an inescapable fact. It is a fact that ought to have practical consequences. The potentialities of Christian influence are great, but the present weight of Christian impact is wholly inadequate. If, in the international field, Christians are to play their clearly indicated part, their churches must have better organization, more unity of action, and put more emphasis on Christianity as a world religion. That, we pray, will come from the Amsterdam Assembly and the final realization of the World Council of Churches.

19

Leadership for Peace

W E MEET at a time that is reminiscent of 1939. In January of that year the President, in a message to Congress, warned that "freedom of religion has been attacked" and that "the attack has come from sources opposed to democracy." He called for increased Armed Forces because the "probability of attack is mightily decreased by the assurance of an ever-ready defense," and he said that we must make effective protest against aggressors although, he said, "obviously along practical, peaceful lines." Two years later we were in the thick of World War II.

Many today feel that history is repeating itself and that forces beyond our control are irresistibly dragging us into another war.

War is not inevitable, but thinking that it is can make it so. Concededly, there are in the world today, as in 1939, forces that oppose religious freedom and democracy and that are aggressively disposed. But there always have been, and always will be, such forces in the world. International peace, like

Address opening the National Study Conference on the Churches and World Order, Cleveland, Ohio, March 8, 1949.

domestic peace, does not have to await the total eradication of evil.

Already in 1940 our churches foresaw that the destruction of the Nazi regime would not end for all time such evils as were in nazism and automatically bring lasting peace. They knew that such evils were recurrent. So they set up a special organization to help them bring new elements into being so that, after World War II, it might be possible to counter peacefully the forces of disorder. The churches wanted the postwar situation to be different for the very reason that they did not want history to repeat itself.

We have to a large extent succeeded. Today there are assets for peace which were wholly lacking before World War II. The present perils are great, but if it were possible to trade what now is for what then was, none, I hope, would make that barter.

After the First World War it seemed that the nations made peace very quickly. Only seven months after the Armistice, the Treaty of Versailles had been completed, in order, as it is there said, to replace the state of war "by a firm, just, and durable peace." The League of Nations was established. The Washington Conference on Naval Limitation reflected the will of the victors to reduce their armament, and the Kellogg-Briand Pact outlawed war. On the surface, all seemed well. But beneath the sugar-coating of fine words there was much that was unsavory.

The American people, who even then possessed preponderant power in the world, turned soft, sentimental, and undisciplined. We abandoned what Washington called "a respectable defensive posture" not as a matter of principle or considered policy but because we found that posture uncomfortable. We adopted an attitude of illusory aloofness. We refused to join the League of Nations, and we sought to enclose our economy and be an oasis of prosperity in a world of misery. We were without vision and did not see that the revolutionary theories of Marx had found powerful embodiment in Russia and that misery and despair in Germany were breeding nazism. We were fascinated by the beautiful things that could be done with words and thought that great results could be accomplished quickly without hard work.

So in 1939 when our nation belatedly bestirred itself for peace, its leadership was without the moral, economic, and military assets that were needed to make its influence felt. At least that is what our leaders told us.

Today matters are different. The United States has not relapsed into a state of supineness. We are maintaining a powerful military establishment, even though that involves substantial sacrifice. . . .

Our nation has achieved a new level of peacetime productivity and also the willingness to share with others. . . .

The United States took leadership in creating a world organization and is taking a leading part in that organization. Our Government is willing to make the United Nations stronger as quickly as that can be done without destroying its universal character. In the meantime, our country has joined an American hemisphere regional pact that involves some surrender of sovereignty, and a comparable Atlantic Pact is in the making.

Our eyes are open to what is going on in the world. Perhaps sometimes we so strain our vision that it distorts what it sees, but at least we are neither blind nor purely introspective.

We are largely cured of the illusion that words are a substitute for deeds, and we know that a just and durable peace cannot be achieved merely by writing it or by heads of state meeting to proclaim it.

All in all, the American people have gone far to correct what they were told were the deficiencies that made it impossible to prevent World War II. Then, it seemed, the people gave would-be peacemakers only bricks without straw. Now they have given some solid brick. Political leadership thus has possibilities that formerly were denied it — and a correspondingly greater accountability.

Our churches have played a notable part in changing the attitudes of our people.

In 1942, at our First National Study Conference at Delaware, there was drawn up the Statement of Guiding Principles. That emphasized the heavy responsibility that devolved upon the United States. "If the future," we said, "is to be other than a repetition of the past, the United States must accept the responsibility for constructive action commensurate with its power and opportunity."

We next drew up, in application of the Guiding Principles, a Statement of Political Propositions generally known as the Six Pillars of Peace. There we set forth the necessity of creating a world organization and outlined the essential tasks that should be given it. That was at a time when our political leadership had not yet felt that world organization was feasible and when reference to it had deliberately been excluded from the statement of peace aims embodied in the Atlantic Charter.

In 1945, when the Dumbarton Oaks Proposals for world organization had been drafted, our Second National Study

Conference exposed certain basic omissions in those proposals, notably in relation to justice, law, human rights, and self-government for colonial peoples, and we sought and largely obtained a moral reorientation of the Charter. Also, we then committed ourselves to renounce the escapist idealism that had been widely prevalent after World War I. We pointed out that "an idealism which does not accept the discipline of the achievable may lose its power for good."

In 1946, we issued a Statement on Soviet-American Relations. We pointed out the impossibility of compromise on matters of faith, but asserted that "war with Russia can be avoided and it must be avoided without compromise of basic convictions." We went on to show that irreconcilable beliefs could coexist in a peaceful world so long as believers renounced the use of violence, coercion, or terrorism to make their faith prevail. That diagnosis, with its key to peace, has now been widely accepted, as shown by the debates at the last Assembly of the United Nations.

In 1947, before there was a European Recovery Program, we said that "Christian precept and enlightened self-interest call for United States economic aid to a degree not yet understood or accepted by our people." And after the European Recovery Program had been formulated, we rallied our church people to support that program in "the conviction that it can be one of history's most momentous affirmations of faith in the curative power of freedom and in the creative capacity of free men."

In April of last year, at a period of great nervousness, when it seemed to many that war with Russia was imminent and unavoidable, we issued a steadying statement calling upon our people to reject fatalism about war and to contribute, each of them, to a change of mood.

I refer to this series of statements not because I, too, have fallen a victim to the illusion that results are achieved merely by fine words, but because every one of these statements, issued at a decisive moment, was carried into the thinking and acting of millions of our citizens by means of publications, study conferences, national missions on world order, and other denominational and interdenominational efforts. At times we worked side by side with Roman Catholics and with Jews. We did not attempt to intermingle church and state; nor did we seek to have the churches make authoritative pronouncements with respect to detailed action in the political field. But we have tried to make clear what Christian principles meant in terms of the actual problems Christians faced as citizens. We have done that sufficiently, so that what we did has had practical consequences.

If our nation has abandoned political isolation, it is largely because our Christian people took the lead in developing the public opinion that not only permitted but that compelled our Government to work to establish a world organization and to work with it. If our nation has abandoned economic isolation, it is because our Christian people saw that both morality and enlightened self-interest required that we who were strong ought to help those who were weak. If our nation is armed, it is because our Christian people, for the most part, have not sought unilateral disarmament. And if, over the past three years, our nation has dealt with the Soviet Union on a basis that has been firm but that, for the most part, avoided provocation, it is largely because our Christian people have, on the one hand, seen the danger lying behind beguiling communist propaganda, but have also seen that there was no inevitability of war.

◇◇

The fact that Christian influence has affected our national conduct is nothing novel, nor should it be surprising. All students of United States history agree that our institutions became what they are, and that our national conduct has been what it was, primarily because of the religious views of our people respecting such matters as the nature of man, the moral law, and the mission of men and nations. Some of the present generation have not learned their history — or have forgotten it. They seem to think it necessary to devise new ways to make America a force for righteousness. What has counted over the past, and what counts today, is the powerhouse of faith and the transmission lines that connect faith and practices.

I know of my personal knowledge the profound influence that has been exerted upon Government by the public opinion that the churches have created over recent years. Most of our political leaders are themselves God-fearing men, who welcome religious influence. Of course there are a few who fear it. They think that it leads to sentimentality and impracticality. They think that they would like it better if the churches confined themselves to ritualistic worship and left it wholly to Government, through its propaganda, to create the public opinion that it thinks is needed to assure the ends that it thinks best.

No doubt the Christian influence is sometimes unrealistic and it does not always accept the discipline of the achievable. No doubt it sometimes annoys those who have the responsibility for practical action and sometimes it intrudes without good reason. Some will probably be annoyed with what we do here, and others will find it inconvenient to reckon with an opinion inspired by what we believe to be sources higher than Government. But that is petty stuff compared to the great fact that the American people do have a faith. No people are ever great, even in worldly terms, without a faith, and nothing would be more dangerous and destructive than to have the present great material power of the United States rattling around in the world detached from the guiding direction of a righteous faith.

The problem on which we plan to center our thinking at this Conference is how our nation can discharge its tremendous responsibility in the world today. We have, in the past, glimpsed that responsibility, but today we see that its magnitude far exceeds our earlier imaginings. The end of the war left us with economic productivity almost equal to that of all of the rest of the world combined. We are the only non-Communist state capable of balancing the military power of the Soviet Union, which otherwise would be dominant in the world. We have moral authority because it is generally believed that we have no lust for conquest, that we genuinely desire peace, and that we may have the wisdom and self-control needed to bring to the world an assurance of peace. All of the non-Communist nations look to us for leadership, and without that leadership there will be chaos in the world.

There can be little doubt but what our nation must accept the leadership that events press into our hands, and at this National Study Conference we shall consider what that means in terms of our relations toward the Soviet Union, toward Europe, toward the Far East and toward the United Nations. I shall not at this time begin that discussion, but I shall suggest certain basic qualities that, it seems to me, our leadership should possess.

1. *First of all, our leadership should be a leadership of peace, by peace, for peace.* That is not a demand for peace at

any price. There are some things that, to many, are more precious than peace. Our Constitutional Bill of Rights assumes that willingness and ability to use arms "are necessary to the security of a free state." But that is something very different from leadership that is on friendly terms with war.

There are some who talk about war as though it were an unpleasant but necessary remedy for existing ills. The fact is that another world war would plunge all of humanity into a pit too awful to contemplate, and make it almost impossible to achieve the good ends for which, no doubt, the combatants would profess to be fighting. It was World War I that delivered the two hundred million people of Russia to the dictatorship of the Communist Party, and World War II is delivering perhaps seven hundred million more people to that control. In a war climate, human liberty wilts, and totalitarianism spreads like a green bay tree. No one who is sincerely anticommunist can be complacent about war unless passion dominates his reason. . . .

◇◇◇◇

Calm analysis justifies the conclusion that, under present circumstances, war is neither useful nor inevitable and whether or not it comes depends most of all on the quality of United States leadership. With all of the assets, moral and material, of which it now disposes, our leadership ought to be able to assure peace. The old alibis have been swept away and if, today, the world passes into the blackness of another war, our leadership cannot escape a large measure of responsibility. That sobering thought should lift our nation above the sway of passion that makes fools the equals of the wise.

2. *Our leadership must be prepared to take some chances for peace.* Winning peace is not just a matter of good intentions. It involves difficult decisions and hard choices. At times,

it may even be necessary to risk war to win peace. Therefore, military considerations are never negligible. At times, military advantage can be gained at the cost of diminishing somewhat the prospect of peace. Sometimes a given course of action may increase somewhat the prospect of peace, but at the cost of putting our nation in a somewhat less advantageous position to win a war should it come. Peace may depend on who makes such decisions — civilians trained in the art of peace or soldiers trained in the art of war.

There are no finer, more patriotic, more personally peace-loving citizens than most of those in our Armed Services. However, they have a distinctive professional responsibility, and that is to do whatever lies within their power to make sure that if there is war, they will win it. That is their job and that is their training. They do not know how to use, perhaps powerfully, perhaps delicately, the enormous possibilities for peace that reside in moral and economic forces, in organizations like the United Nations and the World Court, and in the resources of diplomacy and conciliation. They do not know how to appraise those possibilities. That, too, is an art, and only those skilled in it are qualified to calculate the risks that must be taken for peace, just as only soldiers are competent, in war, to calculate the risks that have to be taken for victory. If we try to give the military the responsibility of preserving peace, they are apt to muff it because it is not the kind of responsibility for which they are trained.

Furthermore, history shows that whenever a nation has a great military establishment, it is under a powerful temptation to rely on the use, or the pressure, of that power, to gain its ends. The greater a nation's military establishment is, the greater should be the gulf between its military leaders and the making of national policy.

Under present conditions, it may be that a strong U.S. military establishment can serve the interest of peace. But that assumes what General Eisenhower refers to as "the necessary and wise subordination of the military to civil power." That is traditional American principle, and failure to observe it will, I fear, not serve the cause of peace.

I can assure you that the peoples and Governments of other lands who proffer us world leadership, do not do so because they want to help us *win* a war with Russia. They do it in order that there should *not be* a war. We would be false to ourselves and false to the trust that mankind puts in our leadership if we allow military judgments to be dominant in our national policy.

3. *Our peaceful leadership must be positive and not merely negative.* . . . It is not possible, in these matters, to be dogmatic or wholly to ignore strategic considerations, but, generally speaking, we should be selective in our moral and material support. We need not laud or sanctify whatever or whomever communism attacks, and our material support should principally serve to sustain, fortify, and enlarge human freedom and healthy economic and social conditions. We should have our own plan of campaign and not let Soviet Communism make it for us.

There was a time when the Western democracies were supreme in prestige because of their dynamic pursuit of liberty, equality, and fraternity, their great experiments in political freedom, and their Industrial Revolution which multiplied many times the productivity of human effort.

It is time to recapture that initiative and we can, in that connection, welcome President Truman's proposal for a pooling of technological resources for the advancement of backward areas.

There is no policy so barren, so certain to fail, as that of maintaining the *status quo*. If our leadership is to be successful, it must develop constructive and creative programs that will capture the imagination and enlist the support of the multitudes whose interest in battling political, economic, and racial injustice is greater than their interest in defending such injustice merely because communism attacks it.

4. *Our leadership must be one of fellowship and not of mastery*. In much of the world, the word "leader" has acquired an ugly significance. Nazism was founded on the "leader" principle. The Communist Party operates under the principle of iron discipline, with a pitiless purging of all who deviate from what the party leaders prescribe. Throughout the world, millions have been bruised in body and spirit by leadership that has meant the ruthless mastery of a brutal few.

Western leadership, too, is under suspicion. For centuries, the West enjoyed a world-wide political supremacy that had elements of economic exploitation and racial intolerance. That supremacy is now peacefully withering away and giving place to self-government. Within recent years over five hundred million people have passed from colonial to self-governing status, and an equal number have been released from Western ties that, in fact, were political shackles. It is to the honor of Western civilization that its Christian ideals and its economic enterprise made possible this peaceful evolution. Nevertheless, the motives of the West have, in the past, been sufficiently selfish, so that today many of other races and cultures are fearful lest the West take advantage of this crisis and use its superior economic and military power to regain world mastery.

They want us to lead, but they want leadership that combines with fellowship. They accept that we have a certain primacy, but only the kind of primacy that can exist as between equals.

That is where the United Nations comes in. It is organized as a center for harmonizing the actions of nations on the basis of the sovereign equality of all its members. We meet there, and discuss, in fellowship. Ideas are valued on the basis of merit, and not merely on the basis of the power of the nation from which they emanate.

There are some matters that, because of their nature, cannot be effectively or properly dealt with through the United Nations. But experience has shown that the United Nations could be trusted much more than has been the case. We can, and should, make the Charter a framework within which our leadership will be exercised in fellowship.

5. *Finally, our leadership should be compassionately human.* Let us not forget that what our nation *is,* is just as important as what it does. There come times which seem to call for action. The present seems one of those times. . . . We devise machines to calculate flights of missiles that are beyond human calculation. We perform miracles of production through the use of ever more efficient tools. Such action may be necessary, and there are many whose duty it is to engage in it. But there is about all this a certain hardness that can affect the inner soul.

What is our feverishness about? It is presumably to save mankind from falling under the sway of a materialistic rule that holds that man's chief end is to glorify the state and to serve it forever. But we shall not accomplish that great and worthy purpose if we go about it in such a way that we, too, become inhuman and deaf to the cry of the masses that a way be found to save them and their children from the death, the misery, the starvation of body and soul that recurrent war and economic disorder now wreak upon man.

Sometimes our churches try to do that for which they are not equipped, neglecting their own distinctive tasks. Today one of the churches' tasks is to preserve in our nation human sympathy and compassion such as Jesus had when he saw the multitudes.

If our churches perform that task, the other problems that concern our nation will more readily be solved. Then our leadership is bound to be leadership that seeks peace; our programs will assuredly be designed to increase human welfare and our relations with others will be those of fellowship. And then perhaps it may be said to our nation: "Thy faith hath saved thee; go in peace."

20

The Way of Love and Compassion

I AM GRATEFUL to you for inviting me to join with the friends of the Presbyterian Hospital. I am proud of the long identification of my family with this institution of healing, compassion, and loving care.

These are qualities that life compels everyone to need; and when that need arises, as it implacably does, no material wealth, no political power, no brilliance of mind is any substitute for these gifts of the soul which others can bestow.

Of course, material things have their worth. Without money and scientific knowledge we would not have this hospital and its equipment. But material things get their value primarily from the spiritual values that go with them and from dedication to uses, inspired by hearts that are responsive to the two great commandments to love God and to love fellow man.

At first thought, it seems strange that the most valuable things are not things which need be scarce but rather are spiritual qualities which each and every one of us can possess abundantly, and which each can give away and still be the richer. But, on reflection, is it not plain that that is the wondrous miracle of our world and the final proof that the world

Address at the Presbyterian Hospital, Philadelphia, April 14, 1952.

is a spiritual world, not made by man? Would not this world be an unjust world if the most valuable things were so scarce that only a few could possess them? It is typical of a man-made order that the greatest value is put on scarcity. But man cannot change the scale of values that God ordained. He in his infinite wisdom and justice made a world where no accident of birth or circumstance limits the capacity of each person to give and to receive the most precious things of life. No one is so poor, so illiterate, and so low in the social scale that he cannot give; no one is so rich, so brainy, or so powerful that he does not need what even the weakest can give him.

No one has given greatly if he has given only materially, and no one is rich unless he receives from others the spiritual values that they have to give.

Constantly, I am in receipt of letters from those who inquire as to what they can do to make this world a better world. They can, whoever they are, give love, sympathy, and compassionate understanding of their fellow men, near and far. And they can, in turn, attract from others the good will, the sympathetic understanding, which enriches those who receive.

In the intimacy of our family and within our homes we realize and practice these truths. We know that the pains of birth, illness, disappointment, and finally death are made tolerable by loving care, and that the joys of life are intensified by sympathetic sharing. Sometimes we forget that what is true in detail is also true in mass. In the family of nations the needs and the values are the same.

The present extremity of trouble within the nations is not due primarily to a shortage of material things. Of course there are such shortages, but they are relatively less today than ever before in the world's history. The troubles are primarily due to the fact that more than ever before political influence is being exerted by those who think and act in terms that are calculated on a purely material basis.

The great evil of Soviet Communism, which dominates one third of the globe, is that it puts material things first. As Stalin has said in his essay on dialectical and historical materialism, "The material life of society is primary, and its spiritual life secondary." . . .

◇◇◇◇

But we in America, who have leadership in the world that is free, are ourselves not without fault. We are relatively free of the fanatical intolerance which characterizes Soviet Communism. But we are apt to look upon our great material possessions with pride as themselves proving us to be superior people. The fact is that this superiority in material things is not nearly so important as many of us believe, and we learn that to our dismay when we deal with other peoples. We think that they should admire us because we have more automobiles than all of the rest of the world put together. We think they should be grateful to us because in one form or another we have given away nearly fifty billion dollars since the fighting stopped. We think that others are stupid and ungrateful that they do not bow down before such material magnificence.

The fact is that our mechanical gadgets are not in the main what others want. Indeed, these others may possess in greater measure than do we ourselves the values which our Christian religion teaches are supreme.

Among other peoples—the Japanese, the Indians, the Mexicans, to name only a few — there are many who possess a love and appreciation of beauty, a capacity for human understanding, and a richness of sympathy which we might well covet for ourselves. If we apply a true measuring rod, we will approach them humbly and not in a mood of lofty superiority.

Also, while what we have given is important, it has not involved either giving or receiving the spiritual values that count most. We have not given out of compassion or because of love of our fellow men. Our vast public loans and grants to other nations have been made, not because we wanted to make them, but because we have been told that we had to make them in order to achieve certain political objectives. The gifts have not carried a message of sympathy and good will but rather expressions of annoyance, grumbling, and carping criticism. The result is that we have not gotten what we bargained for. Our nation is today less liked, more isolated, and more endangered than ever before in its history.

I recall the moving plea which Charles Malik of Lebanon made at the Japanese Peace Conference on behalf of the Near East: "Believe me, I weigh every word when I say our problems, overwhelming as they are, can be solved, and a wondrous new era can usher in, in the Near East, if only people care enough." Apparently no one has cared enough, for that plea has gone without response for now nearly eight months.

Do we care and shall we act out of caring? That is the vital question that confronts our people. Jesus, when he saw the multitudes, was moved with compassion, and then he gave them some material help. He did not give that help because he had calculated that it would be good political propaganda. That is the way for us to follow, making the spiritual primary and the material secondary. That is indeed the traditional American way, and I believe that the American people are eager to return to that way.

I think they would like to do what they believe is the right thing to do rather than constantly be doing what they are told is an act of political expediency.

If only we care enough and have compassion and act as that spirit directs, then our position in the world would be revolutionized overnight. Then, I predict, we shall get, as a by-product, the security which eludes us so long as we seek it in selfish calculation.

It is everlastingly true that if we seek first the Kingdom of God and his righteousness, these other things will be added unto us.

21

The Significance of Theological Education

Out in Tennessee there is a plant which turns out bombs. Here we have a plant which turns out ministers of the gospel. The two seem remote and unrelated. Actually, the issue of our time, perhaps the issue of all human time, is which of the two outputs will prevail.

Too much these days we forget that men's ability to control the physical depends upon the moral. Nothing that statesmen can contrive will work if it does not reflect the moral conscience of the time. Whenever that limitation is ignored, failure ensues. We need to recall that now when many are panicky and demand something that, on paper at least, will seem to give them security. . . . When war occurs, nations avail themselves of any weapon which they think will make the difference between victory and defeat. No agreements are allowed to stand in the way. Indeed, nations at war would consider such self-restraint to be morally wrong. For in war, nations always identify their cause with righteousness and identify the enemy with the forces of evil. Thus, until govern-

Address delivered on the occasion of the inauguration of the President of Union Theological Seminary, November 15, 1945, and repeated in condensed form to the Board of Directors of Union Seminary on May 27, 1958.

ments take a totally different conception of the moral sanctity of contracts in time of war, it is folly to believe that the destructiveness of war can be limited by agreements not to use certain weapons. . . .

The task of statesmanship is to relate theory to reality. Political institutions ought to be as perfect as is consonant with their vigorous survival in the existing environment. Also, of course, those institutions ought to contain within themselves the possibility of improving the environment and thereby making more perfection possible. The United Nations Charter has that great merit. It does not accept as permanent the existing distrusts. It charges the nations, under the leadership of the General Assembly, to work together on tasks of human welfare. The assumption, and the reasonable assumption, is that if they do that, fellowship between nations will grow.

The central problem is how to get world law. Once we can agree upon a lawmaking body, then it will be possible to put overwhelming force behind it. However, it is not possible to have a lawmaking body until there is greater trust and confidence between the peoples of the world, until there is more widespread acceptance and practice of democratic methods, and until there is more nearly a common moral judgment of what is right and wrong.

There is no political short cut to the safety men want. We must carry through the program of San Francisco. We must use the United Nations Organization to bring about that greater trust and fellowship we need before we can have any world government that will work. Fellowship, and not fear, is the cement with which world order must be built. The urgent task is to increase that fellowship and not to abandon that effort on the ground that increased fear makes it unnecessary.

I realize that such a program as I here outline will not satisfy the many who are panicky and the many who are impatient. They want to be shown a formula for quick and absolute security. It would be easy to write one. It would be impossible to write one that would work. There is no short cut. There is no mechanistic solution. It is not possible by a stroke of the pen to make up for accumulated moral deficiencies. What is possible is to increase steadily the acceptance and practice of the moral law. If we do that, then many other things will become possible.

When I talk along this line, it is often replied that I am impractical and idealistic and that we cannot wait for results until the whole world has become evangelized or at least has become highly moral. Such comment merely shows that I have failed to make my meaning clear. To rely upon the force of the moral law is the most practical thing in the world to-day. It is general acceptance of moral law which gives us 99 per cent of the practical security which we enjoy. It is where the moral law is weakest in its application, namely, in relation to bodies corporate, that the greatest danger comes. There is nothing impractical about attempting to extend the system which practically gives us protection. On the contrary, what is impractical and unrealistic is to depend upon agreements by governments which have no moral sanction behind them. . . .

To seek to extend the rule of the moral law . . . is not a program which will be without results until the millennium is achieved. The most important protection we can get comes, not from where we are, but from the way in which we are moving. If the postwar trend is toward increased fellowship and increasing trust and confidence, then that itself will bring us a large measure of protection as a by-product. So long as the trend is in that direction, nations do not interrupt it to wipe each other out with atomic bombs. It is when the trend is toward increased distrust that we need to be afraid.

We can, therefore, with confidence assert that a peaceful order depends most of all upon intensive use of those methods which have been tried and which have worked in the past. Of those methods, the most successful has been extension of the moral law, and in bringing the people to act toward each other in fellowship and as good neighbors. We must not allow ourselves to be diverted from pushing forward along that line. In that effort our greatest reliance is, of course, upon the great religious bodies of the world. It is they, above all others, which create the moral foundation which, in turn, determines the political structure which can be built. These religious bodies, in turn, are dependent upon their seminaries. So it is that the great theological seminaries, of which Union Theological Seminary is an outstanding example, are in reality the central power plants upon which men must, above all, depend not merely for their spiritual salvation but for their material safety.

V

The Power of Moral Forces

This collection began with an address delivered by Mr. Dulles on August 28, 1949, in the First Presbyterian Church of Watertown, New York, in which he had worshiped throughout his boyhood under his father's ministry.

On October 11, 1953, he returned to Watertown to take part in the celebration of the one hundred and fiftieth anniversary of the church. The address delivered on that occasion gathers into summary many of the central convictions of his life.

22

The Power of Moral Forces

I T WAS nearly two years ago that your minister asked me to come here to speak at this one hundred and fiftieth anniversary of the founding of our church. I accepted that invitation. Since then I have had to make and unmake many plans. But this date has been a fixed point around which other things revolved.

I have looked forward eagerly to being here on this historic occasion. It rightfully means much to all of you here and to this entire area. To me this church is richer in memories than any other earthly spot. My father preached here for sixteen years and radiated a spiritual influence that is still felt here, and elsewhere, as I have learned in my travels about the world. Our family life revolved around this church. Before me is the pew in which we sat three times on Sunday and frequently during weekday evenings.

At times the church services seemed overlong and overfrequent. But through them I was taught of the two great commandments, love of God and love of fellow man. Ordained

Address delivered at the Interdenominational Community Service celebrating the one hundred and fiftieth anniversary of the First Presbyterian Church, Watertown, New York, October 11, 1953.

ministers are uniquely qualified to deal with the relations of man to God. But laymen, who have to deal with national and international problems, are perhaps qualified to make some observations on the relations of man to fellow man.

Let me first recall that our American political institutions are what they are because our founders were deeply religious people. As soon as a community was founded, a church was built. This church is an example. Also, wherever a community was founded, its members developed practices and ways of life which reflected their belief that there is a God, that he is the author of a moral law which all can know and should obey, that he imparts to each human being a spiritual dignity and worth which all should respect.

Our founders sought to reflect these truths in their political institutions, seeking thus that God's will should be done on earth.

The Bill of Rights puts into our supreme law the concept "that all men are endowed by their Creator with certain inalienable rights." Our Constitution says, in unmistakable terms, that men, even in the guise of government, cannot lawfully deny other men their fundamental rights and freedoms.

From the beginning of our nation, those who made its laws and system of justice looked upon them as means to assure what seemed just and right. Thus we became heirs to a noble heritage.

We must, however, remember that that heritage is not inexhaustible. Our institutions of freedom will not survive unless they are constantly replenished by the faith that gave them birth.

General Washington, in his Farewell Address, pointed out that morality and religion are the two pillars of our society. He went on to say that morality cannot be maintained without religion. "Whatever may be conceded to the influence of refined education on minds of peculiar structure, reason and experience both forbid us to expect that national morality can prevail in exclusion of religious principle."

Arnold Toynbee, the great student of civilizations, has recently pointed out that the political and social practices of our civilization derive from their Christian content, and, he says, they will not long survive unless they are replenished by that faith. His profound study convinces him that "practice unsupported by belief is a wasting asset."

Many other nations have modeled their constitutions after ours. But they have not obtained the same results unless there was a faith to vitalize the words.

The terrible things that are happening in some parts of the world are due to the fact that political and social practices have been separated from spiritual content.

That separation is almost total in the Soviet Communist world. There the rulers hold a materialistic creed which denies the existence of moral law. It denies that men are spiritual beings. It denies that there are any such things as eternal verities. As a result the Soviet institutions treat human beings as primarily important from the standpoint of how much they can be made to produce for the glorification of the state. Labor is essentially slave labor, working to build up the military and material might of the state so that those who rule can assert ever greater and more frightening power.

Such conditions repel us. But it is important to understand what causes those conditions. It is irreligion. If ever the political forces in this country became irreligious, our institutions would change. The change might come about slowly, but it would come surely. Institutions born of faith will inevitably change unless they are constantly nurtured by faith.

But, it may be asked, may not aggressive material forces prevail unless met by materialism? It sometimes seems that material power is so potent that it should be sought at any price, even at the sacrifice of spiritual values. Always, however, in the past those who took that path have met disaster. Material aggression often is formidable. It is dynamic, and we must admit that the dynamic usually prevails over the static. But it is gross error to assume that material forces have a monopoly of dynamism. Moral forces too are mighty. Christians, to be sure, do not believe in invoking brute power to secure their ends. But that does not mean that they have no ends or that they have no means of getting there. Christians are not negative, supine people.

Jesus told the disciples to go out into all the world and to preach the gospel to all the nations. Any nation which bases its institutions on Christian principles cannot but be a dynamic nation.

Our forebears felt keenly that this nation had a mission to perform. In the opening paragraph of *The Federalist* papers it is said that "it seems to have been reserved to the people of this country, by their conduct and example," to show the way to political freedom. Our Declaration of Independence meant, as Lincoln said, "liberty, not alone to the people of this country but hope for the world for all future time. It was that which gave promise that in due time the weight should be lifted from the shoulders of all men and that all should have an equal chance."

What our forebears did became known as "the great American experiment." They created here a society of material, intellectual, and spiritual richness the like of which the world had never known. It was not selfishly designed, but for ourselves and others. We sought through conduct, example, and influence to promote everywhere the cause of human freedom. Through missionaries, physicians, educators, and merchants, the American people carried their ideas and ideals to others. They availed of every opportunity to spread their gospel of freedom, their good news, throughout the world.

That performance so caught the imagination of the peoples of the world that everywhere men wanted for themselves a political freedom which could bear such fruits.

The despotisms of the last century faded away largely under the influence of that conduct and example. There is no despotism in the world which can stand up against the impact of such a gospel. That needs to be remembered today. Our best reliance is not more and bigger bombs but a way of life which reflects religious faith.

Do our people still have that faith which in the past made our nation truly great and which we need today? That is the ultimate testing of our time. Admittedly, some have come to think primarily in material terms. They calculate the atomic stockpiles, the bombers, the tanks, the standing armies of the various nations, and seem to assume that the victory will go to whichever is shown by these scales to have the greater weight of armament.

Unfortunately, under present conditions we do need to have a strong military establishment. We are opposed by those who respect only visible strength and who are tempted to encroach where there seems to be material weakness. Therefore, without military strength, we could not expect to deter aggression which, even though it would ultimately fail, would in the process cause immense misery and loss. But I can assure you that your Government does not put its faith primarily in material things.

The greatest weakness of our opponents is that they are professed materialists. They have forcibly extended their rule over some eight hundred million people, a third of the people of the world. They are seeking to make these people into a pliant, physical mass which completely conforms to the will of the rulers. But these people are religious people and they are patriotic people. They have shown that over the centuries. We believe that the Soviet rulers are attempting the impossible when they attempt to subject such people to their materialistic and repressive rule. We believe that the subject peoples have faith and hopes which cannot indefinitely be suppressed.

I can assure you that your President, your Cabinet, your Congress, recognize the priority of spiritual forces. We do not intend to turn this nation into a purely material fortress and to suppress the freedom of thought and expression of the inmates, so that our people would more and more assume the likeness of that which threatens and which we hate.

There are a few within this nation who do not share their viewpoint. They honestly feel that the danger is so great and of such a kind that we must give an absolute priority to material efforts. There are others who honestly feel that the danger is so imminent that we should impose uniformity of thought, or at least of expression, abolishing diversity and tolerance within our nation and within our alliances.

Such points of view, while often heard, represent a small minority. Certainly there is some confusion of thinking, which needs to be dispelled. But I believe that the great majority of the American people and of their representatives in Government still accept the words of the prophet: "Not by might, nor by power, but by my Spirit, saith the Lord of hosts."

How shall we surely become infused with that spirit? That is my concluding concern.

There is no mystery about that. The way to get faith is to expose oneself to the faith of others. It is not only diseases that are contagious. Faith is contagious. A strong faith, rooted in fact and in reason, inevitably spreads if contacts are provided. If, therefore, we want spiritual strength, we must maintain contact with those who have it and with those who have had it.

That is above all the task of our churches. The Bible is the greatest book because, as Paul pointed out to the Hebrews, it is a story of faith. It recounts lapses from faith and their consequences, and revival and restoration of faith. Most of all, it is a story of men who lived by faith and died in faith, bequeathing it to successors who molded it into something finer, truer, and more worthy.

Our American history, like Hebrew history, is also rich in the story of men who through faith wrought mightily.

In earlier days our homes, schools, and colleges were largely consecrated to the development of faith. They were places of prayer and of Bible-reading. Parents and teachers told daily the story of those who had gone before and who had lived by faith.

Today our schools and colleges and, I am afraid, our homes largely omit this study in faith. That throws a heavier burden on our churches. They today provide the principal means of drawing together the men, women, and children of our land and of bringing to them knowledge of the faith of those who have gone before, so that today's faith is a contagious and vital force.

As our churches, synagogues, and other places of worship thus carry an ever-greater share of vital responsibility, they should be strongly supported by all our citizens, for they all profit from the institutions which faith inspires.

As we meet here today on this anniversary, we feel that we are indeed compassed about by a great crowd of witnesses. Each of us here knows that in terms of loved ones who have gone before. We know it as we have heard read here the great Book of Faith and as we are taught here the lessons drawn from the story of the great prophets and disciples of the past.

Let us maintain spiritual communion with them. Let us draw faith and inspiration from their lives. Let us act as we know they would want us to act. Then we, in our turn, will run with steadfastness the course that is set before us. Then we, in our turn, will play worthily our part in keeping alight the flame of freedom.

I spoke earlier of the spiritual legacy that had been left us by our fathers. Surely it is our duty not to squander it but to leave it replenished so that we, in our generation, may bequeath to those who come after us a tradition as noble as was left to us.

We meet here beneath a spire which is symbolic. It points upward to the Power above us, from which we derive our spiritual strength. It marks this building as the place where we can gather for a communion that renews our faith.

Let us be ever thankful for this church, remembering those who a century and a half ago founded it. Let us remember also those who during the succeeding decades maintained it, enlarged it, beautified it, and enriched it with their Christian labors. Let us dedicate ourselves to follow in their way.

John Foster Dulles

Born: February 25, 1888, Washington, D.C.

Parents: Allen Macy and Edith (Foster) Dulles

Wife: Janet Pomery Avery, married June 26, 1912

Children: John Watson Foster, Lillias Pomeroy (Mrs. Robert Hinshaw), Avery

Died: May 24, 1959

Academic Record

B.A., *magna cum laude* Princeton University, 1908, Valedictorian

Studied at the Sorbonne, Paris, 1908–1909

LL.B., George Washington University, 1911

LL.D., Tufts, 1939; Princeton University, 1946; Wagner College, Northwestern University, 1947; Union College, 1948; University of Pennsylvania, Lafayette, 1949; Amherst, Seoul National University, 1950; University of Arizona, St. Joseph's College, 1951; St. Lawrence University, Johns Hopkins University, Fordham University, Harvard, 1952; Columbia University, Georgetown University, 1954; University of South Carolina, Indiana University, 1955; Iowa State University, 1956.

Career in National and International Affairs

Secretary of The Hague Peace Conference, 1907

Member of the Second Pan-American Scientific Congress

Special Agent, Department of State, in Central America, 1917

Captain and Major, U.S. Army (Intelligence), 1917–1918

Assistant to Chairman, War Trade Board, 1918

Counsel to American Commission to Negotiate Peace, 1918–1919

Member, Reparations Commission and Supreme Economic Council, 1919

Legal Adviser, Polish plan of financial stabilization, 1927

American Representative, Berlin debt conferences, 1933

Member, U.S. delegation, San Francisco Conference on World Organization, 1945, United Nations General Assembly, 1946, 1947, 1950.

Acting Chairman, U.S. delegation, UN General Assembly, Paris, 1948

Adviser to Secretary of State at Council of Foreign Ministers, London, 1945, 1947; Moscow, 1947; Paris, 1949

United States Senator, appointed 1949

Consultant to Secretary of State, 1950

Special representative of President, with rank of ambassador, negotiated Japanese Peace Treaty, 1951

Negotiator of Australian, New Zealand, Philippine, and Japanese Security Treaties, 1950–1951

Secretary of State, 1953–1959

Special Consultant to the President, 1959

Affiliations

Member, Sullivan & Cromwell, attorneys, 1911–1949; head of firm, 1927–1949

Chairman, Board of Trustees, Rockefeller Foundation, Carnegie Endowment for International Peace, General Education Board

Trustee, Bank of New York, New York Public Library

Member, Association of the Bar of the City of New York, New York State Banking Board, Phi Beta Kappa, Phi Delta Phi

Church Relationships

Member, First Presbyterian Church, Watertown, New York, baptized July 1, 1888; received on profession of faith to communicant membership, July 5, 1902

Elder, Park Avenue Presbyterian Church, New York City; Brick Presbyterian Church, New York City, 1937–1959

Delegate, Conference on Church, Community, and State, Oxford, 1937

Delegate, International Conference of Lay Experts and Ecumenical Leaders, convened by the Provisional Committee of the World Council of Churches, Geneva, 1939

Chairman, Commission to Study the Bases of a Just and Durable Peace, Federal Council of the Churches of Christ in America, 1940–1948

Chairman, Committee on Policy, Department of International Justice and Goodwill, 1948–1949; Member of the department, 1951–1952

Director, Union Theological Seminary, New York City, 1945–1953

Member, Commission of the Churches on International Affairs, 1947–1953

Author, statement on "The Christian Citizen in a Changing World" in preparation for the first Assembly of the World Council of Churches, Amsterdam, 1948

Speaker, first Assembly of the World Council of Churches,
Amsterdam, 1948

Books

War, Peace and Change, 1939
War or Peace, 1950